History of the World

Since 1500

J.M. ROBERTS Merton College, Oxford

Alfred A. Knopf  New York

THIS IS A BORZOI BOOK
PUBLISHED BY ALFRED A. KNOPF, INC.

First Edition

9 8 7 6 5 4 3 2 1

Library of Congress Cataloging in Publication Data

Roberts, John Morris, 1928-
   History of the world.

   Bibliography: v. 1, p.   ; v. 2, p.
   Includes indexes.
   CONTENTS: v. 1. To 1500.—v. 2. Since 1500.
   1. World history. I. Title.
D21.R64 1976b   909   75-28018
ISBN 0-394-31970-0 (v. 2)

Manufactured in the United States of America

Cover illustration: An Aztec solar calendar. The year consisted of 365 days, divided into 18 months of 20 days each, with an additional period of 5 "unlucky days." (European Art Color Slides/P. Adelberg, Inc.)

Preface

This book contains one man's view of the history of the world, but many people have contributed to it, some by the books they have written and others, fewer in number but more directly, by the help they have given me. Many of my colleagues have painstakingly answered questions I put to them (sometimes, I fear, without knowing why I was asking them) and for years my pupils have been asking *me* questions which have often clarified my ideas or revealed my ignorance of topics important to this book. To all of them I am grateful; if they are not singled out by name it is only because they are too numerous. More personal recognition, on the other hand, must be given to two who assisted me during the whole course of preparation of this book; without the help of Carole D'Albiac and Nicki Sissons in preparing material, investigating topics, and checking what I had written, I could neither have completed it in time nor would it have escaped many more errors and inadequacies than no doubt survive. I am deeply grateful to both of them for their conscientiousness, enthusiasm, and encouragement when my spirits flagged. I also wish to thank my editor, Suzanne Thibodeau of Alfred A. Knopf. She cannot always have found it agreeable to handle the complicated business of preparing this book for publication by exchanging letters across the Atlantic with a somewhat irritable author. She has always displayed exemplary patience and understanding and by her work has made an important contribution to this book.

No one except the author, of course, should be blamed for any of the shortcomings of the text. When possible, I shall endeavor to correct them in the next edition.

J. M. Roberts

Contents

Preface   v
Introduction   xi

part IV THE EUROPEAN AGE   481

CHAPTER 21   ECONOMY AND SOCIETY IN EARLY MODERN EUROPE   483
Economy   483
Society   494

CHAPTER 22   AUTHORITY AND ITS CHALLENGERS   499
The Growth of State Power   500
The Renaissance State: Strengths and Weaknesses   501
The Reformation   503
Principalities and Powers   510

CHAPTER 23   THE CHANGING STATE PATTERN OF EARLY MODERN EUROPE   525
Diplomacy's Origins   525
Dynastic Map Making in Western Europe   526
A New Eastern Europe   535

CHAPTER 24   EUROPE'S ASSAULT ON THE WORLD   555
A New Phase of History   555
Africa and Asia   559
The Americas   566

CHAPTER 25   THE NEW SHAPE OF WORLD HISTORY   579
The First World Powers   579
Trade, War, and Empire   580
Cultural Interplay   586

CHAPTER 26   IDEAS OLD AND NEW   593
New Intellectual Forces   594
A New Scientific Age   598
The Enlightenment   605

part V THE GREAT ACCELERATION   613

CHAPTER 27   ECONOMIC AND SOCIAL DEVELOPMENT   615
Population Changes   615
Agricultural Revolution   619

A New Scale of Industrialization   623
Towns and Cities   628
Theories of Change   634

CHAPTER 28   AN AGE OF REVOLUTIONS   636
The American Revolution   636
The French Revolution   643
The Return to Monarchy   653

CHAPTER 29   EUROPE TRANSFORMED   661
The Vienna Settlement   661
1848: The Contagion of Revolution   664
New Nations   667
The Ebbing of Revolution   672
Socialism   675
The Conservative Giant: Russia   677

CHAPTER 30   THE ANGLO-SAXON WORLD   682
The Young Republic's Foreign Policy   683
Irrepressible Conflict   688
The War Between the States   693
The English Constitutional Revolution   697

CHAPTER 31   THE EUROPEAN WORLD HEGEMONY   703
Power and Influence   703
European Nations Overseas   710
Imperialism and Imperial Rule   724

CHAPTER 32   ASIA IN THE EUROPEANIZED WORLD   740
China   740
Japan   751
The British in India   760
Southeast Asia   766

part VI THE END OF THE EUROPEANS' WORLD   769

CHAPTER 33   STRAINS IN THE SYSTEM: EUROPE AT THE BEGINNING
OF THE TWENTIETH CENTURY   771
Changes and Challenges   771
Religion and Science   779
International Order   785

CHAPTER 34   THE FIRST WORLD WAR AND ITS AFTERMATH   789
Prologue   789
The Great War   793
Rebuilding Europe   802

CHAPTER 35   A NEW ASIA IN THE MAKING   816
Clashes in the Far East   816
The Western Islamic Lands   831

CHAPTER 36   THE SECOND WORLD WAR   841
 The Post-Liberal Years   841
 The European Imbalance of Power   845
 Expansion of the War   852
 The Balance Sheet   860

CHAPTER 37   SHAPING A NEW WORLD   864
 Postwar Power Structures   864
 Cold War Origins   868
 The Crumbling of Empires   871

part VII   THE POST-EUROPEAN AGE   883

CHAPTER 38   UNDERCURRENTS OF CONTEMPORARY HISTORY   885
 Fundamental Changes   885
 Science and World Civilization   892
 Religion and the State   898

CHAPTER 39   THE ORGANIZATION OF A NEW WORLD   902
 The Cold War at Its Height   902
 Asian Revolution   907
 The Postimperial Era in the Middle East and Africa   920
 Latin America   926

CHAPTER 40   THE END OF BIPOLARITY   933
 The Superpowers Challenged   933
 A More Fluid World   946

CHAPTER 41   IN THE LIGHT OF HISTORY   953
 One World or Several?   954
 A Material Promise   957
 A New Horizon   960

 FURTHER READING   967
 INDEX   *follows page 975*

PICTURE ESSAY

 Man Makes His World—II   *follows page 736*

Maps

Religious Divisions in 16th-Century Europe   506
The Netherlands During the Eighty Year's War   513
The Empire of Charles V   529
The Austrian Empire 1657–1718   537
Russia's 18th-Century Expansion and the Disappearance of Poland   549
Prussia 1721–1772   550

Overseas Possessions 1713   562
Anglo-French Rivalry in India 1754–1763   565
Rivalry in North America and the Caribbean 1754–1763   573
France and Her Satellite Republics 1792–1799   652
Napoleon's Empire 1810   655
Europe after the Treaty of Vienna   662
The Unification of Italy 1859–1920   670
The Unification of Germany 1815–1871   672
The Decline of the Ottoman Empire 1683–1914   679
The Boundaries of the United States to 1819   686
American Expansion into the Southwest   688
The United States: Slave and Free Territory 1850   691
The Export of European Capital before 1914   707
Migration from Europe 1840–1940   711
The Western Hemisphere 1784   714
Africa in 1885   719
The Partition of Africa   733
Imperialism in Asia and the Pacific   741
The Western Front 1914–1918   796
World War I and Its European Aftermath   799
The New Europe 1919–1926   803
The German Problem 1935–1939   850
World War II in Europe   853
World War II in the Pacific   858
Israel and the Middle East   880
The World 1975   904

Excerpts from Source Readings

Elizabeth's Armada Speech   514
Mysterious Russia   541
The Cruelty of Empire   570
Sally in Our Alley   596
The Principle of Benign Selfishness   607
Merry England in the Early Nineteenth Century   622
The Nineteenth-Century Working Day   624
Luddism in Saxony   632
The Revolutionary as Visionary   650
The Special Relationship   684
The White Man's Burden   736
A Chinese Rebuke to the Barbarian West   742
The Japanese Revolution   754
Nazism under Weimar   848
Left Speaks to Left   934
The First Men in the Moon   962

Introduction

I now know what I had previously only guessed: that it is very hard to write a world history. I have nevertheless been confirmed in my initial view that it is well worth doing, and I hope those who use this book will agree. No doubt a one-man attempt will contain certain faults, but without someone taking big risks in areas in which he cannot pretend to expertise, no true history of the world can be written; there will only be anthologies of subordinate histories — of nations or ethnic groups or different sides of human activity or even different periods — by individual experts and without a unifying vision.

The subject matter of world history has always appeared to me to be the story of the processes which have brought mankind from the uncertainties and perils of primitive and precivilized life to the much more complex and very different uncertainties and perils of today. It must focus on man's growing capacity to handle his environment and on his growing interdependence as a species. These assumptions underlie this book and shape it.

Most of the book is organized around the themes provided by the major traditions of civilization, but it could not begin with them. The roots of behavior even in civilized communities lie in the very remote past, beyond history; this is where this work opens. Humans then acquired certain characteristics and not others. Their ability to deal with the simplest and most crushing forms of natural pressure — cold, darkness, hunger — was shaped in some ways and not others. Basically life must have been much the same in all the habitats in which men then lived; in this sense culture was for thousands of years remarkably standardized. The weight of genetic programming and environmental pressure was enormous. This changed with the emergence of civilization. A huge variety of traditions arose, all of them becoming great historical factors in their own right, in due time interplaying with and changing one another. In fairly recent times, one of these traditions, the Western European, began to show an unprecedented dynamism and power and was able finally to initiate the process which led to the world we live in. This, roughly, is the outline of what follows.

These pages do not therefore simply present an anthology of articles about particular nations or dynasties. They make no pretense of furnishing a continuous account in roughly the same detail of the history of every major country or every major field of human activity. In the dictionary sense of the word, this book is not comprehensive; readers will not find in it the names of all the presidents of the United States or every Italian Renaissance painter of note, or the date on which every African state emerged from colonial rule. It is about processes rather than events. The criterion for the inclusion of factual data has therefore been their historical importance – that is, their effective importance to the major processes of history rather than intrinsic interest or any sort of merit.

This means that I have neglected some areas which have great interest to scholars and some others which possess a certain glamour because of what they have left behind. We still gape in amazement at the ruins of Yucatán and Zimbabwe and wonder over the statues of Easter Island. Yet desirable though knowledge of the societies which produced these things is, they remain peripheral to world history. What Europeans later brought back from and did to such societies is a different matter; that has shaped our lives, even if only in small degrees. But nothing in African or American history before the coming of Europeans affected the evolution of the cultural traditions in which the contributions of the Buddha, the Hebrew prophets, Plato, and Confucius were for centuries and still are today living and shaping influences. Because of this I have only briefly sketched the early history of black Africa and pre-Columbian America.

I hope I have also avoided the seduction which the historian must feel when material is plentiful. What matters is whether a topic is important, not that we may be lucky enough to have a lot of information about it. The wars and diplomacy of Louis XIV for instance, though vital at the level of French history, seem to me easier to assess briefly in the context of world history than, say, the Chinese Revolution, which needs lengthier exposition. More could be said about the first because we know more, but there is no point in doing so. The same is true of the most recent period of history down to our own day, where we have the most information of all; it is more than ever important to distinguish the forest from the trees and not to mention a topic simply because it is familiar to us from television newscasts or the daily papers. Or to take an example from cultural history, scholars traditionally emphasize what is called the Romantic Movement in the European literary and artistic tradition and clearly it is central to much of the local history of Europe. But it does not seem to me to matter much or play a direct and principal role in world history and therefore little is said about it. Many other examples could be given.

A last point about our subject matter: Although the account which follows reaches something of a climax in the European tradition, this is not another run of that tried and trusted war-horse, Western civilization. Indeed I have laid much heavier emphasis on the non-European world than in most books with a global scope. On the other hand, the great centers of Asian civilization have taken more overall from the traditions whose roots are to be sought in the ancient Near East and Aegean than vice versa. It therefore still seems proper to give far more space to the foundation eras of these legacies than to those of India and China. Closer to modern times, the latter require more attention if we are to trace their subtle interplay with the forces operating on them from the European world.

Some readers, especially those already familiar with other approaches to world history, will thus find new emphases and new distributions of space in this book. If they are surprised, that is all to the good, for a new perspective is a step in education. Rather more weight is also given to social history than usual; this is the soil out of which culture and politics grow. I hope the structure will be considered as a whole and its omissions, inclusions, and treatment of particular events related to the overall aim of the book. I see it as a beginning rather than an end, and if it only generates reasoned disagreement and provokes rethinking of our past, this will be a great deal.

Much of the writing is narrative but not by any means all, for some kinds of history escape narrative and can be expounded more intelligibly in an analytic framework. I hope nonetheless that it will be possible to read this book straight through with a sense of movement—as one does a story in fact.

History is fundamentally a matter of judgment, not knowledge, and I hope this will be kept in mind by my readers. I have tried to indicate the limits of firm knowledge and occasionally to show where more work is required or conclusions must be tentative while scholarly appraisal continues. Thus I hope readers will have a sense, even if it only comes and goes, of the excitement of history as an art and a discipline in addition to a grasp of the major lines of the story of world civilization. To awake this sense is one of the most important things any historian can do, and it has to be done again and again, for every generation.

part IV
THE EUROPEAN AGE

Only one civilization has ever been successful all around the world and it is our own. The statement does not have to be read as a boast. From the days when Greeks borrowed scientific ideas from the Near East and Christianity emerged from Judaism to the sixteenth century when tobacco and potatoes came to Europe from the Americas, many tributary streams big and small, many alien ideas, and many exotic materials fed and fertilized European civilization. The resulting compound proved in the end to have undreamed of and revolutionary power. Between 1500 and 1900 Europeans initiated and carried through certain changes which not only altered forever their relationship to the rest of the world but replaced a world of alternative civilizations with one in which their own exercised irresistible power over all others. The story of how this happened is the central theme of modern history.

In 1500 Europe was still basically the little peninsula at the end of the Eurasian land mass whose achievements could, at best, stand only doubtfully on an equal footing with those of the East. By the beginning of the twentieth century even those parts of the world which Europe did not rule directly or indirectly were either peopled by her stocks or were trying to follow her example.

The first of these areas peopled by Europeans, together with the European heartland, constituted what is sometimes called the "Western world," or was called that until the violent political antagonisms of the twentieth century fractured its unity. If we add to this those parts of the world which did not have European roots but were seeking to remake themselves on European lines, we have what Westerners often referred to in 1900 as "the civilized world," or "civilized mankind."

Such revealing phrases recognized the huge success of one civilization in imposing itself on others. Modern history is at last truly world history, for from about 1500 there is a continuous, not an occasional and accidental, interconnection between events in all countries. Gradually the world became a single arena in which the forces of economics, imperialism, technology, and culture ground up the divisions between the great cultural traditions. Of course this was a cumulative process. It did not happen suddenly in 1500—or at any other date.

Modern history can be divided into at least two distinguishable epochs and they correspond to two distinguishable stages in Europe's evolution. The first period has been called "early modern," and for working purposes we can say that it came to a close around 1800, though some historians choose as early as 1700. But rather than emphasize exact dates, we are concerned here with the processes at work. What happened in early modern history was that the basic structure—political, economic, and social—of a new civilization whose heart was Europe emerged from the tradition-dominated, agrarian, superstitious world of the Middle Ages. This was far from being a neat or well-defined process. In England it happened very quickly; in eastern Europe it was far from complete by 1800. But by then some countries had already laid the foundation for the achievement of the later world hegemony of European civilization, and that is the story of the next epoch of world history. First, our concern is with the foundations on which this civilization's success rested.

chapter 21

Economy and Society in Early Modern Europe

ECONOMY

For most of human history most people have had little choice about ways of providing themselves and their families with shelter and enough to eat. Even the possibility that this might be otherwise has only recently become conceivable for many. It is one of the striking novelties of modern history. An explanation of it has to begin with the economy of early modern Europe: what that economy could provide was one of the most important determinants of a society which was to transform the world.

A new age of statistics

The historical evidence left by this economy is much more statistical than at earlier times. For all sorts of purposes governments came to want to know more and more about the resources or potential resources at their disposal and they began to compile figures. This began in the Middle Ages, but private records, especially of business, also give us much more numerical information after 1500, partly because the multiplication of copies as paper and printing became more common meant that the chance of survival was enormously increased. Commerce began to require more publication of data—the movements of ships or reports of prices, for example. All this has led to more knowledge about the size and shape of change in early modern society than for any previous period. Moreover, as historians have refined their techniques they have tackled even poor or fragmentary sources with much greater success than was possible even a few years ago.

Yet it is important not to exaggerate the value of the data. Until recently the collection of good statistics was very difficult; even quite elementary questions, about, for example, who lived in a certain place, were not easy to answer. It was only in 1801 that the first official census was held in the United Kingdom—nearly eight centuries after the *Domesday Book*. France did not have hers until 1876, or Russia hers (and her only one) until 1897. This is not really surprising. A census or a survey requires a complex and reliable administrative machine and may arouse strong opposition (when governments seek new information, new taxes often follow). Such difficulties are enormously increased where the population is illiterate, and that was true of much of Europe for the greater part of modern history.

It is also true that statistical material can raise as many historical problems as it solves. It can illuminate facts while throwing no light at all on causes. Nevertheless, after 1500 we are more and more in an age of measurement, and this makes it a little easier to agree about what was happening.

Population change

At the end of the fifteenth century the European population began an age of growth which has continued ever since. It falls roughly into two phases. The increase (with some notable local and temporary interruptions) was relatively slow and steady until about the middle of the eighteenth century; this roughly corresponds to the early modern period and has been considered a characteristic of it. In the second phase population growth began to accelerate rapidly and great changes followed. But only the first phase concerns us here because it regulated the way in which modern Europe took shape.

The general trends are fairly clear though they still rest heavily on estimates. In 1500 Europe had slightly more than 100 million inhabitants, two centuries later she had nearly 150 million, and in 1800 almost 200 million. By 1800 Europe had nearly a quarter of the world's inhabitants and contributed largely to the peopling of new lands overseas. By 1800 a reasonable estimate is that something like 2 million Europeans had gone to America north of the Rio Grande, and to the south about 100,000 had settled.

In the sixteenth and seventeenth centuries there were no startling disparities as would later appear between the rate of population growth in Europe and that in other continents. European and non-European populations were less different than they were to become. The average age of death, for example, was still low in Europe and only began to go up in a few countries before 1800. At birth a French peasant of the eighteenth century had a life expectancy of about twenty-two years and only a roughly one-in-four chance of surviving infancy. He was in much the same position as an Indian peasant in 1900 or an Italian under imperial Rome. Comparatively few people survived their forties; since they were less well fed than nowadays, they would have looked old to us at that age and probably rather small in stature and unhealthy looking. As in earlier times women tended to die before men, and this meant that many men made a second or even a third marriage, not, as today, because of divorce, but because they were soon widowers. The average European couple had a fairly short married life. If they were well off they could afford a large family; the poor had smaller ones. There is evidence that some form of family limitation other than abortion and infanticide was already used in some places in the seventeenth century. No doubt economic pressures were at work, but this remains one of those mysterious areas where a largely illiterate society is almost impossible to penetrate.

Europe in 1500 was a continent of villages in which people lived at a fairly low level of subsistence, and it would have seemed very empty to modern eyes. In 1800 the English population was only about a seventh of today's and yet was one of the most tightly packed in Europe. In eastern Europe there were for centuries huge empty spaces which rulers eagerly sought to populate by encouraging immigration in all sorts of ways. Yet towns and cities were all the time growing in number and size, a few of them spectacularly. Paris probably doubled between 1500 and 1700, reaching slightly less than half a million inhabitants. London shot ahead of Paris by going up from about 120,000 to nearly 700,000 in the same two centuries; since the English population was much smaller to start with, this growth meant that the shift to urban life was proportionately much greater there than anywhere else. (The word "suburb" came into use in English in the eighteenth century.) About medium-sized and smaller towns it is hard to generalize; in 1500 nine European cities had more than 100,000 people and two hundred years later there were at least a dozen. It is not many; Europe's predominance in urbanization was not so marked in these centuries as it was to become, and there were still many greater cities on other continents.

Neither urbanization nor population growth was evenly spread. Some regions underwent checks and possibly setbacks in a series of seventeenth-century demographic disasters. Spain, Italy, and Germany all had bad epidemics in the 1630s, and there were other celebrated and more localized outbreaks, such as the Great Plague of London in 1665. Famine was another sporadic and local check; we hear even of cannibalism in the disastrous middle years of the seventeenth century. Poor nutrition and the lower resistance it led to always threatened disaster when there was a bad harvest. When accentuated by warfare—and there was always a great deal in central Europe—famine and disease could be cataclysmic. They followed in the wake of armies and could quickly depopulate a small area. The situation was always precarious because population growth was not matched for a long time by equally decisive growth in the food supply.

Agriculture

In agricultural change, as in so many things, different countries have different histories. Production began to increase again in the middle of the fifteenth century, one sign being the renewed cultivation of land which had reverted to waste during the depopulations of the fourteenth century. Yet greater output from this source is only notable in a few places before 1550 or so. More significant before then were important improvements in techniques which raised the productivity of land, mainly by the increased application of labor, that is, by intensive cultivation. Yet over most of Europe the medieval past long lingered in the countryside. Money only slowly broke into the near self-sufficiency of some communities. Serfdom was actually extended in eastern Europe while dying out elsewhere in these centuries. There was, nonetheless, enough growth—and therefore change—overall to sustain the continuing rise of population.

The two most obvious trends were a new orientation toward producing for the market and technical progress. They were interconnected. When a large population existed it meant markets nearby and therefore an incentive to profit from them. Because the Low Countries even in the fifteenth century were a densely populated area with many towns, they were the first place where important advances were made in the techniques of intensive cultivation. It was also in Flanders that improved drainage opened the way to better pasture and, therefore, to a larger animal population. Another region with many town dwellers was northern Italy where new crops were introduced into Europe from Asia; rice, for example, an important alternative to cereals, appeared in the Arno and Po valleys in the fifteenth century.

From the Netherlands agricultural improvements spread slowly across the Channel, to be elaborated in eastern England. In the seventeenth century London at last became a grain-exporting port, and in the next other Europeans came to England to learn how to farm. The eighteenth century brought improvements in husbandry and animal breeding which were to continue in a direct line to the yields now customary but then unimaginable.

The appearance of the countryside and its occupants was gradually transformed. It was in agriculture that science first revealed what might be done—by experiment, observation, record, and experiment again—to increase man's control of his environment. Such improvement had social consequences, too, for it favored the reorganization of land into bigger farms, the reduction of the number of smallholders (except on land which especially favored them), the employment of wage labor, and high capital investment in buildings, drainage, and machinery. The complete integration of agriculture with the market economy and the treatment of land as a commodity like any other would have to wait for the nineteenth century, even in England, the leader of world agriculture in 1800. Yet by then the way ahead was already beginning to appear.

These agricultural advances in the end eliminated the recurrent dearths which so long checked demographic advance. Perhaps the last time when a great calamity like that of the fourteenth century seemed to threaten everywhere was at the end of the sixteenth century. In the next bad spell, during the middle decades of the following century, England and the United Provinces escaped the worst. Thereafter famine and scarcity became local and national events, gradually counteracted by the increasing availability of imported grain. By the eighteenth century some Mediterranean countries depended for their flour on the rising grain production of the Baltic lands. However, it would be a long time before importation would be a sure resource; often the grain could not be distributed quickly enough, given the state of land transport. France was one country where population grew faster than production in the eighteenth century and imports were necessary; it is certain that the standard of living of many of the French—perhaps most— actually fell as the century went on.

Long-term population growth was clearly an important stimulus to economic expansion but also put strains on the economy which could only be met with difficulty and by no means everywhere. Partly for this reason, agriculture was bound to dominate the European economy in 1800 as it had in 1500, even in France and England, the two countries where commerce and manufacture had progressed most. Moreover, nowhere was more than a small part of the population earning its living in economic activity entirely unconnected with agriculture, though many of those engaged in agriculture were also doing things which included manufacture or trade. Brewers, weavers, and dyers all depended on agriculture indirectly, while many who grew crops or cultivated land also spun, wove, or dealt in commodities for the market.

The rise of European commerce

The commercial sector nevertheless underwent sweeping change from the second half of the fifteenth century when a quickening tempo can be sensed. Europe was regaining something like the commercial vigor she had shown in the thirteenth century. The growth of towns, which both needed and provided a living for specialists, contributed to this as it did to agricultural improvements.

The great fairs and markets of the Middle Ages still continued; so did medieval laws on usury and the restrictive practices of guilds. Yet by 1800 a whole new economic world came into existence, characterized by the widespread adoption of such devices as joint stock companies, life insurance, stock exchanges, banks, paper money, and checks—to name only a few. These were all expressions of a total change fundamental to modern history, the coming of what, for want of a better word, we call capitalism, or the capitalist economy.

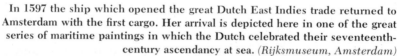

In 1597 the ship which opened the great Dutch East Indies trade returned to Amsterdam with the first cargo. Her arrival is depicted here in one of the great series of maritime paintings in which the Dutch celebrated their seventeenth-century ascendancy at sea. (*Rijksmuseum, Amsterdam*)

Capitalism is a simple word to cover an immensely complicated phenomenon. It was not used as we use it before 1800. Just before that date men talked of "capitalists," but by this they meant men who had accumulated liquid wealth for investment; such an accumulation was a "capital," another word which became common in the eighteenth century. These definitions focus on one of the key elements of capitalism, the prevalence of a money economy, which made possible the accumulation of sums available for investment in commerce or finance, as the owner wished. This meant, of course, that old ideas about what was the morally right or wrong manner to invest money were more and more questioned; it was in the 1630s that modern views about collecting interest—which an earlier time thought the sin of usury—were first put forward.

Along with the free use of liquid wealth in a money economy went a second assumption, that the purpose of all economic activity was private profit; this was a very liberated view in contrast to the medieval position that an individual is defined by social ties and obligations. Together with the new prevalence of money, this emphasis on profit tended to favor large-scale business enterprise. Finally, it should be noted that the money economy from the start more and more linked the power to employ to the chance to accumulate capital, for it was assumed that the controllers of the means of production—buildings, tools, machines—should be those who invested their capital in them, not those who used them.

It was a long time before all this became clear and was recognized, as the delay in arriving at the term "capitalism" perhaps suggests. And it would be long after 1800 before capitalist principles dominated industry as they already dominated commerce and finance before that date. Furthermore, some of the roots of this went back a long way so that the phenomenon is not easily pinned down in historical terms. Nevertheless, when thirteenth-century merchants put money into the Italian textile business, a movement began which would transform the world and make possible the creation of wealth on an undreamed of scale and an expansion of commerce virtually uninterrupted (except by war) until 1930.

Until the end of the seventeenth century little of this revolution was visible; change in the nonagricultural economy was very slow though real. Many authorities agree that this was a period of accumulating wealth, when men put together the fortunes which would generate faster and greater enterprise. With the quickening pace in the sixteenth century the economic center of gravity continued to shift from southern to northwestern Europe, from the Mediterranean to the Atlantic. Part of the explanation of the transfer is political trouble and invasion, such as ruined Italy in the early sixteenth century; another part is comprised of such short-lived but crucial pressures as the Portuguese harassment of Jews, which sent so many of them with their commercial skills to the Low Countries at about the same time.

Antwerp provided the great commercial success story of the early sixteenth century; it collapsed after a few decades in a welter of political and economic troubles, and in the seventeenth century Amsterdam and London were to surpass it. In each case profits from trade with a well-populated

The heart of a new commercial world: the Amsterdam Exchange in the early seventeenth century. *(Museum Boymans-van Beuningen, Rotterdam)*

hinterland provided opportunities for diversification into service and manufacturing industries, and into banking. The old banking supremacy of the medieval Italian cities passed first to the Low Countries and Germany in the sixteenth century and then, finally, to Holland and Belgium. In the seventeenth century the Bank of Amsterdam and in the next the Bank of England were already great international economic forces. About them clustered other smaller banks and merchant houses undertaking operations of credit and finance.

In the eighteenth century the first European paper currencies and checks appeared. By then the joint stock company, which was to prove a uniquely successful way of mobilizing capital for new enterprises, had emerged from older forms of partnership. This further increased the flow of paper and negotiable instruments. People began to buy and sell stock and shares in companies; their prices were quoted in London coffee houses in the seventeenth century. The foundation of the London Stock Exchange soon followed. By 1800 stock exchanges also existed in many other countries. Numerous schemes for accumulating capital were floated in London, Paris, and Amsterdam. Lotteries at one time enjoyed a vogue; so did some spectacular investment ventures, the most notorious being the British South

Sea "Bubble" in which shares rose from £100 to £1,000 before this scheme to finance Pacific trade exploded. All the time the world was growing more commercial, more accustomed to the idea that money could make money; it was acquiring the economic apparatus as well as the economic attitudes of the modern world.

Overseas trade

Diplomats gave much greater attention than before to commercial questions in the seventeenth century. The English and Dutch even went to war over trade in 1652 and 1664, and fears of a French trade monopoly with the Spanish empire contributed to the outbreak of a general European war in 1701; trade was also at issue in the so-called War of Jenkins' Ear between Spain and Great Britain in 1737. Governments also interfered in economic matters (with the best intentions) by granting certain companies monopoly privileges, which made it easier for them to raise capital by offering some security for a return. Though monopolies eventually fell out of favor, commercial considerations increasingly helped to shape both policy and law. The primitive economy of early capitalism benefited as much from government as do modern corporations.

Government's close interest in trade reflected the most important structural development in the commerce of early modern Europe, the rapid expansion from about 1650 of its overseas components. A growing population and some assurance of adequate transport (always cheaper by water than by land) built up an international trade in cereals, while shipbuilding itself promoted the movement of such commodities as pitch, flax, and timber, at first staples of Baltic trade and later important in the economy of North America.

By the late seventeenth century, though the closed trade of Spain and Portugal with their transatlantic colonies was important, overseas commerce was dominated by the Dutch, the first great maritime trading nation, and their rivals, the English. The Dutch were successful because they supplied the salted herrings from the North Sea needed by European markets and had the technical advantage of a particularly suitable bulk-carrying vessel called the flute, or fly-boat. Gradually they were displaced by the English but they maintained a wide spread of colonies and trading stations until the twentieth century. England's maritime supremacy was based in the Atlantic. Fish were important in her trade too. The English caught the immensely nutritious (and therefore immensely valuable) cod on the Newfoundland banks, dried and salted it ashore, and then sold it in Mediterranean countries where demand was great. Gradually, too, both Dutch and English broadened and diversified their carrying trade and became dealers in goods themselves.

All this was taking place in a setting of growing colonial empires. It is really somewhat misleading to speak of Europe when talking of overseas trade, because by the eighteenth century we are in the presence of an oceanic economy, at least in outline. The Portuguese had opened the trade to the Far East in the fifteenth century, and the Dutch, British, and French all followed them there. Around the Atlantic a community had come into being by 1700 which was linked across thousands of miles not only by the ties of government but also by those of trade.

Slaves played an increasingly important part in the developing oceanic economy. Overwhelmingly, they were from Africa. Most were sent across the Atlantic, mainly to the Caribbean colonies, Brazil, and British settlements on the North American mainland. The demographic, economic, and political effects have continued to this day, but here we are only concerned with the importance of slavery to the economy.

It could be seen most obviously in the labor it made available to the Americas, though slavery was not uniformly spread among them for climatic reasons. Most slaves were employed in agriculture or domestic service; Negro craftsmen or, later, factory workers were unusual. Slavery's resulting economic importance, it came to be argued, was so great that the capital invested in slave labor justified the retention of an obvious moral evil. The huge profits involved in the trade itself help to explain another cruelty, the suffering imposed upon the captives packed in the ships which took them across the Atlantic. This could produce appalling death rates, but the cost of slaves in Africa was small and profits in the Americas were great.

Because of its commercial importance the slave trade led to governments competing for a share in it in the seventeenth and eighteenth centuries. The first African slavers were Portuguese; the English entered the trade

The tide turned against slavery in the Western world after 1800. This nineteenth-century print celebrates one accompaniment of the coming of French rule (the tricolor is about to be hoisted while the sailors present arms), the striking off of the wooden fetters of liberated slaves. *(The Bettmann Archive)*

in the reign of Elizabeth I and soon clashed with them. Other nations, such as the Dutch, sought either to break into so lucrative a trade or monopolize it in their own colonies. Slavery was important as one of the generators of profits which sustained commercial expansion and would help in the end to pay for industrialization.

Early industrialization

Before 1800, though there were some examples of industrial concentration in several European countries, the growth of both manufacturing and extractive industry usually meant the multiplication of small-scale artisan production and its technical elaboration. Small workshops, not factories, produced most of Europe's manufactured goods throughout the early modern period.

During the Middle Ages skills had been built up in traditional occupations and extended into new fields. The towns had been the centers where this happened, but the craftsmen often moved about following demand. So much is easy to see, but it is harder to explain what it was in the European mind which pressed the craftsmen forward; it does not seem to have happened elsewhere. By 1500 great numbers of craftsmen were already accustomed to investigating new processes and exploring new techniques. Two centuries of gunnery had brought mining and metallurgy to a high pitch, and scientific instruments and mechanical clocks testified to a wide diffusion of skill in the making of precision goods. This would lead in the end to a reversal of a traditional relationship. For centuries the craftsmen of Asia had astounded Europeans by their skill and the quality of their work. The magnificent textiles and ceramics of the Orient dazzled Western eyes. (Such words as china, muslin, and calico commemorate it.) Then in the fourteenth and fifteenth centuries supremacy in craftsmanship, at least in mechanical and engineering skills, had passed to Europe. By 1500 Asian potentates already sought Europeans who could teach them how to make effective firearms and avidly collected mechanical toys which were the commonplaces of European fairs.

The earliest European industries were closely related to agriculture and they continued to be important long after 1500. Textile manufacture was one, brewing another. Where they developed, concentrations of supporting trades grew up. Antwerp was the great Continental port of entry for English cloth, and so it was there that finishing and dyeing establishments had appeared to work up further the textiles flowing through the port. Wool merchants shaped the early pattern of industrial growth by putting out to isolated rural spinners and weavers the raw materials they needed. The presence of minerals was another locating factor; mining and metallurgy were the first important industrial activities not linked closely to agriculture.

Early industrial complexes grew by accretion, but sometimes they stagnated or even underwent a measure of dissolution because of emigration. This seems to have happened in Italy. Her medieval preeminence in industry disappeared in the sixteenth century (probably because of a series of wars fought on the peninsula by foreign monarchs), while the industrial importance of the Low Countries and western and southern Germany — the old Carolingian heartland — lasted another century or so until England, the Dutch Netherlands, and Sweden became the new industrial leaders. In the eighteenth century Russia's extractive industries would add her to this list. By that time other factors were beginning to enter the equation of economic development.

Economic fluctuation

A long-term picture of expansion and growth requires much qualification. Agriculture's predominance still meant that at any time before 1800 a bad harvest could cause famine and grave demographic damage. Bad harvests, it has been said, made France "one great hospital" in 1708–1709. The margin of agricultural surplus to needs was still narrow, though gradually widening in some countries.

There were also troublesome longer fluctuations in European economic life. Not long after 1500 it began to be noticed that prices were rising with unprecedented speed. Locally this trend could be very sharp, doubling costs in a year. Though nothing like that rate was anywhere maintained, the general effect seems to have been a roughly fourfold rise in European prices in a century. Given twentieth-century rates of inflation, this does not seem very shocking, but in the sixteenth century it was quite novel and had great and grave repercussions. Some landowners were able to raise rents and increase the yields from their feudal dues, but others had to sell out. (In this unpleasant sense, inflation usually makes for social mobility.) Among the poor the effects were almost universally harsh, for though the price of agricultural produce shot up, money wages did not keep pace and real wages therefore fell. This was sometimes made worse by special local factors. In England, for example, high wool prices tempted landlords to enclose common land in order to raise sheep on it. The wretched peasant who had been used to grazing an animal or two on this land could no longer do so and often starved in consequence; thus, as one contemporary commentator put it, sheep ate men. In the 1540s and 1550s there was popular revolt everywhere and disorder of a new sharpness and severity. People did not know what was happening to them, but they did not like it and sought scapegoats and relief in the traditional way.

Much ink has been spent by historians on explaining this century-long price rise. They no longer feel satisfied with the explanation first put forward by contemporary observers, that the essential cause was the new supply of bullion flowing from Spanish mines in the New World; it is clear that inflation was well under way before American bullion began to arrive in any significant quantity. Later, it may have aggravated things, but bullion was probably always supplementary to the fundamental pressure imposed by a growth in population at a time when big advances in productivity still lay in the future.

Prices continued to rise until the beginning of the seventeenth century; then they began to level off and occasionally even showed signs of falling until a slower increase was resumed toward 1700. This halt in the inflationary trend reflected a general crisis in the seventeenth century, which produced the second notable long-term economic fluctuation of the early modern period. Broadly speaking, it was marked by a recession of trade in central and southern Europe (the Dutch more or less escaped this by expanding vigorously their carrying business), a dwindling of the money flow, and falling prices. It, too, emphasized the continuing vulnerability of European economic life.

SOCIETY

Social history is just as fundamental to political change as economics but much more difficult to pin down or be precise about. A society is a group of people with certain characteristics which can be enumerated and studied quantitatively, and it also has certain needs and ways of satisfying them which can be counted. But it is more than this. A society also has certain attitudes and habits and thinks about itself in a particular way. These thoughts (among other things) are very important in determining social structure, which is not limited to the way wealth is distributed or the relative numbers of young and old. It also encompasses the way people treat one another, the duties and obligations they think follow from differences among them which they consider important, and the rules they make as a result of thinking about these things. Furthermore, changes in a society usually occur very gradually, and their outward signs may be confusing and hard to interpret. This makes it difficult to register social change (until very recent times when some acceleration is noticeable) except in the long run, over the passage of a great many years. Even then, though it is easy to be aware that there were important social changes throughout the European world between 1500 and 1800, it would be silly not to expect every generalization to have important exceptions.

Economics and social life

One great change with roots far back in the fourteenth century still operated only very unevenly over Europe by 1800. This was a growing tendency to view agriculture as a matter of business. It was one of the forces bringing changes to the traditional shape of rural society. Even when forms were preserved, the reality crumbled. Although feudal lordship still existed in France in the 1780s, for example, the lord might never see his tenants, might not be of noble blood, and might draw nothing from his lordship except sums of money which represented his claims on his tenants' labor, time, and produce. It had become a purely economic tie. Further east, on the other hand, the feudal relationship remained more real. In part this reflected an alliance between rulers and nobles in eastern Europe to take advantage of the new markets for grain and timber among the growing populations of western and southern Europe. In the seventeenth and eighteenth centuries, they tied their peasants to the land by debt and law, exacting heavier and heavier labor services. In Russia serfdom came to be the very basis of society. In England, at the other extreme, even the commercialized "feudalism" practiced in France had gone by the eighteenth century, though the barbaric kingdom of Scotland, to which it was joined after 1707, was still exacting labor service from serfs in industry. Such variations restrict all possible generalizations about social change, but if distinctions are made within Europe, some trends can be observed.

In the three centuries before 1800 the most prosperous countries and those with the most developed commercial and urban life show a notable change in their notion of what constituted social status and how it might be recognized and provided for, and it was remarked on already in the seventeenth century. This involved a shift from personal ties to market relationships as the definition of individuals: people came to think of themselves less and less as lords and vassals and more and more as employers and employees, landowners and laborers—or simply as rich and poor. Some also began to think of society less as a network of corporations which defined and protected their members' rights and more as a mass of individuals.

Though one country, the United Provinces, was by the mid-seventeenth century in effect ruled by merchants (the oligarchs of Amsterdam, the center of Holland, its richest province), such a change was nowhere quite complete by 1800. Men still respected noble birth and blood, even in Amsterdam, but no longer found it obvious that the distinctions ought to be embodied in laws. Some had begun to think that describing society in terms of social order with legally distinct rights and obligations no longer expressed its reality. They had also ceased to feel so confident that the sanctions and teachings of religion upheld a particular social order. In eighteenth-century England people might still believe that God called men to their stations in life, but this was not quite the same thing as saying that a fixed unchanging order was the expression of God's will—God might intend some industrious and virtuous poor to rise in the world.

In these centuries old hierarchies were under pressure from an increasing social mobility brought about by the rise of towns, the growing predominance of the market economy, the appearance of new commercial opportunities, and the spread of literacy and awareness. But the degree of pressure varied. Broadly speaking, three situations can be distinguished. In the east (in Russia and almost to the same extent in eastern Poland, East Prussia, and Hungary) agrarian society was little disturbed. In a second group of countries clashes between the established order and the new economic and social worlds coming into being provoked demands for change. France is the outstanding example, but in some of the German states, Belgium, and parts of Italy, there were signs of the same sort of strain. A third pattern prevailed in those relatively open societies, such as England, the Netherlands, and colonial North America, where the formal distinctions of society lost much of their legal significance by 1800. Even in the sixteenth century English society seems much more fluid than that of Continental countries, and the

United States Constitution two centuries later would specifically prohibit the conferring of hereditary titles. In such places individualism had a scope almost untrammeled by law, whatever the real restraints of custom and opportunity. Though even in advanced countries there was still much that we could find strange, and the nineteenth century would find its immediate forbears unprogressive, these countries were moving further and faster toward modernity than the great majority in the rest of the world.

Voltaire, a French observer of the early eighteenth century, was struck by the fact that in England a great merchant could be as esteemed as a nobleman. This may have slightly exaggerated things and blurred important nuances, but it is certainly remarkable — and part of the story of Great Britain's rise to world power — that the political class which governed eighteenth-century England was based on land and fiercely reflected landed values, yet constantly asserted the commercial interests of the country and accepted in this area the leadership and guidance of the merchants and bankers of London. Though politics was a matter of disputed places and conflicting traditions within the landed class, somehow interests prospered which in other countries conflicted with inherited rights. It is difficult not to link this with the limited legal privilege of an English peer, which was confined to the right to be summoned to Parliament, to have personal access to the crown, and to trial by his peers. Apart from this, although he might enjoy great wealth and social esteem, an English peer's only other legal distinction was one shared by the majority of Englishmen: he had no vote in the election of members to the House of Commons.

The correspondence between the advanced social evolution of the Netherlands and the United Kingdom and their economic, especially commercial, success is striking. Their economic achievements were once largely attributed to their religion: Protestantism, it was said, provided an ethic for capitalism. This no longer seems plausible. There were too many Catholic capitalists, and France and Spain were still important trading countries in the eighteenth century. Indeed for much of that century France enjoyed something like the same rate of economic growth as the United Kingdom, though she later fell behind.

This should remind us that economic growth after 1500 was most pronounced in countries with Atlantic access. Of course there was more to it than mere geographical position. Mediterranean and eastern Europe differed from the countries of the north and west in more than their locations. But the regional pattern of Atlantic predominance established in the seventeenth and eighteenth centuries was not to be seriously modified until the twentieth.

Above all the European east remained backward. On its southern flank lay the Balkans and the frontier with Turkey, a zone of warfare, banditry, and border raids for most of these centuries. In some areas (Hungary, for example) the effects of Turkish occupation had been so bad as to depopulate the country. When the Turks were driven back and the regions reacquired for Europe, care was taken to tie the peasantry to the land. The serf population of Russia also grew larger as a proportion of the whole in this period, and harsher laws guaranteed their masters control of them. In other eastern countries (Prussia, for example) nobles increased their powers over those on their lands who were not serfs. Kings could not govern in the teeth of their nobles unless they could rely on some other force; even when they wanted to, they dared not side with peasantry against its masters.

The cumulative effect of such differences between eastern and western Europe was to create by 1800 a rough social division on the Oder. To the west lay countries whose institutions were evolving slowly toward a more open society. To the east authoritarian governments presided over agrarian societies where a minority of landholders enjoyed great powers over a largely bound peasantry. Much of later European history was implicit in this distinction.

Women

The division between east and west was even discernible in the ways women were treated, though here another distinction may also be drawn — between Mediterranean Europe and the north. In these centuries the formal legal status of women remained what it had been, only to be questioned at the end of this period. Nevertheless, the real independence of women, especially of upper-class women, seems to have been increased in the more ad-

The Enlightenment in session. One of the most famous pictures of the eighteenth century. It shows an assembly of learned and literary society — among those present are d'Alembert, Helvétius, Buffon, Réaumur, Fontenelle, Turgot, Montesquieu, Diderot, Rameau, Rousseau, and Condillac — in the salon of a lady of intellectual tastes. Voltaire's bust presides over the gathering. *(Musée des Beaux-Arts, Lauros-Giraudon)*

vanced countries. Even in the fifteenth century foreigners had remarked that Englishwomen possessed unusual freedom. Their lead does not seem to have diminished, but by the eighteenth century a well-born woman in France also could enjoy considerable independence.

The improved position of women in the eighteenth century was due in part to the appearance of a society which had room for gatherings independent of religious and family ritual and founded on something other than a royal court. At the end of the seventeenth century Englishmen began gathering in the London coffee houses which were to give birth to the first clubs; the salon, a social gathering in the lady's drawing room of friends and acquaintances, appears in the next. Some French salons were important intellectual centers, which indicates that it had become proper and even fashionable for a woman to show interest in things of the mind. Madame de Pompadour, the mistress of Louis XV, exemplified this when she chose to have a book included in her portrait—Montesquieu's sociological treatise, *De l'Esprit des Lois*. But even when women did not aspire to bluestockings (an expression, significantly, coined in the eighteenth century) the salon and the appearance of a society independent of the court presented them with a real, if limited, escape from the confinement of the family. At the end of the eighteenth century we have reached the age of the female artist and novelist and of the acceptance of the fact that spinsterhood need not mean retirement to a cloister.

Where these changes came from is not easy to see. The English journal *Spectator* addressed itself to women readers as well as men soon after 1700. Perhaps it helped that the eighteenth century produced such conspicuous examples of women with great political influence—an English queen and five empresses (one Austrian and four Russian) who ruled in their own right and did so with success. But the early history of female emancipation still awaits study.

In any case, none of this touched the unchanging roles of the overwhelming majority of women in even the most advanced societies of early modern Europe. The industrial jobs which would provide the first great force to prise apart the unquestioned certainties of traditional life had not yet appeared. Those certainties may have weighed most crushingly in the primitive villages of Poland or in southern Spain where Moorish influences had intensified the subordination and seclusion of women, but they were everywhere still heavy in 1800.

chapter 22

Authority and Its Challengers

The Middle Ages no more came to a sudden end in government and law than in economics and social life. In certain respects and in some places old ideas were strengthened and elaborated after 1500. More and more social facts were forced into what has been called the "corporate" organization of society, the grouping of men in bodies with privileges which protected their members and defined their status. In most countries people also continued to believe that the state should uphold the claims and status of one religious confession; religion and society were everywhere intertwined and the authority of churches established by law. Whatever their reality in terms of power, the Holy Roman Empire still existed in 1800 and so did the temporal power of the pope. Everywhere, continuity was stressed. In 1800 the king of France was still a member of a family claiming direct descent from the Capetians, though he no longer came from the same branch of the family as in 1500 (and indeed was in exile in 1800). In England as late as 1820 a king's champion rode into Westminster Hall in full armor at the coronation banquet of King George IV to uphold that monarch's title against all comers.

While the enormous weight of the past must be given its due, it was nonetheless true that in these three centuries power and authority generally tended to flow away from the institutions of the feudal past, whether they were great or small. This tendency had already begun in the fifteenth century. The idea of Christendom, for example, though it might be important in emotional, even subconscious ways, effectively lost all political reality in this period. Christian princes exposed to the Ottoman onslaught might appeal to their fellow Christians for help, popes might still use the rhetoric of crusade, but the reality, as the Turks well knew, was that Christian states would follow their own interests and even ally with the infidel if necessary. This was the era of realpolitik, of the subordination of principle and honor to intelligent calculation of the interests of the state. Though Europeans came more and more to see the great distinctions of culture which separated them from other civilizations, they hardly recognized that there might be an advantage in creating or reviving institutions which acknowledged their essential unity as empire or papacy had done, however inadequately, in the Middle Ages. Only a few thinkers between 1500 and 1800 advocated the building of institutions which would transcend the state.

The idea of Christendom was undermined by two forces. One of them, for want of a better name, we must call nationalism though it was long mingled with and masked by dynasticism. The second was the great religious upheaval of the sixteenth century which ended the idea of universal papal authority. The Protestant Reformation, of course, did much more than this, but here we are concerned with its political impact. It flowed into the political channels available to it, dynasticism and nationalism, and in the process deepened and broadened them. The only conceivable general authority other than the Church was the Holy Roman Empire, and that institution had been of small account as an authority since the fourteenth century; it came more and more to resemble any other state in that its real power rested on the actual resources available to an emperor from his own hereditary lands.

THE GROWTH OF STATE POWER

While restraints on the state from above all but vanished by 1800, restraints on it from below were also much weakened. Here it is important not to be misled by forms. The general trend of these three centuries was for Europeans to show greater readiness to accept the idea of legislative sovereignty, in other words to think that, provided the authority of the state were in the right hands, there should be no restriction upon its power to make laws.

This idea was rarely grasped clearly, which is not surprising for it was an enormous break with the thinking of the past. A medieval man would have considered it social and juridical as well as theological blasphemy to believe that there might not exist chartered freedoms inaccessible to change by subsequent lawmakers, fundamental laws which would always be respected, or laws of God which could never be traversed by those of men. English lawyers of the seventeenth century floundered in disagreement about what the fundamental laws of the land might be, but all agreed some must exist; a century later the greatest legal minds of France were doing just the same. Frenchmen went on throughout a great revolution trying to write constitutions based on declarations of rights which might not be infringed. Englishmen also tended to act as if there were a special sanctity about property and certainly talked a lot about it. Nevertheless, restraints in both countries proved meaningless. In both England and France by 1800 there was no sphere of life which was thought inaccessible to the law, that is, to the will of the sovereign, whether king, people, or parliament. In the end there emerged in both countries (as to a greater or lesser degree in most others) acceptance of the idea that a legally unrestrained lawmaking power was the characteristic mark of the state.

This took a long time. For most of the history of early modern Europe the process is masked by the fact that the prevalent governmental form was monarchical. Struggles about royal power make up much of European history in these centuries. Some resisted it on the theory that it was wrong for *any* government to have powers such as some monarchs claimed (this might be termed the medieval, or conservative, defense of freedom). Others argued that such powers could properly exist but were being gathered into the wrong hands (this may be called the modern, or liberal, defense of freedom). Confusingly, the two claims were often mixed up.

Unequivocally, the strengthening of the state first manifested itself as the growing power of kings and princes. One indicator in the sixteenth and seventeenth centuries was the decline in most countries of the representative institutions which emerged in the later Middle Ages. By 1789 monarchies little hindered by the existence of effective and continuing representative bodies ruled most of Europe; the main exception was Great Britain. Kings had come to enjoy powers which would have seemed remarkable to medieval barons and burghers. The phenomenon is sometimes described as the rise of absolute monarchy, and providing we do not attribute too great a degree of effective power to the monarchs concerned (for the actual business of governing was very demanding and uncertain), the term is acceptable.

The roots of absolutism lay in the much greater degree of mastery rulers obtained over their subjects in the sixteenth century. Everywhere, or almost everywhere, the relative strength of the crown then greatly improved. New financial resources meant that standing armies and artillery could protect kings against great nobles who did not have such advantages. In some countries the monarchy was able to ally itself with a developing sense of nationhood. In many places, too, in the late fifteenth century people desired an end to the disorder rising from internal strife and were ready to accept the government of someone who would guarantee stability and peace. While there were special reasons in almost every case, nearly everywhere monarchs raised themselves further above the level of the greatest nobles and buttressed their new pretensions to respect and authority with cannons and taxation.

THE RENAISSANCE STATE: STRENGTHS AND WEAKNESSES

In the sixteenth and early seventeenth centuries the growth of monarchical power brought about the apogee of what is sometimes called the Renaissance state. This is a rather grandiose name for a structure that has been called "at bottom, a great and expanding bureaucracy, a huge system of administrative centralization, staffed by an ever-growing multitude of 'courtiers' or 'officers.'" This is clear enough if we remember the implied antithesis: the medieval kingdom whose governmental functions were often in large measure delegated to feudal and personal dependents or to corporations (of which the Church was the greatest).

Of course, neither of these models of political organization ever appeared in a pure form. Royal officials had long existed, and even today states sometimes delegate functions and authority to corporations such as trade unions. Though the multiplication of officials directly dependent upon the crown and the standardization of administrative procedures are both very obvious in the sixteenth century, there was no sudden transition to the modern state: it took centuries. Many obstacles to such an evolution had to be overcome.

One was a simple lack of competent officials. No other monarchy used the English device of delegating local government to resident notables employed as royal justices of the peace. Elsewhere (and in England, too, as Tudor rebellions showed) the provincial nobility had to be treated with care. Rebellion was not an exceptional event but a continuing fact of life for the sixteenth-century statesman. Royal troops might prevail in the end, but no monarch wanted to be reduced to reliance on force—it was too expensive. The French nobility's turbulence right down to the middle of the seventeenth century, the effects of antagonizing local interest in England during the same period, and Habsburg difficulties in unifying their territories at the expense of local magnates all show this. The United Kingdom had its last feudal rebellion only in 1745; other countries had theirs even later.

Because of the danger of rebellion and the inadequacy of machinery, taxation could not be pressed too far, yet officials and armies had to be paid. One way of ensuring officials an income was to allow them to charge fees or extract perquisites from those members of the public who needed their services. For obvious reasons, this was not a complete answer. Rulers still needed to raise greater sums for their own treasuries. Exploiting royal domains might increase revenues somewhat, but all monarchs, sooner or later, were driven to seek new taxation. It was a problem few could solve for there were technical obstacles which could not be tackled until the nineteenth century. But great fertility of imagination was shown for three centuries in inventing new taxes. Broadly speaking, only consumption (through such indirect means as customs, excise, or sales taxes) and real property could be reached by the tax gatherer. In each case the effect bore disproportionately upon the poorest, who spent a larger part of their small disposal incomes on necessities than the wealthy.

Finally, the medieval idea of immunity lay across the path of evolution toward a modern notion of the state and its power. In 1500 it was generally accepted that there were areas, persons, and spheres of action which were especially sacrosanct. They might be defended by an ancient and irrevocable royal grant, such as those guaranteeing the judicial privileges of many cities, by a contractual agreement, such as was said to be the English Magna Carta (a series of concessions forced from a king by his barons in 1215), by immemorial custom, or by divine law. The supreme example was the Church: its properties were not normally subject to lay taxation; it possessed jurisdiction in its courts over matters thus taken out of the hands of royal justice; and it controlled important social and economic institutions. But a province, a town, a group, or a family might enjoy similar immunities, usually from jurisdiction or taxation. Even the French king had to remember, for example, that in Brittany he was not king but duke; his lands were related to one another almost as a collection of little kingdoms. Such were the realities which qualified the power of the Renaissance state, and it often found it hard to do other than accept them. Yet the future in the end lay with the bureaucrats and their files.

THE REFORMATION

The consolidation of state power was accelerated by the great crisis which shook Western Christianity in the early sixteenth century and destroyed forever the old medieval unity of the faith, the Protestant Reformation. Its detonator was yet another calling into question of papal authority, whose form and theory had successfully survived so many challenges. But this time the issues could not be contained, and without anyone expecting it, a constitutional and theological quarrel within the Church became a revolution in secular history and civilization.

There was nothing new about demands for reform. Nor was the encroachment by princes on the pope's authority over local churches unknown. The awareness that papacy and curia did not necessarily serve the interests of all Christians was well grounded by 1500. Some critics had already gone on from this to theological dissent. Fifteenth-century Europe had been marked by a deep, uneasy devotional swell; there had been a sense of looking for new answers to spiritual questions and of looking for them outside the limits laid down by ecclesiastical authority. Heresy had never been blotted out, it had only been contained.

In the fifteenth century there also appeared another current in religious life, one perhaps more profoundly subversive than heresy because it might in the end undercut the traditional religious outlook itself. This was the growth of a learned, humanistic, rational, skeptical style of thought which, for want of a better word, we may call Erasmian after the man who embodied its ideals most clearly in the eyes of contemporaries. Erasmus was profoundly loyal to his faith. He knew himself to be a Christian, and that meant, unquestionably, that he remained within the Church. Of that Church he had a vision which, as his satirical comments on the clergy of his day show, implied reformation. He sought a simpler devotion and a purer pastorate. But the authority of the Church, above all of the papacy, he did not challenge. Nonetheless, his correspondence with colleagues the length and breadth of Europe had a subversive tone. They learnt from him to disentangle the teachings of the faith from the Aristotelian mummifications of scholastic philosophy. In his edition of the Greek New Testament Erasmus made available an instrument which provided a firm basis for argument on doctrine at a time when Greek was again becoming widespread. His learning also exposed the spuriousness of texts on which bizarre dogmatic structures had been raised.

Yet this was only indirect subversion of authority. Erasmus and those who shared his viewpoint did not attack outright the papacy, the ultimate religious authority. The critical attitudes of humanists, like heresy, discontent with clerical behavior, and the cupidity of princes, were in the air at the beginning of the sixteenth century, waiting—as many of these things had long waited—for the man and the occasion. They were turned into religious revolution by the act of a German monk in 1517. What followed was to fragment a Christian unity intact in the West since the suppression of the Arians in the late sixth century.

The Ministry of the Word. Luther holds before him the Bible. The portrait was probably copied from one done from life by Lucas Cranach the Younger. *(Bildarchiv Foto Marburg)*

Luther

Unlike Erasmus, the international man, Martin Luther lived nearly all his life in a small German town, out-of-the-way Wittenberg on the Elbe. He was an Augustinian monk, deeply read in theology, somewhat tormented in spirit, who had already come to the conclusion that he must preach the Scriptures in a new light, to present a forgiving God not a punitive one. This need not have made him a revolutionary; the orthodoxy of his views was not in question until he came into conflict with the papacy.

Luther had been to Rome and had not liked what he saw there: the papal city seemed a worldly place and its ecclesiastical rulers no better than they should be. Thus he was not disposed to feel warmly toward a Dominican monk who arrived in the neighborhood peddling indulgences, papal certificates which assured the possessor that some of the penalties incurred by him for sin would be remitted in payment of a fee (which went toward building the magnificent cathedral of St. Peter then rising in Rome). Accounts of the preaching of this man were brought to Luther by peasants. What the Dominican had said to them was not only misleading but outrageous, and the crudity of the transaction he promoted reflected one of the most unattractive faces of medieval Catholicism. It outraged Luther who was deeply conscious of the overwhelming seriousness of the transformation necessary in a man's life before he could be sure of redemption. He formulated his protests against this and certain other practices of the papacy in a set of ninety-five Latin theses for debate in which he set out his views. In the tradition of medieval scholarly disputation he posted them on the door of the castle church in Wittenberg on October 31, 1517.

Luther got the debate he sought. He sent his theses to the archbishop of Mainz, primate of Germany, who sent them on to Rome asking that Luther be forbidden by his Order to preach on this theme. By this time the theses had been put into German. Technology transformed the situation: they were printed and circulated everywhere in Germany. Soon, only the protection of his ruler, the elector of Saxony, who refused to surrender him, saved Luther. The delay in scotching the chicken of heresy in the egg was fatal. Luther's Order abandoned him, but his university supported him and soon the papacy found itself confronted by a national movement of grievance against Rome. "It is time the glorious Teutonic people should cease to be the puppet of the Roman pontiff," wrote Luther. He had discovered that he was a literary genius of astonishing fluency and productivity, and he was the first to exploit the huge possibilities of the printed pamphlet. Within two years Luther was being called a Hussite, but by then the Reformation had become entangled in German politics.

Even in the Middle Ages, would-be reformers had looked to secular rulers to accomplish what they believed the papacy could not or would not. This did not necessarily mean going outside the fold of the faith; only a little while before Luther the authority of the Catholic Kings had been brought to bear on the problems facing the Spanish church and reformed it. But often secular intervention had encouraged smoldering embers of heresy to break out again. Though kings did not like heretics, an appeal to lay authority was likely to open the way to changes which went further than perhaps their authors had intended.

This, it seems, was the case with Luther, once he had his elector's support. His arguments had soon run beyond questions about the desirability and scope of practical reform and begun to attack papal authority. From there he went on further still and elaborated a theology which said that men were justified—that is, set aside for eternal salvation—not by observance of the sacraments only, but by faith. This was an intensely individualistic position and struck at the root of traditional teaching, which saw no salvation possible outside the Church. Yet it may be noted that when asked for his view Erasmus would not condemn Luther.

In 1520 Luther was excommunicated. Before a wondering audience he burned the bull of excommunication in the same fire as the books of canon law. He continued to preach and write. Summoned to explain himself before the imperial Diet, Luther refused to retract his views, and Germany seemed on the verge of civil war. After leaving the Diet under a safe-conduct, Luther disappeared; he had been kidnapped for his own safety. In 1521 Emperor Charles V placed him under the imperial ban.

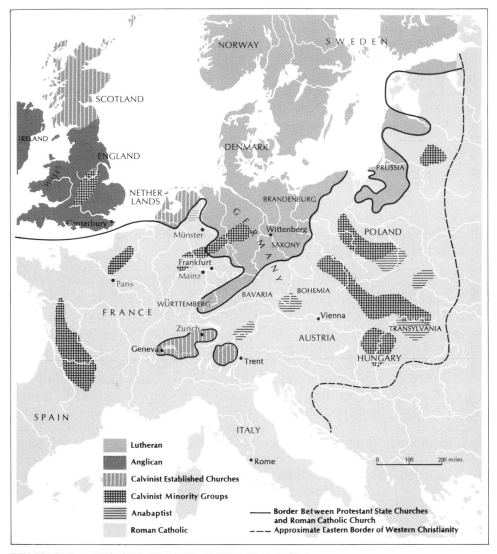

RELIGIOUS DIVISIONS IN 16TH-CENTURY EUROPE
People of different religious denominations were so intermixed after the Protestant
Reformation that a map can only show the division of territory between them on the
theoretical basis of what was legally the established faith. This map shows the
positions on that basis in about 1560, and it should be remembered that thousands of
Catholics and Protestants lived in lands which were officially of a faith they did
not share.

Luther was an outlaw, but Lutheranism had become a German political
fact. Luther's doctrines appealed to the many anticlerical Germans. His followers spread them by preaching and by the dissemination of his German
translation of the New Testament. Lutheranism soon divided the German
princes, who entangled it in their own complicated relations with the em-

peror and his vague authority over them. Wars ensued. It was during this time that the word "Protestant" was first used. By 1548 Germany was irreparably divided into Catholic and Protestant states, and it came to be accepted that the prevailing religion of each state would be that of its ruler. In both Catholic and Protestant Germany religious communities now looked as never before to the political authority to uphold them in a world of competing creeds.

Protestantism elsewhere

Lutheranism took root in Germany and eventually in Scandinavia, but by then other varieties of Protestantism had appeared, some linked with social unrest. One important and socially radical group were the Anabaptists. Their essential theological distinction was that they opposed infant baptism, but when they seized power in Münster in 1534, their leaders introduced communism of property and polygamy, which confirmed their opponents' fears and brought a ferocious suppression down upon them. Religious dissent had long been linked to social subversion in many eyes.

Huldreich Zwingli, a more radical theologian than Luther, briefly led the rejection of Catholicism in Zurich, but Geneva was to be Switzerland's most important Protestant city. John Calvin (1509–1564) was a French theologian who had broken with Catholicism under the influence of Protestant evangelists, and at Geneva he created a theocratic state. It is not easy to

No denomination has a monopoly of bigotry and cruelty. The drawing shows Swiss peasants, newly converted to Protestantism, torturing a monk.
(*Burgerbibliothek Bern*)

understand the attractiveness of his gloomy creed, which insisted on the absolute depravity of man after the fall of Adam and the impossibility of salvation except for those few, the elect, predestined by God to salvation. But the history not only of Geneva but of France, England, Scotland, and British North America was to leave no doubt of its efficacy. The crucial step was to be convinced that one was a member of the elect. As the signs of this were outward adherence to the commandments of God and participation in the sacraments, it was less difficult to achieve such conviction than might be imagined.

Calvin's Geneva was not a place for the easygoing. The punishment imposed for heresy, blasphemy, or witchcraft was death; of course this would not have struck contemporaries as surprising. But though adultery was a crime in most European countries and one punished by ecclesiastical courts, Calvin's Geneva took this offense much more seriously in prescribing the death penalty for those convicted of it. A distinction of sex was respected: guilty women were drowned, men beheaded. (This appears to have been a reversal of the usual penal practice of a male-dominated society; women, believed to be weaker vessels both morally and intellectually, were usually indulged with milder punishments than men.) The most severe punishments, though, were reserved for heretics; like the Inquisition, Calvin had them burned. He was a man of his age.

From Geneva, where its pastors were trained, the new sect took root in France; there it won converts among the nobility and had more than 2,000 congregations by 1561. It also enjoyed great success in the Netherlands, England, and Scotland and also spread to Germany, where it challenged Lutheranism, and thence to Poland, Bohemia, and Hungary. Thus in its first century Calvinism showed a remarkable vigor surpassing that of Lutheranism, which (except in Scandinavia) never spread strongly beyond the German lands which first adopted it and always leaned on existing authority for support.

The English Reformation

The first nation-state to reject papal authority and separate itself from Rome did not need Lutheranism or Calvinism as a spur. In England a unique religious change arose almost by accident. A new dynasty originating in Wales, the House of Tudor, had established itself on the throne at the end of the fifteenth century. The second king of this line, Henry VIII, became embroiled with the papacy over a wish to dissolve his marriage (the first of six he made) in order to remarry and get an heir, a normal preoccupation for a dynastic monarch. After Rome failed to grant the decision he sought in 1534 Henry, with the support of Parliament which obediently passed the required legislation, proclaimed himself head of the Church in England. Doctrinally he conceived no break with the past; the pope, after all, had entitled him Defender of the Faith because he had penned a refutation of Luther (his successor still bears the title). Nevertheless, the assertion of royal supremacy opened the way to the development of an Anglican church separate from Rome.

Henry created a vested interest in the change by dissolving monasteries and some other ecclesiastical foundations and selling their property. Buyers were mainly found among the aristocracy and gentry. In the next reign churchmen sympathetic to new doctrines sought to move the English church significantly toward Continental Protestant ideas. Popular reactions were mixed. Some saw this as the satisfaction of old national traditions of dissent from Rome; some resented innovations and new ceremonies. A long and confused debate brought forth one literary masterpiece, Thomas Cranmer's prayerbook, and in its course gave rise to martyrdom and exile of Catholic and Anglican alike. The first to suffer were Protestants, for England reverted to papal authority in 1553 (and the burning of heretics) when the fourth Tudor, the unfairly named and unhappy Bloody Mary, came to the throne. By that time religion was thoroughly entangled with foreign policy as the states of Europe became more and more divided along religious lines.

Elizabeth I, Mary's half-sister and successor in 1558, had Parliament legislate that she retained the essentials of her father's position; the English Church, or the Church of England as it may henceforth be called, claimed to be Catholic in doctrine but rested on the royal supremacy recognized by act of Parliament. This tied the national cause to the Protestant. Soon England was to be at war with a Catholic king of Spain well known for his determination to root out heresy in his own lands.

The English Reformation is notable not because it was Protestant but because it was carried out by act of Parliament. A constitutional issue was implicit in it; the crown had taken the trouble to express its policy in laws passed by Parliament. As much as any other factor, religion helped the English Parliament survive in the sixteenth century when other representative bodies were going under before the new power of kings.

Wars of Religion in France

There were Catholic martyrs under Elizabeth—though they died because they were traitors not because they were heretics—but England was far less divided by religion than Germany or France. Sixteenth-century France was tormented and torn by two great interests, Catholic and Calvinist, each led by important factions of the nobility. They fought for power in the so-called Wars of Religion (of which nine have been distinguished between 1562 and 1598). At times their struggles brought the power of the French monarchy very low. Yet these divisions ultimately benefited a crown which could use one faction against another. For over thirty years the distinction between war and peace hardly seems discernible, and the wretched population of France had to bear the brunt of disorder and devastation for most of this time. Finally a group known as the *politiques* advocated a measure of toleration as the only solution. With their support a member of a junior branch of the royal family, Henry, king of the little state of Navarre, came to the throne in 1589 after the murder of his predecessor.

As Henry IV of France, he inaugurated the Bourbon line, whose descendants still claim the French throne. He had been a Protestant but accepted Catholicism as the condition of his succession, recognizing that for all the violence and deeply entrenched nature of French Calvinism, Catholicism was the religion most French people would cling to. Protestants were given special guarantees and assured of protection for their religion by a great charter, the Edict of Nantes (1598); it made them a state within a state, for they now possessed fortified towns where the king's writ did not run. This ended civil strife, and Henry and his successors could turn to the business of reestablishing the badly shaken authority of the throne.

Counter Reformation

In the middle of the sixteenth century, religious struggles were further enflamed by a movement of reassessment and innovation within the Roman church which is called the Counter Reformation. Its center was a great papal enterprise, the Council of Trent, which met first in 1545. The council's decisions became the touchstone of Catholic orthodoxy until the nineteenth century and provided a standard to which Catholic rulers could rally. It also initiated important institutional changes, not the least of which provided for the training of priests in diocesan seminaries. Like the Reformation itself, however, the Counter Reformation reached out far beyond definition and reform; it canalized and directed a new devotional intensity and rekindled the ardor of laity and clergy alike.

The desire to put the Catholic house in order also drew on spontaneous fervor among the faithful. One of the most potent instruments of the Counter Reformation was the invention of a Spanish soldier, Ignatius Loyola, who by a curious irony had been a student at the same Paris college as Calvin (it is not recorded that they ever met). In 1534 he and a few companions took vows; their aim was missionary work and as they trained for it, Loyola devised a rule for a new religious order. In 1540 the order was recognized by a papal bull and named the Society of Jesus. The Jesuits, as they soon came to be called, were to have an importance in the history of Roman Catholicism akin to that of the early Benedictines or the Franciscans of the thirteenth century. By Loyola's death in 1556 there were 1,500 of them, working as far away as China and Japan. The Jesuits were the militia of the Church; their warrior-founder made them utterly disciplined and completely subordinate to papal authority through their general, who lived in Rome. They transformed Catholic education and were in the forefront of a renewed Catholic missionary effort. In Europe their intellectual eminence and political skill raised them to places of great influence in the courts of kings.

PRINCIPALITIES AND POWERS

The Counter Reformation state

The Counter Reformation had the paradoxical effect, like the Reformation, of increasing the authority of the state. The new dependence of religion

FILIPE SEGVNDO REY DE ESPAÑA.

Suma ratio pro Religione.

Defender of the Faith: Philip II of Spain depicted in a role with which he would
have undoubtedly identified himself. In the background is the Escorial, the grim
monastery-palace he built outside Madrid. It was planned like a gridiron,
to commemorate the martyrdom by roasting alive of its patron, St. Lawrence.
(Biblioteca Nacional, Madrid)

on political authority — on, in the last resort, organized force — extended the
grip of government further. This was most obvious in Spain where two
forces ran together to create an unimpeachably Catholic monarchy long before the Council of Trent. The Reconquest was one. It was only recently
finished and had been a crusade; the title of the Catholic Kings itself proclaimed the identification of a political process with an ideological struggle.
Another motivating force was the possible threat to the Spanish monarchy
posed by its great numbers of new non-Christian subjects, both Muslim and
Jew. The instrument deployed against them was an old one refurbished: an
inquisition, not under clerical control like the medieval one but under that
of the crown.

Established by papal bull in 1478, the Spanish Inquisition began to operate in Castile in 1480. The pope soon had misgivings; in Catalonia lay and ecclesiastical authorities alike resisted, but to no avail. By 1520 the Inquisition was the only royal institution which exercised authority in all the Spanish domains—in the Americas, Sicily, and Sardinia as much as in Castile and Aragon. It sought out political as well as religious disaffection, and its success encouraged Rome to reestablish the Inquisition (the "holy office") in 1542.

The expulsion and severe persecution of Jews and converted Moors gave Spain a religious unity unbreakable by its few sympathizers with Lutheranism, who were easily dealt with by the Inquisition. The cost to Spain need not be considered here. Already under Charles V, who saw himself as a medieval emperor—"God's standard bearer," in his own phrase—Spain was, in religion as in her secular life, a new kind of centralized, absolutist monarchy, the Renaissance state of theory par excellence. The residues of formal constitutionalism within the peninsula do not affect this. Spain provided the model for the Counter Reformation state and was to impose this form upon much of Europe by force or example in the century after 1558, when Charles V died after a retirement spent largely in devotions in a monastery in Estremadura.

Of all the European monarchs who identified themselves with the cause of the Counter Reformation and saw themselves as extirpators of heresy, none was more determined than Charles' son and successor, Philip II of Spain, widower of Mary Tudor. He received half Charles' empire: Spain, the Indies, Sicily, and the Spanish Netherlands. In 1581 he acquired Portugal as well, and it remained Spanish until 1640.

Philip's methods of government failed most conspicuously in the Spanish Netherlands. Under his father there had already been discontent with the campaign there against heresy. Modern Belgium and the Netherlands by no means correspond to a division between Catholic and Protestant areas, but even in the sixteenth century Protestants predominated in the northern provinces and Catholics in the south. Philip antagonized nobles by centralization, townsmen by taxes, and churchmen by his wish to reform. One nobleman, William of Orange (nicknamed the Silent because of his reputed refusal to be provoked into unguarded anger when he learned of his ruler's determination to bring heretic subjects to heel) took the leadership of what slowly turned into a national rebellion. The Spanish army was successful in holding the southern Netherlands and thus, unwittingly, defined modern Belgium. In the northern provinces revolt continued long after William's death in 1584.

The Dutch (as the northerners may be called after this) had grave disadvantages to overcome. They were divided into many provinces and could rarely come to agreement quickly. But there were also factors working in their favor. In the first place, the formidable Spanish army could not easily subdue an enemy who retired behind town walls and flooded the surrounding countryside by opening the dikes. Furthermore, almost by accident the Dutch transferred their main effort to the sea; there they could do a great deal of damage to the Spanish on more equal terms. Secondly, Spanish

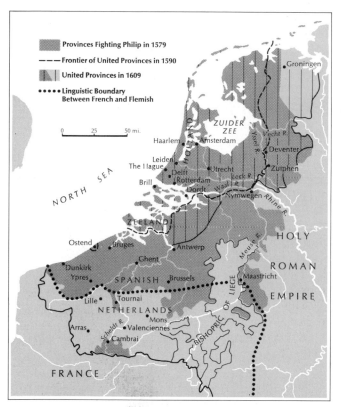

THE NETHERLANDS DURING THE EIGHTY YEARS' WAR

The seventeen provinces making up the Netherlands were detached from the Holy Roman Empire when Charles V abdicated in 1556. As the map indicates, their subsequent division into two states was determined not by linguistic differences but by geography. The great river systems at the mouth of the Rhine eventually proved to be the barrier beyond which the Spanish rulers could not overcome the rebels.

communications with the Netherlands were stretched, and the sea route was harried by the rebels. It was expensive to maintain a big army in Belgium and even more expensive when other enemies had to be beaten off elsewhere on the Continent. This suggests the third factor telling in favor of the Dutch, their acquisition of allies. The Counter Reformation had infected international politics with a new ideological element. Together with England's interest in maintaining a balance of power on the Continent, religious differences led to a diplomatic struggle against Spain which eventually became military and naval and brought assistance to the Dutch.

The beginnings of modern England

The Dutch were to evolve a remarkable republican society and, once their survival was assured, one characterized by religious tolerance and great civic freedom. The only other important country where this happened before 1700 was England, and there it was accompanied by a great strength-

Elizabeth's Armada Speech

On August 8, 1588, Queen Elizabeth went from London to Tilbury, a little further down the Thames, where the feeble army had gathered which was to protect England's capital if the Spanish veterans of the Duke of Parma should cross from the Netherlands. To carry them across was the purpose of the Armada, the great Spanish fleet which had sailed up the English Channel to Calais. In fact, it had been shattered the previous day, after an attack by fire-ships. While at Tilbury Elizabeth made a great speech to her soldiers; like the Gettysburg Address, it was brief and to the point. Yet it was one of the finest expressions of the personality of a great queen and her uncanny skill in exploiting her subjects' love and loyalty. She was fifty-seven at the time and used with unerring skill the sense of nationality and patriotism associated with the Tudors since her great father, Henry VIII. This is the text of the speech as it has reached us:

My loving people: we have been persuaded by some that are careful of our safety to take heed how we commit ourselves to armed multitudes, for fear of treachery; but I assure you, I do not desire to live to distrust my faithful, loving people. Let tyrants fear. I have always so behaved myself that, under God, I have placed my chiefest strength and safeguard in the loyal hearts and good will of my subjects; and therefore I am come amongst you, as you see, at this time, not for my recreation and disport, but being resolved, in the midst and heat of the battle, to live or die amongst you all, to

ening of the state which carried the limitation of legal privilege so far indeed that at the end of the seventeenth century England was regarded with amazement by other Europeans. But for a long time this cannot have seemed a likely outcome.

In the seventeenth century several countries had roughly simultaneous crises of authority, curiously parallel to economic troubles of about the same time. Some historians have argued that the two were inseparably connected. This may be so, but it is not easy to be sure what the nature of the connection was. In England, as elsewhere, there was a breakdown of normal politi-

lay down for my God, and for my kingdom, and for my people, my honour and my blood, even in the dust. I know I have the body of a weak and feeble woman, but I have the heart and stomach of a king, and of a king of England too, and think foul scorn that Parma or Spain, or any prince of Europe should dare to invade the borders of my realm: to which, rather than any dishonour shall grow by me, I myself will take up arms, I myself will be your general, judge, and rewarder of every one of your virtues in the field. I know, already for your forwardness you have deserved rewards and crowns; and we do assure you, in the word of a prince, they shall be duly paid you.

The hint of personal danger was no exaggeration. William the Silent had been assassinated a few years before, Henry IV of France would be a few years later. The pope had authorized Elizabeth's deposition in the interests of the Roman Church, and Protestants in France had been deprived of their leaders in the great St. Bartholomew's Day massacre of 1572. Elizabeth too had signed the death warrant of a fellow-monarch, Mary Queen of Scots. Life was often at stake in sixteenth-century politics.

From J. E. Neale, *Queen Elizabeth I* (London: Jonathan Cape Ltd., 1934), pp. 297–298.

cal life in the sense that existing arrangements were called into question and men were prepared once more to rebel in arms against the crown. It came to a head in civil war, regicide, and the establishment of the only republic in English history.

The heart of the crisis was growing conflict between king and Parliament. The first king of England of the Scotch Stuart dynasty which succeeded the Tudors came to the throne in 1603. This was James I, and if his ambitions and those of his son and successor tended in any direction, it was toward enhancing the power of the monarch along Continental lines. Yet as the experiences of Spain, the Netherlands, and France all show, such an increase in power nowhere went unchallenged. Friction soon developed between James and Parliament over three interconnected issues: money, religion, and foreign policy. The crown was poor and required money; but proposals for taxation were ill-received by Parliament. It voiced criticisms not only of fiscal policy but also religious policy (the king was believed to be unduly sympathetic to Roman Catholics) and foreign policy. An anti-Spanish and Protestant stance in foreign affairs was important to English nationalism in the early seventeenth century.

Thus opened deep constitutional divisions. It was open to argument with whom decision in these matters lay, but Parliament controlled the flow of money necessary to support policy. After some unhappy experiences in the first years of his reign, Charles I, the second Stuart king, took the advice of those who counseled him to do without Parliament altogether. This was just possible—at the cost of curtailing activity abroad and creating antagonism at home by attempts to resurrect obsolete sources of revenue or impose new ones. Under the resulting "Eleven Years' Tyranny," England began to look as if she were on the road to absolutism on the Continental model and loss of the advances made by Parliament under the Tudors. But this did not happen

"This House is to let." Cromwell, dictator of England, dissolves the "Rump" of the "Long Parliament" in 1653. This was what was left of the House of Commons after twelve years without elections and a good deal of political upheaval. It was resummoned, though, six years later. *(The Trustees of the British Museum)*

because a foreign war (with Scotland) forced Charles to reconvene Parliament in 1639. Without new taxation the country could not be defended.

Parliament returned full of grievances, convinced that there had been an attempt to subvert the liberties of Englishmen, and suspicious also that there were royal plans to overturn the Church of England and reintroduce the power of Rome. From this point the quarrel between king and Parliament grew embittered. Parliament harried the king's servants and sent the most conspicuous supporters of the Eleven Years' Tyranny to the block.

In 1641 Charles decided that force was the only way out and the Civil War—or, as royalists called it, the Great Rebellion—began. The king was defeated, but Parliament was uneasy, as were all men, for if you stepped outside the ancient constitution of kings, lords, and commons, where would things end? But Charles threw away his advantage by encouraging a foreign invasion in his support (the Scots were to fight for him this time). Parliament, or those who controlled it, had had enough. Charles was tried and executed in 1649. His son tried to claim his inheritance, was defeated, and went into exile with many of his father's supporters.

There followed in England an interregnum called the Commonwealth during which the dominant figure was one of the most remarkable of all Englishmen, Oliver Cromwell. He was a country gentleman who had risen in parliamentary councils by his genius as a soldier. His military role gave him great power, for providing his army stood by him, he could dispense with the politicians; but it also imposed limitations on him because he would not sacrifice the army's support. The result was an English republic which was astonishingly fertile in new constitutional schemes as Oliver cast about to find a way of governing. Simply to give Parliament unchecked power meant that England would be handed over to intolerant Protestants. The army, the force on which his power rested, knew this and feared such an outcome. But the army would not let him assume a crown and restore the old balance of king and Parliament under which men would feel safe from either. This was "King" Oliver's dilemma, and he never solved it.

Many Englishmen felt (as did Oliver and the leaders of the army) that traditional liberties were threatened by what was called "Puritanism." This had been a growing force in English life since the middle of Elizabeth's reign and had originally signified only a particularly close and austere interpretation of religious doctrine and ceremony. There were Puritans inside the Anglican church as well as among its Protestant critics, but it was to the second group that the name was more and more applied. By the seventeenth century Puritanism betokened, besides rigid doctrine and disapproval of ritual, the reform of manners in a strongly Calvinistic sense. (Many of the early English colonists in America were Puritans of this stamp.) After the Civil War many Puritans who had fought on Parliament's side seemed intent on using its victory to impose their doctrinal and moral ideas on both conservative Anglicans and the dissenting religious minorities—Congregationalists, Baptists, and Unitarians—which were finding their voices under the Commonwealth. There was nothing politically or religiously democratic about Puritanism. Those who were of the elect might freely choose their own elders and act as a community, but to outsiders they were an oligarchy claiming to know God's will for others. Only a few of the untypical minorities brought forth the democratic and leveling ideas which contributed so much to making the Commonwealth a great epoch in English political education and a seedbed of ideas with an important future.

The institutional bankruptcy of the republic became clear after Cromwell's death in 1658. Englishmen could not agree in sufficient numbers to uphold any of its constitutional devices. But most of them would accept the old monarchical structure, and so the story of the Commonwealth ends with the restoration of the Stuarts in 1660. This might suggest that nothing important had happened. Far from it. England took back her king on unspoken conditions: he was restored because Parliament said so and believed he would defend the Church of England. Counter Reformation Catholicism frightened the English as much as did revolutionary Puritanism. Although the struggle between king and Parliament was not over, there would be no absolute monarchy in England; henceforth the crown was on the defensive. The Renaissance state had failed in England.

France and Spain

In France disturbances followed a period of conscious assertion of royal power. Cardinal Richelieu, chief minister of Louis XIII, reduced the privileges of the Huguenots (as French Calvinists were called) and instituted a system of appointing royal officials, the intendants, to reside in the provinces as direct representatives of royal power. Administrative reform brought suffering to the people; a series of fiscal innovations imposed crushing burdens on the poor in the 1630s and 1640s, taxes doubling and sometimes trebling during these years. Rebellions which followed were mercilessly put down. When Richelieu's successors imposed yet more and, it was said, unconstitutional taxation, the role of defender of the rights of Frenchmen was taken up therefore by special interests, notably the Parlement of Paris, the corporation of lawyers who sat in and could plead before the first law court of the kingdom. They led an insurrection in Paris in 1648. A compromise settlement followed when royal troops besieged the city. After an uneasy interval a much more dangerous movement arose among the great nobles. They were supported by the anticentralist feelings of the provincial nobility, as regional rebellions showed. Yet the monarchy weathered the storm because the continuation of disorder cost the rebels the popular and urban support they needed. Although Richelieu's work had suffered a setback, the absolute monarchy of France was still essentially intact when young Louis XIV declared his minority at an end in 1661.

In Spain, too, taxation provoked troubles. An attempt to overcome the provincialism which still persisted in the formally federal structure of the Spanish state led to revolt in Portugal (which had been absorbed into Spain under Philip II with promises of respect for her liberties), among the Basques, and in Catalonia. Portugal was lost in 1640, and it took twelve years to suppress the Catalan revolt. There was also a revolt in 1647 in the Spanish kingdom of Naples; it began as one of peasants against noblemen, but turned into one against the crown before it was suppressed. A tax on fruit had occasioned the actual outbreak in Naples and demands for money loomed large in all these instances of civic turbulence.

Financially the Renaissance state was ceasing to be successful. War was a great devourer of revenues, and the second quarter of the seventeenth century was a time of unremitting conflict. Yet economic factors only partially explain the upheavals which occurred. The burdens of taxation were heavier in France than in England, but it was the English who cut off a king's head and, albeit temporarily, set up a republic. There are too many differences between individual countries to make confident generalizations about the origins of their troubles in the middle of the seventeenth century. England faced a specific challenge to authority from religious forces, which has led to yet another name for its great upheaval, the Puritan Revolution. In Spain religious dissent was nonexistent, and in France it had been contained long before. In fact, the Huguenots had become a vested interest; they saw the French monarchy as their protector and rallied to it in the Fronde, as the disturbances of 1648–1653 were called. Regionalism was important in Spain and to a smaller extent in France where it provided a foothold for conservative interests threatened by governmental innovation, but it seems to have played little part in English events. However, the outcome was the same in all countries: the troubles were surmounted, even if at a cost, and the state continued to gather to itself power and respect above all other authorities.

Parliamentary monarchy

Charles II returned to England in 1660 to take his rightful place on the throne (he had been legally king since his father's execution). The Restoration was something of a turning point in English history. Parliament would again turn a king off the throne, but there was not to be another Civil War. The last English rebellion, by an inadequate pretender and a few thousand deluded yokels in 1685, in no sense revived the dangers with which rebellions under the Tudors had menaced the state. After 1660 even England had a standing army. Yet though the state thus in many ways was steadily growing stronger, men were unwilling to admit the work in which they were engaged. Englishmen in 1688 solemnly legislated a series of defenses of individual liberty in the Bill of Rights, though it was by then hard to argue that what one king in Parliament had done another could not undo and therefore that such rights had any real guarantee at all.

Perhaps the actual success of the English state after the seventeenth-century crisis made it difficult to recognize the principle of legislative sovereignty. Obviously, it would seem most attractive in periods of disorder. The troubles of his time deeply impressed the great English political philosopher Thomas Hobbes with the need to define the location and extent of authority. In his masterpiece, *Leviathan*, published in 1651, he argued that the uncertainty of not agreeing on who has the last word in deciding the law was a disadvantage which clearly outweighed the danger that such power might be tyrannically employed. Even when civil strife was not continuous, disorder was always liable to break out: as Hobbes (roughly) put it, you do not have to live all the time under a torrential downpour to say that the weather is rainy.

Hobbes' contribution to political theory was the proposition that legislative power—sovereignty—rested solely in the state and could not be restricted by appeals to immunities, customs, divine law, or anything else without the danger of falling into anarchy. This idea shocked contemporaries and Hobbes was almost universally condemned. Yet one of the first states to operate on his principles was constitutional England. By the early eighteenth century her rulers accepted, implicitly or explicitly, that there could be no obstacle except a practical one to the operation of law.

This conclusion was embodied in the next great constitutional change after the Restoration. In 1688 England rejected the direct descent of the Stuart male line, pushed James II off the throne, and put his daughter and her consort on it, stipulating that they must rule with respect to certain conventions. With the creation of a contractual monarchy England at last broke formally and finally with her *ancien régime* and began to function as a constitutional state. Effectively government was shared. Its major component lay with a House of Commons which represented the dominant social interest, the landowning classes. The king still had important powers, but his advisers, it soon became clear, had to possess the confidence of the House of Commons. Together the crown and Parliament, expressing their will in statutes, could do anything. The privileged had no special immunity from legislation, as was still the case in Continental countries.

The Glorious Revolution of 1688 (as it is called) brought a foreigner to the English throne. Queen Mary's husband, William III, was Dutch and profoundly aware of the threat presented to other countries by Louis XIV's France. She was a land power as menacing to the independence of the Dutch as the Spain of Philip II had been. To William the major importance of 1688 was that England's power could now be brought into the scale against France. So many interests worked together to make this acceptable to the dominant classes in England that the subsequent series of great wars against Louis XIV cannot be explained in merely ideological terms, as constitutionalism versus despotism. Moreover, the presence of the Empire, of Spain, and of various German princes at different times in the anti-French coalitions would make nonsense of any neat contrast of political principle between the two sides. Nevertheless, it rightly struck some contemporaries that there was an ideological element somewhere in the struggle. England and Holland were more open societies than France. Their constitutions embodied legal protection for the exercise of different religions. They did not censor the press but left it to be regulated by the laws which protected individuals, corporations recognized as possessing legal personality, and the state itself against defamation. They were governed by the classes possessing social and economic power. France was at the opposite pole.

Absolute monarchy

Under Louis XIV absolute government reached its apogee in France and became a model for all European princes. Politics was reduced essentially to administration; royal councils and royal agents in the provinces had still to take into account such social facts as the existence of the nobility and local immunities, but the reign played havoc with the real independence of the political forces hitherto powerful in France. Louis XIV tamed his nobility by tying them to the most glamorous court in Europe; his own sense of social hierarchy made him happy to caress them with honors and pensions, but he always remembered the Fronde and made sure he controlled them. He restricted the parlements to their judicial role and asserted the independence of the French church from Rome to bring it the more securely under his own wing. As for the Huguenots, Louis was determined, whatever the cost, not to be a ruler of heretics and revoked the Edict of Nantes; those who were not exiled were submitted to a harsh persecution to bring them to conversion.

The coincidence—and interdependence—between one of the greatest ages of French cultural achievement and the reign of Louis XIV may obscure the harsh face of his government. It was the triumph of a bigoted, narrow, hierarchical, corporate, theocratic society which looked to the past for its goals. Louis even hoped to become Holy Roman Emperor. He refused to allow a great philosopher and defender of religion, René Descartes, to be given religious burial in France in 1650 because of his dangerous ideas. If logical, this was not magnanimous. Yet for a long time this regime seems to have been what most French people wanted. France was not again to be ungovernable until 1789.

Louis won his European position in large measure by success in war, but he also carried French prestige to a peak where it long remained because of the model of monarchy he presented; he was the perfect absolute monarch, stage manager and leading actor in the finest theatrical spectacle in Europe. The physical setting of the monarchy was a huge new palace he built at Versailles. Few buildings or the lives lived in them can have been so successful as models. Eighteenth-century Europe would be studded with miniature reproductions of the French court, painfully created at the expense of their subjects by pigmy *grandes monarques*.

Enlightened despotism

Except for England, the Dutch United Provinces, the cantons of Switzerland, and the fossil republics of Italy, absolutism was the dominant state form of the eighteenth century, during which it evolved further in style and shape. This phenomenon was soon called "enlightened despotism," a somewhat misleading, though catchy, term. It can no more be confined to a specific reference than political designations like "right" or "left" today. What is clear is that about halfway through the century the wish to carry out practical reforms was growing more obvious in many states. This often resulted in innovations bearing the stamp of the advanced thought of the day. Such reforms were imposed by the absolute monarchs' powers, not through representative bodies. Although humanitarian, the policies of enlightened despots were not necessarily liberal in the political sense. They were, on the other hand, modern: they tended to operate against traditional social and religious authority, they cut across accepted notions of social hierarchy and legal rights, and they clarified the tendency to concentrate lawmaking power of the state and its unchallenged authority over its subjects. But though this general description can be justified by examples, it is almost impossible to find any instance of enlightened despotism which perfectly expresses it.

One set of enlightened despots ruled southern and Mediterranean countries. In Portugal, Spain, Naples, and some other Italian states ministers who promoted reforming policies are conspicuous in the eighteenth century. Even the Papal States showed the trend. But almost all the courts concerned were part of the Bourbon family connection, and when one of the smallest of them, Parma, became involved in a quarrel with the pope, they all mounted a general attack on the Jesuits, the right arm of the Counter Reformation papacy. In 1773 the pope was forced by diplomatic pressure to dissolve the order after its members had already been banished from many of the Bourbon states. This was a great symbolic blow, as important for advanced anticlerical principles as for its practical effects. The other achievements of the reformers in the southern monarchies were most notable in the areas of economic and penal reform, and here the outstanding example is not a Bourbon state but one ruled by a Habsburg, the Grand Duchy of Tuscany.

With the exception of Spain none of the reforming states in the south had any pretension to great power status in the eighteenth century. Of the eastern monarchies which may be thought of as enlightened despotisms, most did. The odd man out was Poland, the sprawling, ramshackle kingdom where attempts at reform came to grief on constitutional rocks. The enlightenment was there all right, but not the despotism. The other three examples, Prussia, the Habsburg empire, and Russia, all expended great effort on reforms shaped largely by the demands of international competition, that is, for the generation of national power. The Russian case is best dealt with elsewhere, in the context of that country's emerging state power, because it was part of a process of modernization which began in the earliest years of the eighteenth century. It is sufficient to note here that enlightened despotism in Russia provided the showy front to a nation achieving great power status without fundamentally affecting the traditional ordering of society.

Eighteenth-century Prussia had a long tradition of efficient, centralized, economical administration which embodied much of what enlightened monarchy meant in other countries, including a religious toleration admired by reformers abroad. Moreover, it had none of the institutions of theocratic monarchy of the Counter Reformation lands. Yet the Prussian state, too, rested on a traditional society of rigidly divided orders which remained virtually unchanged throughout the century. Though Frederick II did not face representative institutions which limited his policy-making power or embodied the corporate rights of the nobility, his power rested on the acquiescence of the nobles of Prussia, and he carefully preserved their legal and social privileges. He remained convinced that only noblemen should be given commissioned rank in the army, and at the end of his reign in 1786 there were more serfs in Prussian territory than there had been at its outset.

Competition with Prussia brought reform to the Habsburg dominions. If the Habsburg rulers were to mobilize the potential of their territories, they had to overcome great obstacles imposed by differences in nationality, language, and institutions. These gave them different legal standing in different places: the emperor was king of Hungary, duke of Milan, and archduke of Austria. Centralization and administrative uniformity were essential if this patchwork empire was to exercise its due weight in European affairs. Another problem: like the Bourbon states but unlike Russia or Prussia, the Habsburg empire was overwhelmingly Roman Catholic, and the power of the Church was deeply entrenched in the Habsburg lands, which included most of Counter-Reformation Europe outside Spain. Economically the Church held great power through its huge properties; legally it was everywhere protected by tradition, law, and papal policy. Finally, it had a monopoly of education.

These facts made modernization in the Habsburg dominions look especially enlightened. Every practical reform there seemed to conflict with the privileges of entrenched social power or of the Church. Maria Theresa, who succeeded her father in 1740, was a far from willing reformer, but her advisers were able to present a persuasive case for change when she was faced by a struggle with Prussia for supremacy in Germany. More money was needed, and once the road to fiscal and consequently administrative reform had been entered upon, it was bound to lead eventually to interference with tradition in both Church and state. This came to a climax under Maria Theresa's son and successor, Joseph II, who did not share the obvious pieties of his mother and flaunted his own taste for advanced views. In his reign reform became especially associated with measures that damaged the interests of the Church. Monasteries lost their property, religious appointments were interfered with, the right of sanctuary was removed, and education was taken out of the hands of the clergy. In the end the leading classes revolted in many parts of his dominions and brought Joseph's measures to a halt. By his death in 1790 he had antagonized into open defiance the nobles of Brabant, Hungary, and Bohemia, and acting through local estates and diets they paralyzed Habsburg government over large areas at the end of his reign.

Reform in France

Differences in the circumstances of states, in the preconceptions of their rulers, and in the degree to which they did not embody enlightened ideas all show how misleading it is to look for a model enlightened despotism. France, certainly touched by reforming policies and aspirations, provides another confirmation of this. Internal obstacles to change, paradoxically, grew stronger after the death of Louis XIV in 1715 because the monarchy tended to lose power. Under Louis XV the nobilitys' influence on government became greater. (The reign began with a minority and a regency.) And increasingly the parlements used their power to register new laws as an opportunity to criticize those which infringed special interest and historic privilege. There was outspoken resistance to the idea that any right of unrestricted legislative sovereignty rested in the crown, and the crown's defenders tended to agree.

As the century wore on France's international role imposed heavier and heavier burdens. The issue of reform tended to crystallize in a search for new sources of tax revenue, an exercise that was bound to bring on conflicts with the privileged. Onto this rock ran most of the reform proposals of the French monarchy. France presented by 1789 the paradox of being the country most associated with the articulation and diffusion of critical and advanced ideas, yet also the one where it seemed most difficult to put them into practice in public life.

The early modern state

Enlightenment created a dilemma which was Europe-wide in the traditional monarchies at the end of the eighteenth century. Wherever reform and modernization had been embarked upon, they had encountered obstacles in vested interests and traditional social structures. In the last resort, it was impossible for absolutism to solve this problem, for it was too much tied to the past itself. A king could not question historical authority too closely – it was also what his office rested upon. Furthermore, whole-hearted acceptance of the idea that legislative sovereignty was unrestricted was still rare in most countries. If historic rights were infringed, could not property be? This was a fair point, but those who expressed it failed to consider how it was that the most successful ruling class in Europe, the English, had managed to accept this theoretical principle with no dire revolutionary consequences.

In spite of important qualifications, enlightened despotism continued to mean growth of the state's power, which is the outstanding general fact of the political history of early modern Europe. Even if only theoretically and implicitly, enlightened despots aspired to control more of their subjects' lives than any earlier monarchs. Yet they had to take account of social forces that today can be ignored, and even the ablest statesmen had to work with machinery of state which to any modern bureaucrat would seem woefully inadequate for its tasks. Though the eighteenth-century state might mobilize much greater resources than the Renaissance state, it had to do so with no revolutionary innovations of technique. Communications at the end of this period depended, just as they had at the beginning, on wind and muscle. Armies could move only slightly faster than in 1500 and at best no faster than their horses. If their weapons were improved, they were not improved out of recognition; the cannons of 1800 were muzzleloaders still. No country had a police force such as exists today, and income tax was still to be introduced. Such increases in the power of the state as had come about in early modern times resulted from changes in ideas and the growing efficiency of well-known institutions rather than because of technical innovation. And before 1789 no state succeeded in so identifying itself with its subjects that it was more concerned with protecting them against foreigners than itself against them.

chapter 23

The Changing State Pattern of Early Modern Europe

DIPLOMACY'S ORIGINS

Rulers have always had to send messages and negotiate with one another, but there were many ways of doing this and interpreting what was going on. The Chinese, for example, used the fiction that their emperor was ruler of the world and that all embassies to him were therefore in the nature of petitions or tributes by subjects. Medieval kings sent heralds to one another, about whom a special ceremonial had grown up and whom special rules protected, or occasional missions of ambassadors. Formal diplomacy as we know it began in the fifteenth and sixteenth centuries. After 1500 it was increasingly the practice to use the standard device we still employ, an ambassador permanently resident in a foreign country through whom all ordinary business is at least initially transacted and who has the task of keeping his own rulers informed about the country to which he is accredited.

The Venetian ambassadors were the first notable examples of this innovation, and it is not surprising that a state so dependent on trade and the maintenance of regular international relationships gave birth to the professional diplomat. More changes followed. Gradually the hazards facing earlier emissaries were forgotten as diplomats were given special status and protected by privileges and immunities. The nature of treaties and other diplomatic forms became more precise and regularized. Procedure became more standardized. All these changes came about slowly, when they were believed to be useful. For the most part, it is true, the professional diplomat in the modern sense had barely appeared by 1800; ambassadors were usually noblemen who had the resources necessary to sustain a representative role, not paid civil servants. Nonetheless, the professionalization of diplomacy was beginning in the sixteenth century. It is one sign that after 1500 a new Europe of relationships between sovereign powers was replacing the old one based on feudal ties between persons and the vague supremacies of pope and emperor.

The most striking characteristic of the emerging European system has remained to this day—the assumption that the world is divided into sovereign states. This idea was by no means wholly clear in 1500. People did not then conceive of Europe as completely divided into independent areas, each governed by a ruler belonging to it alone and to whom alone it belonged. Still less were its political units thought to have any sort of cohesion which might be called national. This was not only because of the survival of such museums of past practice as the Holy Roman Empire. It was also because the dominating principle of early modern Europe's diplomacy was dynasticism.

Dynasticism meant that the political units of Europe were less states than landed estates. They were accumulations of property put together over long or short periods by aggressiveness, marriage, and inheritance—the same processes and forces by which any family's private estate might be built up. As a result, boundaries continually changed as this or that portion of an inheritance passed from one ruler to another. The inhabitants had no more say in the matter than might the peasants living on a farm which changed hands. Dynasticism accounts for diplomacy's monotonous preoccupation with the possible consequences of marriages and the careful establishment and scrutiny of lines of succession.

Besides their dynastic interests rulers also argued and fought about religion and, increasingly, trade or wealth. Overseas possessions gradually became a complicating factor. The old principles of feudal superiority might on occasion be invoked, but there were always map-making forces at work which fell outside the operation of these principles, such as the colonization of new lands or a rising national sentiment. Nevertheless, broadly speaking, rulers in the sixteenth and seventeenth centuries saw themselves as the custodians of inherited rights and interests which they had the duty to pass on.

DYNASTIC MAP MAKING IN WESTERN EUROPE

In 1500 the map of Europe stood at the eve of a great transformation. For the next two centuries, two great dynasties would dispute much of Europe as they were already disputing Italy. They were the ruling house of France—first the Valois family and then the Bourbons, to whom their claim passed by marriage in 1589—and the House of Habsburg. The latter would eventually be confined to Austria, the former's center would always be France, but both would export rulers and the consorts of rulers to much of the rest of Europe. In particular they would contest Spain, Italy, and the Low Countries. Yet when the sixteenth century began, each of them was far from playing a European role. Indeed there was not a great deal in the way of power—though much in antiquity—to distinguish the Valois and Habsburgs from other dynasties, the Welsh Tudors, for example, whose first ruler, Henry VII, had ascended the throne of England as recently as 1485.

Only in England, France, and Spain could there be discerned any real national cohesion and sentiment to sustain political unity at the beginning of the sixteenth century. England, a relatively unimportant power, was in this sense well developed. Insular and secluded from invasion, by 1500 rid of

Continental appendages, her government was remarkably centralized for the age. The Tudors, anxious to assert the unity of the kingdom after a long period of civil strife (the Wars of the Roses), consciously associated national with dynastic interests. France too had already come far along the road to national cohesion, and the dynasty had steadily pressed forward with the centralization of government. The Valois faced greater problems than the Tudors, though, in the continued survival of privileged enclaves within their territories. Nevertheless, France was a national state by the sixteenth century. So was Spain, though to a lesser degree. Her two crowns, of Aragon and Castile, were effectively united only in 1516 when Charles of Habsburg, grandson of the Catholic king, became co-ruler with his insane mother. He still had carefully to distinguish the rights of Castile from those of Aragon, but Spanish nationality grew more self-conscious during Charles' reign in reaction to his tendency to sacrifice Spanish interests to his other dynastic aims.

The last medieval emperor

Charles of Habsburg succeeded his grandfather as Holy Roman Emperor Charles V in 1519. His election was by no means a foregone conclusion. The German rulers feared that German interests would be neglected in the huge Habsburg dominions. Heavy bribery of the electors was needed before he prevailed over the king of France, the only other serious candidate. (Nobody believed that the English king, at first a contender, would be able to pay enough.)

Careful Habsburg marriages in the past had already made Charles the ruler of a territorial empire larger in theory than any predecessor; the title of Holy Roman Emperor only supplied a new crown. From his mother's side he inherited the Spanish kingdoms, the newly discovered Americas, and Sicily. From his father came the Netherlands, which had been part of the old medieval duchy of Burgundy, and from his grandfather the Habsburg lands of Austria and the Tyrol, along with the Franche-Comté, Alsace, and a bundle of claims in Italy. This was the greatest dynastic accumulation of the age. (And it may be remarked here that the crowns of Bohemia and Hungary were held by Charles' brother Ferdinand, who was to succeed him as emperor.) Habsburg preeminence was the central fact of European politics for the first half of the sixteenth century, and Charles' election as emperor the most important milestone. Habsburg pretensions are well shown in Charles' titles when he ascended the imperial throne: "King of the Romans; Emperor-elect; semper Augustus; King of Spain, Sicily, Jerusalem, the Balearic Islands, the Canary Islands, the Indies, and the mainland on the far side of the Atlantic; Archduke of Austria; Duke of Burgundy, Brabant, Styria, Carinthia, Carniola, Luxemburg, Limburg, Athens, and Patras; Count of Habsburg, Flanders, and Tyrol; Count Palatine of Burgundy, Hainault, Pfirt, Roussillion; Landgrave of Alsace; Count of Swabia; Lord of Asia and Africa."

Whatever such a conglomeration was, it was not national. Within it lay two main blocks of influence, the Spanish inheritance, rich through the possession of the Netherlands and irrigated by a growing flow of bullion from the Americas, and the Habsburg lands proper in central Europe, demanding both an active role in Germany to assure preeminence there and the leadership of Europe against the Turks. Charles found this congenial. He saw himself as a medieval emperor and, in a measure, sacrificed dynastic interests to that role. He aspired to make universal empire a reality, a goal beyond the powers of any man given the strains imposed by the Reformation and his inadequate apparatus of communication and administration. His aspiration, nonetheless, is evidence of the way the medieval world still lived on.

The Holy Roman Empire itself (as distinct from the Habsburg possessions) embodied this past but also showed how worm-eaten and unreal it was. Germany was a chaos supposedly united under the emperor and his tenants-in-chief who formed the imperial Diet. The seven electors had been virtually sovereign in their territories since the Golden Bull. There were also a hundred independent princes and fifty-two imperial cities, all independent. As the sixteenth century began, an attempt to reform this confusion and give Germany some measure of national unity failed. Thereafter Habsburg self-interest was virtually the only unifying principle at work in the Empire until it came to an end in 1806.

Competition in Italy

Italy, one of the most striking geographical unities of Europe, had been fragmented into several polities for centuries. The pope ruled the states of the Church. Naples was governed by a king of the House of Aragon, but Sicily belonged to his Spanish relatives. Venice, Genoa, and Lucca were republics. Milan was a large state in the Po valley ruled by the Sforza dukes. Florence was in theory a republic but in the sixteenth century really a monarchy in the hands of the Medici, a former banking family. In northern Italy the dukes of Savoy ruled Piedmont from their own ancestral lands on the other side of the Alps. These divisions made Italy an attractive prey disputed by Habsburg and Valois.

When the French king invaded Italy in 1494 with the aim of conquering Naples, he began a series of wars which lasted until 1559. The early French invasions were reminiscent of medieval adventures and raids, but after the imperial election of 1519 when Charles V defeated Francis I, the lines of the dynastic struggle emerged more clearly. Six Habsburg-Valois wars were fought in Italy. To Charles they were a fatal distraction from the Reformation problem. To the French they meant impoverishment, invasion, and overall defeat; in the end Habsburg Spain became the dominant power in the peninsula.

The wars brought disaster to Italy. An imperial army sacked Rome in 1527. It was the first time since the barbarian invasions that Rome had suffered this fate. Elsewhere in Italy the great days of the city republics were ended forever by Spanish rule and the emigration of skilled craftsmen. Venice was left to face the Turks virtually alone, and a French alliance with the sultan revealed the hollowness of Christendom's unity. At one time French and Turkish ships raided the coasts of Italy together. These were good years

THE EMPIRE OF CHARLES V

for the Ottomans. Charles' expedition against Algiers in 1541 was a disaster, and in 1560 his son Philip was defeated at Tripoli. In 1574 the Turks occupied Tunis; their naval defeat at Lepanto three years before had been only a momentary setback.

Borrowed money had sustained the Habsburg cause well in Italy but left Charles crippled by debt. He abdicated in 1555 and his empire was divided: his brother Ferdinand succeeded him as emperor and took the Austrian inheritance, and his son Philip II became ruler of Spain. Charles, born in the Netherlands, had learned Spanish; Philip was a Spaniard.

Spanish ascendancy

The division of the Habsburg empire marks a watershed in European affairs. What followed was the blackest period for centuries. With a brief lull in the early seventeenth century, European rulers and their peoples indulged in an orgy of hatred, bigotry, massacre, torture, and brutality which had no parallel until science lent a helping hand in the twentieth century. The dominating facts of this scenario were the military preeminence of Spain, the ideological conflict opened by the Counter Reformation, the paralysis of France and Germany by internal religious quarrels, the emergence of new centers of power in England, the Dutch Netherlands, and Sweden, and the first examples of the overseas conflicts of the next two centuries. Toward the middle of the seventeenth century, this epoch drew to a close, the power of Spain dwindled and France inherited her ascendancy.

The great Armada. This tapestry cartoon celebrating the defeat selects for prominence one of the major tactical themes, the outsailing of the rowed Spanish galleys, so unsuited to the Atlantic passage, by the English ships, which used their advantage to rake their enemies' decks with gunfire. *(The National Maritime Museum, London)*

The best starting point is the Dutch revolt against Spanish rule, soon merged in a complex international struggle which mixed religious with more worldly interests. The French monarchy, though often weakened by internal religious conflicts, did not see the dynastic struggle with Habsburg Spain as finished and could not be easy while Spanish armies might invade France from Spain, Italy, or Flanders. This indeed happened in 1598, when Philip II decided to take a hand in the French Wars of Religion and ten years' fighting followed. England's involvement in the revolt arose from other issues. Though Protestant, she was only just Protestant, and Philip II tried to avoid an outright break with Elizabeth I. But national and religious feelings were inflamed in England by Spain's response to English piracy. English prisoners of the Spanish were sometimes treated as heretics and this made it easy to think of them as martyrs. Aware of the danger facing her if she broke openly with Spain, Elizabeth covertly helped the Dutch rebels, whom she did not want to see defeated. At last, with the pope's approval for the deposition of Elizabeth, the heretic queen, Philip mounted the Armada, a great Spanish invasion effort, in 1588. But "God blew and they were scattered" said the inscription on an English commemorative medal: bad weather com-

An allegory of religious competition in the age of the Counter Reformation. In the detail shown here, as the flood goes down, Catholics and Protestants fish for souls — the latter, apparently, having the best of it, which may not be surprising as this was a Dutch picture. *(Rijksmuseum, Amsterdam)*

pleted the work of poor Spanish planning and superior English seamanship to bring the Armada to disaster after it had seemed near to success. Almost incidentally an English naval tradition of enormous importance had received its first encouragement. Spain was long to be regarded as the special enemy of England, and war went on between them until 1604, but the Stuart monarchs strove sensibly to avoid a renewal of the conflict once peace had been made.

The revolt of the Netherlands was reignited by the Spanish after a twelve years' truce (1609–1621). It merged with a much greater struggle, the Thirty Years' War, in which a Franco-Spanish quarrel was only one element. The kernel of this war was a Habsburg attempt to rebuild imperial authority in Germany by linking it with the triumph of the Counter Reformation, a policy which called into question the 1555 agreement at Augsburg that Germany was to be religiously pluralistic. But once again dynastic crosscurrents soon made nonsense of ideological issues. Habsburg and Valois had contested Italy in the sixteenth century; now Habsburg and Bourbon disputed western Germany, with intrusions from an imperialistic Sweden. Dynastic interests divided the Catholic Habsburgs from Catholic France, and France, under the leadership of a Catholic cardinal, allied with Protestant Sweden to assure the rights of German Protestant princes. Cardinal Richelieu has a better claim than any other man to be the creator of the foreign policy of stirring up trouble beyond the Rhine which was to serve France well for over a century. If anyone still doubted it, the age of realpolitik and raison d'état, of simple, unprincipled assertion of the interests of the sovereign, had now clearly arrived.

The Peace of Westphalia

The next good vantage point is 1648. Though the Peace of Westphalia, which ended the Thirty Years' War in that year, registered great changes, it also still showed traces of the fading past. It was the end of the era of religious wars in Europe; this was the last time when European statesmen had the religious allegiance of their peoples as one of their main concerns in a general settlement. The peace also marked the end of Spanish military supremacy on land and the dream of reconstituting the power of Charles V. The Holy Roman Empire, though it lingered in form, had in fact ceased to be a power distinct from the House of Habsburg. From this time, the dynasty's future was an Austrian one. In Germany a new force had appeared in the Protestant electorate of Brandenburg; with it and with Catholic Bavaria the Habsburgs would contend later on, but their recent frustration in Germany had been the work of outsiders, Sweden and France. Here was a sign of the future, the opening of a period when France would dominate Europe west of the Elbe.

There are some negative points about the Peace of Westphalia. It came a century and a half after Columbus, and Spain, Portugal, England, France, and Holland all had important overseas empires. Yet these were not of any interest to the negotiators of the treaty. England was not present at the negotiations and had hardly been concerned with the questions at issue once the first phase of the war was over. Though preoccupied by internal quarrels and troubled by her Scotch neighbors, she directed her foreign policy toward ends as much extra-European as European. England was again to go to war with Spain, her conscience eased by struggle against her traditional and religious enemy, and she would also soon fight the Dutch over questions of trade. Cromwell restored peace between the Protestant republics, telling the Dutch there was room in the world for the trade of both of them. It was significant that England's diplomacy was already showing more clearly than that of other nations the influence of commercial and colonial interests.

French ascendancy

The groundwork of the French ascendancy was laid by Richelieu, but he built on solid natural advantages. His country was the most populous in western Europe, and on this simple fact French military strength rested; until the mid-nineteenth century only an assembly of international forces could match her armies. Though her inhabitants would seem miserable enough to modern eyes, France also possessed great economic resources. They were to sustain a huge efflorescence of French power and prestige under Louis XIV, whose personal rule began in 1661 (though he had come to the throne as a child in 1643). France would often be defeated in the next century and a half, but until 1815 she would be the major power in the west.

Louis XIV was the most consummate exponent of the trade of kingship who has ever lived, and it is only for convenience that his foreign policy should be distinguished from other aspects of his rule. The building of Versailles, for example, both gratified his personal taste and buttressed France's prestige, which was as important a diplomatic weapon as the size of her armies. Similarly, Louis' foreign policy was closely related to his domestic concerns. He might wish to improve the strategical shape of France's northwestern frontier, but Louis also despised the Dutch as merchants (though he bought millions of tulip bulbs from them each year for Versailles), disapproved of them as republicans, and detested them as Protestants. Yet these considerations did not exhaust the matter; Louis was a legalistic man—kings should be—and he felt that he had good legal claims to give respectability to what he was doing even without other grounds. In one way or another, he found convincing grounds for a foreign policy of expansion which, though in the end it cost his country dearly, carried France to a preeminence that would last through the eighteenth century and created a legend to which Frenchmen still look back with nostalgia.

At first Louis' main aim was an improved frontier. This meant conflict with Spain, still in possession of the Spanish Netherlands and the Franche-Comté. The defeat of Spain opened the way to war with the Dutch. The Dutch held their own but had to make peace in 1678, which is usually seen as the peak of Louis' achievement in foreign affairs. In Germany, besides territorial conquest, Louis briefly sought the imperial crown and was willing to ally with the Turks to obtain it. The turning point in the international relations of his reign came in 1688 when William of Orange, the stadholder of Holland, took his wife Mary Stuart to England to join her on the English throne. From this time on Louis had a new and persistent enemy across the Channel. William could now bring into play on the Continent the resources of the leading Protestant power. He had already organized a league (even the pope joined secretly) against France; in King William's War (or the War of the League of Augsburg) Spain, Austria, and the Protestant states of Europe joined together to contain Louis' overweening ambition. The peace which ended it in 1697 was the first in which he had to make concessions.

In 1700 the king of Spain died. It was a long-awaited event for Charles II had been a sickly fellow as well as feeble-minded, and European diplomats had spent years preparing for the great danger and opportunity which his death must present. Charles II was childless. A huge dynastic inheritance was therefore available. The main disputants were bound to be the Habsburg emperor and Louis XIV, who had passed his rights in the matter on to his grandson. But all Europe was interested. The English wanted to know what would happen to the trade of the Indies, the Dutch about the fate of the Spanish Netherlands. And everyone viewed with alarm the prospect of an undivided inheritance going to either Bourbon or Habsburg. The ghost of Charles V's empire walked again. Partition treaties had therefore been made. Unhappily, Louis set them aside. He also offended the English by recognizing the exiled Stuart pretender as James III of England. A Grand Alliance of Habsburg emperor, United Provinces, and England was soon formed, and there began the War of the Spanish Succession in which, after twelve years of fighting, France was driven to terms.

The treaties, known as the Peace of Utrecht, which ended the war in 1713 settled the shape of western Europe for the next eighty years. The crowns of Spain and France were declared forever incapable of being united on the same head, but Louis' grandson was accepted as the first Bourbon king of Spain. With Spain came the Indies but not the Netherlands, which went to the emperor as compensation and to provide a buffer for the Dutch against further French aggression. Austria also made great gains in Italy. France conceded overseas possessions to the United Kingdom, the new political unit formed by the union of England and Scotland in 1707. Louis expelled the Stuart pretender from France and thus recognized the Protestant succession in England.

Eighteenth-century western Europe

Not everyone liked the decisions of Utrecht, but to a remarkable degree the major arrangements of western Europe north of the Alps were to remain as they were in 1714 for the rest of the century. The results were apparent by Louis' death in 1715. Belgium did not yet exist, but the Austrian Netherlands occupied much of the same area, and the United Provinces corresponded to the modern Netherlands. France would keep the Franche-Comté and, except for the years from 1871–1918, Alsace. Spain and Portugal would after 1715 remain separate within their present boundaries; they remained great colonial powers but would never be able to lift themselves above the second rank of powers. There was a new great power in western Europe, the United Kingdom, an island state threatened by no neighbor across a land frontier. The British Isles were, on the other hand, once again attached to the Continent by a personal connection; upon Queen Anne's death without an heir in 1714, the crown had passed to a German prince who was elector of Hanover.

South of the Alps the dust took longer to settle. Italy remained disunited and underwent another thirty-odd years of upheaval as the minor representatives of European royal houses shuffled around it from one state to another trying to seize the leftovers of the age of dynastic rivalry. After 1748 only one important native dynasty remained in the peninsula, that of Savoy, which ruled Sardinia and Piedmont. The Papal States, it is true, could be regarded as an Italian monarchy though only occasionally a dynastic one, and the decaying republics of Venice, Genoa, and Lucca also upheld the tattered standard of Italian independence. Foreign dynasties in the other states and an Austrian viceroy in Milan tied the rest of Italy to non-Italian powers.

Western Europe was thus set in a pattern which was to prove remarkably durable. After 1715 most of the political map of the twentieth century was already visible west of the Rhine, and dynasticism was increasingly relegated to the second rank as a principle of foreign policy. The age of national politics had begun, and also, as Utrecht showed, that of overseas rivalry.

A NEW EASTERN EUROPE

The Ottoman tide turns

In 1500 Europe's eastern frontier powers were Habsburg Austria and a Polish-Lithuanian kingdom formed by marriage in the fourteenth century. These political structures shared with the maritime empire of Venice the burden of resisting Ottoman power. That power could still win victories and make conquests, and was the major concern of eastern European diplomacy and strategy for more than two centuries after the fall of Constantinople in 1453. If the phrase "Eastern Question" had been coined then, men would have meant by it the problem of dealing with the threat from the Turks.

After 1453 a century of naval warfare followed in which the main sufferer was Venice. In 1479 the Ionian islands were conquered, in 1571 Cyprus. Turkish success was interrupted in the early seventeenth century but then resumed, and in 1669 the Venetians had to recognize that they had lost Crete too. Meanwhile, Ottoman advance had also taken place on land. In 1664 Hungary was invaded and the last Turkish conquest of a European kingdom took place. In 1683 the Turks opened a siege of Vienna and Europe seemed in her greatest danger for over two centuries. In fact she was not. This was to be the last time Vienna was besieged. The great days of Ottoman power were already over; the effort which began with the conquest of Hungary was a final rally.

Strains and weaknesses had become apparent in the Ottoman empire early in the seventeenth century. Its army was no longer abreast of the latest military technology; it lacked the field artillery which the Swedes had made the decisive weapon of the seventeenth-century battlefield. At sea the Turks clung to the old galley tactics of ramming and boarding and were helpless against the Atlantic nations' technique of using ships as floating artillery batteries. (Fortunately for the Turks, the Venetians were conservative too.) Their forces, in any case, were stretched; they had always been engaged in Asia as well as in Europe and Africa, and the strain was too much, especially under inadequate or incompetent rulers. A great vizier pulled things together in the middle of the century to make the last offensives possible, but there were weaknesses which he could not correct, for they were inherent in the empire itself.

More a military occupation than a political unity, the Ottoman empire was dangerously dependent on subjects whose loyalty it could not enlist. In Europe the Ottomans followed their general practice of respecting the customs, habits, and institutions of non-Muslims, although non-Muslims were not on equal footing with Muslims (Christians had to pay a special poll tax, for example). Locally, such arrangements were made with communities and their leaders as seemed appropriate for supporting the military machine, the heart of the Ottoman structure.This practice had two disadvantages. It led to over-mighty subjects as pashas feathered their own nests amid incoordination and inefficiency. And it failed to give the sultan's subjects any sense of identification with his rule.

Therefore, although 1683 is a good symbolic date marking the last time Europe stood on the defensive against Islam before going over to the attack, it was a less dangerous moment than it looked. After Vienna the tide of Turkish power ebbed almost without interruption until it was once more (in 1919) confined to the hinterland of Constantinople and the old heartland of the Ottomans, Anatolia. The king of Poland, John Sobieski, soon relieved Vienna. The liberation of Hungary followed; in 1699 that kingdom, though devastated, was once more part of the Habsburg dominions. In the following century Transylvania, the Bukovina, and most of the Black Sea coast were wrested from Turkish control. By 1800 the Russians had asserted a special protection over the Christian subjects of the Ottomans and were thinking about promoting rebellion among them. Ottoman rule had also declined in Africa and Asia; though the forms of supremacy were preserved, the Ottoman caliphate resembled that of the Abbasids in its declining days. Morocco, Algeria, Tunis, Egypt, Syria, Mesopotamia, and Arabia were all in varying degrees independent or semi-independent at the end of the eighteenth century.

Poland

The once great Polish-Lithuanian commonwealth was not among the legatees of the Ottoman heritage, nor did the Poles inflict the most punishing blows as the Ottoman empire crumbled. The Poles instead were approaching a century and a half of eclipse as an independent people. The

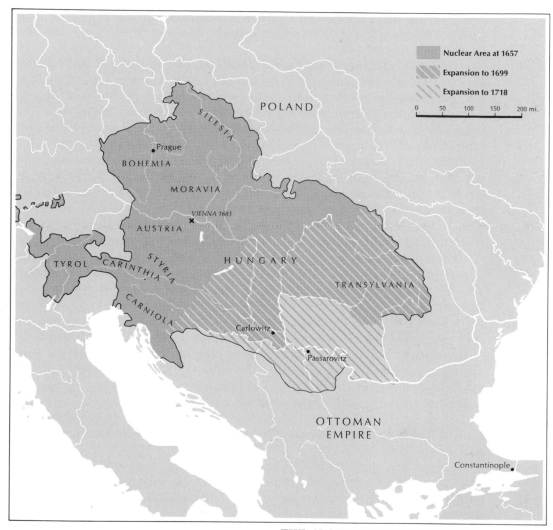

THE AUSTRIAN EMPIRE 1657–1718

union of Lithuania and Poland under a single dynasty which ruled both was turned into a real union of the two countries in 1669, but it was too late to reverse the downward trend.

The throne had become not only theoretically but actually elective when the last king of the Jagellion line died without an heir in 1572. His successor was a Frenchman, and for the next hundred years Polish magnates and foreign kings vied for the crown at each election. Meanwhile Poland was under grave and continuing pressure from Turks, Russians, and Swedes and prospered only when these enemies were embarrassed elsewhere. The Swedes had descended on her during the Thirty Years' War and the last of the Polish coast was given up to them in 1660. Internal divisions also worsened during this period. The Counter Reformation brought persecution of Polish Protestants, and there were Cossack risings in the Ukraine and continuing serf revolts.

John Sobieski was Poland's last great king of Polish blood and his election in 1674 the last not decided by foreign rulers. He won important victories and managed to work with the country's curious and highly decentralized constitutional arrangements which gave the elected kings very little legal power to balance that of the landed proprietors. With no standing army, kings had only their personal following to rely upon when factions of gentry or magnates fell back on the practice of armed gathering (confederation) to get their way. In the Diet, the central parliamentary body of the kingdom, a rule requiring unanimity stood in the way of any reform. Yet without reform a geographically ill defined, religiously divided Poland, ruled by a narrowly selfish rural gentry, could hardly survive. She was a medieval community in a modernizing world. John Sobieski could do nothing to change this situation.

Poland's social structure was bound to clog reform. A few great families of extraordinary wealth divided real power among them. One clan, the Radziwills, owned estates half the size of Ireland and held a court which outshone that of Warsaw; Count Potocki's estates covered 6,500 square miles, equivalent to half the Dutch republic. The smaller gentry had lost ground to such grandees. The *szlachta* of almost a million gentlemen, which was legally the Polish "nation," was in the main poor and dominated by the great magnates, who would not surrender the power to arrange a confederation or manipulate the Diet. At the bottom of Polish society were some of the most miserable peasants in Europe, over whom landlords still had rights of life and death in 1700. The Polish towns hardly counted; after devastation in the wars of the seventeenth century their total population only amounted to half a million or so.

Poland was the only one of the eastern states to go under completely. The principle of an elective crown blocked the emergence of a dynasty which could identify its own instincts of self-aggrandizement with those of the nation and drag it into modernity. Instead Poland entered the eighteenth century under another foreign king, the elector of Saxony, chosen to succeed John Sobieski from a field of ten candidates in 1697. Though Poland got some pickings from the Turkish booty in 1699, the eighteenth century would bring final disaster. Within a few years the signs were obvious: the new king was deposed by the Swedes only to be put back on his throne again by the Russians.

The emergence of Russian power

Russia, whose national identity had barely been a reality in 1500, would in 1800 be one of the most powerful states in the world. But such a future long seemed inconceivable. Ivan IV, crowned in 1547, was the first man to bear the title of Tsar of All the Russias and his ferocious vigor earned him the nickname "the Terrible," but he hardly mattered in European affairs. So little was Russia known even in the seventeenth century that a French king could write to a tsar not knowing that he had been dead for ten years. Though a new Russia was slowly emerging, it did so almost unnoticed in the west. Since the eighteenth century, on the other hand, Russia has loomed enormously large, and we must realize how sudden and even astonishing was her appearance on the world stage.

Even after Ivan the Great, Russia was territorially ill defined and exposed. The Turks had pushed into southwest Europe; between them and Muscovy were the Cossack lands (the modern Ukraine) inhabited by peoples who fiercely protected their independence. In the east the Ural Mountains were a theoretical frontier. Russia's rulers have always found it easy to feel isolated in the middle of their large, hostile space. Almost instinctively they have sought to push out to the natural frontiers or to form a protective buffer of client states.

When Ivan the Terrible came to the throne, Russia had only a small Baltic coast but a vast territory, scarcely inhabited by its scattered and primitive peoples, up to the White Sea. This provided a new route to the west. The English were using it in the 1500s; in 1584 Archangel was founded. Ivan could do little on the Baltic but turned on the Tatars (after they had burned Moscow yet again) and drove them from Kazan and Afghanistan. He won control of the whole length of the Volga, carrying Muscovite power to the Caspian Sea, but could not conquer the Crimea.

The other great thrust of Ivan's reign was across the Urals into Siberia and was less a matter of conquest than settlement. The first Russian colonists in Siberia seem to have been political refugees from Novgorod. Among those who followed were runaway serfs (serfdom did not exist in Siberia) and aggrieved Cossacks. Others had less pressing motives. Soon after Ivan's death in 1584 there were Russian settlements as much as 600 miles beyond the Urals, encouraged by a government anxious to assure itself tribute in furs.

The rivers were the keys to Siberia, more important even than those of the American West. By 1650 a man and his goods could travel by river with only three portages from Tobolsk, 300 miles east of the Urals, to the port of Okhotsk, 3,000 miles away. There he would be only 400 miles by sea from Sakhalin, the northernmost of the major islands of the chain which makes up Japan—a sea passage not much longer than that from New York to Norfolk, Virginia. By 1700 there were 200,000 settlers east of the Urals, and Russia and China had already negotiated a treaty to regulate settlement along the Amur River, their common frontier in the Far East. Some Russians, we are told, talked of the conquest of China.

Siberia was not much affected by the upheavals and dangers of the "Time of Troubles" which followed Ivan's death, though in western Russia there were moments when the outlet to the Baltic was lost and even when Moscow and Novgorod were occupied by Lithuanians or Poles. The rising power of Sweden, too, was thrown against Russia, and the tsars finally regained Smolensk and Little Russia from Poland in 1667.

Maps and treaties now began to define Russia's west in a way which had some correspondence with reality instead of being commentaries on a largely unknown land. By 1700, though Russia still had no Black Sea coast, her southwestern frontier ran west of the Dnieper River for most of its length, embracing the historic city of Kiev and the Cossacks who lived on the east bank. They had appealed to the tsar for protection from the Poles and were granted special semiautonomous governmental arrangements, which they retained until Soviet times. Most Russian gains had been at the expense of Poland, but Russian armies joined the Poles in alliance against the Ottomans in 1687; this was a historic moment, the beginning of what came to be known as the Eastern Question.

Apart from the migration eastward, the making of Russia was overwhelmingly a matter of political calculation. Russia did not grow; she was built. The country had no unity of blood or language and precious little geographical definition to settle her shape. There was only unity in religion and the continuing aggrandizement of tsars whose personal domain and power grew step by step with their conquest of new lands. Autocracy and empire went together. The governmental apparatus was long rudimentary, but Ivan the Terrible was already able to raise an army from feudal levies, which led the king of Poland to warn the English queen, Elizabeth I, that if they got hold of western technical skills, the Russians would be unbeatable. The danger was remote, but the comment was prescient.

Romanov autocracy

Though the Time of Troubles was a bad setback, the survival of Russia was not at stake. The last tsar of the House of Rurik died in 1598. Usurpation and disputing of the throne between noble families and Polish interventionists went on until 1613, when the first tsar of a new house, the noble family of Romanov, emerged. Michael was a weak ruler who lived in the shadow of his dominating father, but in 1613 he founded a dynasty which was to rule Russia for 300 years — until tsardom itself collapsed. His seventeenth-century successors fought off the depredations of rival nobles and humbled the great among them, the boyars, who had attempted to increase a power curbed by Ivan the Terrible.

The crown's only other potential internal rival was the church. It was already weakened by schism before a great step in Russian history was taken when a quarrel led the tsar to depose the patriarch in 1667. There would be no Investiture Controversy in Russia. From 1667 the church was structurally and legally subordinated to a lay official. Plenty of spontaneous doctrinal and moral opposition to current orthodoxy among believers would emerge, and there began the long-lived and culturally very important movement of underground religious dissent called the *raskol* (which would eventually feed political opposition) but Russia never knew the conflict of church and state which was so creative a force in western Europe.

The result of these processes was the final evolution of tsarist autocracy, a semisacrosanct authority unlimited by clear legal checks. It emphasized the service owed to the state by all subjects and the derivation from the state of all institutions within it except the church. They had no independent standing of their own. In practice tsarist government lacked any distinction of

Mysterious Russia

Explaining the ways of Russian government to the outside world has long been a profitable exercise. Defectors are not new, either. Grigorii Karpovich Kotoshikin was a seventeenth-century Russian administrator who did both. His defection was connected with the fact that he had been supplying the Swedish government with information while employed by the tsar. From his memoirs comes the following comment on the official Russian attitude to travel abroad by Russians.

The men of the Russian state are arrogant by nature and untrained in all things, because they do not and cannot receive a good education in their country . . . They do not send their children to foreign lands for education and study, being afraid that a knowledge of the beliefs and customs of foreign lands and the blessed freedom of those lands will change their children's beliefs, and that upon their return the children will have no care and thought for their own homes and kinsfolk. It is forbidden for Muscovites to travel abroad on any occasion, except for those who are sent by order of the tsar or are given travel permits for trading purposes. Although merchants do go abroad for trade, they must produce written pledges from well-born and eminent men, guaranteeing that they will not remain in foreign lands with their goods and possessions but will return home with everything. If a prince, or a boyar, or anyone else, should go abroad himself, or send his son or his brother abroad for whatever purpose without informing and petitioning the tsar, he would be charged with treason, and his patrimonial estates and pomest'ia and possessions would be confiscated by the tsar.

From George Vernadsky et al., eds., *A Source Book for Russian History from Early Times to 1917* (New Haven: Yale University Press, 1972), vol. I, p. 229. Copyright © 1972 by Yale University.

powers and was bureaucratic and military in emphasis. These qualities were not all present at the start, nor were all of them equally operative and obvious at all times. But they decisively mark tsardom off from monarchy in the Christian west, where far back in the Middle Ages towns, estates of the realm, guilds, and other bodies had established the privileges and liberties on which later constitutionalism was to be built. Louis XIV might believe in divine right and aspire to a great concentration of power, but his power was always explicitly restricted by rights, by religion, by divinely-ordained law. Though his subjects knew he was an absolute monarch, they were sure he was not a despot. In England an even more startlingly different monarchy was developing under the control of Parliament. Divergent from each other as English and French governments were, they both bore the stamp of a tradition unknown in Russia and accepted practical and theoretical limitations inconceivable to tsardom. In the west Russian autocracy was to be a byword for despotism for the whole of its existence.

Yet autocracy suited Russia. Perhaps the attitudes which underlay it still exist in some measure, to judge by Russian acceptance of governmental practices unimaginable in western Europe. Eighteenth-century sociologists suggested that big, flat countries favored despotism. This was overly simple, but there were always latent centrifugal tendencies in Russia, embracing so many natural regions and so many different peoples. The tsars' title, significantly, was Tsar of All the Russias, and the empire had always to be held together by a strong pull toward the center if its divisions were not to be exploited by enemies on the borders.

Though the humbling of the boyars left the ruling family isolated in its eminence, it was isolated in a sea of nobles. The Russian nobility was increasingly brought to depend on the crown. The theory was that nobility derived from service, often rewarded in the seventeenth century with land and later with the grant of serfs. Indeed all land was held on the condition of service to the state, and the obligations laid on nobles were very large, often extending over a man's lifetime. A reverse tendency set in around the middle of the eighteenth century, and the duties of the nobility were progressively diminished until almost removed altogether. Nevertheless, service was always the route to an automatic ennoblement, and the Russian nobles were never so independent of their monarch as those in other countries, nor did they ever constitute a closed caste. Instead the Russian nobility grew hugely by new accessions and natural increase and made up nearly the whole socially dominant class. Some of its members were very poor because there was neither primogeniture nor entail in Russia and property could be much subdivided in three or four generations. Most nobles in 1777 had less than a hundred serfs, and for every great man with thousands there were hundreds of lesser gentry with a handful.

Peter the Great

Of all Russia's rulers the one who made the most memorable use of autocratic power and did most to shape its character was Peter the Great. In

1682 he came to the throne a child of ten and by the time he died in 1725 something had been done to Russia which could never be quite undone. He resembles later strong men who have striven ruthlessly to drag traditional societies into modernity. But he was also very much a monarch of his own day, his attention focused on victory in war—Russia was only at peace for one year in his entire reign—and he accepted that the road to that goal would have to run through modernization and westernization. This may owe something to his childhood; he grew up in a quarter of Moscow where foreign merchants lived with their retinues. His own celebrated pilgrimage to the west confirmed his interest in technology. Probably in his own mind Peter did not clearly separate the urge to modernize his countrymen from the urge to free them from the fear of invasion. Whatever the exact balance of his motives, his reforms have ever since served as something of an ideological touchstone; generation after generation of Russians were to look back with awe and ponder what he had done and its meaning for Russia. As one of them wrote in the nineteenth century, "Peter the Great found only a blank page . . . he wrote on it the words Europe and the West."

Peter's territorial achievement is the easiest to assess. Though he sent expeditions off to Kamchatka and the oases of Bokhara, his policy was shaped above all by a driving ambition to reach the sea. Commerce was at the back of his mind in the south. For a while he had a Black Sea fleet and

Peter the Great, craftsman. The tsar gets on with his boat building while dictating letters to his secretary. (*Czar Peter House, Zaandam*)

annexed Azov but it had to be abandoned later because of distractions elsewhere, from the Poles and above all the Swedes. The wars with Sweden for
a Baltic outlet were struggles to the death. Foreigners recognized that something decisive had happened when in 1709 the Swedish army, the best in
the world, was destroyed at Poltava in the middle of the Ukraine (where
they had been trying to find allies among the Cossacks). The rest of his reign
drove home the point, and at the peace which ended the Great Northern
War in 1721, Russia was firmly established in Livonia, Estonia, and the Ka-
relian isthmus. Sweden's seventeenth-century Baltic empire was now a tiny
patch of Pomerania (which she was to keep until 1814) and her days as a
great power were over. She had been Russia's first victim.

A few years before the peace the French *Almanach Royale* for the first
time listed the Romanovs as one of the reigning families of Europe. Victory
had opened the way to easier contact with the west. Peter had already anticipated the successful outcome of the war by beginning in 1703 to build on
captured territory St. Petersburg, the beautiful new city which was to be the
Russian capital for two centuries. It was a deliberate break with the past. The
political and cultural center of gravity passed from the isolation of Muscovy
to the edge of the developed societies of the west.

Muscovy of course had never been completely cut off from Europe. A
pope had helped arrange Ivan the Great's marriage, hoping he would turn to
the Western church. The English merchants who made their way to Moscow
under Elizabeth I are to this day commemorated in the Kremlin by the presence there of a magnificent collection of the work of English silversmiths.
Other traders followed them and the occasional expert also came to Russia

Russian censorship imposed
subterfuge on critics of the regime.
In this attempt religious opponents
give a cat in a folk tale Peter the
Great's features. *(Slavonic Division,
The New York Public Library, Astor,
Lenox and Tilden Foundations)*

from the west. In the seventeenth century the first permanent embassies of
European monarchs were established, but the Russian response was always
tentative and suspicious. As in later times, attempts were made to segregate
foreign residents and they lived in a special quarter of Moscow.

Peter threw tradition aside. He wanted experts—shipwrights, gun
founders, teachers, clerks, soldiers—and granted privileges to get them. He
set up schools to teach technical skills and founded an academy of sciences.
Like many other great reformers he put much energy into what might be
thought superficialities. Courtiers were ordered to wear European clothes,
the old long beards were cut back, and women were told to appear in public
in German fashions. Such psychological shocks to tradition were indispensable in so backward a country. Peter was virtually without allies in his efforts
to drag Russians into a stage of civilization already taken for granted further
west and in the end such things as he achieved had to be driven through by
force. They rested on autocratic power and little else. The old Duma of the
boyars was abolished and a new Senate of appointed men took its place.
Those who resisted were ruthlessly broken, but it was less easy for Peter to
dispose of the conservative force of habit.

The most striking index of successful modernization was Russia's new
military might: the defeated Swedes and Turks were indisputably great military powers. More complicated tests are harder to make. St. Petersburg became the focus of a fairly westernized higher nobility which by 1800 was
largely French speaking and fully in touch with western currents of thought,
but it was often resented by the provincial gentry and formed a cultural island in a backward nation. The mass of the nobility did not benefit from Peter's schools and academies, and further down the social scale the great majority of Russians remained illiterate peasants. Those among them who
fought their way through to literacy did so for the most part at the rudimentary level offered by the teaching of the village priest, often himself only one
generation removed from illiteracy. Russia would not be literate until the
twentieth century.

Serfdom and the Russian economy

Russia's social structure tended more and more to mark her off from the
west. She was not to abolish serfdom until 1861; of the major nations only the
United States kept bonded labor for longer. In most countries serfdom crumbled in the eighteenth century, but in Russia it spread and strengthened itself, largely because labor was always scarcer than land.

The number of serfs had begun to increase in the seventeenth century
when the tsars found it prudent to gratify nobles by giving them land, some
of which already had free peasants settled on it. Debt tied them to their
landlords and many of them entered into bondage to the estate to work it off.
Meanwhile, the law imposed more restrictions on the serf and increasingly
tied the structure of the state to that of the economy. The landlords' power to
restrain the flight of serfs and recapture runaways grew steadily, and land-

lords were responsible too for collecting the poll tax and for military conscription. The estate structure was thus integrated with the service principle; essentially Russian landowners were hereditary civil servants. Economy and administration were more completely united than in any western country.

By the end of the eighteenth century there was little that a lord could not do to his serfs short of inflicting death on them. About half of the Russian people were in bondage to private lords, a large number of the remainder owing almost the same services to the crown and always in danger of being granted away to nobles by the tsar. As new lands were annexed, their populations passed into serfdom even if they had not known it before. The result was a great rigidifying of the social structure. There was a high rate of desertion, serfs making for Siberia or even volunteering for the galleys. Russia's greatest problem for the next hundred years was already in existence: what to do when both economic and political demands made serfdom increasingly indefensible but when its scale presented colossal problems of reform. It was as if a man were riding an elephant; it is all right so long as he keeps going but there are problems when he wants to get off.

Servile labor was the backbone of the Russian economy. Except in the famous "black earth" zone of the Ukraine, only beginning to be opened up in the eighteenth century, Russian soil is by no means rich, and even on the best land farming methods were poor. It seems unlikely that production ever kept pace with population until the twentieth century, and periodic famines and epidemics were the natural restoratives of balance as the Russian population steadily grew. It much more than doubled in the eighteenth century to reach 36 million or so, about 7 million having been acquired with new territories. This was a faster rate of growth than any other European country achieved. But only about one in twenty-five people lived in towns, and Russia was unique in basing industrialization on serfdom.

In spite of backwardness, the economy made striking progress after 1700. Though there had been industrial beginnings under the first two Romanovs, it was Peter the Great who launched official guidance of Russian industrialization. His achievement was real, but Russia's starting point was very low. On the other hand, the economies of other European countries, too, were at that time capable of only very low growth rates. Though grain production rose and the export of cereals (later a staple of Russian overseas trade) began in the eighteenth century, increased agricultural production was obtained by bringing more land under cultivation and perhaps by the more successful extraction of the surplus by the landlord and tax collector. This was to be the story throughout most of the imperial era and sometimes the load was crushing: taxes took an estimated 60 percent of the peasant's crop under Peter the Great. Nonetheless, this agricultural base somehow supported both the military effort needed to make Russia a great power and the first phase of her industrialization.

Perhaps, then, it is not surprising that by 1800 Russia produced more pig iron and exported more iron ore than any other country in the world. Peter, more than any other man, was responsible. He grasped the importance of Russia's mineral resources and built the administrative apparatus to grapple with them. He initiated surveys and imported miners to exploit them. By way of incentive the death penalty was prescribed for landlords who concealed mineral deposits on their estates or tried to prevent their use. Communications were improved to allow access to these resources so that during the century the center of Russian industry shifted toward the Urals. The rivers were crucial, and only a few years after Peter's death river travel easily linked the Baltic to the Caspian.

Around this core of extractive industry which, together with her forests, ensured Russia a favorable balance of trade for the whole century, manufacturing grew up. Less than 100 factories in Peter's reign became more than 3,000 by 1800. After 1754, when internal customs barriers were abolished, Russia was the largest free-trade area in the world, but the state continued to shape the economy; Russian industry did not emerge because of free enterprise but because of regulation.

This was the only way for Russia, since industrialization ran directly against the grain of Russian social fact. There might be no internal customs barriers, but neither was there much internal trade. Most Russians lived in 1800 as they had in 1700, within self-sufficient local communities depending on their own artisans and hardly emerging into a money economy. "Factories" were often little more than agglomerations of artisans under one employer. Over huge areas labor service, not rent, was the basis of land tenure. Foreign trade was still mainly in the hands of foreign merchants. Moreover, though state grants and allocations of serfs encouraged mine owners, the need of such encouragement shows that the stimuli producing growth elsewhere were lacking in Russia. Russia's advance in the eighteenth century to the level of economic development of most of the rest of Europe was a great relative achievement, but did not mean so much in absolute terms; only a tiny proportion of her people were engaged in manufacturing or extractive industry in 1800.

Catherine the Great

The monarchy's contribution to industrialization did not end with Peter the Great but was less clearly marked after his death. In this as in other areas there was a notable flagging of royal energy as the rulers who followed him faced a renewed threat from the great noble families. Peter had had his own son tortured to death and had not named a successor. Though the Romanov dynasty was preserved through female descent, depositions and palace plots weakened the authority of the crown. Then in 1762 Peter III, who had reigned barely six months, was forced to abdicate by a conspiracy among his guards supported by the church and an influential nobleman (whose brother subsequently murdered the deposed tsar). This overmighty subject was the lover of Peter III's widow, a German princess who became Catherine the Great.

The glitter with which Catherine subsequently surrounded herself masked a great deal; it often took in her contemporaries and almost hid the bloody and dubious route by which she had come to the throne. The first part of her reign was a ticklish business; powerful interests existed to exploit her mistakes, and for all her identification with her new country (she had renounced her Lutheran religion to become Orthodox) she was a foreigner. "I shall perish or reign," she once said. She reigned, and to great effect. Her government was even more spectacular than Peter the Great's, but its innovative force was less. She too founded schools and patronized the arts and sciences. But where Peter had been concerned with practical effects, Catherine strove to associate the prestige of enlightened thinkers with her court and legislation; the forms were often progressive while the reality was reactionary. Close observers were not taken in.

Catherine's essential caution was shown by her refusal to tamper with the powers and privileges of the gentry. She was the tsarina of the landed class, and she gave it greater power over the local administration of justice and over serfs, who lost the right to petition against their masters. Only twenty times did the government restrain landlords from abusive use of their serfs in Catherine's thirty-four-year reign. She abolished the nobles' service obligation and in 1785 granted them a charter of rights which sealed a half-century of retreat from the policies of Peter the Great. In return for organizing conscription and collecting the poll tax, landlords were exempted from personal taxation, corporal punishment, and billeting of soldiers; they could be tried (and deprived of their rank) only by their peers, and they were given the exclusive right to set up factories and mines. The landowner became more the partner than the employee of the autocracy. In the long run this did not benefit the state or society. Russia was increasing the inflexibility of her social structure at a time when other countries were beginning to loosen theirs. This would make her more and more unfit to meet challenges and changes.

One sign of trouble was the scale of serf revolts. They had begun in the seventeenth century, but the most frightening and dangerous rebellion was the one led by a Cossack named Pugachev (1773–1775). It was the worst of the regional movements which stud Russian agrarian history. Better policing would contain later outbreaks, but revolt was to continue through almost the whole imperial era. This is hardly surprising. The burden of labor services piled on the peasants in the black earth zone where land was richest rose sharply during Catherine's reign. When critics appeared among the literate class the condition of the peasant would be one of their favorite themes. Their attention to this topic provided an early demonstration of a paradox which appeared in many developing countries over the next two centuries. Modernization was more than a matter of technology and power; if you borrow western ideas, their effects cannot be confined. The first critics of orthodoxy and autocracy were soon to appear.

Yet in 1796 when Catherine died autocracy was still secure, and Russia's place in the world impressive. The most solid ground was the weight of her armies and diplomacy. Catherine once said that she had been well treated by Russia, to which she had come "a poor girl with three or four dresses," but that she had repaid her adopted country with Azov, the Crimea, and the Ukraine. Thus she stood in the line of predecessors who had continued to

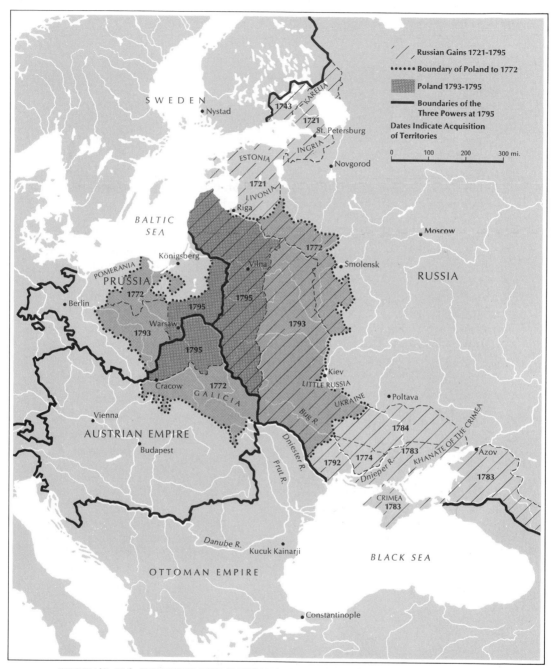

RUSSIA'S 18th-CENTURY EXPANSION AND THE DISAPPEARANCE OF POLAND

press forward with Russian claims in directions pointed out by Peter the Great. The momentum he had provided carried the foreign policy of Russia forward even when the monarchy was weak.

The new Prussia

With Sweden eliminated as a mainland power by Peter, only Prussia or the Habsburg empire could provide a counterweight to balance Russia's new power. Yet for most of the eighteenth century these two were at logger-heads with each other.

Prussia had only become a kingdom, with the consent of the emperor, in 1701 when the elector of Brandenburg took the new title of Frederick I, king of Prussia. Hitherto, Prussia had been a duchy united to Brandenburg in the sixteenth century. The electorate's history went back to a Polish king who had taken Prussia from the Teutonic Knights and secularized it in the early sixteenth century. Soon after, the elector of Brandenburg added it to his own dominions as a fief of the Polish crown. The Hohenzollern family to which he belonged had provided a continuous line of electors since 1415 and had steadily added to their ancestral domains. Religious toleration was the rule in them after one elector turned Calvinist in 1613 but his countrymen re-mained Lutheran. The electors ruled a disparate and dispersed collection of

PRUSSIA 1721–1772

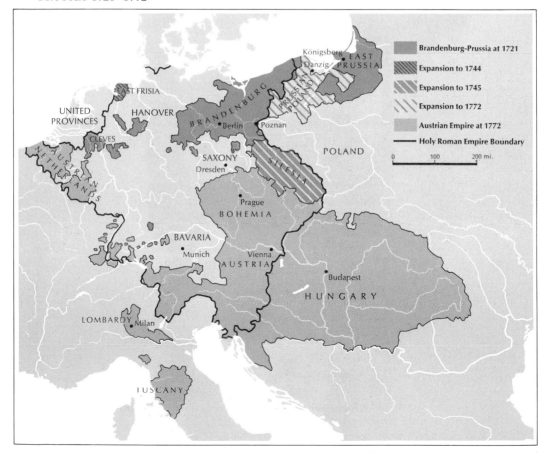

lands stretching from East Prussia to Cleves on the Rhine. The Swedes provided most of the infilling of this scatter of territories in the second half of the seventeenth century when the Great Elector, Frederick William, established the standing army and won the victories which were the basis of the finest military tradition in modern European history.

Frederick William exploited his position as a Protestant by appealing to anti-Catholic sentiment in other states of the Empire. He also talked the language of German patriotism against the foreigners who abused Germany in the Thirty Years' War and the Swedish war which followed. At home he pressed forward to create an effective bureaucracy. He was willing to shed blood to assert the authority of a centralized state, and subsequent electors were not troubled by opposition. Arms and diplomacy carried his successor Frederick I to the kingly crown he coveted and to participation in the Grand Alliance against Louis XIV. But the war imposed a heavy cost, and at Frederick I's death in 1713 Prussia badly needed a period of careful housekeeping to set her affairs in order. This is exactly what was provided by the next king, Frederick William I, a personally unattractive monarch who nevertheless left his son the means to make Prussia a great power—the best army and the best-filled treasury in Europe.

Frederick II is known as the Great because of the use he made of these assets, largely at the expense of the Habsburgs and the kingdom of Poland, though his own subjects also paid through heavy taxation and foreign invasion. He did not create the Prussian tradition, but he was the greatest exploiter of it before the nineteenth century. It is difficult to decide whether he was more or less attractive than his father (whom he hated) for Frederick was malicious, vindictive, and completely without scruple. But he was highly intelligent and much more cultivated, playing and composing for the flute and enjoying the conversation of clever men. He was also utterly devoted to the interests of his dynasty and the magnification of its prestige. He gave up some remote western lands but added to Prussia the rich Habsburg province of Silesia and later Poznan from Poland and the principality of East Frisia.

The opportunity for the conquest of Silesia arose when the emperor died in 1740 leaving a daughter, whose succession he had sought to assure but whose prospects were uncertain. This was Maria Theresa, who became Frederick's most unforgiving opponent. Her intense personal dislike of him was reciprocated. A general European war "of the Austrian Succession" in which Prussia twice intervened lasted until 1748. At the end Frederick held Silesia. The subsequent Seven Years' War did not wrench it from his grasp though this was Austria's principal aim. There was one more war between the two rulers, an unimportant exercise in which no battle was fought.

The conflict between Frederick and Maria Theresa holds more significance for European history than might be thought to lie in competition for a province, however rich, or for the leadership of the princes of Germany. For one thing, it is a reminder of how alive the dynastic preoccupations of the past still were in the eighteenth century. More important is the emergence of a century-long theme with great consequences for Europe as a whole: the struggle between Habsburg and Hohenzollern for the mastery of Germany.

A royal musician. Frederick the Great (who also composed music) performs on the flute for his guests at Sans Souci. *(Radio Times Hulton Picture Library)*

To the winner would go the power to sway the destinies of Europe. There would be periods of good relations between the two, but a long contest opened in 1740.

During Maria Theresa's reign the overstretching of Habsburg interests became very obvious. The Austrian Netherlands were an administrative nuisance rather than a strategic advantage. But the worst distractions from German problems arose in the east, as the second half of the century revealed the likelihood of a long and continuing confrontation with Russia over the fate of the Ottoman empire.

Austro-Russian tensions and the partitions of Poland

For thirty years or so Russo-Turkish relations had slumbered with only occasional minor eruptions before Catherine fought her most successful war against Turkey (1768–1774). Paradoxically, the Turks had rushed into it. In an obscure Bulgarian village called Kuchuk Kainarji Russia and Turkey signed a peace which was one of the most important of the whole century. The Turks gave up their suzerainty over the Crimean Tatars, and Russia received the territory between the Bug and Dnieper rivers, the right of free navigation on the Black Sea and through the Straits, and a right to negotiate with the Turks the interests of "the church to be built in Constantinople and those who serve it." This last provision was in some ways the most pregnant of all with future opportunity because it recognized the Russian government as the guarantor and protector of new rights the sultan granted to his Greek— that is, Christian—subjects. In the following century it was to prove a blank check for Russian interference in Turkish affairs.

Almost at once it became clear that Kuchuk Kainarji was a beginning not an end. In 1783 Russia annexed the Crimea, and another war with the Turks carried her frontier to the Dniester River. The next obvious boundary was the river Prut, which meets the Danube a hundred miles or so from the Black Sea, and the possibility of a Russian army at the mouth of the Danube was to remain an Austrian nightmare.

Meanwhile a new danger had appeared for Austria on another front. It seemed likely that Russia would absorb Poland. With the eclipse of Sweden, Russia had her own way in Warsaw. In support of a puppet king, Russian armies invaded Poland in 1733. The factions and quarrels of the Polish magnates blocked the road to reform and without reform Polish independence was bound to be a fiction.

Not that there was any shortage of reform programs. When a former lover of Catherine the Great became king of Poland in 1764, there seemed for a moment a chance of a real improvement. But the opportunity was checkmated by skillful Russian exploitation of religious divisions to produce confederations which speedily reduced the country to civil war.

The end of Poland's independence came when the Turks declared war on Russia in 1768. To avoid the danger of an Austrian declaration of war on the Russians (who were so successful that they seemed likely to make big gains at the expense of the Turks), Frederick the Great proposed that everyone should have a prize at Poland's expense. The Russians agreed since it looked as if the old system of indirect control in Poland would no longer secure their interests. The result was the first partition of Poland.

In 1772 Russia, Prussia, and Austria shared between them about onethird of Poland's territory and one-half of her inhabitants. The next stage in the process of demolition came in 1793; only Russia and Prussia shared in this second partition which did not leave much for the third (1795) in which Austria once more joined. That was the end of Poland for a century and a quarter. Russia did best overall in terms of territory, gaining something like 180,000 square miles; in the next century it would become obvious that her population of dissident Poles was by no means clear gain. Nevertheless, the transformation of eastern Europe since 1500 was complete and the seal set on the rise of Russia to great power status. The stage was set for the nineteenth century when there would be no Polish booty left to divert Austria and Russia from the Ottoman problem. The Ottoman empire itself was forever gone as a serious competitor for power in eastern Europe; a future in which it would be the victim of others lay ahead—some thought it might follow Poland into partition. The fourth eastern power, Prussia, was only indirectly concerned with the Turkish prospects, but its new stature, too, announced a new age in eastern Europe.

The changes in the east had unrolled while the world the diplomats had to deal with had been changing in other ways too. Not all the changes had lasted, disturbing though they had been in their day. The future international importance of the United Provinces and Sweden had been unimaginable in 1500, but their glory had been brief and had waned by 1800; though both still had great economic success ahead, they were by then nations of second rank. France was to be as much a first-rank power in the age of nation states as she had been in the days of dynastic rivalry; indeed her strength was relatively greater in 1800 than in 1500 and its peak was still to come. But she faced a new challenger, and one which had already defeated her. From the little English kingdom of 1500, cooped up in an island off the coast of Europe under an upstart dynasty, had emerged the world power of Great Britain in the eighteenth century. This had happened almost as surprisingly and suddenly as the rise of Russia and transcended the old categories of European diplomacy quite as dramatically. It was another indication of the way issues had changed in 300 years. European conflicts and disputes had migrated from the old battlegrounds of Italy, the Rhine, and the Netherlands to central and eastern Germany, the Danube valley, Poland and Carpathia, the Baltic, and even across the oceans. With Russians on the Amur and British and French struggles in the Americas, the beginnings of world politics could dimly be seen.

chapter 24

Europe's Assault on the World

A NEW PHASE OF HISTORY

From the earliest times great areas of civilization had grown more and more dissimilar. After 1500 the tide began slowly to turn as one culture spread over or came to influence the whole globe. This had never happened before and it revolutionized world history.

The first signs of this revolution took the form of direct European expansion. By 1800 European nations had laid claim to more than half the world's land surface and in varying degree actually controlled about a third of it. In the Western hemisphere they had transplanted enough settlers to constitute new centers of civilization. From former British territory in North America a new nation had emerged, and to the south the Spaniards had destroyed two mature cultures to implant their own. Eastward the story was different but equally impressive. Once past the Cape of Good Hope (where something like 20,000 Dutch lived) an Englishman traveling on an East Indiaman would not touch at a European colonial settlement like those of the Americas unless he wandered as far off course as Australia, just beginning to receive her settlers. But throughout East Africa, Persia, India, and Indonesia he would find numbers of Europeans who had come to do business and then, in the long or short run, return home to enjoy the profits. They could even be found in Canton and a very few were allowed to live in the closed island kingdom of Japan. Only the African interior, protected still by disease and climate, seemed impenetrable.

The remarkable transformation thus begun (and to go much further) was a one-way process. Europeans went out to the world, it did not come to them. Few non-Europeans other than the Turks entered early modern Europe except as exotic imports or slaves. The Arabs and Chinese were by no means unskillful sailors; they had made oceanic voyages and knew about the compass. And the simple island peoples of the Pacific for centuries made long sea crossings on their mysterious errands. In spite of this, though, the ships which sailed around the Horn or the tip of Africa to Atlantic ports until well into the nineteenth century were European ships homeward bound, not Asian ones.

Through Eastern eyes: a Portuguese vessel
from Macao arrives in seventeenth-century Japan. *(Museum of Fine Arts, Boston,
Fenollosa-Weld Collection)*

The trend toward European domination seemed irreversible by the end
of the eighteenth century, and so it was long to prove. No civilization had expanded more rapidly and dramatically, untroubled by any but temporary and
occasional setbacks. This success was based on its great initial advantages.

Powerful motives to succeed were an important asset. The great thrust
behind the Age of Discovery had been the wish for easier and more direct
contact with the Far East, the source of goods badly wanted by Europeans.
Yet the Far East wanted virtually nothing from Europe. When Vasco da
Gama showed the gifts he had brought for a king, the inhabitants of Calicut
laughed at him; he had nothing to offer which could compare with what

Arab traders already brought to India from other parts of Asia. Indeed it was the known superiority of so much of Oriental civilization that spurred the Europeans to try to reach it on a regular and assured basis; China, India, and Japan were at something like their cultural peaks in the sixteenth and seventeenth centuries. The land blockade of Europe by the Turk made these rich societies even more attractive than they had been before. By 1500 enough had been done for the business of exploration and new enterprise to be attacked confidently; each successful voyage added both to knowledge and to the certainty that more could be done. As time went by, sizable profits accumulated to finance further expansion.

There was also the psychological asset of Christianity. This found a vent in missionary enterprises, but in a more general sense it assured the European that he was at least in one way superior to the "heathen" cultures he began to encounter. This was liable of course to have disastrous effects on the peoples he met. Confident in their possession of the true religion, Europeans overseas were reckless, impatient, and sometimes contemptuous of the values and achievements of the societies they disturbed. It is also true that religious zeal could easily blur into less avowable motives. As the greatest Spanish historian of the American conquests put it, he and his colleagues had gone to the Indies "to serve God and his Majesty, to give light to those who sat in darkness, and to grow rich as all men desire to do."

Greed for gain quickly led to domination and exploitation by force. The outstanding examples of this would be the eventual destruction of whole societies and the huge traffic across the oceans in black slaves, but the theme of dominance was there from the beginning. The adventurers who first penetrated the coasts of India were soon boarding Asian merchant ships, looting their cargoes, torturing and slaughtering their crews and passengers, and burning the ravaged hulks. The Europeans could exact what they wanted because of a technical superiority which exaggerated the power of their tiny numbers.

There was a fitting symbol in the action of the next Portuguese captain after da Gama to visit Calicut: he bombarded it. A little later when the Portuguese first arrived at Canton in 1517, they fired a salute as a gesture of friendship and respect, but the noise of their guns terrified the Chinese. There had long been guns in Asia, and the Chinese had known about gunpowder centuries before Europe, but their technology in artillery had then stood still. In contrast, European craftsmanship and metallurgy had made great strides in the fifteenth century, producing weapons superior to any available elsewhere in the world. There were still more dramatic improvements to come, and the relative advantage of Europeans would increase right down to the twentieth century.

Europe's expertise in artillery was paralleled in other fields, notably by the developments in shipbuilding and navigation already touched upon. When combined, such advances produced the remarkable weapon with which Europe would open up the world, the sailing ship which was a gun carrier. Again evolution was far from complete in 1517, but by then the Portuguese had been able to fight off the Turkish fleets attempting to bar them from the Indian Ocean. The Turks had more success in keeping control of the Red Sea because in those narrower waters the oar-propelled galley which closed in on its enemies to grapple and board retained some of its usefulness. But even there the Portuguese had penetrated as far as the Suez isthmus. The Chinese war junk would do no better than the rowed galley. Abandoning the oar for propulsion and mounting large numbers of guns broadside enormously multiplied the value of Europe's scanty manpower.

European technical advantage was obvious to contemporaries. The Dutch in the seventeenth century were very anxious to keep the secrets of gun manufacture from passing into the hands of Asians. Yet pass they did. There had been European and Turkish gunners in India in the fourteenth century, and before the Portuguese reached China they were supplying the Persians with cannon and teaching them how to cast more in order to embarrass the Turks. In the seventeenth century the Jesuits' knowledge of gun founding and gunnery was one of the attractions which kept them in favor with Chinese authorities. But Chinese artillery remained inferior to Europe's in spite of the Jesuits' training. More than mere know-how separated the two societies.

Europe possessed not only knowledge but an attitude toward knowledge different from that of other cultures. There was a readiness to bring new knowledge to bear upon practical problems, a technological attitude. In it lay the roots of another European characteristic, a new confidence in the power to change things. Here was perhaps the most fundamental difference between Europe and the rest of the world. Europe was open to the future and its possibilities in a way that other cultures were not. Even in 1500 Europeans had seen some of the future — and it worked.

AFRICA AND ASIA

Portuguese explorers figured so largely and successfully in the opening of routes to the East at the beginning of the sixteenth century that their king took the title (confirmed by the pope) "Lord of the conquest, navigation, and commerce of India, Ethiopia, Arabia, and Persia." This sufficiently indicates both the scope and the Eastern bias of Portuguese enterprise but is slightly misleading in its reference to Ethiopia, with which Portugal's contacts were small. Any real penetration of Africa was impossible. The Portuguese suggested that God had intentionally set a barrier around the African interior in the form of its mysterious and noxious diseases. (These would in fact hold Europeans at bay until the end of the nineteenth century.) Even the coastal stations of West Africa were not healthy and were tolerated only because of their commercial importance. Portugal's successors in Africa would also leave the interior alone, and its history would move largely to its own obscure rhythms for another two centuries, except where its inhabitants felt the stimulating and corrosive contact with Europeans at its fringes.

Of course, at the opening of the European Age none of the powers concerned was primarily interested in the subjugation or settlement of large areas of Asia either. European imperialism there down to the middle of the eighteenth century is a story of the multiplication of trading posts, concessions in port facilities, protective forts, and coastal bases; these would assure the only thing it initially sought in Asia — secure and profitable trade.

Portuguese empire in the eastern seas

Portuguese trading supremacy roughly coincided with the sixteenth century. Their fire power enabled the Portuguese to sweep all before them, and they rapidly built up a chain of bases and trading posts. Twelve years after Vasco da Gama's arrival at Calicut, they established their main Indian Ocean trading station at Goa, some 300 miles further up the western coast of

India. It was to become a missionary center as well as a commercial one; the Portuguese empire strongly supported the propagation of the faith. The Franciscans played a leading part in this, and one consequence is modern India's large Roman Catholic population. In 1513 the first Portuguese ships reached the Moluccas, the legendary spice islands; the incorporation within the European world of Indonesia, southeast Asia, and islands as far south as Timur had begun. Four years later the Portuguese opened direct trade with China. In 1555 they were allowed a permanent settlement at Macao, which belongs to Portugal to this day.

When Charles V gave up Spanish rights in the Moluccas, keeping only the Philippines in the Far East and renouncing any interest in the Indian Ocean area, Portugal had nearly a monopoly of Eastern empire. It was not only a trading monopoly with Europe; there was much business to be done between Asian countries. Persian carpets went to India, cloves from the Moluccas to China, copper and silver from Japan to China, Indian cloth to Siam in European ships. Both the Portuguese and their successors found this profitable; it helped offset the unfavorable balance of Europe's trade with Asia, which for a long time wanted little from the West except silver.

The only serious competitors at sea were the Arabs who for centuries had traded between East Africa, the Persian Gulf, India, and Indonesia. They were soon mastered by Portuguese squadrons operating from East African bases, from Socotra at the mouth of the Red Sea, from Ormuz at the entrance to the Persian Gulf, and from Goa. The Portuguese eventually pushed into the Red Sea as far as Massawa and up to the head of the Persian Gulf, where they established a "factory" or trading depot at Basra. They also secured trading privileges in Burma and Siam and in the 1540s were the first Europeans to land in Japan. This network of stations and privileges was supported by diplomatic agreements with local rulers and the superiority of Portuguese fire power at sea.

The Dutch seaborne empire

Portugal's supremacy disguised her fundamental weaknesses: a lack of manpower and a shaky financial base. By the end of the century she was surpassed by the Dutch, the trading imperialists par excellence. Their opportunity arose when Portugal was united with Spain in 1580. This change provided a stimulus, for it brought to an end the profitable reexport trade of Oriental goods from Lisbon to northern Europe which had been mainly in the hands of Dutch seamen at a time when the Netherlands' revolt encouraged them to enter areas where they might make profits at the expense of Spain. They had important advantages in the pool of naval manpower, ships, wealth, and experience built up by their ascendancy in fishing and transport in northern waters. Their commercial strength at home made it easy to mobilize resources for new enterprises. The Dutch were assisted too by the simultaneous resurgence of the Arabs, who won back the East African stations north of Zanzibar as Portuguese power wavered in the aftermath of union with Spain.

In the first decades of the seventeenth century Dutch power replaced Portuguese in many places in the East. The main objective was the Moluccas, the source of nutmeg and cloves. A brief period of voyages by individual venturers (sixty-five in seven years, some around the Strait of Magellan and some around Africa) ended in 1602. In that year the States General, the government of the United Provinces, took the initiative in the setting up of the Dutch United East India Company, which was to prove the decisive instrument of Dutch commercial supremacy in the East. Like the Portuguese before them, the company's servants worked through trading stations and diplomacy with native rulers to exclude competitors. How unpleasant the Dutch could be to rivals was shown when they executed ten Englishmen at Amboina in 1623; this ended any attempt by England to intervene directly in the spice trade.

Amboina had been one of the first Portuguese bases seized by the Dutch, but it was not until a resident governor general was sent to the East in 1609 that they could begin taking over the major Portuguese forts. The center of these operations was the Dutch headquarters at Jakarta, renamed Batavia, in Java. Some Dutch planters settled in this area where they could rely upon the company to back them up in their ruthless control of the native labor force. The early history of the Dutch colonies is a tragic one of insurrection, deportation, enslavement, and extermination. The trade of native shippers and of Chinese junks was deliberately destroyed.

The spice trade to Europe was the focus of Dutch attention and was a huge prize. During most of the seventeenth century it accounted for over two-thirds of the cargo sent back to Amsterdam. But the Dutch also set about replacing the Portuguese in the lucrative inter-Asian trade. Since they could not dislodge the Portuguese from Macao, despite expeditions against them, they set themselves up in Formosa, from which they built up an indirect trade with China. In 1637 the Portuguese were expelled from Japan and the Dutch succeeded them there. In the next two decades they also replaced the Portuguese in Ceylon. Their successful negotiation of a trade monopoly with Siam, on the other hand, was overtaken by France, whose connection with Southeast Asia was opened by accident in 1660 when circumstances took three French missionaries to the Siamese capital. A French diplomatic and military mission followed in 1685. But these promising beginnings ended in civil war and failure there, and Siam moved back out of the sphere of European influence for another two centuries.

In the early eighteenth century the nerve center of Dutch supremacy in the Eastern seas, which to a remarkable degree reproduced the earlier Portuguese one, was the Malacca Strait. From there Dutch power radiated through Malaysia and Indonesia, reaching north to Formosa and the trading links with China and Japan and southeast to the crucial Moluccas, where their spice monopoly had never been shaken. This area was enjoying an internal trade so considerable that it was beginning to be self-financing; bullion from Japan and China provided its flow of currency rather than European bullion as in the early days. To the west the Dutch were also established at Calicut, in Ceylon, and at the Cape of Good Hope and had set up factories

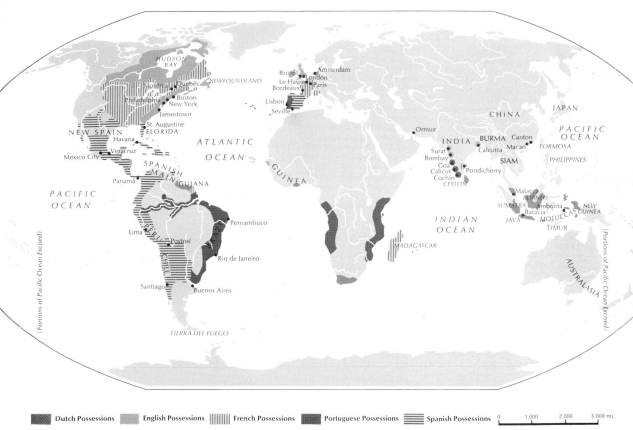

Dutch Possessions   **English Possessions** ||||| **French Possessions**   **Portuguese Possessions**   **Spanish Possessions**   0   1,000   2,000   3,000 mi.

OVERSEAS POSSESSIONS 1713

in Persia. Although Batavia was a big town and the Dutch had plantations to grow the goods they needed, their commercial empire was still a littoral one, not based on domination of the interior mainland. It rested on naval power in the last resort and would succumb, though not disappear, as Dutch naval power was surpassed.

India: beginnings of the Raj

In the last decades of the seventeenth century the Dutch encountered an unlikely challenger, England. An English East India Company had tried to get into the spice trade under James I, and its merchants had gotten bloody noses for their pains, whether they tried to cooperate with the Dutch or fight them. The English therefore needed to change course. The upshot was that by 1700 they had in effect drawn a line under their accounts east of the Malacca Strait. There was to follow the most momentous event in British history before the onset of industrialization, the acquisition of supremacy in India, where their main rivals were not the Dutch or the Portuguese but the French.

The creation of the Raj, as British rule in India came to be called, began in 1612 when the first factory of the East India Company was set up at Surat by permission of native authorities. In the middle of the seventeenth century England acquired Bombay from Portugal as part of the dowry of Charles II's queen. For a long time it was the only Indian territory the English held in full sovereignty and it became the company's main base. Since the 1640s there had also been a factory operating at Madras on the Carnatic coast. This was the limit of English penetration in India until the end of the century.

From these footholds the East India Company of London conducted a trade in coffee and textiles less glamorous than the Dutch spice trade but of growing value (as the establishment of coffee houses in London showed). Another profitable step was taken when ships stopping at India began to be sent on to China for tea; by the end of the seventeenth century the English had found their national beverage in what a poet would soon commemorate as "cups that cheer but not inebriate." Military domination was not necessary for this prosperity. Though an important acquisition was made when the company was allowed to occupy a post at Calcutta, where Fort William was built, the directors rejected in 1700 as quite unrealistic the idea of acquiring fresh territory or planting colonies in India. But all this was to change. The Mogul empire began to collapse after the death of Aurangzeb in 1707. The

A factory, or trading settlement, in seventeenth-century India. It was a warehouse, place of residence, and a defensible site, with a church of its own. (*The Bettmann Archive*)

consequences for British and French alike emerged slowly as India dissolved into a collection of autonomous states with no paramount power.

The Mogul empire had been in trouble before 1707. Popular discontent and the authorities' tendency to lose control of peripheral areas had always favored the nawabs, or provincial governors. Real power had been increasingly divided between them and the Mahrattas. The Sikhs provided a third focus of power. Originally appearing as a Hindu sect in the sixteenth century, they had turned against the Moguls but had also drawn away from orthodox Hinduism to become virtually a third major religion in India. The Sikhs were a military brotherhood, had no castes, and were well able to look after their own interests in a period of disunion. Eventually a Sikh empire appeared in northwest India which would endure until 1849. Meanwhile there were signs in the eighteenth century of an increasing polarity between Hindu and Muslim. The Hindus withdrew more into their own communities, hardening the ritual practices which publicly distinguished them. The Muslims reciprocated. On this growing dislocation, presided over by a Mogul military and civil administration which was conservative and unprogressive, there fell also a Persian invasion in the 1730s which resulted in losses of territory.

There were great temptations to foreign intervention in this situation. In retrospect it seems remarkable that both British and French waited so long to take advantage of it; even in the 1740s the East India Company of London was still less wealthy and powerful than the Dutch. When the British did begin to intervene, moved largely by hostility to the French and fear of what they might do, they had several important advantages. They possessed a station at Calcutta which placed them at the door to India's potentially richest prize, Bengal and the lower Ganges valley. They had assured sea communications with Europe thanks to their naval power, and governments in London listened to the East India merchants as French merchants were not listened to at Versailles. Although France was the most important competitor, her government was often distracted by European commitments. Finally, the British lacked missionary zeal: not only in the narrow sense that Protestant interest in missions awakened much more slowly than Catholic and the company could legally exclude missionaries, but also, more generally, the British had no wish to interfere with native customs or institutions. Somewhat like the Moguls, they sought only to provide a neutral power structure while commerce prospered in peace.

The way into an imperial future was intervention in Indian politics. The British and the French provided support for Indian princes in their rivalries with one another and this was the first, indirect form of competition between the two European powers. By 1744 this had led to armed conflict between British and French forces in the Carnatic. India was thus gradually sucked into the worldwide power struggle between Great Britain and France, and fighting went on there even while the two nations were officially at peace after 1748. The French cause prospered under a brilliant governor, Dupleix. He extended French power by force and diplomacy and greatly alarmed the British, but he was recalled to France. The French company was not to en-

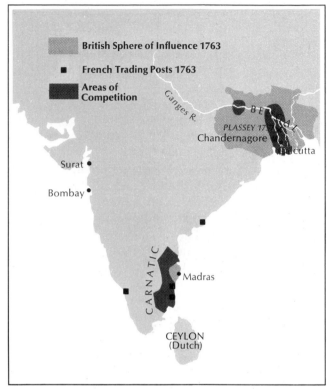

ANGLO-FRENCH RIVALRY IN INDIA 1754–1763

joy the whole-hearted support of the home government which it needed to emerge as the paramount power in India. When the Seven Years' War broke out in Europe in 1756, the nawab of Bengal attacked and captured Calcutta. His brutal treatment of his British prisoners, many of whom were suffocated in the soon legendary "Black Hole," gave additional offense. The company's army, commanded by a young Scotch employee, Robert Clive, retook the city, seized the French station at Chandernagore, and then on June 22, 1757, won a battle over the nawab's much larger armies at Plassey about a hundred miles up the Hooghly River from Calcutta.

Plassey was not a very bloody battle (the nawab's army was suborned), but it was a decisive one in world history. It opened the road to British control of Bengal and its revenues and the destruction of French power in the Carnatic; ahead lay the future British monopoly of the whole of India. London had begun to grasp what was at stake and sent out a battalion of regular troops to help the company; this gesture is revealing, not only because Britain recognized that a national interest was involved but also because only a tiny scale of military effort was needed. A very small number of European troops with European field artillery could be decisive. The fate of India turned on the diplomacy of the company's agents and the handful of European and European-trained soldiers in its employ. Upon this narrow base and the necessities of government in a disintegrated India the British Raj was built.

The Seven Years' War was decisive in India; the peace of 1763 left the French with only five unfortified trading posts. In 1764 the British East India Company became the formal ruler of Bengal. This had by no means been the intention of the company's directors, who sought not to govern but to trade. However, if Bengal could be taxed enough to pay for its own government, then the burden could be undertaken. In 1769 the French company was dissolved. Soon after the British took Ceylon from the Dutch, and the way was cleared for a unique example of imperialism.

The road would be a long one and for some time reluctantly followed, but the company was gradually compelled by its revenue problems and by the disorder of native administrations in contiguous territories to extend its own governmental role. The obscuring of the company's primary commercial role was not good for business. It also gave its employees even greater opportunities to feather their own nests. Before the end of the eighteenth century this began to draw the interest of British politicians, and gradually legislation cut into the company's independence in governing. The outcome was a system of dual control by the British crown and company in India which was to last until 1858. There were also provisions against further interference in native affairs; the British government hoped as fervently as the company to avoid being dragged any further into the role of imperial power in India. But this was what happened in the early nineteenth century as many more acquisitions followed.

The effect was revolutionary. India was quite unlike any other dependency so far acquired by a European state in that hundreds of millions of subjects were joined to a colonial power without any conversion or assimilation being envisaged. The character of the British empire would be profoundly affected as a result. So would British strategy, diplomacy, external trade patterns, and even ideology. It was revolutionary for India too. In the long run the British would leave; unlike earlier conquerors they were not in India to stay. It would not be India's astonishing assimilative power which defeated them as it had done their predecessors, though. And they would leave behind as deep an imprint as conquerors of historical times.

THE AMERICAS

Columbus' landing in the New World was followed by a fairly rapid and complete exploration of the major West Indian islands and some settlement, particularly in Hispaniola and Cuba. At first Spain had no competitors in this zone, and with the exception of Brazil the story of the opening up of Central and South America remains virtually Spanish until the end of the sixteenth century. The colonists as agriculturalists wanted land and as speculators sought gold. The settlers in the islands were often Castilian gentry—poor, tough, and ambitious. Those who went on to the mainland were out for booty though they spoke also of the message of the Cross and the greater glory of the crown.

Spanish imperialism

The first penetration of the mainland had come in Venezuela in 1499. Then Balboa crossed the isthmus of Panama in 1513, and Europeans for the first time saw the Pacific. His expedition built houses and sowed crops; this was an announcement that the Spaniards were on the mainland to stay. The age of the conquistadors had begun. The one among them whose adventures would best capture and hold the imagination of posterity was Hernán Cortés. In 1519 he left Cuba with an expedition of a few hundred men. He was deliberately flouting the authority of its governor and subsequently justified his acts by the spoils he brought to the crown. Upon landing at Vera Cruz he burned the ships he and his men had come in to ensure that they could not go back and then began the march to the high central plateau of Mexico which is one of the most dramatic tales of the whole history of imperialism. When the Spaniards reached Mexico City, they were astounded by the civilization they found there. Besides its wealth of gold and precious

Mexico City in the sixteenth century. The Indian causeways and ceremonial sites have been incorporated into the Spanish city. *(Rare Book Division, New York Public Library, Astor, Lenox and Tilden Foundations)*

stones, moreover, it was situated in a land suitable for cultivation in a manner familiar to Castilians at home.

Though Cortés' followers were few and their conquest of the Aztec empire which dominated the central plateau has appeared heroic, they enjoyed great advantages. The people upon whom they advanced were technologically primitive and easily impressed by the gunpowder, steel, and horses of the conquistadors. The Aztecs hesitated to resist because of an uneasy feeling that Cortés might be an incarnation of their god, whose eventual return they were expecting. They were also very susceptible to imported diseases. Finally, they were themselves an exploiting race and a cruel one, whose priests exacted human sacrifices from their subjects; the other Indians they ruled welcomed the conquerors as liberators or at least a change of masters. Nevertheless, the explanation of the conquest ultimately lies in the toughness, courage, and ruthlessness of the Spaniards.

In 1531 Francisco Pizarro set out upon a similar conquest of Peru. This was an even more remarkable achievement and, if possible, displayed more vividly the rapacity and ruthlessness of the conquistadors. Settlement of this new empire began in the 1540s and almost at once produced one of the most important mineral discoveries of historical times—a mountain of silver at Potosí, which would be the main source of bullion for Europe for the next three centuries.

By 1700 the Spanish empire in the Americas formally covered a huge area stretching from today's New Mexico south to the Plata River. By way of Panama and Acapulco it was linked by sea to Spanish ports in the Philippines. This extent was misleading. The lands north of the Rio Grande—California, Texas, and New Mexico—were very thinly inhabited; for the most part Spanish occupation meant a few forts and trading posts and a large number of missions. Nor was Chile to the south well settled. The most important and most densely populated regions were New Spain (as Mexico was called); Peru, the most civilized part of Spanish America and valuable for its mines; and some of the larger Caribbean islands colonized earlier. The colonial administration long neglected areas unsuitable for settlement by Spaniards.

The Indies were governed by viceroys at Mexico City and Lima who represented the crown of Castile. There was a royal council of the Indies, too, which imposed a high degree of centralization in theory; in practice geography and topography made nonsense of such a pretense. It was impossible to exert close control over New Spain or Peru from Europe with the communications available. The viceroys and captains-general under them enjoyed an important and real independence in their day-to-day business. But the colonies could be run by Madrid for fiscal advantage; indeed for over a century Spain and Portugal were the only powers colonizing in the Western hemisphere which managed to make their American possessions not only pay for themselves but return a net profit to the home country. This was largely because of their wealth of precious metals. After 1540 silver flooded across the Atlantic, to be dissipated in the wars of Charles V and Philip II.

The Spanish colonial system

Spain shared with other colonizing powers of the age the belief that only a limited amount of trade was available and that trade with imperial possessions should be reserved for their rulers by regulation and force of arms. She also endorsed another commonplace of early economic theory, the view that colonies should not be allowed to develop industries which might compete with those of the home country. But Spain was less successful than other powers in putting these ideas into practice. Though there were regulations to prevent the development of any but extractive or handicraft industries in Spanish America, the colonial authorities found it increasingly hard to exclude foreign traders, interlopers as they came to be called, from their territories. Spanish planters wanted things Spain could not supply—slaves especially.

Apart from mining, the economy of the islands and New Spain rested on agriculture. The islands would come to depend on black slavery; in the mainland colonies a Spanish government unwilling to countenance the enslavement of the conquered populations evolved other devices for ensuring compulsory labor. The earliest was a kind of feudal lordship, started in the islands and extended to Mexico: a Spaniard would be given an encomienda, a group of villages over which he extended protection in return for a share of their labor. The general effect was not always easily distinguishable from serfdom or even slavery. The practice was strongly attacked by churchmen, among them one of the first great humanitarian critics of settler society, the Dominican Bartolomé de las Casas. He not only urged the duty of church and royal government to protect Spain's Indian subjects but was one of the few within the Catholic church to denounce all forms of slavery. He had some success in influencing legislation and administration but not enough to protect the Indians when a decline in their population was creating a grave labor shortage.

The presence of large native populations to provide labor was just as crucial as the nature of Spanish rule in differentiating the colonial experience of Central and South America from that to the north. Several centuries of Moorish occupation in their peninsula had accustomed the Spanish and Portuguese to the idea of living in a multiracial society, and they lacked the concern for purity of blood which was shown by the English and French. Consequently there was soon a large population of mixed blood in the southern colonies. When the Portuguese finally secured Brazil from the Dutch after thirty years' fighting, they interbred with the growing Negro population whose origins lay in imported slaves. (In Africa too the Portuguese did not worry about racial mixing, and their lack of a color bar remained to the last days of their empire one of its most striking features.)

Though the establishment of racially mixed societies over huge areas was an enduring legacy of the Spanish and Portuguese empires, these societies were nonetheless stratified in ways that ran along racial lines. The governing classes were the Iberian-born and the creoles, persons of European blood born in the colonies. As time passed, the latter came to feel that the

The Cruelty of Empire

It is one of the glories of the Spanish Church that it provided at a very early date criticism and rebuke of what its countrymen were doing in the New World. The sermon from which this extract is taken was preached in 1511 on Hispaniola (the modern Cuba) by a Dominican, Antonio de Monterinos, to a congregation of the leading colonists. It appears to have been the first protest against the way the Indians were treated and to help them enlists the menace of hellfire for their oppressors.

In order to make your sins against the Indians known to you I have come up on this pulpit, I who am a voice of Christ crying in the wilderness of this island, and therefore it behooves you to listen, not with careless attention but with all your heart and senses, so that you may hear it; for this is going to be the strangest voice that ever you heard, the harshest and hardest and most awful and most dangerous that ever you expected to hear . . . This voice says that you are in mortal sin, that you live and die in it, for the cruelty and tyranny you use in dealing with these innocent people. Tell me, by what right or justice do you keep these Indians in such a cruel and horrible servitude? On what authority have you waged a detestable war against these people, who dwelt quietly and peacefully on their own land? . . . Why do you keep them so oppressed and weary, not giving them enough to eat nor taking care of them in their illness? For with the excessive work you demand of them they fall ill and die, or rather you kill them with your desire to extract and acquire gold every day. And what care do you take that they should be instructed in religion? . . . Are these not men? Have they not rational souls? Are you not bound to love them as you love yourselves? . . . Be certain that, in such a state as this, you can no more be saved than the Moors or Turks.

former, called *peninsulares*, excluded them from key posts and antagonism grew between the two. Below them flowed blurred graduations of blood down to the poorest and most oppressed—the pure Indians. Though local tongues survived, Spanish and Portuguese became the dominant languages on the continent. Language and religion were the great formative influences making for the cultural unification of what was later called Latin America.

The Catholic church played an enormous part in creating Spanish and Portuguese America and acquired an enduring place there. The mission stations of the frontier determined the shape of countries born only centuries later. For good or ill (and its paternalism has been seen as damaging to the Indians' culture and independence) the church saw itself as the protector of the Indian subjects of the crown. Certain important effects of this would only be felt after centuries had brought shifts in the demographic center of gravity within the Roman communion, but many implications were visible much earlier. The church was, for example, virtually the only access the Indians had to European culture, and they found some features of Catholicism, in particular the cult of the Virgin, sympathetic and comprehensible.

The Catholic monopoly also meant an identification of the church in some measure with the administrative and political structure. Although certain priests were later to play important parts in the revolutionary and independence movements of South America, the church as a whole could not easily adopt a progressive stance. The Inquisition was soon set up in New Spain, and it was the church of the Counter Reformation which shaped Catholicism south of the Rio Grande. In the long run this meant that clericalism would become an issue in the politics of independent Latin American states just as it would in Catholic Europe. This was all in marked contrast to the religiously pluralistic society which appeared in British North America.

The Caribbean colonies

For all the spectacular inflow of bullion from the mainland colonies, the part of the New World which mattered most to the Old in the early modern period was the West Indies. Their importance was based on their agricultural produce, sugar above all. Both the Caribbean and Brazil were transformed economically by this crop. Medieval man had sweetened his food with honey; by 1700 sugar though still expensive was a European necessity. Along with tobacco, hardwood, and coffee it gave the planters great importance in the affairs of their respective mother countries.

Commercial agriculture arrived in the Caribbean with the early Spanish settlers, who were soon growing fruit (brought from Europe) and raising cattle. They also introduced rice and sugar cane, but production of these was held back for a long time by a shortage of labor. The native population of the islands succumbed with alarming swiftness to European mistreatment and disease. The next economic phase was the establishment of parasitic industries: piracy and smuggling. The Spanish occupation of the larger islands—the Greater Antilles—still left hundreds of unoccupied smaller ones, mostly on the Atlantic fringe, which attracted the attention of English, French, and

Dutch sea captains. They used them as bases from which to prey on Spanish ships and for contraband trade with Spanish colonists. Some European settlements also appeared on the Venezuelan coast where there was salt available for preserving meat. Where individuals led, governmental enterprises followed in the seventeenth century, in the form of English and French royal concessions and the Dutch West India Company.

The English had for decades been looking for suitable places for "plantations," that is, settler colonies, in the New World. They already had colonies on the North American mainland when in the 1620s they established their first successful settlements in the West Indies — on St. Christopher in the Leeward Isles and on Barbados. Both prospered and their success was based on tobacco. These colonies rapidly became of great importance to England because they supplied customs revenue, and their growth stimulated demand for English exports and provided fresh opportunities for interloping in the trade of the Spanish empire. The French soon joined the English in this lucrative business, occupying the Windward Isles while the English took over the rest of the Leewards. In the 1640s there were about 7,000 French in the West Indies and over 50,000 English.

In the middle of the century the tide of English emigration to the New World shifted to North America, and the number of white settlers in the English colonies in the West Indies began to fall. This was partly because sugar cane joined tobacco as a staple crop. Tobacco can be produced on small as well as large plantations; it had helped to multiply small farms and build up a large immigrant population of whites. Sugar cane is only profitable if cultivated in large units; it suited the big plantation worked by large numbers of slaves, and big plantations meant fewer white landowners. The Dutch supplied the slaves and aspired to a general commercial monopoly in the Western hemisphere such as they were winning in the Far East, working out of a base at the mouth of the Hudson River, New Amsterdam. Sugar production initiated a great demographic change in the Caribbean. In 1643 Barbados had 37,000 white inhabitants and some 6,000 Negro slaves; by 1660 there were over 50,000 of the latter.

With the appearance of sugar the French colonies of Guadeloupe and Martinique took on a new importance and they too wanted slaves. A complex process of expansion was under way. The Caribbean's huge and growing market for slaves and imported European goods added to the commercial opportunities and the Spanish empire was increasingly unable to defend its economic monopoly. This determined the role of the West Indies in the relationships of the powers for the next century. They were long a prey to disorder; the Caribbean was an area where colonial frontiers met, policing was poor, and there were great prizes to be won (one year a Dutch captain captured the great fleet bearing home to Spain the year's treasure from the Indies). Not surprisingly the Caribbean became the legendary hunting ground of pirates, whose heyday was the last quarter of the seventeenth century. Gradually the great powers fought out their disputes until they arrived at acceptable agreements, but this took a long time. Throughout the eighteenth century the West Indies remained the great market for slaves and also became involved in another economy, that of British North America.

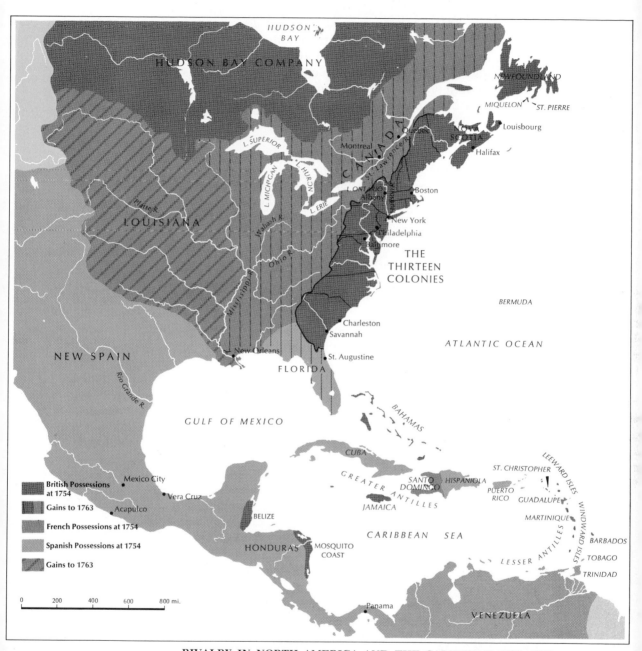

RIVALRY IN NORTH AMERICA AND THE CARIBBEAN 1754–1763

Map legend:
- British Possessions at 1754
- Gains to 1763
- French Possessions at 1754
- Spanish Possessions at 1754
- Gains to 1763

Scale: 0   200   400   600   800 mi.

North American beginnings

For a long time North American settlement was a poor second in attractiveness to what was going on in the Caribbean and Latin America. The continent did not seem to have any precious metals and except for furs in the north offered little that Europe wanted. Yet there was nowhere else to go, given the Spanish monopoly to the south, so a great many nations tried settling there. Spain was not one of them: her expansion north of the Rio Grande was less an occupation than a missionary exercise, and Spanish Florida's importance was strategical, protecting communications with Europe by the northern outlet from the Caribbean. The real efforts at colonization were made on the Atlantic coast, where even a New Sweden briefly appeared beside New Netherland, New England, and New France.

The motives for settling North America were for the most part those which operated elsewhere. During the sixteenth century English explorers hoped to discover mines there to rival those of the Spanish Indies, and were also lured by the possibility of finding a northwest passage to Asia. Other Europeans felt that population pressures at home made emigration necessary, and increasing knowledge revealed ample land in temperate climates with very few native inhabitants. By 1600 these impulses had produced much exploration but only one (unsuccessful) settlement north of Florida, at Roanoke, Virginia. The English were too weak, the French too distracted to achieve more. The seventeenth century brought more strenuous efforts and a revolutionary transformation of the Atlantic littoral. The stage was set in the first decade.

Spain still claimed North America in 1600, but this had long been contested by the English on the ground that "prescription without possession availeth nothing." The Elizabethan adventurers had explored much of the coast and given the name Virginia, in honor of their queen, to all the territory north of 30 degrees latitude. In 1606 James I granted a charter to the Virginia Company to establish colonies, and in 1607 the first English settlement which would survive in America was established at Jamestown, Virginia. It only just came through its early trials, but by 1620 its "starving time" was over and it began to prosper.

The year after Jamestown's foundation the French explorer Samuel de Champlain built a small fort at Quebec. The colony was so insecure that for years its food had to be brought from France, but it was the beginning of Canada. A curious anticipation of the future soon occurred; the French established good relations with the Huron Indians while the settlers at Jamestown were allying with the Iroquois, the hereditary foes of the Huron. When the two areas of settlement impinged on one another and the two European nations began to conflict later in the century, their Indian allies would gladly join in the struggle.

The Dutch arrived in 1609. They had sent an English explorer, Henry Hudson, to find a northeast passage to Asia. When he was unsuccessful, he turned completely around and sailed across the Atlantic to look for a northwestern one. Instead he discovered the river that bears his name and established a preliminary Dutch claim by doing so. Within a few years there were Dutch settlements along the river and on Manhattan and Long Island.

English and French colonization

The English were in the lead in settlement and remained so. They prospered for two reasons. One was their method of colonization: they were the

Reconstructions of the wigwams built by early English settlers in New England. They borrowed the design from the local Indians. Later the log cabin was adopted. *(Society for the Preservation of New England Antiquities)*

first and most successful exponents of the technique of transporting whole communities—men, women, and children. They set up agricultural colonies, worked the land with their own labor, and were soon independent of the mother country for their livelihood. The second was the discovery of tobacco, which became a profitable export crop first for Virginia and then for Maryland, a colony chartered in 1632. Farther north land which could be cultivated on European lines assured the prosperity of the New England colonies. Although interest in this area had originally been aroused by the possibilities of fur trading and fishery, the settlers were soon producing a small surplus of grain for export. This was an attractive prospect for the land-hungry English, and something like 20,000 of them went to New England in the 1630s.

The distinctive feature of the New England colonies was their association with religious dissent and Calvinistic Protestantism. Although the usual economic motives were at work in the settlements, the Puritanism of the first immigrants to Massachusetts in the 1630s resulted in the evolution of a group of colonies whose constitutions varied from theocratic oligarchy to democracy. They shed more rapidly than the southern colonies their inhibitions about radical departures from English social and political practices, and their religious nonconformity did much to bring this about. At some moments during the English constitutional troubles in the middle of the century the colonies of New England seemed likely to escape from the crown's control altogether, but they remained loyal.

A victorious peace in 1667 awarded England the Dutch settlements in what was subsequently called New York, and by 1700 the North American littoral from Florida north to the Kennebec River was organized into twelve English colonies. (A thirteenth, Georgia, appeared in 1732.) This vast area contained some 400,000 whites and perhaps a tenth as many Negro slaves. The wilderness of 1600 had become an important center of civilization. In many places settlement went as far inland as the mountain barrier of the Alleghenies. Farther north lay still disputed territory and then lands that were definitely French.

The French population in North America was comparatively tiny in 1700, numbering perhaps 20,000 in all. There had been no large immigrations of communities as in the English colonies; indeed many of the French settlers were hunters and trappers, missionaries, and explorers, strung out over the length of the St. Lawrence River and dotted about in the Great Lakes region and even beyond. New France was a huge area on the map, but outside the St. Lawrence valley and Quebec it was in reality a scatter of strategically and commercially important forts and trading posts. These were closely supervised from Paris; in 1663 direct royal rule had replaced a company structure, and Canada was ruled by a governor with the advice of an intendant much as a province in France was governed. There was no religious liberty; the Catholic church was monopolistic and missionary. Its history in Canada is full of glorious examples of bravery and martyrdom and also of bitter intransigence. The farms of the settled area were grouped in seigneuries or feudal lordships, a device which had some value in decentralizing administrative responsibility. Social life therefore reproduced the forms of the Old World much more rigidly than in the English settlements, even to the extent of throwing up a nobility with Canadian titles.

Colonial identity and independence

The territories which would eventually form the United States of America represented in their origins a wide range of motives and methods of foundation. They were also becoming ethnically diverse by 1700; Scots-Irish, German, Huguenot, and Swiss emigrants had begun to arrive in appreciable numbers after 1688, though the predominance of the English language and the relatively small numbers of non-English-speaking immigrants would maintain a culture overwhelmingly Anglo-Saxon. Though the close association of some colonies with specific denominations remained marked, in most of them there was a larger measure of effective religious toleration than in Europe, and a religiously pluralistic society existed long before the English territories began to think of themselves as one country.

Strung out as they were over almost the whole Atlantic seaboard, the colonies embodied great differences of climate, economy, and terrain. They were never to have a common local center; the crown and the mother country were the foci of their collective life as Anglo-Saxon culture was still their background. Yet it was already obvious that England's American colonies offered opportunities for individual advancement which were not available either at home or in the more strictly and closely regulated society of Canada. And some of them had already shown a tendency to grasp at independence from royal control.

It is tempting to look back a long way for evidence of the spirit of independence which would later play so big a part in popular tradition, but it would be a misconception to read the early history of the United States in those terms. The Pilgrim fathers were not rediscovered and given their prominent place in the national mythology until the end of the eighteenth century. What can be seen much earlier than the idea of independence is the emergence of factors which would in the future make independence and unity seem good ideas.

One such development was the strengthening of the system of representation in the first century of settlement. Despite their initial variety, all the colonies in the early eighteenth century worked through some sort of representative assembly which spoke for the colony to a royal governor appointed by London. Some colonies had also cooperated with one another against the Indians at an early date, and in the French wars joint action became even more important. The French threat helped create a sense of common purpose which at least at times transcended the interests of the individual colony. Furthermore, economic diversity brought a measure of interdependence. The middle and southern colonies produced plantation crops of rice, tobacco, indigo, and timber; New England built ships, refined and distilled molasses and grain spirits, grew corn, and fished. There was a growing and apparent logic in thinking that the colonies, including those in the West Indies, might perhaps be able to run their economic affairs better than the mother country, and in their own interests instead of hers.

In the eighteenth century the British colonies made great progress in wealth and civilization. Their population was well over a million halfway through the century, and by 1763 Philadelphia could rival many European cities in size. In the 1760s it was beginning to appear that the mainland colonies were going to be worth more to Great Britain than the West Indies had been. By 1763 too a great uncertainty had been removed: Canada had been conquered in the Seven Years' War and seemed likely to remain British. This gave many colonials a more favorable outlook toward both the value of the protection afforded by the imperial government and the question of further expansion to the west.

The British colonies had about filled up the coastal plain by the middle of the century and were pressing inland against the mountain barrier, particularly in the Ohio River valley and in the northwest. After 1763 the French were no longer a danger there, but the westward movement posed other problems for the British government. It had to consider the rights and likely reactions of the Indians. To antagonize them would be to court frontier warfare. But if Indian wars were to be avoided by holding the colonists back, then English troops would have to police the frontier for that purpose. Unfortunately all this was coming to a head in the last decade in which the makers of imperial policy in London accepted without demur the old assumptions about the economics of colonial dependencies and their relationship to the mother country.

The first effects of transatlantic empire

Two and a half centuries of settlement in the New World had an immense effect upon Europe but the results are far from easy to define. All the colonial powers by the eighteenth century had been able to extract economic profit from their colonies, though they did so in different ways. Most obvious was the flow of silver to Spain, and this of course had implications for Europe's economy as a whole and even for Asia. Large populations of colonists had also helped stimulate European exports and manufacturers as well as attract an increasing flow of European emigrants which would culminate in great migrations in the nineteenth century. To the growth of colonies must also be linked the enormous rise in European shipping and shipbuilding. Whether engaged in slaving, contraband trading, legal import and export, or fishing to supply new consumer markets, ship owners and captains benefited. These effects were everywhere incremental and incalculable, and it is hard to guess at all the consequences.

Of the political and cultural importance of Europe's colonial role in the Americas it is easier to speak with confidence. One fact is paramount: the Western hemisphere was to become part of the European cultural world. It would speak Europe's languages, and from Hudson Bay to Tierra del Fuego it would eventually be organized in a series of sovereign states based on her legal and administrative principles. It would also be fundamentally Christian in religion; Hinduism and Islam would come as the faiths of minorities not as rivals to a basically Christian culture.

Perhaps most important politically was what had been done in British North America. Two great transforming factors had still to operate: the westward movement across the continent and a vast tide of multinational immigration. But these forces would flow into and around molds set by the English inheritance, which was as decisive in shaping the future of the United States as Byzantium had been in shaping Russia's. Nations do not shake off their origins, they only learn to see them in different ways. Sometimes outsiders observe this most clearly. It was a German statesman who remarked toward the end of the nineteenth century that the most important international fact was that Great Britain and the United States spoke the same language.

chapter 25

The New Shape of
World History

Europe very quickly began to weave her affairs into those of the rest of the globe and the result was the first phase of European hegemony. By the second half of the eighteenth century the first world powers had appeared, the five Atlantic nations to which the Age of Discovery had given new opportunities and offered historical destinies distinct from the rest of Europe. Their emergence laid the foundations of a new international system and involved all lands except Australasia (and even this was on the eve of settlement). Furthermore, Europe had already begun to grow wealthy faster than the other great traditional centers of civilization, and in fact her new wealth (small though it may seem by later standards) was derived from the fact that she had begun already to lock other parts of the world into her economy. On these new political and economic structures would be based the next phase of European hegemony, which would express itself in the first world-wide civilization.

THE FIRST WORLD POWERS

Spain and Portugal, the only great colonial powers in the sixteenth century, were long past their zenith when the Peace of Paris was signed in 1763 and the Seven Years' War ended. This treaty is a convenient marker of a new world order which transcended Europe. It established Great Britain's ascendancy in the overseas rivalry with France which had preoccupied her for nearly three-quarters of a century. The duel was not quite over, and the French could still hope to recover lost ground. But Great Britain was the imperial power of the future. The British and French had eclipsed the Dutch, whose empire had been built, like theirs, in the seventeenth century, in the era of declining Portuguese and Spanish power. But Spain, Portugal, and the United Provinces all still held huge colonial territories and had left enduring marks on the world map.

The imperial histories of these five nations had differentiated them from both the landlocked states of central Europe and the Mediterranean lands so important in earlier centuries. This had been reflected in the increasing importance of their colonial and overseas interests in their relations with other states and with one another. Overseas expansion gave Europe's courts and chanceries new causes and places over which to quarrel.

Though medieval states had defended or extended their commercial interests through diplomacy, particularly in the Near East, they had rarely defined their interests in extra-European terms, as happened more and more after 1600. Most states were slow in recognizing that they had overseas interests as important as those in Europe. Spain fought grimly for European supremacy in the Thirty Years' War and wasted the treasure of the Indies in the process. France was often worsted in her long duel with Great Britain because of the diversion of her energies and resources to Continental ends. This was a major factor in helping the British take and hold their lead in imperial expansion.

Yet questions which were essentially European, whether dynastic, religious, or national, gradually became entangled with the regulation of trade to Spanish colonies or the treaties agreed to by Asian princes. Such entanglement was inevitable because all nations shared the same theory of imperialism. It gave primacy to the interests of the European power, which were always seen as paramount: it held that colonies existed to produce—from their natural resources or their balance of trade—a net advantage and if possible economic self-sufficiency for the mother country, and that trading bases were to give her the profits of international traffic. Since there was only so much trade to go around, one country could only gain at the expense of another.

TRADE, WAR, AND EMPIRE

In the early sixteenth century extra-European issues were not very important in diplomacy once the Spanish and Portuguese had demarcated their interests satisfactorily. Other European nations could do little to contest the vague claims of Spain to the whole of North America. The fate of a French Huguenot settlement in Florida or the legality of English voyages to Virginia hardly troubled European politics. This situation began to change when pirates and adventurers countenanced by Elizabeth I inflicted damage on Spanish fleets and colonies. Once the Dutch joined in, one of the great themes of the early modern era of diplomacy existed: a French minister under Louis XIV wrote, "trade is the cause of a perpetual combat in war and in peace between the nations of Europe." So much had things changed since the rivalry of Habsburg and Valois began.

One great issue was always Spain's claim to a monopoly of trade with her colonies. After the defeat of the Armada and the successful resistance of the Dutch, Spanish sea power no longer commanded the respect it had earlier. Philip II and his successors were caught in a dilemma to puzzle many Continental rulers. On the one hand, the struggle with France, the eighty years' war which grew out of Dutch revolt, and the Counter Reformation all claimed resources in Europe; on the other, safety in the Indies required Spanish sea power and the organization of effective means to supply the colonists' needs. They chose to try to keep the empire but use it to pay for European policies. In an attempt to reserve the wealth of the Indies for Spain alone, they organized regular sailings in convoy, concentrated colonial trade in a few authorized ports, and policed the Caribbean with coast guard squadrons.

The Dutch first made it clear that they were prepared to fight for a share of such prizes and thus European diplomats were forced to turn their attention and skills to regulating matters outside Europe. For the Dutch, predominance in trade overrode most other considerations. What they would do for it was quickly made clear by successes in the East Indies and the Caribbean. They also engaged great fleets against the Spanish-Portuguese defense of Brazil, the world's chief producer of sugar, but suffered their only serious setback there; in 1654 the Portuguese expelled the Dutch garrison and reestablished their supremacy. Thereafter the Dutch made no further attempts to establish themselves in Brazil.

The Dutch quest for commercial wealth also cut across the wishes of the most Protestant of English seventeenth-century governments. Cromwell would have liked nothing better than to lead a Protestant alliance against Catholic Spain but instead found himself fighting a war against the Dutch in the 1650s essentially over trade. The conflict arose when England restricted her imports to goods traveling in English ships or those of the producing country, a policy which struck at the European carrying trade which was the heart of Dutch prosperity. The Commonwealth had a good navy and won. The English also seized Jamaica from Spain in this period. Though this capture from the old Catholic enemy woke memories of Elizabethan days, the era of ideological foreign policy was over for England.

Cromwell's policies seem in retrospect to mark a parting of the ways. Under him England took the decisive turn toward empire and governments which would seek to protect it. The returned Stuarts kept and strengthened the Navigation Act passed under the Commonwealth for the protection of

Drawings by John White, the artist of the Roanoke expedition, of wonders seen in the Caribbean. These are among the early examples of many animals and plants which were to become familiar to Europeans. *(The Trustees of the British Museum)*

shipping and colonial trade, continued to recognize the new importance of the West Indies, and chartered the Hudson's Bay Company to contest with the French the fur trade of North America. Above all Charles II and his in other ways inadequate successor, James II, maintained (if with some setbacks) English naval strength.

The second Anglo-Dutch war came in 1665 after the English had further provoked the Dutch by seizing New Amsterdam; the Dutch and their allies had the best of it at sea. The Treaty of Breda, which ended the war, is important as the first multilateral European peace settlement to say as much about the regulation of extra-European affairs as European. By it France (Louis XIV had supported the Dutch) surrendered valuable West Indian islands to England, which in turn recognized French possession of the uninhabited and uninviting but strategically important territory of Acadia. The English also kept New Amsterdam.

There is no need to trace the detailed changes of the next hundred years during which the new imperial emphasis of British diplomacy came to maturity. The whole epoch was dominated by the slowly emerging rivalry of England and France. The War of the League of Augsburg at the end of the seventeenth century brought much fighting in the colonies but no great changes. The War of the Spanish Succession, which quickly followed, was very different. It was from the start a war about the fate of the Spanish empire as well as about French power. At its close in 1713 Great Britain not only acquired Acadia (henceforth Nova Scotia) and much else in the Americas from France but also the right to supply slaves to the Spanish colonies and to send one merchant ship a year to trade with them. After this, overseas matters loomed larger and larger in British foreign policy under the new Hanoverian dynasty installed in 1714. The goals of British commerce were often best served by maintaining general peace, sometimes by exerting diplomatic pressure, and occasionally by fighting to keep privileges or a strategical advantage.

The first time that two European powers ever went to war over a purely colonial issue was in 1739 when Britain began hostilities with Spain over, in essence, Spanish interference with British trade in the Caribbean—or, as the Spanish might have put it, over the steps Spain properly took to secure her empire against abuse of the trading privileges won in 1713. This war (picturesquely named the War of Jenkins' Ear) was soon caught up in the War of the Austrian Succession and therefore became an Anglo-French struggle too. The peace of 1748 did not change the respective territorial positions of the two rivals. Nor did it end fighting in North America where the French appeared about to cut off the British colonial settlements from the west by a chain of forts.

Britain sent contingents from her regular army to America for the first time to meet this danger, but it was not until the Seven Years' War began (badly, in 1756) that a British minister grasped that the chance of a final decision in the long colonial duel existed because of France's European commitments. Once British resources were allocated accordingly, sweeping victories in North America and India were followed by others in the Caribbean, some at the expense of Spain, which had joined the French. A British force even seized the Philippines. It was the first global war.

The peace of 1763 did not cripple France and Spain as imperial powers as many of the English had wanted, but it eliminated French competition in North America and (virtually) in India. The primacy of commerce appeared even in the treaty terms: when it was a question of keeping Canada or Guadeloupe, a sugar-producing island, one consideration in British eyes in favor of Canada was that other Caribbean growers already under the British flag feared increased competition within the empire. Though governed by landowners Great Britain continually sustained in her foreign affairs a posture determined by the interests of commerce.

This consistent foreign policy had created a huge empire by 1763. The whole of eastern North America was British including the Gulf Coast as far west as the mouth of the Mississippi River. Canada's conquest had blown away the nightmare—or the dream—of a French empire stretching from the St. Lawrence River to New Orleans, which had been born in the feats of the great seventeenth-century French explorers. Off the continental coast the Bahamas were the northern link of a British island chain that ran down through the Lesser Antilles to Tobago and all but enclosed the Caribbean. Within it, Jamaica, Honduras, and the Belize coast were British too. The limited legal right of the British to trade slaves with the Spanish empire was now pressed far beyond its intended limits. In Africa there were only a few British posts on the Gold Coast, but these were the bases of the huge African slave trade. In Asia the direct government of Bengal was about to initiate the territorial phase of British expansion in India.

Sea power

Imperial supremacy had to rest on sea power. The origins of British naval might can be traced to the ships built by Henry VIII, among the greatest warships of the age, but this early start was then neglected until the reign of Elizabeth I. Her sea captains, with little help from the crown or commercial investors, built a fighting tradition and improved the design of ships on the profits made from operations against the Spanish. Interest and effort in such adventures ebbed under the early Stuart kings; the royal administration could not afford ships. (Indeed taxes to pay for new ones were one of the things Parliament raged over when recalled after the Eleven Years' Tyranny.) The Commonwealth, ironically, inaugurated the serious and continuing attention to naval power which would sustain the Royal Navy of the future. By that time the British well understood the connection between the Dutch superiority in merchant shipping and their rival's naval strength. A strong merchant marine was a nursery of seamen for fighting vessels and one could only be built upon transporting the goods of other nations. Hence the importance of competing, if necessary with gunfire, for entry into such reserved areas as the Spanish American trade.

The ships developed to do the fighting in this competition underwent steady improvement and specialization but no revolutionary change be-

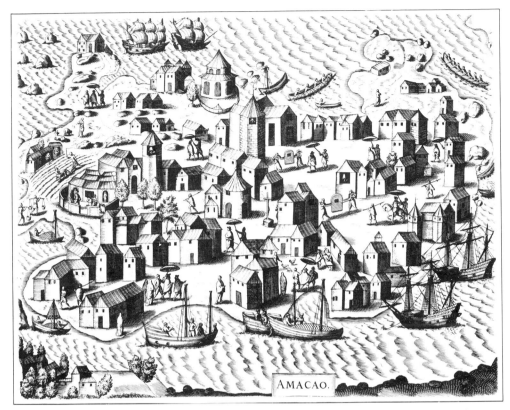

Seventeenth-century Macao. The artist obviously found it harder to render the characteristics of Chinese building than of European, but some contrasts can be detected. (*Rare Book Division, The New York Public Library, Astor, Lenox and Tilden Foundations*)

tween the fifteenth and nineteenth centuries. Once square rigging and broadside firing had been adopted, the essential shape of vessels was determined though individual design could still do much to give sailing superiority. The French often built better ships than Great Britain during the long naval duel between the two countries. Under English influence ships grew longer in proportion to their width in the sixteenth century. And the height of the forecastle and poop gradually came down over this whole period.

Specialization of function and design between warships and merchant vessels was accepted by the middle of the seventeenth century though the line was still somewhat blurred by the existence of older vessels and the practice of privateering. This latter was a way of obtaining naval power cheap. In time of war governments authorized private sea captains or their employers to prey upon enemy shipping, taking profits from the prizes they captured. It was a form of regularized piracy and the English, Dutch, and French all successfully employed it at various times against one another's traders.

Other seventeenth-century innovations were tactical and administrative. Signaling became standardized and the first "Fighting Instructions" were issued to the Royal Navy. Given equality of skill and the limited damage even heavy guns could inflict, numbers of ships were likely to be decisive, and so recruitment became more important. The press gang appeared in England and naval conscription in the maritime provinces of France.

From this seminal period of development in the seventeenth century there emerged a naval supremacy which would last over two centuries and underpin a worldwide Pax Britannica. Dutch competition dropped away as the republic bent under the strain of defending its independence against the French armies. England's important maritime rival was France, and here it is possible to see that a decisive point had been passed by 1700. Faced with the choice of being great on land or sea, the French had decided in favor of land, though French shipbuilders and captains would still win victories by their skill. The British were less and less distracted from oceanic power; rather than maintain great armies themselves they more and more paid to keep their Continental allies in the field. British maritime strategy sought to ensure command of the sea so that friendly ships could move on it in safety while those of the enemy could not. To defeat the enemy fleet in battle was therefore the supreme aim of British naval commanders throughout the eighteenth century, producing almost uninterrupted command of the seas and a formidable offensive tradition.

The growing importance and size of navies fed imperial enterprise indirectly as well. Though sailing ships depending on wind for propulsion are in principle more independent of land than modern ones depending on oil, a maritime strategy increased the need for bases from which they could operate. This aspect of territorial acquisition was particularly important in the history of the British empire. The loss of much of its settled territory in the 1780s would emphasize the fact that European hegemony outside of the New World was still a matter of trading stations, island plantations and bases, and the control of carrying trade rather than the occupation of large areas.

World trade

In under three centuries European imperialism had effected a revolutionary change in the world's economic structure. The more or less self-supporting and self-contained economies of 1500 linked by only thin threads of trade, if any, had been brought together in the first world-wide network of exchange. Even Japan was involved in a limited way, and central Africa, though still mysterious and unknown, was drawn in by slaving and the Arabs. Its first striking expressions had been the new volume of Asian trade with Europe along the sea routes dominated by the Portuguese and the flow of bullion from America to Europe and then, in part, on to Asia. Indeed, without the exploitation of America's mineral wealth there could hardly have been much trade with Asia. This may have been the most important consequence of the bullion flow, which reached its peak at the end of the sixteenth century and in the early decades of the seventeenth.

Although the flow of precious metals was the first and most dramatic effect of Europe's early interplay with Asia and America, it was less important than the general growth of trade, including slaving. The ships engaged in the slave trade usually sailed back to Europe from the Americas loaded with the colonial produce which became more and more a necessity to Europe. First Amsterdam and then London surpassed Antwerp as international ports, in large measure because of the huge growth of trade in the colonial goods which were carried by Dutch and English ships. Shipbuilding, textile manufacturing, and later financial services, such as insurance, all prospered in the general development of overseas trade. This prosperity reflected a great expansion in sheer volume. During the eighteenth century the number of ships sent out by the British East India Company increased threefold. Moreover these ships, thanks to improvements in design, carried more goods and were worked by fewer men than those of earlier times. The Dutch trade with the Far East in the second half of the eighteenth century formed a quarter of their external commerce.

CULTURAL INTERPLAY

Complex and far reaching though they were, the economic consequences of Europe's new involvement with the world are easier to measure than others, for certain material manifestations have lasted ever since. The variety in European diet today originated in the early modern age. The increased consumption of tobacco, coffee, tea, and sugar constituted minor revolutions in taste, habits, and housekeeping. The potato changed the history of some countries by making larger populations possible. Scores of drugs, mainly from Asia, were added to the European pharmacopoeia. Such acquisitions also had a cultural content. Europeans did not discover the potato or the tobacco plant growing wild but cultivated and used by native inhabitants of the New World. Their knowledge and skill were a part of the package Europe received. In such ways societies unable to resist the European challenge left an enduring legacy to it.

Beyond such material effects it is harder to proceed. Men's minds were also changing. Books about discoveries and voyages greatly increased in number as early as the sixteenth century, and Oriental studies was founded as a science in the seventeenth. The printing press intensified the repercussions of Europe's growing knowledge of the world, and by the early eighteenth century there are signs that this new awareness was having a deep intellectual impact.

Idyllic descriptions of savages who lived lives which seemed to be morally admirable without the help of Christianity provoked reflection. One thinker used the evidence of other continents to show that human beings did not share any god-given innate ideas and might even have different ideas of right and wrong. China in particular furnished examples for speculating on the relativity of social institutions, while the penetration of Chinese literature (much aided by the studies of the Jesuits) revealed a chronology whose length made nonsense of traditional calculations of the date of the Flood (described in the Bible as the second beginning of all men).

These rather attractive cannibals, drawn about 1500, represent an early German attempt to make sense of the reports arriving in Europe of what the Portuguese found in Brazil. *(The I. N. Phelps Stokes Collection of American Historical Prints, The New York Public Library)*

China also provoked, as its products became more easily available, most of the eighteenth-century craze for Oriental styles in furniture, porcelain, and dress. As an artistic and intellectual influence this has remained more obvious than the deeper perspective given to European life by an interest in different civilizations with different standards. But while some comparisons had disquieting aspects, such as the revelation that Europe had perhaps less to be proud of in her attitude to other religions than China, others reflecting exploits such as those of the conquistadors fed the notion of European superiority.

The interplay of Europe with the rest of the world is thus not easy to encapsulate in a few simple statements but some of its manifestations are dramatically obvious. It is an appalling fact that almost nowhere in the world can the inhabitants of non-European countries be shown to have benefited materially from the first phase of Europe's expansion and often they suffered terribly. The European colonists were not always to blame—unless they should be blamed for being there at all. In an age with almost no knowledge of infectious disease, Europeans could not have anticipated the impact of smallpox and other diseases they brought to the Americas. But it was disastrous. It has been calculated that the population of Mexico fell by three-quarters in the sixteenth century and some Caribbean islands lost all their native inhabitants. The ruthless exploitation of those who survived and whose labor was so much more valuable after this demographic collapse is a different matter and expresses that leitmotiv of subjection and domination which runs through well-nigh every instance of Europe's impact on the rest of the world.

Different colonial environments and different European traditions resulted inevitably in gradations of oppression and exploitation. Not all colonial societies were based on the same extremes of brutality and horror, but all were tainted with them. The United Provinces' magnificent seventeenth-century civilization was nourished partly by roots which lay in bloody ground in the spice islands and Indonesia. In North America the good relations between the first English settlers of Virginia and their native neighbors quickly soured, and extermination and eviction of the Indians followed. The populations of Spanish America had some measure of state protection against the encomienda system, but this did not prevent their reduction to peonage and the destruction of their culture. The fate of the Hottentot in South Africa and the aborigine in Australia would repeat the lesson that European culture was devastating to those it touched unless they had the protection of an old and advanced civilization such as that of India or China. Even in those countries great damage would be done, but the colonies show most clearly the pattern of domination. Moreover their prosperity long depended on one of the most striking expressions of Europe's aggressiveness, the African slave trade.

Slavery

European enslavement of Africans has long obsessed people who have seen in it the most blatant example of an inhumanity they deplored, whether that of white to black, of European to non-European, or of capitalist to labor. It has properly dominated much of the historiography of Europe's expansion and American civilization for it was a major fact in both. Less properly it has diverted attention from other forms of slavery at other times—or even alternative fates to slavery, such as the extermination, intentional or unintentional, which overtook other peoples. African slaves are by no means the only ones to have played an important part in history, nor were Europeans the only slavers. But black slavery based on the Europeans' purchase from Africans of other Africans and their sale to other Europeans in the Americas is something with more recent repercussions than, say, the enslavement of Europeans by Ottomans or Africans by Arabs.

The story begins after slavery had withered away in Europe but while Europeans were still being enslaved by other peoples. In 1434 the Portuguese brought the first consignment of African slaves to Lisbon. Their enslavement was the work of other Africans; they were members of tribes from the interior sold to the Portuguese by their captors, peoples of the West African coast. Before long the probable importance of this trade dawned on the Portuguese. As they moved down the African coast, they set up a base at Arguim in 1448 to serve as a slaving center.

The settlement of colonies in the Caribbean where indigenous labor was scarce caused the first significant growth in the trade, and later settling of the southern Caribbean shores and the mainland of North America expanded it further. Portuguese captains imported slaves directly to Brazil as the sixteenth century wore on. Elsewhere other Europeans joined in. The English "seadogs" of Elizabeth I who fought their way into Spanish colonial commerce were among the first. Early in the seventeenth century the Dutch founded a company to ensure a regular supply of slaves to the West Indies. By 1700 their strong position had been overtaken by French and English traders who had their own posts on the "slave coast" of Africa.

The consequences became enormous as the volume of the traffic grew. Perhaps 9 or 10 million black slaves altogether were sent to the Americas, between 6 and 7 million of them in the eighteenth century. European ports like Bristol and Nantes found a new prosperity based on slaving. New lands would be opened because black slave labor made it possible to work them. The production of new crops on a much greater scale would in turn bring great changes in European demand, manufacturing, and trading patterns.

We live with the results of slavery still; what has disappeared and now can never be measured is the human misery involved—not merely in physical hardship (a black might live only a few years on a West Indian plantation, assuming he survived the horrible conditions of the voyage) but in the almost unrecorded damage to African societies and the psychological and emotional tragedies of this forced migration. Historians still debate whether slavery "civilized" blacks by bringing them into contact with higher cultures or retarded them in quasi-infantile dependence. It is probably as insoluble a question as that of the degree of cruelty to which Negroes were subjected. On the one hand is the evidence of the fetters and whipping block; on the other the fact that these were common in Europe too and self-interest ought to have prompted a planter to look after his investment. That it did not, slave rebellions show, but such resistance was remarkably infrequent. The debate is not likely to end.

The arguments with which Christians resisted any restriction of this traffic retain a certain gruesome fascination to this day, but gradually feelings of responsibility and guilt began to emerge in the eighteenth century, mainly though not exclusively in England. (As one expression of concern, English philanthropists founded Sierra Leone in 1787 as a refuge for Negro slaves freed in England.) A favorable political and economic juncture would in the end help these sentiments destroy slavery, but this is part of a different story. In the era of unfolding European world power slavery was a huge social and economic fact, and would become the outstanding embodiment of the triumph of power and cupidity over humanity.

Ambiguous gifts

Some believed that whatever the evils their fellow Europeans committed abroad, they were outweighed by what was offered to the rest of the world in Christianity. The missionary impulse was present in the Spanish and Portuguese possessions almost from the start. Jesuits began working in Goa in 1542, and their influence radiated from there all over the Indian Ocean and southeast Asia, even reaching Japan. Like the other Catholic powers, France too emphasized missions, even in areas where she was not economically or politically involved. The new vigor of missionary enterprise in the sixteenth and seventeenth centuries was one result of the Counter Reformation. In the Portuguese and Spanish possessions another result was the Inquisition — persecution followed the missions. At least formally Roman Catholicism took in more converts and covered greater tracts of territory in the sixteenth than in any earlier century. The real impact of the new religion is harder to assess, but it must be allowed that the church, although often unable to achieve much in practice, provided such protection as the native had against his Spanish conquerors and kept alive, however dimly at times, the only notion of trusteeship toward subject peoples which existed in early imperial theory.

Protestantism lagged behind. The Dutch did hardly anything. The English colonists in North America were better at enslaving Indians than converting them (the Quaker colony of Pennsylvania was a laudable exception), and England's great overseas missionary movement did not get under way until the end of the seventeenth century. But even the spread of Christianity

Cortés and his men land their goods and livestock — an Indian picture drawn after the conquest. *(Courtesy of The American Museum of Natural History)*

contained a tragic ambiguity. Not only were missionaries often bound to act as the instruments of European domination, the Gospel itself had enormously corrosive potential, challenging and undermining traditional structures and ideas, threatening social authorities, legal and moral institutions, family and marriage patterns.

Perhaps Europeans could bring nothing with them which was not double-edged. New plants introduced to the Americas became the means of feeding slaves on sugar plantations or gave excuses to drive North American Indians from their hunting grounds. Innocent innovation could also be ecologically disastrous: in the nineteenth century Australia would be devastated by rabbits and Bermuda plagued by toads after both had been brought from England. Europeans introduced many things: they carried wheat to the Americas, bananas to the West Indies, cassava, corn, and sweet potatoes to Africa, coffee to Java and Jamaica. Following success at Madeira, the Spanish established vineyards in South America and Mexico before 1600 and in California a century later. In Asia not long after 1800 tea shrubs from China were transplanted to Java and Ceylon. Probably the most important animal migrants were cattle and horses. Between them they would revolutionize the life of the Plains Indians and eventually make South America a great meat exporter. But almost the whole menagerie of Europe's domesticated animals accompanied settlers to the Americas. The British would later introduce domestic livestock to New Zealand and take to Australia the sheep they originally brought from Spain.

The Europeans brought human stock too. In Latin America, Goa, and Portuguese Africa the effects were profound in that large populations of mixed ethnic origin resulted. The Dutch for a long time did not encourage the mixing of races, but Eurasians soon appeared in India because Englishmen before 1800 often married or kept Indian women as concubines. In British North America racial intermarriage was insignificant, and the nearly exact coincidence of color and legal status bequeathed an enormous legacy of political, economic, social, and cultural problems to the future.

The creation of large colonial populations shaped a future map but also presented European governments with difficulties they were unequipped to solve. Most British colonies had some form of representative institution which reflected parliamentary tradition and practice, while France, Portugal, and Spain all followed a straightforward authoritarian and monarchical institutional system. None of the powers envisaged any sort of independence for their colonists or provided any effective means to safeguard their interests against those of the mother country. This would in time cause trouble, and at least in the British North American colonies there were signs that it might be on lines reminiscent of the conflict in seventeenth-century England between crown and Parliament. Moreover, when drawn into the rivalries of Europe, the colonists always showed a lively sense of their own interests. Even when the United Provinces and England were formally allied against France, their sailors and traders would fight in colonial waters.

This problem of conflict between colonial communities only arose seriously where there were relatively large populations of European stock. By far the majority of these were to be found in the Americas; it is striking to reflect how much the first phase of imperialism was weighted toward the Western hemisphere. Elsewhere in the world in 1800 trade still mattered more than possession, and important areas had yet to feel the full impact of Europe. As late as 1789 the British East India Company was sending only twenty-one ships a year to Canton; the Dutch were allowed two a year to Japan. Central Asia was at that date still only approachable by the long land routes used in the days of Genghis Khan, and the Russians were still far from exercising effective influence over their Asian hinterland. Africa was protected by climate and disease. There, as in the Pacific, discovery and exploration had to complete the world map before European hegemony could become a reality. But this was already happening in the South Seas.

A voyage in 1699 opened a century of exploration which added Australasia, the last unknown area, to the map. Voyages in the 1760s and 1770s brought Tahiti, Samoa, eastern Australia, New Zealand, and Hawaii to the last new world to be opened. The great explorer Captain Cook, the outstanding scientific navigator of modern times, even penetrated the Antarctic Circle. In 1788 the first shipment of convicts, 717 of them, landed with their guards in New South Wales, in southeastern Australia. British judges were calling into existence a new world to redress the balance of the old, where problems of disposal had arisen because the American colonies were no longer available after 1783 for dumping English undesirables. In 1797 the first missionaries arrived in Tahiti, and with them the blessings of European civilization may be considered to have asserted themselves, at least in preliminary and embryonic form, in every part of the world.

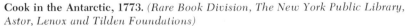

Cook in the Antarctic, 1773. *(Rare Book Division, The New York Public Library, Astor, Lenox and Tilden Foundations)*

chapter 26

Ideas Old and New

Although the twentieth century has done great damage to them, the leading ideas adumbrated by Europeans between 1500 and 1800 were the heart of the civilization Europe was beginning to export to the rest of the world and still provide many of our guideposts. Her culture acquired a secular foundation; it was then that there took hold a progressive notion of historical development as movement toward an apex, at which stood European society, and then that there grew up the confidence that scientific knowledge would make possible limitless advance. In short, the civilization of the Middle Ages came to an end.

Many Europeans were hardly aware of that end in 1800. Over most of Europe the traditions of monarchy, hereditary status, and religion still held sway. Eighteenth-century English and French monarchs touched their superstitious subjects to cure the King's Evil, a skin complaint, as had their medieval predecessors. In both Europe and North America the seventeenth century had brought an epidemic of witch-hunting far more widespread than any in the Middle Ages; it had ebbed, but a Swiss Protestant was legally executed by his countrymen for witchcraft as late as 1782 and the last heretic to be burned in Poland died only two years earlier. At Naples an important local cult made it still of political importance whether a phial of a saint's blood liquefied or not on his feast day. Some crimes such as parricide were still thought so atrocious as to merit punishment of exceptional ferocity; an attempted assassin of Louis XV died under abominable torments in 1757, just a few years before the publication of the most influential book ever written on penal reform. In societies which produced art of exquisite refinement, popular amusements focused on bear baiting, cockfighting, or pulling the heads off geese. There are no neat chronological divisions in cultural history.

Until the end of these three centuries much of the formal and institutional apparatus which upheld the past also remained intact. The most striking example to modern eyes is the obviousness of organized religion almost everywhere during the eighteenth century. Until nearly the end of this period everyone, even ecclesiastical reformers, assumed in Catholic, Protestant, and Orthodox countries alike that religion should be upheld and protected by the law and the coercive apparatus of the state. In much of Europe there was still no toleration for views other than those of the established church. The coronation oaths taken by French kings imposed on them the obligation to stamp out heresy. Only in 1787 did French non-Catholics gain the right to legitimize their children by being allowed legal non-Catholic marriages.

Although the Counter Reformation spirit had ebbed, the Index of prohibited books and Inquisition were maintained, and the censorship (often far from effective) was still supposed and sometimes strove to stifle writing inimical to Christian belief and the authority of the church. The universities everywhere were in clerical hands; even Oxford and Cambridge in England were closed to nonconformist dissenters and Roman Catholics. Religion also determined much of their teaching and the studies they pursued. But the church and universities no longer monopolized the intellectual life of Europe.

NEW INTELLECTUAL FORCES

From the middle of the seventeenth century onward academies and learned societies appeared in many countries and often under the highest patronage. The English Royal Society was given a charter in 1662 and the French *Académie des Sciences* founded four years later. In the eighteenth century such bodies greatly multiplied; they were diffused through smaller towns and founded with more limited and special aims. A common one was the promotion of agriculture. Clubs and societies of all sorts, most common in Great Britain and France, were a characteristic of an age no longer satisfied by the intellectual and social institutions of the past.

Some associations did not have as their sole end literary, scientific, or agricultural activity but provided gatherings and meeting places at which general ideas were debated, discussed, or merely chatted about. The most remarkable of these was the international brotherhood of Freemasons, which achieved a huge success within the half-century or so after it was introduced from England to continental Europe in the 1720s. The masons were later to be the object of much calumny; the myth was propagated that they had long sought revolutionary and subversive aims. This was not true of the Craft (as its members liked to call it) however true it may have been of a few individual masons, but masonic lodges certainly helped to circulate and publicize new ideas and thus to break the ice of tradition and convention.

Literacy

The increased circulation of ideas and information is one striking difference between modern and medieval history. Some have summed it up as the change from a culture focused on the image to one focused on the word. The words were to be found overwhelmingly in printed materials, at first books, then broadsheets, pamphlets, gazettes, and finally newspapers and intellectual journals. One of the crucial transformations of early modern Europe was that her society became more literate. For all the large pools of illiteracy which still existed in 1800, Europe had by then produced the first civilization in which reading and writing (especially the former) were widespread. This was a critical historical change. The printed word eventually superseded the spoken word and images as the primary means of education, information, and social direction. This supremacy was to last until the twentieth century when oral and visual communication again became dominant through radio, movies, and television.

The new power of the press. A print seller in Paris during the French Revolution, offering for sale pamphlets about politics. *(Phot. Bibl. Nat. Paris)*

All the evidence for assessing literacy suggests that improvement was cumulative but uneven from about 1500 on. There were important differences between countries, between the same countries at different periods, between town and country, between the sexes, and between occupations. The first signs of the underlying educational effort appear before the invention of printing as part of the revival and invigoration of urban life that occurred in the twelfth and thirteenth centuries. Some of the earliest evidence of cities providing for schoolmasters and schools comes from the Italian cities of that era, which first recognized literacy to be an essential qualification for certain kinds of office. There we first find, for example, the requirement that judges must be able to read—which has interesting implications for the history of earlier periods.

In the seventeenth century the lead in literacy passed from the Italian cities to England and the Netherlands, both highly urbanized for the age. These were the European countries with the highest levels of literacy in 1700, and their leadership illustrates the geographical unevenness of the advance. Moreover, although literacy rates were higher in England and the United Provinces, France may well have possessed a larger reading public because her total population was so much greater.

The Protestant Reformation was one force making for increased literacy. Almost universally the reformers stressed the importance of teaching believers how to read; it is no coincidence that New England, Scotland, Germany, and Scandinavia all reached high levels of literacy by the nineteenth century. The Reformation made it important in particular to read the Bible, rapidly available in print in the vernaculars which were thus standardized in the process. Bibliolatry, for all its more obviously unfortunate manifestations,

Sally in Our Alley

Henry Carey was a minor English poet and musician of the early eighteenth century. He wrote one masterpiece which deservedly became one of the most popular songs of the day. It has a gentleness and perception which still make it one of the most charming of English poems. It conjures up a vivid picture of eighteenth-century London—in whose streets, Carey said, he had found his subject by following a young apprentice and his girl, watching him treating her to the pleasures they could afford on his day off and dreaming of the end of his "seven long years" as apprentice.

Of all the girls that are so smart
  There's none like pretty Sally;
She is the darling of my heart,
  And she lives in our alley.
There is no lady in the land
  Is half so sweet as Sally;
She is the darling of my heart
  And she lives in our alley.

Her father he makes cabbage-nets,
  And through the streets does cry 'em;
Her mother she sells laces long
  To such as please to buy 'em:
But sure such folks could ne'er beget
  So sweet a girl as Sally!
She is the darling of my heart,
  And she lives in our alley.

When she is by, I leave my work,
  I love her so sincerely;
My master comes like any Turk,
  And bangs me most severely:
But let him bang his bellyful,
  I'll bear it all for Sally;
She is the darling of my heart,
  And she lives in our alley.

Of all the days that's in the week
  I dearly love but one day —
And that's the day that comes betwixt
  A Saturday and Monday;
For then I'm drest all in my best
  To walk abroad with Sally;
She is the darling of my heart,
  And she lives in our alley.

My master carries me to church,
  And often am I blamed
Because I leave him in the lurch
  As soon as text is named;
I leave the church in sermon-time
  And slink away to Sally;
She is the darling of my heart,
  And she lives in our alley.

When Christmas comes about again,
  O, then I shall have money;
I'll hoard it up, and box and all
  I'll give it to my honey:
And would it were ten thousand pounds,
  I'd give it all to Sally,
She is the darling of my heart,
  And she lives in our alley.

My master and the neighbors all,
  Make game of me and Sally,
And, but for her, I'd better be
  A slave and row a galley;
But when my seven long years are out,
  O, then I'll marry Sally;
O, then we'll wed, and then we'll bed —
  But not in our alley.

was a great force for enlightenment both as a stimulus to reading and as a focus for intellectual activity. In England and Germany its importance in the making of a common language and therefore culture can hardly be exaggerated. In each country bibliolatry produced a literary masterpiece in a translation of the Bible, a formative influence of great power.

Innovating monarchies in the eighteenth century also strove to promote education through primary schools; thus secular authority helped literacy. Austria and Prussia were notable in this respect. Across the Atlantic the Puritan tradition had from the start imposed in the New England communities the obligation to provide schooling. Elsewhere too, even when education was left to the informal and unregulated operation of private enterprise and charity (as in England) or to the church, there was a new vigor to be seen. From the sixteenth century begins the great age of Catholic religious orders devoted to teaching and in 1800 secondary education was still dominated by them in most Catholic countries.

The invention of printing was of outstanding importance in the dissemination of knowledge and ideas. It permitted the wide distribution of texts previously scarce and expensive. By the seventeenth century truly popular publishing existed: fairy stories, tales of true and unrequited love, almanacs, books of astrology, and biographies of the saints. The existence of this material is evidence of the demand for it. Printing also created other reading publics; technical information could now be made available very quickly and this meant that specialists had to read in order to maintain their skills.

An important consequence and promoter of increased literacy was the rise of periodicals; journals of regular publication began to replace broadsheets and occasional printed newsletters. Newspapers originated in the seventeenth century. A daily newspaper was published in London in 1702, and by the middle of the century there was an important English provincial press and millions of papers were being printed each year. Magazines and weekly journals began to appear in the first half of the eighteenth century in England; the most important of them, *The Spectator*, set a model for journalism by its conscious effort to shape taste and behavior, of women readers as well as men.

Only in the United Provinces did journalism have such success as in England. In continental Europe learned and literary journals appeared in increasing numbers, but political reporting or comment was rarely available because of the existence of censorship in most countries. Even in eighteenth-century France the authors of works embodying advanced ideas usually circulated them in manuscript. In retrospect it may well seem that the greater opportunity literacy and printing gave for the criticism and questioning of authority was their most important effect. Yet it was by no means the most obvious.

A NEW SCIENTIFIC AGE

What has been called a "scientific revolution" in the seventeenth century must be attributed in part to the cumulative effect of more rapidly and widely circulated information, but its deepest sources lie in changed intellectual attitudes and a changed view of man's relation to nature. It was a great step from observing the natural world with bemused awe as evidence of God's mysterious powers to consciously searching for ways to manipulate it. Although the work of medieval scientists was by no means as primitive and uncreative as it was once the fashion to believe, it has two grave limitations. One was that it could provide very little that was of practical use. This inhibited attention to it. The second was theoretical; medieval science rested on assumptions which were untested, in part because the means of testing them could not be grasped, in part because the wish to test them did not exist. Such dogmatic assertions as the theory that the four elements—fire, air, earth, and water—were the constituents of all things long went unexamined by experiment. Although experimental work of a sort went on within the alchemical and hermetic traditions, it was directed by mythical, intuitive conceptions.

This remained broadly true until the seventeenth century though the Renaissance had its scientific manifestations. They usually found expression in descriptive studies (an outstanding example is Vesalius' human anatomy of 1543) and in solutions to practical problems in the arts (such as those of perspective) and in mechanical crafts. Its greatest achievements in science were provided by one branch of this descriptive and classificatory work, that addressed to making sense of the new geographical knowledge revealed by explorers and cosmographers. In geography, said a French physician of the early sixteenth century, "and in what pertains to astronomy, Plato, Aristotle, and the old philosophers made progress, and Ptolemy added a great deal more. Yet were one of them to return today, he would find geography changed past recognition." New knowledge was one of the stimuli for a new intellectual approach to the world of nature. Yet it was not a stimulus quick to operate.

Only a tiny minority of educated Europeans in 1600 did not accept the medieval world picture based on Aristotle and the Bible—that the whole universe centered on the earth, and the life of the earth upon man, its only rational inhabitant. The intellectual achievement of the next century was to make it impossible to hold this view.

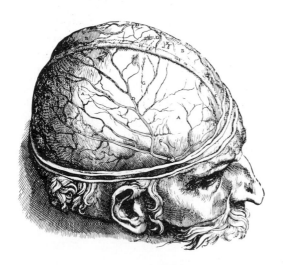

An engraving by Vesalius, this one of the brain. (*Library, The New York Academy of Medicine*)

A new view of science

Changes which manifested themselves early in the seventeenth century amounted to a critical departure in the cultural history of the modern world; an intellectual barrier was crossed and the nature of civilization was altered forever. A new attitude appeared in Europe; it was deeply utilitarian, encouraging men to invest time, energy, and resources to master nature by systematic experiment. Men of a later age saw the beginnings of this outlook in the work of Francis Bacon (1561–1627), sometime Lord Chancellor of England, fondly supposed by later admirers to be the author of the plays of Shakespeare, a man of outstanding intellectual energy and many unlikable personal traits. In a series of works which seem to have had little or no contemporary impact he rejected the authority of the past and advocated a study of nature based upon observation and experiment instead of deduction from a priori principles, and such study should be directed toward harnessing nature for human purposes. "The true and lawful end of the sciences," he wrote, "is that human life be enriched by new discoveries and powers." Through them could be achieved "a restitution and reinvigorating (in great part) of man to the sovereignty and power . . . which he had in his first state of creation." This was ambitious, but Bacon was sure it was possible if scientific research were effectively organized; this too was a prophetic concept, precursor of later scientific societies and institutes.

The modernity of Bacon tended to be exaggerated after his death; a century later he had already become a mythological figure. He is even said to have achieved scientific martyrdom, having caught cold while stuffing a fowl with snow one cold March day in order to observe the effects of refrigeration upon the flesh. Forty years later his central ideas were the commonplaces of scientific discourse. "The management of this great machine of the world," said an English scientist in the 1660s, "can be explained only by the experimental and mechanical philosophers." These were ideas Bacon would have understood and approved and they are still at the heart of the views of most men today. Ever since the seventeenth century it has been a characteristic of the scientist that he ask questions by means of experiment.

At first research concentrated on physical phenomena which could be observed and measured by the techniques available and on the theories needed to make sense of the resulting observations. This accounts for the mechanical, mathematical, astronomical, and cosmological stress of the scientific revolution. The invention of logarithms and calculus was part of an improved instrumentation which among other things built better clocks and optical instruments. The solution of such practical problems in turn permitted the solution of more general ones. In the seventeenth century, for example, the clockmaker's art took another great stride forward with the introduction of the pendulum as a controlling device; the measurement of time with more precise instruments in its turn made astronomy much easier. With better lenses came the telescope and new opportunities to scrutinize the heavens; the new microscope allowed William Harvey to explain the circulation of the blood.

Scientists

For a long time there was no precise line of demarcation between the scientist and the philosopher. Yet a new world of scientists came into being after 1600, a true international scientific community. Here we come back to the importance of printing and the rapid diffusion of new knowledge. This was not limited to scientific books; the *Philosophical Transactions* of the Royal Society were published and so were the reports and proceedings of other learned bodies. Scientists also kept up huge private correspondences with one another, and some of these were later printed and published; they were more widely intelligible and read than would be the exchanges of leading scientists today.

One feature of the scientific revolution especially striking to the modern eye is the big part that laymen played. The learned societies which began to appear more widely about the middle of the century were full of gentleman-ly dabblers who could not by any stretch of imagination have been called professional scientists but who lent to those bodies the indefinable but important weight of their social prestige and respectability. This association of society with science may be one of the most important factors explaining why progress occurred in Europe while in China stagnation was not over-come even by outstanding technical achievement.

By 1700 specialization between different branches of science already existed but was by no means as important as it would later become. Nor was science then so demanding of time; scientists could still make major contri-butions to their disciplines while writing books on theology or holding ad-ministrative office.

Understanding the universe

The techniques available to science in the seventeenth century allowed great advance in some fields but inhibited it in others. Chemistry, for exam-ple, made relatively small progress, while physics and cosmology went ahead rapidly to achieve nothing less than a new view of the cosmos. Its major characteristic was the replacement of the idea of a divinely directed universe with a mechanical one, in which change proceeded regularly from laws of motion acting uniformly and universally. This was still quite compat-ible with belief in God. His majesty was not perhaps shown in daily direct intervention but in His creation of a great machine; in the most celebrated analogy God was the Great Watchmaker.

The scientific outlook of the seventeenth century was neither antireli-gious nor antitheocentric. Though new views on astronomy displaced man from the center of the universe and thus implicitly challenged his unique-ness (in 1686 a book appeared arguing that there might be more than one inhabited world), this was not what preoccupied the men who made the cosmological revolution. For them it was only an accident that the authority of the church became entangled with the proposition that the sun went around the earth. The ideas they put forward, they thought, merely empha-sized the greatness and mysteriousness of God's ways. They assumed the

Optics and astronomy quickly became fashionable crazes in the sixteenth century, partly because effective equipment became more easily available, and partly because of the possible practical applications. *(Photo Deutsches Museum, Munich)*

new knowledge of science would eventually be christened as Aristotle had been in the Middle Ages.

Nikolaus Copernicus, the Polish cleric whose book *On the Revolutions of the Celestial Orbs* appeared in 1543, was a Renaissance humanist not a scientist. Largely for philosophic and aesthetic reasons, he hit upon the idea of a universe where the planets moved around the sun. It was (so to speak) a brilliant guess for he had no means of testing his hypothesis by observation or experiment and most commonsensical evidence told against it. Therefore he worked out a mathematical model to prove that heliocentricity (the orbiting of planets around the sun) was possible. Though he thought he had created a new cosmology, not much public notice was taken of it for half a century. The first true scientific data in support of heliocentricity was in fact provided by a man who did not accept it. This was the Danish astronomer Tycho Brahe, who began to record the movements of planets in the 1560s with elementary instruments and later built the best-equipped observatory of his day. His German assistant, Johann Kepler, went on to make even more careful observations of his own and provided a second great step forward. In 1609 he showed that the orbits of planets could be explained as regular if they followed ellipses around the sun at irregular speeds. This broke at last with the Ptolemaic framework within which cosmology had been more and more cramped.

Galileo Galilei was the first exponent of these views who did not share the mystical, alchemical, and astrological interests of his three great predecessors. He was an academic, professor at Padua of two subjects characteristically linked in early science: physics and military engineering. His use of the telescope, unavailable to Copernicus, finally shattered the Aristotelian scheme: Copernican astronomy was made visible. But Galileo's major work was to describe the physics which made a heliocentric system possible. This produced a new science, statics and dynamics, the mathematical treatment of the movement of bodies. What is more, Galileo formulated it as a result of systematic experiment.

Galileo published his findings in 1632, and his *Dialogue on the Two Great Systems of the World* (that of Ptolemy and Copernicus) has been seen as the first statement of the revolution in scientific thought. It is also significant that he wrote the book not in Latin but in Italian and that he dedicated it to the pope. Galileo was undoubtedly a good Catholic. Yet the *Dialogue* provoked an uproar for it meant the end of the Christian-Aristotelian world view which was the cultural triumph of the medieval Church. Galileo's trial followed. He was condemned by the Inquisition and recanted, but this did not diminish the effect of his work. Copernican views would henceforth dominate scientific thinking (though we have not yet absorbed them in our daily language and speak still of the "rising" and "setting" of the sun).

In 1642, the year Galileo died, Isaac Newton was born; his achievement would be the physical explanation of the Copernican universe whose laws Galileo had demonstrated. This was essentially a matter of a new mathematics which provided a way of calculating the positions of bodies in motion. Newton did not invent infinitesimal calculus, which he called the "method of fluxions," but he was the first to apply it to physical phenomena. In 1687 his conclusions were embodied in a book which was to be the most important and influential scientific work since that of Euclid. The *Principia* (the full title in English is *The Mathematical Principles of Natural Philosophy*) demonstrated how gravity sustained the physical universe. The key demonstration was of the formula that the force of gravity between two bodies varies inversely with the square of the distance between them.

The general cultural consequences of Newton's discovery were comparable in scale with others within science; perhaps they were even greater. That a single law, discovered by observation and calculation, could explain so much was an astonishing revelation of what the new scientific thinking could achieve. The English poet Alexander Pope has been quoted to excess, but his epigram still best summarizes the impact of Newton's work on educated men, exaggerated though his idolatry was:

> *Nature and Nature's laws lay hid in night,*
> *God said "Let Newton be!" and all was light.*

Newton thus joined Bacon as the second canonized saint of the new learning.

The *Principia* completed the revolution begun by Copernicus. A dynamic conception of the universe had replaced a static one. The achievement was great enough to provide the physics of the next two centuries and all the other sciences with a new cosmology. What was not anticipated by Newton and his predecessors was that this might presage an insoluble conflict between science and religion. Newton even seems to have been pleased to observe that the law of gravity did not adequately sustain the view that the universe was a self-regulated system, self-contained once created. He welcomed a logical gap which he could fill by postulating divine intervention.

Religion and science

Churchmen, especially Catholic ones, did not find it easy to come to terms with the new science, as Galileo's treatment shows. In the Middle Ages clerics had made important contributions to science, but from the seventeenth century to the nineteenth they produced almost no first-rank scientific work. In the seventeenth century originated the split between organized religion and science which has haunted European intellectual history ever since, whatever efforts have from time to time been made to patch it up. When people came to look back they found a symbolic figure in a sixteenth-century thinker, the Neapolitan Giordano Bruno, who accepted the Copernican revolution but also dabbled in a magical "secret science" supposedly derived from ancient Egypt. He had been a Dominican monk but broke with his order and wandered about Europe publishing controversial works. In time the Inquisition arrested him, and in 1600 he was burned at Rome for heresy. His execution became one of the foundations of the later historical mythology surrounding the development of free thought, of the struggle between progress and religion as it would come to be seen.

In the seventeenth century scientists and philosophers felt the antithesis between progress and religion much less than churchmen. Newton, who wrote copiously on theology, seems to have believed that Moses knew about the heliocentric theory and urged his readers to "beware of Philosophy and vain deceit and oppositions of science falsely so-called" and to have recourse to the Old Testament. The French philosopher René Descartes formulated what he thought to be satisfactory philosophical defenses of religious belief and Christian truth which were also consistent with a technically skeptical approach. Yet he and the Cartesian philosophical movement (which took its name from him) attracted the hostility of the Catholic church, because the traditional defenders of religious belief were concerned not only with the conclusions people arrived at but the way they reached them. A rationally argued acceptance of religious belief which started from principles of doubt and demonstrated they could satisfactorily be overcome and which divided so completely the Great Watchmaker from His invention was a poor ally for a church which taught that truth was declared by authority. Rome quite logically set aside as irrelevant Descartes' own devotion and Christianity and correctly (from its own point of view) put all his works on the Index.

The argument from authority was in fact disposed of by a French Protestant of the late seventeenth century, Pierre Bayle, who pointed out its unsatisfactory open-endedness. What authority prescribed the authority? In the end it seemed to be a matter of opinion. Every dogma of traditional Christianity, he suggested, might be refuted if not in accordance with natural reason. Bayle expounded his ideas both in a periodical (published in the Netherlands) and in a great encyclopedic dictionary which ridiculed accepted views. These works announced a new phase in the history of European thought.

THE ENLIGHTENMENT

The word "enlightenment" (or a similar one) was used in the eighteenth century in most European languages to characterize the thinking which men felt distinguished their own age from what had gone before. They thought of letting in light upon what was dark, but when the German philosopher Immanuel Kant asked the question "what is enlightenment?" in a famous essay he gave a different answer: liberation from self-imposed tutelage. A questioning of authority was involved. The great heritage bequeathed by the Enlightenment was the idea that nothing was sacred except the critical attitude itself; from this time on, everything was exposed to scrutiny. Yet Enlightenment had its own authority and dogmas. It was as much a bundle of attitudes as a collection of ideas. Many streams flowed into it and by no means did they all flow the same way. The roots of Enlightenment are as confused as its development, which always resembled a continuing debate — sometimes a civil war — much more than the advance of a united army of the enlightened.

Descartes had taught that systematic doubt was the beginning of firm knowledge but had assumed men knew right from wrong. Later in the seventeenth century the English philosopher John Locke reduced the primary constituents of knowledge to the impressions conveyed by the senses to the mind. There were not, he argued against Descartes, ideas innate in man's nature; in his mind were only sense-data and the connections he made between them. This of course implied that mankind had no fixed ideas of right and wrong; moral values, Locke taught, arose as the mind experienced pain and pleasure. There was to be an enormous future for the development of such ideas; from them would eventually flow theories about education and the social consequences of material conditions as well as many other aspects of environmentalism. Yet at the time people found they could fit Locke's philosophy into the framework of Christian belief.

Such incoherences run throughout the Enlightenment but the general trend is clear. The new discoveries of science seemed to promise that the observations of the senses were indeed the way forward to knowledge, and knowledge whose value was proved by its utilitarian efficacy. Science could make possible the improvement of the world in which men lived. Its techniques could unlock the mysteries of nature and reveal their logical, rational foundations in the laws of physics and chemistry. All this was an optimistic creed. The world was getting better and would continue to do so.

In earlier times things had been very different. The Renaissance worship of the classical past had combined with the turmoils of war and the always latent feeling of religious men that the end of the world could not long be delayed to produce a pessimistic mood and a sense of decline from a great past. In a great literary debate over whether the achievements of the ancients excelled those of modern times the writers of the late seventeenth century crystallized the idea of progress which emerged from the Enlightenment.

It was also a creed for nonspecialists. In the eighteenth century it was still possible for an educated man to tie together in a manner satisfactory at least to himself the logic and implications of many different studies. Voltaire was famous as a poet and playwright but wrote at length on history (he was for a time the French royal historiographer) and expounded Newtonian physics to his countrymen. Adam Smith was renowned as a moral philosopher before he dazzled the world with his *Wealth of Nations,* a book which may reasonably be considered to have founded the modern science of economics.

Though religion found a place in all this, enlightened thought had less and less room for the divine and the theological. It was not just that some people no longer felt hell gaping beneath them or that the world was becoming less mysterious; life also promised to be less tragic for the educated. Though there were still appalling natural disasters, such as earthquakes, more and more troubles seemed man-made and therefore remediable. But if the solution of most problems was possible, if, as one thinker put it, "Man's proper business is to seek happiness and avoid misery," what was the relevance of the dogmas of salvation and damnation? God could still be included in a perfunctory way in the philosopher's account of the universe, as the First Cause which had started the whole thing going and the Great Mechanic who prescribed the rules on which it ran, but was there any place for His subsequent intervention in its workings either directly by incarnation or indirectly through His church and the sacraments it conveyed? Inevitably the Enlightenment brought revolt against the church, the supreme claimant to intellectual and moral authority.

Reform

Advanced thought in the eighteenth century tended to express itself in fairly practical and everyday recommendations which are probably best summarized in terms of the fundamental beliefs which underlay them. At the basis of all was a new confidence in the power of mind; enlightened society looked forward to the improvement of humanity's lot by the manipulation of nature and the unfolding to man of the truths which reason had written in his heart. Innate ideas bundled out by the front door crept in again by the back stairs.

The Principle of Benign Selfishness

Adam Smith's book Wealth of Nations *not only set out an economic theory but also a way of looking at human nature and behavior which conflicted with much traditional teaching. The central mechanism of his argument was the harnessing of self-love to socially useful purposes. Here is part of his discussion of how the division of labor arises.*

In almost every other race of animals each individual, when it is grown up to maturity, is entirely independent, and in its natural state has occasion for the assistance of no other living creature. But man has almost constant occasion for the help of his brethren, and it is in vain for him to expect it from their benevolence only. He will be more likely to prevail if he can interest their self-love in his favour, and show them that it is for their own advantage to do for him what he requires of them. Whoever offers to another a bargain of any kind, proposes to do this. Give me that which I want, and you shall have this which you want, is the meaning of every such offer; and it is in this manner that we obtain from one another the far greater part of those good offices which we stand in need of. It is not from the benevolence of the butcher, the brewer, or the baker that we expect our dinner, but from their regard to their own interest. We address ourselves, not to their humanity but to their self-love, and never talk to them of our own necessities but of their advantages.

Optimism was qualified only by the realization that there were grave obstacles to be overcome. The first of these was simply ignorance, which the combination of reason and knowledge promised to dispose of. The greatest literary embodiment of the Enlightenment had precisely this aim. The *Encyclopédie* of Diderot and d'Alembert was a huge compilation of information and propaganda in twenty-one volumes published between 1751 and 1765. As some of its articles made clear, another great obstacle to enlightenment was intolerance—especially when it interfered with freedom of publication and debate. Parochialism too was a barrier to happiness. The values of the Enlightment, it was assumed, were those of all civilized people. They were universal. Never, perhaps, has the European intellectual elite been more cosmopolitan or shared more of a common language than in the eighteenth century.

Once the obstacles of ignorance, intolerance, and parochialism were removed, it was assumed that the operation of the laws of nature, uncovered by reason, would promote the reform of society in the interest of everyone except those wedded to the past by their blindness or their enjoyment of indefensible privilege. The *Lettres persanes* of the French author Montesquieu began the tradition of suggesting that the institutions of existing societies—in his case those of France could be improved by comparison with the laws of nature.

In their vision of themselves as critics and reformers eighteenth-century thinkers invented the idea of the intellectual with us ever since. Their term for such people was simply "philosophers." This came to connote not the specialized pursuit of philosophical studies but the acceptance of a common outlook and critical stance. The archetypal philosophers were a group of French writers soon lumped together in spite of their differences and referred to as the "philosophes." Their numbers and celebrity suggest correctly the preponderance of France in the central period of Enlightenment thought. Yet the movement was international.

The first heroes of the Enlightenment were English: Bacon, Newton, and Locke. It might reasonably be claimed too that the philosopher Jeremy Bentham expressed one of the most extreme developments of its ideals and methods and that its greatest historiographical monument is *The Decline and Fall of the Roman Empire* by another Englishman, Edward Gibbon. Scotland also had a cultural efflorescence in the eighteenth century and produced in David Hume one of the most engaging as well as the most acute of the Enlightenment's technical philosophers, who combined extreme intellectual skepticism with good nature and social conservatism. His friend and countryman was Adam Smith, best known as the author of *Wealth of Nations*.

On the Continent Italy was (outside France) most prolific in her contribution to the Enlightenment in spite of the predominance there of the Catholic church. The Italian Enlightenment would be assured of remembrance even if it had left behind only Cesare Beccaria's *On Crimes and Punishments*, the book which founded penal reform. Beccaria gave currency to one of the major slogans of modern times, "the greatest happiness of the greatest number." The German Enlightenment was slower to unroll and less productive of figures who won universal acclaim (possibly for linguistic reasons), but produced in Immanuel Kant a thinker who, if he consciously sought to go beyond the Enlightenment, nevertheless embodied in his moral recommendations much of what it stood for. Only Spain lagged conspicuously behind. This is not an unfair impression even allowing for the work of one or two enlightened statesmen; Spanish universities in the eighteenth century were still rejecting Newton to study Aristotle.

However important the work of other Europeans might become in the history of civilization, the French Enlightenment struck contemporaries most forcefully. There were many reasons. One was the simple fascination of power; France under Louis XIV had acquired a prestige long to endure. Another was the magnificent instrument for the diffusion of French culture which lay in her language. French was the lingua franca of Europe's intellectuals and people of fashion alike in the eighteenth century; Maria Theresa and her children exchanged their family correspondence in it and Frederick II wrote French verses. A European audience was assured for any book written in French, and it seems likely that the success of that language actually held back cultural advance in the German tongue.

What followed from this common language was international discussion and critical comment. But what would actually be achieved by way of practical reform in the short term was bound to depend largely on political circumstances. This was obvious when enlightened despotisms ran into opposition from vested interests and conservatism. Ideology was at stake in enforcing educational reform at the expense of the church in the Habsburg dominions, or in Voltaire's attacks, written at the brief a royal minister, against the Parlement of Paris when it stood in the way of fiscal innovation. Some rulers, like Catherine the Great of Russia, ostentatiously paraded the influence of enlightenment ideas on their legislation; in her case the results were in practice unimpressive whatever their paper formulation. On the other hand, enlightened reform went very far in Tuscany under Grand Duke Leopold.

Anticlericalism

Religious questions always had a unique attraction for the philosophes. The church and the effects of its teaching were inseparable from every side of European life. It not only claimed great authority but existed as a huge corporate interest, both social and economic, involved in some measure in every aspect of society which interested reformers. Whether it was because the abuse of sanctuary or clerical privilege encumbered judicial reform, or ecclesiastical property impeded economic improvement, or a clerical monopoly of education limited the training of administrators and technicians, the church seemed to find itself always at odds with the Enlightenment, especially in Catholic countries. But this was not all that drew the fire of the philosophes. Religion could also lead, they thought, to crime. One of the last great scandals of this era of religious persecution was the execution of a Protestant at Toulouse in 1762; charged with converting Catholics to heresy, he was tortured, tried, convicted, and broken on the wheel. Voltaire made this a cause célèbre. He could not change the law, but his attacks did much to make it impossible for such a judicial murder ever to be repeated. Yet France did not give Protestants even limited legal toleration until 1787 (and then did not extend it to Jews).

In the end Enlightenment thinking created an important political force: liberal anticlericalism. Criticism of what the church did and taught led lay authorities to support attacks upon ecclesiastical organizations and authority. The struggles of church and state could always be presented as a part of a war of enlightenment and rationality against superstition and bigotry. The papacy in particular attracted criticism and contempt; Voltaire seems to have once believed that because it was so corrupt it would in fact disappear before the end of the century. The papacy was seen as the keystone of the edifice of superstition, the sower of obscurantism, bigotry, and intolerance, an institution which had long outlived the usefulness it possessed in a more barbaric age. The greatest success of the philosophes in the eyes of many was the dissolution of the Jesuits which enlightened rulers forced on the pope.

Some philosophes carried their assault on the church beyond institutions to an attack on religion itself. Out and out atheism and deterministic materialism were both given their first serious expression in the eighteenth century. But such views were unusual. During the Enlightment most people who thought about these things may have been skeptical of the dogmas of the church but kept up a vague theism. Certainly they believed in the importance of religion as a social force. As Voltaire said, "One must have religion for the sake of the people." He continued throughout his life to assert the existence of God.

Limits to Enlightenment

For all their revolutionary power the ideas of the Enlightenment were those of men who took for granted much we could not now accept. These ideas also had to operate within a still very restrictive institutional and moral framework. The relationship with despotism was ambiguous: critics might struggle against censorship or denounce religious intolerance, but they depended on despotic power to carry out reform. Nor, it must be remembered, were enlightened ideas the only source of reform. The institutions Voltaire admired in England did not stem from the Enlightenment, and many of the eighteenth-century improvements in that country owed more to religion than to "philosophy."

The greatest political importance of the Enlightenment lay in its legacies to the future. It clarified and formulated many of the key principles of liberalism, though here too its legacy is ambiguous, for the thinkers of the Enlightenment sought not freedom for its own sake but freedom for the consequences it would bring. Their clearest contribution to the future European liberal tradition was in indicating new general aims—happiness and rationality—and denouncing specific ills—bigotry and intolerance.

The Romantic vision

The most prophetic figure of the eighteenth century was a Genevan who quarreled bitterly with many of the leading figures of the Enlightenment, Jean Jacques Rousseau. His importance in the history of thought lies in his impassioned pleas that due weight be given to man's feelings and moral sense, both, it seemed to him, in danger of eclipse by rationality, calculating self-interest, materialism, and much else that Enlightenment stood for. He believed the men of his day were stunted creatures, partial and corrupt beings deformed by the influence of a society which encouraged this eclipse.

Although Rousseau shared many of the assumptions of his era, nevertheless there is a great contrast between his ideas and those of his contemporaries, and European culture owes an enormous debt to Rousseau's vision. There can be found in his writings a new attitude to religion (which was to revivify it), a new psychological obsession with the individual which was to flood into art and literature, a new and sentimental approach to nature and natural beauty, the origins of the modern doctrine of nationalism, a new child-centeredness in education, and much else besides. Much of this legacy was to prove pernicious. Yet Rousseau was an innovator, even one of genius,

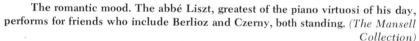

The romantic mood. The abbé Liszt, greatest of the piano virtuosi of his day, performs for friends who include Berlioz and Czerny, both standing. *(The Mansell Collection)*

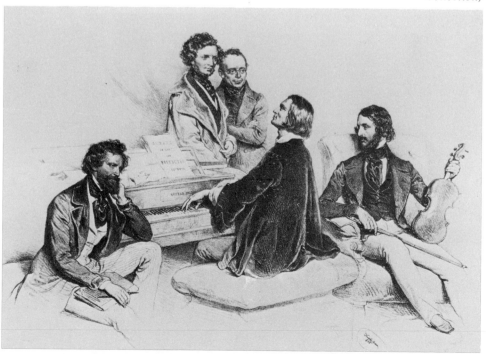

though some of his ideas were shared by other men. For example, Rousseau's distaste for the Enlightenment's erosion of community, its sense that men were brothers and members of a common moral whole, was expressed just as eloquently by the Irish author Edmund Burke, who drew conclusions from it very different from Rousseau's.

Rousseau thus in some measure voiced ideas beginning to be held by others as the Age of Enlightenment passed its zenith. Yet of his central and special importance there can be no doubt. He is the key figure in the making of what has been called Romanticism. This is a much used and misused term. It can be properly applied to things which seem diametrically opposed. Soon after 1800, for example, some people would deny any value to the past and seek to overthrow its legacies; others would strive equally tenaciously to uphold historic institutions. Both groups can be called Romantics because in each moral feeling counted for more than intellectual analysis.

The clearest link between such antitheses lay in the new emphasis on feeling, intuition, and above all the natural. The manifold expressions of Romanticism started almost always from some objection to enlightened thought or from a revulsion against rational self-interest. Romanticism sought authenticity, self-realization, honesty, and moral exaltation. Its great effects were to reverberate through the culture of the nineteenth century, usually with painful results.

part V
THE GREAT ACCELERATION

In the middle of the eighteenth century most Europeans could still believe
that the world would continue much as it always had. The weight of
the past in Europe itself was still enormous; elsewhere it was even greater.
Yet within a century and a quarter irreversible changes in Europe and in
the world of European settlement and empire had cut off much of the
traditional past. Moreover, India, China, and Japan were committed to
fundamental change by their new relations with Europe and North
America.

Rapid transformation was the leading characteristic of a period
running from somewhere about 1750 to somewhere about 1870. There is
nothing sacred about these dates; they are only conveniences. All that can
be said with confidence is that they encompass a transition from a world
regulated by tradition to one whose destiny was to be continuing and
accelerating change. A man born in 1800 who lived to the psalmist's
allowance of three-score years and ten would see the world more altered in
his lifetime than it had been in the previous thousand years.

Central to this upheaval and one its driving motors was the
consolidation of a European world hegemony. Between 1750 and 1870 war
and revolution reshaped Europe and the Americas. At the same time
population growth in these areas became more rapid and led to new and
important differences between countries. There were also further economic

transformations: a market economy became general and so did the new social relationships which went with it. This was especially marked in England, whose industrialization cut her off from the past much more decisively than any experience since the barbarian invasions.

With all this went big political changes. By 1871, the year a newly united Germany took her place among the great powers, virtually the whole of western Europe was organized in states based on the principle of nationality. The Americas too were for the most part already divided into nation states. Within the political framework established by nationalism other forces were making headway. Terms like democracy and liberalism do not help very much in defining them but must be used in default of better ones. In most countries there was a general trend toward associating more and more subjects with the operation of the state through the representative institutions asked for by liberals and democrats. Such institutions could shelter both the progress of individualism and the growing power of the state. The individual increasingly became the basis of political and social organization, the only alternative to the nation as a focus of rights and duties. The individual's membership in communal, religious, occupational, and family units was thought less and less important; his identity lay in being a subject of the state and an economic unit. In some ways this meant greater theoretical and practical freedom, in other ways less. The state was much more powerful in relation to its subjects in the nineteenth century than in the preceding one. A great revolution had occurred both in the technical resources of governments and in the acquiescence of those they ruled.

The triumphs of science and technology opened new grounds for questioning religious and traditional attitudes to life. Often this accompanied an assumption that change must be for the best; more and more people took a progressive and optimistic view of the future, expecting further beneficial advances to follow those already won. That of course is far from the whole story; some people were pessimistic too. But so far as mentality is subject to generalization, it seems safe to say that thinking men and women in the nineteenth century were more confident than ever that superstition was declining and that rationality was winning a long battle with it. Within the European world this attitude registered a huge transformation which, however far into the past some of its particular manifestations may be traced, at last meant in every way the end of the Middle Ages.

chapter 27

Economic and Social Development

POPULATION CHANGES

The most influential study of population ever written appeared in 1798. This was the *Essay on Population* by Thomas Malthus, an English clergyman. He sought to describe the laws of population growth, but much was to flow from this apparently limited task. The book's impact on, for example, economic theory and biological science was to be enormous. What matters here is its importance as a symptom of a change in ideas about population.

Roughly speaking, for two centuries or so statesmen and economists had believed that rising population was a sign of prosperity. Kings should seek to increase the number of their subjects, they agreed, not merely because this would provide more taxpayers and soldiers but also because this was a sign of wealth. The great Adam Smith had said in his *Wealth of Nations*, another book of huge influence, that an increase in population was a good rough test of economic prosperity.

Malthus doused this view with very cold water. Whatever might be judged to be the consequences for society as a whole, he concluded that a rising population sooner or later spelled disaster and suffering for most of its members—the poor. In a famous demonstration he argued that the produce of the earth had finite limits set by the amount of land available for growing food. This in turn set a finite limit to population. As population expanded, it would press increasingly upon a narrowing margin of subsistence. When this margin was exhausted, famine must follow. The population would then fall to a level that could be maintained by whatever food was available. This mechanism could only be kept from operating if people abstained from having children (and a prudent awareness of the consequences might help here by encouraging late marriage) or if such horrors as disease and war imposed natural checks.

This gloomy thesis provoked huge argument and counterargument, but somehow the growth of population had already begun to worry people a little so that even prose as unattractive as Malthus' had great success. People became aware of the dangers of increasing numbers as they had never been

A humorous artist tries to make his countrymen laugh at the new problems of overcrowding in nineteenth-century London. A picture of a future in which boats and balloons are enlisted to meet the new need for space. *(The Mansell Collection)*

before, at the beginning of a century whose population history was to continue to be growth, on a much accelerated scale and to a point hitherto inconceivable.

Its measurement is best taken by a long view and tracing the trend beyond 1870 and into the twentieth century. If we include Russia (whose population must be estimated from very poor statistics), a European population of about 190 million in 1800 climbed to about 420 million a century later. As the rest of the world seems to have been growing rather more slowly, Europe's share of the world's population rose (approximately) from one-fifth to one-quarter even though many Europeans were emigrating during this period. In the 1830s emigration overseas passed the figure of 100,000 a year; in 1913 it would exceed 1.5 million. Taking an even longer view, perhaps 50 million people left Europe between 1840 and 1930, most of them for the Western hemisphere. All these people *and their descendants* were part of the new rapid growth of the European peoples.

The geographical unevenness of population growth affected the standing of great powers. Numbers were for a long time the decisive factor in military strength, and it was a crucial change when Germany overtook France in population in the second half of the nineteenth century. A dramatic increase had appeared earlier in the United Kingdom, whose population grew from about 8 million when Malthus wrote to 22 million by 1850. It was to reach 42 million by 1914, which was by then bigger than that of France; yet in 1800 the British population was less than a third of the French. To make another type of comparison, between 1800 and 1900 Russia's share of Europe's total population grew from 21 to 24 percent and Germany's from 13 to 14 percent, while France's share fell from 15 to 10 percent and that of Austria from 15 to 12 percent.

The basic mechanism of population increase in this period was a fall in mortality. Never in history has there been so spectacular a fall in death rates as in the past century or so, and it showed first in the advanced countries of Europe. It is roughly true that before about 1850 most continental European countries had similar birth rates which slightly exceeded similar death rates. Little impact had been made by then upon the fundamental determinants of men's life in a still overwhelmingly rural society. In the second half of the century this rapidly changed. The annual death rate in advanced European countries fell pretty steadily, from about 35 per 1,000 in 1850 to about 28 in 1900 and thereafter to about 18 by 1950. Less advanced European countries still maintained annual rates of 38 per 1,000 down to 1900 and 32 down to 1950. This produced a striking inequality between two Europes and a fresh accentuation of older divisions between them. In the richer west, north of the Alps and Pyrenees, life expectancy was much higher than in the more backward east and south.

Other factors besides lower mortality helped forward population growth; earlier marriage and a rising birth rate had appeared in the initial phase of expansion as economic opportunity increased. But children had not been as likely to survive in early modern times as they increasingly were from the mid-nineteenth century onward, thanks to better medicine and engineering and growing wealth. Beginning around 1870 doctors first came to grips with the child killers: diphtheria, scarlet fever, whooping cough, and typhoid. But even earlier social reformers and engineers had done much to reduce both their incidence and that of other diseases (though not their fatality) by building better drains and devising better cleaning arrangements for the growing cities. Though cholera devastated London and Paris in the 1830s and 1840s, it was eliminated in industrial countries by 1900. No western European country would have an important plague outbreak after 1899.

As similar progress was felt in more and more countries, the general tendency was everywhere to produce a sharp rise in population. Though it was usually soon coupled with falling birth rates, the fall in death rates proceeded more rapidly. Thus population grew as life expectancy at birth greatly increased. By the second quarter of the twentieth century, men and women in North America, the United Kingdom, Scandinavia, or industrial Europe could expect to live two or three times as long as their medieval ancestors. Immense consequences flowed from this.

Just as rapid population increase began first in the countries which were economically the most advanced, so did the slowing down of that growth which was the next discernible trend. This was produced by a drop in the number of births, invariably appearing first among the better-off members of society. Fecundity, as a rough rule, varies to this day inversely with income – celebrated exceptions among wealthy American political dynasties notwithstanding. In some societies births declined in the nineteenth century because of the postponement of marriage to an older age than hitherto, in others as a result of contraceptive techniques.

It seems likely that some knowledge of contraception goes back a long way, but the nineteenth century brought improved techniques (some made possible by scientific and technical advance in manufacturing the necessary devices) and public propaganda which spread awareness and knowledge of them. Once more a social change reflects many influences; it is difficult not to connect such spreading knowledge with, for example, greater literacy and rising expectations. Although Europeans were enjoying more wealth than their ancestors, they were all the time adjusting their notion of what was a tolerable life – and therefore a tolerable family size. Cultural factors then determined whether they put off the date of marriage (as French and Irish peasants did) or adopted contraceptive techniques (as the English and French middle classes seem to have done).

Effects of population growth

Changes in the way men died and in the way they lived in their families transformed the structures of society. The western European countries in the nineteenth and twentieth centuries had absolutely more young people than ever before, for example. At times, too, they were present in a greater proportion than ever in the past and it is difficult not to think that the expansiveness, buoyancy, and vigor of nineteenth-century Europe owed much to this. Later the young became relatively fewer, and there appeared societies with an unprecedentedly high number of elderly persons. This increasingly strained the social mechanisms which had in earlier times maintained the old and those incapable of work. By 1914 there would be no country in Europe or North America where much thought had not gone into the problems of poverty and dependence, however great the differences in scale and success of efforts to cope with them.

Absolute population growth has continued to be the general rule in the Western world. It is one of the most important themes in the history of the modern era for to it is linked almost every other. Its material consequences can be seen in unprecedented urbanization and the rise of huge consumer markets for large-scale manufacturing industry. Its social consequences ranged from strife and unrest as people competed for a living to the adoption of institutions for the deliberate amelioration of some of its results.

There were international repercussions in the nineteenth century as statesmen took into account population figures in deciding what risks they could or had to take and as people became more and more alarmed about the consequences of overcrowding. The United Kingdom was worried by the prospect of too many poor and this led to the encouragement of emigration, which in turn did much to shape people's thinking and feelings about empire. But some policy makers forgot the gloomy prophecies of Malthus. The Germans discouraged emigration because they feared the loss of military potential, while the French and Belgians pioneered the award of children's allowances for the same reason.

There were still demographic calamities in the nineteenth century: Ireland and Russia had spectacular famines, and famine or near-famine conditions occurred with some frequency in many places. But such things grew rarer as the century passed and the damage they did was local and limited. Instead of verifying Malthus' diagnosis, the facts seemed to refute it because the rise in numbers was actually accompanied by higher standards of living, as a rising life expectancy seemed to show. Pessimists could reasonably reply that Malthus had not been disproved, only that there had turned out to be much more food available than had been feared.

In the eighteenth century European agriculture was capable of obtaining about two and a half times the yield on its seed normal in the Middle Ages. Yields went up to still higher levels in the next century and, even more important, European industry and commerce made it possible to tap huge larders in other parts of the world. A world economy made food cheaper than ever too. Both of these changes were aspects of a single process, the accelerating investment in productive capacity which made Europe and North America by 1870 the greatest concentrations of wealth on the face of the globe.

AGRICULTURAL REVOLUTION

Provided agricultural revolution is not thought of as implying rapid change, it is an acceptable term to describe the impact of the huge increase in output after 1750. This increase was not a simple matter of a few innovations but a process of great complexity. It drew on many different sources and was linked to the other sectors of the economy, and it involved not only Europe but the Americas and Australasia as well.

In 1750 the most advanced techniques were available in Great Britain, and she was to maintain this lead for another century or so. European farmers came to England to observe methods, buy stock and machinery, seek advice. Meanwhile the British farmer, benefiting from peace at home (that there were no large-scale and prolonged military operations on English soil after 1650 was literally of incalculable advantage to the economy) and a rising population to buy his produce, made profits to provide capital for further improvement.

In England the rewards of better farming went to individuals who owned their own land or held it as tenants on secure leases with terms which reflected market realities. English agriculture was a part of a capitalist market economy in which land was even in the eighteenth century treated almost like any other commodity. Restraints on its use familiar in other European countries had disappeared faster and faster ever since Henry VIII's sequestration of monastic property. The last great stage of this process came with a spate of enclosure acts at the turn of the century (significantly coincident with high prices for grain) which mobilized for the larger farmer's private profit the English peasant's traditional rights to pasture, fuel, or other economic benefits. One of the most striking contrasts between English and Continental agriculture in the early nineteenth century was that the traditional peasant all but disappeared in England. England had wage laborers and farmers but nothing like the Continent's huge rural populations with some, if minuscule, legal rights linking peasants to tiny pieces of soil.

The tendency for land to be grouped in economically profitable units was fed by the sales of land by small owners as the capital cost of successful farming grew. Technical progress was expensive but continuous, though for a long time much of it was hit or miss. Early breeders of better animals succeeded not because of a knowledge of chemistry, which was in its infancy, or of genetics, which did not exist, but because they backed hunches. Even so, the results were remarkable. The scraggy medieval sheep whose backs resembled, in section, the Gothic arches of the monasteries which bred them evolved into the fat, square animals familiar today. "Symmetry well covered" was an eighteenth-century farmer's ideal. Just as significant was the change in the appearance of farmland as draining and hedging progressed. The sprawling, common medieval fields divided into narrow strips, each cultivated by a different peasant, gave way to enclosed fields worked on rotations which made a broad patchwork of the English countryside. In some of them machinery could be seen at work by 1750, but it only became really productive in relation to cost as more large fields became available after 1800. The appearance of steam engines for driving threshers in English fields early in the new century opened the way which would run eventually to the almost complete replacement of muscle by machine power.

Agricultural improvements and changes in the ownership of land spread, *mutatis mutandis* and with a lag in time, to continental Europe but did not there transform rural society so completely. On the Continent preliminary changes were needed in social institutions which went much further than anything required in England. The French formally abolished serfdom in 1789; this probably did not mean much for there were few serfs in France at that date, but the abolition of the "feudal system" (as the relevant law put it) in the same year was a much more important matter. By this vague term, what was meant was the destruction of the whole mass of traditional and legal usages and rights which stood in the way of the exploitation of land by individuals as an investment like any other. Almost at once many of the peasants who had thought they wanted this reform discovered that they did not altogether like it in practice; it was fine to stop paying the customary dues to the lord of the manor but far from pleasant to lose customary rights to common land. At the same time a big redistribution of property occurred when lands belonging to the church were sold to private individuals. The upshot was both an increase in the number of people owning land outright and a growth in the average size of holdings. This should, on the English analogy, have led to a period of great agricultural advance for

France, but it did not. There was steady progress but, for example, no consolidation of properties as across the Channel. The French peasant survived.

This suggests, rightly, that generalizations should be cautious and qualified. Yet the abolition of medieval structures and all that was loosely called feudalism was at the heart of agricultural improvement everywhere in Europe. The process was accelerated in some places by French occupation (which introduced French law) during the wars of 1792–1814 and after this by other forces including deliberate reform from above. By 1850 peasants tied to the soil and obligatory labor service had disappeared from most of Europe. The major exception was Russia where serfdom persisted until 1861. Attitudes lingered long after this. Prussian and Polish landlords seem, for good and ill, to have maintained much of their patriarchal authority on the manor even after its legal supports had vanished, and as late as 1914. The Junker accepted the implications of the market in planning his own estate management but not in his relations with his tenants. This was important in preserving conservative aristocratic values in a much more intense form in these areas than in western Europe.

Russia's emancipation edict of 1861 closed an era of European history. It marked the end of a system which had been passed from antiquity to western Christendom during the barbarian invasions and had formed the basis of Europe's civilization for centuries. From the Urals to the Atlantic, whatever the practical and local qualifications, the working of land on the basis of legally obligatory labor services by peasants bound to landlords whom they could not leave had gone. Instead a rural proletariat everywhere worked for wages or tilled land as tenants; the pattern which had begun to spread in England and France during the fourteenth-century agricultural crisis had become universal.

Agriculture overseas

Formally, the medieval practice of binding labor to the estate lasted longest in the United States. In some parts of it obligatory labor in its most unqualified form was legal until the end of a great civil war in 1865; then the abolition of slavery promulgated two years earlier became effective throughout the whole territory of the republic.

The war was in some measure a distraction from the already rapid agricultural development of the country. The very operation which had been the center of debates over slavery, cotton growing, had also indicated how the New World would supplement European agriculture on a scale almost large enough to be indispensable. After the war the way was open to supplying Europe not merely with products such as cotton which she could not easily grow but also with much more food.

The United States—and soon Canada, Australia and New Zealand, Argentina, and Uruguay—could provide much of Europe's food more cheaply then she could grow it herself. Two things made this possible. One was immense agricultural resources; the American plains, the huge stretches of pasture in the South American pampas, and the temperate regions of Australasia offered vast areas for growing grain and raising livestock. The second

Merry England in the Early Nineteenth Century

Joseph Arch was the founder of the trades union movement among English agricultural workers. In his autobiography he recalled the atmosphere of the English rural community of his childhood early in the nineteenth century, notably the alliance of squire and parson to keep their inferiors in the station to which God had been pleased to call them.

When they [the agricultural laborers] did start a sick benefit fund . . . the parsons, the farmers, and the leading men of the parish did their very best to put it down, to stamp it out with their despotic heels. The parson refused point blank to preach a sermon in aid of funds for it . . . That a labourer, who had fallen out of work through illness, should be supported, even for a time, from a common fund over which the rectory had no direct control, was gall and wormwood to the parson. Worse still, the labourer's wife would not be so ready to come to the rectory back-door, humbly begging for help. Worse and worse still, she and the children might slip out of the yoke of Church attendance altogether, if rectory charity were no longer a necessity. No; this sick club was the thin edge of a bad wedge, and it must be pulled out and broken up without delay.

We labourers had no lack of lords and masters. There were the parson and his wife at the rectory. There was the squire, with his hand of iron overshadowing us all. There was no velvet glove on that hard hand, as many a poor man found to his hurt. He brought it down on my father because he would not sign for a small loaf and a dear one; and if it had not been for my mother, that hand would have crushed him to the earth, maybe crushed the life right out of him. At the sight of the squire the people trembled. He lorded it right feudally over his tenants, the farmers; the farmers in their turn tyrannised over the labourers; the labourers were no better than toads under a harrow. Most of the farmers were oppressors of the poor; they put on the iron wage-screw, and screwed the labourers' wages down, down below living point; they stretched him on the rack of life-long abject poverty.

From *The Life of Joseph Arch by Himself* (1898 ed.), in Patricia Hollis, ed., *Class Conflict in Nineteenth-Century England* (London: Routledge & Kegan Ltd., 1973), pp. 124–125.

was a revolution in transport which made these resources exploitable for the first time. Steam-powered trains and ships came into service in increasing numbers after 1860 and quickly brought down transport costs. Cheaper food meant greater demand, generating further profits to be put into more capital investment on the ranges and prairies of the new worlds.

Even in this elementary sketch the story of agricultural expansion bursts its banks. A growing food supply was the foundation of the most obvious expression of the increasing wealth of advanced countries, their greater life expectancies. The demand of the spreading cities, the coming of railways, and the availability of capital all point to the interconnection between agriculture and other sides of a thriving transoceanic economy between 1750 and 1870. For all its chronological primacy and its huge importance as a generator of investment capital, the revolution in agriculture is inseparable from the wide story of overall growth.

A NEW SCALE OF INDUSTRIALIZATION

Growth was registered in the most obvious and spectacular way by the appearance of a new kind of society based on the new phenomenon of large-scale industrialization. This change is a colossal subject. It is not even easy to see just how big it is. It was the most complete change in European history since the barbarian invasions, but it has been seen as even more important, as the biggest innovation in human history since the coming of agriculture or of the wheel. Even to define it is by no means easy though the processes which come together in it are obvious around us. One is the replacement of human or animal labor by machines driven by power from fossil fuels. Another is the organization of production in larger units. Another the increasing specialization of productive work. All these things have far-reaching ramifications and do not make up a tidy pattern. Conscious decisions by countless entrepreneurs and customers made up a blind force sweeping across social life with transforming power, one of the "senseless agencies" detected by a philosopher as half the story of revolutionary historical change. Industrialization meant new kinds of urbanization, new educational requirements, new patterns of social relationships, and these must also be part of its definition.

The origins of so complex a change go back well beyond the early modern period. The creation of capital for investment was made possible by agricultural and then commercial changes occurring slowly over centuries and then accelerating after 1600. The technologists of the Industrial Revolution (as a Frenchman of the early nineteenth century named his epoch) stood on the shoulders of innumerable craftsmen and artificers of preindustrial times who built up the skills and experience on which later development rested. In the fourteenth century, for example, Rhinelanders learned to cast iron — an important advance in European metallurgy. The use of blast furnaces, which lowered the cost of iron, spread in the eighteenth century. Once cheap iron was available (even in what were by later standards small quantities), new ways of using it were more freely experimented with and further changes quickly followed.

The Nineteenth=Century Working Day

P. Leroy-Beaulieu was a French sociologist who published a book in 1881 on the tendency for inequality to diminish. In the course of his argument he discusses the hours worked in industry. The passage is a revealing one, both for what it assumes to be a tolerable daily burden of toil and also for its misgivings about Asian threats to the economic well being of the West. It also of course illustrates what real progress had already been made in the material well being of the industrial worker.

In the recent past, for we are referring to a situation which existed only 30 or 40 years ago, a working day of 14 or 15 hours was not unusual, both in domestic as well as in factory production. Nowadays the duration of work is not more than 12 effective hours, and it is much too long. French law has fixed it at this figure; Swiss law has reduced it to 11 hours; in England it is down to 9½ hours; in Paris and in nearly all the cities, in innumerable occupations it does not exceed 10; in the mines it is generally below this and in most of the factories it varies between 10½ and 11 hours. Thus out

Iron lay so much at the heart of industrialization that its history is worth pursuing a little further. Its production on a large scale gave new importance to areas where the ore was first found. With the development of smelting techniques which used fossil rather than vegetable fuel, the location of supplies of iron and coal became a major factor in determining the later industrial geography of Europe and North America. Much of the world's discovered coal supply lies in a great belt running from the basin of the Don, through Silesia, the Ruhr, Lorraine, the north of England, and Wales across to Pennsylvania and West Virginia. This was one source of a difference to grow increasingly marked between the Atlantic world and Asia and between the northern and southern hemispheres.

of 24 hours of a day the worker has 13 for his own needs and if we deduct sleep and meals, he has three to four hours to attend to his own affairs, for family life, amusements, conversation, and reading, in addition to having the whole of Sunday free. Contrary to what is often claimed, this can in no sense be regarded as slavery; and it is probable that soon, in the whole of Europe, the effective working day will be everywhere reduced to 10 hours or to 60 hours out of the 168 in the week, not through legislation, but at the request of the parties concerned; deducting 9 hours per day for sleep and meals, the worker will be free to enjoy 45 hours per week. Any further improvements could only be achieved by incurring great disadvantages; there is a need to be on guard against the yellow race, the Chinese and the Japanese, without mentioning the Indian, who, when they possess our mechanical arts and industrial discoveries will perhaps show European workers and those in the United States, by a course of cruel lessons, the need for hard work, sobriety and temperance.

From Sidney Pollard and Colin Holmes, eds., *Documents of European Economic History* (New York: St. Martin's Press, Inc., 1972), vol. II, pp. 477–478. Reprinted by permission of St. Martin's Press, Inc., and Edward Arnold Ltd.

Steam power

Better metal and richer fuel made their decisive contribution to early industrialization with the invention of a new source of power, the steam engine. That steam could be used to produce movement had been known in ancient Alexandria. What was lacking was the technology to develop this knowledge and the economy to make the effort worthwhile. The eighteenth century brought a series of technical refinements so important that they really deserve to be considered as fundamental changes. The result was a source of power rapidly recognized as a revolutionary force.

Steam engines were not only the product of an economy based on coal and iron, they also consumed them, both directly as fuel and materials used

A Yorkshire collier of 1813, with two steam engines at work behind him. *(The Mansell Collection)*

in their construction and indirectly by making possible other processes such as the building of railways which led to increased demand for them. In most countries the railway consumed coal, and it required huge quantities of first iron and then steel for rails and rolling stock. But it also lowered the cost of transporting goods—including coal and ore. As these became cheaper away from the regions in which they were mined, new industrial areas grew up. From them trains could carry manufactured goods to distant markets.

The railway was not the only means by which steam changed movement. The first commercially successful steamboat voyaged up the Hudson River in 1807. By 1870, though there were still many sailing ships at sea and shipyards were still building battleships with a full spread of sail, steamships were commonplace. The "shrinkage" of space which steam thus produced overturned men's ideas of the possible. The domestication of the horse, the invention of the wheel, and the digging of canals had enabled man to convey himself and his goods over considerable distances at speeds which varied, according to local roads, between one to five miles per hour. Faster travel was possible at sea and this had perhaps increased somewhat as ships underwent quite considerable modification. But such improvement was only slight in thousands of years. It was dwarfed when a man could witness in his lifetime the change from travel on horseback to trains capable of speeds of 40 or even 50 miles an hour for long periods.

We have now lost one of the pleasantest of industrial sights, the long plume of steam streaming from the funnel of a speeding locomotive and

An English locomotive of the 1830s. *(The Mansell Collection)*

hanging for a few seconds behind it against a green landscape. It was a sight which greatly struck those who first saw it and so did other visual aspects of industrialization. One of the most terrifying to them was the industrial town, whose characteristic feature was the factory with smoking chimneys, as that of the preindustrial town had been the spire of church or cathedral.

So dramatic and novel was the factory that it has often been overlooked that it was not the typical expression of the early stages of industrialization but an unusual one. Even in the middle of the nineteenth century the majority of English industrial workers were employed in units of less than fifty. It was only in textiles that great agglomerations of labor were to be found, and the huge Lancashire cotton mills which first gave that area a visual and urban character distinct from earlier manufacturing towns were unusual. Yet it was apparent long before 1870 that the trend in more and more manufacturing processes was toward centralization under one roof.

The workshop of the world

In the middle of the nineteenth century only one country, Great Britain had a mature industrial society. The inhabitants of "the workshop of the world," as they liked to call it, could observe all around them the transformation of British wealth and power which had already followed upon industrialization. In 1850, for example, the United Kingdom owned half the world's ocean-going ships and contained nearly half the world's railway mileage. On those railways trains ran with a precision and regularity ("time-table" was a word just invented for them) and even a speed not much improved upon for a hundred years after. The railways already employed the electric telegraph and they were ridden by men and women who had a few years before traveled in stage coaches. In 1851, the year a great international exhibition in London advertised her supremacy, Great Britain smelted 2.5 million tons of iron. It does not sound like a lot today, but it was five times as much as the United States and ten times as much as Germany. In the same year British steam engines could produce more than 1.2 million horsepower, over half that of all Europe together.

By 1870 Germany, France, Switzerland, Belgium, and the United States were also industrial nations, and a change had started to appear in relative positions. Great Britain remained in most ways in the lead, but less decisively. She still had more steam power than any other European country, but the United States had long been ahead of her and Germany was coming up fast. In the 1850s both Germany and France had made the important transition (effected earlier in Great Britain) from smelting a majority of iron by charcoal to smelting with fossil fuels. Though Britain's pig iron output had gone on rising, it was now only three and a half times that of the United States and four times that of Germany. But these were still huge superiorities; the age of British industrial dominance had not yet begun to close.

TOWNS AND CITIES

The early industrial societies were puny creatures in comparison with what they were to become. Only Great Britain and Belgium had most of their population living in towns in the middle of the nineteenth century, and the census of 1851 showed that agriculture was still the biggest single employer of labor among British industries (equaled only by domestic service). But in all the industrializing countries the steady increase in the numbers of those engaged in manufacturing, the rise of new concentrations of wealth, and a new scale of urbanization made very visible the changes which were going forward. The growth of towns was particularly obvious. They grew at a spectacular rate in the nineteenth century, particularly in its second half. The appearance of big centers that would be the nuclei of what a later age would call megalopolis was then especially marked.

There are difficulties in reckoning other indices of urbanization, largely because different countries defined urban areas in different ways, but they do not conceal the main lines of what was happening. In 1800 London, Paris, and Berlin had, respectively, about 900,000, 600,000, and 170,000 inhabitants. In 1900 the corresponding figures were 4.7 million, 3.6 million, and 2.7 million. By then Glasgow, Moscow, St. Petersburg, and Vienna also had more than a million inhabitants each. These were the giants; just behind them were sixteen more European cities with populations over 500,000—a figure only surpassed by London and Paris in 1800. These great cities and many smaller ones (which were still immeasurably bigger than those of earlier centuries) were fed by immigration from the countryside. Urbanization was most marked in the relatively few countries where industrialization had made headway because it was the wealth and employment generated by industry which above all drew people to urban centers. Of the twenty-three cities of more than 500,000 in 1900, thirteen were in four countries: the United Kingdom (6), Germany (3), France (3), and Belgium (1).

Opinions about cities have often changed. As the eighteenth century ended, something like a sentimental rediscovery of rural life was in full swing among romantics. This coincided with the first phase of industrialization, and thus the nineteenth century opened with the tide of aesthetic and moral comment turned against an urban life which was about to reveal a new and often unpleasant face. Cities were distrusted places, destroyers of traditional patterns of behavior and crucibles of new social forms and ideas. Long after European governments had demonstrated the ease with which they could control urban unrest, cities were still regarded suspiciously as likely nests of revolution.

There were two reasonable grounds for this distrust. One was that conditions in many of the new metropolitan centers were often terrible. The east end of London could present shocking evidence of poverty, filth, disease, and deprivation to anyone who chose to penetrate its slums. In 1845 a young German businessman, Frederick Engels, wrote one of the most influential books of the century, *The Condition of the English Working Class,*

Foreign visitors were appalled — but also awed — by the bustle and scale of life in Victorian London. This rendering by a French artist of traffic in the 1870s suggests that some problems recur in every age. *(Prints Division, The New York Public Library, Astor, Lenox and Tilden Foundations)*

which alleged appalling facts about the Manchester poor. It was not illogical to suppose that such conditions could breed resentment and hatred of the beneficiaries and rulers of society and that the urban poor were a potentially revolutionary force. In France the phenomenon of the "dangerous classes," as the Parisian poor were called, preoccupied governments for the first half of the nineteenth century.

It was also reasonable to think the city made for ideological subversion. It was a huge and anonymous thicket in which men and women easily escaped the scrutiny of priest, squire, and neighbors which had regulated rural communities. Moveover (and this was especially true as literacy slowly spread downward) it was a place where new ideas were brought to bear upon long unchallenged assumptions. Nineteenth-century society was particularly struck by what it believed to be the tendency of city life to atheism and irreligion. More was at stake in this, people felt, than merely sound doctrine. Religion was the great sustainer of morals and a major support of the established social order. Karl Marx sneered that it was "the opium of the people"; the possessing classes would hardly have put it in quite the same terms, but they acknowledged the importance of religion as social cement.

There was a long-continued series of attempts in both Catholic and Protestant countries to find a way of recapturing the cities for Christianity. The effort was misconceived insofar as it presumed that the churches had ever had any footing in the new urban areas, which had long since swamped the traditional parish structures and religious institutions of the old towns and villages at their hearts. But it led to the building of new churches in industrial suburbs and the creation of missions combining evangelism and social service. By the end of the century religious-minded people were well aware of the challenges they faced in an urban society. In 1890 a great English evangelist titled of one of his books *Darkest England* to emphasize the parallel with missionary work in pagan lands overseas. His answer was to found a unique instrument of religious propaganda, the Salvation Army, designed specifically to appeal to a new kind of population and to combat the ills of industrial society.

Labor

Industrialization reshaped society in many ways. One great influence was the creation of a new work pattern. For the whole of history economic behavior had been regulated fundamentally by the rhythms of nature. In an agricultural or pastoral economy they imposed an annual pattern which dictated the kinds of work which could or should be undertaken at different times of year. Operating within the seasonal rhythm were the subordinate ones of light and darkness, fair weather and foul. But by the middle of the nineteenth century many people's lives followed quite different rhythms. These were dictated by the means of production and their demands — by the need to keep machines economically employed, by the cheapness or dearness of investment capital, and by the availability of labor. The symbol of industrial rhythm was the factory. Its gas lights made night shifts possible. Its machinery set a pattern of work in which accurate time keeping was essential. People began to think about time in a quite new way as a consequence.

Industry also related the laborer to his work in new ways. Formerly people had lived in great intimacy with their tools, their animals, and the fields in which they won their bread. It is important to avoid sentimentalizing this past in assessing the change that occurred. Af first sight the disenchantment of the factory worker with his monotonous routine, with its exclusion of personal involvement and its sense of working for another's profit, justifies the hard things said about it. But the life of the medieval peasant had also been monotonous and much of his time, too, had been spent working for another's profit. Nor is an iron routine necessarily less painful because it is set by sunset and sunrise instead of an employer. What is certain is that the new disciplines involved a revolutionary transformation of the ways people earned their livelihood, however we may evaluate the results by comparison with what had gone before.

One of the most notorious evils of early industrialism was its use of child labor. A generation of Englishmen morally braced by the abolition of slavery and intensely aware of the importance of early religious training was disposed to be sentimental about children in a way previous generations had not been. This helped create an awareness of the brutal exploitation of children in factories, which in fact was only one part of a total transformation of employment patterns. Child labor in itself was not new. Children had for centuries been swineherds, bird scarers, gleaners, maids-of-all-work, cross-

Title page of an 1853 book attacking the inhumanity of employers of child labor. (*Economics Division, The New York Public Library, Astor, Lenox and Tilden Foundations*)

Luddism in Saxony

Luddism got its name in England, but there were manifestations of the machine breaking, which was one of its expressions, in most industrializing countries in nineteenth-century Europe. Here is an example from Saxony, in 1848, a year whose disturbances reflected much more than the liberal and national demands which seized the headlines.

On 28 March, 1848, it came to the notice of Jahn, the owner of a machine-made nail manufactory at Mittweida near Scheibenberb in the Erz Mountains that a nailmaker from Elterlein had been going about the district around Mittweida and had incited the nailmakers there to "demolish" his manufactory. . . . Jahn thereupon began to make preparations; he hid the "firm's books, documents and cash box" in the cellar, sent a message to the District Governor for "the most urgent military assistance," and to the mayor for some volunteers. When news came from Elterlein that in the factory of Zimmerman and Leinbrock "all had been broken up and destroyed," Jahn called together his workmen and armed them with scythes and fire-arms. In addition he got ready barrels of nails, cast iron articles and old machine parts to drop on the attackers from above. At 2 P.M. the attack began. After the nailmakers had been

ing sweepers, and casual drudges. The terrible lot of unprotected children painted by the French novelist Victor Hugo in *Les Misérables* (published 1862) is a picture of their life in a *pre*industrial society. The institutional forms of the factory only regularized and gave a new sort of harshness to their plight.

Whereas the work of children in an agricultural society had perforce been clearly differentiated from that of adults by their inferior strength, the tending of machines offered a whole range of activities in which child labor competed directly with that of adults. In a labor market normally oversupplied this put irresistible pressures upon parents to send their children into the factory to contribute to the family income as soon as possible. This was sometimes at the age of five or six. The consequences were not only often terrible for the victims but also transformed the relation of children to soci-

repulsed twice, and one woman had been shot in the fighting, the attackers withdrew in order to call up reinforcements. Meanwhile the manufacturer Breitkopf had come to the assistance of Jahn with about twenty of his machine workers, and when the nailmakers returned, the attacks were renewed and pursued with greater vigour. The latter succeeded in entering the factory first at one, and later at several points, whereupon Jahn saw the hopelessness of further resistance and fled . . . The destruction which Jahn found on his return to Mittweida, he describes as follows: "the yard was full of stones . . . in the factory buildings nearly all the machines had been destroyed by axes and crowbars. Nothing was left undamaged. Most of the stocks had been stolen or thrown into the river. In the living quarters, all the furniture and even all items of clothing had been stolen or destroyed, all stoves, doors and windows smashed, even the window frames had not been spared . . . In the rooms, which were full of stones of such a size that it was amazing how they could have been thrown up to the first floor, the floorboards had been partially torn up—probably in order to search for hidden treasure. The cellars, which met the brunt of the first attack, were completely ransacked."

From Sidney Pollard and Colin Holmes, eds., *Documents of European Economic History* (New York: St. Martin's Press, Inc., 1968), vol. I, pp. 530–531. Reprinted by permission of St. Martin's Press, Inc., and Edward Arnold Ltd.

ety and the structure of the family. This was one of the "senseless agencies" of history at its most dreadful.

Such problems were too pressing to remain without attention and men quickly made a start in taming the more obvious evils of industrialism. By 1850 the law of England had begun intervening to protect, for example, women and young children in manufacturing work: children under eight were not to be employed in factories and those under twelve were not to work more than eight hours a day. This may sound woefully inadequate, but in all the millennia of agriculturally based economies it had been impossible by the same date to eradicate slavery. Given the unprecedented scale and speed with which social transformation was upon them, the inhabitants of early industrial Europe should not be blamed without qualification for not acting more quickly to remedy ills whose outlines they could only dimly grasp.

THEORIES OF CHANGE

Many Europeans were disposed to see the absence of social regulation as the explanation of the enormous new wealth being generated. Although very few economic theorists or publicists of the early industrial period advocated absolute noninterference in the economy, there was a broad, sustaining current of informed opinion which favored the view that much good would result from allowing market forces to operate without the help or hindrance of politicians and civil servants. One influence in this direction was the teaching of economists, which has often been summed up in a phrase made famous by a group of eighteenth-century Frenchmen: laissez faire. Broadly speaking, theorists said with growing consensus that the production of wealth would be accelerated and therefore the general well-being would increase if the use of economic resources followed the "natural" demands of the market. Another reinforcing trend was individualism; the assumption that people knew their own business best and the increasing organization of society around the rights and interests of the individual both told against collective interference in the economy through law.

These were the sources of the long-enduring association between industrialism and liberalism; they were deplored by conservatives who regretted a hierarchical, agricultural order of mutual obligations and duties, settled ideas, and religious values. Yet liberals who welcomed the new age were by no means taking their stand merely on a negative and selfish base. The creed of Manchester, as the celebration of laissez faire was called (because of the symbolic importance of cotton spinning in English industrial and commercial development) was for its leaders much more than a matter of mere self-enrichment.

Protection and free trade

In the early nineteenth century Great Britain was preoccupied by a great political battle over the repeal of what were called the Corn Laws, a tariff system originally imposed to protect the British farmer from imports of cheaper foreign grain. The repealers, whose ideological and political leaders were businessmen, Richard Cobden and John Bright, argued that the duties on grain demonstrated the grip upon the legislative machinery of the agricultural interest, the traditional ruling class, which ought not to be allowed a monopoly of power. The national economy ought to be free from such distortions in the interest of a particular group. Back came the reply of the anti-repealers: the manufacturers were themselves a special interest and only wanted cheap food imports in order to pay lower wages. If they wanted to help the poor, let them accept regulation of the conditions under which they employed women and children in factories. To this the repealers responded that cheap food would mean cheaper goods for export. And in this, for someone like Cobden, much more than profit was involved. He believed that from an expansion of free trade between nations would spring international progress both material and spiritual; trade brought peoples together, exchanged and multiplied the blessings of civilization, and increased the power of progressive forces in each country.

There was much more to the free trade issue (of which the Corn Laws were the focus) than a brief summary can encompass. The more it is expounded, the more it becomes clear that industrialism involved a creative, positive ideology which implied intellectual, social, and political challenge to the past. This is why the free trade debate and the broader issues of laissez faire should not be the subject of simple moral and nonhistoric judgments, though both conservatives and liberals thought they could be at the time. Yet the same man might resist legislation against long hours while proving himself a model employer in his treatment of his own workmen, actively supporting educational and political reform, and fighting the corruption of public interest by privileged birth. His opponent might struggle to protect children working in factories and act as a benevolent patriarch to his tenants while bitterly resisting the extension of the franchise to those not members of the established church or any reduction of the political influence of landlords. It was all very muddled. In the specific issue of the Corn Laws the outcome was also paradoxical because a conservative prime minister was in the end convinced by repeal arguments; when Sir Robert Peel had the opportunity to do so without too obvious an inconsistency, he persuaded Parliament to make the change in 1846. His party contained men who never forgave him, and this great climax of Peel's political career (for which he was to be honored by his liberal opponents) came shortly before he was dismissed from power by his own followers.

England was the only country where the issue of free trade was so fought out. On the Continent protectionists tended to have the best of it, as the setting up of a customs union (the Zollverein) between German states illustrates; it created an enlarged area of free trade inside Germany but provided in the process a firmer basis for tariff protection against other countries. Only in the middle of the century, a period of great expansion and prosperity, did free trade ideas attract much support outside the United Kingdom. There the prosperity of the times was regarded by anti-protectionists as evidence of the correctness of their views. At any rate, it mollified their opponents, and free trade became a British political fetish untouchable until well into the twentieth century. Because it was attached to the prestige of British economic leadership, it gained a brief popularity elsewhere in Europe. The prosperity of expansion probably owed as much to other influences as to this ideological triumph, but the belief added to the optimism of economic liberals. Their creed was the culmination of the confident, progressive view of man's potential born during the Enlightenment.

There was plenty of ground for optimism. In assessing the impact of industrialization we labor under the handicap of not having before us the squalor of the past it left behind. For all the poverty and the slums, the people who lived in the great cities of 1870 consumed more and lived longer than their ancestors. This of course does not mean they were either tolerably off by later standards or contented. But the way people look at their world and decide whether or not they are satisfied is a matter of much more than material facts.

chapter 28

An Age of Revolutions

In the eighteenth century the word "revolution" changed its meaning. It had once meant only a change in the composition of government and not necessarily a violent one. After 1789 it had a different meaning. People came to see that year as the beginning of a new sort of revolution characterized by violence and by limitless possibilities for fundamental change — social, political, and economic. They began to think too that it might be international. Both those who welcomed such a revolution and those who feared it agreed that it was fundamental to the politics of their age. There were indeed within a century or so after 1750 numerous upheavals which could properly be called revolutions in the new sense even though many of them failed and others brought changes far different from those people expected.

THE AMERICAN REVOLUTION

The first and most obvious change in this era was the dissolution of the first British empire, and the central episode of this drama later became known as the American Revolution.

In 1763 British imperial power in North America was at its height. Canada had just been taken from the French and the future seemed secure. Yet some prophets had suggested even before the French were defeated that their removal might weaken rather than strengthen the British grasp on North America. The British colonies, after all, already had more inhabitants than many sovereign states of Europe, and a large number of these subjects were not of English descent. Moreover the colonies had economic interests not necessarily congruent with those of the imperial power, at least within the framework of accepted colonial theory. The grip of the British government was bound to be slack simply because of the huge distances which separated London from the colonies. Once the threat from the French (and from the Indians whom they had egged on) had been removed, it was argued, the ties of empire would have to be relaxed still more.

One difficulty appeared at once in the wake of the French expulsion. This was the problem of the West. How was it to be organized? What relation was it to have to the existing colonies? How were the new Canadian subjects of the crown to be treated? These questions were given urgency by the revolt of an Indian confederacy led by an Ottawa chief, Pontiac, in the Ohio valley in 1763 in response to pressure by the colonists. The imperial government immediately barred the area west of the Alleghenies to settlement. This offended many colonials who saw the West as their proper domain for settlement and trade, and their irritation grew as British administrators negotiated treaties with Indians and worked out arrangements for a garrisoned frontier to separate and protect from one another the colonists and the Indians.

This was the beginning of ten years during which the dormant potential for American independence matured and came to a head. Grumbles about grievances turned first into resistance, then rebellion. The pace throughout was set by London's initiatives; colonial leaders used provocative British legislation to radicalize American politics by making the colonists believe that the liberty they already enjoyed was in danger. Paradoxically Great Britain was ruled at this time by a succession of ministers anxious to carry out reforms in colonial affairs. Their excellent intentions helped destroy a status quo which had previously proved workable.

One principle firmly grasped in London was that the Americans ought to pay a proper share of the taxes which contributed to their defense and the common good of the empire. The first attempt to put this into practice took

The American Revolution owed much to the printing press. Pamphlets and prints gave wide circulation to radical propaganda. This one depicts a mock burial (coffin on the left) of the Stamp Act, at which an effigy of the Stamp Master for New Hampshire was also paraded. *(The Metropolitan Museum of Art, Bequest of Charles Allen Munn, 1924)*

the form of the Sugar Act of 1764 and the Stamp Act of 1765. The important thing about these laws was not the amounts they proposed to raise or even the novelty of taxing the internal transactions of the colonies (which was much discussed) but rather that they were, as both English politicians and American taxpayers clearly saw, unilateral acts of legislation by the imperial Parliament. Hitherto the colonists had usually handled their affairs and raised revenue by haggling with their own assemblies. What the new taxes now brought forward was a question hardly even formulated before: whether the undoubted legislative sovereignty of the Parliament of the United Kingdom also extended to its colonies.

Riots, nonimportation agreements, and angry protests by the colonists followed. The unhappy officials who held the stamps (which were to be affixed to commercial and legal documents, thus automatically raising revenue from the ordinary transaction of business) were given a bad time. Ominously, in 1765 representatives of nine colonies attended a Stamp Act Congress in New York. The act was repealed the next year.

London then took a different tack, turning to external duties on paint, paper, glass, and tea. As these were not internal taxes and the imperial government had always regulated trade, they seemed more promising. This proved an illusion. Americans were by now being told by their radical politicians that no taxation should be levied on them by a legislature in which they were not represented. As King George III clearly saw, it was not the crown but Parliament whose power was under attack. There were more riots and boycotts and one of the first of those influential scuffles which make up so much of the history of decolonization, the death of five rioters mythologized by agitators into the Boston Massacre.

Once more the British government retreated. In 1770 it withdrew three of the duties, keeping only the one on tea. Unfortunately, the issue was by now out of hand; it transcended taxation, as London knew, and had become a question of whether or not Parliament could make laws enforceable in the colonies. As George III put it a little later, "We must either master them or totally leave them to themselves." Resistance was focused in one city, though it was evident throughout the colonies. After radicals destroyed a cargo of tea in 1773 at the Boston Tea Party, the crucial question for the British government was: could Massachusetts be governed?

There were to be no more retreats: George III, his ministers, and the majority of the House of Commons were agreed on this. A number of coercive acts were passed to bring Boston to heel. The New England radicals were heard all the more sympathetically in the other colonies at this juncture because the Quebec Act of 1774, providing for the future of Canada, stirred up wide resentment. Some disliked the privileged position it gave to Roman Catholicism (a sensible, humane measure designed to leave French Canadians as undisturbed as possible by their change of rulers), and others saw its extension of Canada's boundaries south to the Ohio River as another block to expansion westward.

In September of that year delegates from the colonies met at Philadelphia to form the Continental Congress, which proclaimed the severing of

The year 1775 through British eyes. America burns, the national credit vanishes, the Constitution is trampled underfoot, and only the hated Scotchmen (whose mythical leader, Lord Bute, rides as footman to the king) prosper. The vainly protesting figure on crutches is Lord Chatham, formerly William Pitt, the "Great Commoner." *(The John Carter Brown Library, Brown University)*

commercial relations with the United Kingdom and demanded the repeal of much existing legislation, including the Quebec Act. By this time recourse to force was probably inevitable. The radical colonial spokesmen had brought out into the open the practical sense of independence already felt by many Americans. But it is unlikely that any eighteenth-century imperial government could have grasped this. The British government was remarkably reluctant to act on its convictions or to rely simply on force, until disorder and intimidation of law-abiding and moderate colonists had already gone very far. At the same time, it made it clear that it would not willingly bend on the principle of sovereignty.

The colonists began gathering arms in Massachusetts. In April 1775 a detachment of British soldiers sent to Lexington to seize some of them fought the first action of the American Revolution. It took a year more for the feelings of colonial leaders to harden into the conviction that only complete independence from Great Britain would rally an effective resistance. The result was the Declaration of Independence of July 1776 and the debate was transferred to the battlefield.

The British lost the war which followed because of the difficulties imposed by geography, because the Americans succeeded in avoiding superior forces long enough to preserve an army capable of victory at Saratoga in 1777, because the French entered the war soon after in search of revenge for the defeat of 1763, because the Spanish followed them and thus tipped the balance of naval power against Great Britain, and because of the generalship of the allies in the final brilliant campaign. The British had a further handicap: they dared not fight the kind of war which might win military victory, that is, by terrorizing the American population to encourage its cooperation in cutting the supplies and freedom of movement which General Washington's army enjoyed. They could not do this because their overriding aim had to be to keep open the way to a conciliatory peace with colonists willing to accept British rule once again.

The military end came in 1781 when a British army found itself trapped at Yorktown between the Americans on land and a French squadron at sea. Only 7,000 or so soldiers were involved, but their surrender, besides being the worst humiliation yet undergone by British arms, was also the end of an era of imperial rule. Yorktown opened the way for peace negotiations and two years later the Treaty of Paris was signed. In it Great Britain recognized the independence of the United States, whose territory the British negotiators had already agreed should run to the Mississippi River—a concession of immense importance in shaping a new nation. The French, who had envisaged a recovery for themselves in the Mississippi valley, were disappointed; it appeared that only Spain and Great Britain would share the northern continent with the American republic.

The new nation

For all the loose ends which took decades to tie up, the appearance of a new state of great potential resources in the Western hemisphere was by any standard a revolution. If it was often seen as something less than this by contemporary foreign observers, that was because at the time the weaknesses of the new nation were more apparent than its potential. Indeed, it was far from clear that this was a nation at all; in 1783 it seemed weak and divided. Many expected the colonies to fall into quarreling and disunion. Their one advantage was their remoteness; they could work out their problems virtually untroubled by foreign intervention. This was crucial to much that was to follow.

As after all civil wars and wars of independence, deep divisions accentuated political weakness. Among these, that between loyalists and rebels was, for all its bitterness, perhaps the least important. The problem was solved, brutally, by emigration of the defeated; something like 80,000 loyalists left the rebel colonies for a variety of motives, from intimidation and terror to simple loyalty to the crown. Other divisions likely to cause more trouble in the future were those of economic interest between farmers, merchants, and plantation owners. Finally, there were differences between regions or sections of the country, and one of them, that imposed by the economic importance of black slavery to the southern states, was to take decades to work out.

The war against the British had imposed a certain self-discipline among the colonists. Victory was followed by a half-dozen critical years during which decisions shaping much of the future history of the world were taken by a handful of American politicians. The Articles of Confederation agreed upon by the former colonies came into force in 1781. In them appeared the name of the new nation, the United States of America. But peace brought a growing sense that these arrangements were unsatisfactory. Two pressing problems revealed their limitations. One was civil disturbance arising fundamentally from disagreement about what the Revolution ought to mean in internal affairs. To many Americans the central government appeared far too weak to deal with disaffection and disorder. The other was a postwar economic depression which particularly affected trade and was linked to currency problems stemming from the independence of the individual states. To deal with these, too, the central authority seemed ill equipped. It was accused of neglecting American domestic and economic interests in its conduct of relations with other countries. Whether true or not, this was widely believed.

The result was the Constitutional Convention of 1787. Fifty-five delegates from the thirteen states met at Philadelphia to draft a new basis of government. After four months' work they submitted their plan to the individual states for ratification. The required nine had accepted it by the summer of 1788, and the Constitution went into effect the following year. In April 1789 George Washington, the former commander of the American forces in the war against the British, took the oath of office as the first president of the new republic, thus inaugurating a series of presidencies which has continued unbroken to this day.

The Constitution

Much was said about the need for simple institutions and principles clear in their intention, yet the new Constitution would still be revealing its potential for development over a hundred and fifty years later. For all the determination of its drafters to provide an unambiguous document which would resist reinterpretation, they were (fortunately) unsuccessful. The United States Constitution was to prove capable of spanning a historical epoch in which a nation made up of a scatter of largely agricultural societies changed into a giant industrial and world power. In part this was because of the provision for amendment, but in larger measure would be due to continuous interpretation of what the Constitution meant.

To begin with its most obvious feature: the Constitution was republican. This was by no means unsurprising in the eighteenth century and should not be taken for granted. Some Americans felt that republicanism was so important and so easily threatened that they even disapproved of installing a president as the head of the executive because it "squinted toward monarchy," as one of them put it. The republics of ancient times were as famous for their tendency toward decay and faction as for their legendarily admirable morals. The history of the Italian republics was no more encouraging and even less edifying. In eighteenth-century Europe republics were few and apparently unflourishing; furthermore they seemed to persist only in small countries. Though it was conceded that the remoteness of the United States might protect republican forms which would elsewhere ensure the collapse of a large state, foreign observers were not sanguine about the new nation. Yet European advocates of political change would soon look to America for inspiration, and before much longer the influence of republican example would spread from the northern to the southern half of the New World.

The second significant characteristic of the Constitution was that its roots lay in British political experience. This was true of the actual arrangement of government as well as the jurisprudence of the new state, which rested on the principles of English common law. The founding fathers had all grown up in a colonial system in which their own elected assemblies had debated the public interest with the royal governors. They therefore instituted in the Constitution a bicameral legislature on the English model (although they excluded any hereditary element in its composition) to offset a president. They then followed the theory of English constitutionalism in putting a monarch, albeit an elected one, at the head of the executive machinery of government (though this was not the way the British constitution actually worked). The Americans took the best constitution they knew, purged it of its corruptions (as they saw them), and modified it to fit their own political and social facts. They did not emulate the alternative principle of government available in contemporary Europe, monarchical absolutism, even in its enlightened form. The Americans wrote a constitution for free men because they believed that the British already lived under one: it had failed only insofar as it had been improperly employed to deprive Americans of the rights they too possessed under it.

Federalism was another way the United States differed from most other existing states and one in which it diverged consciously from the British constitutional model. Indeed, only large concessions to the independence of individual states had made union possible at all. The former colonies had no wish to set up a new central authority which could bully them as they believed the government of King George had done. The federal structure provided an answer to the problem of diversity — *e pluribus unum*. It also dictated much of the form and content of American politics for the next eighty years. Question after question, which might be economic or social or ideological in substance, would be pressed into the channels of a continuing debate about what were the proper relations between the central government and the individual states. In the end this debate would come within an ace of destroying the union. It would also promote a major readjustment within the Constitution, the rise of the Supreme Court as the authority on what was and what was not constitutional. Federalism would later appeal to many other countries impressed by what it appeared to have achieved in America.

Finally, there is the significance of the opening words of the Constitution: "We the People." Political arrangements in some of the states were not democratic in 1789, but the principle of popular sovereignty was enunciated clearly from the start. In whatever form the mythology of a particular historical epoch might cloak it, the popular will was to remain the ultimate court of appeal in American politics. Here was a fundamental departure from the British tradition, and it owed something to the political theories of seventeenth-century colonists who had sometimes given themselves constitutions. Yet even these had been conceived within the overall framework of kingship. British constitutionalism was prescriptive; the sovereignty of king in Parliament existed not because the people had once decided it should, but because it was there and was unquestioned. The new Constitution broke with this and every other prescriptive theory. But even this was not quite a clean break with British political thinking for Locke had said that governments held their powers on trust and that the people could overturn governments which abused that trust.

The United States' adoption of the democratic theory that all governments derive their just powers from the consent of the governed was not new but it was epoch marking. In practice though it by no means solved the problems of political authority at a stroke. Many Americans feared democracy and sought to restrict the element of popular will in the political system right from the start.

The problem of defining political authority was suggested too by the Bill of Rights, added to the Constitution in 1791 to secure individual liberties. Yet the fundamental rights set out in the first ten amendments were presumably as much subject to revision at the hands of popular sovereignty as any other part of the Constitution. Here was an important source of confusion for the future: whether democratic principles consist in following the wishes of the majority or in upholding certain "inalienable" rights.

Despite its ambiguities, nevertheless, the adoption of the democratic principle in 1787 was immensely important for the future and justifies the consideration of the Constitution as a revolutionary landmark in world history. For generations to come the new nation would be the focus of the aspirations of people longing to be free the world over—"the world's last, best hope," as one American said. Even today, when the United States has become a great conservative power, the democratic ideal it preserved and exemplified for so long retains its glamour in many countries, and the institutions it fertilized are still working.

THE FRENCH REVOLUTION

Paris was the center of Europe's social and political debates, and to it returned some of the French soldiers who had fought for the young American republic. Thus it is hardly surprising that the French were more aware of the transatlantic revolution than most Europeans. American example and the hopes it raised contributed in some measure to the huge release of forces which is still, in spite of later upheavals, called *the* French Revolution.

Politicians and scholars have offered many different interpretations of the essence of the Revolution; they have disagreed about how long it went on, what its results were, and even when it began. What is certain is that it was very important and that it changed the whole concept of revolution. Yet there was much in the French experience that looked to the past rather than the future. In the great boiling over of the pot which occurred at the end of the eighteenth century, there was the same sort of jumbled mixture of conservative and innovating elements present in the 1640s in England and also much the same blend of consciousness and unconsciousness of direction and purpose. This confusion was the symptom of big dislocations and maladjustments in the material life and government of France.

The French crisis

France was the greatest European power. Her ruler neither could nor wished to relinquish her international role. The first way in which the American Revolution had affected France was by providing an opportunity for revenge; Yorktown was the return match for her defeat at the hands of the British in the Seven Years' War. To deprive them of the thirteen colonies was some compensation for the French loss of India and Canada. Yet the effort was costly. For no considerable gain beyond the humiliation of a rival, France added yet another layer to a huge and accumulating debt piled up since the days of Louis XIV by efforts to maintain her European supremacy.

Attempts to liquidate this debt and free the monarchy from the cramping burden it imposed (which after 1783 was sharply narrowing France's real independence in foreign affairs) were made by a succession of ministers under Louis XVI, the young, somewhat stupid but high-principled and well-meaning king who came to the throne in 1774. None of them succeeded even in arresting the growth of the debt, let alone in reducing it. The essential difficulty was that the whole social and political structure of France stood in the way of tapping the wealth of the better-off, the only sure means of emerging from the financial impasse. In practice a due weight of taxation could not be levied on those who possessed the most wealth unless the government was prepared to resort to force. The paradox of eighteenth-century government appeared in France at its purest: a theoretically absolute monarch could not really act to infringe the mass of liberties and rights (i.e., privileges) which made up the essentially medieval constitution of the country because monarchy itself rested on the same footing.

To more and more Frenchmen it appeared that a complete renovation of the governmental and constitutional structure was needed. Some went further. They saw the failure to share fiscal burdens equitably between classes as the extreme example of a whole range of abuses blocking desirable reform. The issue was increasingly stated in terms of polarities: of reason and superstition, of freedom and slavery, of humanitarianism and greed. Above all it tended to concentrate on the symbolic question of legal privilege. The anger this aroused was directed toward the nobility, an immensely diverse and very large body (there seem to have been between 200,000 and 250,000 noble males in France in 1789) about which generalization is impossible beyond the fact that all its members enjoyed a legal status which in some degree conferred privileges, special immunities, and prescriptive rights.

Although the logic of financial extremity pushed the government of France more and more toward conflict with the privileged classes, there was a natural unwillingness on the part of many royal advisors, themselves usually noblemen, and the king himself to proceed except by agreement. In 1788 a series of failures to obtain agreement on reform nerved the government to act, but it still sought to confine the inevitable clash to legal channels by reviving the nearest thing to a national representative body that France had ever possessed, the Estates General. This assembly of nobles, clergy, and commoners had not met since 1614, and the hope was that it would command enough moral authority to squeeze agreement to higher taxes from the fiscally privileged. This was unimpeachably constitutional, but it had the disadvantage of arousing great expectations without anyone's knowing quite what the Estates General could legally do. Some immediately assumed that it would be able to legislate for the nation even if historic legal privileges were at issue.

This very complicated political crisis was coming to a head at a time when France was also under other strains. The underlying problem was population pressure. Since the second quarter of the century population had been rising sufficiently fast to outstrip increases in food production. This meant a long-run inflation of prices, which bore most painfully upon the vast majority of Frenchmen who were landless or nearly landless peasants. Between the demands of the government (which for a long time staved off the financial crisis by raising the direct and indirect taxes which fell most heavily on the poor) and the demands of landlords seeking to protect themselves in inflationary times by holding down wages and raising rents and dues, the poor French peasant grew poorer and more miserable for nearly all the century.

In addition to this general impoverishment special troubles from time to time afflicted particular regions or classes, and these intensified at the end of the 1780s. Bad harvests, cattle disease, and a recession which seriously affected textile production (which peasants often engaged in to supplement their income) all hit the precarious economy in rapid succession and sometimes together. The sum effect of this was that the elections to the Estates General in 1789 took place in a very excited atmosphere. Millions of Frenchmen were desperately seeking some way out of their troubles; they were eager to find scapegoats and had quite unrealistic notions of what their good and trusted king could do for them.

The complex interplay of governmental impotence, social injustice, economic hardship, and reforming aspiration brought about the French Revolution. But before this complexity is lost to sight in the subsequent political battles and the simplifying slogans they generated, it is important to emphasize that almost no one either anticipated the overthrow of the monarchy or desired it. There was much social injustice in France, but no more than many other eighteenth-century states were able to live with. There was a welter of expectant and hopeful advocates of particular reforms, ranging from the abolition of censorship to the prohibition of immoral and irreligious literature, but no one doubted that such changes could easily be carried out by the king once he was informed of his peoples' wishes and needs. What did not exist was a party of revolution clearly confronting a party of reaction.

1789

Parties only came into existence when the Estates General met. This is one reason why the day it convened, May 5, 1789 (a week after George Washington's inauguration), is a date in world history; it opened an era in which to be for or against "the Revolution" became the central political question in most continental countries and even affected the very different politics of Great Britain and the United States.

What happened in France was bound to matter elsewhere. At the simplest level, the internal affairs of the greatest European state affected international life; the Estates General would either paralyze her (as many foreign diplomats hoped) or liberate her from her difficulties to play again a forceful role. Beyond this, France was also the cultural leader of Europe. What her writers and politicians said and did was immediately accessible to people elsewhere because of the universality of the French language and it was bound to be given respectful attention because people had the habit of looking to Paris for intellectual guidance.

In the summer of 1789 the Estates General turned itself into a national assembly claiming complete sovereignty. Breaking with the assumption that it represented the great medieval orders of society, it now claimed to represent without distinction all Frenchmen. It was able to make this revolutionary assertion because popular violence had frightened the government and members of the assembly who opposed such a change. Revolts in the countryside and riots in Paris had alarmed a government no longer sure that it could rely upon its armed forces. This led to many concessions by the crown to the radical leaders of the new National Assembly. At the same time disturbance created a fairly clear-cut division between those who were for the Revolution and those who were against it, soon identified as "left" and "right" because of the places where they sat in the Assembly.

This body saw the writing of a constitution as its main task, but in fact transformed the whole institutional structure of France. By the time it dispersed in the autumn of 1791, it had nationalized the lands of the church, abolished the "feudal system," ended censorship, created a system of centralized representative government, obliterated the old provincial and local divisions and replaced them with the departments under which Frenchmen still live, instituted equality before the law, and separated the executive from the legislative power. These are only the most outstanding accomplishments of one of the most remarkable bodies the world has ever seen. Broadly speaking, the National Assembly removed the legal and institutional checks on the modernization of France. Its failures tend to mask this huge achievement; they should not be allowed to do so. Popular sovereignty, administrative centralization, and individual legal equality were from this time on poles toward which French political life would always return.

The Revolution speeds up

Many Frenchmen did not like all the Assembly did; some liked none of it. By 1791 the king had clearly shown his own misgivings; the good will which had at first supported him was gone and he was suspected as an anti-revolutionary. Some nobles had already disliked enough changes to emigrate, and the fact that they were led by two of the king's brothers did not improve the outlook for royalty. But the revolutionary settlement of church affairs had created the most important division so far. Much in this settlement had appealed to many French people, churchmen among them, but the pope had rejected it. This forced French Catholics to choose whether the authority of the pope or that of the Constitution was supreme for them. This deeply embittered revolutionary politics.

In 1792 a great crisis occurred. France had gone to war with Austria and Prussia at the beginning of the year. The issue was complicated, but many Frenchmen believed that foreign powers wished to destroy the Revolution and put the clock back to 1788. The war went badly, shortages and suspicion mounted at home, and by the summer the king had been discredited. A Parisian insurrection in August overthrew the monarchy and led to the summoning of a new assembly to draw up a republican constitution. This body, called the Convention, was the center of French government until 1796. Despite civil and foreign war and economic and ideological crisis it achieved the survival of the Revolution.

Most of the Convention's members were not much more advanced in their political views than their predecessors. They believed in individualism, in the sanctity of property (they prescribed the death penalty for anyone proposing a law to introduce agrarian communism), and that the poor are always with us, though they allowed them a say in affairs by supporting direct universal suffrage. But they were willing to go rather further to meet emergencies than their predecessors had been (especially when frightened by the possibility of defeat), and they sat in a capital city manipulated by more extreme politicians, which pushed them into somewhat democratic measures and very democratic language. Consequently they frightened Europe much more than the politicians of the early Revolution had done.

The symbolic break with the past came when the Convention voted for the execution of the king in January 1793. The judicial murder of kings had hitherto been believed to be an English aberration; now the English were as shocked as the rest of Europe. They too went to war with France with easier consciences, though their reason for doing so was their fear of the strategical and commercial impact of French success against the Austrians in the Netherlands. But the war began to look more and more like an ideological struggle. To win it, the French government appeared increasingly bloodthirsty at home.

A new instrument for humane execution, the guillotine (a characteristic product of prerevolutionary enlightenment, combining as it did technical efficiency and benevolence in the swift, sure death it afforded its victims) became the symbol of the Terror. This was the name soon given to a period during which the Convention strove to preserve the Revolution by intimidation of its domestic enemies. It is somewhat misleading. Some of the Terror was only rhetoric, the hot air of politicians trying to keep their own spirits up and frighten their opponents. In practice it often reflected a jumble of patriotism, practical necessity, muddled idealism, self-interest, and petty venge-

One of the victims of the Terror was the duke of Orléans, head of the junior branch of the French royal family. His own violently revolutionary views (he voted for the death of the king) did not save him. *(Phot. Bibl. Nat. Paris)*

fulness as old scores were settled in the name of the republic. Many people died of course — something over 35,000 — and many emigrated to avoid danger. Yet the guillotine killed only a minority of the victims. Most of them died in the provinces, often in conditions of civil war and sometimes with arms in their hands. In eighteen months or so the Frenchmen whom contemporaries regarded as monsters killed about as many of their countrymen as would die before firing squads in ten days during the upheavals of the Paris Commune in 1871. To take a different but equally revealing measure, those who died in the Terror number roughly twice the British fatalities on the first day of the battle of the Somme in 1916.

The Terror of course deepened divisions within France, but even these should not be exaggerated. Noblemen probably lost most in the Revolution, but only a small minority of them found it necessary to emigrate. Indeed the total emigration from France during the Revolution was much less than from the United States after the War of Independence; in contrast to the Americans, a much larger proportion of Frenchmen could live with their Revolution, even with the Terror.

The Revolution secured

The Convention won victories and put down insurrection at home. By 1797 only Great Britain among France's enemies had not made peace, the

Terror had been left behind, and the republic was ruled by something much more like a parliamentary regime under a constitution whose adoption had closed the Convention era at the end of 1795. The Revolution was safer than ever. But it did not seem so. Abroad, royalists strove to get allies with whom they could return and intrigued with malcontents inside France. The restoration of the old order was a prospect which few Frenchmen would welcome though. On the other hand, there were those who argued that the logic of democracy should be pressed further, that there were still rich and poor and that this was as offensive as the old division by legal privilege had been, and that the Parisian radicals should have a greater say in affairs. This was almost as alarming as the threat of restoration to those who had benefited from the Revolution or simply wanted to avoid further bloodshed.

Thus pressed from right and left, the Directory (as the new government was called) was up to a point in a good position, though it made enemies who found the somewhat zig-zag middle road it tried to follow unacceptable. In the end the Directory was destroyed from within when a group of politicians intrigued with soldiers to bring about a coup d'état; a new regime was instituted in 1799 with the announcement: "Citizens, the Revolution is established upon its original principles. It is over."

Ten years after the meeting of the Estates General most observers could see that France had broken forever with the medieval past. In law this had happened very rapidly. Nearly all the great reforms were legislated at least in principle in 1789. The formal abolition of feudalism, legal privilege, and theocratic absolutism and the organization of society on individualistic and secular foundations were the heart of what were called the "principles of '89." They were expressed in the Declaration of the Rights of Man and the Citizen, which prefaced the Constitution of 1791. Legal equality and the legal protection of individual rights, the separation of church and state, and religious toleration were the results. Popular sovereignty acting through a unified national assembly, before whose legislation no privilege of locality or group could stand, was the basis of the jurisprudence which underlay them.

Other Europeans had watched aghast or at least amazed as the Revolution overturned and rebuilt institutions at every level of French life. Law, currency, bureaucracy, even measurement were transformed; it was a democratic version of enlightened despotism. Judicial torture came to an end, and so did titular nobility and the old corporate guilds of French workmen. But incipient trade unionism was scotched in the egg by legislation forbidding association by workers or employers for collective economic ends.

Such great changes were bound to be divisive; men's minds change more slowly than their laws. Peasants who eagerly welcomed the abolition of feudal dues were much less pleased by the disappearance of the beneficial communal usages which were also part of the feudal order. It was especially hard to assess the importance of such conservatism in religious affairs, yet it was very important. During the Terror the authorities publicly destroyed the holy vessel kept at Rheims from which the kings of France had been anointed since the Middle Ages, an altar to Reason replaced the Chris-

The Revolutionary as Visionary

Certainly the most principled and idealistic — if also possibly the most priggish and repellent — of the great revolutionary leaders of the Convention was Maximilien Robespierre, a lawyer from Arras, who envisaged the creation in France of a Republic of Virtue in which men would live in harmony on Rousseauist principles. Unfortunately the path to virtue led across the scaffold; Robespierre was ruthless in the destruction of those he saw as enemies of virtue and the Revolution. Their ranks came to include almost anyone who disagreed with him about the need for ruthlessness in defending his vision of the Revolution. This contributed very much to the consolidation of opposition which eventually sent Robespierre too to the guillotine. A few weeks before this happened, he delivered a speech on the principles which should animate the internal government of the Republic; it is one of the best examples of the theme of moral regeneration through government which has so often been the goal of puritan revolutionaries.

We seek an order of things in which all base and cruel passions are enchained, all the beneficent and generous passions awakened by the laws; where ambition becomes the desire to merit glory and to serve our country; where distinctions are born only of equality itself; where the citizen is subject to the magistrate, the magistrate to the people, and the people to justice; where our country assures

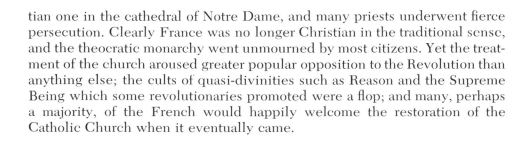

tian one in the cathedral of Notre Dame, and many priests underwent fierce persecution. Clearly France was no longer Christian in the traditional sense, and the theocratic monarchy went unmourned by most citizens. Yet the treatment of the church aroused greater popular opposition to the Revolution than anything else; the cults of quasi-divinities such as Reason and the Supreme Being which some revolutionaries promoted were a flop; and many, perhaps a majority, of the French would happily welcome the restoration of the Catholic Church when it eventually came.

the well-being of each individual, and where each individual proudly enjoys our country's prosperity and glory; where every soul grows greater through the continual flow of republican sentiments, and by the need of deserving the esteem of a great people; where the arts are the adornments of the liberty which ennobles them and commerce the source of public wealth rather than solely the monstrous opulence of a few families.

In our land we want to substitute morality for egotism, integrity for formal codes of honor, principles for customs, a sense of duty for one of mere propriety, the rule of reason for the tyranny of fashion, scorn of vice for scorn of the unlucky, self-respect for insolence, grandeur of soul for vanity, love of glory for the love of money, good people in place of good society. We wish to substitute merit for intrigue, genius for wit, truth for glamor, the charm of happiness for sensuous boredom, the greatness of man for the pettiness of the great, a people who are magnanimous, powerful, and happy, in place of a kindly, frivolous, and miserable people—which is to say all the virtues and all the miracles of the republic in place of all the vices and all the absurdities of the monarchy.

We want, in a word, to fulfill nature's desires, . . .

From Richard T. Bienvenu, ed., *The Ninth of Thermidor: The Fall of Robespierre* (London: Oxford University Press, 1968), pp. 33–34.

The export of revolution

The divisions aroused by revolutionary change in France could no more be confined within her borders than could the principles of '89. Though these commanded much admiration at first and not much explicit condemnation in other countries, this soon changed as French governments began to export their principles by propaganda and war.

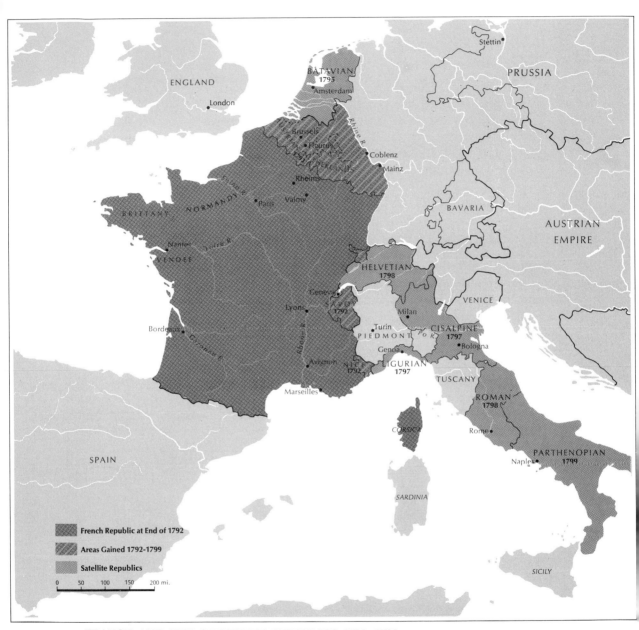

FRANCE AND HER SATELLITE REPUBLICS 1792–1799

Some Frenchmen advocated the acceptance by other nations of the recipes they employed for solving of their own problems. This was not entirely arrogant. All countries in preindustrial Europe had much in common; all could learn something from France. Conscious propaganda and missionary effort reinforced the forces making for French influence. In this way France gave her politics to Europe.

Modern European politics began in the revolutionary decade and the terms right and left have been with us ever since. Liberals and conservatives (though it was to be a decade or so before these terms were used) came into political existence when the French Revolution divided people between, on the one side, republicanism, a wide suffrage, individual rights, free speech, and free publication and, on the other, order, discipline, an emphasis on duties rather than rights, respect for hierarchy, and a wish to temper market forces by morality.

The unprecedented challenge of the Revolution crystallized the political thinking of conservatism. Many of the constituent elements were already lying about in such phenomena as irritation over the reforming measures of enlightened despotism, clerical resentment of "advanced" ideas, and the emotional reaction against the modern and consciously rational which is at the center of Romanticism. Such forces were especially prevalent in Germany, but the first and in many ways the greatest statement of the conservative, antirevolutionary argument appeared in England. This was the *Reflections on the Revolution in France*, published in 1790 by Edmund Burke, who had earlier defended the rights of American colonists. Burke shook off the legalistic defense of institutions and expressed his conservative stance in a theory which saw society as much more than a conscious contrivance freely entered into by men.

The polarization of Europe's politics also promoted the new idea of revolution as a radical, comprehensive upheaval, perhaps even tending to the subversion of such basic human institutions as the family and property. According to whether people felt heartened or dismayed by this prospect, they sympathized or deplored revolution wherever it occurred as a manifestation of a universal phenomenon. In the nineteenth century they even came to speak of "The Revolution" as a universally, eternally present force. This kind of thinking expressed an ideological form of politics which is by no means yet dead and whose mythology has produced much misery. First Europe and then the world she transformed have had to live with those who respond emotionally to this mythological way of seeing politics, just as earlier generations had to live with the follies of religious divisions. Its survival is testimony to the enduring impact of the French Revolution.

THE RETURN TO MONARCHY

An end to the Revolution is as artificial as a beginning. The year 1799 nonetheless was an important punctuation mark. The coup d'état which swept the Directory away brought to power a man who quickly inaugurated a dictatorship which was to last until 1814 and turn Europe upside down. This was Napoleon Bonaparte, formerly a general of the republic, now First Consul of the new regime, and soon to be the first Emperor of France.

Like most of the leading figures of his time, Bonaparte was still a young man. He had already shown exceptional brilliance and ruthlessness as a soldier. His victories combined with a shrewd political sense and a readiness to act in an insubordinate manner to win a glamorous reputation. In 1799 he had personal prestige and popularity; no one except the defeated politicians regretted it much when he shouldered them aside and assumed power with the title of First Consul. He immediately justified himself by defeating the Austrians (who had joined again in a war against France) and making a victorious peace as he had already done once before. This removed the threat to the Revolution; no one doubted Bonaparte's own commitment to its principles. His consolidation of them was to be his most enduring achievement.

Although Napoleon (as he was called officially after he proclaimed himself emperor in 1804) reinstituted monarchy in France, it was in no sense a restoration. The new symbolism was republican, Roman, Merovingian, Carolingian, but not Bourbon. Indeed he took care to so affront the exiled royal family that any reconciliation with it was inconceivable. He sought popular approval for the Empire and got it in a plebiscite. This was a monarchy Frenchmen had voted for; it rested on popular sovereignty and it assumed the consolidation of the Revolution which the Consulate had already begun.

All the great institutional reforms of the Revolution were confirmed or at least left intact; there was no disturbance of the land sales which had followed the confiscation of church property, no resurrection of the old corporations, and no questioning of the principle of equality before the law. Some of the Revolution's measures were even taken further, notably centralization of the administrative structure; Napoleon gave each department an administrative head, the prefect, who was in his powers something like one of the emergency emissaries of the Terror (many former revolutionaries served as prefects). In governmental practice, it is true, Revolution principles were often infringed. Like every government since 1793, Napoleon controlled the press by a punitive censorship, locked up people without trial, and in general gave short shrift to the Rights of Man so far as civil liberties were concerned. Though there were representative bodies under Consulate and

Napoleon's coup d'état of 1799. A nineteenth-century print from a popular pictorial life of the emperor. It purports to show the dissolution of the parliamentary body of the Directory, the end of constitutional government in France for fifteen years. *(Phot. Bibl. Nat. Paris)*

French Empire
Satellite Kingdoms
Nominal Allies of Napoleon
Hostile to Napoleon
Confederation of the Rhine Boundary

0   100   200   300   400 mi

NORWAY

SWEDEN

GREAT BRITAIN

DENMARK

BORODINO 1812 ✗

Moscow•

•Smolensk

Tilsit•

Vilna•

RUSSIA

Amsterdam•

PRUSSIA
Stettin•

•London

Brussels•
✗
WATERLOO 1815

HANOVER

•Berlin

Vistula R.

•Warsaw

GRAND DUCHY OF WARSAW

WESTPHALIA

SAXONY
LEIPZIG 1813 ✗

•Paris •Rheims

Rhine R.

BADEN

BAVARIA

Vienna•

AUSTRIAN EMPIRE

✗ AUSTERLITZ 1805

SWITZERLAND

Geneva•
Lyons•

Trieste•

Danube R.

•Milan

Turin•

ILLYRIAN PROVINCES

•Corunna

Genoa•

ITALY

PYRENEES

ELBA

CORSICA

Rome•

NAPLES

OTTOMAN EMPIRE

PORTUGAL

•Madrid

SPAIN

Naples•

SARDINIA

CAPE TRAFALGAR 1805 ✗

BALEARICS

SICILY

NAPOLEON'S EMPIRE 1810

Empire, not much attention was paid to them. But it seems that this was what Frenchmen wanted, as they had wanted Napoleon's most creative act of statesmanship, a concordat with the pope which reconciled French Catholics to the regime.

All in all, this amounted to a great consolidation of the Revolution and one guaranteed by firm government at home and by military and diplomatic strength abroad. Napoleon's huge military efforts for a time gave France the dominance of Europe; her armies fought their way to Moscow in the east and Portugal in the west and garrisoned the Atlantic and northern coast from Corunna to Stettin.

The cost of this dominance was too great; France could not sustain it against the coalition of all the other European powers which Napoleon's arrogant supremacy aroused. His invasion of Russia in 1812 was the beginning of the end. When the greatest army he ever led crumbled into ruins in the snows of the winter, he was doomed to defeat unless his enemies should fall out with one another. This time they did not. Napoleon himself blamed the British, who except for one short break had been at war with him—and before him with the Revolution—since 1792. There is some truth in this for many English and French saw the struggle as the most important of the Revolutionary era just because it transcended it as French wars with the land powers of continental Europe did not. They saw the conflict as the last

The battle of Borodino, September 7, 1812. This was the major defensive action fought by the Russians as they fell back to Moscow. It was one of the bloodiest of the Napoleonic wars. The French lost about 30,000, the Russians about one and a half times as many. (*Musées Nationaux, Paris*)

and most important round in a century of Anglo-French rivalry as well as a war of constitutional monarchy against military dictatorship. The sea power brought to bear at Trafalgar in 1805 confined Napoleon to Europe, Great Britain's money financed her allies when they were ready to come forward against France, and from 1809 on a British army in the Iberian peninsula kept alive there a front which drained French resources and gave hope to other Europeans.

By the beginning of 1814 Napoleon could only defend France, and although he did so at his most brilliant, sufficient resources were not available to fight off Russian, Prussian, and Austrian armies in the east and a British one in the southwest. At last his generals and ministers were able to set him aside and make peace without a popular outcry, even though this meant the return of the Bourbons. But it could not by then mean the return of anything else of significance from the years before 1789. The concordat with the pope remained, the departments remained, equality before the law remained, a representative system remained; the Revolution in fact had become part of the established order in France. Napoleon had provided the time, the social peace, and the institutions for that to happen. Nothing survived of the Revolution except what he had confirmed.

The Napoleonic stamp on Europe

Napoleon was a democratic despot whose authority came from the people, both in the formal sense of the plebiscites and in the more general one that he had needed (and won) their good will to keep his armies in the field. This makes him very different from a traditional monarch, even the most enlightened. He is nearer to twentieth-century rulers than to Louis XIV though he shares with that monarch the credit for carrying French international power to unprecedented heights. Both of them have because of this retained the admiration of their countrymen, who like to have a good opinion of themselves. But there is an important and twofold difference: Napoleon dominated Europe as Louis XIV never did and his hegemony represented, because the Revolution had taken place, more than mere national supremacy.

The Napoleonic hegemony should not be sentimentalized. Napoleon the great European was the creation of later legend. The most obvious impact of his dominance in Europe between 1800 and 1814 was the bloodshed and misery he brought to every corner of it, often as a consequence of megalomania and personal vanity. But there were also side effects, some intentional, some not, which added up to the further spread and effectiveness of the principles of the French Revolution.

The most apparent result was a new map. The patchwork quilt of the European state system of 1789 had already been revised before Napoleon took power, when French armies set up new satellite republics in Italy, Switzerland, and the United Provinces. But these had proved incapable of survival once France's support was withdrawn, and it was not until after the Consulate reestablished French hegemony that there appeared a new pattern of states which would have enduring consequences in some parts of

Europe. Most important were the big consolidations of political units in Germany and Italy which took place under the aegis of Napoleon.

Germany's political structure was revolutionized and its medieval foundations swept away. German lands on the left bank of the Rhine were annexed to France from 1801 to 1814, and this began the destruction of historic German polities. East of the river France set up the plan of a reorganization which secularized the ecclesiastical states, abolished nearly all the free cities, gave extra territory to Prussia, Hanover, Bavaria, and Baden to compensate them for losses elsewhere, and abolished the independent imperial nobility. The practical effect was to diminish the Catholic and Habsburg character of Germany while strengthening the influence of the larger princely states, especially Prussia. Though the Holy Roman Empire was reorganized to take account of these changes, it lasted in its new form only until 1806 when another Austrian defeat brought the end of the institutional structure which, however inadequately, had given Germany her only political bond since Ottonian times. A Confederation of the Rhine was now set up to be a third force balancing Prussia and Austria.

This was by no means the end of the Napoleonic changes, but a great work of destruction was complete by 1806. Richelieu and Louis XIV would have liked to contemplate a frontier on the Rhine and beyond it a Germany divided into interests likely to hold one another in check. But there was also another side to the changes: the old structure had been a hindrance to German consolidation, and no further rearrangement would ever contemplate its resurrection. The complicated structure of 1789 had contained over 300 political units with different principles of organization; these were reduced to thirty-eight states in 1815. When the victorious allies finally came to settle post-Napoleonic Europe, they too provided for a German Confederation (though different from Napoleon's not least in that Prussia and Austria were members of it insofar as their territories were German) and the Napoleonic consolidations remained.

Consolidation was less dramatic in Italy and its effects less revolutionary. There the Napoleonic system created in the north and south two large units which were nominally independent, and a large part of the peninsula (including the Papal States) was formally incorporated into France and organized in departments. None of this survived in 1815, but neither was there a complete restoration of the old pattern. The ancient republics of Genoa and Venice were left in the tombs to which the armies of the Directory had first consigned them and their lands were absorbed by bigger states—Genoa by Sardinia, Venice by Austria.

By 1812, at the height of his power, Napoleon had annexed to France and governed directly a huge block of territory with coasts running from the Pyrenees to Denmark in the north and almost without interruption to the boundary between Rome and Naples in the south. Beyond Italy a large piece of modern Yugoslavia was also under direct rule of the Empire. Satellite states and vassals with varying degrees of real independence, some of them ruled by members of Napoleon's own family, controlled the rest of Italy, Switzerland, and Germany west of the Elbe. Isolated in the east was another satellite, the grand duchy of Warsaw, created from former Russian territory.

Imperial government

Most of these countries experienced government by institutions and ideas which embodied the principles of the Revolution. These forces hardly reached beyond the Elbe except in the brief Polish experiment, and thus the French Revolution came to be another of those great shaping influences which again and again have helped to differentiate eastern and western Europe.

In the territories of the French Empire, Germans, Italians, Illyrians, Belgians, and Dutch were all governed by the Napoleonic legal codes. Napoleon's own initiative and insistence had brought these to fruition, but the work was essentially that of revolutionary legislators who had been unable in the troubled 1790s to promulgate the new, coherent body of law so many Frenchmen had hoped for in 1789. The codes spread French concepts of family, property, the individual, public power, and many other institutions generally through Europe. They replaced and supplemented a chaos of local and customary procedures and a jumble of Roman and ecclesiastical law. Similarly the departmental system of the Empire imposed a common administrative practice, and service in the armies of France, a common discipline and military regulation. French weights and measures and the decimal system replaced scores of local oddities. Such changes took time to produce their full effect, but it was a deep one and revolutionary.

French innovations also exercised an influence beyond the actual limits of imperial rule, providing models and inspiration to modernizers in other countries. The models were all the more easily assimilated because French officials and technicians worked in many of the satellites, and many different nationalities were represented in the Napoleonic service.

In a different way a more subtle revolution resulted from the Napoleonic impact; this lay in the reaction and resistance it provoked. To follow conquest by the introduction of revolutionary principles meant that the French were often laying up trouble for the future. Popular sovereignty lay at the heart of the Revolution and it is an idea closely linked to nationalism. French principles taught that peoples ought to govern themselves and that the proper unit in which they should do so was the nation: the revolutionaries had proclaimed their own republic "one and indivisible" for this reason. Manifestly, Italians and Germans did not live in national states, and they began to think that perhaps they should. But this was only one side of the coin.

French Europe was run for the benefit of France. Other Europeans saw their interests sacrificed to French economic policy, found they had to serve in the French armies, or received at the hands of Napoleon a French king. When even those who had welcomed the principles of the Revolution felt such things as grievances, it is hardly surprising that those who had never liked the new ideas began to think in terms of national resistance. European nationalism was given an immense fillip by the Napoleonic era even if governments distrusted it and felt uneasy about employing it. Germans came to think of themselves as more than Westphalians or Bavarians, and Italians as more than Romans or Milanese, because they discerned a common interest against France. In Spain and Russia the identification of patriotic resistance with resistance to the Revolution was virtually complete.

Napoleon's empire proved brief. So did the dynasty he had hoped to found. Yet the Napoleonic era was of great importance because of the processes which it allowed to mature. Napoleon unlocked huge reserves of energy in other countries just as the Revolution had unlocked them in France, and afterward they could never be entirely shut up again. He ensured the legacy of the Revolution its maximum effect.

The unconditional abdication of Napoleon in 1814 was not quite the end of the story. Just under a year later he returned to France from Elba, where he had lived in a pensioned exile, and the restored Bourbon regime crumbled at a touch. The allies nonetheless determined to overthrow him for he had frightened them too much in the past. His attempt to anticipate the gathering of overwhelming forces against him came to an end at Waterloo on June 18, 1815, when Anglo-Belgian and Prussian armies destroyed the threat of a revived French Empire. This time the victors sent Napoleon to St. Helena, thousands of miles away in the South Atlantic, where he died in 1821. The final alarm that he had given them strengthened their determination to make a peace that would avoid any danger of a repetition of the twenty years of almost continuous war which Europe had undergone in the wake of the Revolution. Thus Napoleon still shaped the map of Europe by the fear France had inspired under his leadership.

chapter 29

Europe Transformed

After 1815 the French Revolution was still to exercise influence outside France as a source of world politics. Although South Americans were stirred by the revolutionary example and principles, the immediate impact was first felt in Europe where between 1815 and 1870 the legacy of the Revolution was being worked out in other countries and old institutions were swept away as they had already been swept away in France.

The revolutionary tradition expressed itself mainly in three ways: in the belief that Europe was, for good or ill, in a state of potential revolution on the lines of 1789; in the operation of the doctrine of nationalism; and in what, for want of a better word, must be called liberalism, an attitude which strove at different times for many different goals but which always promoted the liberation of the individual from restraints laid upon him by traditional society or political authority. Liberalism was the political creed of market society, and its principles had powerful success. They did not achieve all that was hoped or feared, but they provide the best guiding lines in the rich and turbulent history of nineteenth-century Europe, the powerhouse which was changing the rest of the world.

THE VIENNA SETTLEMENT

The foundation deed of the nineteenth-century international order was the Treaty of Vienna of 1815. It closed the era of the French wars and its central purpose was to prevent their repetition. To contain France and avoid revolution the peacemakers prescribed both the principle of legitimacy, or respect for the right of established rulers, which was the ideological core of conservative Europe, and practical territorial arrangements to provide strong barriers to future French aggression. Thus Prussia was given large territories on the Rhine, a new northern state appeared under a Dutch king ruling both Belgium and the Netherlands, the kingdom of Sardinia got Genoa, and Austria not only recovered her former Italian possessions but kept Venice (taken by her briefly in 1797) as well and was allowed a virtually free hand in keeping the other Italian states in order. In most of these cases legitimacy bowed to expediency; those states despoiled in the revolutionary and Napoleonic eras did not obtain a restoration of the old order. But the powers still talked legitimacy with some success. For nearly forty years the Vienna settlement provided a framework within which disputes were settled without war.

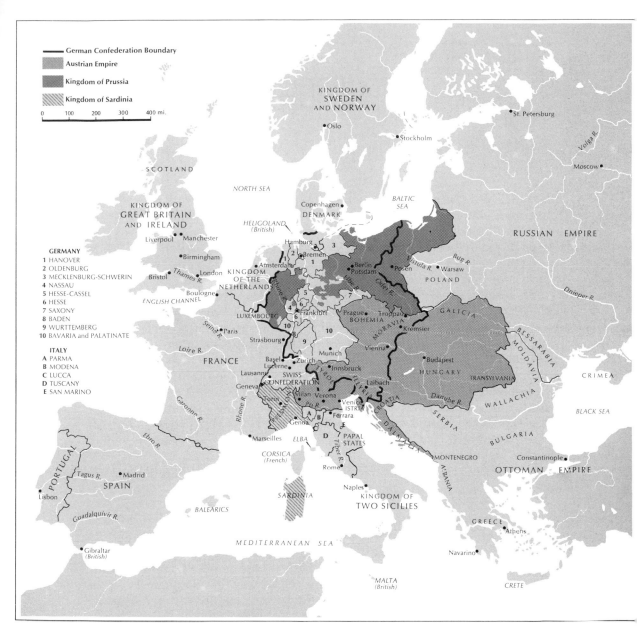

EUROPE AFTER THE TREATY OF VIENNA

This continent-wide peace owed much to the salutary fear of revolution. In all the major states the restoration era (as the years after 1815 have been termed) was a great period for policemen and plotters alike. But no subversive threat arose that could not be handled easily enough. Austrian troops dealt with attempted coups in Piedmont and Naples, French soldiers restored the power of a reactionary Spanish king hampered by a liberal constitution, and the Russian empire survived a military conspiracy and a Polish revolt. The Austrian predominance in Germany was not threatened at all, and it is difficult in retrospect to discern any very real danger to any part of the Habsburg monarchy before 1848. Russian and Austrian power—the first in reserve, the second the predominant force in central Europe and Italy from 1815 to 1848—were the two rocks on which the Vienna system rested.

Liberalism and nationalism were regarded as inseparable revolutionary forces; this was to prove terribly short-sighted later but was then broadly true. Those who sought revolution before 1848 did so in the name of the political principles of the French Revolution, which linked representative government, popular sovereignty, and freedom of the individual and the press to nationality. Many revolutionaries confused liberalism and nationalism too; the most famous and admired of those who did so was Giuseppe Mazzini. By advocating an Italian unity most of his countrymen did not want and conspiring unsuccessfully in support of it, he became an inspiration and model for nationalists and democrats in every continent for over a century. But the age of the ideas he represented did not come in the restoration era.

France after 1815

To the west of the Rhine, where the writ of the Holy Alliance (as the three conservative powers, Russia, Austria, and Prussia, were called) did not run, the story was different; there legitimism was only briefly successful. Even the restoration of the Bourbon dynasty in 1814 had been a compromise with the principle of legitimacy. Louis XVIII was supposed to have reigned like any other king of France since his nephew and predecessor, Louis XVII, died in prison in Paris in 1795. But in fact, as everyone knew but legitimists tried to conceal, he came back in the baggage trains of the allied armies which had defeated Napoleon and had been able to do so only on terms acceptable to the French political and military elites of the Napoleonic period and to the mass of Frenchmen. The restored monarchy was regulated by a charter which made it a constitutional state, albeit with a limited suffrage.

Nevertheless, there was uncertainty for years about the future; battle between right and left began with arguments about the charter itself—was it a contract between king and people or a simple royal gift which might therefore be withdrawn as easily as it had been granted?—and went on over a whole range of issues which raised questions of principle (or were thought to) about ground won for liberty and the possessing classes in the Revolution. The uncertainty persisted until 1830 but was then resolved at the hands of Charles X, the last king of the direct Bourbon line. He foolishly attempted to break out of the constitutional limitations which bound him by staging what was virtually a coup d'état. Paris rose against him. Liberal politicians hastily put themselves at the head of the revolt, and, to the chagrin of republicans, ensured that a new king replaced Charles on the throne.

Louis Philippe was head of the junior branch of the Bourbons, the Orleans family, but to many conservative eyes he was the Revolution incarnate. His father had voted for the execution of Louis XVI (but himself went to the scaffold soon after). Louis Philippe had fought as an officer in the republican armies and had even been a member of the infamous Jacobin club, widely believed to have been the conspiracy at the heart of the Revolution and certainly a hotbed which produced some of its most prominent leaders. To liberals he was attractive for much the same reasons; he reconciled the Revolution with the stability provided by monarchy. He also understood business and liked wealthy men. To people on the left wing he was a disappointment; they had wanted a republic.

The regime over which Louis Philippe presided for eighteen years did indeed prove remarkably conservative, but it was also unimpeachably constitutional. It fostered the interests and upheld the ideals of the well-to-do. It suppressed urban disorder (of which poverty produced plenty in the 1830s) and preserved the essential freedoms which enabled its citizens to take the advice of a prominent politician and enrich themselves; the man who said *enrichissez vous* was telling Frenchmen that the way to gain the vote was to obtain the wealth which was the qualification for it. This is an indicator of the restrictions on the regime's liberalism; the suffrage was so narrow that in 1830 only about a third as many Frenchmen as Englishmen could vote for their parliament although the population of France was about twice that of England. Nevertheless, the theory of the July Monarchy (as the new regime was termed) was that the state rested once more on popular sovereignty, which caused it to be regarded with suspicion by the orchestrator of European conservatism, the Austrian chancellor, Count Metternich.

In the 1830s there was a very evident division in Europe between the constitutional states—England, France, Spain, and Portugal—and the legitimist, dynastic states of the east, with their Italian and German satellites. The conservative powers were alarmed when the Belgians rebelled against their Dutch king in 1830 but were not able to support him because the British and French favored the Belgians and Russia was embarrassed by a Polish rebellion. It still took nine years to secure the establishment of an independent Belgium, and this was the only important change before 1849 in the state system created by the Vienna settlement, though a revolt by the Greeks against their Turkish rulers in 1821 had led to the emergence of a new kingdom of Greece in 1830. This announced not only that the nineteenth-century Eastern Question had opened but that it was going to be additionally complicated by the forces of nationalism.

1848: THE CONTAGION OF REVOLUTION

In 1848 a burst of rebellion made it appear for a time that the whole 1815 settlement was at last in jeopardy. Social strains coincided with a wide range of different political exasperations in many countries which came to a head at the same time. Once a revolution detonated this in one place, a chain reaction followed. Each revolt moreover weakened the ability of the general security system to deal with the next. By summer the government in every major capital except London and St. Petersburg appeared to be in retreat. Then the revolutionary movements began to reveal their own weaknesses and divisions, and by the end of 1849 the formal structure of Europe was again much what it had been in 1847, though there had been important changes within some countries.

The 1840s were years of economic hardship, food shortages, and distress. In Ireland there was a great famine in 1846, followed the next year by dearth in central Europe and France, where a trade recession particularly affected the cities. Unemployment was widespread and this gave new edge to urban radical movements everywhere. When Louis Philippe realized in February 1848 that the middle classes, on whom he had hitherto relied, would not support his resistance to a broader suffrage, he abdicated. This was the February Revolution. A republic then emerged in France and with its installation every revolutionary in Europe took heart. The dreams of thirty years' conspiracies and the plans of countless exiles now seemed realizable. France was great again and the armies of the Revolution might march once more to uphold its principles in other countries.

Hard times in old Ireland. A contemporary print depicting the ransacking of a potato store by hungry peasants in the 1840s. The famine which struck Ireland in this decade, together with its accompanying diseases, brought about a terrible loss of life. It also caused huge emigration. Thus, unhappily, a situation Malthus had predicted was remedied by the harsh operation of the "natural checks" on population he had been fearing. (*Radio Times Hulton Picture Library*)

But this was far from what happened. In the end the Second Republic made diplomatic noises of sympathy for Poland, the classic focus of the nationalist cause, but the only military operations it undertook were in defense of the pope, an unimpeachably conservative cause. The reasons for this were complicated, not the least being the very divergent and confusing paths followed by revolutionaries in 1848.

In most of Italy and central Europe there were revolutions against governments which were regarded as oppressive because illiberal; the great symbolic demand was for constitutions to guarantee essential freedoms. When such a revolution occurred in Vienna itself, Metternich, the embodiment of the conservative order, was driven into exile. Successful revolution at Vienna meant the paralysis of Habsburg monarchy and therefore the dislocation of the whole of central Europe. The German states could now have their revolutions without fear of Austrian intervention. So could other nationalities within the Austrian dominions; Italians turned on the Austrian armies in Lombardy and Venezia, Hungarians revolted at Budapest, and Czechs at Prague. This complicated matters. Many of these revolutionaries were as much for national independence as for constitutionalism, though constitutionalism seemed for a time the way to independence because it attacked the principles of dynastic autocracy.

If constitutional governments were installed in all the capitals of central Europe and Italy, then, it followed, there would actually come into existence nations hitherto without a state structure of their own. If Slavs achieved their own national liberation, it had to follow that states previously thought of as German would be shorn of huge tracts of territory, notably in Poland and Bohemia. It took some time for this to sink in, though the German liberals suddenly fell over this problem in 1848 and quickly drew their conclusions; they chose nationalism.

The German revolutions of 1848 failed essentially because German liberals decided that they could not do without a strong Prussia; they would accept her terms for the future of Germany because their nationalism required the preservation of German lands in the east. Before the end of 1848 there were already other signs that the tide had turned. The Austrian army mastered the Italians. A Parisian rising to take the Revolution further in the direction of democracy was crushed with great bloodshed in June, and it was evident that the new republic was going to be a conservative one. In 1849 the end came. The Austrians defeated the Sardinian army, which was the only shield of the Italian revolutions, and monarchs all over the peninsula began to withdraw the constitutional concessions they had made while Austrian power was in abeyance. German rulers did the same, led by Prussia. For a time pressure on the Habsburgs was kept up by the Croats and Hungarians, but then the Russian army came to its ally's help.

Later, liberals saw in 1848 a "springtime of the nations." If it was one, the shoots had not lived long before they withered. Nationalism had certainly been very important in 1848, but it had also demonstrated that it was neither strong enough to sustain governments nor necessarily a progressive force. Its failure in 1848 shows that the charge that the statesmen of 1815 neglected to give it due attention is false; no new nation emerged from 1848 for none was ready to do so. The basic reason was that nationalism was an abstraction; only relatively few and well-educated or at least half-educated people cared much about it. Where national differences also embodied social issues there was certainly effective action by national groups, but it did not lead to the setting up of new nations; the Ruthene peasants of Galicia had happily murdered their Polish landlords in 1847 when the Habsburg administration allowed them to do so, thus satisfying themselves and in consequence remaining loyal to the dynasty in 1848.

There were some genuinely popular revolutions in 1848, but they had many and diverse ends. It Italy they were usually revolts of townsmen rather than peasants; the Lombard peasants cheered the Austrian army when it returned because they saw no good for themselves in a revolution led by the aristocrats who were their landlords. In parts of Germany, over much of which the traditional structures of landed rural society remained intact, the peasants went as their French counterparts had done in 1789 to burn their landlords' houses, not merely out of personal animus but in order to destroy the hated and feared records of rents, dues, and labor services. Such violence frightened urban liberals as much as the outbreak of despair and unemployment in Paris, known as the June Days, frightened the French middle classes. But in France the peasant had been (speaking broadly) a conservative since 1789, and thus it was soldiers from the French provinces who crushed the Parisian poor on whom extremists relied.

The revolutions probably achieved most in relation to social issues in the countryside of eastern and central Europe. There liberal principles and the fear of popular revolt went hand in hand to impose change on the rural nobility. Almost everywhere where they survived outside Russia obligatory peasant labor and bondage to the soil were abolished as a result of 1848. The rural social revolution launched in France in 1789 had come to central and eastern Europe. The way was now open for the reconstruction of agricultural life in Germany and the Danube valley on individualist and market lines. Though many of its practices and habits of mind were still to linger, feudal society had in effect now come to an end all over Europe.

NEW NATIONS

Nationalism, in spite of 1848's failures, did not have to wait long. A dispute over Russian influence in the Near East, where Turkish power was visibly declining, led in 1853 to the first war between great powers since the Vienna settlement. The Crimean War, in which the French and British fought as allies of the Turks against the Russians, was in many ways a notable struggle. Fighting took place in the Baltic, in southern Russia, and in the Crimea, the last theater attracting most attention. There the allies succeeded in their aim of capturing Sevastopol, the naval base which was the key to Russian power in the Black Sea.

Some of the results were surprising. All the armies fought gallantly, but the British force had to cope with its own commanders as well as the enemy

The beginnings of modern warfare. This print shows the railway built
for the British army in the Crimea in 1854, the first ever constructed
for a military purpose. (*The Mansell Collection*)

and was especially distinguished by the inadequacy of its administrative arrangements; the scandal provoked a wave of radical reform at home. Another
indirect result was the founding of a new profession for women, that of nursing, for the collapse of British medical services had been particularly striking. The work of Florence Nightingale with the army and still more her efforts to stir up politicians and public opinion were of great importance in
bringing about the first major extension of the occupational opportunities
available to European women since the creation of female religious communities in the Dark Ages. The war is also noteworthy in another way: it
was the first between major powers in which steamships and a railway were
employed.

Yet these things, however portentous, mattered less in the short run
than the war's effect on international relations. At its close in 1856 France
was again a victorious power. Russia was defeated and her power to intimidate Turkey bridled. A step was taken with the approval of Russia and
France toward the establishment of another new nation, Rumania. Once
more nationality triumphed in former Turkish lands. But the crucial diplomatic significance of the war was that it ended the Holy Alliance. The old
eighteenth-century rivalry between Austria and Russia over what would
happen to the Turkish inheritance in the Balkans had broken out again when
Austria warned Russia not to occupy the Danube principalities (the future
Rumania) during the war and then occupied them herself. This was five
years after Russia had intervened to restore Habsburg power by crushing the

Hungarian revolution, and it was the end of friendship between the two powers. The next time Austria faced a revolutionary threat, she would have to do so without the policeman of conservative Europe at her side.

Few people can have anticipated in 1856 how quickly that time would come. Within ten years Austria had lost in two short, sharp wars her hegemony in both Italy and Germany, and those countries were united as national states. Thus nationalism was indeed to triumph and at the cost of the Habsburgs (as had been prophesied by enthusiasts in 1848), but in a totally unexpected way. Not internal revolution but the ambitions of two traditionally expansive monarchical states, Sardinia and Prussia, had led each to set about improving its position at the expense of Austria. Austria's isolation was complete.

Ironically, revolution in France had also told against Austrian interests, for from it had emerged a regime certainly conservative but presided over by a Bonaparte. In 1852 France was ruled once more by an emperor, Napoleon III, the nephew of the first Napoleon. He had been elected president of the Second Republic, whose constitution he had then set aside by coup d'état. His very name was a program of international reconstruction — or revolution. He stood for the destruction of the anti-French settlement of 1815 and therefore of the Austrian predominance which propped it up in Italy and Germany. He talked the language of nationalism with less inhibition than most rulers and seems to have believed in it. With arms and diplomacy he forwarded the work of two great diplomatic technicians: Camillo Cavour, prime minister of Sardinia, and Otto von Bismarck, prime minister of Prussia.

In 1859 Sardinia and France fought Austria; after a brief war the Austrians were left with only Venezia in Italy. More important, Cavour now had a field free from Austrian intervention when he incorporated other Italian states into Sardinia. As part of the price of her support France received Sardinian Savoy on the northern slopes of the Alps. Cavour died in 1861, and debate still continues over the extent of his real aims, but by 1871 his successors had produced a united Italy under the house of Savoy, the rulers of Sardinia.

In that same year Germany was united. Bismarck had begun by rallying German liberal sentiment in a nasty little war against Denmark in 1864. Two years later Prussia defeated Austria in a lightning campaign in Bohemia, thus at last ending the Hohenzollern-Habsburg duel for supremacy in Germany begun in 1740 by Frederick II. The war itself was rather a registration of an accomplished fact than its achievement, for Austria was already much weakened in German affairs. The German liberals of 1848 had not offered a German crown to the Austrian emperor but to the king of Prussia. Nevertheless, some states had still looked to Habsburg leadership and patronage, and they were now left alone to meet Prussian bullying.

After the war the Habsburg empire became truly Danubian, its foreign policy preoccupied with southeast Europe and the Balkans. It had retired from the Netherlands in 1815 and now left Germany to her own devices. Moreover the Prussians had exacted Venezia for the Italians in 1866. Immediately after the peace the Hungarians seized the opportunity to inflict a fur-

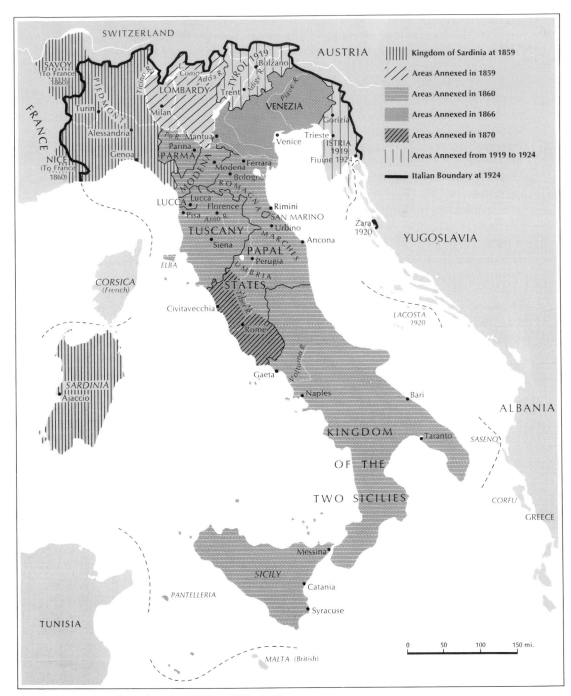

THE UNIFICATION OF ITALY 1859–1920
The essential work of uniting Italy was completed by 1870 and was accomplished by annexation of the formerly independent or dependent states to the
Kingdom of Sardinia. Its king became King of Italy but surrendered Savoy
and Nice, part of his inheritance, to France in return for military and
diplomatic support.

ther defeat on the humiliated monarchy by obtaining virtual autonomy for the lands of the Hungarian crown. The empire thus became in 1867 the Dual or Austro-Hungarian Monarchy, divided rather untidily into two halves linked by little more than the dynasty itself.

The completion of German unification required one further step. It had gradually dawned in France that the assertion of Prussian power beyond the Rhine was not in the French interest; instead of a disputed Germany, she now faced one dominated by an important military power. Bismarck used this new awareness, together with Napoleon III's weaknesses at home and his regime's international isolation, to provoke France into a declaration of war in 1870. Prussia's victory in this war set the keystone of the new edifice of German nationality; she had taken the lead in "defending" Germany against France—and there were still Germans alive who could remember what French armies had done in Germany under an earlier Napoleon. The Prussian army destroyed the Second Empire in France (it was to be the last monarchical regime in that country) and created a new one in Germany, the Second Reich as it was called, to distinguish it from the medieval empire. In practice it was Prussian domination cloaked in federal forms, but it was a German national state, which satisfied many German liberals. In the palace of Louis XIV at Versailles, the king of Prussia accepted the crown of a united Germany from his fellow princes in 1871, which his predecessor had refused to take from the liberals in 1848.

There had thus been in fifty years a revolution in international affairs. Germany had replaced France as the dominant land power in Europe as France had replaced Spain in the seventeenth century. This fact would dom-

Milan in 1859; the troops of the king of Sardinia enter the city after its abandonment by the Austrians. (*Museo del Risorgimento, Milan; Scala New York/Florence*)

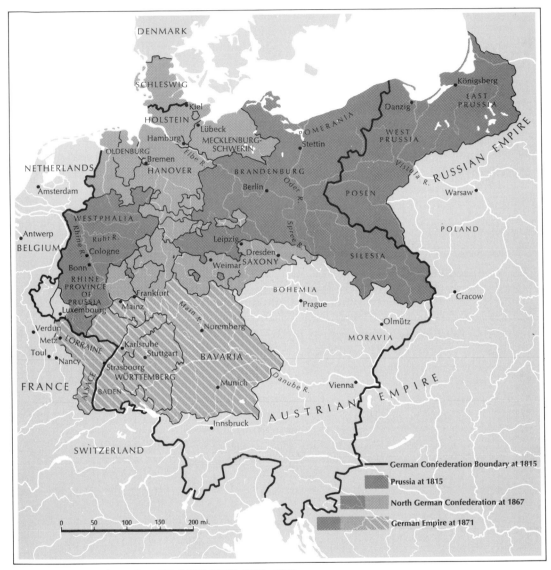

THE UNIFICATION OF GERMANY 1815–1871
A series of successful wars led to the construction in 1871 of a Germany dominated
by Prussia.

inate Europe's international relations until they ceased to be determined by
forces originating within her.

THE EBBING OF REVOLUTION

The conscious revolutionaries of the nineteenth century did nothing to
alter Europe which could be compared with the work of Cavour, Bismarck,
and (half in spite of himself) Napoleon III. In fact revolution achieved little

except at the fringes of Europe and had even begun to show signs of flagging by 1850. Down to 1848 there had been plenty of revolutions, to say nothing of plots, conspiracies, and *pronunciamentos* which did not justify the name. After 1848 there were very few. Another Polish revolution against the tsar took place in 1863, but that was the only outbreak of note in a large state until 1871.

An ebbing of revolutionary effort in the 1850s and 1860s is understandable. Revolutions had achieved so little except in France and had even there brought disappointments. Some of their goals were being realized in other ways. Though greatly to the chagrin of Mazzini, Cavour and his successors had after all created a united Italy, and Bismarck had done what many of the German liberals of 1848 had hoped to do by creating a Germany which was indisputably a great power. Other ends were being achieved by economic progress. For all the horrors of poverty which abounded in its slums, nineteenth-century Europe was getting richer and was giving more and more of her peoples a larger share of her wealth. Even quite short-term factors helped here. The great gold discoveries in California provided a flow of bullion to stimulate the world economy in the 1850s and 1860s; confidence grew and unemployment fell in these decades and this was good for social peace.

A more fundamental reason why revolutions were fewer was that they had also become more difficult to conduct. Governments grappled more easily with them, largely for technical reasons. The nineteenth century created modern police forces. Better communications by rail and telegraph gave new power to central authorities in dealing with distant revolt. Above all, armies had a growing technical superiority over rebellion. As early as 1795 the French government had shown that as long as it had control of the regular armed forces and was prepared to use them it could master Paris. During the long peace from 1815 to 1848 many European armies in fact became much more instruments of security, directed potentially against their own populations, than means of international competition. It was the defection of important sections of the military which permitted successful revolutions in Paris in 1830 and 1848. When the army remained loyal to the government, battles like the June Days of 1848 in Paris—which one observer called the greatest slave war in history—could only end, as that uprising did, with the defeat of the rebels. From that year no popular revolution was ever to succeed in a major European country against a determined government whose control of its armed forces was unshaken by defeat in war or by subversion.

This was vividly and bloodily demonstrated in 1871 when the French government once again crushed a rebellious Paris. This time the cost in lives, in a little more than a week, was as savage as that exacted by the Terror of 1793–1794. A popular regime which attracted a wide range of radicals and reformers had set itself up in the capital and proclaimed itself the Commune of Paris, a name evocative of traditions of municipal independence going back to the Middle Ages and, more important, to the Revolution in which the commune (or city council) of Paris had often been the focus of revolutionary fervor. The Commune of 1871 was able to take power because the government was too enfeebled in the aftermath of defeat by the Germans to disarm the capital of the weapons with which it had successfully withstood a siege and because that defeat had inflamed many Parisians against a government they believed to have let them down. During its brief life the Commune did very little, but it produced a lot of left-wing rhetoric and was soon seen as the embodiment of social revolution. This gave additional bitterness to the efforts to suppress it. Once the government had reassembled its army from returning prisoners of war, the Commune was doomed. Paris became the scene of brief but bloody street fighting as regularly constituted armed forces overcame workmen and shopkeepers manning hastily improvised barricades.

The ghastly failure of the Paris Commune should have killed the revolutionary myth, both in its power to terrify and its power to inspire. Yet it did not. If anything, it strengthened it. Conservatives found the Commune an excellent example of the dangers lurking always ready to burst out from under the surface of society. Revolutionaries had a new set of heroes and

The Janus-like face of the new power of the state. These British policemen of 1851 were bitterly resented in many working-class districts but soon established themselves as admirable figures in the eyes of the middle class. They turned out to be one of the most important instruments by which the power of the state over its citizens was increased in the nineteenth century.
(*The Mansell Collection*)

martyrs to add to an apostolic succession begun in 1789. But the Commune also revivified revolutionary mythology because of a new factor whose importance had already struck both left and right.

SOCIALISM

The words socialism and socialist have meant a great many different things almost from the start. They were first widely used in France around about 1830, when they were applied to the theories and the men who opposed a society run on market principles and an economy operated on laissez-faire lines, of which the main beneficiaries were supposed to be the wealthy. Economic and social egalitarianism is fundamental to the socialist idea. Most socialists have been able to agree up to that point. They have usually believed that in a better society no one class could oppress another through advantages derived from the ownership of wealth. They welcomed the thought that one day no wealth would give a man power over the lives of others. All socialists could agree too that there was nothing sacred about property, whose rights buttressed injustice. Many sought its abolition. "Property is theft" was one very successful slogan.

Such ideas were understandably frightening but not entirely novel. Egalitarian ideas have fascinated people throughout history, and the Christian rulers of Europe had managed without difficulty to reconcile social arrangements resting on sharp divisions of wealth with the practice of a religion one of whose greatest hymns praised God for filling the hungry with good things and sending the rich empty away. What happened in the early nineteenth century was that egalitarian ideas seemed to become at once more dangerous and more popular—hence the need for new terms to label them.

There were several reasons for this change. One was that the success of liberal political reform soon made some people feel that legal equality was not enough if it was deprived of content by dependence on other men's economic power or denatured by poverty and attendant ignorance. Another was the view already voiced by a few thinkers in the eighteenth century that big discrepancies of wealth were irrationalities in a world which should be regulated to produce the greatest good for the greatest number. In the upheavals of the French Revolution some writers and agitators had pressed forward demands in which later generations would see socialist ideas, but egalitarian theories only became socialism in a modern sense when they began to grapple with the nineteenth-century problems of economic and social change, above all with those presented by industrialization. This required great perspicacity because these changes were very slow in making their impact outside Great Britain and Belgium. Yet perhaps because the contrast they presented with traditional society was so stark, even the small beginnings of concentration in capitalist finance and manufacturing were remarked.

One of the first men to grasp their implications for social organization was a French nobleman, Claude Saint-Simon. His contribution to socialist thought was to take into consideration in the ordering of society the new facts of technology and science. Saint-Simon recognized that they not only made planned organization of the economy imperative but also implied great changes in society. They demanded, he thought, the replacement of the traditional ruling classes, aristocratic and rural in their outlook, by elites representing new economic and intellectual powers.

After his death in 1825 Saint-Simon's ideas influenced many thinkers (most of them French) who in the 1830s advocated fundamental changes in society to produce greater equality. Their theories made enough impact and were enough talked about to terrify the French possessing classes in 1848, who thought they saw in the June Days a "socialist" revolution. Socialists usually willingly identified themselves with the tradition of the French Revolution and hoped its next stage would be the realization of their ideals. It was then, in 1848, that there appeared a pamphlet which is perhaps the finest of the century and certainly the most important document in the history of socialism.

Karl Marx

The *Communist Manifesto* was largely the work of a young German Jew, Karl Marx, and it marks the point at which the "prehistory" of socialism can be separated from its history. Marx proclaimed a complete break with what he called the "utopian socialism" of his predecessors. He maintained that nothing could be hoped for from arguments to persuade people that change was morally desirable. Everything depended on the actual creation of a new working class by industrial society, the rootless wage earners of the new industrial cities whom he termed the proletariat. This class was bound, according to him, to act in a revolutionary way. History was working upon its members so as to generate revolutionary mentality and capacity. It would present them with conditions to which revolution was the only logical outcome, and that revolution was, because of those conditions, guaranteed success.

Utopian socialists attacked industrial capitalism because they thought it was unjust; Marx claimed that this was beside the point. What mattered was not that capitalism was morally wrong but that it was already out of date and therefore historically doomed. In his view a particular society had a particular system of property rights and class relationships, and these accordingly shaped its particular political arrangements. Politics and political structures were bound to express economic forces. They would change as the organization of society changed under the influence of economic developments, and therefore sooner or later (and Marx seems to have thought sooner) the revolution would sweep away capitalist society and its forms as capitalist society had already swept away feudal.

There was much more to Marx than this (and scholars still argue about what much of it means) but the confidence expressed in the *Communist Manifesto* that history was already on their side was a great revolutionary tonic. Socialists learned with gratitude that the cause to which they were impelled anyway by motives ranging from a sense of injustice to the promptings of envy was predestined to triumph. This was essentially a religious faith. For all the importance of the doctrine as an analytical instrument and the complex development of Marx's own thinking, Marxism came to be a popular mythology with two main tenets: one was a view of history which said that people were bound by economic necessity because their institutions were determined by the evolving methods of production; the other was a faith that the working class were the Chosen People whose pilgrimage through a wicked world would end in the triumphal establishment of a just society where necessity's iron law would cease to operate. Social revolutionaries could thus feel confident of scientifically irrefutable arguments for irresistible progress toward the socialist millennium while clinging to a revolutionary creed such arguments seemed to make unnecessary. Marx himself seems to have applied his teaching more cautiously, only to the broad, sweeping changes in history which individuals are powerless to resist and not to its detailed unfolding. Perhaps it is not surprising that, like many masterminds, he did not recognize all his children: he later came to protest that he was not a Marxist.

This new religion was an inspiration to working-class organization. Trade unions and cooperatives already existed and their members grew in number as the century went on. The first International Workingmen's Association appeared in London in 1864. Though it included many who did not subscribe to Marx's views, he was its secretary and his influence was paramount. Its name soon had the power to frighten conservatives, some of whom blamed the Paris Commune on it, without justification. Nevertheless, their instincts were right, for in the years after 1848 socialism had captured the revolutionary tradition from the liberals. The future ideology of an industrial working class as yet barely in existence (let alone predominant in most European countries) was tacked onto the tradition which held that, broadly speaking, revolution could not be wrong. Marx even snapped up the Commune for the socialist cause in a powerful tract though Paris was not one of the great manufacturing centers in which he predicted that proletarian revolution would mature. The Commune was actually the last and greatest example of traditional Parisian radicalism and its greatest failure. Socialism suffered from the repressive measures it provoked, yet Marx made it an important episode in socialist mythology.

THE CONSERVATIVE GIANT: RUSSIA

Only Russia seemed (except in her Polish lands) long immune to the French Revolution. Although Alexander I, Napoleon's opponent, for a time indulged himself with liberal ideas and even thought of a constitution, nothing came of this. The liberalization of Russian institutions did not begin until the 1860s, and then its source was not revolutionary contagion.

True, liberalism did not quite leave Russia untouched in the first half of the century. There was a small group of critics of the regime who found models in the West. Also even under Alexander the effect of experiences in the West upon some Russian officers who went there with the armies which pursued Napoleon to Paris prompted them to make unfavorable comparisons with their homeland. This was the beginning of Russian political opposition, and in an autocracy it was bound to be conspiratorial. A number of these officers took part in the organization of secret societies which attempted a coup amid the uncertainty caused by Alexander's death in December 1825. Their movement collapsed but only after giving a big fright to the new tsar, Nicholas I, who decisively affected Russia's historical destiny at a crucial moment by ruthlessly crushing political liberalism.

The immobility which Nicholas imposed upon Russia was as formative an influence (though a negative one) as the reforms of Peter the Great had been. A dedicated believer in autocracy, he confirmed the Russian tradition of authoritarian bureaucracy, the management of cultural life, and the rule of the secret police just when the other great powers were (unwillingly in some cases) beginning to move in precisely the opposite direction. There was of course much to build on already in the historical legacies which differentiated Russian autocracy from western European monarchy. But the forces of change which were at least being felt in other dynastic states in the first half of the nineteenth century were simply not allowed to operate in Russia. In the long run this was bound to exclude also certain possibilities of modernization. In the short run, however, it was highly successful. Russia passed through the whole century without a revolution, and those which erupted in Russian Poland in 1830 and 1863 were ruthlessly suppressed, the more easily because Poles and Russians cherished traditions of mutual dislike.

The other side of the coin was almost continuous rural disorder and a mounting and ever more violent tradition of conspiracy. This perhaps incapacitated Russian society for an easy transition to normal politics, which depend upon a measure of shared assumptions. Instead, Russian problems were seen in terms of irreconcilable opposites, with little scope for the emergence of moderate men. Unfriendly critics variously described Nicholas' reign as an ice age, a plague zone, and a prison, but not for the last time in Russian history the preservation of a harsh and unyielding despotism at home was not incompatible with a strong international role.

This role was based on Russia's huge military superiority at a time when armies contended with muzzle-loaders and no important technological differences distinguished one from another. In these conditions numbers were decisive, and the antirevolutionary security system rested on Russian military strength, as the crushing of the Hungarian rebellion in 1849 showed. There were also successes outside Europe. Pressure on the central Asian khanates and China was consistently kept up. The left bank of the Amur River became Russian, and Nicholas exacted great concessions from Persia. During the early nineteenth century Russia obtained Georgia and part of Armenia, and in 1860 Vladivostok was founded. For a time there was even a determined effort to pursue Russian expansion in North America; there were forts in Alaska and settlements in northern California until the 1840s.

The major effort of Russian foreign policy, nevertheless, was directed to the southwest, toward Turkish Europe. This had been true since Catherine's day. War in 1806–1812 and in 1828 (when the Greek revolution obliged

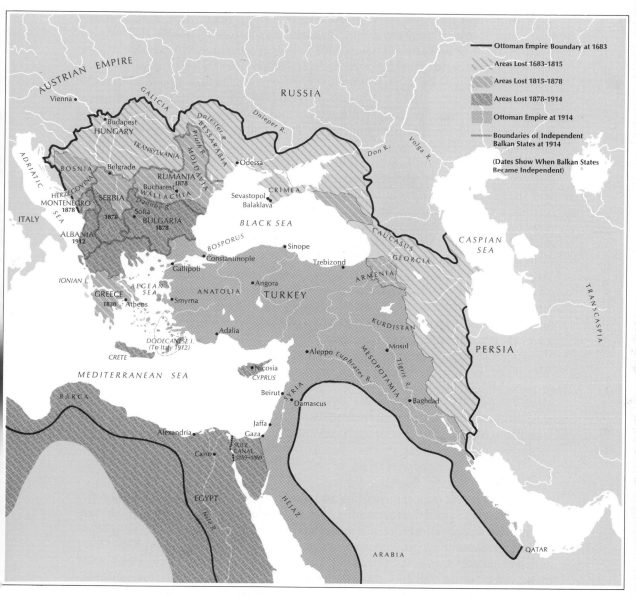

THE DECLINE OF THE OTTOMAN EMPIRE 1683–1914

Russia to side with rebels if she was to support the Christian subjects of the Ottomans and maintain her national interests) carried the Russian frontier across Bessarabia to the mouth of the Danube. It was by then clear that the Eastern Question of the nineteenth century would be the partition of Turkey as that of the previous century had been the partition of Poland, but there were important differences. The interests of more powers were involved this time, and the complicating factor of national sentiment among the subject peoples of the Ottoman empire would make an agreed outcome much more difficult. As a result Turkey survived far longer than might have been expected. Some of these factors led to the Crimean War, which revealed that the military colossus of 1815 no longer enjoyed an unquestioned superiority. Russia was defeated on her own territory and had to accept a peace in 1856 which involved the renunciation for the foreseeable future of her traditional goals in the Black Sea area.

In the middle of the war Nicholas I had died. This simplified the problems of his successor. Defeat made it clear that change must come in Russia and that it must involve some degree of practical liberalization of her institutions if she was to generate again a national power commensurate with her potential. This had always been vast but had become more and more unrealizable within the framework of her institutions and the backwardness they corseted. Before the war there had been no Russian railway south of Moscow. The once important Russian contribution to European industrial production had hardly grown since 1800 and was now well outstripped by that of the Western countries. Russian agriculture remained one of the most unproductive in the world, and yet the population steadily rose and pressed upon its resources.

In these circumstances Russia at last underwent radical change under Alexander II, who had succeeded Nicholas in 1855. Though less dramatic in form than much that had happened in the rest of Europe, it was in fact more of a revolution than what often went by that name elsewhere. What was being disturbed was an institution which lay at the very roots of Russian life—serfdom.

Emancipation

The growing importance of bond labor had been the leading characteristic of Russian social history since the seventeenth century. It had already been seen as an evil hindrance under Catherine the Great, and its disadvantages had become so obvious in the nineteenth century that even Nicholas I agreed that serfdom was the central problem of Russian society. From 1827 onward his reign had been marked by increasingly frequent serf insurrections, attacks on landlords, burning of crops and maiming of livestock. The refusal of dues was probably the least alarming form of popular resistance. Yet it was an appallingly difficult problem to tackle. The vast majority of Russians were serfs. Mere legislation could not transform them overnight into wage laborers or smallholders, nor could the state accept the administrative burden which would suddenly be thrown upon it if the services discharged by the manorial system were withdrawn and nothing put in their place. Nicholas had not dared to proceed. His successor did.

The one card Russian government could always play was the unquestioned authority of the autocrat and it was now put to good use. After years of studying the evidence and possible advantages and disadvantages of different forms of abolition, Alexander II issued in 1861 the edict which marked an epoch in Russian history and won him the title of Tsar Liberator. The edict gave the serfs personal freedom and ended bond labor. It also gave them allotments of land, but these were to be paid for by redemption dues intended to make the change acceptable to the landowners. To secure the repayments and offset the dangers of suddenly introducing a free labor market, the peasant remained to a considerable degree subject to the authority of his village community which was also charged with distributing the land allotments on a family basis.

Before long much would be heard about the shortcomings of this settlement. Yet there is much to be said for it and in retrospect it seems a massive achievement. A few years later the United States would emancipate its Negro slaves. There were far fewer of them than there were Russian peasants and they lived in a country of much greater economic opportunity, yet the effect of throwing them on a labor market dominated by laissez-faire economic liberalism would exacerbate a color problem with whose ultimate consequences the United States still has to grapple. In Russia the largest measure of social engineering in recorded history to date was carried out without grievous social and economic dislocation and opened the way to modernization for what was potentially one of the strongest nations on earth.

Emancipation began an era of reform; it was the first and greatest of a series of measures which by 1870 had given Russia a representative system of local government and a reformed judiciary. When the Russians took advantage of the Franco-Prussian war in 1871 to denounce some of the restrictions placed on their freedom in the Black Sea in 1856, there was almost a symbolic warning to Europe in what they did. After tackling her greatest problem and beginning to modernize her institutions, Russia was announcing that she would after all be mistress in her own house. The resumption of the oldest, most successful, and most consistently pursued policy of expansion to be found in modern European history was only a matter of time.

chapter 30

The Anglo=Saxon World

The United States of America and the United Kingdom had more in common in the nineteenth century than the bickering and back talk of their politicians and journalists allowed to appear. For one thing, their politics were different from those of continental Europe. Both countries escaped first the absolutist and then the revolutionary traditions. Anglo-Saxon politics of course changed quite as radically as those of any other country in the nineteenth century. But they were not transformed by the same political forces as those of Continental states nor in the same way.

Their similarity was in part because the two countries shared more than they usually admitted, and one aspect of their curious relations was that the United States could still without a sense of paradox call England the "mother country." The heritage of English culture and language was for a long time paramount in the United States; the influence of other European countries became overwhelmingly important only with the immigrations of the second half of the nineteenth century. Though many Americans—perhaps most—already had the blood of other European nations in their veins by the middle of the century, they did not elect a president who did not have an English, Scotch, or Irish surname until 1837. (The next would not be until 1901, and there have been only four such down to the present day.)

Post-colonial problems made, as they did in much later times, for emotional, sometimes violent, always complex relations between the United States and the United Kingdom. But they were also much more than this. They were, for example, shot through with strong economic connections. Far from dwindling (as had been feared) after independence, commerce between the two countries had gone on from strength to strength. English capital found the United States an attractive place for investment even after repeated and unhappy experiences with the bonds of defaulting states. British money was heavily invested in American railroads, banking, and insurance. Meanwhile the ruling elites of the two countries were at once fascinated and repelled by each other. Englishmen commented acidly on the vulgarity and rawness of American life; Americans found it hard to come to terms with monarchy and hereditary titles.

But more striking than the huge differences between them was that the United Kingdom and the United States had much in common when considered from the standpoint of continental Europe. Above all both were able to combine liberal and democratic politics with spectacular advances in wealth and power. They did this in very different circumstances for the most part, but at least one was common to both, the fact of isolation: if the United States had the Atlantic between it and Europe, Great Britain had the Channel.

Other nations too besides the United States shared the English heritage. There were growing British communities in Canada, Australia, New Zealand, and South Africa, though the first and last had other important components also. No other European nation had seeded nations on the same scale since the Spanish empire. But the two great Atlantic powers were the heart of the Anglo-Saxon world, both exercising world-shaping influence by force and example.

THE YOUNG REPUBLIC'S FOREIGN POLICY

For a long time the international potential of the United States was masked by its physical remoteness and the immense opportunities facing Americans in the West. At the peace of 1783 the British had defended American frontier interests to such effect that there would inevitably be a period of expansion ahead, but it was not clear at that time how far it might carry or what other powers it might entangle. This was partly a matter of geographical ignorance; it was not known in 1800 what the western half of the continent might contain. For some time the huge spaces just across the eastern mountain ranges provided a big enough field of expansion. The new republic was still psychologically and actually very much a matter of the Atlantic seaboard and the Ohio valley in 1800.

Its ill-defined frontiers nonetheless imposed relations with France, Spain, and the United Kingdom. The only other interests which might involve America in foreign affairs were trade and the protection of her nationals or foreign intervention in her internal affairs. The French Revolution appeared briefly to pose the chance of the latter and a quarrel with France ensued in 1793, but for the most part frontiers and trade preoccupied American diplomacy in the first quarter-century of the young nation.

American hopes of nonentanglement with the outside world led in 1793 to the Neutrality Proclamation rendering citizens of the United States liable to prosecution if they took any part in the Anglo-French war. The bias behind it received a classical formulation three years later in Washington's Farewell Address to his "Friends and Fellow-Citizens" as his second term as president drew to a close. In this he commented on the objectives and methods of a successful republican foreign policy in phrases which were to be deeply influential. Their predominantly negative and passive tone is now more striking than ever. "The great rule of conduct for us," he began, "in regard to foreign nations is, in extending our commercial relations, to have with them as little political connection as possible." "Europe has a set of primary interests," he continued, "which to us have none, or a very remote

The Special Relationship

*The European habit of going to the United States and returning to
write a book about its shortcomings was soon matched by the
American equivalent. England was an especial irritant to American
visitors, for obvious reasons. In the 1830s the novelist James
Fenimore Cooper came to England. Here is an extract from*
England, With Sketches of Society in the Metropolis, *which he
published on his return to the United States. As can be seen, he
tried to make distinctions which would ensure his (generally
unfavorable) judgments were fair.*

The comparison between the condition of the common English
house-servant, and that of the American slave, is altogether in
favour of the latter, if the hardship of compelled servitude be kept
out of view. The negro, bond or free, is treated much more kindly
and with greater friendship, than most of the English domestics; the
difference in colour, with the notions that have grown up under
them, removing all distrust of danger from familiarity. This is not
said with a view to turn the tables on our kinsmen for their
numberless taunts and continued injustice; for, with such an object,
I think something more original and severe might easily be got up;
but simply because I believe it to be true. Perhaps the servants of
no country have more enviable places than the American slaves, so
far as mere treatment and the amount of labour are concerned.

relation . . . Our detached and distant situation invites and enables us to
pursue a different course . . . It is our true policy to steer clear of permanent
alliances with any portion of the foreign world." Washington also warned his
countrymen against assumptions of permanent or special hostility or friendship with any foreign power.

In all this there is no trace of America's destiny as a world power. Washington had not even considered non-European relations; the nation's future
Pacific and Asian role was inconceivable in 1796. By and large a pragmatic

One prominent feature of poverty, in England, is dependent on causes which ought not to be ascribed to the system. If a man can be content to live on a few grapes, and a pound of coarse bread, and to go without a coat, or a fire, in a region like that of Naples, it does not necessarily follow, that another ought to be able to do the same things in a country in which there are no grapes, in which a fire is necessary, and a coat indispensable. The high civilization of England unquestionably contributes also to the misery of the very poor, by augmenting their wants, though it adds greatly to the comforts of those who are able to sustain themselves. As between the Americans and the English, it is not saying much, under the peculiar circumstances of their respective countries, that the poor of the former are immeasurably better off than the poor of the latter; but, apart from certain disadvantages of climate in favour of the south of Europe, I am not at all certain that the poor of England, as a body, do not fare quite as well as the poor of any other part of Christendom. . . . I think I should prefer being a pauper in England, to being a beggar in France. I now speak of physical sufferings altogether, for on all points that relate to the feelings, admitting that the miserable still retain sentiment on such points, I think England the least desirable country, for a poor man, that I know.

From Henry Steele Commager, ed., *Britain Through American Eyes* (New York: McGraw-Hill, Inc., 1974), pp. 169–170. Copyright © 1974 by Henry Steele Commager. Reprinted by permission of McGraw-Hill Book Company.

approach to foreign relations within a framework of cautions and even suspicious isolationism would be the policy pursued by Washington's successors in the presidency for more than a century.

Before 1917 the United States' only war against a great power was that with Great Britain in 1812. Besides contributing to the growth of nationalist feeling in the young country (Uncle Sam made his appearance as the caricature embodiment of the nation and *The Star-Spangled Banner* was composed), it marked an important stage in the evolving relations between the

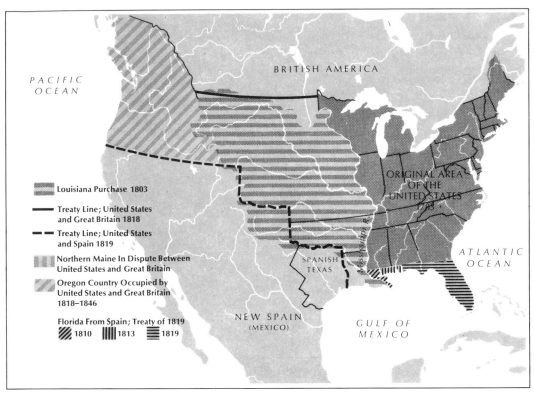

THE BOUNDARIES OF THE UNITED STATES TO 1819

two nations. Though the war rearoused anglophobia in the United States, the fighting (which had its humiliations for both sides) cleared the air. It was henceforth tacitly understood that neither American nor British governments were willing to consider war except under the most extreme provocation. In this setting the northwestern boundary of the United States was soon defined as far west as the "Stony Mountains" (as the Rockies were then called); in 1845 it was carried further to the Pacific and by then the disputed Maine boundary had also been settled.

A far greater change in American territorial definition had been brought about by the Louisiana Purchase of 1803. Roughly speaking, Louisiana was the area between the Mississippi River and the Rocky Mountains and it was theoretically in French possession, the Spanish having ceded it to them in 1800. This change had aroused American interest; New Orleans, which controlled the mouth of the river down which so much American commerce already passed, was of vital importance. The United States entered a negotiation which ended with the buying of an area larger than the total area of the republic itself. On the modern map it includes Louisiana, Arkansas, Iowa, Nebraska, both the Dakotas, Minnesota west of the Mississippi, most of Kansas, Oklahoma, Montana, Wyoming, and a big piece of Colorado. The price was $11,250,000.

This was the largest land sale of all time and its consequences were appropriately huge. It changed American domestic history by opening the way to the trans-Mississippi West: the social result would be a shift in demographic and political balance of revolutionary import. This shift was already beginning in the second decade of the century when the population living west of the Alleghenies more than doubled. With the acquisition of Florida from Spain the United States had by 1819 legal sovereignty over territory bounded by the Atlantic and Gulf coasts from Maine to the Sabine River, the Red and Arkansas rivers, the Continental Divide, and the 49th parallel. It was thus incontrovertibly the most important state in the Americas.

Alarm about a possible restoration of Spanish power in Latin America and concern with Russian activity in the Pacific northwest next led to a statement of American determination to rule the roost in the Western hemisphere. This was the Monroe Doctrine, enunciated in 1823, which said that no future European colonization could be envisaged in the hemisphere and that intervention by European powers in affairs there would be seen as unfriendly to the United States. As this suited British interests and no European state could conceivably mount an American operation if opposed by British sea power, the Monroe Doctrine remained the bedrock of American hemisphere diplomacy.

One consequence was that other American nations could not use European support to defend their own independence against the United States.

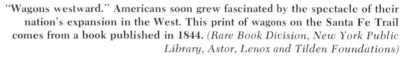

"Wagons westward." Americans soon grew fascinated by the spectacle of their nation's expansion in the West. This print of wagons on the Santa Fe Trail comes from a book published in 1844. *(Rare Book Division, New York Public Library, Astor, Lenox and Tilden Foundations)*

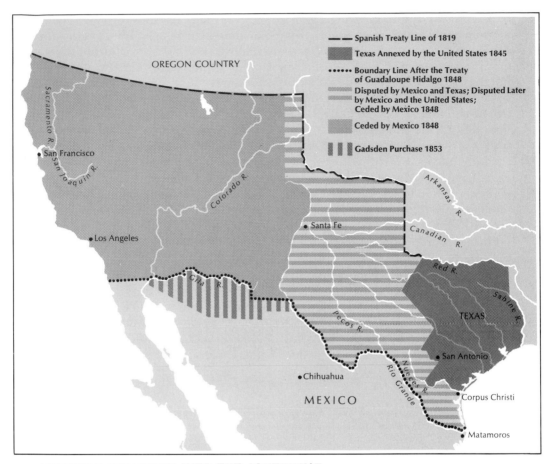

AMERICAN EXPANSION INTO THE SOUTHWEST

The main sufferer before 1860 was Mexico. American settlers in Mexican territory set up an independent Texan republic which was subsequently annexed by the United States. In the war that followed Mexico did very badly, and the peace of 1848 stripped her of what would become Utah, Nevada, California, and most of Arizona. With one small purchase of other Mexican land in 1853, the continental territory of the United States was rounded off to its modern form. Seventy years after the Peace of Paris the republic filled half a continent.

IRREPRESSIBLE CONFLICT

There was expansion too in other ways. About 4 million people in 1790 had become nearly 24 million by 1850. Most of them still lived east of the Mississippi and New Orleans was the only city with more than 100,000 inhabitants west of the Alleghenies, but the nation's center of gravity was moving westward. From the moment settlers entered the Ohio valley a Western interest had been in existence; Washington's Farewell Address had already recognized its importance. It had growing political impact.

Expansion and economic growth shaped American society as profoundly as the democratic bias of her political institutions. A notable example was the changing importance of slavery. When Washington began his presidency there were a little under 700,000 Negro slaves within the territories of the republic. This was a large number, but the framers of the Constitution only took special note of them when deciding that a slave could count as three-fifths of a free man in fixing how many representatives each state should have. Within the next half-century three things revolutionized the context in which the founding fathers had seen slavery.

The first was its enormous extension, largely as a result of technical change and a huge rise in the world's consumption of cotton (especially by English mills). The crop doubled in the 1820s and then doubled again in the 1830s; by 1860 cotton provided two-thirds of the value of the total exports of the United States. This growth was achieved mainly by planting new land, and new plantations meant more labor. By 1820 there were already 1.5 million Negro slaves, by 1860 about 4 million. As slavery became the foundation of the economic system in the Southern states, Southerners felt their civilization to be more and more distinct from that of other parts of the Union. Their "peculiar institution," as slavery was called, came to be regard-

Richmond, Virginia, on the eve of the Civil War; a slave auction.
(Courtesy of The New-York Historical Society, New York City)

ed as the essential core of a particular society, and by 1860 many of its members thought of the South as a distinct nation with a way of life which they idealized. Moreover they believed it to be threatened by tyrannous interference from the outside because of the growing hostility of Congress to slavery.

This had been the second development changing slavery's importance in American life. The early politics of the republic had reflected what were later called sectional interests and the Farewell Address itself had drawn attention to them. Roughly speaking, they produced political parties reflecting, on the one hand, mercantile and business interests which tended to look for strong federal government and protectionist legislation and, on the other, agrarian and consumer interests which asserted the rights of individual states and cheap money policies. At this stage slavery was hardly the stuff of politics. But this political world gradually gave way to a more modern one. Judicial interpretation gave a national and federal emphasis to the Constitution, and Congress became more responsive to American democracy; the presidency of Andrew Jackson has traditionally been seen as especially important in this. The growing democratization of politics reflected among other things the increase of population in an industrializing North and the westward expansion made possible by the Louisiana Purchase. The opening of the West inevitably brought slavery into politics, for there was great scope for dispute about the terms on which new territories should be joined to the Union.

The third great change was the rise of a fierce antislavery movement in the North. This dragged the slavery issue to the forefront of American politics and kept it there until it overshadowed every other question. The campaign for the abolition of the slave trade and the eventual emancipation of the Negro stemmed from much the same forces which produced such demands in other countries toward the end of the eighteenth century. But the American movement was confronted with a *growth* in slavery at a time when it was disappearing elsewhere in the European world. Moreover the issue involved deep constitutional questions, above all one which lay at the heart of the Constitution and indeed of the political life of every European country too: who was to have the last word? The people were sovereign, that was clear; but were "the people" the majority of their representatives in Congress or the populations of individual states acting through their legislatures and asserting their rights even against Congress? By mid-century slavery was entangled with almost every side of American life.

These great issues were contained so long as the balance of power between the Southern and Northern states remained roughly the same. Although the North always had a slight preponderance of population, the crucial equality in the Senate was maintained for some time. Down to 1819 new states were admitted to the Union on an alternating system, one slave, one free; there were by then eleven of each.

The first crisis came over the admission of the state of Missouri. In the days before the Louisiana Purchase French and Spanish law had permitted slavery there and her settlers expected this to continue. They were indignant, and so were representatives of the Southern states, when a Northern congressman proposed restrictions upon slavery in the new state's constitution. There was great public stir and debate about sectional advantage; there was even talk of secession from the Union, so strongly did some Southerners feel. Yet the moral issue was muted. It was still possible to reach a political answer to a political question by the Missouri Compromise of 1820, which admitted Missouri as a slave state but balanced her by admitting Maine at the same time and also prohibited any further extension of slavery in the United States territory north of a line of latitude 36° 30'. This settled the question for a generation, but some had already seen the future it promised. Thomas Jefferson, a former president and the man who had drafted the Declaration of Independence, wrote that he "considered it at once as the knell of the Union," and another (future) president wrote in his diary that the Missouri question was "a mere preamble – a title page to a great, tragic volume."

The tragedy did not come to its climax for forty years. In part this was because Americans had much else to think about and in part because no question arose of incorporating territories suitable for cotton growing (and therefore requiring slave labor) until the 1840s. But there were soon forces at work to agitate public opinion. In 1831 a newspaper was established in Boston to advocate the unconditional emancipation of Negro slaves. This was the beginning of the abolitionist campaign which generated increasingly bitter propaganda, electoral pressure upon politicians in the North, assis-

THE UNITED STATES: SLAVE AND FREE TERRITORY 1850

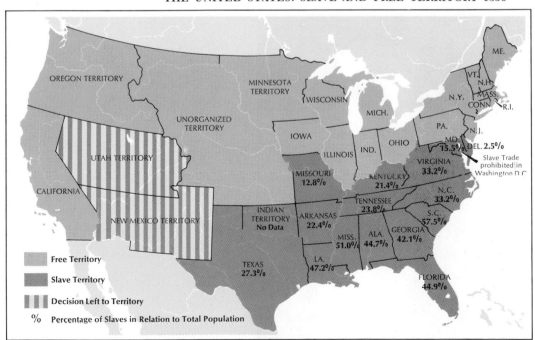

tance to runaway slaves and opposition to returning those recaptured to their owners, even when the law courts said they must be sent back. Against this background a struggle in the 1840s over whether to permit slavery in the territory won from Mexico ended in 1850 in a new compromise but one destined not to last long. From this time on Southern leaders showed an increasing sense of persecution and a growing arrogance in the defense of their region's way of life. Political allegiances were now affected; the Democratic party declared its stand that the 1850 settlement was final.

The next decade brought the descent to disaster. The need to organize Kansas for statehood blew up the truce which rested on the 1850 compromise and brought about the first bloodshed as abolitionists strove to bully proslavery Kansans into accepting their views. The Republican party emerged in protest against the proposal that popular sovereignty *in the territory* should decide whether Kansas would be slave or free: Kansas was north of the 36° 30′ line. The anger of abolitionists now mounted too whenever the law supported the slaveholder, as it did in 1857 in a notable Supreme Court decision returning a Negro to his owner. Southerners on the other hand saw such outcries as incitements to disaffection among the slaves and as determination to use the electoral system against Southern liberties—a view which was of course justified because the abolitionists were not men who would compromise. In fact, the Republican party did not support their demands; its presidential candidate in the election of 1860 campaigned on a program

Abraham Lincoln, five months before his election as President of the United States in November 1860. (*Courtesy Chicago Historical Society*)

which envisaged only the exclusion of slavery from all territories to be brought into the Union in the future.

Even this was too much for many Southerners. Although the Democrats were divided, the country voted on strictly sectional grounds in 1860; the Republican Abraham Lincoln, the greatest of American presidents, was elected by the Northern and the two Pacific coast states. This was the end of the line for many Southerners. South Carolina formally seceded from the Union as a protest against the election. In February 1861 six other states joined her, and the Confederate States of America which they set up had its provisional government and president installed a month before President Lincoln was inaugurated in Washington.

THE WAR BETWEEN THE STATES

Each side accused the other of revolutionary designs and behavior. It is very difficult not to agree with both. The heart of the North's position, as Lincoln saw, was that democracy should prevail, a claim of potentially limitless revolutionary implication. In the end the North would achieve a social revolution in the South. On the other side, what Southerners were asserting in 1861 (and three more states joined the Confederacy after the first shots were fired) was that they had the same right to organize their region's life as had, say, revolutionary Poles or Italians in Europe. It is unfortunate, but generally true, that the coincidence of nationalist claims with liberal institutions is rarely complete, or even close.

Behind these issues of principle were concrete personal and local forces which make it very difficult to draw clearly the actual lines along which the republic divided for the great crisis of its history and identity. They ran through families, towns and villages, religions, and sometimes around groups of different colors. It is the tragedy of civil wars to be like that.

War has a revolutionary potential of its own. Much of the particular impact of what some called a rebellion and others the War between the States grew out of the necessities of the struggle. It took four years for the Union forces to win and in that time an important change had occurred in Lincoln's aims. At the beginning of the war he spoke only of restoring the proper order: there were things happening in the Southern states, he told the people, "too powerful to be suppressed by the ordinary course of judicial proceedings" and thus would require military operations. This view broadened into a consistent reiteration that the war was being fought to preserve the Union. Lincoln's aim was to reunite the states, and for a long time he failed to satisfy those who sought from the war the abolition of slavery. In 1862 he could still say in a public letter: "If I could save the Union without freeing any slave, I would do it; and if I could save it by freeing all the slaves, I would do it; and if I could save it by freeing some and leaving others alone, I would also do that," but by then he had already decided that he must proclaim the emancipation of slaves in the rebel states. It became effective on New Year's Day 1863. Thus the nightmare of Southern politicians was a reality at last, thanks to the war they had courted. Emancipation transformed the nature of the struggle though not very obviously. The final step in 1865 was an amendment to the Constitution which prohibited slavery anywhere in the United States. By that time the Confederacy was defeated, Lincoln was dead, and the cause which he had imperishably summed up as "government of the people, by the people, for the people" was safe.

In the aftermath of its military victory that cause could hardly appear as an unequivocally noble or righteous one to all Americans, but its triumph was pregnant with the future not only of America but of mankind. The Union's survival settled the destiny of the continent; one great power would continue to dominate it and exploit the resources of the richest untapped domain yet open to man. That fact in due course would determine the outcome of two world wars. The Union victory also meant that the democratic system would prevail in American politics; this might not perhaps always be true in the sense Lincoln meant but the political institutions which in principle provided for the rule of the majority were henceforth secure from direct challenge. This was to have the incidental effect of linking democracy and material well-being closely in the minds of Americans, for the institutions under which the United States grew richer seemed to explain its growing prosperity. Industrial capitalism would have a great pool of ideological commitment to draw upon when it faced its later critics.

The war's most obvious domestic consequence was the creation of a new color problem. In a sense there had been no color problem while

The price of defeat: ruins of a flour mill in Richmond, Virginia, at the end of the war. *(The Library of Congress)*

slavery existed. Servile status had been the barrier separating the over-whelming majority of blacks (there had always been a few free among them) from whites and nothing else was necessary. Emancipation swept away the framework of legal inferiority and replaced it with the framework, or myth, of democratic equality when very few Americans were ready to make this a social reality.

Millions of Negroes in the South were suddenly free. They were also for the most part uneducated, largely untrained except for field labor, and vir-tually without leaders of their own race. When the occupying Union armies withdrew from the South, blacks soon disappeared from positions in the legislatures and public offices which they had briefly held. In some areas they disappeared from the polling booths too. Legal disabilities were re-placed by a social and physical coercion which was sometimes harsher than the old regime of slavery. Competition with impoverished whites in a free labor market at a time when the economy of large areas of the South was in ruins was disastrous for the black. By the end of the century he had been driven by a poor and bitterly resentful white population into social subordi-nation and economic deprivation. From this was to stem emigration to the North in the twentieth century and the racial problems of our own day.

As another consequence of the war the United States retained a two-party system. Despite occasional threats from third parties, Republicans and Democrats have continued to divide the presidency ever since. There was

Former Confederate soldiers take the oath of allegiance to the Union, 1865.
(The Library of Congress)

nothing to make this probable before 1861. Many parties had come and gone down to that time. But the war riveted upon the Democratic party a commitment to the Southern cause which at first was a grave handicap because it carried the stigma of disloyalty to the Union (no Democrat was president after the war until 1885). Correspondingly, the Republicans kept the loyalty of Northern states and the hopes of radicals who saw them as the saviors of the Union and democracy and the liberators of the slave. Before the inadequacy of these stereotypes became clear, both parties were so deeply rooted in certain states that their predominance in them was unchallengeable. Twentieth-century American politics would transform these two parties internally, not reject them in favor of others.

Progress resumed

The impact of Republican policies upon a South both defeated and devastated made the Reconstruction years bitter ones. In striving honestly to ensure democratic rights for the blacks in the South, radical Republicans guaranteed the future hegemony there of the Democrats. But the South was forgotten as the great expansion interrupted briefly by the war resumed; it was about to produce another revolution. America's advance to the point where her citizens would have the highest per capita income in the world was the work of an era which began in the 1870s. In a huge blossoming of confidence and expectation all political problems seemed for a while to have been solved. Under Republican presidents the country turned, not for the last time, to comforting reflection that the business of America was business.

The South remained largely untouched by the new prosperity, but the North and West could look forward with confidence that the changes of the previous seventy years promised even better times ahead. Foreigners felt this too and came to the United States in ever growing numbers — 2.5 million in the 1850s alone. They fed a total population which had grown to nearly 40 million in 1870, about half living west of the Alleghenies and the majority in rural areas. The building of railroads was opening the Great Plains for settlement and exploitation which had not yet really begun before. In 1869 the driving of the golden spike marked the completion of the first transcontinental railroad. Already, thanks to the labor shortage of the war years, farm machines were being used in numbers which pointed to a quite new scale of farming and an agricultural revolution that would end with North America becoming the granary of Europe. Great years lay ahead for industry too. The United States was not yet an industrial power to compare with Great Britain (in 1870 there were still less than 2 million Americans employed in manufacturing), but the groundwork was done. With a large, increasingly well-off domestic market the prospects for American industry were bright.

Poised on the brink of their most confident and successful era, Americans were not being hypocritical in forgetting the losers. They understandably found it easy to do so because of a general sense that the American system worked well. The blacks and poor whites of the South had now joined the Indian (who had been a steady loser for two and a half centuries) as the forgotten failures of the United States. The poor of the growing cities need not be regarded, comparatively, as losers; they were probably better off than the poor of Manchester, Skibbereen, or Naples whose willingness to come to the United States showed what a magnet it was. Nor was its attraction only material. Besides the "wretched refuse" there were the "huddled masses yearning to breathe free." The United States in 1870 was still an inspiration to political radicals elsewhere, though perhaps American political practice and forms had most impact in Great Britain where people linked (both approvingly and disapprovingly) democracy with the "Americanization" of British politics.

THE ENGLISH CONSTITUTIONAL REVOLUTION

Great Britain underwent a constitutional revolution in the nineteenth century as the United States did not. During a time of unprecedented social change, some of it dislocating, which created the world's first industrialized urban society within a single lifetime, Great Britain maintained a remarkable continuity in her constitutional and political forms but transformed their working. At the same time she was also acting as a world and European power and ruling a great empire.

In a social sense (if the blacks are set aside as a special case) the United Kingdom was still a far less democratic country than the United States in 1870. A social hierarchy, reflecting when possible birth and land but otherwise money, stratified the nation. Yet political democracy had come a long way since 1800. Even though universal male suffrage, long established in the United States, would not be law until 1918, the democratic revolution in English politics was past the point of reversibility.

For all its liberal institutions—equality in law, personal liberty, a representative system—the English constitution of 1800 did not rest on democratic principles but on the representation of individual and historic rights. The accidents of the past which had created these rights produced an electorate in 1832 large by contemporary European standards, but the word "democratic" was then still a pejorative one. Democracy meant the French Revolution and military despotism to most Englishmen. Yet in that year a great revision of the representative system became law. Previously, the franchise had been based on a jumble of different principles in different places; the Reform Act of 1832 now gave the vote to freeholders in the rural areas and to most middle-class householders in the towns. The man with property (and thus with a stake in the country) was the model elector; the others did not count

The immediate result was an electorate of about 650,000 and a House of Commons which did not look very different from its predecessor and was still dominated by the landed gentry. But the 1832 reform nonetheless began the slow democratization of British politics, because if the constitution had been changed once in this way, then it could be changed again, and the House of Commons more and more claimed the right to say what should be done without being thwarted by the House of Lords or the crown. In 1867 another act produced an electorate of about 2 million, and in 1872 an act prescribed that voting should take place by secret ballot—a great step.

Electoral reform brought other changes in British politics. Slowly and somewhat grudgingly the traditional ruling class began to organize parties which were something more than family connections or personal cliques of members of Parliament. The extension of the franchise in 1867 greatly speeded up this process, but its implication—that there was a public opinion to be courted which was broader than the old landed interest—had by then already been grasped. All the great parliamentary leaders in the nineteenth century derived their success from their ability to catch not only the ear of the House of Commons but also that of important sections of society outside it. The great political duelists of the 1860s and 1870s, Benjamin Disraeli and William Ewart Gladstone, both did this in their different ways; so did Lord Palmerston, the idol of the British public in foreign affairs. But the first and possibly most significant example was Sir Robert Peel, who created English conservatism. By accepting the verdicts of public opinion, he gave the Conservative party a pliability which saved it from the intransigence into which the right was tempted in so many European countries.

Reform

The great political crisis of Corn-Law Repeal demonstrated the Conservatives' flexibility. The debate was not only about an economic policy but about who should govern the country, and before 1832 the fight for repeal in some ways complemented the struggle for parliamentary reform. The disappearance of the corn laws meant that landed society no longer had the last word. The Conservative party, the stronghold of country gentlemen who considered the agricultural interest the embodiment of England, turned on Peel and rejected him soon after he carried the crucial debate in 1846. They were right in sensing that the whole tendency of Peel's policy had been directed to the triumph of the free trade principles which they associated with middle-class manufacturers. But the Conservative party accepted free trade and did not attempt to reverse the achievement any more than it attempted to reverse the Reform of 1832.

The redirection of tariff and fiscal policies toward free trade was one side, in some ways the most spectacular, of a general alignment of British politics toward reform and liberalization between 1840 and 1870. During this time a beginning was made with local government reform (significantly, in the towns, not in the countryside where landed interests were still strong), a new poor law was introduced, factory and mining legislation was enacted and began to be effectively policed by official inspectors, the judicial system was reconstructed, disabilities on Protestant nonconformists, Roman Catholics, and Jews were removed, a postal system was set up which became the model for others, and efforts were even made to tackle the scandal of English educational neglect. All this was accompanied by an unprecedented growth in wealth, symbolized by the Great Exhibition of the world's industrial wares held in London in 1851 under the patronage of the queen and the

A LEAP IN THE DARK.

Britannia flinches at a leap into the unknown. The horse has the face of Disraeli,
who, while a conservative prime minister, nonetheless introduced a radical
set of proposals for extending the franchise in 1867 and then presided
over what was probably the most important single step toward political
democracy in Great Britain in the nineteenth century. *(Courtesy, PUNCH)*

direction of her consort. If the English were inclined to bumptiousness, as
they seem to have been in the central decades of Victoria's reign, it may
be said that then they had grounds.

In spite of the evidence of extremes of wealth and poverty as great as
any other country's, some Englishmen feared reform. The state invaded
more and more areas which had previously been immune and at the same
time developed more effective means for intervention. England in the nineteenth century was very far from centralizing power in her state apparatus in
a modern sense, but some people worried that she might be going the way of
France, a country whose highly centralized bureaucracy was believed to
explain Frenchmen's failure to achieve liberty and success in establishing
equality.

Yet the general mood was still confident and progressive in 1870. In
spite of the appalling conditions of her factory towns and the social unrest in

the early decades of the century, England had somehow navigated the shoals of popular demands which had proved fatal to orderly government in other states. She had deliberately undertaken huge reconstructions of her institutions at a time when the dangers of revolution were clearly apparent elsewhere, and she had emerged unscathed, her power and wealth enhanced and the principles of liberalism even more apparent in her politics. She did not have the advantages of geographical remoteness and almost limitless land enjoyed by the United States—and even the United States had fought one of the bloodiest wars in human history to contain a revolution. How then had the English done it?

Popular demands

It may be that there never had been a potentially revolutionary threat in this rapidly changing society. Many of the basic reforms which the French Revolution brought to Europe had been modeled on institutions familiar in Great Britain for centuries. The constitution had always offered quite large possibilities. Even in unreformed days the House of Commons and House of Lords were not the closed corporate institutions which were all that were available as representative bodies in many European states. They had shown their capacity to meet, even if slowly and belatedly, new needs; the first factory act (admittedly not a very helpful one) had been passed as early as 1801. After 1832 there were good grounds for thinking that if Parliament were only pressed hard enough from the outside, it would eventually carry out any reforms that were required. Certainly there was no legal restraint on its power to do so. The oppressed and angry seem to have realized this. There were many outbreaks of desperate violence and many revolutionaries about in the 1830s and 1840s (which were especially hard times for the poor), but the most important popular movement of the day, the great spectrum of protest gathered together in what was called Chartism, asked in the People's Charter which embodied its program for measures which would make Parliament more democratic and responsive to society's needs, not for its abolition.

It was also important that the great reforms of Victorian England, with the possible exception of factory legislation, affected the interests of the middle class as much as the masses. The English middle class came to share in political power as its Continental counterparts did not and could therefore use constitutional processes to obtain change; its members were not tempted to ally with revolution, the recourse of desperate men to whom other avenues were closed.

But in any case it does not seem that the English masses were themselves very revolutionary. The traditional patterns of behavior died hard; England was long to remain a country with habits of deference to social superiors which much struck foreigners—especially Americans. Furthermore working-class organizations provided alternatives to political violence. They were often very unrevolutionary in their emphasis on self-help, caution, prudence, sobriety. Of all the elements which have made up the great English labor movement, only the political party which bears that name was not in existence before 1840, and the others were mature by the 1860s. The "friendly societies" for insurance against misfortune, the cooperative associations, and especially the trade unions all provided channels for personal participation in the improvement of working-class life. Their early maturity was to underlie the paradox of English socialism: its later dependence on a very conservative and unrevolutionary trade union movement, the largest and best organized in the world.

Once the 1840s were over, improved economic conditions may have helped allay discontent. At any rate working-class leaders often said so, almost regretfully. When the international economy picked up in the 1850s, good times came to the industrial cities of an England which was the workshop of the world, and its merchant, banker, and insurer too. As employment and wages rose, the support which the Chartists had mustered crumbled away and they were soon only a reminiscence.

Ireland

There was only one sphere in which the capacity for imaginative change seemed always to fail the British people. This was in their dealings with Ireland, the one place where England faced a real revolutionary danger and had had to put down a rebellion in 1798. In the 1850s and 1860s Ireland was quiet. But the reason was in large measure an appalling disaster which overtook the island in the middle of the 1840s when the failure of the potato crop was followed by the famine and disease which Malthus had prophesied would be the result of overpopulation. For the moment despair muted both the demand for repeal of the Act of Union, which had joined Ireland to Great Britain in 1800, and the dislike of her predominantly Catholic population for an alien and established Protestant church.

The problems nonetheless remained, and the Liberal government of Gladstone which took office in 1868 addressed itself above all to them. What emerged from his efforts was a new Irish nationalist movement demanding home rule. This demand was to haunt British politics and overturn their combinations and settlements for the rest of the century. Through capacity of this issue to wreck British liberalism, Ireland again became of importance in world history after over a thousand years of obscurity. She made another indirect impact upon it at about the same time in heavy emigration to the United States.

Victoria Regina

Even Irish discontent could not puncture British confidence and complacency in the middle decades of the nineteenth century. It was then that Englishmen began to use the adjective "Victorian" and thus showed their awareness that they lived in a unique era. It was one which seemed above all remarkable for its combination of revolutionary technological and economic change with the maintenance of social peace and of age-old traditions and habits. The symbols of the unchanging forms which contained so much change were the central institutions of Parliament and the crown. When the Houses of Parliament burned down and new ones were built, a mock-medieval design was chosen to emphasize the antiquity of the Mother of Parliaments. In such ways the changes of this most revolutionary era of English history were draped in the robes of custom and tradition.

Above all the monarchy continued; when Victoria ascended the throne in 1837, it was second only to the papacy in antiquity among the political institutions of Europe. Although it had been brought very low in public esteem by the last two kings, Victoria and her husband were to make it again unquestioned. This went somewhat against the grain for the queen herself; she did not find easy the political neutrality appropriate to a constitutional monarch when the crown had withdrawn above the political battle. Yet this withdrawal was made in her reign. She also domesticated the monarchy; for the first time since the days of George III the "Royal Family" was a reality and could be seen to be one. Its creation was one of many ways the queen's German husband Prince Albert helped her adapt the institution of hereditary monarchy to a liberal state, though he got little thanks for it from an ungrateful English public.

chapter 31

The European World Hegemony

POWER AND INFLUENCE

In 1900 Europe and the nations of European stocks overseas dominated the affairs of most of the globe. It was not always to the disadvantage of non-Europeans, but their usual role was as underdog. If not ruled directly by Europe, they were either helplessly involved in her commerce or had to give individual Europeans a big share in the direction of their affairs or (perhaps most important of all as a demonstration of the prestige of European civilization) succumbed to the attractive force of European ideals. Such things make it reasonable to speak of a European world hegemony. The United States played a big part, at certain times and places, in advancing this dominance, which may also be termed "Western" if it is remembered that the rest of the world hardly distinguished American from European and that the Americas stood in the tradition of European civilization. Given the current use of the phrase "Western world," it will be clearer and more accurate to talk here of European civilization and hegemony, making a distinction from American when it is necessary to do so.

One reason for this civilization's success in the nineteenth century was that it was already rich and getting richer all the time. It possessed a self-feeding capacity to open up and even create new resources as industrialization proceeded; the obvious example was the United States, more and more revealing itself as a treasure house. Furthermore the power generated by new wealth made it possible to appropriate many of the resources of other parts of the world. Not for a long time would the profits of Congo rubber, Burmese teak, or Persian oil be reinvested in the capital improvement of those countries. The poor of Europe and North America benefited from low prices for raw materials, and mortality rates tell the story of an industrial civilization finding it possible to give its peoples a richer life. European peasants could buy cheap manufactured clothes and tools while their contemporaries in Africa and India still lived in the Stone Age.

Material advantage was not the whole story. Ideas and attitudes mattered because they provided ways to approach the world which enabled Europeans to deal with it with confidence. This has been noted in considering the begin-

A VILLAGE IN PUKAPUKA, UNDER HEATHENISM

THE SAME VILLAGE, UNDER CHRISTIANITY.

The blessings of Christian civilization. Two engravings from a book by a Victorian missionary showing the effects of Christianity on a village in the Cook Islands. *(Rex Nan Kivell Collection, National Library of Australia, Canberra)*

nings of Europe's expansion. Success fed further success; it was taken to be another demonstration of the inherent superiority of European ideas and values. Americans and Europeans spoke naturally of the "civilized world" and meant by it their own.

This was certainly arrogant. The people who used the phrase could not easily see that anything in the world beyond the countries which shared their institutions, technology, and beliefs deserved to be called civilization, even if some cultures had deserved so in the past. Much had been added to the earlier simple faith in the superiority of Christianity. "Civilized" by 1900 meant what we now call Westernized or modernized and embodied a whole repertoire of progressive ideas.

The result was a sort of secular missionary activity. Europeans responded to the unintelligible barbarities they found elsewhere by exporting their own form of education, their ideas about sanitation and health, their emphatic attention to the individual, their desire to raise the status of women and protect children, even their wish to be kind to animals. They were confident that the values of their civilization were better than indigenous ones and were usually oblivious to the disruptive effect they might have. Even anti-imperialists who opposed European rule thought that the remedy for that rule was a dose of Europeanization in the form of a free press and the vote.

In the nineteenth century science and enlightenment seemed to show that Europeanization and progress were the same thing, but so did Christianity, still one of the most important formal channels by which European civilization reached the non-European world. In terms of the growing territorial spread of the churches and their numbers of official adherents, the nineteenth century was the greatest era of Christian expansion since apostolic times. Much of this was the result of a renewed wave of missionary activity; the Roman Catholic church set up new orders and Protestant countries created new societies for the support of overseas missions. The paradoxical effect was to intensify the European flavor of what was supposedly a creed for all humanity. In most of the receiving countries Christianity was long seen as just one more aspect of European civilization rather than as a spiritual message which might express itself in many different local forms. An interesting if trivial example is the concern missionaries often showed about dress. Whereas the Jesuits in seventeenth-century China had discreetly adopted the costume of their hosts, nineteenth-century missionaries set to work with zeal to put Bantus and Solomon Islanders into European garments which were often freakishly unsuitable.

Christian missionaries thus diffused more than a creed. Often they brought important material benefits: food in time of famine, agricultural techniques, hospitals, and schools. Such patronage was also provided by some colonial governments and was in such cases the expression of a new paternalism which had developed under the impact of eighteenth-century progressive thought. Whatever the reality or the degrees of difference between them, European governments at least said they wanted to govern for the well-being of their subjects. Thus the assumptions of a progressive civilization filtered through colonial administration.

Nonetheless, such agencies only operated at all because in the last resort they could not be kept away; Europeans had force on their side. By 1900 only Ethiopia had successfully resisted; there barefoot levies massacred an Italian army in 1896. Except for Tibet, still considered all but inaccessible, there was no part of the world where Europeans could not, if they wished, impose themselves by armed strength. Nineteenth-century weapons gave them an even greater relative advantage than they had enjoyed when the first Portuguese broadside was fired at Calicut. Even when their opponents had modern arms, they could rarely use them effectively. At the battle of Omdurman in the Sudan in 1898, a British regiment opened fire on its Dervish opponents at a range of 2,000 yards with the army's ordinary magazine rifle of the day. A few minutes later shrapnel shells and machine guns were shredding to pieces the masses of the Dervish army, which never reached the British line. By the end of the day about 10,000 of them had been killed; 48 British and Egyptian soldiers had died. It was not simply, as an Englishman put it soon afterward, that

> Whatever happens, we have got
> The Maxim gun, and they have not,

for the Dervish leader had machine guns in his armory at Omdurman. He also had telegraph apparatus to communicate with his forces and electric mines to blow up the British gunboats on the Nile. But none of these things was properly employed; a mental as well as a technical transformation was required before non-European cultures could use the Europeans' instrumentation to defeat them.

Force was at the base of European hegemony in another, less unpleasant way. The maritime Pax Britannica throughout the whole nineteenth century stood in the way of European nations competing by war for mastery of the non-European world. The colonial wars of the seventeenth and eighteenth centuries were not repeated during what was the greatest extension of direct colonial rule in modern times. Peace meant that traders of all nations could move without interference on the surface of the seas and they were key figures in the spread of European influence.

The first world economy

By 1900 the whole world formed an economic structure with Europe at its center. Though there had been temporary disruptions of it, a world economy transcended those of particular continents. At the heart of this structure was a broad distinction of roles between industrial and nonindustrial countries: the second tended to be primary producers meeting the needs of the increasingly urbanized populations of the first. But this crude division requires much explanation and qualification, and individual countries often do not fit the pattern; the United States, for example, was both a great primary producer and the world's leading manufacturing power in 1914, producing as much as Great Britain, Germany, and France together. Nor is this distinction one which ran exactly between nations of European and non-European

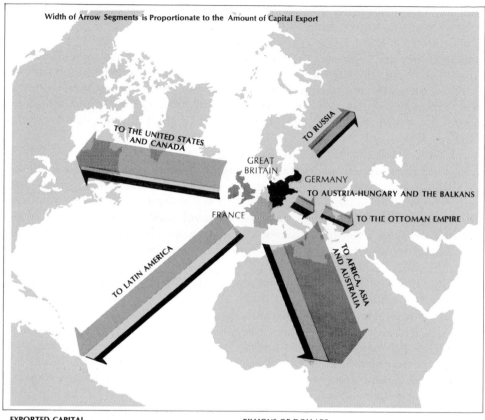

Width of Arrow Segments is Proportionate to the Amount of Capital Export

TO THE UNITED STATES AND CANADA

TO RUSSIA

GREAT BRITAIN

GERMANY

TO AUSTRIA-HUNGARY AND THE BALKANS

FRANCE

TO THE OTTOMAN EMPIRE

TO LATIN AMERICA

TO AFRICA, ASIA AND AUSTRALIA

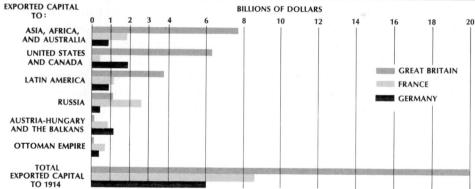

EXPORTED CAPITAL TO:

BILLIONS OF DOLLARS

0 1 2 3 4 5 6 8 10 12 14 16 18 20

ASIA, AFRICA, AND AUSTRALIA

UNITED STATES AND CANADA

LATIN AMERICA

RUSSIA

AUSTRIA-HUNGARY AND THE BALKANS

OTTOMAN EMPIRE

TOTAL EXPORTED CAPITAL TO 1914

GREAT BRITAIN

FRANCE

GERMANY

THE EXPORT OF EUROPEAN CAPITAL BEFORE 1914

Great Britain, France, and Germany were the major sources of capital for investment
before 1914, and this chart illustrates the proportions in which this capital went to
different parts of the world. From Great Britain the greatest sums by far went to the
United States, South America, South Africa, and Australia — territories ruled by
Europeans and developing fast; little went to the new colonial possessions acquired
at the end of the nineteenth century in the last imperialist wave. French and
German investors were more active in eastern and southeastern Europe.

culture. Japan and Russia were both undergoing industrialization in a much greater measure than China or India in 1914, but Russia, though European, Christian, and imperialist, could certainly not be regarded as a developed nation in economic or social terms. Nor could one be found in Balkan Europe. Yet clearly in 1914 a group of advanced countries with highly developed social and economic structures formed the core of an Atlantic community which was increasingly the world's main producer and consumer. The rest of the world was dominated economically by the influence of this central bloc.

London was the world's financial center, providing the services which sustained the flow of world trade. A huge amount of the world's business was transacted by means of the sterling bill of exchange; it rested in turn upon the international gold standard which ensured fairly steady relationships among the main currencies. World travel was possible with a bag of gold sovereigns, five-dollar pieces, gold francs, or any other major medium of exchange without any doubts about their acceptability. Usually not even a passport was needed.

England was in another sense the center of the economic world; although the United States and Germany had overtaken her in gross output by 1914, she was still the preeminent trading nation. The bulk of the world's shipping and carrying trade was in British hands. She was also the greatest importing and exporting nation and the only one which sent the major portion of its manufactures to non-European nations. She was still the largest exporter of capital and drew a huge income from her overseas investments, notably those in the United States and South America.

The world economy worked on a roughly triangular system of international exchange. The British bought goods, manufactured and otherwise, from Europe and paid for them with their own manufactures, cash, and overseas produce. To the rest of the world they exported manufactures, capital, and services, taking in return food, raw materials, and cash. This complex system illustrates that Europe's economic relationship with the rest of the world was far from being a simple exchange of manufactures for raw materials. And there was of course always the great exception of the United States, little involved in export and still a capital importer, but gradually commanding a greater and greater share of its own domestic market for manufactured goods.

Most British economists still believed in 1914 that the prosperity which this system enjoyed and the increasing wealth which it made possible demonstrated the truth of free trade doctrines. Great Britain's own wealth had grown most rapidly in the heyday of such ideas. By 1800 a majority of British exports were already going outside Europe, and the greatest expansion of trade in India and China still lay ahead. Understandably, British imperial policy was directed not to the potentially embarrassing acquisition of new colonies but to the penetration of closed trading areas, for that was where prosperity was deemed to lie. As the outstanding example of this policy, the Opium Wars of 1840 and 1841 opened five Chinese ports to trade and gave Great Britain a base at Hong Kong for her commercial activities.

The high tide of free trade ideas came in the middle of the nineteenth century when for a couple of decades more governments seemed willing to act upon them than ever before or after. The British retained their comparative advantage during this phase, but the climate changed in the 1870s and 1880s. The onset of a worldwide recession of economic activity and falling prices meant that by 1900 Great Britain was again the only major nation without protective tariffs, and even some British economists were beginning to question the old free trade dogmas as competition from Germany grew fiercer and more alarming.

Nevertheless, the economic world of 1914 must seem by comparison with today's to be one of astonishing freedom. A long peace had provided the soil in which trading connections could be built. Stable currencies assured great flexibility to a world price system; exchange control existed nowhere in the world. Russia and China were as completely integrated into this market as any other country. Freight and insurance rates had grown cheaper and cheaper. Food prices had shown a long-term decline and wages a long-term rise. Interest rates and taxation were low. It seemed as if a capitalist paradise might be achievable.

As this system had grown to incorporate Asia and Africa, it too had spread ideas and techniques originally European but soon acclimatized elsewhere. Joint stock companies, banks, and commodity and stock exchanges spread around the world and began to displace traditional structures of commerce. The building of docks and railways, the infrastructures of world trade, together with the beginnings of local industry created in some places the rudiments of an industrial proletariat. Sometimes integration with the international market had bad effects on local economies; the cultivation of indigo, for example, more or less collapsed in India when synthetic dyes became available in Germany and Great Britain. Isolation, first disturbed by explorers, missionaries, and soldiers, was destroyed by the arrival of the telegraph and the railway; in the twentieth century the automobile, which had already appeared in Europe and the United States, would take this further.

Economic integration thus brings the story back to cultural diffusion and cannot be separated from it. The formal instruments of missionary religion, educational institutions, and government policy had as much indirect as direct importance. European languages, when used officially, carried with them European concepts and opened to educated elites in non-European countries the heritage of both Christian civilization and secular and "enlightened" European culture. Missionaries meanwhile provoked the natives' criticism of their own traditional society. In some colonies too they criticized the colonial regime because its performance did not match up to the pretensions of the culture it imposed.

It can now be seen how important such unintended, ambiguous effects were. The common urge to imitate might express itself ludicrously in the adoption of European dress or much more importantly in the conclusion drawn by many that to resist Europe's influence it was necessary to adopt her ways. Almost everywhere radicals and reformers advocated Europeanization. The most dramatic effects were to be seen in Asia and have not yet ceased; the ideas of 1789 and 1848 still have power in the non-European world.

This is an extraordinary outcome too often taken for granted and overlooked. Of its full unraveling 1900 provides only a vantage point, not the end of the story. The Japanese are a gifted people who have inherited exquisite artistic traditions, yet they have adopted not only Western industrialism (which is perhaps explicable) but Western art forms, Western dress, and even Western drink in preference to their own. The Chinese nowadays revere the name of a German Jew who articulated a system of thought rooted in nineteenth-century German philosophy and English social and economic facts. This suggests another curious fact: the balance sheet of cultural influence is overwhelmingly one-sided. The world gave back to Europe occasional fashions but no idea or institution of comparable effect to those she gave to the world. The teaching of the European Marx is a force throughout Asia today; the last non-European whose words had any comparable authority in Europe was Jesus Christ. For centuries, thousands of European ships sailed to Calicut, Nagasaki, Canton. During those same centuries not one Indian, Japanese, or Chinese ship ever docked at Tilbury, Genoa, or Amsterdam.

EUROPEAN NATIONS OVERSEAS

Outside the United States, the two most important groups of European communities overseas are in Latin America and in the former British colonies of white settlement which, though formally subject to London's direct rule for much of the nineteenth century, were in fact oddly hybrid—not quite independent nations but not colonies either. All of them continued to be shaped by the ideas and institutions of the Europeans who first settled in them and laid their foundations. Of course there were other formative influences. Each nation had its frontiers, each had to face special environmental challenges. But so had the settlers of eastern Europe in the Middle Ages. What they had in common were ways of dealing with these challenges, institutions which different frontiers would reshape in different ways. They were all formally Christian (no one ever settled new lands in the name of atheism until the twentieth century), all regulated their affairs by European systems of law, and all had access to the great cultures of Europe with which they shared their languages.

Emigration

Both groups were fed during the nineteenth century by the same great diaspora of European peoples which also fed the United States, and its scale does much to justify the name which has been given to this era of European demography: the Great Resettlement. Before 1800 the only big emigrations had been from the British Isles. Since that date something like 60 million Europeans have settled overseas, and this tide began to flow strongly (at

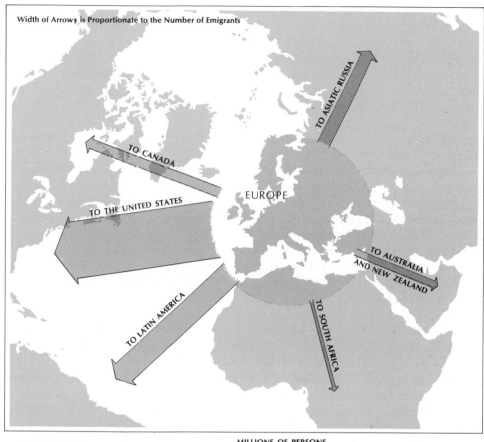

Width of Arrows is Proportionate to the Number of Emigrants

TO ASIATIC RUSSIA

TO CANADA

TO THE UNITED STATES

EUROPE

TO AUSTRALIA AND NEW ZEALAND

TO LATIN AMERICA

TO SOUTH AFRICA

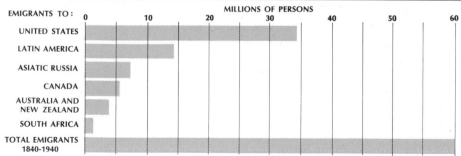

EMIGRANTS TO:	MILLIONS OF PERSONS
	0 10 20 30 40 50 60
UNITED STATES	
LATIN AMERICA	
ASIATIC RUSSIA	
CANADA	
AUSTRALIA AND NEW ZEALAND	
SOUTH AFRICA	
TOTAL EMIGRANTS 1840-1940	

MIGRATION FROM EUROPE 1840–1940
The pattern of emigration which established the location of European stocks
familiar today.

over 100,000 a year) for the first time in the 1830s. Most of it in the nineteenth century went to North America; Latin America (especially Argentina
and Brazil), Australia, and South Africa were the next most popular goals. At
the same time a concealed emigration was also occurring across land inside
Russia; peasants and political deportees both played a part in this eastward

movement. The peak of overseas emigration actually came on the eve of World War I, in 1913, when over 1.5 million people left Europe; over a third of these were Italians, nearly 400,000 were British, and just over 200,000 were Spanish. Fifty years earlier Italians had figured only to a minor degree; Germans and Scandinavians had loomed much larger. All the time the British Isles contributed a steady flow; 8.5 million Britons went overseas between 1880 and 1910. The Italian figure for this period was just over 6 million.

Most British emigrants went to the United States (about 65 percent of those who left between 1815 and 1900), but large numbers went also to the self-governing colonies. This changed after 1900 and by 1914 more than half went to the latter. Italians and Spaniards went to South America in great numbers though Italians preferred the United States. That country remained the major receiving nation: between 1820 and 1950 it benefited by the arrival of over 33 million Europeans.

The explanation of this striking demographic evolution is not hard to find. Rising numbers in Europe always pressed upon economic possibilities, as the discovery of the phenomenon of unemployment (a word invented in the nineteenth century) shows. In the last decades of the century European farmers were hard hit by overseas competition. There were better opportunities in other lands and also cheap means of getting there. The steamship and railroad changed demographic history after 1880. They permitted much greater local mobility too, and temporary migration and movement inside Europe increased. Great Britain exported great numbers of Irish peasants, Welsh miners and steelworkers, and English farmers; at the end of the century she received an influx of Jews from eastern Europe who long remained a distinguishable element in British society. Labor had always moved across border districts in Europe, but now Poles went to France to work in coal mines and Italian waiters and ice cream vendors became part of British folklore. North Africa was also changed by emigration from Europe. Italians, Spaniards, and Frenchmen were drawn there to settle or trade in the coastal cities and thus created a new society with its own distinct interests.

It was not only Europeans who moved. Chinese and Japanese flocked to the Pacific coast of North America, and the first act to restrict this was passed in 1882 (frightened Australians meanwhile sought to preserve a "White Australia" by limiting immigration by ethnic criteria). The British empire provided a framework within which Indians spread around the world. Chinese migrants moved down into southeast Asia, Japanese to Latin America. But these movements were subordinate to the major phenomenon of the nineteenth century, the last great *Völkerwanderung* of the European peoples.

Latin America

Southern Europeans could find much that was familiar in Latin America. There was a Catholic framework to life and Latin languages and social customs. Law and some political institutions had persisted through an era of political upheaval at the beginning of the nineteenth century when events in Europe had led to a crisis which ended Spanish and Portuguese colonial rule.

The imperial decline in Latin America was not for want of effort, at least on the part of Spain. In contrast to the British in North America, the Spanish government had carried out sweeping reforms in the eighteenth century. Though it took some decades to become apparent, a new era of imperial development had begun when the Bourbons replaced the last Habsburg on the Spanish throne in 1701. When changes came, they led first to reorganization and then to "enlightened" reform. The two viceroyalties of 1700 became four, new ones appearing in New Granada (Panama and the area covered by Ecuador, Colombia, and Venezuela) and La Plata, which ran from the mouth of that river across the continent to the border of Peru. Structural rationalization was followed by relaxation of the closed commercial system; this stimulated the economy in both the colonies and those parts of Spain (notably the Mediterranean ports) which benefited from the ending of Seville's monopoly of colonial trade.

Nonetheless these healthy tendencies were offset by weaknesses which they could not touch. Occasional disturbances did not amount to a revolutionary danger, but some outbreaks (especially in Peru in 1780) required special military efforts to contain them. One response was to raise levies of colonial militia, a double-edged solution which provided the creoles with military training. The deepest division in Spanish colonial society was between the Indians and the colonists of Spanish descent, but this did not have the immediate political importance of the rift between creoles and peninsulares. It had not narrowed but widened with the passage of time. Resentful of their exclusion from high office, the creoles noted with attention the success of the British colonists of North America in shaking off imperial rule. At first, too, the French Revolution suggested possibilities rather than dangers in resistance. One of those it inspired was the Venezuelan creole Francisco de Miranda, who went to seek the support of European powers for the liberation of the Spanish empire.

As these events unrolled, the position of the Spanish government grew more embarrassed. In 1790 a quarrel with Great Britain led at last to Spain's surrender of the remnants of her old claim to sovereignty throughout the Americas. Then came wars, first with France, then with Great Britain (twice), and finally (in fact though not in law) with France again during the Napoleonic invasion. These wars not only cost her Santo Domingo, Trinidad, and Louisiana but also her dynasty, which was forced to abdicate by Napoleon in 1808. Spanish sea power had already been destroyed at Trafalgar, and soon Spain herself was engulfed by French invasion. The creoles decided the time had come to break loose and in 1810 the wars of independence began.

The creoles were not at first successful, and in Mexico they found that they had a racial war on their hands when the Indians took the opportunity to turn on all whites. But the Spanish government could not muster sufficient strength to crush them. Since British sea power guaranteed that no other conservative European state could step in to help Spain, a collection of

THE WESTERN HEMISPHERE 1784

republics emerged from the fragments of her former empire, most of them ruled by soldiers.

In Portuguese Brazil the story had gone differently. A French invasion of Portugal had in 1807 driven her prince regent and mad queen from Lisbon to Rio de Janeiro, which thus became the effective capital of the Portuguese empire. When the prince went back to Portugal as king in 1821, he left behind his son, who took the lead in resisting a attempt to reassert control by Lisbon and with relatively little fighting became in 1822 Pedro I, emperor of an independent Brazil.

No United States of Latin America was to emerge from the wars of independence. Although the great hero and leader of independence, Simón Bolívar, hoped for much from a congress of the new states which met in Panama in 1826, nothing came of it. The former British North American colonies, with many advantages absent in Latin America, had found it hard enough to unite. It is hardly surprising that the republics to the south could not achieve continental unity.

In any case the Latin Americans of the early nineteenth century faced no danger or opportunity which made unity desirable. Great Britain and the United States protected them against the outside world. Their domestic problems of postcolonial evolution were far greater than had been anticipated and were unlikely to be tackled more successfully by the creation of an artificial union. Indeed, as in Africa a century and a half later, the removal of colonial rule revealed that geography and community did not always make for political units which corresponded to the old colonial administrative divisions. The huge, thinly populated states which emerged from the wars of independence were constantly in danger of fragmentation as the urban minorities who had guided the independence movement found it impossible to control their followers. Some did break up. There were racial problems too, and the social inequalities they spawned were not removed by independence. Not every country experienced the same difficulties. In Argentina, for example, there were few Indians, and Argentine society was celebrated by the end of the century for the extent to which it resembled Europe. At the other extreme, more than half of Brazil's population was black and at the time of independence much of it was still enslaved; slavery was not totally abolished there until 1888.

The new states could not draw on any tradition of self-government to deal with their problems, for the absolutist Spanish administrations had not permitted representative institutions. The leaders of the republics usually looked to the French Revolution for their political principles, but these were advanced ideas for states whose tiny elites did not even agree about accepted practice. Revolutionary principles could hardly produce a framework of mutual tolerance; worse still, they quickly brought the Catholic church into politics, a development which was perhaps in the long run inevitable given its huge power and wealth as a landowner but unfortunate in adding anticlericalism to the woes of the continent. During most of the century each republic found that its affairs tended to drift into the hands of caudillos, military adventurers and their cliques who controlled armed forces sufficient to give them power until even stronger rivals came along.

The cross currents of civil war and wars between Latin American states — some very bloody — led by 1900 to a map which is substantially that of today. Mexico had lost land in the north to the United States. Four mainland Central American republics had appeared and two island states, the Dominican Republic and Haiti. Cuba was on the point of achieving independence. To the south were ten independent states on the continental mainland. All of these countries were republican (Brazil having given up her monarchy in 1889), but they represented very different degrees of stability and constitutional propriety. In Mexico an Indian had become president to great effect in the 1850s, but everywhere there remained the social division between Indians and mestizos (those of mixed blood) on the one hand and those of European blood (much reinforced by large-scale immigration after

1870) on the other. The Latin American countries had contained about 19 million people in 1800; a century later they had 63 million.

This rise in population argues an increase in wealth. Most of the Latin American countries had important natural assets in one form or another, and these tended to become more valuable as Europe and the United States became more industrialized. Argentina had space and some of the finest pasture in the world; the invention of refrigerator ships in the 1880s made her England's butcher and later her grain grower as well. Chile had nitrates and Venezuela had oil; both would grow more important in the twentieth century. Brazil had coffee and Mexico oil. The list could be continued but would confirm that the growing wealth of Latin America came above all from primary produce. The capital to exploit this came from Europe and the United States and produced new ties between these European nations overseas and Europe herself.

Latin America's prosperity had two related drawbacks. One was that it did little to reduce the disparities of wealth to be found in these countries; indeed they may have increased. In consequence social (like racial) tensions remained. An apparently Europeanized urban elite enjoyed lives wholly different from those of the Indian and mestizo masses. This was accentuated by the second drawback, the dependence of Latin America on foreign capital. Not unreasonably, foreign investors sought security. They by no means always got it, but the search tended to divert some of their resources to the support of existing social and political authorities, who thus enhanced still further their own wealth. Soon after the turn of the century conditions resulting from this sort of thing would produce social revolution in Mexico.

Hemisphere relations

After the war with Mexico the relations of the United States with its neighbors had never been easy (nor are they today). Too many complicating factors have always affected them. The Monroe Doctrine expressed the basic wish of the United States to keep the hemisphere politically uninvolved with Europe. The first Pan-American Congress, organized by Washington in 1889, was another step in this direction. But economic links with Europe could not be cut off and European capital was put into both private investment and the public finances of Latin American states. Sometimes this created political tension, for the instability of some regimes led to defaulting or to a failure to make the payments due to creditors. When this happened, Europeans usually applied diplomatic pressure to collect debts, and occasionally armed intervention followed. In 1902, for example, Great Britain, Germany, and Italy all joined in a blockade of Venezuela to force payment of money owed to their subjects.

To Washington such intervention had come to seem all the more undesirable because during the nineteenth century the strategic situation which underlay the background of the Monroe Doctrine was slowly changing. Steamships and the growth of American interests in the Far East made the

United States much more sensitive to developments in the Caribbean and Central America, the zone where an interoceanic canal seemed more and more likely to be built. This helps to explain the greater heavy-handedness shown by the United States toward its neighbors in the early twentieth century. A brief war with Spain in 1898 had allowed Washington to assure Cuba's independence; one price exacted from the Cubans was the imposition of clauses in the new republic's constitution which ensured that it would remain a satellite of the United States. Next, the territory of the Panama Canal was obtained by intervention in the affairs of Colombia. The Venezuelan debt affair brought an even more remarkable assertion of American strength—a "corollary" proposed by President Roosevelt to the Monroe Doctrine. This was the announcement (almost at once given practical effect in the Dominican Republic) that the United States had a right of intervention in the affairs of any state in the Western hemisphere whose internal affairs were in such disorder that they might tempt European intervention. A later American president sent marines to Nicaragua in 1912 on this ground, and another occupied the Mexican port of Vera Cruz in 1914 as a way of coercing the Mexican government.

These unhappy events were symptomatic of the ambiguous standing of the Latin American states in relation to Europe. Rooted in her culture and tied to her by economics, they nonetheless were constrained to avoid political entanglement with her by their powerful neighbor to the north. Of course this did not mean that they did not stand, so far as Europeans were concerned, on the "white man's side," the great distinction more and more being drawn between those within the pale of European civilization and those outside it. When the European thought of Latin Americans, he thought of those of European descent, the urban, literate, privileged minority, not the majority, who were Indians and blacks.

The British dominions

At the end of the nineteenth century the British magazine *Punch* printed a patriotic cartoon in which the British lion looked approvingly at rows of little lion cubs, armed and uniformed, who represented the colonies. They stood for the contingents sent from other parts of the empire to fight for the British in a war they were then engaged upon in South Africa. But in 1800 no one would have expected a single colonial soldier to be available to the mother country a century later. The events of 1783 had burned deep into the consciousness of British statesmen. Colonies, they thought they had learned, were tricky things. They cost money, conferred few benefits, engaged the mother country in fruitless strife with other powers and native peoples, and in the end turned around and bit the hand that fed them. This distrust of colonial entanglements helped swing British imperial interest toward the East, to the possibilities of Asian trade; the absence there of complications caused by European settlers, and the confidence that in Eastern seas most problems could easily be met by the Royal Navy made this seem the attractive area for future overseas enterprise.

Broadly speaking, this thinking underlay official attitudes during the whole nineteenth century. It led to colonial policy which sought, above all else, economy and the avoidance of trouble. In Canada and Australia it produced the eventual uniting of the individual colonies which had appeared in their huge spaces into federal structures responsible for their own government. In 1867 the Dominion of Canada came into existence, and in 1901 there followed the Commonwealth of Australia. In both cases union was preceded by the grant of responsible government to the original colonies and in both there were special difficulties in unification. In Canada the outstanding one was the existence of a French Canadian community in the province of Quebec; in Australia it was the clash of interests between convicts (the last consignment was delivered in 1868) and settlers. Moreover each country was huge and thinly populated and would only gradually be pulled together by communications. The generation of a sense of nationality was slow because of this: the last spike was not driven on the transcontinental line of the Canadian Pacific Railway until 1885, and for a long time the use of different gauges in different states delayed transcontinental railway travel in Australia. In the end nationalism benefited from a growing awareness of potential external threats—United States economic strength and Asian immigration—and of course from bickering with the British.

New Zealand also achieved responsible government in the nineteenth century. This colony was acquired reluctantly. Europeans had settled there from the 1790s onward and had found a native people with an advanced and complex culture, the Maori, whom they set about corrupting. Missionaries followed and did their best to keep out settlers and traders, but they arrived just the same. When it seemed that a French entrepreneur was likely to establish a French interest, London at last gave way to the pressure of missionaries and some of the settlers and proclaimed British sovereignty in 1840. In 1856 the colony began to run its own affairs and only wars with the Maoris delayed the withdrawal of British soldiers until 1870. In the later years of the century the New Zealand government showed a remarkable independence of mind in the pursuit of radical social policies, and the colony achieved dominion status, that is, full self-government, in 1907.

That was the year after a colonial conference in London had decided that the name "dominion" should in the future be used for all the self-governing dependencies, which meant in effect the colonies of white settlement. One more remained to be given this status before 1914, the Union of South Africa, which came into existence in 1910. This was the end of a long and unhappy chapter—the unhappiest in the history of the British empire. Unfortunately it closed only to open another which now looks just as bleak.

South Africa

There were no British colonists in South Africa until after 1814, when Great Britain for strategical reasons retained Cape Colony, the former Dutch possession at the Cape of Good Hope. Soon some thousands of British set-

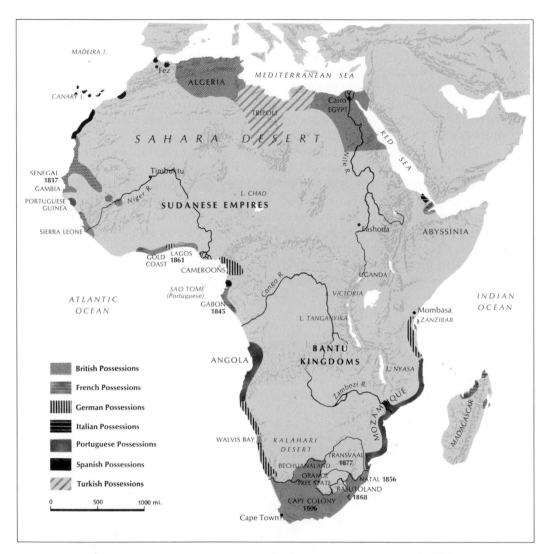

AFRICA IN 1885

Compare with the map on p. 733 to see how rapidly partition proceeded in the next twenty years.

tlers arrived. Though outnumbered by the Dutch, they had the backing of their government in introducing British habits and law and began whittling away the privileges of the Boers, as the Dutch farmers were called. The Boers were particularly irked by the replacement of their own officials by British who did not speak Dutch and by the limitations placed on their freedom to deal with native Africans as they wished. Their special indignation was aroused when, as a result of the abolition of slavery in British territory in 1833, some 35,000 blacks were freed with, it was said, inadequate compensation. Convinced that the British would not abandon policies that the Boers thought unduly favorable to the native African — and indeed this was a realistic view — they began an exodus from Cape Colony in 1835. Their migration north across the Orange River, known as the Great Trek, was of the first importance in forming the Boer consciousness. It was the beginning of a long period during which Anglo-Saxon and Boer struggled to live in Africa, sometimes apart, sometimes together, but always uncomfortably, their decisions dragging in their train the fate of the black African.

A Boer republic in Natal was soon made a British colony in order to protect the Africans, and another exodus of Boers took place, this time north of the Vaal River. This was the first extension of British territory in South Africa; the pattern was to be repeated. Besides humanitarianism, the British government and the British colonists on the spot were stirred by the need to establish good relations with the African peoples, who would otherwise (as the Zulus had already shown against the Boers) present a continuing security problem not unlike that posed by the Indians in the American northwest in the previous century. By mid-century two new Boer republics existed in

The Boer republics of South Africa had equipped themselves with artillery from France and Germany before the Anglo-Boer war broke out in 1899. As it proceeded they increasingly adopted guerrilla tactics and used these heavy weapons less and less. These Boers still wear uniforms, another indication that this picture was taken at an early stage of the war. *(South African Information Service, New York)*

the north, the Orange Free State and the Transvaal; to the south Natal and Cape Colony were under the British flag and governed by elected assemblies for which black men who met the required economic tests could vote. There were also native states under British protection; in one of these, Basutoland, Boers were actually under black jurisdiction, an especially galling subjection for them.

Happy relations were unlikely in these circumstances, and in any case London was often in disagreement with the colonists at the Cape, who had, after 1871, responsible government of their own. New facts arose too. The discovery of diamonds led the British to annex a piece of territory north of the Orange, which angered the Boers. British support for the Basutos, whom the Boers had defeated, was another irritant. Finally, the governor of Cape Colony committed an act of folly by annexing the Transvaal republic. After a successful Boer rising and the nasty defeat of a British force, London had the sense not to persist and restored independence to the Transvaal in 1881, but by then Boer distrust of British policy in South Africa was probably insurmountable.

Two further unanticipated changes would lead to war within twenty years. One was a small industrial revolution in the Transvaal. A gold strike there in 1886 brought a huge influx of miners and speculators, the involvement of outside financial interests in the affairs of South Africa, and the possibility that the Boer republic might develop sufficient financial resources to escape from the British suzerainty. The index of what happened was Johannesburg, which grew in a few years to a city of 100,000 – the only one of this size in Africa south of the Zambezi River. The second change was that other European powers were swallowing up large sections of Africa in the 1880s and 1890s and the British government reacted by stiffening in its determination that nothing must shake the British presence at the Cape. The general effect was to make it view with concern any possibility of the Transvaal's obtaining independent access to the Indian Ocean. The pressure of an oddly assorted crew of idealistic imperialists, Cape politicians, English demagogues, and shady financiers finally provoked a confrontation with the Boers in 1899 which ended in the outbreak of the Boer War.

The fighting amply sustained the highest traditions of the British army of Victorian times, both in the ineptness and incompetence shown by some of its higher commanders and the administrative services and in the gallantry displayed by regimental officers and their men in the face of a brave and well-armed enemy whom their training had not prepared them to meet. But of the outcome there could be no doubt. South Africa was isolated by British sea power; no other European nation could help the Boers, and it was only a matter of time before greatly superior numbers and resources were brought to bear upon them. This cost a great deal – over a quarter of a million soldiers were sent to South Africa – and aroused great bitterness in British domestic politics. Furthermore it did not present a very favorable picture to the outside world, which regarded the Boers as an oppressed nationality. So they were, but the nineteenth-century liberal obsession with nationality in this case as in others blinded observers to some of the shadows it cast.

Fortunately British statesmanship recovered itself sufficiently to make a generous peace in 1902 when the Boers had been beaten in the field. This was the end of the Boer republics, but concessions rapidly followed. By 1906 the Transvaal had its own government which the Boers soon controlled in spite of the large non-Boer population brought there by mining. Almost at once they began to legislate against Asian immigrants, mainly Indians. When in 1909 a draft constitution was agreed upon for the Union of South Africa, it provided for elected government but for each province to decide its own electoral regulations. In the Boer provinces the franchise was confined to white men.

When people spoke of a racial problem in South Africa at this time, they meant the problem of relations between the British and the Dutch, which seemed in urgent need of improvement. The defects of the settlement would take some time to appear. When they did, it would be not only because the historical sense of the Boer proved to be tougher than people had hoped but also because the transformation of South African society begun by the industrialization of Transvaal could not be halted.

All the other British white dominions were caught up in the world economy which Europe dominated. With the unrolling of the railroad across her plains, Canada became one of the great granaries of Europe. Australia and New Zealand first exploited their huge pastures to produce wool for which European factories were increasingly in the market, then with the invention of refrigeration they used them for meat and in the case of New Zealand for dairy produce as well. In this way these new nations found staples to sustain their economies. South Africa was different in that she revealed herself only gradually (as much later would Australia) as a producer of minerals. The beginning of this was the diamond industry, but the great step forward was the Transvaal gold discovery of the 1880s, which sucked in capital and expertise to make possible the eventual exploitation of other minerals. The return which South Africa provided was not merely in the profits of European companies and shareholders; there was also an augmentation of the world's gold supply which stimulated European commerce much as did the California discoveries of 1849.

The native peoples

The growth of humanitarian and missionary sentiment in England and the well-founded Colonial Office distrust of settler demands made it harder for the white dominions to forget the native populations than for Americans to sweep aside the Indian. In all these countries nineteenth-century society made its impact not upon ancient civilizations but on primitive societies, some Neolithic, some Paleolithic, even if they had access to gadgets from the white man's technology. The Canadian Indians and Eskimos were a smaller problem than the American Indian; they were fewer and offered no resistance comparable to the Plains Indians' efforts to keep their hunting grounds. The story in Australia was far bloodier. Settlement disrupted the hunting and gathering society of the aborigine, the uncomprehending brutality of white Australians antagonized the tribes and provoked them into violence, and new diseases cut fast into their numbers. The early decades of each Australian colony are stained by the blood of massacred aborigines and perhaps no other population inside former British territory underwent a fate so like that of the American Indian. The first white men in New Zealand gave guns to the Maoris, who employed them first on one another. Later came the wars with the British, which arose from the settlers' encroachment on Maori lands. At their conclusion the government took steps to safeguard tribal territories from further expropriation, but the introduction of English notions of individual ownership led to the disintegration of the tribal holdings by the end of the century. The Maoris, too, declined in numbers but not so considerably or irreversibly as the Australian aborigines.

As for Africa, the story is a mixed one. British protection enabled some native peoples to survive into the twentieth century living a life on their ancestral lands which changed only slowly. Others were driven off or exterminated. In all cases, though, the crux of the situation was that in Africa, as elsewhere, the fate of the native inhabitants was never in their own hands. They depended for their survival upon the local balance of governmental interest and benevolence, settler needs and traditions, economic opportunities and exigencies. Although in the short run they could sometimes present formidable military problems (as did the Zulus and Matabeles in Africa and the guerrilla warfare of the Maoris), they could not in the end generate from their own resources the means of effective resistance any more than the Aztecs had been able to resist Cortés. For non-European peoples to do that, they would have to Europeanize. The price of establishing the new European nations beyond the seas always turned out to be paid by the native inhabitant, often to the limit of his ability.

Yet this should not be quite the last word. There remains the problem of self-justification: Europeans witnessed these things happening and did not stop them. It is too simple to explain this by saying they were all bad, greedy men, and in any case there were humanitarians among them. The answer must lie somewhere in the European mentality. Though they might recognize that something damaging was happening to the native populations even when the white contact with them was benevolent in intention, Europeans could rarely understand the corrosive effect of their culture on established structures. And of course much native culture was simply savagery and the missionary confidence of the European was strong. He *knew* he was on the side of Progress and Improvement and might well still see himself as on the side of the Cross too. This confidence ran through every side of European expansion—the white settler colonies, the possessions directly ruled, and the arrangements made with dependent societies. The assurance of belonging to a higher civilization was not only a license for predatory habits, as Christianity had earlier been, but the nerve of a faith akin in many cases to that of crusaders. The certainty that they brought something better all too often blinded men to the consequences of substituting individual freehold for tribal rights and of turning the hunters and gatherers whose possessions were what they could carry about into wage earners.

IMPERIALISM AND IMPERIAL RULE

The ruling of alien peoples and other lands was the most striking evidence of European hegemony. In spite of the enormous argument about what imperialism was and is, it is helpful to confine the notion to such direct and formal overlordship. In this sense imperialism is not the manifestation of only one age, nor is it peculiar to Europe's relations with non-Europeans overseas, for it has been observable all through history. Nonetheless, the word came to be used much more in the nineteenth and twentieth centuries in association with Europe's expansion overseas because her direct domination over the rest of the world was then much more obvious than ever before. Down to about 1870 some of the old imperial powers continued to enlarge their empires impressively while others stood still or found theirs reduced. The second group included the Dutch, Spanish, and Portuguese. The still growing empires were the Russian, French, and British.

Russian imperialism had something in common both with the American experience of filling up a continent and dominating its neighbors and with the spread of British rule in India. The difference was that in one direction — the west — Russia faced matured, established European states where there was little hope of successful expansion. The same was only slightly less true of expansion into the Turkish territories of the Danubian regions because there the interests of other powers were likely to come into play against her in the end. Russia's main freedom of action lay to the south and east, and the first three-quarters of the century brought great successes in both these directions. A war against Persia (1826–1828) led to the establishment of Russian naval power in the Caspian Sea as well as territorial gains in Armenia. In Central Asia there was almost continuous advance into Turkestan and toward the oases of Bukhara and Khiva which culminated in the annexation of the whole of Transcaspia in 1881. In Siberia aggressive expansion was followed by the exaction of the left bank of the Amur River from China and the founding in 1860 of Vladivostok, the Far Eastern capital. Soon after, Russia liquidated her commitments in America by selling Alaska to the United States, thus indicating that she would be an Asian and Pacific power but probably not an American one.

British imperialism

The cases of France and Great Britain were different in that their imperialism took them overseas. The British empire expressed a maritime supremacy which was without serious challenge after 1805, the year of the annihilating victory won at Trafalgar over the combined French and Spanish fleets by the greatest of English admirals, Horatio Nelson. It was not that resources did not exist elsewhere which, had they been assembled, could have wrested this supremacy from Great Britain. But to do so would have demanded a huge effort. There were even advantages to other nations in having the world's greatest commercial power undertake the policing of the seas from which all trading ships could benefit.

Many of Great Britain's gains were made at the expense of France in the Revolutionary and Napoleonic wars, which were in this respect the final round of the great Anglo-French contest for colonial power in the eighteenth century. As in 1714 and 1763, Great Britain increased her empire in 1815. Besides Mauritius, Tobago, and St. Lucia, she kept also Malta, the Ionian islands, the Cape of Good Hope, and Ceylon.

These acquisitions illustrate the changed flavor of British imperialism, which now gave greater importance to the Eastern than to the Western hemisphere, as was soon shown in the growth of Asian trade. This rested upon naval bases and secure communications. Naval supremacy guarded the circulation of trade which gave the British colonies participation in the fastest growing commercial system of the age. The colonies grew in number in the teeth of a general prejudice against new possessions because they supported commerce by serving as naval bases. With the coming of steam, considerations of the convenience of coaling began to be taken into account in acquiring yet further stations.

The obvious new scale of the British empire was in part comparative; no other imperial structure appeared to rival it in extent, nor was any other European country founding new colonies of settlement—and the white colonies looked just the same color on the map and were formally as much a part of the empire as those with non-white populations, despite their growing command over their own affairs. New territories were added after 1815 by conquest and annexation as well as by settlement. In 1839 an internal upheaval in the Ottoman empire, to which Arabia belonged, gave the British the opportunity to take Aden, a base of strategic importance on the route to India. This was an example of a process which revealed more and more clearly as the decades went by the unique and central place which India had in the whole British imperial system. Both strategically and commercially much of the rest of the empire existed by 1850 because of India.

The Raj

In 1784 the British government had moved nearer to assuming direct responsibility for the affairs of the East India Company by the institution of dual control which shared the government of the subcontinent between the two. It had then also taken steps to resist any further acquisition of Indian territory in line with the prevailing view that new governmental responsibility was to be avoided. Yet there was a continuing problem: through its management of revenue the company inevitably became entangled in Indian administration and native politics. This made it more important still to prevent excesses by its individual officers, such as had been tolerable in the early days of private trading. Slowly it dawned on British politicians that London had a responsibility for the good government of Indians. A notion of trusteeship began to emerge.

The British government set the terms on which the company's charter was periodically renewed. In 1813 the renewal made London's control tighter and also abolished the company's monopoly of trade with India. The wars with France had led to the gradual extension of British power over southern India through annexation and the negotiation of treaties with native rulers which secured control of their foreign policy. By 1833, when the company's charter was again renewed, the only important block of territory not ruled directly or indirectly by the company was in the northwest. The annexation of the Punjab and Sind followed in the 1840s, and with British paramountcy established in Kashmir, British India had filled up virtually the whole geographical unity of the subcontinent.

The company had ceased to be a commercial organization and had become a government, but one whose powers were checked more and more by London. The 1833 charter took away its trading functions (not only in India but in China too); in sympathy with current thinking, Asian commerce was henceforth to be conducted on a free trade basis and the company confined to an administrative role. The way was open to the consummation of many real and symbolic breaks with India's past and the final incorporation of the subcontinent in a modernizing world. It was symbolic that the name of the Mogul emperor was removed from the coinage, but more than symbolic that Persian ceased to be the legal language of record and justice. The advance of English as the official language disturbed the balance of forces between Indian communities. Anglicized Hindus would do better than less enterprising Muslims. In a subcontinent divided in so many ways, the adoption of English as the lingua franca of administration was complemented by the important decision to provide primary education in English.

At the same time successive governors general exercised an enlightened despotism which pressed forward with material and institutional improvements. Roads and canals were built and in 1853 India's first railway. The government introduced legal codes. A college was established to train English officials for the company's service. The first three universities in India were founded in 1857 and were based on academic institutions in existence long before this. Much of the transformation India underwent arose from the increasing freedom of operation granted to nongovernmental agencies. Missionaries were at work from 1813 onward and their arrival gradually built up another constituency in England with a stake in what happened in India.

The coming of the steamship also brought India nearer to England. More Englishmen began to live in India and make their careers there. This gradually transformed the nature of the British presence. The comparatively few officers of the eighteenth-century company had been content to live the lives of exiles, seeking rewards in their commercial opportunities and relaxation in a social life closely integrated with that of the Indians. They often lived much in the style of Indian gentlemen, some of them taking to Indian dress and food, some to Indian wives and concubines. In the nineteenth century reform-minded officials intent on the eradication of the backward and barbaric in native practice (and infanticide and suttee were good cause for concern), missionaries with a creed to preach which was corrosive of the whole structure of Hindu society, and especially the Englishwomen who arrived to make permanent homes in India for two and three years at a time all radically changed the temper of the British community. While govern-

The mingling of East and West. In the late eighteenth century an Indian painted this picture of a British officer being carried, Indian-style, in state on an elephant. His ladies, presumably, are in the litter in the foreground. *(Victoria and Albert Museum)*

ment was offending powerful interests by its legislation and more and more confining the educated Indian to the lower ranks of the administration, individual Englishmen were thus reducing their social contacts with Indians and withdrawing into an enclosed, but conspicuously privileged, life of their own. They grew consciously more alien from those they ruled. In essence this change increased the British sense of superiority and sanctioned the ruling of Indians as cultural and moral inferiors.

Earlier conquerors had been absorbed by Indian society in greater or lesser measure; the Victorian Englishman and Englishwoman, thanks to a modern technology which constantly renewed their contacts with the homeland and their complete confidence in their intellectual and religious superiority, remained immune and increasingly aloof. Yet they could not be quite untouched by India, as many legacies to the English language and dinner table still testify. They created a society that was neither Indian nor wholly English; in the nineteenth century an Anglo-Indian was an Englishman who made his career in India, not a person of mixed blood, and the term indicated a cultural and social distinctiveness

The isolation of Anglo-Indian society was made virtually absolute by the appalling damage done to British confidence by the rebellions of 1857 called the Indian Mutiny. Essentially, this was a chain reaction of outbreaks initiated by a mutiny of sepoys in Bengal who feared the polluting effect of using a new type of cartridge greased with tallow. The facts are unclear; it is likely that the fat of both cows and pigs was used, but whichever was, both Hindus and Muslims were outraged. This detail is significant. Much of the revolt was the spontaneous and reactionary response of traditional society to innovation and modernization. Reinforcing popular sentiment were the irritations of native rulers, both Muslim and Hindu, who regretted the loss of their privileges and thought that the chance might have come to recover their independence—the British were after all very few. The response of those few was prompt and ruthless. With the help of loyal Indian soldiers they crushed the rebellions, but not before there had been some massacres of British captives and three columns had been sent to relieve Lucknow, where the most important British force in rebel territory held out under siege for several months.

The Mutiny and its suppression were disasters for British India though not quite unmitigated ones. It did not much matter that the British at last formally abolished the Mogul empire (because the Delhi mutineers had proclaimed the emperor their leader). Nor was there, as later Indian nationalists would suggest, a crushing of a national liberation movement whose end was a tragedy for India. Like many episodes that have contributed to the making of nations, the Mutiny became a myth and an inspiration; what it was later believed to have been was more important that what it actually was, a jumble of essentially reactionary protests. Its really disastrous effect lay in the wound it gave to British good will and confidence. Whatever the expressed intentions of imperial policy, the consciousness of the British in India after the Mutiny was suffused by the memory that Indians had once proved almost fatally untrustworthy. Among Anglo-Indians as well as Indians the mythical importance of what had happened grew with time. The atrocities actually committed were bad enough, but imaginary ones were alleged as grounds for a policy of repression and social exclusiveness. Immediately and institutionally, the Mutiny closed an epoch because it brought to an end the rule of the East India Company. The governor general now became the queen's viceroy, responsible to a British cabinet minister. This structure would provide the framework of the British Raj for the whole of its life.

The Mutiny changed Indian history but perhaps only by thrusting it more firmly in a direction to which it already tended. Equally revolutionary for India though much more gradual in its effects was the nineteenth-century flowering of the British economic connection. Commerce was the root of the British presence in the subcontinent and continued to shape its destiny to the very end. The first major development occurred when India became the essential base for the China trade whose greatest expansion came in the 1830s and 1840s when for a number of reasons access to China became much easier. At about the same time there was a rapid rise in British exports to India, notably of textiles, so that by the time of the Mutiny many more Englishmen and English firms were involved in Indian commerce than had ever been under the company.

Anglo-Indian trade was now locked into the general expansion of British manufacturing and world commerce. The opening of the Suez Canal in 1869 brought down the costs of shipping goods to Asia by a huge factor, and the volume of British trade with India more than quadrupled over the next three decades. The effects were felt not only in Great Britain; in India a check was imposed on an industrialization which might have gone ahead more rapidly without British competition. Paradoxically the growth of trade thus delayed India's modernization and alienation from her past. But there were other forces at work which pointed toward the future and influenced especially the attitudes of Indian elites; by the end of the century the framework provided by the Raj and the stimulus of the cultural influences it permitted had already made impossible the survival of a totally unmodernized India.

The French empire

By 1870 the French had made substantial additions to the empire they had been left with in 1815. They did not lose sight of France's interests elsewhere (in West Africa and the South Pacific, for example), but the major expression of a reviving French imperialism came in Algeria, whose conquest began uncertainly in 1830. A series of wars with both the inhabitants of Algeria and the sultan of Morocco followed, and by 1870 the French controlled most of the country. They then turned their attention to Tunis, which accepted a French protectorate in 1881. Large numbers of Europeans settled in both countries, coming not only from France but also from Italy and later Spain. This built up substantial non-native populations which were to complicate the story of French rule. The day was past when the African Algerian could be exterminated or all but exterminated, like the Aztec, American Indian, or Australian aborigine. His society in any case was more resistant, formed in the crucible of an Islamic civilization which had successfully contested Europe's. Nonetheless he suffered, particularly from the introduction of land laws which broke up traditional usages and impoverished the peasant by exposing him to the full blast of market economics.

The whole of North Africa was in a measure open to European imperialism because of the decay of the Ottoman sultan's formal overlordship. All around the southern and eastern Mediterranean coasts the possibility was posed of a Turkish partition. French interest in the area was natural; it went back to a great extension of the country's Levant trade in the eighteenth century and Bonaparte's expedition to Egypt in 1798. The latter had detonated the national awakening of Egypt and led to the emergence there of the first great figure of nationalism outside the European world, Mehemet Ali, pasha of Egypt. Called upon by the sultan for help against the Greek revolution, Mehemet Ali subsequently attempted to seize Syria as his reward. This threat to the Ottoman empire provoked an international crisis in the 1830s, in which the French took his side. They were not successful, but thereafter French policy continued to interest itself in the Levant and Syria, an interest which was eventually to bear fruit in the twentieth century.

Late nineteenth-century imperialism

The feeling that Great Britain and France had made good use of their opportunities in the early part of the nineteenth century was no doubt one of the sentiments inspiring other powers to try to follow them from 1870 onward. But this hardly explains the extraordinary suddenness and vigor of what has sometimes been called the "imperialist wave" of the late nineteenth century. Between 1870 and 1914 European powers divided up the continent of Africa so that no part of it remained independent except Ethiopia and Liberia, a West African state established in 1847 by emancipated slaves. In the same period China lost much more of her empire, was forced to lease or concede ports or special areas in them to European administration, and surrendered to foreigners the control of her own finances. Of the other Asian states only Siam and Japan kept any real independence, and the United States established itself in the Far East by taking the Philippine Islands from Spain. The Ottoman empire lost control of even more of its lands and Persia was demarcated into spheres of influence by two imperial powers. Outside Antarctica and the Arctic, there remained by 1914 less than a fifth of the world's land surface which was not under a European flag or that of a country of European settlement, and of this small fraction only Japan, Ethiopia, and Siam enjoyed real autonomy.

Clearly a part of the explanation is the sheer momentum of accumulated forces; European hegemony became more and more irresistible as it built upon its own strength. The theory and ideology of imperialism were in a measure rationalizations of the huge power the European world suddenly found in its possession. For example, as medicine began to master tropical infection and steam provided quicker transport, it became easier to establish permanent bases in Africa and to penetrate the interior; the Dark Continent had long been of interest but its exploitation began to be feasible for the first time in the 1870s. Thus technical and scientific developments made possible and attractive an extension of European rule which could promote and protect trade and investment.

The hopes such possibilities aroused were often ill founded and disappointed in the event. Whatever the appeal of "underdeveloped estates" in Africa (as one British statesman liked to put it) or the supposedly vast market for consumer goods constituted by the penniless millions of China, industrial countries still found their best customers and trading partners in other industrial countries, and existing colonies or former ones were always more attractive for overseas capital investment than new ones. By far the greatest part of British investment abroad, for example, went to the United States and South America; French money preferred Russia to Africa, and German money, Turkey.

Economic expectation nevertheless excited many individuals who introduced into the imperial expansion of this period a random factor which accounts for much of the difficulty of generalizing about it. Explorers, traders, and adventurers—often made into popular heroes—took steps which occasionally led willing or unwilling governments to new extensions of territory.

One of the most famous meetings of the nineteenth century. The Welsh journalist Stanley, engaged by an American newspaper to find the celebrated missionary Dr. Livingstone, comes upon him at Ujiji in October 1871. It was then, allegedly, that the famous words were spoken: "Dr. Livingstone, I presume?" *(The Mansell Collection)*

The most active phase of European imperialism coincided with a new popular participation in public affairs. By voting or cheering in the streets the masses were more and more involved in the political process at a time when imperialism was seen as a projection of national rivalries. A new mass press often pandered to this or stimulated interest in imperial advance by focusing attention on heroic deeds of exploration or colonial warfare. All sorts of social dissatisfactions at home might be soothed by contemplating the expanding rule of the flag over new areas, even though statesmen knew that nothing was likely to be forthcoming except expense.

A final complication is the role of idealism, which undoubtedly inspired some imperialists and salved the consciences of many more. To rule others for their good was a duty to men who believed that they alone possessed true civilization. In countries such as India or French Africa, governments, missionaries, and businessmen tried to bring the blessings of railways, Western education, hospitals, law and order to colonial territories which were assumed to be governed for their own good as much as for that of the imperial power. Some of the British in India saw themselves as their classical education had taught them to admire the Romans, as exiles in alien lands, resigned to hardship and loneliness in order to bring peace to the warring and law to peoples without it. Kipling did not urge Americans to pick up the White Man's Booty but the White Man's Burden, for civilization was seen as a precious gift justifying self-sacrificial labors to convey it to others.

All these elements were tangled together in the imperialist wave of the late nineteenth century and further complicated the story of international relations, but two continuing themes were especially important. One reflected Great Britain's world-wide imperial power; she had possessions everywhere and therefore almost every other imperialist nation quarreled with her at one time or another. The center of her concerns was India; this was shown by both her acquisition of African territory to safeguard the Cape and Suez routes and her tendency to show alarm over dangers to the lands on India's borders. Between 1856 and 1914 the only occasions when crises over non-European issues made war seem possible were when Russian power threatened to predominate in Afghanistan and when the French tried to establish themselves on the upper Nile. For much of the rest of the period British relations with France and Russia turned on the issues of French penetration of the Sudan and Indochina and Russian influence in Persia.

These facts indicate the second continuing theme, and it is a negative one. When the great war broke out in 1914, Great Britain, Russia, and France, long thought colonial rivals, would be on the same side; it was not overseas colonial rivalry which brought about war. Though the nations of Europe quarreled about what happened overseas for forty years or so and the United States went to war with one of them, the partition of the non-European world was achieved with amazing ease and without war. Only Morocco once presented a real danger, and here the issue was not really influence on the spot but whether Germany could bully France without fear of her being supported by others. Indeed quarrels over non-European affairs were a positive distraction from the more dangerous rivalries within Europe. Such quarrels did, however, have their own momentum. When one power got a concession or a colony, it almost always spurred on another to catch up.

The partition of Africa

The results of colonial rivalry were most striking in Africa. By 1870 the activities of explorers, missionaries, and campaigners against slavery had prepared the public to see the extension of European rule there as a spreading of enlightenment and humanitarianism—the blessings of civilization. Centuries of experience on the African coasts had revealed that desirable products were available in the interior. At the Cape there were white communities with a disposition to push farther inland. This explosive mixture was set off in 1881 when the British sent a force to Egypt to secure that country's government against a nationalist revolution which seemed to pose a threat to the Suez Canal. Thus European culture—for it was the source of the Egyptian nationalists' ideas—touched off another stage in the decline of the Ottoman empire (of which Egypt was still a part) and began the "scramble for Africa."

The British government had hoped soon to withdraw its forces from Egypt. In 1914 they were still there; the British were by then virtually running the administration of the country and would soon, when Turkey went to war, proclaim a protectorate over it. To the south Anglo-Egyptian rule had pushed deep into the Sudan. To the west Turkey's provinces in Tripoli had

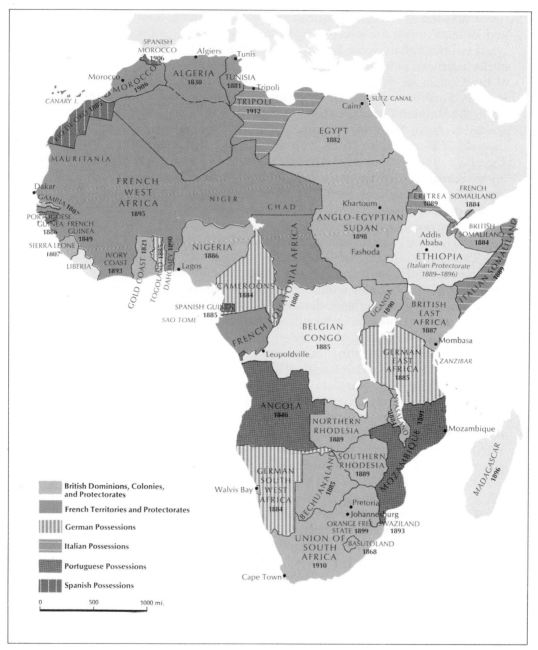

THE PARTITION OF AFRICA

been taken by the Italians, who felt unjustly squeezed out of Tunisia by the French protectorate there. Algeria belonged to France, and she enjoyed a virtually free hand in Morocco except where the Spanish were installed. Southward from Morocco to the Cape of Good Hope the coastline was entirely divided between the British, French, Germans, Spanish, Portuguese, and Belgians with the exception of the isolated state of Liberia. The empty wastes of the Sahara were French; so was the basin of the Senegal and much of the northern side of the Congo River. The Belgians were installed south of the Congo, in what was to prove one of Africa's richest mineral-bearing regions. Farther east British territories ran up from the Cape through Rhodesia to the Belgian Congo border. On the east coast they were cut off from the sea by German Southwest Africa and Portuguese Angola. From Mombasa, the port of British East Africa, a belt of British territory stretched up through Uganda to the borders of the Sudan and the headwaters of the Nile. Isolated by Somalia and Eritrea (in British, Italian, and French hands) was Ethiopia, the only other independent African country. The monarch of this ancient but Christian polity was the only non-European ruler of the nineteenth century to remove the threat of colonization by military success, which he did by wiping out an invading Italian army in 1896.

This colossal extension of European power transformed African history. The bargains of European negotiators, the accidents of discovery, and the convenience of colonial administrations determined the channels and the influences which brought modernization to that continent. The various colonial regimes operated in quite different ways. When they strove to improve the lot of their subjects, they did so with different cultural and economic impacts. Eventually distinctions were very remarkable between countries where, say, French administrative ideas or British judicial forms had long enough to take root. But everywhere Africans found their patterns of employment changed, could learn something of Europe's ways through European schools or service in colonial regiments, could see things to admire and things to hate in the governments which now came to regulate their lives. What they did not have the power to do was to resist by force, as the French suppression of Algerian revolt in 1871, the British destruction of the Zulu and Matabele, and worst of all the German massacre of the Herrero in South West Africa all showed. When these corroding influences had done their work, a later generation of Africans would find that their decisions too were being shaped by the formative years which followed the scramble. Even when (as came to be British practice) great emphasis was placed on rule through traditional native institutions, these had to work in a context which was new. Tribal and local unities would reassert themselves in the twentieth century but often only against the grain of what had been created by colonialism.

There were also to be results of European rule which took longer to become apparent. The suppression of intertribal warfare and the introduction of even elementary medical services permitted the African population in some areas to begin growing as it had not done before. As in America centuries earlier, the introduction of new crops made it possible to sustain greater numbers. In the end this would also affect the balance of races in the areas of white settlement.

Europe was less momentously changed by her African adventure. Some European countries—Russia, Austria, Hungary, the Netherlands, and Scandinavia—were not involved at all. To those that were, the easily exploitable wealth was clearly important; there was more than a touch of the conquistador about some of the late nineteenth-century adventurers. King Leopold's administration of the Belgian Congo and forced labor in Portuguese Africa were notorious examples, but there were other places where Europeans ruthlessly exploited or despoiled Africa's natural resources—human and material—in the interests of profit and with the connivance of imperial authorities. Some colonial powers recruited African soldiers, though only the French hoped to employ them to offset the weight of numbers in Europe. Others hoped for colonies of settlement even though the possibilities Africa presented for European residence were very mixed. The two large blocks of settlement were in French North Africa and in the south from which British colonists spread into East Africa and Rhodesia, but Portuguese Africa also had a significant number of settlers. The hopes entertained of Africa as an outlet for Italians, on the other hand, were disappointed, and German immigration was tiny and almost entirely temporary.

The Far East

Africa was the centerpiece of the new imperialism but far from the whole story. The Pacific was partitioned in a less conspicuous way but so as to leave no independent political unit among its island peoples. There was also a big expansion of British, French, and Russian territory in Asia. The French established themselves in Indochina, the British in Malaya and Burma, which they took to safeguard the approaches to India. Siam retained her independence because of the convenience to both powers of having a buffer between them. The British also asserted their superiority in Tibet, with the same consideration of Indian security in mind. Most of these areas, like many of the territories into which Russia was expanding overland, were formally under Chinese suzerainty, and their absorption is a part of the story of the crumbling of the Chinese empire, a story which paralleled, but with much greater importance for world history, the erosion of other empires by European power. At one moment it looked as if a partition of China might follow the partition of Africa, but events took a different course. The imperialist wave in the Pacific and Asia was in one other important way different from that in Africa: the United States was now a participant.

American imperialism

The general response of the citizens of the United States to overt imperialism has always been uneasy and distrustful. Even at its most blatant, the message of American imperialism has had to be muffled and muted in a way unnecessary in Europe. The creation of the United States had followed upon a successful rebellion against an imperial power. The Constitution contained no provision for the ruling of colonial territories, and Americans found it very difficult to determine the legal position of peoples who could not be envisaged as eventually moving toward full statehood. On the other hand,

The White Man's Burden

In 1899 the United States took the Philippines from Spain. The English poet Rudyard Kipling celebrated the occasion with a poem in which he coined a phrase that would live—"the White Man's Burden." The poem expressed perhaps better than any other piece of writing the mixture of conscientious responsibility, arrogance, and philanthropy which was the ideal of late nineteenth-century white imperialism.

Take up the White Man's Burden—
  Send forth the best ye breed—
Go bind your sons to exile
  to serve your captives' need;
To wait, in heavy harness,
  on fluttered folk and wild—
Your new-caught, sullen peoples,
  Half-devil and half-child.

Take up the White Man's burden—
  In patience to abide,
To veil the threat of terror
  And check the show of pride;
By open speech and simple,
  An hundred times made plain,
To seek another's profit,
  And work another's gain.

Take up the White Man's burden—
  The Savage wars of peace—
Fill full the mouth of Famine
  And bid the sickness cease;
And when your goal is nearest
  The end for others sought,
Watch Sloth and heathen Folly
  Bring all your hope to nought.

Man Makes His World =II

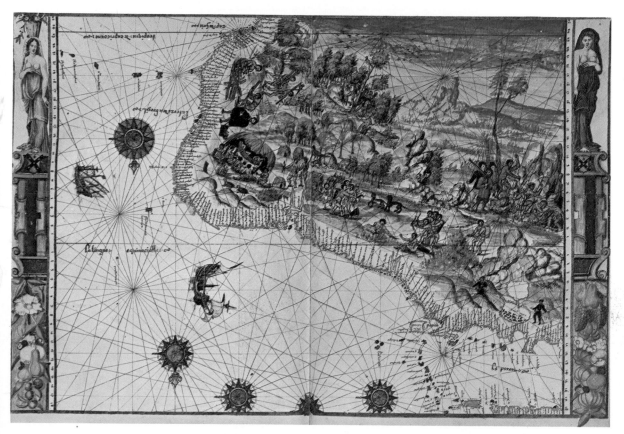

A sixteenth-century Spanish map of the northeastern coast of South America
(Courtesy of the Huntington Library, San Marino)

One of the most dramatic expressions of a new human power to control and manipulate the environment was the rapid extension and integration of geographical knowledge. With the exception of Australasia and the South Pacific, knowledge of the geographical structure of the globe was carried to an extraordinary degree of near-completeness within a very short time, a century or so after 1500. Maps of remarkable accuracy were soon being produced in great numbers and this knowledge was, thanks to the printing press, swiftly and widely diffused, even among those who would have no opportunity to make use of it. Those who did prospered from the new information. For all the perils with which seafaring continued to be fraught, the Europeans who undertook it after 1600 were immeasurably better prepared than their predecessors even a century before, if only because they more frequently knew where they *meant* to be going.

Alcazar, the palace of the Moorish kings at Seville; view of the Patio de Palacio Arabe *(Mas)*

The interplay of cultures and civilizations had never been totally blocked by obstacles of terrain and mentality, even if it had long been difficult. In some places, such as Islamic Spain, it was not only vigorous and fruitful in its day, but left great legacies to the future, in monuments, knowledge, custom, and behavior. Subsequently, interchange, even when it was uncomprehending, was to be much more frequent and more fruitful still. Printing, together with the great discoveries and explorations of the fifteenth and sixteenth centuries, opened the way to an age of world civilization. Unfortunately, it was a civilization which only too soon displayed the harshness implicit in its exploitative nature and, in the long run, a great potential for self-destruction and self-frustration.

The Western European civilization often showed itself to be a brutal one, with violence all too frequently justified by the assumption of moral superiority. Spanish treatment of the Indians soon became a byword for cruelty and oppressiveness, but it

**Spaniards burning Indians at the stake; an illustration from a book
by the French explorer Samuel de Champlain** *(The John Carter Brown Library, Brown University)*

Leonardo da Vinci's design for a cannon *(Reproduced by permission from Bern Dibner,*
Leonardo da Vinci—Machines and Weaponry)

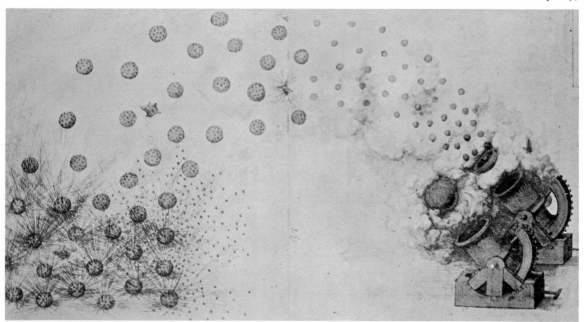

was only the opening of three centuries during which European peoples showed an uncompromisingly aggressive face toward other traditions. It was one part, though not the whole, of the story by which one civilization came to impose itself right round the world, and the attitudes it encouraged are still shaping events in the twentieth century. Perhaps the self-confidence of a culture which for so long proved itself successful in mastering nature could not allow itself a dangerous respect for other traditions.

Europe's technological supremacy was obvious in growing degree in the arms which gave her mastery over other traditions. Much ingenuity and industry went into the development of the possibilities of gunpowder, even if the result was usually seen in more orthodox weapons than the mortar designed by Leonardo da Vinci; it was intended to fire a shell which released many smaller shells which in their turn would fragment on impact. Into the perfection of new weapons went much of an accumulated intellectual and technological capital; this story seems dismally familiar. The cumulative effect was to add more and more to the advantages already enjoyed by Europeans as a result of their mental habits, their expectations and assumptions, and the ill-preparedness of other humans to meet the challenges they offered.

Dutch countryside of the seventeenth century; *The Avenue*, *Middelharnis* by **Hobbema**
(Reproduced by courtesy of the Trustees, The National Gallery, London)

A Pit Head, **anonymous eighteenth-century painting of the British School**
(The Walker Art Gallery, Liverpool)

Europe's growing wealth and power in the seventeenth century did not arise merely from the pillaging of other peoples but also from the exploiting of her own resources and the generation of capital from them. These resources were, economically speaking, for a long time overwhelmingly agricultural. Even though the great revolution of providing everyone with enough to eat did not take place until the nineteenth century, long before then a growing agricultural surplus was available to sustain the growing might of Europe. It became bigger thanks to the efforts of improving farmers and landlords. The Dutch were foremost among them, and the neat Dutch countryside of the seventeenth century provided testimony in its carefully dug and cleaned ditches, ordered fields, and closely tended orchards.

Other resources besides agricultural land were always and, from the seventeenth century increasingly, exploited by Europeans. Where minerals were easily found they provoked industrial growth and the beginnings of a process which in the end transformed the European landscape and the world's life. In the early days of that transformation there must have been a few scenes like the one above, in which the first simple machines of a new industrial age were set incongruously to work in a still rural setting. From these simple beginnings followed revolutionary changes and the creation of industrial regions dominated by the machine, its needs and its rhythms, in which nature—even human nature—seemed crushed almost beyond recognition.

From the feudal and dynastic polities of Western Europe grew nation states which were to dominate its history until the twentieth century and provide a model which in the end spread all over the world. To capacities for the organization of power which European governments inherited from the past they added commitment by their subjects. The new religion of patriotism was fostered by nothing so much as success in war. The process can be seen at work as early as the Middle Ages, and for centuries conflicts were plentiful enough. It became a commonplace of royal adulation to depict kings in attitudes of martial glory, sometimes amid evocations of a classical and mythological past. No king more assiduously cultivated such a view of his role than Louis XIV of France. In so doing, he in fact fed the new mythology of nationalism, for later Frenchmen would look back to his reign as one of national, not dynastic, splendor and glory.

Louis XIV in martial glory, from the Salon de la guerre, Versailles
(Lauros-Giraudon)

From the *Demolition of the Bastille* by **Herbert Robert, 1733–1808** (*Giraudon*)

As the sunshine of the revolution breaks through history's clouds, the people of Paris embark upon the systematic destruction of the Bastille, symbol of monarchical tyranny and the obscurantism of the past. After the events of 1776 and 1789 another myth was added to the myth of nationalism and powerfully reinforced it, that of democracy. It was not liberal in tendency. In retrospect one of the most striking facts about the great revolutions of modern times—French, Russian, and Chinese—is that they all strengthened, rather than weakened, the state as an institution. It was not quite the same on the other side of the Atlantic, where the young United States came into existence by throwing off a feeble state power exercised from three thousand miles away. For a long time the pressures upon the new nation were not sufficient to lead it to concede much to the national government. In the end, nevertheless, the central authority waxed in America too, and did so for similar reasons. The triumph of the federal government in 1865 was just such a triumph of democratic nationalism over local liberties as other revolutions had been.

If there was a modern turning point in the history of conflict, it came with the American Civil War, the first industrial and democratic war. Yet its lessons—of the ferocious economic and ideological demands of a new kind of war and of the huge killing power possessed by technologically advanced armies—went almost unnoticed in

The American Civil War: *Battle of the Crater* **by John Elder**
(Commonwealth Club; photo by Colonial Studios, Richmond)

Europe. Even in the United States where it was fought, as the painting shown here suggests, it was difficult not to think of the war in traditional terms of personal encounter and the morality of heroism. Yet wars between whole societies have become almost the normal pattern. Their increasing violence and growing cost are another aspect of what some see as the tendency for technical mastery to jump out of human control, inflicting in an age of nuclear and biological weapons perhaps irreparable damage.

In its self-consciousness and confidence the nineteenth century was the era in which European civilization reached its peak. The men of the Western world were then proudly and deeply aware that they stood at the spearhead of history. There could be few better illustrations of that fact, they thought, than the actual domination of physical nature which that civilization had achieved. In 1897, when the glorious reign of Queen Victoria came to a climax in the Diamond Jubilee (the celebration of her sixty years on the throne), a popular British illustrated magazine laid out on one of its pages the technological contrast between the beginning and the end of her reign. It had seen the transition from the early paddle-driven steamship, still carrying a full spread of sail, to the Cunarder; from the stagecoach of *The Pickwick Papers* to the railway train; from a London of gas lamps and unpaved streets to one of electrically-lit and asphalted highways along which bowled hansom cabs, lady bicyclists, and the first motorcars.

The sources of at least some of the world's new wealth lay in an injustice which took many forms, and it was not only the non-European world which suffered. In the great

"The Triumph of Steam and Electricity"; progress during the reign of Queen Victoria
(Guildhall Library, City of London)

new industrial and commercial cities of rich countries lay a pool of cheap labor which was often exploited. Argument has gone on ever since about whether this was an inevitable cost of industrialization, but about the wide spectrum of social evils it presented there is little disagreement. The age discovered a new fear in the phenomenon of unemployment, a terrible threat in an age without welfare support. It forced the acceptance of low wages in factories or the underpaid and grueling piecework of the "sweatshop" which was the last, tragic stage of the decline of a long-familiar figure, the domestic industrial worker.

A New York sweatshop at the turn of the century *(The Bettmann Archive)*

Shooting buffalo on the Kansas-Pacific Railroad, 1871 (*The Bettmann Archive*)

From the beginnings of agriculture man has destroyed the environment by exploiting and changing it; it has even been suggested that the pastoralists of Tassili did much to ruin their feeding grounds by destroying its forests. The pace with which damage was done nevertheless quickened notably with the coming of industrialism and the large demands it created and could supply. Destruction was another of the costs, long hidden, of mankind's growing mastery of the planet. Sometimes it was an unobserved by-product, such as the diseases taken to parts of the world where they had never been known, with terrible results. Sometimes it was a matter of careless greed, as forests were felled to provide cheap timber or strip mining disfigured the landscape and ruined the topsoil. But sometimes it was merely wanton. The beginnings of the near-extermination of the North American buffalo lay in a wasteful exploitation of their herds for food; there were so many that an animal was sometimes killed merely to provide one man's steak. But even this implausible justification and its minimal restraints vanished at times. The shooting of these noble beasts could become pure savagery.

For all the damage done by conscious exploitation, many people now think that the subtlest and seemingly most implacable threats to the continuation of a civilization based on unprecedented manipulation of nature lie in the consequences of its own successes. The overcrowding and poverty that follow from a population growth which presses up to the margin of subsistence can now be seen in many parts of the world.

A street in Bombay (*Raghubir Singh/Woodfin Camp*)

Together with its successes, the Western European civilization has exported the most intolerable of its own evils just as it began to be able to conquer them in its own societies. In the background loom more frightening possibilities still of an overuse of world resources, of famine and its attendant evils.

From ancient times, huge images of rulers and gods have shown man's recurrent need to abase himself before a reassuring majesty. The twentieth century has only replaced old gods by new. The age of inhuman colossi returned with the totalitarian systems which appeared after the First World War. They were to prove more powerful than any earlier political structures. Through the manipulation of the economy and the new technological advances which benefited systems of terror, they brought the control of their subjects to an unprecedentedly high level. They were legitimized in the eyes of millions of those who lived under them by their seeming capacity to meet the terrifying challenges posed by the twentieth century. Yet they were successful in the long run only in a few underdeveloped countries. Such systems leave no room for self-assertion by the individual against the state except by crime or subversion. This can hardly be felt as a deprivation, though, in countries where the individual has never counted for much and where the magic of what is promised by a new messiah is often compelling.

Lenin's image dwarfing Russian passersby *(Bert Glenn/Magnum)*

Billboards in Shanghai (*Jørgen Bitsch/Black Star*)

At a moment when many doubts are felt about the shortcomings of a culture of exploitation and manipulation, it can still prove paradoxically attractive. China's long history of subordinating the individual to society and its demands has proved a ready ally of communism. Consequently, a modernizing creed of science, anti-super-naturalism, technological improvement, and economic egalitarianism has been fitted into Chinese society (albeit with bloodshed and brutality at times) as Western-style billboards are fitted into the traditional framework of a Chinese arch in Shanghai. But there is an ambiguity about such juxtapositions; it is hard to see why consumer goods should be advertised in a controlled economy. Moreover, pride in the production of goods equivalent to those of the disliked and despised West may awake a demand for them and bring its own dialectical strains. And at bottom, Marxist communism is itself a product of the rationalizing, exploitative civilization of the West, as inimical to traditional ways as any other European ideological artifact.

It is hard to be sure exactly what we mean when we refer to a general decline of religion. Certainly the ebbing of some of the power of organized and traditional religious authorities has meant that men have looked elsewhere for a focus for their awe and a sense of transcendent authority. Even when, within the Christian traditions, growing control of the physical world has resulted in a narrower and narrower definition of the field of action open to divine intervention, the religious sense has continued to express itself in different forms. It has also sought to redefine itself—in the worship of a Supreme Being who was not the God of the Christian Church, for example, or in the embodiments of supposed historical processes such as nations or classes, or even in a crude belief in human saviors.

Worshipping a new god (the statue on the crag): crowds honoring the diety
invented by Robespierre. Detail from the *Festival of the Supreme Being* by Thomas Charles Naudet, 1794
(Musée Carnavalet, Paris)

A new world for man and his machines *(NASA)*

In the end, for all its appalling injustices and evils, the Western European civilization which still dominates the world in which we live has shown its own power more strikingly and startlingly than ever in this latest age. As the human environment expands into interplanetary space, immense new possibilities appear. When the first men on the moon looked out to see the planet earth they had left not long before, they not only provided a supreme demonstration of mankind's capacity to manipulate the environment by simply being there but also symbolized the colossal promise this still holds out. There is no reason to think mankind to be in a dead end from which it cannot break out. Man may be confronting only the end of the beginning of his history.

Earth rising above the lunar horizon *(NASA)*

Take up the White Man's burden—
   No tawdry rule of kings,
But toil of serf and sweeper—
   The take of common things.
The ports ye shall not enter,
   The roads ye shall not tread,
Go make them with your living,
   And mark them with your dead!

Take up the White Man's burden—
   And reap his old reward:
The blame of those ye better,
   The hate of those ye guard—
The cry of hosts ye humour
   (Ah, slowly!) towards the light:—
"Why brought ye us from bondage,
   Our loved Egyptian night?"

Take up the White Man's burden—
   Ye dare not stoop to less—
Nor call too loud on freedom
   To cloak your weariness;
By all ye dry or whisper,
   By all ye leave or do,
The silent, sullen peoples
   Shall weigh your Gods and you.

Take up the White Man's burden—
   Have done with childish days—
The lightly proffered laurel,
   The easy, ungrudged praise.
Comes now, to search your manhood
   Through all the thankless years,
Cold-edged with dear-bought wisdom,
   The judgement of your peers!

From *Rudyard Kipling's Verse: Definitive Edition* (1899). Reprinted by permission of Doubleday & Company, Inc.

there was much that was imperial or barely distinguishable from it in the territorial expansion of the United States in the nineteenth century, though Americans might not recognize it under the label of "Manifest Destiny." The most blatant examples were the War of 1812 and the treatment of Mexico in the middle of the century. But the dispossession of the Indian must also be considered and the assertive implications of the Monroe Doctrine.

In the 1890s the overland expansion of the United States was complete, the continuous frontier of settlement no longer existed. This was a moment when economic growth gave business interests great influence in government, which was sometimes expressed in terms of an economic nationalism, for example, in the imposition of high tariff protection. Some of these interests directed the attention of American public opinion to Asia, where they feared the United States was in danger of being excluded from trade by the European powers. The dawning of an era of Pacific awareness, as California grew in population and a half-century's talk of a canal across Central America came to a head, also stimulated interest in the doctrines of strategic planners who suggested that the United States might need oceanic possessions if the Monroe Doctrine were to be maintained.

These currents flowed into a burst of expansion which has remained to this day a unique example of American overseas imperialism. The beginnings must be traced to the opening of China and Japan to American commerce in the 1850s and 1860s and participation with the British and the Germans in the administration of Samoa, where a naval base obtained in 1878 has remained a United States possession. This was followed by two decades of increasing intervention in the affairs of Hawaii; the United States had extended its protection to the monarchy there in the 1840s, and American traders and missionaries had established themselves in the islands in large numbers. In the 1890s, benevolent supervision decayed under the efforts of these American residents to achieve annexation to the United States. The United States government already had the use of Pearl Harbor as a naval base but was led to land marines in Hawaii when internal affairs produced a revolution there. Washington finally gave way to the forces set in motion by the settlers and annexed the short-lived Hawaiian republic, which it had briefly recognized, as a territory in 1898.

In that year a mysterious explosion which destroyed an American cruiser, the U.S.S. *Maine*, in Havana harbor led to the outbreak of war with Spain. In the background was Spain's long failure to master a revolt against her rule in Cuba, where American business interests were prominent and American sentiment was aroused, and the growing awareness of the importance of the Caribbean approaches to a future canal across the isthmus. The conflict spread to the Pacific when the United States intervened in the Philippines to support a rebel movement against the Spaniards. When American rule replaced Spanish, the rebels turned against their former allies and began a guerrilla war. This was the first troublesome phase of the long and difficult process of disentangling the United States from its first Far Eastern colony. For the moment, given the probability of the collapse of the Chinese empire, Washington thought it best not to withdraw. In the Caribbean, Span-

ish empire in the Western hemisphere at last came to an end; Puerto Rico passed to the United States and Cuba obtained independence on terms which guaranteed American domination. United States forces were back in occupation of the island under these terms from 1906 to 1909 and again in 1917.

The Spanish-American War was the prelude to the last major development in this wave of American imperialism, the securing of the Panama Canal Zone. The building of an isthmian canal had been in the air since the middle of the nineteenth century and the completion of Suez gave it new plausibility. After American diplomacy negotiated the obstacle of possible British participation, all seemed plain sailing. But a snag arose in 1903 when Colombia rejected a treaty providing for the acquisition of a canal zone across her territory. The United States engineered a revolution in Panama, where the canal was to run, and prevented its suppression by the Colombian government. A Panamanian republic emerged and gratefully bestowed upon the United States the necessary territory, jurisdiction within it, and the right to intervene in the affairs of Panama to maintain order. Thus secured, the work began and the canal was opened in 1914. It caused a great change in American naval strategy because it permitted the rapid transfer of ships from one ocean to another. The canal scheme had also been the background to the Roosevelt Corollary to the Monroe Doctrine. The zone became the key to the naval defense of the hemisphere and therefore it became more important than ever to assure its protection by the maintenance of stability and United States predominance in the Caribbean countries.

Though the motives and techniques were different—and there was virtually no American settlement in the new possessions—the actions of the United States were part of the last great seizure of territories carried out by European powers. Almost all of them had taken part except the Latin Americans; even the Australians had pushed forward in New Guinea. By 1914 a third of the world's surface was under the flags of two nations, the United Kingdom and Russia (though how much Russian territory should be regarded as colonial is arguable). To take a measure which excludes Russia, in 1914 the United Kingdom ruled 400 million people outside its own borders, France over 50 million, and Germany and Italy about 14 million each. This was an unprecedented aggregation of formal authority, but there were signs by then that imperialism overseas had run out of steam, if for no other reason than that there was little left to divide. The most probable area for further imperial expansion was the decaying Ottoman empire, whose dissolution at last seemed imminent. The Italians had seized Tripoli in 1912 and a Balkan coalition had taken away almost all that was left of its European territories the following year. But the anticipated Turkish partition did not seem likely to be as free of conflict as the division of Africa had been; in it crucial issues would be at stake for the European powers.

chapter 32

Asia in the Europeanized World

Asia's own traditions of civilization were rich and deeply-rooted at the outset of the European age. Yet by the end of the nineteenth century European mastery of them seemed complete. However it was packaged—whether in political, economic, or cultural forms—this mastery was even more striking than in Africa or the Americas just because it was deployed over so much richer a heritage of native civilization. But there was an illusion in this. For all their pride, the rule of Europeans in Asia was to disappear more quickly than it arose, and this would owe much to what they had brought with them. In time Asia, like the Americas more than a century earlier, was to cast off Europe with ideas and weapons borrowed from her.

CHINA

Under the immediate successors of K'ang-hsi the Manchu empire was already past its peak; a slow and eventually fatal decline could be expected, given the cyclical pattern of dynastic rise and fall in the past. What made the fate of the Manchu dynasty different from that of its predecessors was that it survived long enough to face a quite new threat, one from a culture stronger than that of traditional China. For the first time in nearly two thousand years it would be Chinese society which would change in the end, not the imported culture of the new barbarians. The Chinese revolution was about to begin.

The beginning of the Western onslaughts

When England's George III sent Lord Macartney to ask for equality of diplomatic representation and free trade in 1793, Chinese confidence was still intact; the first Western advances and encroachments had been successfully rebuffed or contained. Macartney had to take back messages which refused his master's applications to what the Chinese emperor was pleased to call "the lonely remoteness of your island, cut off from the world by intervening wastes of sea." George III was patted on the back for his "submissive loyalty in sending this tribute mission" and encouraged to "show even great-

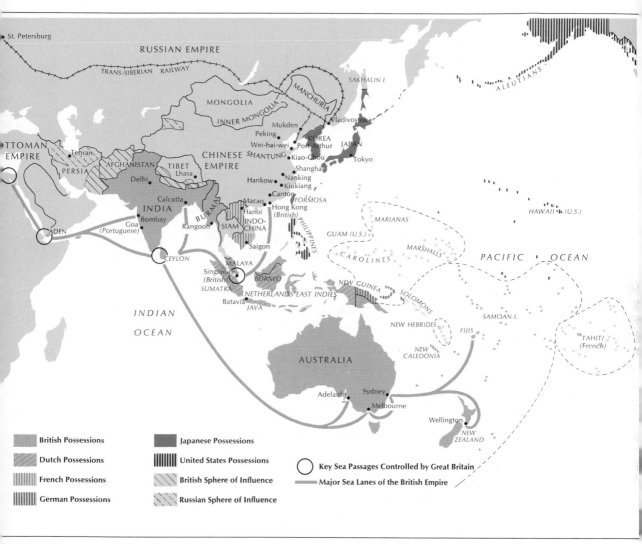

IMPERIALISM IN ASIA AND THE PACIFIC

er devotion and loyalty in future." This was not merely pomposity and arrogance. Educated Chinese took for granted their cultural and moral superiority just as European and American missionaries and philanthropists took their own for granted a century later. The Chinese believed that all nations paid tribute to the holder of the Mandate of Heaven, and that China, which already had the highest civilization, would only waste her time and energy if she indulged in relations with Europe going beyond the limited trade tolerated at Canton, where by 1800 there were perhaps 1,000 Europeans. This attitude was by no means nonsensical. During nearly three centuries of direct trade the Chinese had wanted no manufactured goods from Europe ex-

A Chinese Rebuke to the Barbarian West

In 1839 the Chinese minister Lin Tsê-Hsü addressed Queen Victoria on the attitude she should have taken (in Chinese eyes) about the East India Company's import of opium to China. It was a blend of moral argument and veiled threat; the hint that China might cut off England's supplies of rhubarb, for example, was not merely to suggest economic warfare but that the wretched islanders might suffer the pangs of constipation in consequence. Such was the Chinese belief, at any rate. The English were unimpressed; it is not recorded whether the young Queen Victoria was amused by the appeal to her moral sense or by the threat.

Let us ask, where is your conscience? I have heard that the smoking of opium is very strictly forbidden by your country; that is because the harm caused by opium is clearly understood. Since it is not permitted to do harm to your own country, then even less should you let it be passed on to the harm of other countries — how much less to China! Of all that China exports to foreign countries, there is not a single thing which is not beneficial to people: they are of benefit when eaten, or of benefit when used, or of

cept a few mechanical toys and clocks, which they found amusing. Instead European traders had brought China mainly either silver or the products of other Asian countries.

Nonetheless, the seeds of future difficulties were already present in China's internal affairs in the eighteenth century. The secret societies and cults which had provided foci for a smoldering nationalist resentment against the dynasty, for social war, and for resistance to the central power still survived and even prospered. They mattered more because the surge of population was becoming uncontainable; numbers seem to have more than doubled in the century before 1850 to reach by then about 430 million. Pressure on cultivated land became much more acute because the area worked could only be increased by a tiny margin; times grew steadily harder and the lot of the peasantry became more and more miserable. There were warning

benefit when resold: all are beneficial. Is there a single article from China which has done any harm to foreign countries? Take tea and rhubarb, for example; the foreign countries cannot get along for a single day without them. If China cuts off these benefits with no sympathy for those who are to suffer, then what can the barbarians rely upon to keep themselves alive? Moreover, the woolens, camlets and longells [i.e., textiles] of foreign countries cannot be woven unless they obtain Chinese silk. If China, again, cuts off this beneficial export, what profit can the barbarians expect to make? As for other foodstuffs, beginning with candy, ginger, cinnamon, and so forth, and articles for use, beginning with silk, satin, chinaware, and so on, all the things that must be had by foreign countries are innumerable. On the other hand, articles coming from the outside to China can only be used as toys. We can take them or get along without them. Since they are not needed by China, what difficulty would there be if we closed the frontier and stopped the trade?

From Ssu-yü Teng and J. K. Fairbank, *China's Response to the West* (Cambridge, Mass.: Harvard University Press, 1954), pp. 24–26.

signs in the 1770s and 1780s when a century's internal peace was broken by great revolts, so often an indicator of dynastic decline. In the first decades of the nineteenth century they grew more frequent and destructive. To make matters worse, inflation brought a crushing new burden to the poor at the same time.

Rising prices resulted from a change in China's trading relations with the outside world which within a few decades had made nonsense of the reception given to Macartney. By 1830 the terms of trade with Europe had been reversed because British traders had at last found a commodity the Chinese wanted: opium. Naval expeditions forced the Chinese to open their country to the sale (albeit at first under certain restrictions) of this drug, but the Opium Wars of the 1840s only registered the completion of a change in China's economic relations with the West. The Canton monopoly and the tributary status of the foreigner came to an end together. Now that they had kicked it ajar, the British would struggle to open still further the door to Western trade. Others were to follow them through it.

Thus, unwittingly, Europe launched the Chinese revolution. The aggression of the 1840s had detonated a chain reaction of upheaval and repudiation which took over a century to come to completion. It was the beginning of a revolution which would slowly reveal itself as a double repudiation, of both the foreigner and of Chinese tradition. The first would increasingly express itself in the nationalist modes and idioms of the progressive European world but because such ideological forces could not be contained within the traditional framework, they would in the end prove fatal to it. More than a century after the Opium Wars the revolution would at last finally shatter the social system which had been the framework of Chinese life for thousands of years.

For thirty or forty years after the Opium Wars Western encroachment usually produced only a xenophobic hostility, and even this was not universal since the foreigners' arrival for a long time affected very few Chinese in an obvious way. A few (notably Canton merchants involved in the foreign trade) even sought accommodation with them. Hostility was a matter of anti-British mobs in the towns after the Opium Wars and of the rural gentry. Chinese officials at first saw the problem as a precise one: the addiction of the empire's subjects to a dangerous drug. They were humiliated by the weaknesses this revealed in their own people and administration; there was much connivance and corruption involved in the opium trade. They do not seem to have sensed the deeper issue of the future, the questioning of the entire traditional order. Yet there was already a portent in the 1840s when the imperial government had to concede that missionary activity was legal. Officials in the Confucian mold soon realized its corrosive influence. Their stirring up of popular feeling against missionaries — whose efforts made them easy targets — produced hundreds of riots in the 1850s and 1860s. Sometimes foreign consuls would be drawn in; occasionally a gunboat would be sent. The Chinese government's prestige would then suffer in the ensuing exchange of apologies and punishment of culprits. Meanwhile the missionaries were steadily undermining traditional society by preaching an individualism and egalitarianism alien to it and by attracting more and more converts to whom Christianity offered economic and social advantages.

Social upheaval

Chinese authorities did not always resist the presence of the foreigners. First the gentry of the areas immediately concerned and then the Peking government came around to feeling that foreign soldiers might not be without certain value for the regime. Social disorder was growing and threatened to be worse as China entered a cycle of peasant revolts which proved the greatest in human history. In the middle of the century the familiar symptoms multiplied: banditry, peasant uprisings. In the 1850s the secret society called Red Turbans was suppressed only at great cost. Such internal troubles threw the regime onto the defensive, leaving it with little spare capacity to resist the steady gnawing of the West.

The great nineteenth-century rebellions were fundamentally caused by hunger for land as the population grew and conditions worsened. The most important and distinctive of them was the Taiping Rebellion or, as it may more appropriately be called, Revolution, which lasted from 1850 to 1864 and cost the lives of more people than the First World War. The heart of this huge convulsion was a traditional peasant revolt which hard times and a succession of natural disasters had helped to provoke. It drew on land hunger, hatred of tax gatherers, social envy, and national resentment against the Manchus (though it is hard to see exactly what this meant in practice because the bulk of the officials who actually administered the empire were of course themselves Chinese). It was also at least initially a regional outbreak, beginning in the south and even there promoted by an isolated minority of settlers originally from the north.

A new feature behind the Taiping revolt which made it ambiguous in the eyes of both Chinese and Europeans was that its leader, Hung Hsiu-ch'üan, had a superficial but impressive acquaintance with the Christian religion in the form of American Protestantism and this led him to denounce the worship of other gods, destroy idols — including the Confucian ancestor tablets — and talk of establishing the kingdom of God on earth. Within the familiar framework of one of the periodic peasant upheavals of old China, a new ideology was at work subversive of the traditional culture and state. Thus the rebellion can realistically be seen as another epoch in the Western disruption of China.

The Taiping army at first had a series of spectacular successes. By 1853 it had captured Nanking and established there the court of Hung Hsiu-ch'üan, now proclaimed the Heavenly King. In spite of alarm farther north, this was as far as the revolution was to get and after 1856 it was on the defensive. Nevertheless, it announced important social changes (which made it a source of inspiration for later Chinese reformers); and although it is by no means clear how widely these were effective or even appealing, their disruptive ideological effect was considerable. The basis of Taiping society was communism; there was no private property but communal provision for general needs. In theory the land was distributed in plots graded by quality to provide just shares. Even more revolutionary, the Taipings extended social and educational equality to women and prohibited the traditional binding of their feet. Also an important degree of sexual austerity marked the movement's aspirations (though not the conduct of the Heavenly King himself). These things reflected the mixture of religious and social elements which lay at the root of the Taiping cult and the danger it presented to the traditional order.

Foreign pressure continued while the imperial government grappled with the Taipings. Treaties with France and the United States which followed that with Great Britain guaranteed the toleration of Christian missionaries and began the process of reserving jurisdiction over foreigners to consular and mixed courts. The success of the Taiping revolution brought yet more concessions: a fresh burst of fighting resulted in the opening of more Chinese ports to foreign trade, the take-over of Chinese customs administration by foreigners, the legislation of the sale of opium, and the cession to the

Russians of the province in which Vladivostok was to be built. It is hardly surprising that in 1861 the Chinese decided for the first time to set up a special department to deal with foreign affairs. The old myth that all the world recognized the Mandate of Heaven and owed tribute to the imperial court was dead.

The Taiping movement had benefited from the demoralization in Manchu forces after the disasters of the Opium Wars and from the central government's usual weakness in a relatively distant and distinct region. As time passed and the government troops received abler commanders, the bows and spears of the Taipings proved insufficient. In the end the Europeans joined in against them—a response by no means illogical, given that the revolution was strongly against opium. Whether foreign help was by then needed by the imperial government may never be known; there is evidence that the Taiping movement was already failing. In 1864 Hung died and shortly afterward Nanking fell to the Manchus.

This was a victory for traditional China: the rule of the bureaucratic gentry had survived one more threat from below. Nonetheless, Chinese history had reached an important turning point. A rebellion had offered a revolutionary program in which there was a discernible Western contribution. The Europeans had joined in suppressing that revolution, but it had announced a new danger, that the old challenge of peasant revolt might be reinforced by foreign ideology deeply corrosive of Confucian China. The potential of this danger was shown by the fact that the end of the Taiping Rebellion did not mean internal peace; continuously from the middle of the 1850s until well into the 1870s there were great Muslim risings in the northwest and southwest and other rebellions elsewhere. The problem of internal weakness and disorder continued to threaten a declining dynasty.

Semicolonialism

Immediately, the obvious legacy was even greater Chinese weakness in the face of the West. Large areas had been devastated in the fighting; in many of them the soldiers were more powerful than ever and threatened the control of the bureaucracy. If the enormous loss of life did something to reduce pressure on land, this was probably balanced by a decline in the prestige and authority of the dynasty. Concessions had already been made to the Western powers under and because of these disadvantageous conditions; there would be more. The methods which had drawn the sting of nomadic invaders were not likely to be efficacious with the confident Europeans whose ideological assurance and increasing technical superiority protected them from the seduction of Chinese civilization.

In the middle decades of the century the spate of concessions to the foreigner went on to admit trade in more "treaty ports," to the establishment of resident diplomatic representation at Peking, and to the removal of restraints on the travel of Europeans. When Roman Catholic missionaries were given the right to buy land and put up buildings, Christianity was linked to economic penetration; soon the wish to protect converts meant involvement in the internal affairs of public order and police. It was impossible to contain the slow but continuous erosion of Chinese sovereignty. Never formally a colony, China was beginning nonetheless to undergo a measure of colonialization.

The empire lost more territory as the century wore on. In the 1870s the Russians seized the Ili valley (though they later handed much of it back); and in the next decade the French established protectorates over Indochina. Loosely asserted but ancient Chinese suzerainty was being swept away as the French next began to absorb Indochina themselves and the British annexed Burma. Another Asian state delivered the worst blow; in the war of 1894–1895 the Japanese took Formosa and the Pescadores and briefly the Liaotung peninsula which European pressure later forced them to return, while China had to recognize explicitly the independence of Korea, which had paid tribute to her since the seventeenth century. Still further encroachments by other powers followed the Japanese success. Provoked by the Russians who took Port Arthur, England, France, and Germany all extracted long leases on ports at the end of the century; the Portuguese, who had been in China longest, had earlier converted their tenure of Macao into outright ownership. Even the Italians were in the market though they did not actually get anything. And all the time the Western powers were exacting concessions, loans, and agreements to protect and foster their own economic interests. It is hardly surprising that a British prime minister spoke at the end of the century of two classes of nations, "the living and the dying." China was an outstanding example of the second class and statesmen began to envisage her partition.

Reform movements

Before the end of the nineteenth century many Chinese intellectuals and civil servants recognized that the traditional order could not generate the energy necessary to resist the new barbarians. Attempts to work along the old lines had failed. New tendencies began to appear. A "Society for the Study of Self-Strengthening" was founded to consider Western ideas and inventions which might be helpful. Its leaders cited the achievements of Peter the Great and, more significantly, of contemporary reformers in Japan. Yet the would-be reformers still hoped that they could root change in the Confucian tradition, albeit one purified and invigorated. They were members of the gentry class and by 1898 had succeeded in obtaining the ear of the emperor; they were thus working within the traditional framework and machinery of power to obtain administrative and technological reform without compromising the fundamentals of Chinese culture and ideology.

Unfortunately this involved them in court politics and meant that the Hundred Days of Reform of 1898 (as it came to be known) was almost at once tangled up in the rivalry between the emperor and the dowager empress, to say nothing of Chinese-Manchu rivalries. A stream of reform edicts was swiftly overtaken by a coup d'état staged by the empress, who locked up the emperor. The basic cause of the reformers' failure was the provocation offered by their inept political behavior. The movement had failed. Yet it

had importance simply by having existed at all. It was to be a great stimulus to wider and deeper thinking about China's future.

For the moment, as the dramatic episode of the Boxer Rebellion showed, China seemed to have turned back to old and unsuccessful methods of confronting the threat from outside. The Boxer movement was essentially backward-looking and xenophobic; it was encouraged by the empress and resulted in attacks on Europeans and a siege (unsuccessful) of the foreign legations at Peking. It was unable to stand up to Western fighting power. The uprising revealed again the hatred of foreigners which was waiting to be tapped but also how little could be hoped for from the old conservative forces. It was suppressed by a military intervention which provides the only

天津城埋

The Boxers drive the barbarians of
the West fleeing before them—a
hopeful Chinese print from the early
days of the rebellion of 1899–1900.
(The Trustees of the British Museum)

example in history of the armed forces of all the great powers operating in
the field of combat under the same commander (a German, as it happened,
though he arrived after the most serious fighting was over). The sequel was
yet another diplomatic humiliation. An enormous indemnity was settled on
the Chinese customs system.

The revolutionary movement

The ending of the Boxer movement made the internal situation still
more unstable. Reform had failed in 1898; now reaction had too. Perhaps only
revolution lay ahead. Officers in the parts of the army which had undergone

reorganization and training on Western lines began to think about it. Students in exile had already begun to meet and discuss their country's future, above all in Tokyo. The Japanese were happy to encourage subversive movements which might weaken their neighbor; already in 1898 they had set up the East Asian Cultural Union from which emerged the new slogan: "Asia for the Asians." The Japanese had great prestige in the eyes of young Chinese radicals as Asians who were escaping from the trap of traditional backwardness which had been fatal to India and seemed about to engulf China. Japan could confront the West on terms of equality. Other students looked elsewhere for support, some to the secret societies which had long endured in China. Among them was a young man called Sun Yat-sen. His achievement has often been exaggerated; nevertheless, he attempted revolution ten times altogether, and constitutional monarchy (which was all he was asking for in the 1890s) was a very radical political demand at the time.

Discontented exiles could also draw on a considerable measure of support from Chinese businessmen abroad. Some of them helped to promote the formation by Sun Yat-sen of a revolutionary alliance in Japan in 1905. This Combined League Society sought the expulsion of the Manchus and the initiation of Chinese rule, a republican constitution, and land reform; it was also conciliatory to foreigners, at this stage a wise tactical move. This was the beginning of the party eventually to emerge as the dominant clique in the Chinese republic. The influence of Western liberal and radical thinkers was apparent in the new program; once again the West provided both the stimulus and some of the ideological baggage of a Chinese reform movement.

The formation of revolutionary groups, though, may well be thought less important than another event of 1905, the Manchu government's abolition of the traditional examination system. This was part of a series of constitutional and administrative reforms carried out since 1901, and possibly the one of the greatest importance. More than any other institution, this system had continued to hold Chinese civilization together by providing the bureaucracy with internal homogeneity and cohesion through the inculcation of Confucian principles. These would now quickly wane. Moreover the reform removed the distinction between the mass of Chinese subjects and the privileged ruling class. Meanwhile students returning from abroad, dissatisfied with what they found and no longer under the necessity of going through the examination procedure if they wished to enter government service, were now a new force for change. They much increased the rate at which Western ideas permeated Chinese society. Together with the soldiers in a modernized army, more and more of them looked to revolution for a way ahead.

There were a number of rebellions (some directed by Sun Yat-sen from Indochina with French connivance) before the empress and the emperor both died in 1908 on successive days. A child emperor succeeded to the throne. These events raised new hopes, but the Manchus continued to drag their feet over reform. On the one hand they made important concessions of principle, notably by giving Chinese a bigger role in government and promoting the flow of students abroad; on the other the dynasty showed that it could not achieve a decisive break with the past or surrender any of the imperial privileges of the Manchus. Perhaps more could not have been asked for.

By 1911 the situation had deteriorated still further. The gentry class showed signs of losing its unity; it would no longer back the dynasty in the face of subversion. Governmentally, there existed a near stalemate, the dynasty relying in effect upon divisions between its monarchist and republican opponents to offset its own weakness. In October a revolutionary headquarters was discovered at Hankow. There had been revolts earlier in the year which had been more or less contained. This discovery precipitated one by the plotters who decided to act before the government could seize them and it turned into a successful revolution. Sun Yat-sen, whose name was used by the rebels, was taken by surprise: he was in the United States at the time.

The defection from the regime of its military commanders largely set the course of the revolution. The most important of these officers was Yüan Shih-kai; when he turned on the Manchus, the dynasty was lost. The Mandate of Heaven had been withdrawn and on February 12, 1912, the last Manchu emperor (aged six) abdicated. A republic had already been proclaimed with Sun Yat-sen its president, and a new nationalist party soon appeared behind him. In February Sun resigned the presidency the day after the imperial edict was issued which established the republic and ended the empire officially. He was succeeded by Yüan Shih-kai, a sign where power really lay. A new phase of Chinese government now began in which an effective constitutional regime at Peking disputed the practical government of China with war lords. This alone meant that China still had a long way to travel before she would be a modern nation-state. Nonetheless, she had begun the march. Within another half-century she would regain the reality of an independence anciently and still formally hers but actually lost in the nineteenth century to the West.

JAPAN

In the early nineteenth century Japan was, like any other preindustrial society, deeply conservative. Yet much had already changed since the establishment of the Tokugawa shogunate in the early seventeenth century and there were signs that the changes would cut deeper and faster as the years went by. Paradoxically this was in part attributable to the success of the Tokugawa clan itself. It had brought peace, and an obvious result was that Japan's military system became old-fashioned and inefficient. The samurai themselves became a parasitic class; as warriors there was nothing for them to do except cluster in the castle towns of their lords, consumers without employment. Nor were they the only economic problem posed by prolonged peace. It led also to a money economy, to the beginnings of quasi-capitalism in agriculture which eroded the old feudal relationships, and to the growth of towns. Osaka, the greatest mercantile center, had between three and four hundred thousand inhabitants in the last years of the shogunate; Yedo probably had a million. These great centers of consumption were sustained by financial and mercantile arrangements which had grown enormously in scale and complication since the seventeenth century and made a mockery of the old notion of the merchant order's inferiority. Even their sales techniques were modern; the eighteenth-century shops of the House of Mitsui (still today one of the pillars of Japanese capitalism) gave free umbrellas marked with their trademark to customers caught inside by the rain.

Many of these changes registered the creation of new wealth, but the shogunate had not itself benefited, largely because it was unable to tap new resources at a rate which kept pace with its own growing needs. The main revenue was a rice tax which flowed through the lords. It did not take away the new wealth arising from better cultivation and land reclamation; this remained in the hands of the wealthier peasants and village leaders and led to sharpening contrasts in the countryside. The poorer peasants were often driven to the towns at a time when the better-off prospered, another sign of the disintegration of feudal society. In the towns, which suffered from an inflation made worse by the shogunate's debasement of the coinage, only the merchants seemed to prosper. A last effort of economic reform failed in the 1840s. The lords grew poorer and their retainers lost confidence; before the end of the Tokugawa some samurai were beginning to dabble in trade. Their share of their lord's tax yield was often still only that of their seventeenth-

Among the things brought by Perry's "black ships" on his second visit to Japan was a miniature railway. It was set up on shore to impress the Japanese and is here shown in a contemporary Japanese print.
(The Library of Congress)

century forerunners. Regional differences existed, but everywhere could be found impoverished, politically discontented swordsmen—and some aggrieved families of great lords who recalled the days when their predecessors had stood on equal terms with the Tokugawa.

The opening of Japan

Insulation against Western ideas had long since ceased to be complete. A few learned men had soon become interested in European books, which entered Japan through the narrow aperture of the Dutch trade in the seventeenth century. In an important respect Japan was very different from China—its technical receptivity. A sixteenth-century Dutchman observed, "The Japanese are sharp witted and quickly learn anything they see." They had soon grasped and exploited as the Chinese never did the advantages of European firearms and began to make them in quantity. They copied the European clocks which the Chinese treated as toys. They were eager to learn from the foreigners, as unhampered by their traditions as the Chinese seemed bogged down in theirs. On the great fiefs there were notable schools and research centers of "Dutch studies." The shogunate itself authorized the translation of foreign books, an important step in so literate a society. It also

The Japanese Revolution

The autobiography of one of Japan's first Westernizing intellectuals, Yukichi Fukuzawa, provides vivid evidence of the psychological atmosphere in which the revolutionary transformation of Japan was begun in the nineteenth century. The following extract reveals the enthusiasm with which Western techniques were taken up and the pride felt in national success even before the Meiji Restoration itself.

It was in January, the first year of Manen (1860), when our ship, the Kanrin-maru, left Yedo . . . In winter, on the rough seas, with her diminutive steam engine of one hundred horse power, which was to be used only in manoeuvring about ports, she had to face the voyage under sail. And so hard was the weather on the voyage that we lost two of the four life-boats overboard. . . .

We with the entire crew of ninety-six men reached land at San Francisco after thirty-seven days . . . I am willing to admit my pride in this accomplishment for Japan. The facts are these: it was not until the sixth year of Kaei (1853) that a steamship was seen for the first time; it was only in the second year of Ansei (1855) that we began to study navigation from the Dutch in Nagasaki; by 1860, the science was sufficiently understood to enable us to sail a ship across the Pacific. This means that about seven years after the first sight of a steamship, after only about five years of practice, the Japanese people made a trans-Pacific crossing without the help of foreign experts. I think we can without undue pride boast before the world of this courage and skill. . . . Even Peter the Great of Russia, who went to Holland to study navigation, with all his attainments could not have equalled this feat of the Japanese. Without doubt the famous emperor was a man of genius, but his people did not respond to his leadership in the practice of science as did our Japanese in this great adventure.

From Eiichi Kiyooka, tr., *The Autobiography of Yukichi Fukuzawa* (New York: Columbia University Press, 1966.

permitted medical students to study Dutch, which caused a sudden expansion of numbers at the medical school set up in Osaka in 1838. Education in Tokugawa Japan had been almost too successful; there was a high degree of literacy and even young samurai were beginning to inquire about Western ideas. The islands were relatively small and communications good, so new ideas got about easily. This was the situation in which Japan had suddenly to face a new and unprecedented challenge from the West.

The first and more or less uncontrolled period of Western contact with Japan had ended in the seventeenth century with persecution and the exclusion of all but a few Dutchmen. Europe had not then been able to challenge this outcome. But the situation had changed by the nineteenth century, and Japan's rulers observed with increasing alarm what was happening to China. The Europeans (who might at any moment be joined by the North Americans) had, it was clear, both a new interest in breaking into Asian trade and new and irresistible strength to do it. The king of the Netherlands warned the shogun in the 1840s that exclusion was no longer a realistic policy. But there was no agreement among Japan's rulers about whether resistance or concession was better. Then in 1851 the president of the United States commissioned a naval officer to open relations with Japan. The second American squadron to sail into Japanese waters entered Edo Bay under Commodore Perry in 1853 (an earlier visit had ended with the Americans' withdrawal to avoid hostilities). In the following year Perry returned and the shogunate signed the first of a series of treaties with foreign powers.

The Meiji Restoration

Within a few years the success of the Western nations was embodied in and symbolized by a series of so-called "unequal treaties." Commercial privileges, extraterritoriality for their resident nationals, diplomatic representation, and restrictions on the Japanese export of opium were the main concessions won from the shogunate by the United States, Great Britain, France, Russia, and the Netherlands. Soon afterward the shogunate came to an end; its inability to resist the foreigner was one contributing factor and another was the threat from two great aggregations of feudal power which had already begun to adopt Western military techniques. There was fighting between the Tokugawa and their opponents, but this was followed not by a relapse into disorder and anarchy but by the resumption of imperial power in 1868, known as the Meiji Restoration.

It cannot be doubted that the reemergence of the emperor and the widespread acceptance of the revolutionary renewal which followed were attributable above all to the passionate desire of most literate Japanese to escape from a "shameful inferiority" to the West which might have ended in their sharing the fate of the Chinese and Indians. Japan dropped antiforeign agitation in order to learn from the West the secrets of its strength. There was a paradox in this because, as in Europe, a nationalism rooted in a conservative view of society was to prove in the end a huge solvent of the tradition in whose name it was developed.

Westernizing Japan. The Imperial Diet meets in 1890, in a chamber modeled on
those of Western parliaments, wearing Western dress, and seated on Western chairs.
(*Radio Times Hulton Picture Library*)

The transference of the court to Yedo (renamed Tokyo) was the symbolic opening of the Meiji Restoration; its indispensable first stage was the abolition of feudalism. What might have been a difficult and bloody business
was made simple by the four greatest clans' voluntary surrender of their
lands to the emperor. In a memorial addressed to their sovereign they explained that they returned to him what had originally been his, "so that a
uniform rule may prevail throughout the empire. Thus the country will be
able to rank equally with the other nations of the world." This expressed a
patriotic ethic which was to inspire Japan's leaders for the next fifty years.
Nationalism was a widespread phenomenon in the nineteenth century and
such expressions were not uncommon. What was peculiar to Japan was the
urgency which observation of China's fate lent to the program, the emotional
support given to the idea by Japanese social and moral tradition, and the fact
that the throne, with its great reserves of moral authority, was not committed
to maintaining the past and could be brought into play on the side of reform.
These conditions made possible a conservative revolution opening the way
to radical change.

Japan rapidly adopted the institutions of European government. A
prefectorial system of administration, a daily newspaper, a ministry of
education, a postal system, military conscription, the first railway, religious
toleration, and the Gregorian calendar all arrived within the first five years.
Representation entered local government in 1879, and ten years later a new
constitution set up a bicameral parliament (after a peerage had been created to
furnish the upper house). In fact this document was somewhat less revolutionary than might appear, given its strong authoritarian strain. At about this
time the innovatory passion was showing signs of flagging; the first craze for

things Western was over, and no such enthusiasm would be seen again until the second half of the twentieth century. In 1890 an imperial Rescript on Education, to be read on great days to generations of Japanese schoolchildren, enjoined them to observe the traditional duties of filial piety and obedience and the sacrifice of self to the state if need be.

Much—perhaps the most important part—of old Japan clearly survived the Meiji revolution and this is part of the fascination of the story of modern Japan. But much, too, had gone by 1900. Feudalism could never be restored, generously compensated with government stock though the lords might be. The old class system had also come to an end. The government showed care in removing the privileges of the samurai; some of them could find compensation by the opportunities offered to them in the new bureaucracy, in business (no longer to be a demeaning activity), and in the modernized army and navy. For their military the Japanese sought foreign instruction of proven excellence. Characteristically, they dropped their French advisers and employed Germans after the Franco-Prussian War. Young Japanese were sent abroad to learn at first hand other secrets of the wonderful and threatening puissance of the West. It is still hard not to be moved by the ardor of many of these young men and their elders and impossible not to be impressed by their achievement. It went far beyond Japan and their own time. The shishi (as the activists of reform were called) inspired national leaders right across Asia, from India to China. Their spirit was still at work, with unfortunate consequences, in the young officers of the 1930s who were to launch the last and most destructive stage of Japanese imperialism.

The crudest indexes of the reformers' success are the economic ones, but the accomplishments by 1914 are very striking: the creation of the infrastructure of a modern state, an indigenous arms industry, a credit rating usually high in the eyes of foreign investors, and a huge expansion of cotton spinning and other textiles. These achievements grew out of the work of the nineteenth century, which released in Japan a current of growth observable in no other non-European state.

The basis of economic advance was a great increase in agricultural production, though the peasants who made up four-fifths of the population in 1868 benefited little from it. Japan managed to feed her growing population in the nineteenth century by bringing more land under cultivation. Though the government's dependence on the land tax lessened as a bigger portion of revenue could be found from other sources, the cost of the new Japan continued to fall most heavily upon the peasant. (This would remain true right down to 1941.) As there were few other natural resources, the tax on land made increasingly productive had to pay for investment. Consumption remained low. A high rate of saving (12 percent in 1900) removed dependence on foreign loans but, again, restricted consumption. This was the other side of the balance sheet of expansion whose credit entries were clear enough.

Eventually it was to become clear that a heavy spiritual price had been paid for modernization. Even while seeking to learn from the West, Japan turned inward. The upholders of the state Shintoist cult attacked the foreign religious influences of Confucianism and even, at first, Buddhism. Under the shogunate Shintoism had begun to stress and enhance the role of the emperor as the embodiment of the divine. In the Meiji era the demands of loyalty to the emperor as the focus of the nation came to override the principles embodied in the new constitution, which might have been developed in liberal directions in a different cultural setting. The quality of the regime was shown less in liberal institutions than in the repressive actions of the imperial police. Yet it is difficult to see how an authoritarian emphasis could have been avoided given the two great tasks facing the statesmen of the Meiji Restoration. Modernization of the economy did not mean planning in the modern sense but a strong governmental initiative and harsh fiscal policies. The other problem was order. The imperial power had once before gone into eclipse because of its failure to meet the threat on this front, and now there were new dangers because not all conservatives could be reconciled to the new Japan. Discontented ronin (the retainers of great men) were one source of trouble. Another was peasant misery; there were scores of agrarian disturbances in the first decade of the Meiji era. In the Satsuma rebellion of 1877 the government's new conscript forces showed their competence. This was the last of several rebellions against the Restoration and its last great challenge from conservatism.

Aggressive nationalism

Although the energies of the discontented samurai were gradually siphoned off into the service of the new state the process was not purely beneficial for Japan. Their values intensified in certain key sectors an assertive nationalism which would lead eventually to disaster. Modernization at home and adventure abroad were often in tension in Japan after the Meiji Restoration, but their long-term tendency was to pull in the same direction. Even popular and democratic movements felt the tug of imperialism. Immediately, this found expression in expansion on the nearby Asian mainland.

China was the predestined victim and she was to be served as harshly by her fellow Asians as by any of the Western states. At first, however, she faced only indirect aggression. Just as Europeans challenged Chinese supremacy in Tibet, Indochina, and Manchuria, so the Japanese menaced it in the ancient empire of Korea, long claimed as a dependency by Peking. Japan's interest in Korea went back a long way. In part this was strategic: the mainland was nearest to her across the Tsushima Straits. In 1876 the Japanese made an overt move. Under the threat of military and naval action (which was very much like that used on China by the Europeans and on Japan by Perry) the Koreans agreed to open three of their ports to the Japanese and to exchange diplomatic representation.

Some Japanese already wanted more. They remembered invasions and successful piracy on the Korean coast by their ancestors and pointed to the mineral and natural wealth of the peninsula. The statesmen of the Restoration did not at once give way to such pressure, but in a sense they were only making haste slowly. In the 1890s another step forward led to war with China. The Japanese forces were sweepingly successful but their victory was followed by an appalling national humiliation. At the end of 1895 the alarmed Western powers forced Japan to accept a settlement much less advantageous than the one she had originally imposed on the Chinese, which had included a declaration of Korea's independence.

Popular resentment of the unequal treaties had been running high in Japan and the disappointment over the outcome of the Chinese war brought it to a head. Bitterness toward the West fused with expansion in Asia. The Japanese government had its own interests in backing Chinese revolutionary movements and the East Asian Cultural Union provided a means of doing so. It was also clear to the Western powers that dealing with Japan was going to be a very different matter from bullying China. The great symbol of the change was their relinquishing in 1899 of extraterritoriality, throughout the world one of the most humiliating signs of European predominance. Then came the greatest of all marks of Japan's acceptance as an equal by the West, the Anglo-Japanese alliance of 1902. Japan, it was said, had joined Europe.

The greatest European power in the Far East was Russia. Her role had been important in 1895, and her advance since then made it clear that the longed-for prize of Korea might elude the Japanese if they delayed for long. The building of railways, the development of Vladivostok, and the activities of Russian businessmen and agents in Korea all looked alarming. Most serious of all, in 1898 Russia leased the naval base of Port Arthur from the enfeebled Chinese. In 1904 the Japanese struck at the Russians in Manchuria. The result, after a year of war, was a humiliating defeat for the tsarist forces. For the first time since the seventeenth century a non-European power had defeated a European one in a major war (though it had been done with European arms and training). The implications were colossal. The immediate consequences, too, were far reaching. It was the end of Russian pretensions in Korea and southern Manchuria, where Japanese influence was henceforth dominant, and other territories passed into Japanese possession to remain there until 1945. In 1910 Korea was at last annexed.

A coming age in Asia

With the Japanese annexation of Korea and with the Chinese revolution of 1911 and the end of the Manchu dynasty, the first discernible phase of Asia's response to the West can be given a boundary. The two states which were to be the great Asian powers of the second half of the twentieth century had behaved very differently in the century preceding this. One of them had been able to inoculate herself against the threat of modernization by accepting the virus; the other had not. In each case the West provided both direct and indirect stimulus to upheaval, but in one it was successfully contained and in the other it was not. In each case, too, the fate of the Asian state was decided not only by the response it could itself generate but by relations among the Western powers. Western rivalries in China produced the scramble there which so alarmed and tempted the Japanese, and it was the Anglo-Japanese alliance which assured them that they could strike at their great enemy, Russia, and find her unsupported. A few years more and

Japan and China would both be participants as (formally) equals with other powers in the first world war.

Japan's example and above all her victory over Russia inspired other Asians. That victory was the greatest single reason for them to ponder whether European domination was bound to be their lot. What Japan had done, they might do. Japan had turned Europe's skills against her; the disturbance brought by an aggressive civilization had provoked imitation. In other Asian countries, too, European agencies launched changes which in time contributed to the crumbling of Europe's political hegemony. They brought assumptions about nationalism and humanitarianism, the Christian missionary's dislocation of local society and belief, and the experience of an exploitation not sanctioned by tradition. All these set in motion important economic and social changes. Primitive, almost blind responses, such as the Indian Mutiny or Boxer Rebellion, were the most obvious consequences of the European impact, but there were others which had a much more important future ahead.

THE BRITISH IN INDIA

In 1877 Parliament bestowed the title of Empress of India upon Queen Victoria; some Englishmen laughed and a few disapproved, but it does not seem that many did either. Most assumed the British supremacy there would be permanent or nearly permanent. They would have agreed with their compatriot who said "we are not in India to be pleasant" and held that only a severe and firm government could be sure of preventing another Mutiny. Others would have agreed with the British viceroy who declared as the twentieth century began that "As long as we rule India, we are the greatest power in the world. If we lose it, we shall drop straightway to a third-rate power." There was more than just fear, greed, or lust for power to this outlook. Human beings do not find it easy to pursue collective purposes without some sort of myth to justify them, and this was true of the British in India. Besides an idealism of service and missionary zeal, many British were convinced of the superiority of their civilization and, in some cases, of their stock. In the later nineteenth century such convictions were especially reinforced by the then fashionable currency of racialist ideas and notions derived from nineteenth-century biological science.

Such theories helped justify the much greater social separation of British residents from native Indians after the shock of the Mutiny. Although there was a modest intake of nominated Indian landlords and native rulers into the legislative branch of government, not until the very end of the century were these joined by elected Indians. Moreover, though Indians could compete to enter the civil service, there were important practical obstacles to their doing so. And in the army Indians were kept out of the senior commissioned ranks.

The largest single part of the British army was always stationed in India, where its reliability and monopoly of artillery combined with the officering of the Indian army by other British soldiers to ensure that there would be no repetition of the Mutiny. The coming of railways, telegraphs, and more advanced weapons also told in favor of government in India as much as in any European country. But armed force was no more the explanation of the self-assuredness of British rule than was a conviction of racial superiority. The Census Report of 1901 recorded that there were just under 300 million Indians. These were governed by about 900 white civil servants. Usually there was about one British soldier for every 4,000 Indians. As an Englishman once picturesquely put it, had all the Indians chosen to spit at the same moment, his countrymen would have been drowned.

The Raj rested also on carefully administered policies. One assumption underlying them after the Mutiny was that Indian society should be interfered with as little as possible. Female infanticide might be forbidden, but there was no attempt to prohibit polygamy or child marriage (though after 1891 it was not legal for a marriage to be consummated until the wife was twelve years old). The line of British law usually ran outside what was sanctioned by Hindu religion. This conservatism was reflected in a new attitude toward the native Indian rulers. The Mutiny had shown that they were usually loyal; it was believed that those who turned against the government had been provoked by British annexation of their lands. Their rights were therefore scrupulously respected after the Mutiny; the princes ruled their own states independently and virtually irresponsibly, checked only by their awe of the British political officers resident at their courts. The native states included over a fifth of the population. Elsewhere the British cultivated the Indian aristocracy and landlords. Enlightened despotism at their expense and in the interests of the peasantry (such as had been shown in the early nineteenth century) now disappeared. These were all among the unfortunate consequences of the Mutiny.

The Raj was no more able than any other imperial government to ensure itself permanently against change. Its very success told against it. The suppression of warfare favored the growth of population — and one consequence was more frequent famine. But providing ways of earning a living other than by agriculture as possible relief for the overpopulated countryside was made very difficult by the obstacles placed in the way of Indian industrialization. These arose in large measure from a tariff policy directed in the interests of British industry. A slowly emerging class of Indian industrialists therefore did not feel warmly toward the government but antagonized by it. The ranks of opposition also included many of the growing number of Indians who had received an education along English lines and subsequently been irritated in comparing its precepts with the practice of the British community in India. Those who had studied at Oxford, Cambridge, or the Inns of Court found the contrast especially galling: in nineteenth-century England there were even Indian members of Parliament, but in India a native graduate might be slighted by a British private soldier, and there was an outcry from British residents in the 1880s when a viceroy wished to remove the "invidious distinction" which prevented a European from being brought before an Indian magistrate. Many had also pondered what they read in their studies; the English radical John Stuart Mill and the Italian nationalist Mazzini were thus to have a huge influence in India and, through her leaders, in Asia.

Resentment was especially strong among the Hindus of Bengal, an area where European influence had long operated and the historic center of British power — Calcutta was the capital of India. In 1905 this province was divided in two for administrative reasons. The partition was an important landmark because it brought the Raj for the first time into serious conflict with something not existing in 1857, the Indian nationalist movement.

Indian nationalism

At every stage nationalism had been fed and stimulated by non-Indian forces. British orientalists at the beginning of the nineteenth century had begun the rediscovery of classical Indian culture, which was essential to the self-respect of Hindu nationalism and to overcoming the subcontinent's huge divisions. Under European guidance Indian scholars began to examine the neglected Sanskrit texts; through them they could formulate a conception of a religion and culture far removed from the rich and fantastic, but also superstitious, accretions of popular Hinduism. By the end of the nineteenth century this recovery of the Aryan and Vedic past — Islamic India was virtually disregarded — had gone far enough for Hindus to meet with confidence the reproaches of Christian missionaries and offer a cultural counterattack. A Hindu emissary to the 1893 Parliament of Religion in Chicago not only achieved great personal esteem and obtained serious attention for his assertion that Hinduism was a great religion capable of revivifying the spiritual life of other cultures, but he actually made converts.

Such success justified a Hindu national consciousness. Like the political activity it was to reinforce, it was for a long time confined to a few. The proposal that Hindi should be India's language seemed wildly unrealistic when the hundreds of languages and dialects which fragmented Indian society were considered; it could only appeal to an elite seeking to strengthen its links across the subcontinent. The definition of this elite was one of education rather than of wealth or birth: its backbone was provided by those Hindus, often Bengali, who felt especially disappointed at the failure of their educational attainments to win them an appropriate share in the running of India. The Raj seemed determined to maintain the racial predominance of Europeans and to rely upon such conservative interests as the princes and landlords to the exclusion and, possibly even more important, the humiliation of the babu, the educated, middle-class, urban Hindu.

A new cultural self-respect and a growing sense of grievances over rewards and slights were the background to the formation of the Indian National Congress. The immediate prelude was a flurry of excitement over government proposals, subsequently modified because of the outcry of European residents, to equalize the treatment of Indians and Europeans in the courts. Disappointment led an Englishman, a former civil servant, to take steps which culminated in the first conference of the Indian National Congress in Bombay in December 1885. Viceregal initiatives, too, had played a part in this, and British would long be prominent in the administration of the congress and even longer patronize it with protection and advice from London. It was an appropriate symbol of the complexity of Europe's impact on India that some Indian delegates attended in Western dress, improbably attired in morning suits and top hats of comical unsuitability to the climate of their country.

The congress soon declared its commitment to the principles of national unity and regeneration, but it did not at first aspire to self-government. It sought only to provide a means of communicating Indian views to the viceroy and proclaimed its "unswerving loyalty" to the British crown. Only after twenty years, in which much more extreme nationalist views had won adherents among Hindus, did the congress begin to discuss the possibility of independence. During this time its attitude had been soured and stiffened by the vilification it received from British residents who declared it unrepresentative and by the unresponsiveness of an administration which endorsed this view and preferred to work through more traditional and conservative channels. Extremists grew more insistent, and in 1904 came the inspiriting victories of Japan over Russia.

The partition of Bengal in 1905 provided the issue for a crucial change. The purpose of the partition was twofold: it was administratively convenient and it would possibly weaken Bengal's nationalism. It produced a West Bengal where there was a Hindu majority and an East Bengal with a Muslim majority. This detonated a mass of explosive materials long accumulating.

The Indian National Congress began to discuss independence. The extremists were heartened by antipartition riots, but at first moderates and radicals avoided a split in the nationalist movement by agreeing on the aim of swaraj, which in practice might mean independent self-government such as that enjoyed by the white dominions: their example was suggestive. A new weapon was deployed against the British, a boycott of goods, which it was hoped might be extended to other forms of passive resistance, such as nonpayment of taxes and the refusal of soldiers to obey orders. Within a few years extremism was producing terrorism. Again foreign models were important. Russian revolutionary terrorism now joined the works of Mazzini and the biography of Garibaldi, the heroic guerrilla leader of the Italian wars of nationhood, as formative influences on an emerging India; the extremists argued that political murder was not ordinary murder. The British met assassination and bombing with special repressive measures, and in 1908 the extremists were excluded from the congress.

Communalism

Perhaps the most momentous consequence of partition was that it brought out into the open the division between Muslim and Hindu. Ever since the Arabian Wahhabi sect had generated an Islamic reform movement a century earlier, Indian Muslims had felt more and more distinct from Hindus. Distrusted by the British because of attempts to revive the power of the Mogul emperor in 1857, they had little success in winning posts in government or on the judicial bench. Hindus had responded more eagerly than Muslims to the educational opportunities offered by the Raj; they had more

The blood of the martyrs continued into recent times to be the seed of the Church. This Vietnamese print depicts the martyrdom of a Roman Catholic priest and two catechists in 1840. *(Missions/Trangeres de Paris)*

commercial weight and more influence on government. But Muslims had also found British helpers, who had launched a new Islamic college to give them the English education they needed to compete with Hindus and had helped set up Muslim political organizations. Some English civil servants began to grasp the potential for balancing Hindu pressure which Muslim nationalism could give the Raj. Intensifications of Hindu practice, such as a cow protection movement, could only increase the separation of the two communities.

Nevertheless, it was only in 1905 that the split became, as it would remain until 1947, one of the fundamentals of Indian politics. The antipartitionists campaigned with a strident display of Hindu symbols and slogans. The British governor of East Bengal favored Muslims against Hindus and strove to give them a vested interest in the new province. He was dismissed, but his inoculation had taken: Bengal Muslims deplored his removal. An Anglo-Muslim entente was suspected and further inflamed Hindu terrorists. To make things worse, all this was taking place during five years (from 1906 to 1910) in which prices rose faster than at any time since the Mutiny.

A set of governmental reforms in 1909 merely changed somewhat the terms of political forces which were henceforth to dominate the history of India until the Raj came to an end nearly forty years later. Indians were for the first time appointed to the council which advised the British minister responsible for India; more important, further elected places were provided for Indians in the legislature. But the electorates were to have a communal

A French print extolling the bravery of French soldiers in the Indochina campaign of 1885. Although the year began badly with a grave defeat for the French at Hanoi, it was in fact the beginning of the last phase of the pacification of Indochina which brought a treaty with China recognizing the French presence there.

(Phot. Bibl. Nat. Paris)

basis; the division of Hindu and Muslim India, that is to say, was institutionalized.

In 1911, for the first and only time, a reigning British monarch visited India. A great imperial durbar or court was held at Delhi, the old center of Mogul rule, to which the capital of British India was now transferred from Calcutta. The princes of India came to do homage; even the Indian National Congress did not question its duty to the throne. George V's accession earlier that year had been marked by the conferring of real and symbolic benefits, the most notable and politically significant being the reuniting of Bengal. The Raj seemed at its apogee.

Yet India was far from settled. Terrorism and seditious crime continued. The policy of favoring Muslims had made Hindus more resentful while Muslims now felt that the government had gone back on its understandings with them in withdrawing the partition of Bengal, where they feared the resumption of Hindu ascendancy. Hindus, on the other hand, took the concession as evidence that resistance paid off and began to press for abolition of the communal electoral arrangements which the Muslims prized. The British had therefore already somewhat alienated Muslim support when a further strain appeared.

The Indian Muslim elites which favored cooperation with the British were increasingly under pressure from their lower-class brethren, who were susceptible to the violent appeal of a growing pan-Islamic movement. The pan-Islamists could point to the fact that the British had let the Muslims down in Bengal. Soon they noted that in Tripoli (which the Italians attacked in 1911) and the Balkans (in 1912 and 1913) Christian powers were attacking Turkey, which was the seat of the caliphate, the institutional embodiment of the spiritual leadership of Islam. Great Britain was indisputably a Christian power. The suspicions of lower-class Indian Muslims were excited to the point where agitators could present even the involvement of a mosque in the replanning of a street as part of a deliberate plot to harry Islam. When Turkey went to war with Great Britain in 1914, Muslim political organizations remained loyal, but some Indian Muslims accepted the logical consequence of the caliphate's supremacy and began to prepare revolution against the Raj. They were few. What was more important for the future was that by then three forces were operating in Indian politics: British, Hindu, and Muslim. Here was the origin of the future partition of the subcontinent.

SOUTHEAST ASIA

Most of Southeast Asia was under European sovereignty by 1900, but this is a huge area and generalizations about it are rarely easy and hardly ever safe. Perhaps the soundest is to say that no European possession there was as much transformed before 1914 as India, though all of them showed evidence of the impact of modernization and the decline of local tradition. The same forces were at work there as elsewhere: European aggression, the example of Japan, and the impact of Western culture. But the first and last of these had operated in the region for a shorter time than in China and India. In 1880 most of Southeast Asia was still ruled by independent native princes though they had usually already made concessions in unequal treaties with European powers. In the following decade the situation rapidly changed. Great Britain annexed Burma in 1885 and France swallowed Indochina in stages. The sultans of Malaya acquired British residents at their courts who directed policy through the native administration. By 1900 only Siam was still independent among the kingdoms of this region.

Most of them had been shaped by cultural influences of Indian origin. The only one which was more closely linked to China was Vietnam, that part of Indochina known in the early stages of French imperial expansion as Annam. Vietnam had the longest tradition of national identity and a history of national revolt long before the European imperial era. It is therefore not surprising that resistance to Europeanization was most marked in this part of the French *Union Indochinoise.*

French missionary interest in the area went back to the seventeenth century, and the persecution of Christianity in the nineteenth century led France to intervene again in southern Vietnam in the 1850s. This of course brought about diplomatic conflict with China, which then claimed sovereignty over the country. A war between the two imperial powers (1883–1885) established the French as paramount. They set about the creation of a structure which disguised a centralized regime behind a system of protectorates. Though this meant the preservation of native rulers (the emperor of Vietnam and the kings of Cambodia and Laos), the aim of French colonial policy was always assimilation. French culture was to be brought to new French subjects, and their elites were to be Gallicized because this was believed to be the best way to modernization and civilization.

The centralizing tendencies of French administration soon showed that the formal native structure of government was a sham. The French thus eroded local institutions without replacing them with others enjoying the loyalty of the people. This was a dangerous course. There were other important by-products of the French presence. It brought with it, for example, French tariff policy, which was to slow down industrialization and eventually lead Indochinese businessmen to wonder in whose interests their country was run. Additional problems arose from the conception of Indochina as an integral part of France whose inhabitants should be turned into Frenchmen. The colonial administration had to grapple with the paradox that access to French education could lead to reflection on the motto adorning official buildings and documents: liberty, equality, and fraternity. Finally, French law and notions of property broke down the structure of village landholding and threw power into the hands of moneylenders and landlords. With population rising in the rice-growing areas, a revolutionary potential for the future was being built up.

The examples of Japan and China provided catalysts for these grievances and the legacy of traditional Vietnamese nationalism. The Japanese victory over Russia brought several young Vietnamese to Tokyo, where they met Sun Yat-sen and the Japanese sponsors of "Asia for the Asians." After the Chinese revolution of 1911 one of these young men organized a society to work for a Vietnamese republic. None of this much troubled the French, who were well able to contain such opposition before 1914, but it curiously paralleled conservative opposition to them among the Confucian scholar class. This important section of Vietnamese opinion was deeply alienated by French rule within a couple of decades. Though the French opened a university in 1907, they had to close it almost at once. It remained closed until 1918 because of fears of unrest among the intellectuals.

Indonesia

Sixty million Indonesians had ancestors who for much longer than the Vietnamese had experience, sometimes bitter, of foreign rule. In the nineteenth century there were times when nearly half the Dutch national budget was met by what was called a "surplus" from Indonesian revenues. The workings of the agricultural system had led to exploitation of the peasant, which in the second half of the nineteenth century began to awaken among Dutchmen an uneasiness about the conduct of their colonial governments. This culminated in a great change of attitude toward Dutch Indonesia. A new "ethical policy" announced in 1901 was expressed in decentralization and a campaign to achieve improvement through village administration. But this program sometimes proved so paternalistic and interventionist that it stimulated yet more hostility, which was utilized by the first Indonesian nationalists.

Inspired by India, some Indonesians formed an organization in 1908 to promote national education. Three years later an Islamic association appeared. Its early activities were directed as much against Chinese traders as against the Dutch, but by 1916 it had gone so far as to ask for self-government while remaining in union with the Netherlands. Before this, however, a true independence party had been founded in 1912. It opposed Dutch authority in the name of native-born Indonesians of any race; a Dutchman was among its three founders and others followed him. In 1916 the Dutch took the first step toward meeting the demands of these groups by authorizing a parliament with limited powers for Indonesia.

Though nationalism was an observable general trend in almost all Asian countries by the early years of the twentieth century, it took different expressions from the different possibilities presented by history. Not all colonial regimes behaved in the same way toward it. The British encouraged nationalism in Burma while the United States doggedly pursued a benevolent paternalism in the Philippines, where it had inherited an insurrection originally directed against the Spanish. Americans had the additional peculiarity of governing the only predominantly Christian country of Asia, thanks to their predecessors, though French missionary fervor produced important Christian communities in Vietnam. But history not only operated through different colonial traditions; these regimes played upon different social structures. Too much history was present already for the last phase of European expansion alone to explain the later course of twentieth-century Asia. The catalytic and liberating power of that expansion, nonetheless, was what brought Asia into the modern era and gave her history redirection on the course it still follows.

part VI THE END OF THE EUROPEANS' WORLD

In 1900 Europeans could look back on two, perhaps three, centuries of astonishing growth. Most of them would have said too that it was growth for the better, that is, progress. Their history since the Middle Ages—and that of Europeans settled overseas—looked very much like a continuing advance to goals evidently worthwhile. Fewer and fewer people questioned them. Whether the criteria were intellectual and scientific or material and economic (even if they were moral and aesthetic, some said, so persuasive was the gospel of progress), a look at their own past assured Europeans that they were set on a progressive course, which meant that the world was set on a progressive course for their civilization was spread world wide. What was more, limitless progress seemed to lie ahead. Europeans showed in 1900 much the same confidence in the continuing success of their culture as the Chinese had shown in theirs a century earlier. The past, they were sure, proved them right.

Even so, there were a few who did not feel so confident. It was not that they were struck by the rapid collapse of Chinese pretensions and felt that nemesis might lie in wait for Europe's overweening pride in the same way. They felt rather that the very past which looked so encouraging to optimists could equally well imply a pessimistic conclusion. Though there were far fewer pessimists than optimists, they numbered in their ranks men of acknowledged standing and powerful minds. Some of them argued *that the civilization in which they lived had yet to reveal its full self-destructive potential and sensed that the time when it would do so might not be far away. A half-century earlier Thomas Macaulay, the archpriest of an optimistic interpretation of history, had suggested that there would come a day when a New Zealander would sit contemplating the ruins of London in much the spirit that a Victorian tourist contemplated those of Rome. The true pessimists went much further. At worst they saw a civilization more and more obviously drifting away from its moorings in religion and absolute morality, carried along by the tides of materialism and barbarity probably to complete disaster.*

As it turned out, neither optimists nor pessimists were very exact prophets, perhaps because their eyes were glued too firmly to what they thought were the characteristics of European civilization. They looked to its own inherent powers, tendencies, or weaknesses for guidance about the future; very few of them paid any attention to the way Europe was changing the world in which her own ascendancy had been built and was thus ultimately changing once more the balance between different historic centers of civilized traditions. Few looked farther than Europe and Europe beyond the seas except the unbalanced cranks who fussed about the "Yellow Peril"; yet Napoleon had a century earlier warned that China was a sleeping giant best left undisturbed.

It is tempting to say in retrospect that the pessimists have had the best of the argument and it may be true. But hindsight is sometimes a disadvantage to the historian and in this instance makes it difficult to see how the optimists could once have felt so sure of themselves. Yet we should try to do so. For one thing, there were men of vision and insight among them; for another, optimism was for so long an obstacle to the solution of certain problems in this century that it deserves to be understood as a historical force in its own right. And much of what the pessimists said was wrong too. Appalling though the disasters of the twentieth century have been, they fell on societies more resilient than those shattered by lesser ones in earlier times, and they were not always the disasters feared seventy years ago. Optimists and pessimists alike in 1900 had to work with data which could be read in more than one way. We are not so successful with better data as to be in a position to condemn them. It is not reprehensible, merely tragic, that so few people could judge what lay ahead at the beginning of this century. What they saw quite correctly was that for good or evil its possibilities were immense.

chapter 33

Strains in the System: Europe at the Beginning of the Twentieth Century

CHANGES AND CHALLENGES

One of the most obvious facts of 1900 was the continuing growth of population in the European world. Europe then had about 400 million inhabitants, a quarter of them Russians, the United States about 76 million, and the British overseas dominions about 15 million altogether. This kept the dominant civilization's share of world population high. On the other hand, growth was slowing down in some countries early in the twentieth century. In the advanced societies which were the heart of western Europe, growth depended more and more on falling death rates as the conscious restriction of family size spread downward through society. A traditional contraceptive knowledge had long been available, but the nineteenth century had brought more effective techniques to the better-off. When these spread to the most numerous classes of society (as they soon appeared to be doing), their impact on population structure would be very great.

In eastern and Mediterranean Europe such effects were far away. There, rapid growth was just beginning to produce its greatest strains. Only emigration made it possible to surmount these, and trouble might develop if the outlets overseas ceased to be so easily available. Another pessimistic reflection looked farther afield, to a time when the agencies reducing the death rate in Europe would spread to Asia and Africa. In the world civilization the nineteenth century had created, this could not be prevented. Europe's success in imposing herself guaranteed the eventual loss of the demographic advantage she had long enjoyed. The "Yellow Peril" would become a reality. So might the once feared Malthusian crisis.

Malthus' warnings had been overtaken in the nineteenth century by the first "economic miracle"—the greatest expansion of wealth the world had ever known. Its sources lay in the industrialization of Europe and the United States. There had been a vast and accelerating production of commodities available only in tiny quantities a century earlier, and whole new ranges of goods had come into existence. As sources of energy, oil and electricity had joined coal, wind, and water. A chemical industry unimaginable in 1800 had been born. Growing power and wealth had tapped seemingly inexhaustible natural resources, both agricultural and mineral. Railways, steamships, the first automobiles, and even bicycles gave millions a new control over their environment by accelerating travel for the first time since animals had been harnessed to carts thousands of years before. In many countries a growing population had been easily supported by an even faster increase in the production of wealth; for example, between 1870 and 1900 Germany's output of pig iron increased sixfold, but her population rose only by about a third. In terms of consumption, the services to which they had access, and even the enjoyment of better health, the masses in developed countries were much better off in 1900 than their predecessors a hundred years before. Though people like the Russian or Andalusian peasants had not yet benefited, it looked as if the way ahead was promising even for them.

In spite of this cheerful picture, doubts could still arise about the cost of the new wealth and the social justice of its distribution. Even in rich countries most people were very poor, and increasing numbers were more struck by the apparent illogicality and inequity of this than in earlier times. Poverty was all the more afflicting when society showed such obvious power to create new wealth. Here was the beginning of a change in expectations of revolutionary import. Another change in the way people thought about their condition concerned their ability to earn a livelihood at all. It was not new for men to be without work, but now the operation of blind forces of boom and slump could suddenly produce millions of workers without jobs concentrated in great towns. This was a new phenomenon for which a new word was needed and found—unemployment. Some economists thought it might be an inevitable concomitant of capitalism.

Nor were the cities yet rid of the evils which had struck the first observers of industrial society. By 1900 the majority of western Europeans were town dwellers; in 1914 Europe had more than 140 cities of over 100,000 inhabitants. Millions of people were cramped together, ill housed, lacking adequate schools and fresh air, let alone amusement other than that of the streets, and this often in sight of the wealth their class helped produce. "Slums" was another word invented by the nineteenth century. Two converging conclusions were often drawn from contemplating them. One was that of fear: many sober statesmen at the end of the nineteenth century still distrusted cities as centers of revolutionary danger, crime, and wickedness. The other was hopeful: the slums gave grounds to some for assurance that revolution was inevitable. What these responses neglected was both the evidence of experience that revolution in western Europe was in fact less and less likely and the dogged and successful attempts of reformers to make things better.

Revolution and reform: the alternatives

The most alarming evidence of revolutionary danger was in the east. In Russia reform had not modified autocracy enough to stifle a continuing revolutionary movement. It broke out in terrorism—one of the victims was a tsar—and was supplemented by spontaneous agrarian unrest. Peasant attacks on landlords and their bailiffs reached a peak in the early years of this century. When defeat in war momentarily shook the regime's confidence, the result was a revolution in 1905.

Russia was clearly a special case. But Italy, too, experienced outbreaks in 1898 and 1914 that some observers thought of as barely contained revolutions, and one of Spain's great cities, Barcelona, exploded into bloody street fighting in 1909. Strikes and demonstrations could become violent even in industrialized countries without revolutionary traditions; in Great Britain deaths resulted from them before 1914. Such events kept policemen and respectable citizens on their toes. The anarchists were especially successful in pressing themselves on the public imagination during the 1890s by their acts of terrorism and assassination; their deeds (which transcended their immediate context because of the growth of the press) had shown that a bomb or a dagger stroke could produce a great sensation. Not all anarchists shared the same aims, but they were children of their epoch: they protested not only against the state in its governmental aspect but also against a whole society they judged unjust.

Socialist principles easily explained. Four Dutch cartoons of 1895 contrasting the defects of absolute monarchy, constitutional government, and free enterprise capitalism with a socialist paradise. *(New York Public Library, Astor, Lenox and Tilden Foundations)*

Socialists contributed most to the rhetoric which sustained the fear of revolution, and by 1900 socialism usually meant Marxism. An important alternative to Marxist socialism existed only in England, where the early growth of a broad trade union movement and the possibility of working through one of the established political parties produced a less overtly revolutionary brand of socialism. The supremacy of Marxism among Continental socialists was formally expressed in 1896. In that year the Second International, an organization set up in 1889 to coordinate socialist action in all countries, expelled the anarchists who would not accept its discipline. Four years later the International opened a permanent administrative center in Brussels.

Numbers, wealth, and theoretical contributions gave the German Social Democratic Party practical preponderance within the International. This party had prospered during Germany's rapid industrialization in spite of police persecution. By 1900 it was an established fact of German politics, the country's first truly mass organization. Numbers and wealth alone would have made it likely that Marxism, the official creed of the German party, would be predominant in an international socialist movement. But Marxism had its own intellectual and emotional appeal; it gave socialists the assurance that the world was going the way they hoped and the emotional satisfaction of participating in a class struggle which must end in revolution. Marxism was as much a religious faith as an intellectual approach.

Though such a mythology confirmed the fears of the established order, some intelligent Marxists had noticed that after 1880 or so the facts by no means obviously supported it. Great numbers of people had obtained a higher standard of living within the capitalist system. Nor was the unfolding of that system in all its complexity simplifying and sharpening class conflict in the way Marx had predicted. In some countries, capitalist political institutions had actually served the working class; in Germany and England especially, important advantages had been won for the poor. When the vote was available as a weapon, workers were not disposed to ignore it while waiting for the revolution. These trends led some socialists to attempt to restate official Marxism; they were called revisionists and their conclusions seemed to point to a peaceful advance toward the transformation of society. Their views provoked a conflict in socialism which came to a head at the end of the nineteenth century.

The debate took years to settle. What emerged in the end was explicit condemnation of revisionism by the International, but national parties, notably the Germans, continued to act on it in practice while using the rhetoric of revolution. Many socialists hoped that the revolution would become a reality if workers refused to fight as conscripts when their governments tried to make them to go to war. One socialist group, the majority in the Russian party, continued vigorously to denounce revisionism and advocate violence; no doubt this stance recognized the peculiarity of the situation in Russia, where there was little opportunity for parliamentary activity and a deep tradition of revolution and terrorism. These men were called Bolsheviks, from the Russian word signifying a majority, and more would be heard of them.

By 1900 many conservatives worried that further advances by liberalism and democracy might well prove irresistible except by force. A few of these were still living in a mental world which was pre-nineteenth rather than pre-twentieth century. Especially in eastern Europe quasi-patriarchal relationships and an almost absolute authority of the landowner over his estates could still be found. Such societies produced aristocratic conservatives who were opposed in spirit not merely to encroachments upon their material privileges but also to the secularism, individualism, and materialism of market society. But this rejection of market society was more and more blurred; for the most part, conservative thinking tended to fall back upon the defense of capital, a position which in many places a half century earlier would have been regarded as radically liberal because individualist.

The new form of capitalist, or industrial, conservatism opposed more and more vigorously the state's interference with its wealth, an interference which had grown steadily with the state's acceptance of a larger role in the regulation of society. There was a crisis in England on the issue which led to a final revolutionary transformation of what was left of the 1688 constitution in 1911 by the legislative crippling of the House of Lords' power to thwart an elected House of Commons. In the background were many political issues, but prominent among them was payment for further extensions of social services. The fear of new taxes on wealth was all the greater because international competition was imposing heavy bills for armaments on the European great powers. Even France had by 1914 accepted the principle of an income tax.

Women's challenge

By 1914 universal male suffrage existed in France, Germany, and several smaller European countries, and Great Britain and Italy had electorates big enough to come near to meeting this criterion. It brought forward another disruptive question: should not women too have the vote in national politics? This was already causing uproar in Great Britain. But in Europe only Finland and Norway had women in their national electorates by 1914, and the issue would not be settled in many countries for another thirty years.

The vote was only one side of the whole question of women's rights in a society whose entire bias, like that of every other great civilization which had preceded it, was toward the interests and values of men. A woman's right to education, to employment, to control of her own property, to moral independence, even to wear more comfortable clothes had increasingly been in debate in the nineteenth century. Henrik Ibsen's play *A Doll's House* was interpreted as a trumpet call to the liberation of women (though the author intended it as a plea for the individual). Female emancipation was real revolution. It threatened assumptions and attitudes institutionalized not for centuries but millennia. The new claims of women awoke complex emotions because they touched deep-seated notions about the family and sexuality, and they troubled some people—men and women alike—more than the threat of social revolution or political democracy. People were right to see the question in this dimension. In the early European feminist movement was the seed of something whose explosive content would be even greater when transferred (as it soon was) to other cultures and civilizations.

The politicizing of women and political attacks on the legal and institutional structures they considered oppressive, nonetheless, probably did less to undermine traditional family patterns than other changes. Two of these were of slowly growing and eventually gigantic importance. The first was the development of the advanced capitalist economy. By 1914 there were great numbers of jobs for women in some countries—as typists, secretaries, telephone operators, factory workers, department store assistants, and teachers. Almost none of these had existed in 1800. This meant a huge practical accession of economic power to women, and if they could earn their own living, they were at the beginning of a road which would eventually transform family structures. For growing numbers of women a job already spelled some degree of liberation from parental regulation and the trap of married drudgery. Most women did not yet benefit by 1914, but an accelerating process was at work because these developments would stimulate other demands, for example, for education and professional training.

A "suffragette" (as women who sought the vote in England were called) being led away from a demonstration outside Buckingham Palace in 1914. (*Radio Times,Hulton Picture Library*)

The second great transforming force was even further from showing its full potential in 1914. This was contraception. It had already decisively affected demography. What lay ahead was a revolution in power and status as more women absorbed the idea that they could control the demands of child bearing and rearing, which throughout history had determined most women's lives. Beyond that lay an even deeper change, only beginning to be discerned in 1914, as women came to see that they could pursue sexual satisfaction without necessarily entering into the obligations of life-long marriage.

Nationalism and mass politics

The need to organize the new voting masses had by 1900 given birth to the modern political party, with its simplification of issues to present clear choices, its apparatus for arousing political awareness, and its cultivation of special interests. It would spread around the world. Old-fashioned politicians deplored the new model of party because these parties reponded to public opinion and they deplored that.

English politicians had begun to take note of public opinion early in the nineteenth century, and it had been thought decisive in the struggles over the Corn Laws. Its influence soon spread to the Continent. In 1870 the French emperor could not resist the popular clamor for a war he feared and which he was to lose. Bismarck, the quintessence of conservative statesmen, responded to the demand of public opinion in the 1880s to promote Germany's colonial interests. The manipulation of public opinion, too, seemed to have become possible (or so many newspaper owners and statesmen believed). Growing literacy had two sides to it. Investment in mass education was necessary to civilize the lower classes for the proper use of the vote, yet rising literacy created a market for a new cheap press which often pandered to emotionalism and sensationalism and for the devisers of advertising campaigns (another invention of the nineteenth century).

The political principle which undoubtedly still had the most mass appeal was nationalism. Moreover, in many places it kept all its revolutionary potential. In Turkish Europe from the Crimean War onward the successes of nationalists in fighting the Ottoman empire and establishing new nations had never flagged. Serbia, Greece, and Rumania were solidly established by 1870. By the end of the century they had been joined by Bulgaria and Montenegro. In 1913, in the last wars of the Balkan states against Turkey before a European conflict swallowed the Turkish question, Albania appeared, and by then an autonomous Crete already had a Greek governor. These nationalist movements had at several times dragged greater states into their affairs and always presented a potential danger to European peace.

Less important international consequences followed from nationalism within the Russian empire, where Poles, Jews, Ukrainians, and Lithuanians felt oppressed by the Russians. Perhaps it produced its worse strains in the Austro-Hungarian empire; it was a real revolutionary danger in the lands within the Hungarian half of the monarchy. Slav majorities there looked across the border to Serbia for help against Magyar (Hungarian) oppressors.

UNCLE SAM: "My, Johnny, but it dew please me to have you on my side for once."

Anglo-Saxon attitudes: the national stereotypes of Uncle Sam and John Bull were diffused more widely than ever before by the cheap press of the nineteenth century. In this American cartoon of 1898 Uncle Sam alludes to British diplomatic support over the Spanish-American war. (*Radio Times Hulton Picture Library*)

Elsewhere in the Habsburg lands—in Bohemia and Slovakia, for example—feeling was less high, but nationalism was still a dominant question. Great Britain faced no comparable danger, but even she had a similar problem—in Ireland. Indeed, she had two. That presented by the Catholic Irish was for most of the nineteenth century the more obvious. Important reforms and concessions had been granted though they fell short of the autonomous Ireland of home rule to which the British Liberal party came to be committed. By 1900, however, better economic conditions had done much to draw the venom from Irish nationalism insofar as that was a matter of Catholic Ireland. It was reinserted, unhappily, by the appearance of *another* Irish nationalism, that of the Protestant majority of the province of Ulster, which was excited by politicians to threaten revolution if the government in London gave home rule to the Catholic Irish nationalists. Partition would be one outcome.

These were all expressions of national groups which with greater or less justification believed themselves to be oppressed. But the nationalism of the great powers was also a disruptive force in Europe. France and Germany were psychologically deeply sundered by the former's loss of two provinces, Alsace and Lorraine, to Germany in 1871. French politicians whom it suited to do so assiduously cultivated the theme of revanche (revenge). Nationalism in France gave special bitterness to her domestic political quarrels because they seemed to raise questions of loyalty to great national institutions. Even the supposedly sober British from time to time grew excited about national symbols. There was a brief but violent enthusiasm for imperialism and always great sensitivity over the preservation of British naval supremacy. More and more the latter appeared to be threatened by Germany, whose obvious economic dynamism also caused alarm because it challenged British supremacy in world commerce. It did not matter that the two countries were each other's best customers; what was noticed was that they appeared to have interests opposed in many specific ways.

Additional color was given to this by the stridency of German nationalism during the reign of the emperor Wilhelm II. Conscious of Germany's potential, he sought to give it not only real but symbolic expression. His enthusiasm for building a great navy especially annoyed the British, who could not see it as intended for use against anyone but themselves. But there was a generally growing impression in Europe, far from unjustified, that the Germans were prone to throw their weight about unreasonably in international affairs. National stereotypes helped to impose terrible simplifications upon public reactions and are part of the story of the disruptive power of nationalist feeling at the beginning of this century.

RELIGION AND SCIENCE

Once religion had exercised some restraint, even if not a completely effective one, over the behavior of kings and states, but its power had collapsed with the idea of Christendom which underlay it. In the nineteenth century religion was only a palliative of conflict feeding a general humanitarianism which had other and secular sources too. This was one reflection of the marked decline in the status of religion within European civilization after the French Revolution. Although millions of Europeans and Americans in 1900 still kept their religious practices, misgivings had by then long been felt about the state of religion both as a system of belief and as a regulator of behavior.

These misgivings had not arisen because another faith challenged the traditional churches of Christendom in their homelands. They had developed because almost all the Christian communions seemed to suffer from one or another of the intellectual and social advances of the age. The Catholic Church was the most obvious victim because the papacy had especially and specifically lost both prestige and power. It had openly proclaimed its hostility to progress, rationality, and liberalism in statements (the most famous being the Syllabus of Errors of 1864) which became part of the dogmas of the church. The whittling away of Rome's temporal power had begun in the 1790s, when the French armies brought revolutionary principles to Italy. Later infringements of the papacy's rights were justified in terms of the master ideas of the age: democracy, liberalism, nationalism. Finally in 1870 the new kingdom of Italy absorbed the last of those territories which had constituted the Papal States, and the papacy became a purely spiritual and ecclesiastical authority.

To some this seemed an inglorious end for a centuries-old state; in fact it was to prove advantageous, a new beginning. Nevertheless, this spoliation confirmed both the papacy's hostility to the forces of the century and the derision in which it was held by many progressive thinkers. Their contempt reached new heights in 1870 when it became a part of Roman Catholic dogma that the pope, when he spoke *ex cathedra* on faith and morals, did so with infallible authority. There followed two decades in which anticlericalism and priest baiting were more important in the politics of Germany, France, Italy, and Spain than ever before. Persecution bred intransigence. But the fact emerged that whatever view might be taken of the abstract teachings of the Roman church, it could still draw on vast reservoirs of loyalty among believers. Moreover, it was still gaining converts in the mission field overseas. Though Catholicism did not make much progress among the new city dwellers of Europe, untouched by an inadequate ecclesiastical machine and paganized by the slow stain of an increasingly industrial culture, it was far from dying, let alone dead, as a political and social force. Indeed, the liberation of the papacy from its temporal role made it easier for some Catholics to feel uncompromised loyalty toward it as the century ended.

The Roman Catholic Church had been the most demanding of the Christian churches and was in the forefront of religion's battle with the age, but the claims of revelation and the authority of priest or clergyman were everywhere being questioned. This was one of the most striking features of the nineteenth century, all the more so because so many Europeans and Americans still retained simple and literal beliefs in the dogmas of their churches and the story contained in the Bible. They felt great anxiety when these beliefs were threatened, yet this happened increasingly and in all countries.

The threat to traditional belief appeared first among an intellectual elite often consciously holding ideas drawn from Enlightenment sources: "Voltairean" was a favorite nineteenth-century adjective which implied antireligious and skeptical views. As the century proceeded, these ideas were reinforced by two other currents, both also at first a matter of elites but increasingly unlikely to be limited in their effect in an age of growing mass literacy and cheap printing.

The first challenge came from biblical scholars, the most important of them German, who from the 1840s onward not only demolished many assumptions about the value of the Bible as historical evidence but also, and perhaps more fundamentally, brought about a psychological change of attitude toward the scriptures. In essence this consisted of making it possible henceforth to regard the Bible simply as a historic text like any other, to be approached critically. An immensely successful (and scandal provoking) *Life of Jesus* published by a French scholar in 1863 brought such an attitude before a wider public than ever before. The book which had been the central text of European civilization since its emergence in the Dark Ages was never to recover its unquestioned position.

The challenge from science

The second source of ideas damaging to traditional Christian faith — and therefore to the morality, politics, and economics for so long anchored in Christian assumptions — was science. Enlightenment attacks on internal and logical inconsistencies in the teaching of the church became much more alarming when science began to produce empirical evidence that certain things said in the Bible (and therefore based on the same authority as everything else in it) were plainly not in accordance with observable fact.

The starting point was geology. Ideas which had been about since the end of the eighteenth century were given a much wider public in the 1830s by the writings of an English geologist, Charles Lyell. His *Principles of Geology* explained landscape and geological structure in terms of forces still at work, that is, not as the result of a single act of creation but of wind, rain, and so on. Moreover, Lyell pointed out that the presence of fossils of different forms of life in different geological strata implied the creation of new animals in each geological age. If this were so, the biblical account of creation was clearly in difficulties.

It is an oversimplification, but not a grossly distorting one, to say that the questions thus raised were brought to a head over twenty years later in one of the seminal books of modern civilization, the work by Charles Darwin called, for short, *The Origin of Species*. Much in this book was owed without acknowledgment to predecessors. Its publication in 1859 also came at a moment when and in a country where the issue of the rightfulness of the traditional dominance of religion (for example, in education) was in the air. The word "evolution" with which Darwin's name came especially to be connected was by then already familiar (and he tried to avoid using it). This background explains some of the interest shown in Darwin's ideas. Nevertheless, *The Origin of Species* was the greatest single statement of evolutionary hypothesis—namely that living things were what they were because their forms had undergone long evolution from simpler ones. This of course included man. Views differed on how evolution had occurred. Darwin, impressed by Malthus' vision of the murderous competition of mankind for food, took the view that the qualities which made success likely in hostile environments ensured the "natural selection" of those creatures embodying them, a hypothesis to be vulgarized and terribly distorted by the misuse of the phrase "survival of the fittest." But important though many aspects of his work were to be in inspiring fresh thought, it is relevant here that Darwin dealt the most widely publicized blow so far against the biblical account of creation (as well as against the assumption of the unique status of man). In combination with biblical criticism his book made it impossible for any conscientious and thoughtful person to accept the Bible as literally true.

Religious beliefs were also affected by the vague general prestige science was coming to have as the supreme instrument for the manipulation of nature, which was seen as increasingly powerless to resist it. This would later grow into a mythology of science, and its essence lay in the fact that while the great achievements of seventeenth-century science had not often resulted in changes in the lives of ordinary men and women, those of the nineteenth century increasingly did. Men who understood not a word written by Joseph Lister, who established the need and technique of using antiseptics in surgery, or Michael Faraday, who more than anyone else made possible the generation of electricity, still knew that the medicine of 1900 was different from that of their grandparents and saw electricity being used in their work and homes. By 1914 radio messages could be sent across the Atlantic, flying machines which did not need the support of bags of gas lighter than air were common, aspirins were easily available, and an American manufacturer had produced the first cheap mass automobile. The objective achievements of science were by no means adequately represented by such practical applications, but it was material advance of this sort which impressed the average man with its power. This is to say that his awareness of science came through technology. Respect for it therefore usually grew in proportion to spectacular results in engineering or manufacture.

Science is so interwoven with modern society that it is difficult to come to grips with its rapid growth. It has affected every part of life while people are still trying to grapple with some of its most elementary philosophical implications. At least three aspects must be taken into account in trying to assess science's impact on civilization: its status as a social and material phenomenon in its own right, its direct material effects, and its importance as a source of mythology.

From the moment when the great advances in physics were made in the seventeenth century, science was already a social fact. Institutions quickly arose in which men came together to study nature in a way a later age could recognize as scientific. Even then rulers sometimes employed scientists to bring their expertise to bear on specific problems. And in the useful arts— and they were more usually called arts than sciences—such as navigation or agriculture, experiments by those who were not themselves practitioners made valuable contributions. But terminology helps put this first great age of science in perspective and establish its remoteness from the nineteenth century and after: scientists in the seventeenth and eighteenth centuries were still called "natural philosophers."

The word "scientist" was invented about a third of the way through the nineteenth century when men felt the need to distinguish a rigorous experimental and observational investigation of nature from speculation on it by unchecked reason. About the same time science gained acceptance as a specialized field of study conferring professional standing. Its new status was marked by the much larger place given to it in education, whether by the creation of new departments at existing universities or by the establishment in some countries, notably France and Germany, of special scientific and technical institutions. This process accelerated as the results of science on social and economic life became increasingly obvious. The sum effect was to carry much further an already long-established trend, a steady and exponential increase in the world population of scientists which has been marked since about 1700. Their numbers have doubled roughly every fifteen years (which explains the striking fact that since then there have always been more scientists alive than dead).

This social phenomenon underlay the increasing control of environment and the improvement of daily life so easily grasped by laymen. By 1914

A Boston telephone exchange in 1883. Besides its technical interest, the photograph also provides evidence of the difference technology made to the employment of women; if we count the gentleman with the cigar as an employee, the sexes were employed in equal numbers in this exchange, it seems.
(American Telephone and Telegraph)

western Europeans and Americans lived in a world of technology which had not existed a century previously. Although there had never been a time since the seventeenth century when scientific activity had not produced some obvious practical fall-out, it was only in the nineteenth century that science really began to play an important role in sustaining and changing society. This was by no means merely a matter of its striking and spectacular accomplishments. Much nineteenth-century research into the chemistry of dyeing, for example, contributed to the development of drugs, explosives, antiseptics, and many other things. In addition the production of new fast dyes had all sorts of unspectacular but important economic and social repercussions: the unhappy Indian grower of indigo saw his market drying up, and the industrial working classes of the West found they could buy marginally less drab clothes. In time mass production and man-made fibers would all but obliterate visible differences between the clothes of different classes.

This already takes us across the boundary between sustaining life and changing it. Fundamental science was to go on changing society in other ways. One area in which effects are comparatively easy to measure is medicine. By 1914 huge advances had been made; what had been a skill a century earlier had become a science. Great bridgeheads had been driven into the theory and control of infection; antiseptics, introduced by Lister in the 1860s, were taken for granted a couple of decades later, and he and his friend Louis Pasteur, the great French chemist, had laid the foundations of bacteriology. Queen Victoria had been a pioneer in publicizing new medical methods; the use of anaesthetics during the birth of a prince or princess was important in giving quick social acceptance to techniques still in their infancy in the 1840s. Fewer people were aware of the importance of such achievements as the discovery of the drug Salvarsan in 1909, a landmark in the development of selective treatment of infection, or the identification of the carrier of malaria, or the discovery of x-rays. Yet all these advances were affecting people's lives and gradually the view they took of science itself.

Enough impact was made by science even before 1914 to justify using the word "mythology" to describe one of its results. In this context "mythology" implies no connotations of fiction or falsity. It is simply a convenient way of calling attention to the fact that science, the vast bulk of its conclusions no doubt validated by experiment and therefore "true," has also acted as an influence shaping the way people look at the world, just as great religions did in the past. That is to say, it has come to be important as more than a method for exploring and manipulating nature. People look to science for guidance about metaphysical questions, the aims they ought to pursue, the standards they should employ to regulate behavior. All this of course has no intrinsic or necessary connection whatsoever with science as the pursuit of scientists. But the upshot is a civilization whose elites, except vestigially, have no dominant religious belief or transcendent ideals. The core of this civilization, whether articulated or not, is a belief in the promise of what can be done by controlling nature. It affirms that no problem is insoluble given sufficient resources of intellect and money; it has room for the obscure but not for the essentially mysterious. Many scientists have drawn back from this conclusion and the implications are still far from being grasped. But on such assumptions a dominant world view now rests, and it was formed in essentials before 1914.

Confidence in science in its crudest form has been called "scientism," but probably very few people have ever experienced this confidence with complete clarity and lack of qualification. The prestige of the scientific method, though, is shown by the wish of intellectuals to extend it beyond the natural sciences. One of the earliest attempts to found "social sciences" appeared among the utilitarian followers of the English reformer and intellectual Jeremy Bentham. He wished to base the management of society upon calculated use of the principles that men respond to pleasure and pain and that pleasure should be maximized and pain minimized, always taking into account the sensations of the greater number and their intensity. Later in the nineteenth century Marx (who was greatly impressed by the work of Darwin) also exemplified the desire to found a science of society. The French philosopher Auguste Comte supplied a name for one: sociology. Attempts to emulate the natural sciences proceeded on the basis of a search for general quasi-mechanical laws. That the natural sciences were just then abandoning the search for such laws does not signify; the method still testified to the prestige of the scientific model.

By 1914 science obviously was contributing to an ill-defined sense of strain in European civilization. The most apparent manifestation of this was the problems it posed to traditional religion. But it also operated in a more subtle way; the determinism derived from evolutionary theories and the relativism suggested by anthropology or science sapped confidence in the values of objectivity and rationality, which had been so important to European civilization since the eighteenth century. There were signs that liberal, rational, enlightened Europe was under strain just as much as traditional, religious, conservative Europe had been for a century or so.

INTERNATIONAL ORDER

Those who felt confident about the future could point to the diminution of international violence in the nineteenth century; there had been no war between European great powers since 1871 (unless Turkey was counted as one: she fought Russia in 1876). The summoning of congresses in 1899 and 1907 to halt competition in armaments, though they failed in their aim, seemed hopeful too. The practice of arbitration had grown and some restrictions on the brutality of warfare had resulted. A significant phrase was used by the German emperor when he sent off his contingent to the international force fielded against the Chinese Boxers. Stirred to anger by reports of Chinese atrocities against Europeans, he urged his soldiers to behave "like Huns." It was a phrase which would stick in people's memories. Though thought excessive at the time, its real interest lies in the fact that he should have felt such a recommendation was needed. Nobody would have had to tell a seventeenth-century army to behave like Huns, because they would have done so anyway. So far had war been humanized. "Civilized warfare" was a nineteenth-century concept and far from a contradiction in terms. In 1899 it had been agreed to forbid, albeit for a limited period, the use of poison gas and dum-dum bullets and even the dropping of bombs from the air.

The great powers

Although many Europeans might be skeptical or fearful about the future, it was almost never suggested that Europe would not continue to be the center of the world's affairs, the greatest concentration of political power and usually the maker of the world's destiny. Diplomatically and politically, the European statesman could ignore the rest of the world for all important matters except in the Western hemisphere, where another nation of European origins, the United States, was paramount, and in the Far East, where Japan was increasingly important and the Americans had interests which they might require others to respect. European governments essentially directed their attention on their relationships with one another. And in this realm there was evidence early in the twentieth century that the international situation was growing dangerous.

Some of the major states had internal problems. For all the huge differences between them, united Germany and united Italy were new nations; they had not been in existence at the beginning of 1870. This made their rulers especially sensitive to internal divisive forces and willing to court nationalist feeling. Nationalism led Italy into disastrous colonial ventures, continuing suspicion and unfriendliness toward Austria-Hungary (formally her ally but the ruler of territories still regarded in Italy as "unredeemed"), and finally to war with Turkey. Germany had the advantages of huge industrial and economic success to help her, yet after the cautious Bismarck had been sent into retirement, her foreign policy was conducted more and more with an eye to winning respect and prestige—a "place in the sun," as it was summed up. Germany also had to face the consequences of industrialization. One problem was a set of new economic and social forces increasingly difficult to reconcile with a constitution which gave too much weight in imperial government to a semifeudal, agrarian aristocracy.

Internal tension was not the monopoly of new states. The two great dynastic empires of Russia and Austria-Hungary still stood out best among the nations of Europe as the embodiments of the assumption of the Holy Alliance era, that governments were the natural opponents of their subjects. Yet both states had undergone great changes in the past century. The Habsburg monarchy in its new, hyphenated form was itself the creation of a successful nationalism, that of the Magyars. In the early years of the twentieth century there were signs that it was going to be more and more difficult to keep the two halves of the monarchy together without provoking other nations inside it beyond endurance. Moreover industrialization in Bohemia and Austria was beginning to add new tensions to the old.

Russia actually exploded in political revolution in 1905, but the reshaping of her structure had begun before this. Autocracy and terrorism between them brought to an end the liberal promise of Alexander II's reforms but did not prevent industrial growth at the end of the century. This was the beginning of an economic revolution to which the serf emancipation had been the essential preliminary. Fiscal policies designed to exact grain from the peasantry provided a commodity for export to pay for the foreign loans which financed capital investment. With the twentieth century Russia began to show a formidable rate of economic growth. The quantities were still small: in 1910 Russia produced less than a third as much pig iron as the United Kingdom and only about a quarter as much steel as Germany. But this production had been achieved very quickly. Probably more important, there were signs by 1914 that Russian agriculture might at last have turned the corner and be capable of producing a grain harvest which would grow faster than population. In a determined effort to create a class of prosperous, independent farmers whose self-interest was linked to raising productivity, the government removed the last of the restraints on individualism imposed by the terms of emancipation.

At this stage Russia was potentially a giant great power but one still entangled with her past. The autocracy governed badly, reformed unwillingly, and opposed all change, even after 1905. The general level of culture was low and unpromising; industrialization would demand better education and that would provoke new strains. Liberal traditions were weak; terrorist and autocratic traditions were strong. In 1914 less than 10 percent of the Russian people lived in towns and only about 3 million out of a total population of more than 150 million worked in industry. Russia was still dependent on foreign suppliers for capital, and most of it came from her ally, France.

With the United Kingdom and Italy the French Third Republic represented liberal and constitutional principles among the great powers of Europe. Socially conservative, France in spite of her intellectual vitality was uneasy and conscious of weakness and division. In part this was superficial, a matter of bitter exchanges between politicians; in part it was because of a militant socialist and working-class movement weak in numbers but striving to keep alive the revolutionary tradition and its rhetoric. Actually the Republic was more stable than many states but had a weakness of which Frenchmen were very aware—military inferiority. The war in 1870 had shown that the French did not have the numbers to beat the German army. Since then the disparity between the two countries had grown even greater. France had fallen still further behind Germany in manpower, and in economic development she had been dwarfed by her neighbor. Just before 1914 France was producing about a sixth as much coal as Germany, less than a third as much pig iron, and a quarter as much steel. If there was ever to be a return match for 1870, the French knew they needed allies.

An ally was not in 1900 to be looked for in Great Britain, the other major constitutional state. This was mainly because of colonial issues; France (like Russia) came into irritating conflict with Great Britain at a great many places around the globe. For a long time the British found it possible to remain clear of European entanglements; this was an advantage, but they too had troubles at home. The first industrial nation had to face working-class agitation and, increasingly, uncertainty about her relative strength. By 1900 some British businessmen were sure that Germany was a major rival, and there were plenty of signs that in technology and method German industry was greatly superior to British. The old certainties began to give way; free trade itself was called into question. There were even signs that parliamentarianism might be threatened in the violence of Ulster and the suffragettes or in embittered struggles over social legislation with a House of Lords determined to safeguard the interests of wealth. Yet there was a solidity about British institutions and political habits. Parliamentary monarchy had proved able to carry through vast changes since 1832 and there was little reason for serious doubt that it could continue to do so.

The new great powers

A perspective from Japan or the United States, the two great extra-European powers, reveals the fundamental change in the position of the United Kingdom within half a century or so. Japan's new role was shown by her military victory over Russia. That the United States would shortly emerge as the most powerful nation in world politics was much less conceivable; yet there were some signs.

The great nineteenth-century expansion of the United States had come to a climax with the establishment of its unquestioned supremacy in the Western hemisphere. The war with Spain and the building of the Panama Canal rounded off the process. American domestic, social, and economic circumstances were such that the political system proved easily able to handle the problems it faced once the great mid-century crisis had been surmounted. Some of the gravest difficulties resulted from industrialization. The confidence that all would go well if the economically strongest were simply allowed to drive all others to the wall began to be questioned toward the end of the nineteenth century. But this was after an industrial machine of immense scale had already matured. It would be the bedrock of future American power. By 1914 the United States produced more than twice the pig iron and steel of Great Britain and Germany together and mined almost enough coal to outpace them in that respect too. At the same time the standard of living of its citizens continued to act as a magnet to immigration. Abundant natural resources and a stream of cheap, highly motivated labor were two major sources of America's economic might. Another was foreign capital. The United States was the greatest of debtor nations.

Though its political constitution was older in 1914 than that of any major European state except Great Britain and Russia, immigration gave the United States some of the characteristics of a new nation. The need to integrate new citizens often led to the expression of strong nationalist feeling. But because of its geography, its tradition of rejecting Europe, and the continuing domination of American government and business by elites formed in the Anglo-Saxon tradition, this did not take violent forms outside the Western hemisphere. The United States in 1914 was still a young giant waiting in the wings of European history.

chapter 34

The First World War and Its Aftermath

Though neither the bloodiest nor the most prolonged in history, the war which began in 1914 was the greatest in intensity and geographical extent to have occurred down to that time. Every continent was involved, although the major theaters were Europe and the Near East. On the battlefronts of these areas and on the seas the fighting was more continuous and also more costly than in any earlier war and made unprecedented demands upon resources. Whole societies were mobilized for it. Another novelty was its transformation by science; it was the first war in which machines played an overwhelmingly important part.

It was also the first of two world wars in which the central issue was the control of German power. Between them they so damaged Europe as to end her political, economic, and military supremacy. Both of these conflicts began in essentially European issues and the First World War always retained a predominantly European flavor; like the Second, nevertheless, it sucked into it other quarrels and jumbled together a whole anthology of conflicts.

PROLOGUE

The European balance which had kept the peace between great states for over forty years was dangerously disturbed by 1914. Too many people had come to feel that the chances of war might offer them more than a continued peace. This was especially true in Germany, Austria-Hungary, and Russia. Those who were in a position to make the major decisions had reached this conclusion gradually. By the time they did so, there already existed a complicated set of ties, obligations, and interests between states which so involved them with one another that it was unlikely that any conflict could be limited to two or even a few of them. One force making for instability in this system was the existence of special relations between small countries and larger ones; some minor states could act with confidence that they would be backed up by their protectors and were thus in a position to take important decisions out of the hands of those who would have to accept responsibility for a war.

The psychological atmosphere in which statesmen had to work by 1914 made this delicate situation all the more dangerous. It was an age when mass emotions were easily aroused, in particular by nationalist and patriotic stimuli. Moreover there was widespread ignorance of the dangers war would bring. All but a tiny minority thought in terms of France in 1870, not of Virginia and Tennessee in the 1860s. Though everyone knew that wars were destructive, they also thought that in the twentieth century they would be swiftly over. The very cost of armaments made it inconceivable that civilized states could sustain a prolonged struggle such as the Napoleonic Wars; the complex world economy and the taxpayer, it was said, could not survive one. This perhaps diminished misgivings about courting danger.

There are also signs that many Europeans were bored by their lives in 1914 and saw in war an emotional release to purge their sense of decadence and sterility. Revolutionaries of course welcomed international conflict because of the opportunities they thought it might bring. Finally, it is worth remembering that the long success of diplomats in negotiating grave crises was itself a danger. Their machinery had worked so many times that the possibility of its failure for a time seemed to escape many of those who had to deal with the events of July 1914. On the very eve of war statesmen were still wondering whether another conference of ambassadors or even a European congress might not extract them from their difficulties.

Balkan problems

One of the conflicts which came to a head in 1914 went back a very long way. This was the rivalry of Austria-Hungary and Russia in southeastern Europe. Its last phase was dominated by the accelerated collapse of the Ottoman empire in Europe from the Crimean War onward. Thus from one point of view the First World War is well described as the war of the Ottoman succession. The Congress of Berlin in 1878 had pulled Europe through one dangerous moment when Russian pressure on Turkey had seemed likely to provoke a general conflict, and by the 1890s Habsburg and Romanoff had settled down to a sort of understanding. This lasted until Russia's interest in the Danube valley revived after the Japanese checked her imperial ambition in the Far East. At that moment a new aggressiveness was appearing in Austro-Hungarian policy too.

At the root of this change at Vienna was revolutionary nationalism. A "Young Turk" movement of reform and national regeneration looked for a while as if it might pull the Ottoman empire together again, and this both provoked the smaller Balkan nations to try to undo the status quo established by the great powers and stirred up the Austrians to look to their own interests in a situation once more looking fluid. They offended the Russians by annexing the Turkish province of Bosnia in 1909 (Russia had not received a corresponding and compensating gain). Another consequence of this annexation was more Slav subjects for the Dual Monarchy. There was already discontent among the empire's subject peoples, in particular the Slavs who lived under Magyar rule. More and more under the pressure of Magyar interests, the government in Vienna had shown hostility toward Serbia, a nation these Slav subjects might look to for support; some Slav idealists saw Serbia as the nucleus of a future state embracing all South Slavs.

The Serbian government seemed unable to restrain South Slav revolutionaries, who used Belgrade as a base for terrorism and subversion in Bosnia. Lessons from history are often unfortunate; the Vienna government was only too ready to conclude that Serbia might play in the Danube valley the role that Sardinia had played in Italy. Having been excluded from Germany by Prussia and from Italy by Sardinia, the Habsburgs were now threatened with exclusion from the lower Danube valley by a potential Yugoslavia. This would finish the Dual Monarchy as a great power. It would also end Magyar supremacy in Hungary because such a state would insist upon a fairer treatment of Slavs who remained in Hungarian territory. The continuing collapse of the Ottoman empire could then only benefit Russia, the power which stood behind Serbia, determined that there should not be another 1909.

The alliances

Into this complicated situation other powers were pulled by interest, choice, sentiment, and formal diplomacy. Of these the last was perhaps less important than was once thought. Bismarck's efforts in the 1870s and 1880s to ensure the isolation of France and the supremacy of Germany had spawned a system of alliances unprecedented in peacetime. Their common characteristic was that they defined conditions on which countries would go to war to support one another. The alliances seemed to cramp diplomacy, but in the end they by no means operated as planned. This does not mean that they did not contribute to the coming of war, but simply that formal arrangements can only be effective if people want them to be and other factors decided the issue in 1914.

At the root of the whole business was the German seizure of Alsace and Lorraine in 1871 and French restlessness for revenge. Bismarck guarded against this at first by building on the common ground of dynastic resistance to revolutionary and subversive dangers, which France, the only republic among the major states, was still supposed to represent; it was after all only eighty-odd years since 1789. He gave up this strategy in the 1880s, essentially because he felt he must back Austria-Hungary in the last resort if a conflict between her and Russia proved unavoidable. Italy then joined Germany and the Dual Monarchy to form the Triple Alliance in 1882. Bismarck still kept a separate "reinsurance" treaty with Russia, but he seems to have felt uneasy about the prospect of maintaining peace between that power and Austria-Hungary, given the fuss the Magyars were now making about any extension of Russian influence in the Balkans.

A conflict between the two powers did not again look likely until after 1909. By then Bismarck's successors had allowed his reinsurance treaty to lapse and Russia was since 1892 an ally of France. From that alliance the road led away from Bismarck's Europe, where everyone else had been kept in equilibrium by Germany's central role, to a Europe divided into two camps. German policy made the situation worse. In a series of crises Germany appeared determined to frighten other nations with her displeasure and make herself esteemed. In particular she directed her irritation in 1905 and 1911 against France and used commercial and colonial issues as excuses to show by displays of force that the French had not won the right to disregard German wishes by making Russia an ally. By 1900 German military planners had already worked out the strategy for a war on two fronts; it called for a quick overthrow of France before the resources of the ponderous Russian war machine could be fully mobilized.

Within a few years after 1900 it had therefore become probable that if an Austro-Russian war broke out, Germany and France would join in. The Germans soon made this outcome more likely by patronizing the Turks. This was very alarming to the Russians because a growing export trade in grain from Russia's Black Sea ports had to pass through the straits of Constantinople. The Russians began to improve their fighting power. One essential step was the completion of a railway network to make possible the mobilization of Russia's vast armies and their delivery to the battlefields of eastern Europe.

The end of British isolation

In all this there was no obvious concern for Great Britain, had not German policy perversely antagonized her. At the end of the nineteenth century Great Britain's quarrels were above all with France and Russia. They arose where imperial ambitions clashed, in Africa and Central and Southeast Asia. Anglo-German relations were more easily managed, if occasionally prickly. As Great Britain entered the new century, she was still preoccupied with imperial issues, not with Europe. Her first peacetime alliance was with Japan, to safeguard her interests in the Far East. Then came a settlement of long outstanding disputes with France in 1904; this was in essence an agreement about Africa, where France was to be given a free hand in Morocco in return for British predominance in Egypt—a way of settling another bit of the Ottoman succession—but it rounded up other colonial quarrels the world over, some going back as far as the Peace of Utrecht in 1713. A few years later Great Britain made a similar (though less workable) agreement with Russia about spheres of interest in Persia.

But the Anglo-French settlement grew into something much more than a clearing away of grounds for dispute. It became what was called an entente, or special relationship. This was largely Germany's doing. Irritated by the Anglo-French agreement, she decided in 1905 to show France that she would have to have her say in Morocco's affairs at an international conference. She got it, but bullying France solidified the entente; the British began to realize that they would have to concern themselves for the first time in decades with the Continental balance of power. If they did not, Germany would dominate Europe. Secret military talks with the French explored what might be done to help France against a German invasion through Belgium. This was not going far, but it was the first step toward Great Britain's adoption of a role as a major military power on land, a change of assumptions in the strategy she had followed since the days of Louis XIV, the last time she had put her main weight into an effort on the Continent.

Germany then threw away the chance to reassure British public opinion by pressing forward with plans to build a great navy. It was inconceivable that such a step could be directed against any power except Great Britain. The result was a naval race which the British were determined to win (if they could not end it) and therefore the further inflammation of popular feeling. In 1911, when the gap between the two countries' fleets was narrowest and felt most keenly in Great Britain, German diplomacy provoked another crisis over Morocco. This time a British minister said publicly something that sounded very much like an assertion that Great Britain would go to war to protect France.

THE GREAT WAR
Sarajevo and after

Yet when war came it was in the South Slav lands. Serbia did well in the Balkan Wars of 1912–1913, in which the young Balkan nations first despoiled Turkey of most that was left of her European territory and then fell out over the booty. But Serbia might have gotten more had the Austrians not objected. Behind Serbia stood Russia, launched on a program of rebuilding and expanding her armed forces which would take three or four years to bring to fruition. If the Dual Monarchy wished to humiliate Serbia and thus show the South Slavs that they could not hope for her support, then the sooner the better. Given their alliance with Germany, the Austrians were unlikely to draw back from fighting Russia while there was still time to be sure of winning.

The crisis came when a Bosnian terrorist assassinated an Austrian archduke at Sarajevo in June 1914. The Austrians decided that the moment had come to teach Serbia her lesson and kill forever pan-Slav agitation. The Germans supported them. The Dual Monarchy declared war on Serbia on July 28. A week later all the great powers were at war, though ironically the Austro-Hungarians and Russians were not yet at war with each other; it was only on August 6 that the Dual Monarchy at last declared war on its old rival. Before that date German military planning had decided the timetable which shaped events. The key decision to attack France before Russia had been made years before; German strategy required such an attack to be made through Belgium, whose neutrality the British among others had guaranteed. When Russia mobilized to bring pressure on Austria-Hungary for Serbia's protection, the Germans declared war on Russia. Thereafter the sequence of events fell almost automatically into place. According to their plans the Germans had to attack the French and so declared war on them. (Thus the Franco-Russian alliance never actually operated.) Germany's violation of Belgian neutrality gave the British government, uneasy about an attack on France but not seeing clear grounds to justify intervention, an issue to unite the country and take it into war against Germany on August 4.

Just as the duration and intensity of the war were to outrun all expectations, so did its geographical spread. Japan and the Ottoman empire came in soon after the outbreak; the former on the side of the Allies (as France, Great Britain, and Russia were called) and Turkey on that of the Central Powers (Germany and Austria-Hungary). Italy joined the Allies in 1915 in return for promises of Austrian territory. There were other efforts to pick up new allies by offering checks to be cashed after a victorious peace; Bulgaria joined the Central Powers in September 1915 and Rumania the Allies in the following year. Greece became another Allied state in 1917. Portugal's government had been unable to enter the war in 1914 because of internal troubles but was finally faced with a German declaration of war in 1916. By the end of that year the original issues of Franco-German and Austro-Russian rivalry had been thoroughly confused by other struggles. The Balkan states were fighting a third Balkan war (the war of the Ottoman succession in the European theater), the British a war against German naval and commercial power and another which was the Asiatic side of the Ottoman succession conflict, and the Italians the last war of the Risorgimento, while the Japanese were pursuing another highly profitable and cheap episode in the assertion of their hegemony in the Far East.

A new sort of war

One reason why allies were sought in 1915 and 1916 was that the war then showed every sign of bogging down in a stalemate no one had expected. The nature of the fighting surprised almost everyone. The German sweep into northern France had not achieved the lightning victory which was its aim. In the east Russian offensives had been stopped by the Germans and Austrians. Thereafter, though more noticeably in the west than the east, the battlefields settled down to siege warfare on an unprecedented scale, the Germans occupying almost all Belgium and much of northeastern France. The huge killing power of modern weapons favored defense over offense. Magazine rifles, machine guns, and barbed wire could stop any attack not preceded by pulverizing bombardment. The casualty lists demonstrated this. By the end of 1915 the French army had lost 300,000 dead; in 1916 one seven-month battle before the French fortress of Verdun added another 315,000 to this total. In the same battle 280,000 Germans died. While it was going on, another struggle further north, on the Somme, cost the British 420,000 casualties and the Germans about the same. The first day of that battle, July 1, remains the blackest in the history of the British army: it suffered 60,000 casualties, more than a third of them fatal.

Yet these tragic figures did not shorten the struggle. This was a reflection of another surprise, the enormous war-making power of industrial societies. By the end of 1916 the warring states had amply demonstrated an unforeseen capacity to organize and conscript their peoples as never before to produce unprecedented quantities of material and furnish the recruits for new armies. Whole societies were fighting one another; the international solidarity of the working class and the international interests of ruling classes against subversion had both disappeared.

Front line, 1916. A British trench on the Somme, four men asleep while one is posted as a sentry. By the standards of the winter months, this trench must have been a comfortable one. Men lived in such conditions for two weeks or so at a time, until their unit was relieved. Significantly, the only indisputably clean thing in the picture is the sentry's rifle and bayonet, the infantryman's "best friend," as every Small Arms Manual reminded him. (*Imperial War Museum, London*)

While diplomats sought new allies to break the deadlock, generals looked for new fronts. In 1915 the Allies mounted an attack on Turkey at the Dardanelles in the hope, not to be realized, of knocking her out of the war and opening up communication with Russia through the Black Sea. The same search for a way around the stalemate in France later produced a new Balkan front at Salonika; it replaced the one which had collapsed when the Austrians overran Serbia. Colonial possessions had ensured from the first that there would be fighting all around the globe. British command of the seas meant that the German colonies could be picked up fairly easily, though the African ones provoked some lengthy campaigning. The most important extra-European operations were in the eastern and southern parts of the Turkish empire. A British and Indian army entered Mesopotamia. Another British force advanced from the Suez Canal toward Palestine. In the Arabian desert an Arab revolt against the Turks provided some of the few romantic episodes relieving the brutal squalor of industrial war.

The expansion of the war in terms of technique was most noticeable in its industrial effects. The American Civil War a half-century before had pre-

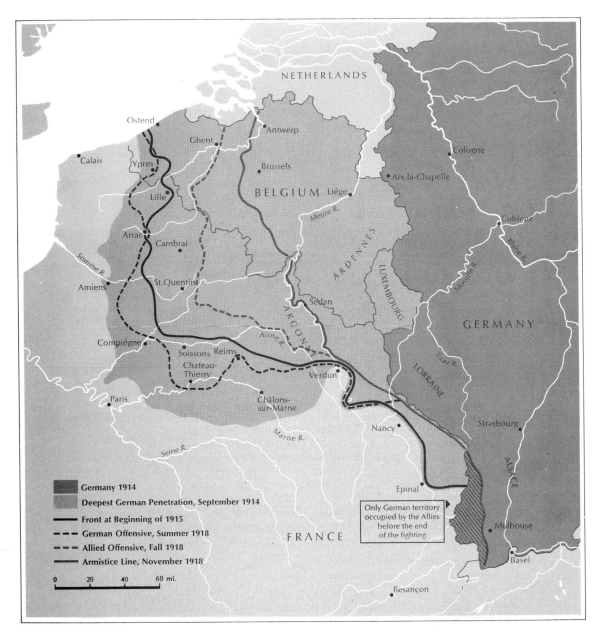

THE WESTERN FRONT 1914–1918

figured the economic demands of mass war in a democratic age. The mills, factories, mines, and furnaces of Europe now worked as never before. So did those of the United States and Japan, the former accessible to the Allies but not to the Central Powers because of British naval supremacy. The maintenance of millions of men in the field required not only arms and ammunition but food, clothing, medical equipment, and machines in huge quantities. Though millions of animals were still needed, it was the first war of the internal combustion engine; trucks and tractors swallowed gasoline as avidly as horses and mules ate their fodder.

The repercussions of this vast increase in demand rolled outward through society, leading in all countries in varying measure to government control of the economy, the conscription of labor, a revolution in women's employment, and the introduction of new health and welfare services. They also flowed overseas. The United States ceased to be a debtor nation; the Allies liquidated their investments there to pay for what they needed and became debtors in their turn. Indian industry received the fillip it had long

New weapons, new defenses. Poison gas called forth countermeasures. These cumbersome gas masks of impregnated flannel were worn by Indian soldiers in 1917. *(Gernsheim Collection, Humanities Research Center, The University of Texas at Austin)*

required. Boom days came to the ranchers and farmers of the Argentine and the British dominions. The latter also sent soldiers to Europe or fought in the German colonies.

Its technical expansion also made the war more frightful. This was not only because machine guns and high explosives made possible such terrible slaughter. It was not even because of new weapons, such as poison gas, flame throwers, or tanks, all of which made their appearance as soldiers strove to find a way out of the deadlock of the battlefield. It was also because the fact that whole societies were engaged in warfare brought with it the realization that whole societies could be targets for warlike operations. Attacks on the morale, health, and efficiency of civilian workers and voters became desirable. The possibilities of mass literacy and the recently created motion-picture industry supplemented and in time overtook such old standbys as pulpit and school in propaganda warfare. To British charges that the Germans who carried out primitive bombing raids on London by airship were "babykillers," Germans retorted that the same could be said of the sailors who maintained the British blockade.

The rising figures of German infant mortality bore them out. Because of this slow British success and its own unwillingness to risk the fleet whose building had done so much to poison the prewar atmosphere, the German high command turned to a weapon which had been underrated in 1914—the submarine. Early in 1915 they launched their U-boats at Allied shipping and the ships of neutrals who were supplying the Allies, attacks often being made without warning and on unarmed vessels. But few submarines were then available and they did not do much damage. There was an international outcry that year when a great British liner, the *Lusitania*, was torpedoed with the loss of 1,200 lives, many of them Americans, and the Germans called off unrestricted attacks on shipping.

1917: the hinge of modern history

By the beginning of 1917 it was clear that if Germany did not starve Great Britain first, she herself would be choked by the British blockade. During that winter there was famine in the Balkans and people starved in Vienna. Food riots and strikes were becoming more frequent in Germany, where infant mortality was approaching a level 50 percent higher than that of 1915. Though the French had suffered 3.35 million casualties so far and the British over a million, the Germans had lost nearly 2.5 million men and were still fighting a war on two fronts. There was no reason to suppose that the German army would be any more likely to achieve a knockout blow in the west than the British and French forces had been. In these circumstances the German general staff chose to resume unrestricted submarine warfare in February. This decision brought about the first great transformation of the war in 1917, the entry of the United States in April. The Germans expected this but gambled on bringing Great Britain to her knees—and thus France to hers—before American weight could be decisive.

American public opinion, by no means favorable to one side or the other in 1914, had come a long way since then. Allied propaganda and purchases

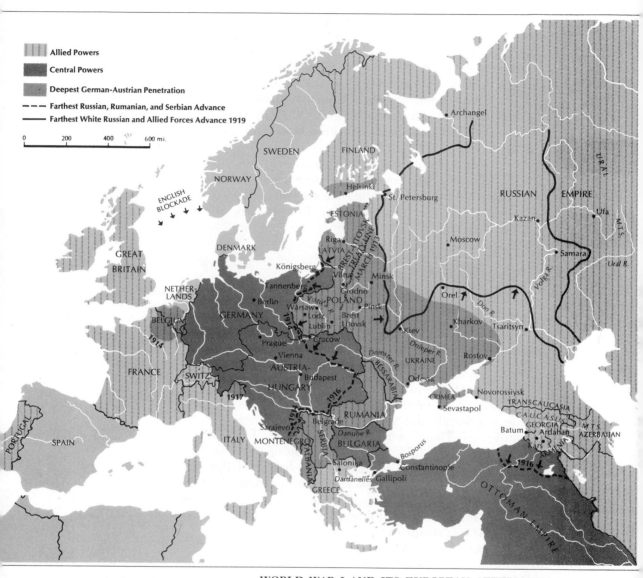

WORLD WAR I AND ITS EUROPEAN AFTERMATH
Although the most intense fighting of the war took place in the West,
the Eastern theater both then and after the armistice saw operations
of far greater territorial scope.

had helped; so had the first German submarine campaign. The fact that Allied war aims came to include the reconstruction of Europe on a basis that would safeguard the interests of nationalities had an appeal to some "hyphenated" Americans. The resumption of unrestricted submarine warfare was decisive; it was a direct threat to American interests and the safety of American citizens. When Washington learned that Germany hoped to negotiate an alliance with Mexico and Japan against the United States, the hostility aroused by the U-boats was confirmed. Soon after an American ship was sunk without warning, the United States declared war.

The impossibility of breaking the European deadlock by means short of total war had thus sucked the new world into the quarrels of the old. The Allies were delighted: victory was now assured. Yet immediately they faced an even blacker year than 1916. The U-boat campaign was almost successful, and a terrible series of battles in France (usually lumped under one name, Passchendaele) cost Great Britain another 400,000 men to gain five miles of mud and left an ineffaceable scar upon the British national consciousness. The French army, worn out by its heroic efforts in 1916, underwent a series of mutinies. Worst of all, the Russian empire collapsed and consequently the eastern front. Russia ceased to be an ally and even, by the end of the year, a great power.

Revolution in Russia

The Russian state was destroyed by the war. The makers of revolution in Russia in February 1917 were the German armies, which had in the end broken the hearts of even the long-enduring Russian soldiers. Defeated Russian armies had behind them cities starving because of the breakdown of the transport system and a government of incompetent and corrupt men who feared constitutionalism and liberalism as much as defeat. At the beginning of 1917 the state could no longer depend upon its security forces. Food riots were followed by mutiny and the autocracy was suddenly seen to be defenseless. Liberals and socialists formed a provisional government and the tsar abdicated. Then the new government itself failed, in part because it attempted the impossible, the continuation of the war; the Russians wanted peace and bread, as Nikolai Lenin, the leader of the Bolsheviks, saw. His determination to take power was the second reason for the moderates' failure. Presiding over a disintegrating country, administration, and army while still facing the unsolved problems of privation in the cities, the provisional government was swept away by the October Revolution.

Both the Bolshevik seizure of power and America's entry into the war mark 1917 as a break between two eras. Previously Europe had settled her own affairs; now the United States would be bound to have a large say in her future. Furthermore, there now existed a state which was committed by the beliefs of its founders to the destruction of the whole prewar European order, a truly and consciously revolutionary center for world politics.

The immediate and obvious consequence of the establishment of the Soviet state—the Workers' and Soldiers' Soviet (council) had become Russia's basic political institution—was a new strategic situation. The Bolsheviks consolidated their coup d'état by dissolving (since they did not control it) the only freely elected, representative body Russia has ever had and by bidding for the peasants' loyalties by assurances of land and peace. Peasant support was essential to the regime's survival; the backbone of the new ruling party was the very small industrial working class of a few cities. Only

Outside the Winter Palace, Petrograd, 1917. One of the units guarding the
Provisional Government was a women's battalion. Whatever step forward
in female emancipation this may have marked, the unhappy members of this
unit were among those guarding the Palace on the night of the Bolshevik
coup commemorated as the "October Revolution." *(Sovfoto)*

peace could provide a safer and broader foundation. Consequently the
Bolsheviks signed the Treaty of Brest-Litovsk with Germany in March 1918.
It cost severe losses of Russian territory but gave the new government the
peace and time it desperately needed to tackle its internal troubles.

The Allies were furious. They saw the Bolsheviks' action as a treacherous defection. Their attitude toward the regime was not softened by its intransigent revolutionary propaganda, directed at their citizens. The Russian
leaders looked for a revolution of the working class in all the advanced capitalist countries. This knowledge gave an extra dimension to a series of Allied
military interventions in Russia. Their original purpose was strategic, to stop
German exploitation of Russia's departure from the war, but many people in
the capitalist countries and all Bolsheviks quickly interpreted them as anticommunist crusades. Worse still, the Allies became entangled in the civil
war which had followed the Revolution and seemed near to destroying the
new regime.

Even without the doctrinal background of Marxist theory, which provided the interpretative scheme of Lenin and his colleagues, these episodes
would have been likely to sour relations between Russia and the capitalist
world for a long time; viewed against Marx's historical vision, they seemed to
confirm an essential and ineradicable hostility. Their recollection has
dogged Russian attitudes ever since. The interventions also helped justify

the Russian Revolution's turn toward authoritarian government. Fear of the invader as a restorer of the old order and patron of landlords combined with Russian traditions of autocracy and police terrorism to stifle any liberalization of the regime.

The revolutionized war

The Russian Communists' conviction that revolution was about to occur in central and western Europe was justified in an ironic way. In 1918 the war's revolutionary potential indeed became plain, but in national not class forms. The Allies were provoked (in part by the Bolsheviks) to a revolution strategy of their own. The military situation was bleak for them at the end of 1917. It was obvious that they would soon face a major German attack alone, or virtually alone, since the Italian front required reinforcement by British and French troops. They had lost the advantage of a Russian front to draw off their enemies in the east, and it would be a long time before American troops arrived in large numbers to help them in France. But they could appeal to the nationalities of the Austro-Hungarian empire. This had the additional advantage of emphasizing in American eyes the ideological purity of the Allied cause now that it was no longer joined with tsardom. Accordingly, propaganda was directed to the Austro-Hungarian armies and encouragement given to Czechs and South Slavs in exile. Before Germany gave in, the Dual Monarchy was already dissolving under the combined effects of this barrage and a Balkan campaign which at last began to provide victories in the autumn. This was the second great blow to old Europe. The political structure of the whole area bounded by the Urals, the Baltic, and the Danube valley was now in question as it had not been for centuries. There was even a Polish army in existence by 1918, patronized by the Germans as a weapon against Russia, while the American president Woodrow Wilson announced that an independent Poland was an essential of Allied peace making. All the certainties of the past century seemed to be in the melting pot.

It was against this increasingly revolutionary background that the crucial battles were fought in 1918. By summer the Allies had managed to halt a last great German offensive. It had made great gains, but not enough. When the Allied armies began to move forward victoriously in their turn, the German leaders sought an end. They too thought they saw signs of revolutionary collapse at home. When the kaiser abdicated, the third dynastic empire had fallen. A new German government requested an armistice and the fighting came to an end on November 11.

REBUILDING EUROPE

The cost of this huge conflict has never been adequately computed. One rough figure indicates its scale: about 10 million men died as a direct result of military action. But even this horrible total does not indicate the physical cost in maiming, blinding, the loss to families of parents and husbands or the

THE NEW EUROPE 1919–1926
The new states carved out of the former dynastic empires.

spiritual cost in the destruction of ideals, confidence, and good will. Europeans looked at their huge cemeteries and were appalled at what they had done. The economic damage was immense too. Over much of Europe people starved. A year after the war manufacturing output was still nearly a quarter below that of 1914; Russia's was only 20 percent of what it had then been. In some countries it was almost impossible to procure transport. Moreover all the complicated, fragile machinery of international exchange was smashed and some of it could never be replaced. At the center of this chaos lay, exhausted, a Germany which had been the economic dynamo of central Europe. "We are at the dead season of our fortunes," wrote J. M. Keynes, a British economist, in 1919. "Our power of feeling or caring beyond the immediate questions of our own material wellbeing is temporarily eclipsed. . . . We have been moved beyond endurance, and need rest. Never in the lifetime of men now living has the universal element in the sole of man burnt so dimly."

The terms of Versailles

At the end of 1918 delegations from the Allied countries assembled in Paris to begin drawing up the greatest peace settlement since 1815. They had to reconcile great expectations with stubborn facts. The power to make the crucial decisions was remarkably concentrated: the British prime minister, Lloyd George, the French premier, Clemenceau, and the American president, Woodrow Wilson, dominated the negotiations. These took place between the victors; the defeated Germans were subsequently presented with their terms. In the diverging interests of France, aware above all of the appalling danger of any third repetition of German aggression, and of the Anglo-Saxon nations, conscious of standing in no such peril, lay the central problem of European security, but many other issues surrounded and obscured it. The Allied statesmen were drafting a world settlement. It not only dealt with territories outside Europe — as some earlier treaties had done — but many non-European voices were heard in its making. Of the twenty-seven states whose representatives would sign the treaty, seventeen lay in other continents. The United States was the greatest of these; with Japan, Great Britain, France, and Italy it formed the group described as the "principal" victorious powers. No representative of Russia, a great power with both European and Asian interests, was present.

Technically, the peace settlement consisted of several treaties — with Germany, Bulgaria, Turkey, and the "succession states" which claimed the divided Dual Monarchy. Within this last group the Allies drew an important distinction. A resurrected Poland, an enlarged Serbia, renamed Yugoslavia, and an entirely new Czechoslovakia were treated as victors, while a much reduced Hungary and the Germanic heart of old Austria were considered defeated enemies. But the main concern of the peace conference was the settlement with Germany embodied in the Treaty of Versailles signed in June 1919.

This was a punitive peace and explicitly stated that the Germans were responsible for the outbreak of war. But most of the harsh terms arose not from the issue of moral guilt but from the French wish to make a third war with Germany inconceivable. This was the purpose of economic reparations, by which Germany was supposed to pay for the damage she had done. They angered Germans, made acceptance of defeat even harder, and were economic nonsense. Yet the penalizing of Germany was not supported by arrangements to ensure that she might not one day try to reverse the decision by force of arms, and this angered the French. Germany's territorial losses, it went without saying, included Alsace and Lorraine but were otherwise greatest in the east, to Poland. In the west the French did not get much more reassurance than an undertaking that the German bank of the Rhine would be demilitarized.

The second leading characteristic of the peace was its attempt where possible to follow the principles of self-determination and nationality. This particularly affected the area occupied by the old Dual Monarchy. After outlasting even the Holy Roman Empire, the Habsburgs were gone at last, and in their place appeared states which, though not uninterruptedly, have all survived to this day. The Allies also followed the principle of self-determination in providing that certain frontier zones should have their destinies settled by plebiscite.

The principle of nationality could not always be applied. Geographic, historic, cultural, and economic realities cut across it. When it prevailed over them—as in the destruction of the Danube's economic unity—the results could be bad; when it did not, they could be just as bad because of the aggrieved feelings left behind. Eastern and central Europe was studded with national minorities embedded resentfully in states to which they felt no allegiance. A third of Poland's population did not speak Polish; a third of Czechoslovakia's consisted of minorities of Poles, Russians, Magyars, and Ruthenes; an enlarged Rumania now contained over a million Magyars. In some places the infringement of the principle was felt with special acuteness as an injustice. Germans resented the existence of a "corridor" to connect Poland with the Baltic across German lands; Italy was disappointed of Adriatic spoils held out to her by the Allies when they had needed her help; and the Irish had still not gotten home rule after all.

The most obvious non-European question was the disposition of the German colonies. Here there was an important innovation. Old-fashioned colonial greed was not acceptable to the United States; instead, the device of trusteeship was to provide tutelage for non-European peoples formerly under German or Turkish rule. Mandates to administer these territories while they were prepared for self-government were given to the victorious powers (though the United States declined any) by the League of Nations, itself the most imaginative idea to emerge from the Versailles settlement.

The League of Nations owed most to the enthusiasm of Woodrow Wilson. He secured its creation and gave its covenant (constitution) pride of place as the first part of the peace treaty. It was the one instance in which the settlement transcended the idea of nationalism. It also transcended Europe; twenty-six of the original forty-two members of the league were countries outside Europe. Unfortunately, because of Wilson's neglect of domestic politics, the United States was not among them. This was the most fatal of several grave weaknesses. Nonetheless, the league was to have some successes in handling matters which might without its intervention have proved dangerous. If exaggerated hopes were entertained that it might do more, this does not mean it was not a valuable and imaginative idea.

Russia was absent from the league as she was from the Versailles settlement. Probably the latter was the more important. The political arrangements to shape the next stage of European history were entered into without consulting her though the boundaries being drawn in eastern Europe were bound to be of vital interest to any Russian government. It was true that the Bolshevik leaders did all they could to provide excuses for being excluded from consultation on these matters. They envenomed relations with the major powers by revolutionary propaganda and were convinced that the interventions had always had as their purpose the overthrow of their government. Lloyd George and Wilson were in fact more flexible — even sympathetic — than many of their colleagues and electors in dealing with Russia. Clemenceau, on the other hand, was passionately anti-Bolshevik and in this had the support of many French ex-soldiers and investors. Versailles was the first great European peace to be made by statesmen all the time aware of the dangers of disappointing democratic electorates. But however the responsibility is allocated, the failure to consult Russia in making a new Europe was bound to drive her into the ranks of those who wished to revise the settlement or overthrow it.

In spite of its manifest failures, the peace of 1919 has been too fiercely condemned; it had many good points. When it failed, it was for reasons which were for the most part beyond the control of the men who had made it. In the first place, the days of European world hegemony in a narrow and political sense were over. The peace terms could do little to fix the future outside Europe. The old imperial policemen, France and Great Britain, were too weakened to do their job inside Europe, let alone outside. They were left to their own affairs by the isolationism of the United States and by the Bolsheviks' ideological preconceptions which made relations with Russia sterile and unproductive. When no revolution broke out in Europe, the Russians turned in on themselves; when Wilson gave Americans the chance to be involved in Europe's peacekeeping, they refused it. Both decisions are comprehensible, but their combined effect was bad. Finally, the settlement was to fail largely because of the economic fragility of the new structures it presupposed. Here its terms are more in question: self-determination and new boundaries often made nonsense of economics.

The problems of democratic Europe

The situation in Europe was all the more likely to prove unstable because so many illusions persisted and so many new ones arose. To many it appeared that there had been a great triumph of liberalism and democracy since four autocratic, antinational, illiberal empires had collapsed. This illusion also drew strength from the ostentatious stance taken by Wilson during the war; he had done all he could to make it clear that he saw the participation of the United States as essentially different in kind from that of the other Allies, being governed (he reiterated) by high-minded ideals and a belief that the world could be made safe for democracy if other nations would give up their bad old ways. Some thought he had been proven right; the new states, above all the new Germany, adopted liberal, parliamentary constitutions and often republican ones. There was also the illusion of the league; the hitherto impossible dream of an international authority which was not an empire seemed at last a reality. Finally, there was the expectation that economic life could now return to the pattern of 1914.

This optimism was rooted in fallacy and false premises. The peacemakers had been obliged to leave much unsatisfied nationalism about and had created great resentment in Germany. Perhaps this was inevitable, but it created fertile soil in which things other than liberalism could grow. Further, the democratic institutions of the new states—and the old ones too for that matter—were being launched on a world badly damaged economically. Poverty, hardship, and unemployment existed everywhere, and in many places respect for national sovereignty made things worse by fragmenting former economic units. The war's destruction of old trading relations between states meant a further obstacle to economic recovery. This was a situation revolutionaries could exploit.

The Communists were happy and ready to do so; in fact they believed history had cast them for this role. Each country soon had a revolutionary Communist party. They effected little that was positive but caused great alarm. Because of the circumstances of their birth, they also did much to prevent the emergence of strong left-wing and progressive parties. A Comintern, or Third International, was devised by the Russians in March 1919 to provide leadership for the European socialist movement. For Lenin the test of socialist groups was their adherence to the Comintern, whose principles were deliberately rigid, disciplined, and uncompromising in accordance with his view of the needs of an effective revolutionary party. In almost every country this divided socialists into two camps, those who adhered to the Comintern and took the name Communist and those who, though sometimes claiming still to be Marxist, remained in the rump national parties. The two camps were henceforth usually in bitter competition for working-class support.

The new revolutionary threat on the left was all the more alarming to many Europeans because there were indeed revolutionary disturbances which the Communists sought to exploit. The most conspicuous led to the installation of a Communist government in Hungary. Perhaps more alarming were attempted Communist coups in Germany, whose institutions were threatened also by violence from the right. The German situation was especially ironic because the republican government which had emerged there in the aftermath of defeat was dominated by the Socialists, who were forced into reliance upon conservative forces—notably the professional soldiers of the old army — to prevent a left-wing success. This occurred even before the founding of the Comintern and it gave a special bitterness to the later divisions of the left in Germany. But throughout Europe Communist policy made united resistance to conservatism more difficult while alarming moderates with revolutionary rhetoric and conspiracy.

In eastern Europe the revolutionary social threat was seen also as a Russian threat. The Russian leaders manipulated the Comintern as an instrument of their foreign policy since they assumed that the future of world revolution depended upon the preservation of the first socialist state as its citadel. In the early years of domestic weakness and civil war the Bolsheviks deliberately incited disaffection abroad to preoccupy capitalist governments. But in eastern and central Europe more was involved because territorial boundaries were still in doubt long after the Versailles settlement. The First World War did not end until March 1921 when a peace treaty between Russia and the new Polish republic provided frontiers which would last until 1939. Poland was the largest, the most anti-Russian by tradition, the most anti-Bolshevik by religion, and the most ambitious of the new nations. But all of them felt menaced by a recovery of Russian power in any form, all the more because it was now connected with the threat of social revolution.

Soviet Russia

With peace at last between Poland and Russia and, symbolically, the establishment of orderly official relations between Russia and Great Britain in 1921, there was a noticeable relaxation of tension in Russia. It was connected with the Russian government emerging from a period of acute danger and civil war. Internal security did not much help diplomatic relations, which were all the time cut across by revolutionary propaganda and denunciation of capitalist countries, but the Bolsheviks at last felt their backs were no longer to the wall and that they had time to engineer the recovery of their own shattered land. In 1921 Russian pig-iron production was about one-fifth of its 1913 level, that of coal a tiny 3 percent or so, while the railways had less than half as many locomotives in service as at the start of the war. Livestock had declined by over a quarter and cereal deliveries were less than two-fifths those of 1916. Onto this impoverished economy fell a drought in southern Russia, and more than 2 million died in the subsequent famine. Even cannibalism was reported. Some liberalization of the economy brought a turnaround. By 1927 both industrial and agricultural production were nearly back to prewar levels.

The regime was undergoing in these years great uncertainty in its leadership. This had begun to appear in the early 1920s, but Lenin's acknowledged ascendancy had kept rival forces in balance; his death in 1924 opened a period of evolution and debate in the upper ranks of the Russian Communist party. This was not about the centralized, autocratic nature of the regime which had emerged from the 1917 revolution; none of the main protagonists considered that political liberalization was conceivable or that the use of secret police and party oversight could be abandoned. But they could disagree about tactics, and personal rivalry sometimes gave an extra edge to this.

Broadly speaking, two viewpoints emerged. One emphasized that the Revolution depended on the good will of the mass of Russians, the peasants. They had first been allowed to take the land, then antagonized by attempts to feed the cities at their expense, then conciliated again by the New Economic Policy, known as NEP, of liberalization and the restoration of the market. Lenin had approved the last as an expedient. Under it the peasants had been able to make profits for themselves and accordingly had begun to grow more food and sell it to the cities. From the other viewpoint the same facts were seen in a longer perspective. To conciliate the peasants would slow down industrialization, which Russia needed to survive in a hostile world. Therefore the party's proper course was to rely upon the revolutionary militants of the cities and to exploit the still unbolshevized peasants in their interest while pressing on with industrialization and the promotion of revolution abroad. The Communist who was possibly the most intellectually able of the party's leaders, Leon Trotsky, took this view.

In essence what happened was that Trotsky was shouldered aside, but his view on economic priorities prevailed. Out of the intricate politics of the party eventually emerged the dominant member of its bureaucracy, Joseph Stalin, a man far less attractive than either Lenin or Trotsky but of greater historical importance. Gradually arming himself with a power he used as

The first tractor arrives in Samarkand, 1926. The Soviet regime brought about a huge modernization and Westernization of Russian Asia. *(Tass from Sovfoto)*

ruthlessly against former colleagues and old Bolsheviks as against his enemies, Stalin carried out another revolution. For him the industrialization of
Russia was paramount. A way had to be found of forcing the peasant to pay
for it by supplying the grain he would rather have eaten if not offered a good
profit. The first of two Five-Year Plans to industrialize the country therefore
began in 1928 with the collectivization of agriculture. The party now for the
first time conquered the countryside. In a new civil war millions of peasants
were killed or transported and grain levies brought back famine. But the
towns were fed. The police apparatus kept consumption down to the minimum and real wages fell, but by 1937 80 percent of Russian industrial output
came from plants built since 1928. Russia was again a great power. This
alone should assure Stalin a place in history.

The price in suffering was enormous. Collectivization was only made
possible by brutality on a scale far greater than anything seen under the tsars
and collectivization made Russia a totalitarian state far more effective than
the old autocracy had been. Stalin in this light, nonetheless, looks a fully
Russian figure, a despot whose ruthless use of power is anticipated by Ivan
the Terrible or Peter the Great. He was a somewhat paradoxical claimant to
Marxist orthodoxy. That doctrine had taught that the economic structure of
society determined its politics; Stalin precisely inverted this and demonstrated that political power could revolutionize the economic substructure
by force.

Fascism

Critics of liberal capitalist society in other countries sometimes pointed
to Soviet Russia, of which they had a very rosy picture, as an example of the
way a society might achieve progress and revitalization, but Russia was not
the only model available in the 1920s to those who found the civilization of
the West disappointing. In Italy a movement emerged which was to lend its
name to other radical movements only loosely related to it. This was Fascism.

The world war had brought grave strains to Italy for she was weaker
economically than the other great powers. Her share of fighting had been
very heavy and often unsuccessful; much of it had taken place on Italian territory. Inequalities had accentuated social divisions as the war went on. In
particular, inflation damaged the middle classes and those who lived on investments or fixed incomes. The owners of property, whether agricultural or
industrial, and those who could ask higher wages because of a labor shortage
were more insulated.

Before 1914 the middle classes of Italy had supplied the most convinced
supporters of the unification which had its climax in 1870. They had sustained a constitutional and liberal state while conservative Roman Catholics
and revolutionary socialists had long opposed it. They had seen the war Italy
entered in 1915 as the completion of the Risorgimento, a crusade to remove
Austria from the last soil she still ruled inhabited by those of Italian blood
or speech. Like all nationalism this was a muddled, unscientific notion, but

it was powerful. The Versailles settlement left many of the Italian dreams unrealized and brought deep disillusionment. Moreover, as the immediate postwar economic crisis deepened, the Socialists grew stronger in Parliament and seemed more alarming. In the background was fear of Russian propaganda and an Italian 1917. Disappointed and frightened, angry with antinationalism, many Italians began to cast loose from liberal parliamentarianism and to look for a new way out. They became intransigent nationalists abroad (and applauded an adventurer who seized the Adriatic port of Fiume, which the peace conference had failed to give Italy) and violent anti-Marxists at home.

A Roman Catholic country was likely to be anti-Marxist, but it was not only from the traditionally conservative church that the new leadership against Marxists came. In 1919 a journalist and ex-serviceman who before the war had been an extreme socialist, Benito Mussolini, formed a movement called the *fascio di combattimento*, which may be roughly translated as "union for struggle." It sought power by any means, among them violence, which groups of young thugs directed at first against socialists and working-class organizations and later against elected authorities. The move-

The march on Rome by the Fascists, 1922. Mussolini surrounded by his colleagues strides toward power. His dress, somewhat more formal than theirs, is explained by the need to visit the king; a smart turnout was easier because Mussolini had made the "march" by train. *(UPI)*

ment prospered. Italy's constitutional politicians could neither control it nor tame it by cooperation. Soon the Fascists (as they came to be called) enjoyed a large measure of official or quasi-official patronage and protection from local authorities and police. By 1922 they had not only achieved important electoral success but had made orderly government virtually impossible in some places by terrorizing their political enemies on the left, whether Communist or Socialist (Italian Marxists were as divided as those of other countries by the appearance of the Comintern). In that year, other politicians having failed to master the Fascist challenge, the king called Mussolini to form a government; he did so on a coalition basis and the violence came to an end. This was what later Fascist mythology called the March on Rome, but it did not mean the end of constitutional Italy. Mussolini only slowly turned his position into a dictatorship. It was only in 1925 that he removed the old constitution and in the following year that he suspended elections and began to govern by decree. There was little opposition.

The new regime had terrorism in plenty at its roots, and it explicitly denounced liberal ideals, yet Mussolini's rule was far short of totalitarian and much less brutal than what emerged in other countries where liberalism had failed. He had aspirations to revolutionary change (and many of his followers much stronger ones), but they turned out to mean little in practice; such aspirations reflected Mussolini's own temperamental impatience as much as real radical pressure in his movement. Italian Fascism tended to reflect more and more the power of established social forces. Its greatest domestic step was a diplomatic agreement with the papacy, which in return for substantial concessions to the role of the church in Italian life (which persist to this day) at last recognized the Italian state in the Lateran treaties of 1929. For all Fascism's revolutionary rhetoric, this was a concession to the greatest conservative force in Italy. "We have given back God to Italy and Italy to God," said the pope. Just as unrevolutionary were the results of Fascist criticism of free enterprise, which boiled down to depriving trade unions of their power to protect their members. Few checks were placed on the freedom of employers and Fascist economic planning was a mockery. Only agricultural production notably improved.

The same divergence between style and aspiration on the one hand and achievement on the other would elsewhere mark movements called Fascist. Though they reflected something new and post-liberal — they were inconceivable except as expressions of mass society — they almost all made compromising concessions to conservative influences. This makes it difficult to define Fascism. Many countries had regimes which were authoritarian and even totalitarian in aspiration, intensely nationalist, and anti-Marxist. But Fascism was not the only possible source of such ideas. The governments which emerged in Portugal and Spain, for example, drew as much upon traditional and conservative forces as upon those which arose from the new phenomenon of mass politics. True radicals who thought themselves Fascists were often discontented at the concessions these regimes made to the existing social order. Only in Germany did a Fascist movement succeed in revolutionizing society and mastering historical conservatism.

For such reasons it is best to recognize two separable phenomena of the 1920s and 1930s and confine the term "Fascism" to the one distinguished by the appearance (even in stable democracies, such as Great Britain and France) of ideologists and activists who spoke the language of a new, radical politics, emphasized idealism, willpower, and sacrifice, and looked forward to rebuilding society and the state without respect for vested interests or concessions to materialism. This phenomenon could be found in many places but triumphed in only two major states, Italy and Germany. In both cases economic distress, outraged nationalism, and anti-Marxism were the sources of success.

In other countries, usually underdeveloped economically, it might be better to speak of authoritarian rather than Fascist regimes. Large agricultural populations in eastern Europe faced hard times aggravated by the effects of the peace settlement; often the presence of national minorities was an irritant. Liberal institutions were only superficially implanted and traditional social and religious forces were strong. As in Latin America, where similar economic conditions prevailed, an apparent constitutionalism tended to give way sooner or later to the rule of dictators and soldiers. This was the case before 1938 in the new Baltic states, Poland, and all the successor states of the Dual Monarchy except Czechoslovakia, the one effective democracy in central Europe or the Balkans. These nations' acceptance of authoritarian government demonstrates both the unreality of the hopes entertained in 1918 of their political maturity and the new fear of Marxist communism, especially acute on Russia's borders. The pressures of economic backwardness and the absence of deeply rooted constitutional and liberal principles operated also, though less intensely, in Spain, Portugal, and the new republic of Austria; in these states the influence of traditional conservatism was even stronger and Catholic social thinking counted for as much as Fascist.

Economic recovery and collapse

The failures of democracy were not obvious all at once. In the 1920s it was still possible to feel hopeful. After a bad economic start, most of Europe outside Russia shared in a gradual recovery of prosperity. The years from 1925 to 1929 were on the whole good ones. The appalling postwar inflations had receded and currencies were once more stable; the resumption by many countries of the gold standard was a sign of confidence. In 1925 the production of food and raw materials in Europe for the first time passed the 1913 figure and manufacturing was also making gains. With the help of a worldwide commercial recovery and huge investment from the United States, now an exporter of capital, Europe reached in 1929 a level of trade not to be touched again for a quarter of a century. Yet disaster followed. Economic recovery had been built on insecure foundations. When faced with a sudden depression, the new prosperity crumbled rapidly and contributed to a world economic crisis, the single most important event between the two world wars.

The complex but remarkably efficient economic system of 1914 had been swept away. International exchange was hampered by a huge increase of restrictions immediately after the war as infant economies strove to protect themselves with tariffs and exchange control and the bigger and older nations tried to keep enfeebled economies going. The peace treaty made things worse by saddling Germany, the most important industrial state in Europe, with an indefinite burden of reparations in kind and in cash, which not only distorted her economy and delayed its recovery for years but also took away much of the incentive to make it work. Germany's greatest potential market to the east, Russia, was almost entirely cut off behind an economic frontier which little trade could penetrate; the Danube valley and the Balkans, formerly great areas of German enterprise, were divided and impoverished.

What gradually overcame these difficulties was American money. Though they would not take European goods and retired behind their tariff walls, the Americans were able and willing to lend their dollars. In the 1920s the United States produced nearly 40 percent of the world's coal and over half the world's manufactures. This abundance, enhanced by the demands of war, had transformed the life of many Americans, the first people in the world to take for granted the possession of family automobiles. Unfortunately the domestic prosperity of the United States carried the world. On it depended the confidence which provided American capital for export. Because of this, a swing in the business cycle turned into a world economic disaster.

In 1928 there were signs in the United States that short-term money was harder to get. There were also signs, notably in housing, that the end of the long boom might be approaching. These two factors led American investors to call back their money from abroad. Soon some European borrowers were in difficulties. Meanwhile demand was slackening in the United States as people began to think a severe slump might be on the way. Almost accidentally this detonated a particularly sudden and spectacular stock market collapse in October 1929. A temporary rally failed to restore American business confidence and money for overseas investment dried up. The world slump now began.

Economic growth came to an end because of the collapse of investment, but another factor was soon operating to accelerate disaster. As the industrialized debtor nations tried to put their accounts in order, they cut imports. This caused a drop in world prices so that countries producing primary goods could not afford to buy Europe's exports. World trade shrank. At the center of things both the United States and Europe went into a financial crisis; as countries struggled, unsuccessfully, to cling to the gold standard, they adopted deflationary policies to balance their books. This cut demand still further. By 1933 all the major currencies except the French franc were off gold. Financial chaos was accompanied by a level of unemployment which may have reached 30 million in the combined industrial countries. The index of industrial production for the United States and Germany in 1932, their worst year, was in each case only just above half of what it had been in 1929.

The effects of economic depression rolled outward with a ghastly and irresistible logic. The social gains of the 1920s, when many people's standard of living had improved, were wiped out. No country had a solution to unemployment, and though it was at its worst in the United States and Germany, it existed in a concealed form all around the world in the villages and farmlands of the primary producers. The national income of the United States fell by 38 percent between 1929 and 1932; this was exactly the figure by which the prices of manufactured goods declined, but at the same time prices for raw materials and foodstuffs fell by 56 percent and 48 percent, respectively. Everywhere the poorer nations and the poorer sectors of the mature economies suffered disproportionately. Primary producers suffered more than industrial countries in terms of the proportion by which their incomes decreased. This may not always have been apparent; because they had less far to fall than the town dweller, an eastern European or Argentinean peasant may not have been absolutely much worse off for he was always badly off, but an unemployed German clerk or factory worker certainly was.

There was to be little recovery until another great war. Nations cut themselves off more and more behind tariffs and strove in some cases to achieve self-sufficiency by increasing state control of economic life. The disaster was a promising setting for Communists and Fascists, who expected or advocated the collapse of liberal civilization and now began to flap expectantly about the dying carcass. The gold standard and the belief in noninterference with the economy were dead. This marks the collapse of liberal Europe in its economic dimension as strikingly as the rise of totalitarian regimes and destructive nationalism marked it in its political. It was the most frightening example of the loss of men's power to control events. Many Europeans found this hard to see, though, and continued to dream of the restoration of an age when the values of their civilization had rested on a political and economic hegemony which, for a time, had worked.

chapter 35

A New Asia in the Making

Europe's troubles were not confined to Europe. The nineteenth-century beginnings of the revolutionizing of Asia by European colonialism and Western cultural and economic influences have already been traced. European sources continued to nourish the process they had set in motion, but revolutionary influences also were soon felt from an Asian source too, Japan. Japanese dynamism dominates Asian history in the first forty years of this century. China's revolution had no comparable impact until after 1945 when, together with new forces from outside, she surpassed Japan in importance as a shaper of Asian affairs. Meanwhile the processes of change which stemmed from Europe were also at work in the Islamic lands.

CLASHES IN THE FAR EAST

Japan's dynamism showed itself both in economic growth and territorial aggressiveness. For a long time the first was more obvious and in some measure helped mask Japan's imperialism. Her industrialization (which was the most dramatic feature of her economic development) was part and parcel of an overall process of Westernization, which in the 1920s could still justify a mood of liberal hopefulness about Japanese society and politics. In 1925 universal male suffrage was introduced, and in spite of much available evidence from the West that this had no necessary connection with liberalism or moderation, it seemed to confirm a pattern of steady constitutional progress begun in the nineteenth century.

The First World War had given Japan great opportunities: markets (especially in Asia) in which she had faced heavy Western competition were abandoned to her as their former exploiters concentrated all their efforts on the war in Europe; the Allied governments ordered great quantities of munitions from Japanese factories; a world shipping shortage gave her new shipyards the work they needed. Though the boom collapsed in 1920, expansion was resumed later in the decade and by 1929 the Japanese had an industrial base which (though it still engaged less than one in five of the population) had in twenty years seen its steel production rise almost tenfold, its textile production triple, and its coal output double. Japanese industry reached out to other Asian countries; it imported iron ore from China and Malaya, coal from Manchuria. Though her manufacturing industry was still small by Western standards and though it coexisted with an enduring small-scale and artisan sector, Japan's new industrial strength was beginning to shape both domestic politics and foreign relations in the 1920s. In particular it affected her relations with mainland Asia, where the continuing eclipse of China provided the counterpoint to Japanese ascendancy.

The Chinese republic

The 1911 revolution was of enormous importance to China. It marked an epoch far more fundamentally than the French or Russian revolutions: it was the end of more than two thousand years of history during which the Confucian state had held China together and Confucian ideals had dominated Chinese culture and society. Inseparably intertwined, Confucianism and the legal order fell together, shattering all the standards by which China lived. Yet the revolution was limited, in two ways especially.

In the first place it was destructive rather than constructive. The imperial structure had held together a vast country, virtually a continent, of widely different regions. Its collapse meant that the centrifugal regionalism which had so often appeared in Chinese history could again have full rein. Many of the revolutionaries were animated by a bitter envy and distrust of Peking. Local concentrations of power, secret societies, the gentry, and military commanders were all ready and willing to take a grip on affairs in their own regions. These tendencies were somewhat masked while Yüan Shih-kai remained at the head of affairs (until 1916) but then burst out. The revolutionaries were split between those who upheld the central parliamentary structure at Peking and a group round Sun Yat-sen called the Chinese National People's Party, or Kuomintang. Sun's support was drawn mainly from Canton businessmen and certain soldiers in the south. This was the background to the phenomenon of the warlords, soldiers who happened to have control of substantial forces and arms at a time when the central government was continuously weak. Between 1912 and 1928 there were about 1,300 of them; at times they controlled important areas, and Yüan Shih-kai himself may be regarded as the greatest of them. Some warlords carried out reforms. Some were simply bandits. A few had considerable pretensions to status as plausible pretenders to governmental power. It was a little like the end of the Roman Empire though less drawn out. Nothing took the place of the old scholar-bureaucrats, and the soldiers stepped forward to fill the void.

The second limitation of the revolution of 1911 was its failure to provide a basis of agreement for further progress. Sun Yat-sen had said that the national question—the assertion of China's independence—would have to be solved before the social. But even about the shape of a nationalist future there was much disagreement; the struggle against the common enemy before 1911 had merely delayed its emergence. Although eventually creative, the marked intellectual confusion among the revolutionaries in the first decade of the revolution was deeply divisive and symptomatic of the huge task awaiting China's would-be renovators.

Some attempted to rehabilitate Confucian values, but these values were also the subject of the most bitter attacks by intellectuals. Beginning in 1916 a group of cultural reformers began to gather at the University of Peking. The previous year one of them, Ch'ên Tu-hsiu, had founded a journal called *New Youth*, which was the focus of the debate they ignited. Ch'ên preached to the Chinese youth, in whose hands he believed the revolution's destiny to lie, a total rejection of the old cultural traditions. Like other intellectuals who talked of John Stuart Mill and Herbert Spencer and introduced to their bemused compatriots the works of Ibsen, Ch'ên still thought the key lay in the West; in its Darwinian sense of struggle, its individualism and utilitarianism, it seemed to offer a way ahead. One of his coadjutors, Hu Shih, also emphasized the need to reorient Chinese culture; he had been a pupil of the American educational philosopher John Dewey. But important though such leadership was and however enthusiastic its disciples might be, the emphasis on a Western reeducation for China was a handicap. Not only were many educated and patriotic Chinese sincerely attached to the traditional culture, but Western ideas were only sure of a ready welcome among the most untypical elements of Chinese society—the seaboard, urban merchants and their student offspring, frequently educated abroad. The mass of Chinese could hardly be touched by such ideas and appeals, and the demand for a vernacular literature was one evidence of the reformers' recognition of this fact.

Insofar as they had nationalist feelings, the Chinese were likely to turn against the West and Western-inspired capitalism, which for many of them meant one more kind of exploitation and was the most obvious constituent of the civilization they were urged to adopt. But most Chinese were peasants and they seemed after 1911 to have relapsed into passivity, apparently unmoved by events and unaware of the agitation of angry, Westernized young men. The peasantry grew more miserable throughout the whole first half of this century. As the population steadily increased, nothing was done to meet its hunger for land; instead, the number of the indebted and landless grew, their wretched lives frequently made even more intolerable by war, whether directly or through its concomitants, famine and disease. The Chinese revolution would only be assured success when it could activate these people. The cultural emphasis of some reformers masked an unwillingness to envisage the practical political steps necessary for this.

Japanese aggression

China's weakness remained Japan's opportunity. The latter's nineteenth-century policies had not been abandoned. A world war was the occasion to push them forward again. The Black Dragon Society, an ultranationalist organization, urged that the Europeans' quarrels with one another should be exploited. Japan's allies could hardly object to her seizure of the German ports in China; even if they did they could do little about it while they needed Japanese ships and manufactures. The Allies also hoped that the Japanese might send an army to fight in Europe. Nothing like this happened of course. Instead, the Japanese finessed by arousing fears that they might make a separate peace with Germany and pressed ahead in China.

At the beginning of 1915 the Japanese government presented the Chinese with a list of twenty-one demands and an ultimatum. In their entirety they amounted to a proposal for a Japanese protectorate over China. The United Kingdom and the United States did what they could by diplomacy to have them reduced, but in the end the Japanese got much of what they asked for, including further confirmation of their special commercial and leasehold rights in Manchuria. Chinese patriots were enraged, but there was nothing they could do while their internal politics were in such disorder. Indeed, they were so confused that Sun Yat-sen was himself at that moment seeking Japanese support.

In 1916 Japanese pressure was successfully brought to bear on the British to dissuade them from accepting Yüan Shih-kai's attempt to restore stability by making himself emperor. In the following year came another treaty, this one extending the recognition of Japan's special interests as far as Inner Mongolia. In August 1917 the Chinese government went to war with Germany, partly in the hope of winning good will and support at the peace conference. Yet a few months later the United States formally recognized Japan's special interests in China in return for a Japanese endorsement of the Open Door policy toward foreign trade there and a promise to maintain Chinese integrity and independence. All the Chinese got was the ending of German and Austrian extraterritoriality and agreement to delay payment of Boxer indemnities to the Allies. The Japanese, moreover, secured more concessions from China in secret agreements in 1917 and 1918.

The Versailles settlement deeply disappointed both the Chinese and Japanese. Japan was now indisputably a world power; in 1918 she had the third largest navy in the world. She won solid gains at the peace: the former German rights in Shantung (promised to her by the British and French in 1917), mandates over many of the Pacific islands taken from Germany, and a permanent seat on the council of the League of Nations. But the gain in "face" implied in recognition as a great power was offset in Japanese eyes by the failure to have a declaration in favor of racial equality written into the covenant of the league. The Chinese had much more to feel aggrieved about; in spite of widespread sympathy over Japan's twenty-one demands (notably in the United States) they were unable to obtain a reversal of the Shantung decision. Disappointed of American diplomatic support and crippled by the divisions within their own delegation between the representatives of the Peking government and those of the Kuomintang, the Chinese refused to sign the treaty.

The May 4th movement

An almost immediate consequence of China's disappointment was a development which some commentators have considered as important as the 1911 revolution. This was the May 4th movement of 1919,* which stemmed

---

*It had been planned for May 7, the anniversary of China's acceptance of the 1915 demands, but was moved forward to anticipate action by the authorities.

from a student demonstration in Peking against the peace terms. It escalated, though at first only into a small riot which resulted in the resignation of the head of the university. This then led to a nationwide student movement (one of the first political reflections of the new colleges and universities widely established in China after 1911), which in turn spread to embrace others than students, notably industrial workers and the new Chinese capitalists who had benefited from the war, and to manifest itself in strikes and a boycott of Japanese goods. It was the most important evidence yet to be seen of the mounting rejection of Europe by Asia.

For the first time an industrial China entered the scene. China, like Japan, had enjoyed an economic boom during the war. Though a decline in European sales to China had been partly offset by increased Japanese and American imports, Chinese entrepreneurs in the ports had found it profitable to invest in production for the home market. The first considerable industrial areas outside Manchuria had begun to appear. Progressive Chinese capitalists sympathized with revolutionary ideas all the more when the return of peace brought renewed Western competition and evidence that China had not earned her liberation from tutelage to the foreigner. The workers also felt resentment: their jobs were threatened. Many of them were first-generation town dwellers, drawn into the new industrial areas from the countryside by the promise of employment. An uprooting from the tenacious soil of peasant tradition was even more important in China than in Europe a century before. The migrant to the town broke with patriarchal authority and the reciprocal obligations of the independent producing unit, the household. This was a further great weakening of the age-old structure which even after the revolution still tied China to the past.

The May 4th movement showed what could be made of all these forces. It had created the first widely based Chinese revolutionary coalition. Progressive Western liberalism was not enough for such a movement and implicit in the movement's success was the disappointment of the hopes of many of the cultural reformers. Capitalist democracy on Western lines had been shown up by the Chinese government's helplessness in the face of Japan. Now that government suffered another humiliation from its own subjects: the boycott and demonstrations forced it to release the arrested students and dismiss its pro-Japanese ministers. But this was not the only important consequence of the May 4th movement. For all their limited political influence, the reformers had for the first time, thanks to the students, broken through into the world of social action. This aroused enormous optimism and greater popular political awareness than ever before and this is why contemporary Chinese history begins positively in 1919 rather than 1911.

Chinese communism

By 1919 China's cultural tradition was dissolving fast. The abolition of the examination system, the return of Westernized exiles, and the great literary and cultural debate of the war years had all pushed things too far for any return to the old stable order. The warlords provided no new authority to represent and sustain orthodoxy. An alternative principle was needed. West-ern liberalism had never had mass appeal; now its charm for intellectuals was threatened at a moment when a rival ideological force had appeared on the scene. The Bolshevik Revolution gave Marxism a homeland to which its adherents abroad could look for inspiration, guidance, leadership, and, sometimes, material support. This was a great new factor introduced the world over into an already dissolving historical epoch. Its immediate effect in China was to bring into the open divisions always present in the reform movement though temporarily overcome in the euphoria of May 4th.

Both the Russian Revolution and the Bolshevik victory had been warm-ly welcomed by one of the contributors to *New Youth,* Li Ta-chao, who in 1918 became librarian at Peking University. By 1919 he saw in Marxism the motive force of world revolution and a means to vitalize the Chinese peas-antry. At that moment Russia was very popular among Chinese students. The successors of the tsar had abandoned the old imperialist aims, it seemed, for one of the first acts of the Soviet government had been a formal renunciation of all extraterritorial rights and jurisdictions enjoyed by the tsarist state. In the eyes of the nationalists Russia had, therefore, clean hands. Moreover her revolution—a revolution in a peasant society—claimed to be built upon a doctrine which seemed especially applicable to China in the wake of the industrialization provoked by the war. In 1918 a Marxist study society had begun to meet at the University of Peking; one of its members was a young assistant in the university library, Mao Tse-tung, and others were prominent in the May 4th movement. By 1920 there was an outlet for Marxist ideas in one of the student magazines, and the first attempts had been successfully made to deploy Marxist and Leninist principles by orga-nizing strikes in support of the demands of May 4th.

Marxism accelerated the opening of divisions within that movement. Ch'ên Tu-hsiu threw his energies into organizing the emerging Chinese left around its principles. The liberals were beginning to be left behind as a new split appeared between those who sought cultural and those who sought institutional reform. The Comintern observed its opportunities and in 1919 sent its first man to China to help. The effects were not entirely happy; there were quarrels. Nevertheless, in circumstances still obscure (we know precisely neither names nor dates) delegates from different parts of China formed a Chinese Communist party in Shanghai in 1921. Mao Tse-tung was among them.

So began the last stage of the Chinese revolution and the last example of that curious dialectic which has run through Asia's relations with Europe. Once more an alien Western idea, Marxism, born and shaped in a society totally unlike those of the East, was taken up by an Asian people and put to use not merely against their traditional sources of inertia in the name of the Western goals of modernization, efficiency, and universal human dignity and equality but also against the source from which it came, the European world.

Communism was to benefit enormously from the fact that in Chinese eyes capitalism appeared as the connecting principle behind foreign and imperialist exploitation. In the 1920s nothing happened to weaken this identification. China's divisions were thought to justify treating her as of little account in international affairs. However, nine powers with Asian interests agreed to guarantee her territorial integrity and Japan consented to the return of Kiaochow. This was part of a complicated set of agreements made at Washington in 1922; their core was an international limitation on naval strength (there was great uneasiness about the cost of armaments) which in the end left Japan relatively much better off. The four major powers guaranteed one another's Pacific possessions too, and this allowed the British to abandon the Anglo-Japanese alliance with decency, since its formal purpose was now met by the new guarantee (the Australians were pleased by this). But the guarantee to China, everyone knew, was worth no more than the Americans' preparedness to fight to support it; the British had been obliged by the treaties *not* to build a naval base at Hong Kong. Meanwhile foreigners continued to administer the customs and tax revenues on which the Peking government of an "independent" China depended, and foreign agents and businessmen dealt directly with the warlords when it suited them. Though American policy had further weakened the European position in Asia, it was not apparent on the spot.

The Chinese Communist party and the Kuomintang

Foreign intervention was one reason Marxism's appeal to intellectuals went far beyond the formal structure of the Chinese Communist party. Sun Yat-sen stressed his disagreements with Marxism but adopted views which helped carry the Kuomintang away from conventional liberalism and toward it. His view of the world came to be one in which Russia, Germany, and Asia had a common interest since they were exploited by their oppressors and enemies, the four imperialist powers. (Germany was well regarded after she had undertaken in 1921 to place her relations with China on a completely equal footing.) He coined a new expression, "hypo-colony," to identify the state of affairs in which China was exploited without formal subordination as a dependency. The conclusion was collectivist. "On no account must we give more liberty to the individual," Sun wrote, "let us secure liberty instead for the nation." This gave a new sanction to rejection of the ideal of individual liberty, a rejection always present in the classical Chinese outlook and tradition. Sun even envisaged a necessary period of one-party rule to make possible an exercise in mass indoctrination.

Thus doctrinally no grave obstacle was apparent to cooperation between the Communists and the Kuomintang. The behavior of the Western powers and the warlords provided common enemies. Finally, there were international considerations. For Sun's party, good relations with Russia, the anti-imperialist power with whom China had her longest land frontier, seemed at least prudent and potentially very advantageous, while Comintern policy favored cooperation with the Kuomintang to safeguard Russian interests in Mongolia and constitute some kind of barrier against Japan. Russia was still the great power with the largest territorial interests in the Far East, but she had been left out of the Washington conferences. Her rulers had earlier been

alarmed by the presence of Japanese forces in an Allied intervention in
Siberia. For them, cooperation with the likely winners in China was an obvious course even if Marxist doctrine had not also fitted such a policy. Consequently from 1924 onward the Chinese Communist party was working with
the Kuomintang under Russian patronage in spite of some doubts among
Chinese Communists. As individuals, though not as a party, they could belong
to the Kuomintang. Sun Yat-sen's able young soldier, Chiang Kai-shek, was
sent to Moscow for training, and a military academy was founded in China
to provide ideological as well as martial instruction.

In 1925 Sun Yat-sen died, but the united front endured and made progress. While the Communists in certain provinces won peasant support for
the revolution, the new revolutionary army led by idealistic young officers
made headway against the warlords. By 1927 a semblance of unity had been
restored to the country under Kuomintang leadership. Anti-imperialist feeling resulted in a successful boycott of British goods, which led London,
alarmed by the evidence of growing Russian influence in China, to surrender its concessions at Hankow and Kiukiang. The British had already promised to return the port of Weihaiwei to China and the United States had renounced its share of the Boxer indemnity. Sun Yat-sen's will (which Chinese
schoolchildren learned by heart) had said that the revolution was not yet
complete; such successes added to signs that it was winning.

The full significance of one important aspect of the revolution's advance
went unremarked. Theoretical Marxism stressed the indispensable role of
the industrial proletariat. The Chinese Communists were proud of the progress they had made in politicizing the new urban workers and looked forward to the day when they would provide an effective revolutionary force.
But the mass of Chinese were peasants, still trapped in the Malthusian vise
of rising numbers and too little land. Their centuries of suffering were intensified by the breakdown of central authority in the warlord years. Some
Chinese Communists began to see in the peasantry a revolutionary potential
which, if not easy to reconcile with contemporary Marxist orthodoxy (as re-
tailed by the Moscow theorists), nonetheless embodied Chinese reality. One
of them was Mao Tse-tung. He and those who agreed with him turned their
attention away from the cities to the countryside in the early 1920s and began an unprecedented effort to win over the rural masses to communism.
Paradoxically Mao seems to have cooperated with the Kuomintang longer
than other Chinese Communists just because it was more sympathetic than
his own party to the organization of the peasants.

A great success followed. It was especially marked in Honan, but altogether the Communists had organized some 10 million or so peasants by
1927. "In a few months," wrote Mao, "the peasants have accomplished what
Dr. Sun Yat-sen wanted but failed to accomplish in the forty years he devoted to the national revolution." Organization made possible the removal of
many of the ills which beset the peasants. Landlords were not dispossessed,
but rents were often reduced. Usurious rates of interest were brought down
to reasonable levels.

Rural revolution had eluded all previous progressive movements in
China; the Communist success in reaching this goal was based on the dis-

A peasant unit of the Communist militia raised in China in the 1930s training with spears in default of rifles. *(Eastfoto)*

covery that it could be brought about by using the revolutionary potential of the peasants themselves. This had enormous significance for the future because it implied new possibilities of historical development in the peasant countries of Asia. Mao grasped this and revalued urban revolution accordingly. "If we allot ten points to the democratic revolution," he wrote, "then the achievements of the urban dwellers and the military units rate only three points, while the remaining seven points should go to the peasants in their rural revolution." In the peasant associations he had founded Mao saw the revolutionary future. In his report on the Honan movement he compared the peasants to an elemental force: "The attack is just like a tempest or hurricane; those who submit to it survive, those who resist perish." Even the image is significant; there was here something rooted deeply in Chinese tradition and the long struggle against landlords and bandits. If the Communists tried hard to set that tradition aside by eradicating superstition and breaking down family authority, they nevertheless drew on the Chinese past.

Communism's rural lodgment was the key to its survival in the crisis which followed Sun Yat-sen's death. With him there passed from the scene not only a figure who had commanded the respect of many Communists but also a force reconciling contradictions within the Kuomintang. A rift soon opened between a left and a right wing. The young Chiang Kai-shek, who had been seen as a progressive, now emerged as the military representative of the right, which reflected mainly the interests of capitalists and indirectly landlords. Differences within the Kuomintang were resolved when Chiang, confident of his control of his troops, committed them to destroying the left factions and the Communist party's organization in the cities. They accomplished this with much bloodshed in Shanghai and Nanking in 1927, under the eyes of European and American soldiers who had been sent to China to protect the concessions. The Chinese Communist party was proscribed.

This was not quite the end of cooperation between the Nationalists (as the Kuomintang came to be called abroad) and Chinese Communists. It continued in a few areas for some months, largely because of Moscow's unwillingness to break with Chiang. Russian direction had already contributed to the destruction of the urban Communists. The Comintern myopically pursued in China, as elsewhere, what were believed to be Russian interests, refracted through the mirror of dogmatic Marxism. These interests were for Stalin in the first place domestic. But Stalin also wanted a Chinese government which could stand up to the British, the greatest imperialist power, and the Kuomintang seemed the best bet for that. Finally, theory fitted these choices: according to Marxist orthodoxy the bourgeois revolution had to precede the proletarian. After the triumph of the Kuomintang was clear, the Russians withdrew their advisers from the Chinese Communist party, which gave up open politics to become a subversive, underground organization. Chinese nationalism had done well out of Russian help even if Chinese communism had not.

But Russian policy alone cannot explain this split inside the Chinese revolution. The Kuomintang could hardly have indefinitely resisted the strains within it. It depended on privileged interests, but the revolution needed to satisfy mass demands if it was to survive. For all the apparent triumph of the Kuomintang, the split was in fact a setback. It made it impossible to dispose finally of the warlord problem and, more serious, weakened the antiforeign front—above all against Japan.

Japanese in Manchuria

In Asia as in Europe the world economic depression which began in 1929 marked a revolution. By 1931 half Japan's heavy industry was idle and exports of manufactured goods were running at about a third of their 1929 total. From a base of 100 in 1926, employment fell in five years to 73.1. The hardship in the countryside became intolerable; rents had always been high because of the limited land available and now millions of farmers were ruined or forced to sell their daughters into prostitution to survive. These pressures led to the opening of a new phase in Japanese politics which was to reach its climax with the country's entry into a world war in 1941.

In the 1920s liberal government in Japan led to relaxed pressure on China. For a time military expenditure was actually reduced (though it doubled over the whole decade). This displaced the armed services, who were further antagonized when another naval agreement with the British and Americans in 1930 imposed on Japan what they saw as dangerous and humiliating restraints. The issue was connected with the danger, as the military leaders saw it, of civilian control of the armed forces, which had always been regarded as directly responsible to the emperor.

The economic crisis exacerbated domestic political issues in two ways. In the first place it made an aggressive foreign policy once more seem desirable and perhaps essential. The collapse of markets in Europe and European colonies had produced a shattering effect on Japan's economy. Her outlets on the Asian mainland were now crucial, and anything that seemed to threaten them provoked intense irritation. Nationalist extremism had for a long time been absorbed in the struggle against the unequal treaties. With these out of the way, a new outlet for patriotism would be needed; for this reason too expansion on the Asian mainland which might safeguard markets was more than ever attractive in 1931. The circumstances seemed propitious. The Western colonial powers were clearly on the defensive if not in full retreat. The Dutch had faced rebellions in Java and Sumatra in the 1920s and the French a Vietnamese revolt in 1930; in both places there was the sinister novelty of Communist help to nationalist rebels. The British were not in quite such difficulties in India but were in retreat there; in China they had already shown in the 1920s that they wanted only a quiet life and not too grave a loss of face; and they were even more shaken in their Far Eastern policies after the economic collapse, which had also knocked the stuffing out of American opposition to Japan. Finally, Russian power seemed in eclipse; Moscow's attempt to influence events in China had failed dismally, and the Japanese saw a chance to make gains which would recoup their failure to retain a foothold in eastern Siberia after the interventions of 1918. Chinese nationalism, on the other hand, had won notable successes, showed no sign of retreat, and was beginning to threaten the long-established Japanese presence in Manchuria. All these factors were present in the calculations being made by Japanese statesmen as the depression deepened.

A second and more direct effect of the economic depression on Japanese politics was the resentment against capitalism and the Western progressive ideals which it led to. There was a real revolutionary potential in the distress of 1930 and 1931, and it was especially obvious to junior and middle-ranking army officers, whose ties with the countryside and the peasantry were close both because of their own origins and because most of their men were peasant boys. At the same time as they felt Japan to be threatened by a weak foreign policy, they also believed that her liberal government was not meeting the needs which a capitalist collapse had thrown up. Patriotic and paternalistic, they sought a new path in the ideal of nationalist self-sacrifice and from 1930 on were forming secret societies to promote their ends. When it became clear that overt political change would be difficult, they turned instead to direct action in foreign affairs.

Manchuria was the crucial theater. The Japanese presence there went back to 1905 and heavy investment had followed its establishment. The Japanese position had been guaranteed by subsequent Sino-Japanese agreement but had begun to be questioned by the Chinese in the 1920s. There was armed conflict in 1928 when Japanese forces tried to prevent Kuomintang soldiers from operating against warlords whom the Japanese found it convenient to patronize. The Russians supported China because they feared that the Japanese might push their influence toward Inner Mongolia. Even when in 1929 the Chinese came into conflict with the Russians over control of the railway which ran across Manchuria and was the most direct route to Vladivostok, this can only have impressed Japan with the new vigor of Chinese power. The nationalist Kuomintang was asserting itself in the territories of the old empire. By 1931 the Japanese government was by no means in control of its Manchurian policy. Effective power rested with the commanders of the Japanese forces there. When these organized an incident near Mukden that year and used it as an excuse for taking over the whole province, an area as big as France and Spain combined, those in Tokyo who wished to restrain them could not do so.

The Japanese transformed Manchuria into a puppet state, Manchukuo (ruled by the last Manchu emperor). There was an outcry at the League of Nations against Japanese aggression but no effective action. Assassinations

The high tide of victory—Japanese soldiers cheer after their seizure of Shanghai in 1937.
(Ullstein Bilderdienst)

in Tokyo led to the establishment there of a government much more under military influence and an expansion of the quarrel with China. In 1932 the Japanese replied to a Chinese boycott of their goods by attacking Shanghai. The following year they invaded Jehol, crossing the Great Wall to impose a peace settlement which left Japan dominating a part of historic China herself. A demilitarized zone now ran to within fifty miles of the old Chinese Eastern Railway, and the Japanese unsuccessfully tried to organize a secessionist North China. There matters stood until 1937 when what would prove to be the first campaign of the Second World War began. The failure to discipline the officers of 1931 turned out to have consequences much more grave than had appeared at the time.

Civil war in China

After establishing itself in Peking in 1928, the Kuomintang government had moved to Nanking and from this new capital controlled, it appeared, all save a few border areas. It continued to whittle away at the treaties of inferiority and was helped by the fact that the Western powers saw in it a means of opposing communism in Asia and thus became somewhat more accommodating. Yet these achievements, considerable though they were, masked important weaknesses. This was revealed in 1931 when the Kuomintang proved unable to halt imperialist aggression by Japan in spite of its success against the Western concessions.

Within China too the Kuomintang failed in the early 1930s. The social revolution had come to a stop. The intellectuals withdrew their moral support from a regime which did not provide the social reforms of which a need to do something about land was the most pressing. The peasants had never given the Kuomintang their allegiance as some of them had given it to the Communists. At this juncture Chiang fell back more and more upon direct government through his officers and appeared increasingly conservative at a time when the traditional culture had decayed beyond repair. The regime became tainted with corruption in public finances, often at the highest level. The foundation under the Nationalist government was therefore insecure, and once more a rival was waiting in the wings.

For some time after 1927 the central leadership of the Chinese Communist party had continued to hope for urban insurrection and to show great caution about reliance on the peasants. But in the provinces individual Communist leaders followed the lines indicated by Mao in Honan. They dispossessed absentee landlords and organized local soviets in a shrewd appreciation of the traditional peasant hostility to central government. By 1930 they had even created an army in Kiangsi, the southeastern province where Mao had established himself, and the Chinese Soviet Republic there ruled 50 million people, or claimed to. In 1932 the Communist leadership left Shanghai to join Mao in this sanctuary. Kuomintang efforts were directed toward destroying the Kiangsi army, which meant fighting on a second front at a time when Japanese pressure was strongest. The last great Nationalist drive was a partial success; it forced the Communists to abandon their southern base in 1934 and begin the Long March north to Shensi, the epic of the

A carefully posed picture from the Chinese civil war years. Only one of these defenders of Shanghai in 1927 feels sufficiently involved in what he is doing to close his disengaged eye.
(UPI)

Chinese revolution and the inspiration of Mao's followers ever since. The demands of resistance to the Japanese prevented the Nationalists from doing more; the Communists were safe in their new refuge.

Consciousness of external danger explains why there were tentative essays in cooperation between the Communists and the Nationalists again in the later 1930s. These efforts also owed something to another change in the policies of the Comintern; it was the era of "popular fronts" which elsewhere combined Communists with other parties. The Kuomintang was also obliged to mute its anti-Western line, and this won it a certain amount of easy sympathy in England and even more in the United States. But neither the cooperation of Communists nor the sympathies of Western liberals could prevent the Nationalist regime from being forced upon the defensive when the Japanese launched a new attack on China in 1937. The "China Incident," as the Japanese called what followed, grew into eight years of fighting which did enormous damage to China and in the end opened the last phase of the Chinese revolution.

The "China Incident"

Japan's attack led the Chinese government to remove to the safety of Chungking in the far west. From there it watched the Japanese occupy all the important northern and coastal areas. League condemnation of Japan and Russian deliveries of aircraft equally seemed unable to stem the onslaught.

The only bonus in the first black years was an unprecedented degree of patriotic unity in China; Communists and Nationalists alike saw that the national revolution was at stake, whether the revolution was seen as a matter of social and cultural revolution for its own sake or as a way of building up the strength which would enable China to be once more independent of the foreigners. The Japanese shared both views; they not only sought territory and markets but looked for allies among conservative Chinese. Significantly they encouraged the reestablishment of Confucianism in the areas they occupied.

The Western powers felt deplorably unable to intervene. Their protests, even on behalf of their own citizens, were brushed aside by the Japanese, who soon made it clear that they were prepared to blockade the foreign concessions if recognition of their new order in Asia was not forthcoming. For British and French weakness there was an obvious explanation: they had troubles enough elsewhere. American ineffectiveness had deeper roots; it went back to the long-established fact that, however the United States might talk about mainland Asia, it would not fight for it. When the Japanese bombed an American gunboat near Nanking in 1937, the State Department huffed and puffed but eventually swallowed Japanese "explanations." It was all very different from what had happened after the destruction of the U.S.S. *Maine* forty years before. However, the Americans did send supplies to Chiang Kai-shek.

By 1941 China was all but cut off from the outside world and had suffered enormous social and physical damage. In the long duel between the two Asian rivals, Japan was clearly the winner so far. Her international position had never seemed stronger; she showed it by humiliating Western residents in China and by forcing the British in 1940 to close for a time the Burma Road by which supplies were being sent to Chungking and the French to admit an occupying army to Indochina. Here was a temptation to further adventure, and it was not likely to be resisted while the military's prestige and power in government remained as high as it had been since the mid-1930s. Yet there was a negative side to all this. The economic cost of the struggle in China was high and Chinese resistance was not overcome simply by victories in the field. The Japanese faced large problems of security and government in the areas they controlled because of guerrilla activity. Aggression made it more and more imperative for the Japanese to acquire the resources of Southeast Asia and Indonesia. But it also helped prepare the Americans psychologically for armed defense of their interests. The United States would in the end have to decide whether to be an Asian power at all.

In the background lay an even deeper question. Despite her aggression against China, it was with the window-dressing slogan of "Asia for the Asians" that Japan advanced on the crumbling Western position in the Far East. Just as the defeat of tsarist forces in 1905 had marked an epoch in the psychological relations of Europe and Asia, so did the independence and power which Japan showed in 1938–1941. When followed by conquest of western territories, as it was to be, it would signal the beginning of the era of decolonization, fittingly inaugurated by an Asian power outstandingly successful in its Westernization.

THE WESTERN ISLAMIC LANDS

Japan was not the only successful Westernizing society though she was the most powerful. Far to the west in the region of the oldest civilizations, the Near East, there had been startling transformations well before 1941. Their story has to begin in the nineteenth century when the integrating power of the Ottoman empire all but disappeared in Europe and Africa. The basic causes were the same in each continent: nationalism and the predatory interests of European powers. A revolt in Servia in 1804 and Mehemet Ali's establishment of himself as the governor of Egypt in 1805 opened the final era of Turkish decline. In Turkish Europe the next change was the Greek revolt; from that time its story can be told in the birth dates of new nations until by 1914 Turkey was left with only eastern Thrace.

The birth of modern Egypt

The decline of Ottoman power west of the Sinai desert had been even more rapid; much of North Africa was virtually independent of Constantinople early in the nineteenth century. Consequently nationalism there operated as much against Europeans as against the Ottomans. It was socially and culturally the most revolutionary force in Islam since the seventh century.

The foundations of Egyptian nationalism were laid by Mehemet Ali. Though he was to see little more of Europe than his birthplace (Kavalla, a seaport in eastern Greece), he admired European civilization and thought Egypt could learn from it. He imported technical instructors, employed foreign consultants in the direction of health and sanitation measures, printed translations of European books and papers on technical subjects, and sent boys to study in France and England. He was working against the grain and was disappointed in his practical achievements, but he nevertheless opened Egypt to European influence, especially French, as never before. French became the second language of educated Egyptians, and a large French community settled in Alexandria, one of the great cosmopolitan cities of the Mediterranean.

Through the channels thus established flowed more than technical knowledge. Some young Egyptians began to pick up political ideas; there were, after all, plenty available in French. A fertile soil was forming as the century went on which would in time provide men to transform Egypt's relations with Europe. Egyptians would draw the same lesson as Indians, Japanese, and Chinese: the European disease had to be caught in order to generate the necessary antibodies against it. Modernization and nationalism became inextricably intertwined.

The next landmark was the building of the Suez Canal; this did more (though indirectly) than any other single fact to doom Egypt to foreign intervention because it gave European governments an interest in assuring that the administration of the area was conducted on sound lines. Intervention began under Ismail, the first ruler of Egypt to obtain the title of khedive from the sultan. He liked up-to-date ideas, had been educated in France, and traveled much in Europe. He was very extravagant. When he became ruler in 1863, the price of cotton, Egypt's major export, was high because of the American Civil War. His financial prospects therefore looked good. Unhappily Ismail's management of money was less than orthodox. The results showed in the Egyptian national debt; it rose from £7 million at Ismail's accession to nearly £100 million thirteen years later. The interest charges then amounted to £5 million a year. In 1876 the Egyptian government was bankrupt and ceased to pay its debts.

There could only be one outcome, the management of Egypt by foreigners. Two controllers, one British, one French, were installed to make sure that Ismail's son governed Egypt with the priority of paying off the national debt. Egyptians soon blamed these officials for the huge burdens of taxation laid upon the peasant to provide the revenue to pay interest on Ismail's loans and for unpopular economies, such as the reduction of the army and cuts in government salaries. In the nationalists' eyes, the European financial officials were agents of foreign imperialism. Moreover, there was resentment of the privileged legal position of the many foreigners in Egypt, who had their special courts.

These grievances led to the formation of nationalist groups and eventually to revolution. Some nationalists looked to the reform of Islam, the unity of the Muslim world, and a pan-Islamic movement adapted to modern life; others took a more local view, antagonized by the preponderance of Turks in the khedive's entourage. But their divisions mattered less in frustrating the revolution than British intervention. That intervention became inevitable, but not for financial reasons: British policy, even under a Liberal prime minister like Gladstone who favored nationalism in other parts of the Ottoman empire, could not accept the danger that an unfriendly government at Cairo might jeopardize the security of the Canal route to India.

After a British army defeated Arabi Pasha, the officer who led the revolutionaries, in 1882, the British became the prime targets of nationalist hatred. They were soon bogged down in Egypt. Though they asserted that they wanted to withdraw as soon as a dependable government was available, they could not do so for none acceptable to them was conceivable. Instead British administrators took over more and more of the government of Egypt. This was not wholly regrettable inasmuch as they reduced the debt and carried out irrigation schemes that made it possible to feed a growing population (which doubled between 1880 and 1914), but they antagonized Egyptians by occupying important posts and by imposing high taxes. After 1900 there was growing unrest and violence. The British and the puppet Egyptian government proceeded firmly against agitation but also sought a way out through reform. At first administrative, this led in 1913 to a new constitution providing for much more representative elections to a more powerful legislative assembly. Unfortunately the assembly only met for a few months before it was suspended at the outbreak of war in 1914. The Egyptian government was pushed into war with Turkey, a khedive suspected of anti-British plotting was replaced, and at the end of the year the British proclaimed a protectorate over Egypt, whose ruler now took the title of sultan.

The Young Turks

The only other effective manifestation of reforming nationalism to appear in the Islamic lands of the Ottoman empire was the Young Turk movement. The Young Turks had a complicated history but a simple purpose. As one of them once put it, "We follow the path traced by Europe . . . even in our refusal to accept foreign intervention." The first part of this meant constitutional and liberal government. They wished to end the despotic rule of Sultan Abdul-Hamid and restore the liberal constitution granted in 1876 and subsequently withdrawn. But they wanted this because they thought it would also revive and reform the empire. Both the Young Turks' program and their methods of conspiracy owed much to Europe; they used, for example, Masonic lodges as cover and organized secret societies like those which had flourished among European liberals in the days of the Holy Alliance. Turkish nationalists also resented the increasing interference of Europeans in the internal affairs of the empire, notably in the management of finance; as in Egypt, the government's inability to repay money borrowed for internal development was followed by loss of independence. European domination was also shown (they felt) in the Ottomans' long and humiliating retreat in the Danube valley and the Balkans.

After a series of mutinies and rebellions (which owed something to the fear of European intervention in Macedonia, where revolts had recently taken place) the sultan gave way in 1908 over the constitution. Liberals abroad smiled on the new Turkey; it seemed that misrule was at last to end. But an attempted counterrevolution led to a Young Turk coup which deposed Abdul-Hamid in April 1909. From 1909 to 1914 the Young Turks ruled with increasingly dictatorial means from behind the façade of constitutional monarchy.

They faced problems which many later modernizers in non-European countries encountered, and their violent methods would often be emulated—from necessity or imagined necessity. They threw themselves into reform of every branch of government (importing many European advisers), but they took power in the middle of a shattering succession of humiliations in foreign affairs which weakened their appeal and led them to rely more and more on force. After the Habsburg government annexed Bosnia in 1908, the ruler of Bulgaria won an acknowledgment of his country's independence and the Cretans announced their union with Greece. Next came the Italian attack and conquest of Tripoli and then the Balkan Wars. It was apparent under strain that the unity among the peoples of a reformed empire on which liberalism had relied was a chimera. Religion, language, social custom, and nationality still fragmented even what was left of the empire. The Young Turks were driven back upon the assertion of one nationalism among many, that of the Ottomans. This of course led to further resentment among other peoples. The result was renewed massacre, tyranny, and assassination, the time-honored instruments of rule at Constantinople; from 1913 they were deployed by a triumvirate of Young Turks who ruled as a collective dictatorship until the outbreak of the war.

Though they disappointed many of their admirers, the Young Turks had the future on their side. They represented the ideas which would one day remake the Ottoman heritage: nationalism and modernization. They even contributed (unknowingly) to remaking it by losing almost the last Ottoman possessions in Europe, thus releasing the empire from a burden. It would be easier for a purely Turkish state to be without the heritage of empire in the long run, but that heritage was still too encumbering in 1914. Before them there was no better alternative as a vehicle for reform than nationalism. How little the pan-Islamic ideas of which some Muslim thinkers had dreamed would mean was to be shown by what happened after 1914 in the largest remaining block of Ottoman territory, the largely Muslim provinces of the Near East.

The Ottoman Near East and the First World War

In 1914 the Ottoman empire encompassed a still large and strategically very important area. From the Caucasus its frontier with Persia ran down to the Persian Gulf near Basra, at the mouth of the Tigris. On the southern shore of the gulf Turkish rule ran down the coast as far south as Qatar. But from here right around to the entrance to the Red Sea the coast of Arabia was in one way or another under British influence, although the whole interior and the Red Sea coast were Ottoman. Under British pressure the Sinai desert had been surrendered to Egypt a few years before, but the ancient lands of Palestine, Syria, and Mesopotamia remained Turkish. This was the heartland of historical Islam, and the sultan was still caliph, the spiritual leader. Yet this heritage would also crumble as the strategy and politics of world war played upon it, bringing about in the end a revolutionary disruption as complete as that which had destroyed Ottoman Europe.

In these lands too nationalist forces were at work before 1914. In part they derived from long-established European cultural influences, which operated in Syria and Lebanon even more strongly than in Egypt. The French influence was again strongest, but it was also accompanied by American missionary efforts which led to the founding of schools and colleges to which there came Arab boys, both Muslim and Christian, from all over the Arab world. The Levant was culturally advanced and there was wide literacy. On the eve of the First World War over a hundred Arabic newspapers were published in the Ottoman empire outside Egypt.

The triumph of the Young Turks and their Ottomanizing tendencies crystallized Arab nationalism. Arab exiles, particularly in Paris and Cairo, formed secret societies and open groups of dissidents. In the background to the problem that nationalism was beginning to pose to the Turks was another uncertain factor, the rulers of the Arabian peninsula. The most important of them was Hussein, sherif of Mecca, who by 1914 had lost the confidence of the Turkish government. There had also been the ominous sign of a meeting of Arabs in 1913 in Persia to consider the independence of Iraq. Against the problems and threats they faced, the Turks could do little but hope to benefit from the divisiveness of the different interests represented among the Arabs.

Finally, although it was not an immediate danger, the latest converts to the religion of nationalism were the Jews. Their history had taken a new turn in 1897 when a Zionist congress was founded with the aim of securing a national home in Palestine. Thus in the long history of Jewry, assimilation, barely achieved in many European countries, was now replaced as an ideal by nationalism. Jewish immigration to Palestine had begun before 1914 but was still on a small scale. The unrolling of the war was to change its significance.

Curious parallels existed between the Ottoman and Habsburg empires in 1914. Both sought war, seeing it partly as a solution to their problems. Yet both were likely to suffer from war because too many people inside and outside their borders saw in it an opportunity to score at their expense. Perhaps at the outset only Russia was obviously presented with an opportunity: the chance of at last gaining the great prize of Constantinople. Long opposition to this by the British and French had evaporated. But the French also had interests which might lead to territorial acquisition. Though their irritation over the British presence in Egypt had subsided with the entente and a free hand for France in Morocco, there was the tradition of a special French interest in the Levant. For a hundred years France had exercised a protection of Catholicism in the Ottoman empire—and this was important in Syria—as well as a cultural predominance. French business had much capital invested there too. These were not forces which could be overlooked. Nevertheless, Turkey's main antagonists were likely to be Russia in the Caucasus and Great Britain at Suez.

Defense of the Suez Canal was still the foundation of British strategic thinking in 1914, but it soon became clear that the Turks posed no great danger there. British policy toward Turkey could take into account other possibilities. The two new factors which would in the end turn the Near East upside down were oil and nationalism. At the end of 1914 an Indian-British army landed at Basra to safeguard oil supplies from Persia. So began the interplay of oil and politics in the destiny of this area, but it was not to obtrude until the Ottoman empire had ceased to exist. However, an approach which the British governor of Egypt made to Hussein of Mecca in October 1914 bore fruit very quickly. The weapon of Arab nationalism would be put to use.

The Arab revolt

The attraction of striking a blow against Germany's ally became all the greater as the fighting in Europe dragged on indecisively, but there was a limit to what could be offered to the Arabs. In return for his help, Hussein demanded independence for all the Arab lands south of a line running along the 37th degree latitude; this was about eighty miles north of a line from Aleppo to Mosul and included, in effect, the whole of the Ottoman empire outside the borders of Kurdistan. This was much more than the British could take at a gulp in 1914. They negotiated, consulting the French because of their special interest in Syria. In the end the two European powers reached

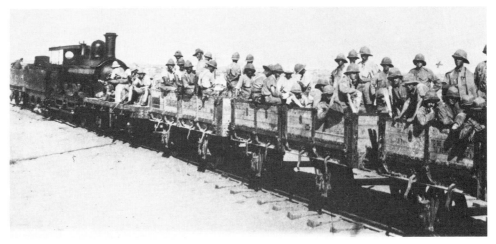

British soldiers on the move in Palestine, 1917. *(UPI)*

an agreement—which left many questions still unsettled—on spheres of influence in a partitioned Ottoman empire.

Such undertakings were put in doubt by the course of the Arab revolt, which began in June 1916 with an attack on the Turkish garrison of Medina. Soon the British felt they must take the Arabs more seriously and recognized Hussein as king of the Hejaz. British troops pressed forward in 1917 into Palestine, taking Jerusalem. In 1918 they would enter Damascus together with the Arabs. But before this two other events further complicated the situation. One was the American entry into the war; President Wilson favored "an absolute unmolested opportunity of development" for the non-Turks of the Ottoman empire. The other was the Bolsheviks' publication of their predecessors' secret diplomacy, which revealed Anglo-French proposals for the Near East; one of them was that Palestine should be administered internationally. A further irritant to the Arabs was added when British policy was declared to be in favor of the establishment of a national home in Palestine for the Jewish people. This was the Balfour Declaration of 1917, which was Zionism's first great success. It was not necessarily incompatible with what had been said to the Arabs, and President Wilson added to the good work of the declaration by introducing qualifications to protect those who were not Jews, but it is almost inconceivable that it could have been made to work. Further British and French expressions of good will toward Arab aspirations followed in 1918. The result was a thoroughly confused situation after the Turkish defeat.

The organization of the Arab lands

King Hussein was at this moment recognized as king of the Arab peoples by Great Britain, but this did little for him. Outside forces—primarily British and French but soon the League of Nations too—were to lay out the main lines of the map of the modern Arab world. It would not be completed until the 1930s, after a confused decade in which the British and French became embroiled with the Arabs, whom they had so recently conjured onto the stage of world politics, while the Arab leaders quarreled among themselves.

Islamic unity had once more disappeared. The British and French distrusted each other but could agree roughly on the basis that if the British had their way in Iraq, the French could have theirs in Syria. The League of Nations subsequently legitimized their "understanding" by awarding mandates to them for Arab lands. Palestine, Transjordan, and Iraq went to Great Britain and Syria to France. The French governed high-handedly from the start, having to install themselves by force after a national congress had asked for independence or a British or American mandate. Subsequently they had to face a full-scale insurrection. They were still holding their position by force in the 1930s, but there were by then signs that they would concede some power to the nationalists. Unfortunately the Syrian situation then showed the dangers of nationalism in the Near East; the Kurdish people of northern Syria revolted against the prospect of being submerged in an Arab state.

The Arabian peninsula was meanwhile wracked by a struggle between Hussein and yet another king with whom the British had negotiated a treaty. To make things more difficult still, religious conflict between Muslims was added to dynastic and tribal rivalry. Hussein lost power and in 1932 the new kingdom of Saudi Arabia emerged in the place of Hejaz. Sons of Hussein were by this time kings of Iraq and Transjordan. The latter had been recognized as independent by the British in 1928 but they retained some military and financial powers there. After heavy fighting in Iraq had shown the difficulties ahead, the British moved as fast as they dared toward ending that mandate as well, seeking only to secure their strategic interests. This was done by preserving a military and air force presence, and in 1932 Iraq entered the League of Nations as an independent and fully sovereign state.

Palestine was the most difficult problem. In 1921 there were anti-Jewish riots by Arabs alarmed over Jewish immigration and acquisition of Arab land, and from then on the unhappy country was never to be long at peace. More was at stake than merely religious or national feeling. Jewish immigration was bound to mean the eruption of a new Westernizing and modernizing force, its operation changing economic relationships and imposing new demands on a traditional society. The British mandatory power was caught between the outcry of Arabs if it did not restrict Jewish immigration and the outcry of Jews if it did. London now had to consider Arab governments which occupied lands economically and strategically important to British security. But world opinion was also becoming involved. The question became more inflamed than ever in the 1930s when the new regime in Germany began to persecute Jews and take away the legal and social gains they had been acquiring since the French Revolution. By 1937 there were pitched battles between Jews and Arabs in Palestine, and a British army was engaged in containing an Arab insurrection.

The collapse of paramount power in the Arab lands had at many times in the past initiated a period of disorder. What was unclear after the First World War was the likelihood of this being followed—as earlier periods of anarchy had eventually been—by the establishment of a new imperial hegemony. The British were not contenders for that role; they wanted only to secure their own fundamental interests in the area—the protection of the Suez Canal and the growing flow of oil from Iraq and Iran. Between 1918 and 1934 a great pipeline had been built from northern Iraq across Transjordan and Palestine to the port of Haifa, which gave yet another new twist to the future of these territories. Europe's consumption of oil was not yet so great that there was any general dependence on this supply, nor had the discoveries been made which would again change the political situation in the 1950s. But a new factor was making itself felt, and the British navy had converted to oil for its ships.

The British believed Suez was best secured by maintaining a garrison in Egypt, but this caused increasing trouble. The war had brought a great growth of national feeling. Armies of occupation are never popular and wartime had sent prices up. Some of the Egyptian nationalist leaders attempted in 1919 to put their case to the Paris peace conference but were prevented from doing so; this led to a rising against the British, which was quickly put down. But the British were on the retreat in Egypt and ended the protectorate there in 1922 in the hope of getting ahead of nationalist feeling. Yet the new kingdom of Egypt had an electoral system which returned nationalist majority after nationalist majority, thus making it impossible for an Egyptian government to come to terms acceptable in London. The result was a long constitutional crisis and intermittent disorder until the British finally agreed in 1936 to a limit on the number of years they would garrison the Canal zone. An end was also announced to the jurisdictional privileges of foreigners. The British concession was part of a general imperial withdrawal from the Near East after 1918, but it was also a reflection of weaknesses elsewhere as British foreign policy began to be preoccupied by other challenges.

Another new external influence on the Islamic lands was communism. During the whole of the period between the wars Russian radio broadcasts to the Arab countries supported the work of the first Arab Communists. But for all the worry this caused, communism showed no sign of being able to displace the strongest revolutionary influence in the area, Arab nationalism. Ominously the focus of pan-Arab feeling came to be Palestine. In 1938 a great congress of Arab states was held in Syria to support the Arab case there. But Arab resentment was also fed by the brutality of the French in Syria and the outcry of Egyptian nationalists against the British. In this resentment lay a force which might in the end override the divisions of the Arab kingdoms.

A new Turkey

Allied wartime agreements also complicated the history of the Ottoman homeland. The British, French, Greeks, and Italians had all agreed on shares of the empire; the only simplification brought by the war was the elimination of a Russian claim to Constantinople and the straits. Faced with Greek and Italian invasions, the sultan signed a ludicrously humiliating peace. Greece received large concessions, Armenia became an independent state, and what was left of Turkey was divided into British, French, and Italian spheres of influence. This was the most blatant imperialism, and as if to make the point European financial control was reestablished together with the humiliating capitulations.

The treaty provoked a Turkish resistance movement and thereafter the first revision of any part of the peace settlement. This was largely the work of one man, Mustafa Kemal, a former Young Turk and an outstanding soldier. He drove out in turn Italians, French, and Greeks and with Bolshevik help crushed the Armenians. The British decided to negotiate and a second peace treaty was concluded in 1923. It was a triumph of nationalism over the decisions made at Paris and the only part of the peace settlement negotiated between equals and not imposed on the defeated. (It was also the only treaty in which Russian negotiators took part and it lasted better than any other part of the settlement.) The capitulations and financial control disappeared. Turkey gave up her claims to the Arab lands and the islands of the Aegean—Rhodes and the Dodecanese—and Cyprus. A big exchange of Greek and Turkish populations followed. So the Ottoman empire outside Turkey was wound up after six centuries, and a new republic began its existence in 1923 as a national state under a dictator who rapidly proved to be one of the most effective of modernizers. Appropriately the caliphate followed the empire, being abolished in 1924.

Kemal, as he tended to call himself (the name meant "Perfection"), was something of an enlightened despot, something of a Peter the Great. His government secularized the law (on the model of the Napoleonic code), abandoned the Muslim calendar, and in 1928 amended the constitution to remove the assertion that Turkey was an Islamic state. Polygamy was forbidden. In 1935 the weekly day of rest, at first Friday, the Islamic holy day, became Sunday and a new word entered the language: *vikend*, the period from 1 P.M. Saturday to midnight Sunday. Schools ceased to give religious instruction. Kemal even outlawed the fez, which had originally come from Europe but was considered Muslim. This act and others like it symbolized a radical transformation, the replacement of traditional Islamic society by a European one. The alphabet was Latinized and this had great importance for education, henceforth obligatory at the primary level. A national past was rewritten in the books and in the schools; it was popularly said that Adam was a Turk.

Kemal—on whom the national assembly conferred the name of Ataturk, or "Father of the Turks"—is an immensely significant figure. He became what Mehemet Ali perhaps wanted to be, the first transformer of an Islamic state by modernization. He remains a strikingly interesting individual, who until his death in 1938 seemed determined not to let his revolution congeal. The result was the creation of a state in some ways among the most advanced in the world. A much greater break with the past was involved in

Turkey than in Europe in giving a new role to women, but in 1934 Turkish women received the vote and they were encouraged to enter the professions.

The revival of Persia

The most important Islamic country not under imperial control, either European or Ottoman, before 1914 was Persia. There had been a measure of interference in her affairs by the British and Russians after their agreement over spheres of influence in 1907, but Russian power had lapsed with the Bolshevik Revolution. British forces continued to operate on Persian territory to ensure that this remained true. Resentment against the British was excited (as it had been in Egypt) when a Persian delegation too was not allowed to state its case to the peace conference. There was a confused period in the early 1920s during which the British struggled to find a way of maintaining resistance to the Bolsheviks after withdrawing their troops. Given the over-taxing of British strength, there could be no question of retaining Persia by force.

A Persian officer, Reza Khan, solved London's dilemma, though hardly in the way anticipated. He carried out a coup d'état in 1921 and at once used the Bolsheviks' fear of the British to get a treaty from them which conceded to Persia all Russian rights and property in the country and promised the withdrawal of Russian forces. Reza Khan went on to defeat separatists who had British support. In 1925 the national assembly gave him dictatorial powers and a few months later proclaimed him Shah of Shahs. The new shah was to rule until 1941, almost an Iranian Kemal. The abolition of the veil and religious schools showed his secularist aims, but these were not pressed so far as in Turkey. In 1928 an important symbolic step was taken when the special privileges and protections for foreigners were abolished. Meanwhile the Persian government pressed forward with industrialization and the improvement of communications and cultivated a close association with Turkey. The shah also won the first notable success in the new diplomacy of oil. He canceled the concession held by the Anglo-Persian oil company in 1933; a new concession was eventually negotiated under the auspices of the League of Nations but on terms much more favorable to Persia. This was Reza Shah's greatest victory and the best evidence of his country's independence. A new era had opened in the Gulf, fittingly marked in 1935 by the change of name from Persia to Iran.

chapter 36

The Second World War

The Second World War demonstrated that the European Age was at last over. The war began in 1939 as a European struggle and then, like its predecessor, became a combination of wars. To a far greater degree than the First World War, it made unprecedented demands; this time they left nothing untouched, unmobilized, undisturbed. It was realistically termed "total" war.

THE POST-LIBERAL YEARS

By 1939 there were already many signs for those with eyes to see that a historical era was ending. Though 1919 had brought a few extensions of territorial control by colonial powers, the behavior of the greatest of them, Great Britain, showed that Western imperialism was far from the dynamic force it had once been. The vigor of Japan meant that Europe was no longer the only focus of the international power system; a prescient South African statesman had said in 1921 that "the scene has shifted away from Europe to the Far East and to the Pacific." His prediction now seems more than ever justified and it was made when the likelihood that China might again exercise her due weight was not yet clear. The economic foundations of Western preponderance had been shaken even more plainly than the political; the United States, greatest of industrial powers, still had 10 million unemployed in 1939. Though none of the European industrial states was quite so badly off by then, confidence in the economic system had evaporated. Industry might be picking up—largely because rearmament was stimulating it—but attempts to find recovery through international cooperation had come to an end in 1933 with the breakdown of a world economic conference. After that each nation had gone its own way; even the United Kingdom at last abandoned free trade. Laissez faire was dead, and governments were deliberately interfering with the economy as they had not done since the heyday of mercantilism in the seventeenth century.

It is more difficult to delineate intellectual and spiritual trends. Though many people still clung to old shibboleths and still attended religious services, they were a minority even in Roman Catholic countries. The masses lived in a post-Christian world in which the physical removal of the institutions and symbols of religion would have made little difference to their daily lives. So did intellectuals; they perhaps faced an even greater problem because many of the liberal ideas which had helped undermine Christianity were now undermined in their turn. In the 1920s and 1930s the great certainties — objective moral criteria, rationality, the authority of parents, and an explicable mechanical universe — all seemed to be going under at the same time as free trade.

This was clearest in the arts. For three or four hundred years, since the age of humanism, it had been presumed that the arts expressed aspirations, insights, and pleasures accessible to ordinary people even if these were raised to an exceptional degree of fineness in execution. It was possible for the whole of that time to retain the notion of the cultivated individual who, given time and study, could discriminate with taste among the arts of his day because they were expressions of a shared culture with shared standards. This idea was first weakened when the nineteenth century, in the wake of the Romantic movement, came to idealize the genius and formulated the concept of the avant-garde. By the first decade of the twentieth century it was very difficult for trained eyes and ears to recognize art at all in many contemporary works. The symbol of this was the dislocation of the image in painting. The flight from the representational kept a tenuous link with tradition as late as cubism, but by then it had long ceased to be apparent to the average "cultivated man" — if he still existed. Artists retired into a less and less accessible chaos of private visions, a trend which reached its climax in the world of dada and surrealism in the 1920s. This decade was something of a culmination of disintegration; in surrealism even the notion of the objective disappeared, let alone its representation. As one surrealist put it in the 1924 *Manifeste du Surréalisme,* the movement meant "thought dictated in the absence of all control exerted by reason, and outside all aesthetic or moral preoccupations." Through chance, symbolism, shock, suggestion, and violence the surrealists sought to go beyond consciousness itself; they used any materials that came to hand, not simply paint or words but random objects and carefully contrived paradoxical combinations: a fur tea cup was a famous one. Whatever their aesthetic value, such phenomena were symptomatic of the decay of the liberal culture produced by the high civilization of the European Age.

It is interesting that disintegratory movements were often prompted by a sense that the traditional culture was too limited because it excluded the resources of emotion and experience in the unconscious. The man who gave the twentieth century a language in which to explore this area of the mind and a belief that the secrets of life lay there was Sigmund Freud, the founder of psychoanalysis, who deserves a place in the history of nonscientific culture beside Newton and Darwin. Like them, he changed the way educated people thought of themselves. His influence quickly spread into literature, personal relations, education, politics. His importance beyond science — where his influence was more profound — was in providing a new mythology. It was to prove highly corrosive.

The message men took from Freud suggested that the unconscious was the true source of most significant behavior, that moral values and attitudes were projections of the influences which had molded this unconscious, that therefore the idea of responsibility was at best a myth and probably a dangerous one, and that rationality was perhaps an illusion. It did not matter much that Freud's own assertions would have been nonsense had some of these propositions been true or that such a view left out the subtlety and science of his work. This bundle of ideas called into question the very foundation of liberal civilization—the idea of the rational, responsible, consciously motivated individual, and this was its general importance.

Freud was not the only intellectual force contributing to the loss of certainty and the sense that men had little firm ground beneath their feet, but he was one of the most talked about in the interwar period. From grappling with the insights he brought, or with the chaos of the arts, or the incomprehensibility of a world of science which had abandoned Newton, men plunged worriedly into the search for new mythologies and standards to give them bearings. Politically, this led to fascism, Marxism, and the most irrational of the old certainties, extreme nationalism. People no longer felt inspired by tolerance, democracy, and the individual freedoms, though continental Europe showed more signs of their weakening than Great Britain or the United States. Such influences made it all the more difficult to deal with the deepening uncertainty and foreboding over international relations in the 1930s.

The German problem

Germany had not been destroyed in 1918; it was therefore logical that one day she would again be a great power. Germans had soon begun to demand a revision of the Versailles Treaty, and in the 1920s this demand had been tackled hopefully. The real burden of reparations was then gradually whittled away. The Locarno Pact of 1925 was seen as a great landmark because by it Germany gave her consent to the territorial settlement in the west. But Locarno left open the possibility of revision in the east, and behind this loomed a larger question: how could a country potentially so powerful be related to its neighbors in a balanced, peaceful way, given the Germans' particular historical and cultural experience?

Most people assumed in the 1920s that the new republican and democratic government in Germany would gently and benevolently reconstruct the nation's society and culture. Their illusions did not last long. Although the constitution of the Weimar Republic (named after the city where the constituent assembly met) was very liberal, too many Germans were out of sympathy with it from the start. That Weimar had solved the German problem was revealed as an illusion when economic depression shattered the narrow base on which the German republic rested and set loose the destructive nationalist and social forces it had masked.

When this happened in the early 1930s, the containment of Germany again became an international problem, and for a number of reasons the prospects were very unpromising. Some of the worst effects of the worldwide depression were in the relatively weak agricultural economies of the new eastern European countries which France looked to for allies. Furthermore, the existence of the new states made it doubly difficult to involve Russia in any scheme to contain Germany. Geography as well as ideology presented barriers. No Russian force could reach Germany without crossing one or more of the east European states whose short lives were haunted by the fear of Russia and communism: Rumania, Poland, and the Baltic states, after all, actually incorporated former tsarist lands. Finally, it appeared unlikely that the United States would again enter a European conflict to redress the balance of power.

Isolationist America

The trend of American policy ever since Wilson's failure to get his countrymen to join the League of Nations had been back toward a traditional, self-absorbed isolation. Americans who had gone to Europe as soldiers did not want to repeat the experience. Justified apparently by boom in the 1920s, isolation was paradoxically confirmed by slump in the 1930s. When Americans did not confusedly blame Europe for their troubles—the European debts from the war years had great psychological impact because they were believed to be tied up with the international financial problems (as indeed they were, though not quite as Americans thought)—they felt distrustful of further entanglement. Anyway, the depression gave them enough to think about.

The election of a Democratic president in 1932, however, opened an era of important change which would in the end make Americans feel they had world obligations as never before. It was to be presided over by Democrats for five successive presidential terms, the first four won by the same man, Franklin Roosevelt. To stand four successive times as presidential candidate was almost unprecedented (Eugene Debs had done so); to win, astonishing. To do so with (on each occasion) an absolute majority of the popular vote was something like a revolution. No Democratic candidate had had one since 1865, and no other would until 1964. An important political transformation followed the 1932 election, which was basically a contest of hope versus despair. Roosevelt offered confidence and the promise of action to shake off the blight of economic depression. Later a Democratic hegemony was built on a coalition of neglected constituencies—the South, the poor, the farmer, the Negro—which attracted further support as it seemed to deliver results.

The Roosevelt administration's New Deal launched a huge program of unemployment relief with insurance, poured millions into public works, introduced new regulation of finance, and began a great experiment in public ownership with a hydroelectric scheme in the Tennessee valley. Though it was still not grappling satisfactorily with the economy by 1939, the New Deal had changed the emphasis of the working of American capitalism and its relationship with government. It gave capitalism a new lease on life, but it also brought the greatest extension of the power of federal authorities over American society and the states that had ever occurred in peacetime and the trend has proved irreversible. Thus American society reflected the same pressures toward collectivism which affected other countries in the twentieth century. In this sense too the Roosevelt era was historically decisive. It changed the course of American constitutional and political history as nothing had done since the Civil War and incidentally offered a democratic alternative to fascism and communism by providing a liberal version of large-scale national economic planning.

THE EUROPEAN IMBALANCE OF POWER

With Russia and the United States unavailable, only the western European great powers remained to contain a revived Germany. Great Britain and France were badly placed to do this and in any case had been much at odds with one another since 1918. They remembered their difficulties in the last war even with Russia as an ally, and they both were militarily weaker than they had been in 1914. France, conscious of her inferiority in manpower, had invested in a program of strategic defense through fortifications which were powerful and looked impressive but effectively deprived her of the power to act offensively. The British navy was no longer the strongest in the world nor, as in 1914, able to concentrate its resources in European waters. Great Britain had long pursued the reduction of military expenditures while world-wide commitments placed a growing strain on her forces. Economic depression reinforced this tendency. Furthermore, many Englishmen believed that Germany had just grievances. They were disposed to make concessions in the name of German nationalism and self-determination, even by handing back German colonies.

The joker in the European pack was Italy. For a time hopes were entertained of her as a force against Germany, but these disappeared under Mussolini. In 1935 Italy made a belated attempt to participate in the scramble for Africa by invading Ethiopia. It was clearly a breach of the covenant of the League of Nations for one of its members to attack another. France and Great Britain, as great powers, Mediterranean powers, and African colonial powers, were bound to take the lead against Italy at the league. But they did so feebly and half-heartedly because they did not want to alienate a possible ally against Germany. The result was the worst possible: the league failed to check aggression, Ethiopia lost her independence, and Italy was alienated after all.

In retrospect the failure to discipline Italy seems a fatal error, but it is really impossible to say at what stage the situation which developed from these facts became unmanageable. Certainly the emergence of a much more radical and ferociously opportunistic regime in Germany was the major turning point. But the depression preceded this and made it possible. Economic collapse had another important effect. It made people think in terms of class conflict, which led many to interpret international relations as if fascism versus communism, right versus left, or democracy versus dictatorship were all the same thing. This was even easier once Mussolini, angered by British and French policy, made an alliance with Germany and began to talk of an anti-communist crusade. All ideological interpretations of international affairs in the 1930s tended to obscure the central nature of the German problem—and therefore made it harder to tackle.

Russian policy

Russian propaganda also fed this confusion. During the 1930s Russia's internal situation was precarious. The industrialization program was imposing grave strains and sacrifices. These were navigated by a savage intensification of dictatorship which turned terrorism against the cadres of the regime itself from 1934 onward. In five years hundreds of thousands of Russians were imprisoned or exiled, often to forced labor. The world looked on amazed as defendants who had been high in the regime groveled with grotesque "confessions" before Soviet courts. Nine out of ten generals in the army went and an estimated 50 percent of the officer corps. A new Communist elite replaced the old one in these years; by 1939 over half the delegates to the party congress of 1934 had been arrested. It was very difficult for outsiders to be sure what was happening, but it was clear to them that Russia was neither a civilized state nor necessarily a very strong potential ally.

The purges directly affected the international situation because of the propaganda which accompanied them. Much of this no doubt arose from the siege mentality inside Russia. Far from being relaxed, the habit of thinking of the world in terms of Us versus Them, which had been born in Marxist dogma and the interventions, was encouraged still more in the 1930s, and the Comintern stressed the doctrine of international class struggle. The reciprocal effect was predictable. The fears of conservatives in other countries were intensified, and it became easy for them to think of any concession to left-wing or even mildly progressive forces as a victory for the Bolsheviks. As attitudes thus hardened on the right, Communists were given new evidence for the thesis of inevitable class conflict and revolution.

Yet there was still not one successful left-wing revolution. The revolutionary danger had subsided rapidly after the immediate postwar years. Labour governments had peacefully and undramatically ruled England for part of the 1920s. One ended in financial collapse in 1931, to be followed by Conservative or Conservative-dominated governments which had overwhelming electoral support. They proceeded to govern with remarkable fidelity to the tradition of piecemeal social and administrative reform which had marked Great Britain's advance into the "welfare state." This development—toward the use of public funds for services and cash benefits to the poor and otherwise needy—had been taken even further in the Scandinavian countries, often lauded for their combination of political democracy and practical socialism and as a contrast to communism. Even in France, where there was a large and active Communist party, its aims were clearly not acceptable to the bulk of the electorate even after the depression. The German Communist party won large numbers of votes before 1933 but was never able to displace the Social Democrats in control of the working-class movement. In less advanced countries communism's success was even smaller. In Spain it competed with both socialists and anarchists, rarely a force in other countries. Spanish conservatives certainly feared it as they feared also the tendency of the republic (established in 1931) to slide toward disorder, but Spanish communism was hardly the real danger facing them.

Nazi Germany

In 1933 there came to power in Germany a new ruler, Adolf Hitler. He still remains a figure whose motives and significance are hard to assess, but it is difficult to deny him political genius. He poured out his obsessive nationalism and anti-Semitism not only in hypnotically effective speeches but in a long, shapeless, semi-autobiographical book which few people read. Though Hitler's messages were simple, his appeal was complex. He preached that Germany's troubles had identifiable sources. The Treaty of Versailles was one. The international capitalists were another. The antinational activities of German Marxists and Jews were others. He also said that the righting of Germany's political wrongs must be combined with the renovation of her society and culture and that this was a matter of purifying the biological stock of the German people by excising its non-Aryan components.

In the early 1920s such ideas had limited appeal, and Hitler was only an unsuccessful nationalist agitator who had failed in an attempt to overthrow the government of Bavaria. Yet in 1931 his National Socialist German Workers' party (Nazi for short) won 107 seats in the German parliament—more than the Communists (who had 77). The Nazis were already the beneficiaries of economic collapse, and it was to grow worse. There are several reasons why they did well but one of the most important was that the Communists spent as much energy fighting the Socialists as their other opponents. This had fatally handicapped the left in Germany all through the 1920s. Another reason was that under the Weimar Republic anti-Semitic feeling (which had deep roots in Germany and Austria) had grown because Jews played a much more prominent part in the state than they had in imperial times. Anti-Semitism, like nationalism, cut across class lines, but naturally antagonized some classes while (it was hoped) attracting others.

By 1930 the Nazis showed they were a power in the land. They attracted more support and won backers among anticommunist, nationalist, and conservative politicians who saw Hitler as a party leader like any other who might now be valuable in their own game. The maneuvers were complicated, but in 1932 the Nazis became the biggest party in the German parliament though without a majority. In January 1933 the president of the republic legally and constitutionally appointed Hitler chancellor as the result of a decision by right-wing politicians. There followed new elections in which the regime's monopoly of the radio and use of intimidation still did not secure an absolute majority for the Nazis, but they had the support of some right-wing members of parliament, who joined them in voting special enabling powers to the government. The most important permitted governing by emergency decree: it thus meant the end of parliament itself. Armed with these powers, Hitler proceeded to carry out a revolutionary destruction of democratic institutions. The conservatives lost too; they soon found that Nazi interference with the independence of traditional authorities went very far. By 1939 there was virtually no sector of German society not controlled or intimidated by the Nazis.

Nazism under Weimar

In the last years of the Weimar Republic, the Nazi movement made much use of provocative displays and street-brawling, both to intimidate opposition and to build up an impression of simple, no-nonsense, commonsense response to the revolutionary threat presented by Marxist parties. Their uniforms and insignia gave them a special glamour, but their deliberate violence was the real distinction between them and other parties. It helped to spread the idea — since the police were rarely used against them — that the democratic republic was incapable of keeping order and hence that it was in decay. In 1932 a reporter for the Manchester Guardian, *a great English liberal newspaper, sent this report from Brunswick, subsequently confirmed by others.*

The Nazi Storm Troops (called S.A. men) have living quarters which they use as barracks. (One of these quarters is in the richest part of the city.) They also have lorries on which they race along at great speed, their flags (red with a white disc, and on the disc the swastika, their anti-Semitic symbol) fluttering over the bonnet. The sides of the lorries can be clapped down so that the inmates can jump out at a moment's notice.

If there is any real or alleged trouble, the lorry dashes to the spot, the storm troops leap down, blows from cudgels, knives, preservers, knuckle dusters are dealt out right and left, heads are cut open, arms raised in self defence are broken or bruised and crouching backs or shoulders are beaten black and blue. Sometimes shots are fired and knives are drawn. In a few moments all is over — the Nazis scramble back into their lorry and are off. The police arrive to find a man lying dead or several lying unconscious with concussion of the brain, or staggering away clasping an abdominal knife wound or holding a broken head from which the blood drips down on the cobbles. The injured are sometimes Reichsbanner men, sometimes there is a Communist too, and sometimes chance passers by — very rarely are they Nazis.

From David Ayerst, ed., *The Guardian Omnibus, 1821–1971* (London: Wm. Collins Sons & Co. Ltd., 1973), p. 487.

The Nazi system, like that of Stalin's Russia, rested in a very large measure on terror. This was used mercilessly against enemies of the regime. It was also unleashed against the Jews, and an astonished Europe witnessed revivals in one of her most advanced societies of the pogroms of the Middle Ages or tsarist Russia. This was indeed so astounding that many people outside Germany could not believe it was happening.

Confusion over the nature of the regime made it even more difficult to deal with it. Some saw Hitler simply as a nationalist leader bent upon regeneration of his country and the assertion of its rightful claims. Others saw him as a crusader against bolshevism or at least thought he might be a useful anti-Bolshevik barrier, which encouraged the left to see him as a tool of capitalism. But no simple formula will contain Hitler or his aims, and there is still great disagreement about what these were. Probably a reasonable approximation of the truth is simply to recognize that he embodied the resentments and exasperations of German society in their most negative and destructive forms and exploited and used them to a monstrous degree. When his personality was given scope by economic disaster and a favorable arrangement of international forces, he released these negative qualities at the expense of all Europeans, his own countrymen included.

Charisma. Hitler, the greatest spellbinder of mass politics, reviews the Hitler Youth at the Nazi party rally at Nuremberg, 1935. Even in these well-disciplined ranks, one lad cannot resist turning his head to look over his shoulder at the Führer.
(Photoworld)

The coming of war

The path which led Germany to war again in 1939 is complicated, and there is still much argument about when, if ever, there was a chance of avoiding the final clash. Clearly one important moment was when Mussolini, formerly wary of German ambitions in central Europe, was reconciled to Hitler after he had been alienated by British and French policy over Ethiopia. Then, in 1936, a mutiny by Spanish generals against the left-wing republic launched a civil war. Hitler and Mussolini both sent contingents to Spain to support the man who emerged as the rebel leader, General Franco. This had two effects: it accelerated the rapprochement of Italy and Germany until it became alliance and it gave an ideological color to Europe's divisions. Hitler, Mussolini, and Franco were now identified as "Fascist." All left-wing parties in Spain tried, without great success, to cooperate to defend the republic and Russian foreign policy soon began to coordinate support for Spain within western countries. Local Communists abandoned their attacks on other left-wing parties and encouraged popular fronts against the fascist threat, which they saw as international. Spain came to be seen as a conflict between right and left in its purest form; this was a distortion, but it had much effect in accustoming people to think of Europe as divided into two camps.

The British and French were by this time well aware of the difficulties of dealing with Germany. Hitler had already announced in 1935 that German rearmament (forbidden at Versailles) had begun. Until their own rearmament was completed, the western powers would remain very weak. Consequently they made no attempt to resist when German troops reentered the demilitarized zone on the eastern bank of the Rhine, where their presence had been forbidden by the Versailles treaty. After the Spanish Civil War had thrown opinion in Great Britain and France into even greater disarray, Hitler seized Austria on a specious pretext in March 1938. The provision of Versailles prohibiting the fusion of Germany and Austria seemed hard to

THE GERMAN PROBLEM
1935–1939

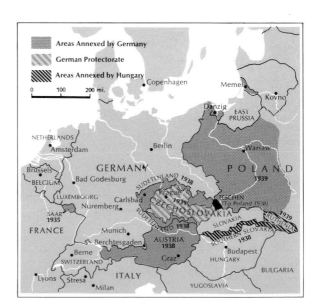

uphold. The Austrian republic had long had internal troubles and its pan-Germans wanted absorption in Germany. To the French and British publics the Anschluss (union with Germany) appeared as a matter of legitimately aggrieved nationalism. In the autumn came the next German aggression, the seizure of part of Czechoslovakia, again justified by the claims of self-determination. The areas involved were so important that their loss crippled the prospect of future Czechoslovak self-defense, but they were areas with many German-speaking inhabitants. Memel, a German town over which Lithuania had sovereign rights, would follow on the same grounds the next year. Hitler was gradually fulfilling the old dream ended when Prussia beat Austria in 1866—the vision of a Great Germany defined as the lands containing all those of German blood.

The dismemberment of Czechoslovakia was something of a turning point. It was achieved by a series of conferences, in which Great Britain and Germany took the main parts, at Munich in September 1938. It was the last great initiative of British foreign policy to try to satisfy Hitler. The British prime minister, Neville Chamberlain, was still too unsure of rearmament to resist but hoped also that the transference of the last substantial group of Germans from alien rule to that of their homeland might deprive Hitler of the motive for further revision of Versailles, which was now somewhat tattered in any case.

He was wrong. Hitler went on to inaugurate a program of expansion into Slav lands. The first step was the absorption of what was left of Czechoslovakia in March 1939. This brought forward the question of the Polish settlement of 1919. Hitler resented the "Polish Corridor" (which gave Poland access to the sea) because it separated East Prussia from Germany and also contained Danzig, an old German city internationalized in 1919. At this point the British government, though hesitatingly, changed tack and offered guarantees against aggression to Poland and other east European countries. It also began a wary negotiation with Russia.

Russian policy remains hard to interpret. It seems that Stalin kept the Spanish Civil War going with support to the republic as long as it seemed likely to tie up German attention but then looked for other ways of buying time against the attack from the west he always feared. He probably believed that Great Britain and France would see with relief the trouble they had so long faced turning eastward. No doubt they would have. But under any circumstances there was little possibility of working with the British or French to oppose Hitler because no Russian army could reach Germany except through Poland—and this the Poles would never permit. Accordingly, as a Russian diplomat remarked to a French colleague on hearing of the Munich decisions, there was now nothing for it but a fourth partition of Poland. This was arranged in the summer of 1939. After all the propaganda directed against Bolshevik-Slav barbarism by the one and against Fascist-capitalist exploitation by the other, Germany and Russia made an agreement in August which provided for the division of Poland between them. Armed with this, Hitler went on to attack Poland and thus began the Second World War on September 1, 1939.

Two days later the British and French honored their guarantee to Poland and declared war on Germany. It was obvious that they could not help Poland effectively. (That unhappy nation disappeared once more, divided by Russian and German forces about a month after the outbreak of war.) But failure to intervene would have meant acquiescing in the German domination of Europe because no other nation would have thought British and French support worth having. So, uneasily, the two major liberal states of western Europe found themselves at war with a totalitarian regime. Neither their peoples nor governments had much enthusiasm for this role, but exasperation with Hitler's long series of aggressions and broken promises made it hard to see what sort of peace could be made which would reassure them enough for them to come to terms. The basic cause of the war was, as in 1914, German nationalism. But whereas then Germany had gone to war because she felt threatened, now Great Britain and France were responding to the danger presented by her expansion. They felt threatened this time.

EXPANSION OF THE WAR

To the surprise of many observers the first six months of the war were almost uneventful once the short Polish campaign was over. It was quickly plain that mechanized forces and air power were to play a much more important part than between 1914 and 1918. The memory of the earlier slaughter on the Somme and at Verdun was too vivid for the British and French to plan anything but an economic offensive; the blockade weapon, they hoped, would be effective against Germany. Hitler was at first unwilling to disturb them because he was anxious to make peace. This deadlock was broken only when the British wished to intensify the blockade in Scandinavian waters, a departure which coincided remarkably with a German offensive to secure ore supplies in that area.

Hitler attacked Norway and Denmark on April 9, 1940, and quickly conquered them. A month later there began a German invasion first of the Low Countries and then of France. A powerful armored attack through the Ardennes divided the Allied armies and opened the way to the capture of Paris. On June 22 France signed an armistice with Germany. By the end of the month the whole European coast from the Pyrenees to the North Cape was in German hands, Great Britain had no ally left on the Continent, and Italy had joined in on the German side. The new French government broke off relations with Great Britain after the British seized or destroyed French warships they felt might fall into German hands. The French Third Republic effectively came to an end with the installation of Marshal Pétain, a hero of the First World War, as head of state.

This rapid succession of victories brought a huge change in the nature of the war. It was not exactly true that Great Britain was left alone. The dominions had all entered the war on her side, and a number of governments in exile from the overrun Continent had small forces of their own. Norwegians, Danes, Dutchmen, Belgians, and Poles were to fight gallantly, often with decisive effect, in the years ahead. Yet all this did not add up to anything

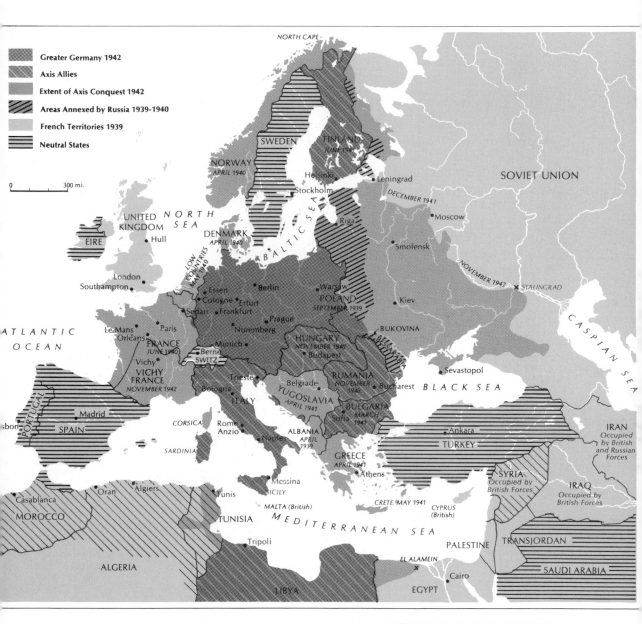

WORLD WAR II IN EUROPE
Besides showing the conquests of Germany and her allies at their
greatest extent, this map also gives dates when these conquests
took place or when Germany's allies entered the war.

like the power lost in France. Some of the largest exiled contingents were
French, but they represented a division within France and not her legal
government (now sited at Vichy, Paris being occupied by the Germans). A
general who had left France before the armistice and was condemned to

death *in absentia* was their leader, Charles de Gaulle. He saw himself as the custodian of his country's interests and honor and soon began to show an independence which was in the end to make him the greatest servant of France in this century.

The British recognized de Gaulle as "leader of the Free French." His position was important because of uncertainties about what might happen to parts of the French empire where he hoped to find sympathizers who wished to continue the struggle under the Cross of Lorraine, the banner of Joan of Arc, which he had chosen as his own. This was one way in which the war was now extended. Another resulted from Italy's entry into the war; her African possessions and the Mediterranean sea lanes now became operational areas. Finally, German control of Atlantic and Scandinavian ports meant that what was later called the Battle of the Atlantic—the struggle to sever British sea communications by submarine, surface, and air attack—was bound to become much fiercer.

Immediately the British Isles faced direct attack. The hour had already found the man to lead the nation against such a challenge. Winston Churchill, after a long and checkered political career, had become prime minister following the Norwegian collapse because no other man commanded certain support in all parties in the House of Commons. To the coalition government which he immediately formed, he gave a vigorous leadership hitherto lacking. More important, he called forth in his people, whom he addressed frequently by radio, qualities they had forgotten they possessed. It was soon clear that only defeat after direct assault would get the British out of the war.

In August and September the fighter aircraft of the Royal Air Force won a great battle over southern England. As Churchill put it in one of his most quoted speeches, "Never in the field of human conflict was so much owed by so many to so few." Englishmen for a moment felt like the Greeks hearing the news of Marathon. This victory made a German seaborne invasion impossible (though a successful one was in any case unlikely). It also showed that Great Britain could not be defeated by air bombardment alone. The islands had a bleak outlook ahead, but the direction of the war had been changed; a variety of influences now turned German planning eastward.

By the winter of 1940 the Soviet government had made several further gains in the east, apparently with an eye to securing buffers against a future German attack. A war against Finland had secured important strategic areas. Russia had also swallowed the Baltic states and taken back Bessarabia, which had gone to Rumania in 1918, together with the northern Bukovina. The last acquisition went beyond tsarist boundaries.

In December 1940 the Germans began specific planning for an invasion of Russia. The decision arose in part because of some disagreements about the future direction of Russian expansion: Germany sought to keep Russia away from the Balkans and the straits of Constantinople. The attack was also aimed at demonstrating, by a quick victory in the east, that further British war making was pointless. But there was a deep personal element in the decision too. Hitler had always sincerely and fanatically detested bolshevism and maintained that the Slavs, a racially inferior group, should provide Ger-

The underground stations of London found a new use as deep and bombproof shelters during the night bombing of 1940–1941. This is the Elephant and Castle station, one morning at about ten to four; at six or seven, the trains would begin to run again, and those sleeping here would roll up their bedding and go off to their day's work.

(*Imperial War Museum, London*)

mans with living space and raw materials. This was a last, perverted vision of the old struggle of Teuton to impose western civilization on the Slav east, and many Germans responded to such a theme. It was to justify more appalling atrocities than any earlier crusading myth.

In a brief spring campaign the Germans overran Yugoslavia and Greece, where Italian forces had been unhappily engaged since October 1940. Crete was also taken in a spectacular airborne assault. One more brief British expedition to the mainland of Europe had been eliminated. Now all was ready for Barbarossa, as the great onslaught on Russia was called, after a crusading emperor of the Middle Ages. It was launched on June 22, 1941, and had huge early successes. The Germans took vast numbers of prisoners and drove the Russian armies back hundreds of miles. Their advance guard came within a narrow margin of capturing Moscow. But that margin was not quite eliminated, and by Christmas the first successful Russian counterattacks had announced that in fact the German army was pinned down. German strategy had lost the initiative. If the British and Russians could hold on and agree, their access to American production would inexorably increase their strength. This did not mean that they could defeat Germany, only that they might bring her to negotiate terms.

America's road to war

President Roosevelt believed from the outset that Great Britain had to be supported up to the limits permitted by his own public and the law of neutrality. In fact he went well beyond both at times, but American opinion was developing fast. A crucial step was the passage in March 1941 of the Lend-Lease Act, which provided American production and services to the Allies without payment. Soon afterward the United States extended further eastward into the Atlantic its operations to defend its shipping against hostile submarines, which could only be German or Italian. By the summer of 1941 Hitler regarded the United States as an undeclared enemy. After the invasion of Russia a meeting between Churchill and Roosevelt resulted in a statement of shared principles—the Atlantic Charter—in which one nation at war and another formally at peace spoke of the needs of a postwar world "after the final destruction of the Nazi tyranny." This was a long way from isolationism.

Extensive Anglo-American cooperation was the background to Hitler's second fateful decision of 1941, his declaration of war on the United States on December 11. This followed a Japanese attack on British and American territories on December 7. Hitler had earlier promised the Japanese he would do this. The war thus became global. Yet Japan's aggression might have left two separate conflicts with only Great Britain engaged in both. Hitler's action threw away the chance that American power could be kept out of Europe and deployed only in the Pacific. Few single acts have so marked the end of an epoch, for this announced the eclipse of European affairs. Europe's future would now be settled not by her own efforts but by the two great powers on her flanks, the United States and Soviet Russia.

The Japanese decision was also a rash one. Japan's ties with Germany and Italy, though they had some propaganda value for both sides, did not amount to much in practice. What mattered in the timing of Japanese policy, which had long pointed toward conflict with the United States, was the resolution of debates in Tokyo about the danger of a challenge to the Americans which must involve war. The crux of the matter was that Japan's needs for a successful conclusion of the war in China included oil, which she could only obtain with the tacit consent of the United States that she might destroy China. This no American government could have given. Instead Washington had imposed an embargo on all trade with Japan in October 1941.

For Japanese military planners the question had by then become purely a strategic and technical one; since they would have to take the needed resources of Southeast Asia by force, all that had to be settled was the nature of the war against the United States and its timing. Such a decision was fundamentally irrational because the chances of ultimate and lasting success were very small. But arguments of national honor had won at this point, and the final calculations about the best place and moment of attack were carefully made. It was decided to strike as hard a blow as possible against American sea power at the outset in order to gain the maximum freedom of movement in the Pacific and South China Sea. The operations of December 7 thus centered around an air attack on the United States fleet at Pearl Harbor, which was one of the most brilliantly conceived and executed assaults in the history of warfare. By mischance it fell just short of complete success. Though it gave the Japanese for months the strategical freedom they sought, it did not destroy American naval air power. This failure was enough; the Japanese faced a prolonged war they were bound to lose in the end. Pearl Harbor united Americans as little else could have done. Isolationism was virtually dead on December 8 and Roosevelt had a nation behind him as Wilson never had.

A world war

When a few Japanese bombs fell on the American mainland,* it was indeed obvious that this was much more truly a world war than the first had been. German operations in the Balkans had by the time of Pearl Harbor left Europe with only four neutral countries—Spain, Portugal, Sweden, and Switzerland. Fighting in North Africa raged back and forth between British, German, and Italian armies in Libya and Egypt. It was extended to Syria by the arrival there of a German mission and to Iraq when a British force removed a nationalist government supported by German aircraft. In East Africa, Ethiopia was liberated and the Italian colonial empire destroyed. With the opening of the Far Eastern war the Japanese wrought equal destruction on the colonial empires there. Within a few months they held Indonesia,

---

*Off the West Coast a Japanese submarine released a number of balloons which drifted over the mainland and then (by a timing device) released bombs.

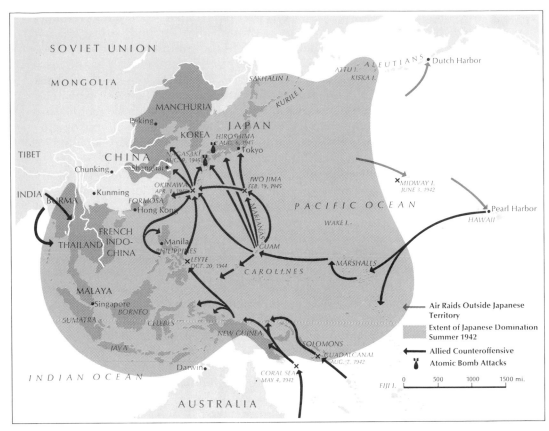

WORLD WAR II IN THE PACIFIC

Indochina, Malaya, and the Philippines. They pressed through Burma toward the Indian border and were soon bombing the Australian port of Darwin from New Guinea. Their naval and air forces were engaged in an operational arc stretching up from the South Pacific to the Aleutians in the north and around to the Bay of Bengal in the west. Meanwhile the naval war with Germany was fought by submarines, planes, and surface ships all over the Mediterranean and Atlantic, Arctic and Indian oceans.

Only a tiny minority of countries were left out of this struggle. Its demands were colossal and carried much further the mobilization of whole societies than had the First World War. Here the role of the United States was decisive. Its huge manufacturing power made the material preponderance of the United Nations (as the coalition fighting the "Axis" powers was called from the beginning of 1942) incontestable. The way ahead was nonetheless a hard one, and the first part of 1942 was very bleak for the Allies.

The turning point came in four great and very different battles. In June a Japanese fleet attacking Midway was broken in a battle fought largely by aircraft. Japan's losses in carriers and crews were such that she never regained the strategical initiative, and the long American counterattack in the Pacific now began to unroll with a landing on the important island of Guadalcanal. At the beginning of November, coincidental with Anglo-American landings in French North Africa, the British army in Egypt decisively defeated its German and Italian opponents at El Alamein and began a march west which ended with the eviction of the enemy from this continent the following May. By the end of 1942 the Russians had bottled up a German army (rashly exposed by Hitler) at Stalingrad on the Volga. The remnants surrendered in February in the most demoralizing defeat yet suffered by German arms. Yet it was only part of three months of winter advance which were the turning point of the war on the eastern front.

The fourth great Allied victory has no specific date but was as important as any of the others. This was the Battle of the Atlantic. Its peak came in the early months of 1942. In March nearly 850,000 tons of shipping were lost and six U-boats were sunk; six months later the figures were 560,000 tons and eleven U-boats. The tide had turned by then though there was still hard fighting ahead. At the end of the year nearly 8 million tons of shipping had

The long way back. An American tank moves in on the survivors of the huge bombardment which preceded landing on Kwajalein Atoll. This kind of operation was repeated many times, often at heavy cost in lives to the attackers, as the United States counteroffensive of 1943–1945 unrolled in the Pacific.
(*Official U.S. Army Photograph*)

been lost for eighty-seven U-boats sunk. In 1943 the totals were 3.25 million tons and 237 U-boats. This was the most crucial battle of all for the Allies because their ability to draw on American production to defeat Germany depended on it.

Command of the sea also made reentry into Europe possible. Roosevelt had agreed to give priority to the defeat of Germany, but the invasion of France could not be managed before 1944. The delay angered the Russians, who wanted a western front to take the strain off their armies. When it came, the Anglo-American invasion of northern France in June 1944 was not only the greatest but the most successful seaborne expedition in history thanks to overwhelming Allied air superiority. More than 4,000 ships and 10,000 air-craft took part. Mussolini had been overthrown by the Italians in 1943 and Italy had already been invaded from the south. Now Germany was fighting on three fronts.

Soon after the landings in Normandy the Russians entered Poland. They advanced faster than their allies, but it still took them until the following April to reach Berlin. In the west Allied forces broke out of Italy into central Europe and from the Low Countries into northern Germany early in 1945. The Rhine was crossed on March 7. Almost incidentally terrible destruction has been inflicted on the German cities by a great air offensive, which until the last few months of the war had no decisive strategic effect. When the man who had ignited this global conflagration killed himself in a bunker beneath the ruins of Berlin on April 30, historic Europe was literally as well as figuratively shattered.

The war in the Far East took a little longer, but by the beginning of August 1945 the Japanese government knew it must be defeated. Many of its former conquests had been retrieved. American forces had fought a series of bloody battles for islands from which their bombers devastated Japanese cit-ies. Japan's sea power, on which her communications and safety from inva-sion depended, was in ruins. Then the United States dropped two nuclear bombs of a destructive power hitherto unapproached with terrible effect on Hiroshima and Nagasaki. Between the explosions Russia declared war on Japan. On September 2 the Japanese government abandoned its plans of a suicidal last-ditch stand and signed an instrument of surrender. The Second World War had come to an end. Argument continues about whether the use of nuclear weapons to achieve this was justified.

THE BALANCE SHEET

In the immediate aftermath it was difficult to measure the colossal changes brought about in six years. Only one clear and unambiguous good emerged at once: the overthrow of the Nazi regime. As the Allied armies ad-vanced into Europe, they uncovered the deepest evils of a system of terror and torture. It became apparent that Churchill had spoken no more than the bare truth when he told his countrymen that "if we fail, then the whole world, including the United States, including all that we have known and cared for, will sink into the abyss of a new Dark Age made more sinister, and

As administration broke down in the last stages of the Nazi defeat, disease was
added to the horrors of the concentration camps' cruelties. Here at Belsen the
liberators bulldozed mass graves, and whenever possible the SS guards were
made to remove the bodies to them for burial.

(Imperial War Museum, London)

perhaps more protracted, by the lights of perverted science." The reality of
this danger could be seen in the Belsen and Buchenwald concentration
camps and the huge extermination factories, such as Treblinka. Distinctions
could hardly be meaningful between degrees of atrocity inflicted on political
prisoners, slave laborers from other countries, and some prisoners of war.
Millions of people, mostly Slavs, died in one way or another and almost incidentally as a result of casual massacre, ill-treatment, starvation, overwork,
and disease. But the world's imagination was most struck by the systematic
attempt to wipe out European Jewry, Hitler's "Final Solution," which was
carried far enough to change the demographic map: the Polish Jews were
almost obliterated and Dutch Jews too suffered heavily in proportion to their
numbers. Overall, though complete figures may never be available, probably
between 5 and 6 million Jews were killed in the gas chambers and cremato-

ria of the extermination camps, by murder on the spot in east and southeast Europe, or by overwork and hunger.

Few people and no state had engaged in the war because they saw it as a crusade against wickedness, though no doubt many were later heartened by the sense that the conflict had a moral dimension. Nevertheless, the war in Europe was a moral struggle in a way no other had ever been. It is important to recognize this because much has been heard of the regrettable consequences of Allied victory. These consequences remain but do not diminish what was achieved, the destruction of the worst challenge to liberal civilization which has ever arisen.

Some far-sighted men could see a deep irony in this challenge. Germany had been one of the most progressive countries in Europe, the embodiment of many of the most central features of her civilization. That Germans should fall prey to collective derangement on this scale suggested that something had been wrong at the root of that civilization itself. The crimes of Nazism were not carried out in a fit of barbaric intoxication with conquest but in a systematic, scientific, controlled, bureaucratic way about which little was irrational except the appalling end it sought.

In this respect the Asian war was importantly different. Japanese imperialism replaced the old Western imperialisms for a time, but sometimes the subject peoples did not have much to regret in the change. Propaganda during the war attempted to give currency to the notion of a "Fascist" Japan, but this was a distortion of so traditional a society's character. No such appalling consequences as faced European nations at the hands of the Nazis would have followed from a Japanese victory.

The second immediately obvious result of the war was its unparalleled destructiveness. It was most visible in the devastated cities of Germany and Japan, where aerial bombing, one of the major innovations of the Second World War, did even more damage than had been feared after the preview given of it in the Spanish Civil War. Yet, although often invaluable in combination with other forms of fighting, air power was in this role disappointing. The British and Americans had built up a huge strategic air offensive against Germany from 1941 onward until their combined efforts could provide a target with continuous day and night bombing, but it achieved very little until the last few months of the war. Nor was the destruction of Japan's cities as important strategically as the elimination of her sea power.

Bombing had not only shattered cities, it had also grievously wounded most of the communications system of central Europe. Millions of refugees were wandering about and there was grave danger of famine and epidemic because of the difficulty of supplying food. The tremendous problems of 1918 were on Europe again but worse, and this time they confronted nations demoralized by defeat and occupation; no European country other than the neutrals and Great Britain had escaped these experiences. Fighting had raged all over the Continent and there were abundant arms in private hands, a potential revolutionary threat. These conditions could also be found in Asia, but there the physical destruction was less intense and prospects of recovery better.

Two Europes

In Europe the revolutionary political impact of the war was more immediately discernible in 1945 than in 1918. The power structure which had been a reality until 1914 and had an illusory prolongation of life between the two world wars was doomed with the events of 1941. Two great peripheral powers now dominated Europe politically and their armies were established in the heart of it. It was already appearing that this meant important new differences would again separate the Continent's eastern and western halves. Once again a division of the continent along a zone running from the Baltic to the Adriatic was given new reality. In all the revived states to the east of it Communist governments or governments in which Communists shared power were set up. All of these had been overrun by the Russian army, which proved itself a far better instrument for the extension of international communism than revolution had ever been.

The line between two Europes ran across Germany, which had effectively ceased to exist. The Russians, Americans, British, and French had partitioned the country into zones of occupation. The other political units of Western Europe had reconstituted themselves after occupation and defeat. Italy (which had changed sides after Mussolini's overthrow) had a much strengthened and enlarged Communist party, which was still committed to the revolutionary defeat of capitalism. So did France.

Only Great Britain retained the stature of 1939 in the world's eyes; indeed it was enhanced. She remained the recognized equal of Russia and the United States, a joint author of victory. Yet her moment was past; there was an element of illusion in this last, finest moment of grandeur. By mobilizing her resources and society to a degree unseen outside Stalin's Russia, she had been able to retain her standing. But she had only been saved strategically by the German attack on Russia and economically by the American adoption of Lend-Lease. Symbolically Great Britain's last major military effort in Europe, the invasion of 1944, had been commanded by an American general; though British forces on the Continent for a few months afterward matched the Americans, they were outnumbered by the end of the war. In the Far East the British had reconquered Burma, but the defeat of Japan was the achievement of American naval and air power. For all his close relationship and sympathy with Churchill, Roosevelt was by 1945 negotiating over his head with Stalin, proposing *inter alia* the dismantling of the British empire. Great Britain had not escaped the shattering impact of the war on Europe's political structure though she had escaped some of its most terrible blows.

Thus was registered the passing of European supremacy. Even at its periphery this was evident. British forces secured Dutch and French territories in time to hand them back to their former owners and prevent the seizure of power by anticolonial regimes. But fighting almost immediately began and it was clear that the imperial powers had difficulties ahead. Therefore 1945 is not a good point at which to pause; reality was still to a degree masked by appearance. Some people could still not discern that at least in political terms the European Age was over.

chapter 37

Shaping a New World

POSTWAR POWER STRUCTURES

During the war many decisions had been made about the postwar world. One of the most important was that there should be an organization with the aim of maintaining peace among nations. The fact that the great powers probably saw such a body in different ways—the Americans as a beginning of regulating international life by law and the Russians as a means of keeping the Grand Alliance in being—did not prevent their pressing forward to help establish the United Nations Organization at San Francisco in 1945.

The United Nations

Naturally much thought had been given to the lessons of the League of Nations, which had not come up to expectations. One of its great defects, at least, was overcome in 1945: the United States and Russia were members of the new organization from the start. The basic structure of the United Nations reproduced that of the league in consisting of two essential organs, a small council and a large assembly. All member states had permanent representatives who sat in the General Assembly. The Security Council at first had eleven members, of whom five were permanent; these were the representatives of the United States, Russia, Great Britain, France (at the insistence of Winston Churchill), and China.

The Security Council was given greater power than the old league council. This was largely the doing of the Russians, who saw a strong likelihood that they would often be outvoted in the General Assembly, where at first fifty-one nations were represented, because the United States could rely not only on the votes of its allies but also on those of its Latin American satellites. Naturally not all the smaller powers liked this strengthening of the body which would have the last word and in which the great powers would carry the day. But despite long wrangles, the great powers got the structure they wanted, as indeed they had to if the organization was to work at all. They agreed less easily with one another about the other main issue which caused grave constitutional dispute, the giving of a veto power to the permanent members of the Security Council. But this too was necessary if the great powers were to accept the organization. Ultimately the veto was restricted somewhat in that one of the permanent members could prevent investigation and discussion of matters which affected it especially unless the debate was likely to lead to action inimical to its interests. The Security

Council thus possessed in theory very great powers, but of course their use was bound to reflect political reality. The Charter of the United Nations envisaged that a call by the Security Council to members to take arms against an aggressor would be mandatory, but it is revealing that no such call has ever been made.

In the end the greatest importance of the United Nations was to prove to lie not in its power to act but in the forum it provided for discussion. For the first time a world public—linked as never before by radio and film and soon by television—would expect sovereign states to justify their actions before the General Assembly. This was something quite new. Sometimes feelings of sterility would develop as increasingly bitter and unyielding views were set out in debates which persuaded no one to change his mind, but an educational force was at work even in these. It was especially important that New York soon became the permanent seat of the General Assembly because this drew American notice to it and helped offset the historic pull of isolation.

The United Nations General Assembly held its first meeting in London in 1946. At once there were bitter debates. Attention was drawn to Russia's failure to withdraw her soldiers from the Iranian territory of Azerbaijan, occupied during the war. The Russians immediately responded with an attack on Great Britain for keeping forces in Greece, where they were supporting a conservative government against a Greek Communist rebellion. Within a few days the first veto was cast, by the Russians. There were to be many more. The instrument which the Americans and British had regarded and continued to use as an extraordinary measure for the protection of special interests became a normal part of Soviet diplomatic technique. The United Nations was already becoming the arena for diplomatic battles between Russia and a still inchoate Western bloc, which her policies would do much to solidify.

The superpowers

It has become fashionable to trace the origins of conflict between the United States and Russia back a very long way, but the British impression in the later years of the war was that American policy made too many concessions to Russia and was overly friendly. Of course a fundamental ideological division existed; if the Russians had not always had a deep preconception about the roots of behavior in capitalist societies, they would certainly have behaved differently after 1945 toward their wartime ally. It is also true that some Americans consistently distrusted the Soviet regime and saw in it a revolutionary threat to their own society, but this is not the same thing as saying that they had significant impact on American policy. When the war ended in 1945, American distrust of Russian intentions was much less than it would later become, and of the two states the more suspicious and wary was Russia.

At that moment these two powers seemed the arbiters of the world. For all the legal fiction of the Security Council's composition, Great Britain was gravely overstrained, France barely risen from the living death of occupation and plagued by internal divisions and a large Communist party which threatened her stability. China had never yet been a great power in the modern era. The Americans and Russians therefore enjoyed immense superiority over any other possible rival.

In the closing stages of the war Russian armies had fought their way before the British and Americans into Prague and Berlin, thanks in part to decisions by the Western commander, General Eisenhower. They now dominated a huge European zone which included Germany's second greatest industrial region. Moscow also had an ally beyond it in Yugoslavia, the only Communist state to emerge from the war without the help of the Red Army. The old traditional barriers to Russian power, provided by the Habsburg empire and a strong Prussia, had gone. No corresponding obstacle could be seen in an exhausted Great Britain and slowly reviving France. Russian armies also stood on the borders of Turkey and Greece, where a Communist rising was under way, and occupied northern Iran. At the end of the war in the Far East they had occupied the naval base of Port Arthur and much of Sinkiang, Mongolia, and northern Korea and had liberated the rest of Manchuria. The only territory the Russians actually took from the Japanese, however, was the southern half of Sakhalin Island and the Kuriles. All the rest of their gains were effectively at the expense of China.

The United States' superiority rested much less on the occupation of territory though it too had a garrison in the heart of Europe and, just as important, naval and air bases around much of the Eurasian land mass. The country had been immune to damage by the enemy during the war and was intact; its industrial power was the greatest in the world. Finally, the United States had just demonstrated at Hiroshima and Nagasaki the power of the new weapon it alone possessed, the atomic bomb.

Appearances may have been deceptive on both sides. For all the power possessed by the United States, there was little will to use it, and the first concern of American military policy after victory was to organize as rapid a demobilization as possible. The cutting off of Lend-Lease arrangements severely weakened American allies, who were faced with grave enough problems of recovery without having to shoulder those of providing a new security system to replace American strength. Nor could the use of the atomic bomb be envisaged except in the last resort: it was too powerful.

About Russia's position it is much harder to judge, but she had obviously suffered appallingly from the war, possibly even more than Germany. No one has ever been able to calculate exactly the Russian war losses, but something like 20 million people may have died. Stalin was probably less aware of his strength than his weakness in 1945. Russian governmental methods relieved him of any need, such as faced Western countries, to demobilize the huge land forces which gave him supremacy on the spot in Europe. But Russia had neither an atomic bomb nor a significant strategic bomber force. Stalin's decision to develop nuclear weapons was bound to put a further grave strain on the Russian economy. The years immediately after the war may have been as grim for Russians as those of the industrialization drive in the 1930s. Nevertheless, in 1949 an atomic explosion took place in Russia, and the following year it was officially announced that she had an atomic weapon.

By then much had changed. Piecemeal, relations between the United States and Russia had deteriorated very seriously. The issues which caused this arose first in Europe, the area most in need of imaginative and coordinated reconstruction in 1945.

Europe in ruins

The destruction has never been accurately measured in the places where it was worst, Germany and Russia. A rough indicator is that about 7.5 million dwellings were destroyed in those countries. Leaving out the Russians, about 15 million Europeans were dead; if the Russians are included, the total might rise as high as 40 million. Those who survived lived amid shattered factories and communications. There was nothing with which to pay for the imports needed to get them running again. Currencies were in ruins; Allied occupation forces found cigarettes and bully beef were better

Purification 1944, after the German defeat. The Frenchwoman with a shaved head, accused of collaborating with the occupying Germans, was accordingly punished in this way by her fellow-townsfolk. There was much such victimization, some justified, some not.
(Robert Capa/Magnum)

than money. Civilized society had collapsed not only under the horrors of Nazi warfare. Occupation had transformed lying, swindling, cheating, and stealing into acts of virtue; they were not only necessary to survival, they could be glorified as acts of "resistance." Resistance itself had bred new divisions. As countries were liberated by the advancing Allied armies, the firing squads got to work in their wake to wipe out old scores. It is said that in France more perished in the "purification" of liberation than in the Terror of 1793.

Above all, as in 1918, the economic structure of Europe was fragmented by politics and the pattern the war had taken. Europe had long been an economic unity even if not a perfect one. Germany was its flywheel. But even if the communications and productive capacity had been there, the Allies were at first bent on holding down German industrial production to prevent her recovery, and the Russians had from the start been carrying off capital equipment to repair their own ravaged lands—as well they might. The Germans had destroyed 39,000 miles of Russian railway track in their retreat, and Russia may have lost a quarter of her gross capital equipment.

COLD WAR ORIGINS

Another division between Eastern and Western Europe appeared before the end of the war. The British in particular had been alarmed by the handling of the question of Poland's future in 1944 because what followed Russian occupation, the imposition of Communist party dominance, seemed to show that Moscow would tolerate only subservient governments in Eastern Europe. This was hardly what American policy considered freedom for nations to choose their own governments, but the United States did not begin to be seriously concerned or to doubt the possibility of coming to reasonable agreement with the Russians until the war was over. Broadly speaking, Roosevelt was convinced that good relations were possible if the Russians were approached on the common ground which he saw in recognizing their fears about a German revival and providing for them, and in an anticolonialism which was bound to be at the expense of their and his allies. Neither he nor the American public understood the historic tendencies of Russian policy in southeastern Europe, and they disapproved strongly of the British intervention in Greece against the Communist guerrilla army which sought to overthrow the monarchy after the German withdrawal. (Stalin on the other hand did not object; he agreed with Churchill that Great Britain should have a virtually free hand in Greece in return for the same for Russia in Rumania.)

President Truman (who as vice-president succeeded to the presidency when Roosevelt died in April 1945) and his advisers came to change their views about the possibilities of cooperation with Russia largely as a result of Stalin's approach to the future of Germany. The beginnings may be sought in the actual behavior of Russians on the spot. Efforts to ensure Russia's security against a future German recovery led to the increasing separation of her zone of occupation from those of the three other occupying powers. No doubt this was intended to provide a solid and reliable (i.e., Communist) core for a united Germany, such as had been foreseen at the last conference of Allied leaders at Potsdam in 1945. Yet the eventual result was a solution to the German problem which no one had envisaged during the war, the partition of the country into two states. The first sign of this was that the Western zones of occupation were integrated for economic reasons. Meanwhile Russian occupation policy aroused distrust because of its methods of ensuring the control of the Communist parties in its zone. The pattern seemed to be the same as in other East European countries. Only in Bulgaria and Yugoslavia were there real Communist majorities; in other countries the Communists shared power in coalition governments. But it increasingly appeared to outsiders that all these governments could in fact do was to behave as little more than Russian puppets. In the negotiations of peace treaties with Italy, Hungary, and Bulgaria, for example, East European states voted steadily for the Russian proposals. Something like a bloc was already appearing in Eastern Europe in 1946.

It is rash to speculate on Russian motives at that moment. While Moscow was acting with apparent anxiety to establish eastern Germany on its side of the European dividing line, Russian policy in China was still officially supporting the Kuomintang. In Iran, on the other hand, Anglo-American concern was aroused by Russia's reluctance to withdraw her forces as had been agreed. When they finally departed, they left behind a satellite Communist republic in Azerbaijan (which the Iranians later obliterated). By 1947 the Americans were giving Iran military aid. In the Security Council the Russians more and more employed the veto to frustrate their former allies' proposals, and it was clear that the Communist parties in France and Italy especially were manipulated to embarrass their governments. Yet Stalin's calculations remain in doubt, though it is likely that he was relying upon an economic collapse in the West.

Yet there was still much good will for Russia in the West. When Winston Churchill, no longer prime minister, drew attention in a speech in the United States in 1946 to the increasing division of Europe by an "iron curtain," he by no means spoke for all his countrymen. The Labour government elected in 1945 was at first hopeful that "left could speak to left," though it soon came to be more skeptical. British and American policy began to draw together during 1946 as it became clear that the British intervention in Greece had in fact made possible free elections and American officials gained more experience of the tendency of Russian ambitions. President Truman did not have the disadvantage of prejudices in favor of Russia which his predecessor had shown during the wartime conferences. The British had also embarked upon a deliberate policy of leaving India, and that counted much with American official opinion.

The Truman Doctrine and the Marshall Plan

In February 1947 Truman made a momentous decision. It arose as a result of a communication by the British government which contained the admission, long resisted, that Great Britain could no longer act as a great military power. Her economy, in spite of Lend-Lease, had been gravely damaged by the huge wartime efforts. There was urgent need for investment at home. Moreover the first stages of decolonization were expensive. In 1947 the British realized that they could maintain their balance of payments only if they withdrew their forces from Greece, and Washington was told so. President Truman at once decided that the United States must fill the gap by giving financial aid to Greece and Turkey to enable them to survive the pressure they were under from Russia. He deliberately drew attention to the implication: much more than propping up two countries was involved. Although only Turkey and Greece were to receive aid, he pointedly offered "the free peoples" of the world American leadership to resist, by efforts which would have American support, "attempted subjugation by armed minorities or by outside pressures." The Truman Doctrine, as these principles came to be called, was a reversal of the independent course which the United States had seemed to wish to pursue in 1945. It resulted from observation of Stalin's methods over the intervening eighteen months. The adoption of a policy of "containment" of Russian power, as it was called, was possibly the most important change in American foreign affairs since Washington's Farewell Address. It held out unrealistic possibilities of deploying American power beyond its effective limits, but this was not seen at the time.

In June 1947 the Truman Doctrine was completed by the offering of American economic aid to European nations which would come together to plan their recovery. The Marshall Plan, named after the American secretary of state who announced it in a public speech, embodied the notion of a nonmilitary, unaggressive form of containment. It surprised everyone, but the British foreign secretary, Ernest Bevin, was the first foreign statesman to grasp its implications and, with the French, to press for the acceptance of this offer by Western Europe. It was made of course to all Europe, but it was unlikely that the Russians would participate. Indeed, they did not, nor did they allow their satellites to do so. More, they bitterly attacked the plan.

When, with obvious reluctance, the coalition government of Czechoslovakia also declined to join in the plan, it was apparent that that country, the only one in Eastern Europe by then without a fully Communist government and not regarded as a Russian satellite, had to toe the line too. Any residual hope of Czechoslovakia's independence disappeared when a Communist coup in February 1948 ended the coalition government.

Another sign of Russian intransigence was the reestablishment in September 1947 of the old prewar propaganda device, the Comintern, now renamed the Cominform. It at once began the denunciation of what its secretary-general termed the United States' "frankly predatory and expansionist course . . . to establish the world supremacy of American imperialism." Finally, in response to the appearance in the West of the Organization for European Economic Cooperation to handle the Marshall Plan, the Russians at the beginning of 1949 organized their own half of Europe with the Council for Mutual Economic Assistance, Comecon for short, which was for a long time largely window-dressing.

The cold war had now begun. In a succession of crises, which would continue well into the 1960s, two groups of states, one led by the United States and one by Soviet Russia, strove to achieve their own security by all means short of war between the principal contenders. Much of the conflict was put in ideological terms, and the cold war therefore appeared in some Western countries as a sort of civil war or as a moral debate about values such as freedom, social justice, and individualism. Some of it was fought in marginal theaters by propaganda and subversion or by guerrilla movements sponsored by the two superpowers, but it always stopped short of the point at which Russia and America would have to fight with the nuclear weapons whose increasing power made the notion of a successful outcome more and more unrealistic.

The cold war also meant economic competition, and in this an important part was played by offers of aid to allies and uncommitted nations. Much opportunism was mixed up with doctrinaire rigidity. In retrospect, for all the violence of the language that attended it, the cold war now begins to look somewhat like the labyrinthine struggles of religion in sixteenth- and seventeenth-century Europe, when the simplicities of ideology could certainly provoke violent emotion but could never wholly contain the complexities and crosscurrents of the day, above all not those introduced by national interest. As had also happened in the religious conflicts of the past, there was soon every sign that, although the cold war might die down and disaster be avoided, the rhetoric and mythology of the struggle would go rolling on long after they had ceased to have much relation to reality.

THE CRUMBLING OF EMPIRES

One of the most important factors which cut across the cold war and continuously influenced its outcome was the existence of numerous states uncommitted to one side or the other. This was a growing number, not least because many new nations were appearing as a result of another shift in international relations and one affecting as many human beings as the cold war. This was decolonization. The United Nations General Assembly was just as important as a platform for anticolonialism as for cold war propaganda.

The nationalist movements which had existed before 1939 in the colonial territories of Asia were guaranteed success, even if not immediately, by the war. It had exploded the cardcastle of European imperialism in Southeast Asia, and the repercussions were great even in areas (such as the Indian subcontinent) where the Japanese did not displace the imperial power. The surrender of 80,000 Commonwealth troops at Singapore in 1942 was the signal that the British empire in Asia was doomed, a new Yorktown. No efforts could retrieve such an appalling loss of face. It did not help matters much that the Japanese behaved badly to their new conquests: when the imperial powers parachuted arms to their former subjects to resist the Japanese, it strengthened the likelihood that the weapons would be used at a later time against the reinstated colonial rulers. Furthermore, if much of life in the villages of Asia went on undisturbed by comparison with the upheavals brought by bombing, fighting, labor conscription, starvation, and disease in Europe, there were notable side effects which offered potential for political change when the Japanese were defeated. Imperial possessions in the Far East would be all but swept away within a few years of 1945.

The last age of British India

In the case of India enough had occurred before 1939 to make it plain that the issue there was no longer the maintenance of imperial rule but the timetable for its replacement and the form of government which would follow it. Most Englishmen who favored Indian independence hoped to keep the country linked to the British Commonwealth of Nations, as it had been increasingly common to term the empire since the Imperial Conference of 1926. That conference had officially defined dominion status as independent association in the Commonwealth, with complete control of internal and external affairs. This set a conceivable goal for India, but it was not one which British governments could see as an immediate aim before 1940. Yet some progress was made before then, and this moderated anti-Western feeling in India.

Indian politicians had been deeply disappointed by their treatment after the First World War. They had for the most part rallied loyally to the crown; India had made big contributions of men and money to the imperial war effort, and Gandhi had been one of those who had worked for it in the belief that this would bring India her due reward. In 1917 the British government had indeed announced that it favored a policy of steady progress toward responsible government for India within the empire, but this was short of the dominion status some Indians were beginning to ask for. Reforms announced in 1918 had seemed meager to most nationalists but satisfied some moderates. Unfortunately even this limited success was soon dissipated.

One of the factors influencing the situation was the continuing isolation of the British community in India. Convinced that Indian nationalism was a matter of a few ambitious intellectuals, the community pressed merely for strong measures against conspiracy, a course which recommended itself all the more to administrators now confronted with the consequences of the Bolshevik Revolution (though the Indian Communist party was not founded until 1923). The result was legislation, against the wishes of all the Indian members of the legislative council, which suspended normal legal safeguards in order to deal with conspiracy. This provoked Gandhi to begin a campaign of strikes and pacifist civil disobedience. In spite of his efforts to avoid violence there were riots. At Amritsar in 1919 some Englishmen were killed and others attacked, and a foolish general decided to disperse the crowd by force. When the firing stopped, nearly 400 Indians had been killed and over 1,000 wounded. This was a bad blow to British prestige, made worse by the very vocal approval of British residents in India and some members of Parliament.

A period of boycott and civil disturbance followed; during it Gandhi's

Gandhi visits the imperial capital, London, 1931. His costume, deliberately chosen to emphasize to his countrymen the importance of using only Indian cloth, always attracted much good-humored but bewildered attention. (*Radio Times Hulton Picture Library*)

program was adopted by the Indian National Congress, which became a mass party. Although he himself emphasized that his campaign was nonviolent, there was much disorder and Gandhi was arrested and imprisoned for the first time in 1922. The British soon released him because of their fear that he might die in prison, a fear so great that it became an important weapon in his hands. In 1927 the British government began to move slowly forward again by sending a commission to India to look into the working of the last series of constitutional changes, but this caused more trouble because no Indians were included in it.

By this time much of the enthusiasm which had sustained unity among the nationalists had evaporated, and there was danger of a rift between those who stuck to the demand for complete independence and those who wanted to work for dominion status. This was just bridged by Gandhi's efforts and prestige. A more serious division was the now deepened one between Hindu and Muslim. Every year there was communal rioting and bloodshed. By 1930 the president of the Muslim League was proposing that the future constitutional development of India include the establishment of a separate Muslim state in the northwest. That year was a violent one. Civil disobedience was resumed after a constitutional conference foundered on the question of minority representation. But the wheels of the India Office were beginning to turn as they absorbed the lessons of the discussions and the 1927 commission.

In 1935 Parliament passed the Government of India Act, which took still further the establishment of representative and responsible government, leaving in the viceroy's sole control only such matters as defense and foreign affairs. The act once more affirmed the principle of separate community representation. Almost immediately its working provoked further hostility between Hindu and Muslim. The Congress party was by now to all intents and purposes a Hindu organization though it refused to concede that the Muslim League should therefore be the sole representative of Muslim Indians. But the Congress party had its own internal problems, divided as it was between those who wished to press forward to independence and those—some of them beginning to be alarmed by Japanese aggressiveness—who were willing to work the new institutions in cooperation with the imperial government.

The Japanese attack at the end of 1941 forced the hand of the British government, but too late. London offered the nationalists autonomy after the war and a right of secession from the Commonwealth, but they now demanded immediate independence. Their leaders were arrested and Great Britain continued to rule India, but the sands were running out if the British wanted to go peacefully. One new factor was pressure from the United States. President Roosevelt discussed confidentially with Stalin the need to prepare for Indian independence (as well as independence for other parts of Asia and trusteeship for French Indochina). As in the First World War, the involvement of the United States implied revolutionary change. But in the end a more important factor was the election victory in 1945 of the British Labour party, which had long had the independence of India and Burma as part of its program.

On March 14, 1946, while India was torn with Hindu-Muslim rioting and her politicians were squabbling over the shape of the future, London offered full independence. Nearly a year later, to force a decision, it put a pistol to the heads of Indian leaders by announcing that it would hand over power not later than June 1948. The British actually and legally did so on August 15, 1947, leaving as their heirs two new dominions, India and Pakistan. The cutting of the tangle of communal rivalries was achieved by the partition of the subcontinent. Its cost was enormous. The psychic wound to many nationalists was symbolized by a Hindu fanatic's murder of Gandhi for his part in it. Huge massacres occurred in areas where there were minorities. Something like 2 million people died; about the same number fled to where their coreligionists were in control. The only unity ever enjoyed by the whole subcontinent was ended. Pakistan was Muslim and itself divided into two slabs of land, at the east and west extremities of northern India. The princely states also survived, to make their own terms with the new regimes.

Both India and Pakistan soon became republics. Both also faced grave problems. In neither country could independence of itself do anything about natural disaster or structural backwardness. There was a basic threat in a continuing rise in population. Though Indian industrialization had made important advances, especially during the Second World War, this hardly offset the problem of providing subsistence for a fast-growing population, and Pakistan had little industry. In 1951 there was famine again in India, and in 1953 in Pakistan. Nor, in spite of the outlawing of "untouchability" in the last days of the Raj, had India been able to tackle successfully the enormous problems of modernizing Hindu society. She remained in 1947 a country where marriage outside one's caste was still virtually unthinkable and where auspicious days could determine the calendar of a businessman or a public servant. On the other hand, the Hindu-Muslim problem was solved for the time being by the bloodletting and transfer of populations. Furthermore, the new states inherited a civil service most of whose members were already native-born and an important infrastructure of institutions and services.

The completion of the Chinese revolution

China had been engaged in fighting off a different sort of imperialism and the Second World War made possible the completion of her long revolution. The political phase of this transformation began in 1941 when the war with Japan merged into a world conflict. The change gave China both powerful allies and a new standing. Significantly, the last vestiges of the unequal treaties with Great Britain, France, and the United States were then swept away. This was more important than the military help the Allies could give; for a long time they were too busy extricating themselves from the disasters of early 1942 to do much for China. Instead a Chinese army came to help defend Burma against the Japanese. Still hemmed into the west, though supported by American aircraft, the Chinese had to hold out as best they could. Nonetheless, a decisive internal change had begun.

China had at first responded to the Japanese invasion with a sense of national unity long desired but never hitherto forthcoming except perhaps in the May 4th movement. There had been friction between the Communists and the Nationalists, sometimes breaking out into open conflict, but on the whole this unity lasted until 1941. Then the awareness that the United States was now Japan's major enemy and would eventually destroy her subtly transformed the attitude of the Nationalist government. Since ultimate victory was certain, it came to feel that there was no point in using up men and resources fighting the Japanese when they might be husbanded for the struggle against the Communists after the peace. Soon the Kuomintang was fighting the Communists again.

Two Chinas rapidly appeared. Nationalist China was marked more and more by the lethargy, self-seeking, and corruption which had from the early 1930s tainted the Kuomintang because of the nature of the support on which it drew. The regime was repressive and stifled criticism. It alienated the intellectuals. Its soldiers, sometimes badly officered and undisciplined, terrorized the peasants as much as did the Japanese. Meanwhile in large areas under their control (often behind the Japanese lines) the Communists made a deliberate attempt to gain the support of as wide a spectrum of interests as possible by moderate but unambiguous reform and disciplined behavior. Outright attacks on landlords were usually avoided, but peasant good will was cultivated by enforcing lower rents and abolishing usury. At the same time Mao published a series of theoretical writings designed to prepare the new Communist cadres for the task that lay ahead. There was a need for political education as the party and the army grew steadily in numbers; by the time Japan surrendered in 1945 there were about a million Chinese Communist soldiers.

The suddenness of the Japanese collapse was the second decisive factor in the last stage of the Chinese revolution. Huge areas of China were suddenly free of the invader and waiting to be reincorporated in the Chinese state. But the Communists were already effectively in control of many of them, and Nationalist forces could not possibly reach many others before the Communists established themselves there. The Americans did what they could by sending soldiers to hold the ports until the Nationalists could take them over. In some places the Japanese were told to remain in control until the Nationalist government could reestablish its authority. But when the final military stage of the revolution opened, the Communists held much more territory than ever before and held it in the main with the support of the population, who found that Communist rule was by no means as bad as they had heard.

The approach to Communist victory in China. Mao on the march with his men in Shensi province in 1947. *(Eastfoto)*

Thus the Japanese, by launching their destructive attack on the Kuomintang regime, had unwittingly brought about the triumph of the Chinese revolution they had long striven to avoid. A Nationalist government undistracted by foreign invasion and not suffering the crippling damage it inflicted might have been able to master Chinese communism in the short run. In 1937 the Kuomintang could still draw on good will resting on the belief that it was the authentic carrier of the revolution. The war destroyed such a possibility. It enabled China to resume her long march toward world power from which she had been deflected first by Europeans and then by fellow Asians. The long frustration of Chinese nationalism was over, and the beneficiary was communism.

The displacement of the Kuomintang took three years. Together with territory the Communists acquired large stocks of arms in many places when the Japanese surrendered, in spite of attempts by the Americans (who sometimes kept armed Japanese forces in being until the Nationalists could arrive). The Russians cooperated by allowing the Communists access to Manchuria and the Japanese arms there. It was against this background that Mao made deliberately moderate policy pronouncements and continued to push forward with land reform, which gave him a great advantage in the rekindled civil war. His victory in 1949 would be essentially a triumph of the countryside over a city-based regime.

The United States became increasingly disillusioned by the revealed inadequacy and corruption of the Chiang Kai-shek regime and in 1947 withdrew its forces. At the same time Washington abandoned the efforts it had hitherto made to mediate between the two Chinas. In the following year, with most of northern China lost to the Communists, the Americans began to cut down their financial and military aid to the Kuomintang. From then on the Nationalist government's course was militarily and politically clearly downhill. More and more of its servants sought to make terms while they might with the Communists as the conviction spread that a new era was dawning. By the beginning of December 1949 no important Nationalist military force remained intact on the mainland, and Chiang withdrew to Formosa (Taiwan). The Americans cut off their aid while this withdrawal was under way and publicly blamed the inadequacies of the Nationalist regime for the debacle. Meanwhile the largest Communist state in the world had come into existence on October 1, 1949, when the People's Republic of China was officially inaugurated at Peking. Once again the Mandate of Heaven had passed.

Indonesia and Indochina

In Southeast Asia and Indonesia the Second World War was equally decisive in bringing colonial rule to an end though the pace was faster and the going rougher in Dutch and French colonies than British. The grant of genuine representative institutions by the Dutch in Indonesia had not checked the growth of a nationalist party before 1939, and there was also a flourishing Communist movement by then. Some nationalist leaders, among them Achmed Sukarno, collaborated with the Japanese when they occupied the islands in 1942. These nationalists were in a favorable position to act when Japan surrendered, and they proclaimed an independent Indonesian republic before the Dutch could return. Fighting and negotiation followed for nearly two years until agreement was reached for an Indonesian republic still linked to Holland under the Dutch crown; this arrangement did not work. Fighting began again, the Dutch pressing forward vainly with their "police operations" in one of the first campaigns by a former colonial power which attracted the full blast of Communist and anticolonial stricture at the United Nations. Both India and Australia, which had concluded that she should conciliate the independent Indonesia which must eventually emerge, took the matter to the Security Council. Finally the Dutch gave in. The story begun by the East India Company of Amsterdam three and a half centuries before thus came to an end in 1949, and the United States of Indonesia emerged, a mixture of more than 110 million people of scores of races and religions scattered over hundreds of islands. A vague union under the Dutch crown subsisted but was dissolved five years later.

The French in Indochina for a time seemed to be holding on better than the Dutch. The area's wartime history was somewhat different from that of the British Malay States or Dutch Indonesia; although the Japanese had exercised complete military control of the area since 1941 French sovereignty was not formally displaced until early 1945. The Japanese then amalgamated Annam, Cochin-China, and Tonkin to form the new state of Vietnam under the emperor of Annam. As soon as the Japanese surrendered, the chief of the local Communist party, the Vietminh, installed himself in the government palace at Hanoi and proclaimed a Vietnamese republic. This was Ho Chi Minh, a man with long experience in the Communist party and also in Europe. The revolutionary movement quickly spread and it was evident that it would not be easy for the French to reestablish themselves. A large expeditionary force was sent there and a degree of concession was made when the French recognized the Republic of Vietnam as an autonomous state within the French Union. But then there arose the question of giving Cochin-China separate status and on this point all attempts to agree broke down. Meanwhile anti-French activity mounted as soldiers were sniped and convoys attacked by the Vietminh and their nationalist allies. At the end of 1946 there was an attack on residents in Hanoi and many deaths. French troops relieved Hanoi and Ho Chi Minh fled.

This was the beginning of a war in which the Communists were to struggle essentially for the nationalist aim of a united Vietnam while the French tried to retain a diminished Vietnam which, with the other Indochinese states, would remain inside the French Union and would satisfy nationalists by having a native head of state—the man who had been appointed to rule Annam by the Japanese in 1945. By 1949 France had come around to including Cochin-China in Vietnam and recognizing Cambodia and Laos as "associate states" of the French Union. But outsiders were now interested. Moscow and Peking recognized the government of Ho Chi Minh; London and Washington that of the Annamese emperor whom the French had set up.

In Asia the processes of decolonization had quickly escaped from the simple forms Roosevelt had envisaged. A Communist-supported guerrilla war had begun in 1948 in Malaya; though it was to be unsuccessful and would not impede progress toward independence in 1957, it presented paradoxes to American policy. The developing antagonism toward the Communist world began to cut across American anticolonialism.

The Middle East

As in other parts of the world, the war greatly changed things in the Middle East. In 1939 the French still held mandates in Syria and Lebanon (their original mandate had been divided into two); the British had retained theirs in Palestine, but elsewhere in the Islamic lands they exercised varying degrees of influence or power according to treaties negotiated with individual states. The most important were Iraq, where a small British force (mainly air force units) was maintained, and Egypt, where a substantial garrison protected the Suez Canal. The security of the Canal became a more and more important matter in the 1930s as Mussolini showed increasing hostility to Great Britain, and the Canal zone became one of the most vital areas of British strategy after Italy's entry into the war, which brought the fighting to Egypt's western border. Egypt remained neutral until it was almost over. The war also made it critical to assure the supply of oil from the Persian Gulf. This increased the importance attached to Iraq and led to British intervention when the Iraqi government threatened to move in a pro-German direction. Another country suspected of German sympathies was Iran, and she too was occupied by British and Russian forces, though mainly with the aim of opening up a land route of communication between the Western allies and their partner.

Nationalism made some progress in some Middle Eastern countries while the war went on. A British and Free French invasion of Syria to keep the country out of German hands led to a proclamation of independence in 1941. Soon afterward Lebanon also proclaimed her independence. The French tried to reestablish their authority at the end of the war but were unsuccessful, and during 1946 these two new countries saw the last foreign garrisons leave. The French also had difficulties farther west, in Algeria, where fighting broke out in 1945. The nationalists were at that moment asking only for autonomy in federation with France. The French went some way in that direction in 1947, but this was far from the end of the movement.

In the lands where British influence was paramount, anti-British sentiment was still a good rallying cry for nationalists, and in both Egypt and Iraq there was much hostility to the presence of British troops in the postwar years. In 1946 Great Britain announced that she was prepared to withdraw her forces from Egypt, but negotiations after a new treaty that year broke down so badly that Egypt referred the matter (unsuccessfully) to the United Nations. By this time the whole question of the future of the Islamic lands had been overtaken by the appearance of the issue which has dogged the politics of the area ever since, the Jewish decision to establish a national state in Palestine by force.

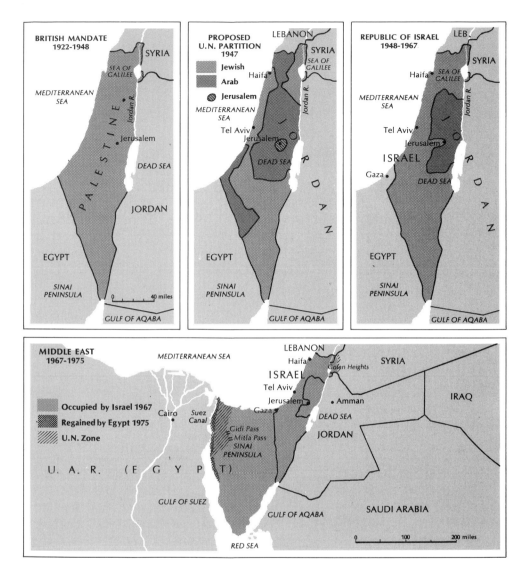

ISRAEL AND THE MIDDLE EAST

Israel

The decisive change in the Palestine problem had come with the Nazi revolution in Germany. At the time of the Balfour Declaration there had been 600,000 Arabs in Palestine and 80,000 Jews, whose presence was already felt by Arabs to be threateningly large. In some of the years which followed, Jewish emigration actually exceeded immigration, and there was ground for hope that the problem of reconciling the promise of a national home for Jews with respect for "the civil and religious rights of the existing non-Jewish communities in Palestine" (as the declaration had put it) might be resolved. Hitler changed this. The numbers of those who wished to come to Palestine rose as soon as the Nazi persecution began, and the extermination policies of the war years made nonsense of British attempts to restrict immigration.

Limitations on immigration were the side of British policy unacceptable to Jews; the other side—to partition Palestine—was rejected by the Arabs. The issue was dramatized as soon as the war ended by the demand of the World Zionist Congress that a million Jews be admitted to Palestine at once. New factors now began to operate. One owed something to the British who earlier in 1945 had looked benevolently on the formation of an Arab League of Egypt, Syria, Lebanon, Iraq, Saudi Arabia, Yemen, and Transjordan. There had always been in British policy a strand of hopefulness that pan-Arabism might prove a stabilizing force in the Middle East and that the coordination of Arab policies might open the way to solution of many problems. But the league was soon preoccupied, to the virtual exclusion of other affairs, with the Palestine question.

The other new factors arose from Russian and American policies. In the immediate postwar era Stalin seems to have been impressed still with the earlier Communist view that Great Britain was the main imperialist power and prop of the international capitalist system. Attacks on her position and influence therefore followed. In the Middle East they coincided with traditional Russian interests and went hand-in-hand with simultaneous pressure on Turkey at the straits of Constantinople. Accordingly, Russian policy was deployed continuously to support Zionism, the most disruptive element in the situation. At just the same time American policy became very anti-British or, rather, pro-Zionist. This could hardly have been avoided. The votes of American sympathizers with Zionism were important in the congressional elections of 1946. In any case, since the Roosevelt revolution in domestic politics, a Democratic president could hardly envisage an anti-Zionist position as a possibility.

It was in this setting that the British sought to disentangle themselves from the Holy Land. From 1945 they faced terrorism and guerrilla warfare from both Jewish and Arab organizations in Palestine. Unhappy Arab, Jewish, and British policemen struggled to hold the peace while London once more strove to find a way of bringing the mandate to an end acceptable to both sides. On one occasion it even enlisted American help, but to no avail: Truman wanted a pro-Zionist solution. In the end the British took the matter to the United Nations. It too recommended partition, still a non-starter for the Arabs. Warfare between the two communities grew fiercer and the British decided to withdraw. On the day that they did so, the state of Israel was proclaimed and almost at once was attacked by the forces of the Arab League. The Israelis fought off their attackers, and both sides agreed to a truce supervised by the United Nations (during which a Zionist terrorist assassinated the United Nations mediator). Both the United States and Russia had almost at once recognized the new state, a remarkable fact because they were not to agree about much else in the Middle East in the next quarter-century.

In 1949 the Israeli government moved to Jerusalem, once more a national capital for the first time since the days of imperial Rome. Half of the city was still occupied by Jordanian forces, but this was almost the least of the problems created by the new nation. Through American and Russian diplomatic support and American private money, Jewish energy and initiative had successfully established a new national state where no basis for one had existed twenty-five years before. This had been done at enormous cost. The disappointment and humiliation of the Arab states assured their continuing hostility, and this inevitably meant opportunities for great-power intervention in the future; here was the fruition of the unhappy and tangled policies followed by Great Britain in the Middle East since 1914. Moreover, the deliberate terrorism of some Zionist extremists and the by no means conciliatory behavior of Israeli forces in 1948–1949 led to an exodus of Arab refugees. Soon there were 750,000 of them in camps in Egypt and Jordan, a social and economic problem, a burden on the world's conscience, and a potential military and diplomatic weapon in Arab hands.

Thus many currents flowed together in a curious and ironic way, to swirl in confusion in an area always a focus of world history. After being persecuted for centuries, the Jews could now be seen by some as persecutors in their turn. The problems with which the peoples of the Middle East now had to grapple had been brought together by many forces: the dissolution of Ottoman power, the rivalries of successor imperialisms, the horrifying experience of centuries of European anti-Semitism culminating in the "Final Solution" of Nazism, the rise of two new world powers, the interplay of nineteenth-century European nationalism and ancient religion, the strategical needs of European states, and the first effects of the revolution implied in the growing dependence of developed nations on oil. There are few moments in the twentieth century so soaked in history as that of the establishment of Israel.

part VII
THE POST=EUROPEAN AGE

One of the decisive and distinguishing facts of contemporary history is that it is world history. The meaning of this is at first sight far from obvious. Until recently world history has been a skein of distinct threads, the histories of many more or less independent and important processes. Within the last century—perhaps since 1900—it has become one process. The affairs of the world are now meshed together in an interdependent system at every level in a way never apparent before. This trend dwarfs even great nations so that their individual stories are no longer useful guides to the major courses of change. Even the great traditions of civilization, which have provided the fundamental architecture of this study, are no longer satisfactory as a basis for organizing our material.

Out of the simplicities of prehistory the paths of civilization led to diversity for many thousands of years. They began to move back together once again when a pattern of life that first evolved in Europe gradually spread around the world. From the nineteenth century onward the pattern has expressed itself more and more in the process called modernization or Westernization. There are signs that the material carriers of this process have led to more generally shared assumptions than ever before because they have provided a common ground of experience to more and more people. It is now beginning to be possible to discern something of a world pattern of civilization.

This does not mean that huge divisions between men do not persist. Although the great powers have been able to avoid fighting one another openly for most of the time since 1945, there has been no return to what from this distance seems the almost Augustan peace of the nineteenth century, despite all the hopes and rhetoric which clustered about the infant United Nations Organization. Enough conflict continues (and there are enough frequent reminders of persistent divisions) to make the world seem more fragmented than ever. Nationality, ideology, and economic interest still cut across it with irresistible force as debates at the United Nations show. Yet there has never been a time when world civilization was more of a reality.

This paradox is the central problem of organizing what follows. It is not easy to see the forest from the trees. There is a vast amount of information, but it is impossible even to scan it in a confident manner because of much we still remain ignorant. Moreover the pace of change is enormously faster. The acceleration of historical evolution in almost every aspect of society has been remarkable. In part this has been unexpected— some technical advances, for example, have very quickly had far-reaching application and power—in part it has been consciously willed, especially in political and economic life. The Second World War released all sorts of currents which put new force behind the urge to modernize. Contemporary history is difficult to expound, therefore, not only because of the vastness which makes it hard to distinguish major trends from accidental details but also because the perspective of the last quarter-century changes almost day by day. A war in the Middle East in 1973 which lasted only a few weeks is in one perspective merely another of the many indecisive conflicts which have followed the collapse of Ottoman power. But in another perspective it is the first to reveal a reversal since 1945 of the relations of some great industrial societies to the area. Their stance changed because of their dependence on Arab oil. The fact of that dependence was already there ten years ago; the 1973 war gave it new significance.

Nevertheless an effort has to be made to understand changes historically: this is almost a definition of the responsibility of the historian. In the vast field of available data some general trends can be discerned which form the beginnings of a structure. But it is perhaps best to look first at some recent transformations which underlie them. Their beginnings lie well in the past though their full weight is only now becoming apparent.

chapter 38

Undercurrents of Contemporary History

FUNDAMENTAL CHANGES

World population

A vast amount of information is now available about demography, but it is not easy to decide where to begin tracing the movements which have underlain so much of politics and economics since the Second World War. The trends which operate in our own world have to be followed back far beyond 1945 to be comprehensible. Another problem (which surprises some people) is that our data are far from satisfactory. Accuracy is still a relative business in computing population; we can only estimate the present population of the world to within one or two hundred million. The degree of error in our estimates, nonetheless, cannot distort the overall trend. In round numbers a world population of about 730 million in 1750 more than doubled by 1900, when it stood at about 1,500 million. Thus approximately 850 million people were added in a century and a half. It took only fifty years to add the next 850 million and more; by 1950 the population of the world was about 2,500 million. Even more striking, another 850 million were added by the middle of the 1960s — in another fifteen years. Here is the phenomenon of acceleration in historical change at its most violent and obvious.

This population growth has generated much alarm. The specter of Malthusian disaster has been revived. Both national governments and international organizations have made efforts to control population increase. They have sometimes seemed to have success, sometimes not; it may be too early to assess them. It is interesting, nonetheless, that many societies have come to accept for the first time the possibility of consciously controlling their shape and size. In one sense this is not a new idea; infanticide and abortion have in many societies long played a part in controlling demands upon scarce resources. What is new is that simpler means are now being provided with the authority of society behind them to make possible positive economic improvement instead of merely the avoidance of family disaster.

Population growth, though a world-wide fact, does not take the same forms everywhere or produce the same effects. It is approximately true to say that in the twentieth century some tendencies visible in Europe have also spread to other parts of the world: death rates have fallen without there being a corresponding fall in reproduction rates. It would be rash to prophesy either that the next phase of population history in developed countries will now be mirrored elsewhere or that it will not, because what makes populations grow at different rates is still largely unknown. The limits set by man's control of nature are not all that is involved; equally important are social and personal attitudes — a very tricky area.

If the experience of developed countries can be taken as a guide to what will happen elsewhere, the outlook is gloomy. They seem to have begun reducing their birth rate as they achieved a prosperity which made it attractive to individuals to have smaller families. This is a long way from the present state of many fast-growing countries where there is still plenty of scope for medicine — which has made huge strides in the last thirty years — to cut into mortality without a corresponding economic growth following. One of the best rough indicators of population trends is infant mortality. In a century, from 1870 to 1970, this fell from an average of about 225 per thousand live births to under 20 per thousand in developed countries; in 1967 the comparative figures for Mexico, the United States, and Great Britain were 63.1, 22.1, and 18.8. Such discrepancies exist — sometimes they are much greater — between many of the poorer countries and the richer. They make it likely that the steam will not go out of population growth for some time yet.

Such differentials are also to be seen in life expectancy. In developed countries life expectancy at birth rose from rather more than forty years in 1870 to slightly over seventy a hundred years later. This is a revolution. People are living three-quarters longer than they used to. There is by now a remarkable evenness among developed countries; life expectancy at birth in the United States, Great Britain, and Russia in 1967, for example, was 70.5, 71.6, and 70.0. In India it was 41.3 and in Haiti 32.6. The last figure is rather better than India's at the beginning of this century or that of France in 1789. This longevity trend produces different age distributions within the populations of developed and undeveloped countries. For most of human history societies have resembled pyramids, with very large numbers of young people and a few old; now developed societies, with a larger proportion of older people than in the past, are beginning to look like slowly tapering columns.

Economic, political, and cultural divergences are all likely to follow from different population structures, but they do not derive only from them. Whether a society makes large or small, social or individual provisions for the care of its aged, for example, is the result of a complicated interplay of attitudes, resources, and institutions (it matters a lot for example whether or not politicians need the votes of the elderly). Such differences are too complicated for discussion here but illustrate that the fact of overall population growth tells us very little by itself; although there is certainly a continuing gross increase, the differences in the way it operates produce different historical effects.

Changes in population balance between countries are among the most obvious results of recent growth. In 1968 the distribution of world population was calculated to be roughly as follows:

Area	Population (millions)	Percentage
Europe	693	20.6
Asia	1,883	56.0
Africa	290	8.6
Latin America	258	7.7
North America	223	6.6
Australasia and Oceania	16	0.5

This table combines a Russian population of perhaps 215 million with Europe and Asia; it is reasonable to count about 75 million as the population of European Russia.

The fall in Europe's share of world population is striking, particularly as this followed a period in which, until the 1920s, Europe was an exporter of manpower to other continents, notably the Americas. This emigration was cut by the United States' restrictions in the 1920s and dwindled even more during the Great Depression. It has never recovered its importance (though more Britons still emigrate each year than are needed to balance an inflow from other countries). Instead Europe now attracts North Africans, Asians, and West Indians who seek employment lacking at home.

Asia now contains over half mankind and one country, China, more than one-fifth of it. Huge as the Asian rates of growth have been, they are not so fast as those of Latin America. World growth runs at an average of about 2 percent per annum while that of Brazil, for example, was running at about 3.5 percent in the early 1960s. In some Latin American countries standards of living and life expectancy are also high, approximating the European levels of the first quarter of this century, but rapid population growth has continued. The factor differentiating Latin American countries from the European pattern is that a high level of births has continued even when mortality has fallen. The Roman Catholic Church exercises great influence in all these countries and there has long been great resistance to contraception in them. In other parts of the globe experiencing rapid population growth, governments have begun to promote population control; China and Russia are notable exceptions. But present data do not provide grounds for believing that the Western answer to overpopulation, contraception, will prove efficacious everywhere else (Indian attempts seem so far ineffective) or that population stability may not be achieved by other means.

World food supply

Differences in population growth imply, other things being equal, differences in power, but among the things which have to be equal is access to wealth. In many countries the benefits of modernization have been held back because a rising population has consumed extra production. This is another example of the differential effects of population growth. The crucial question has been food. Here it is at least obvious that though many have starved, many others have lived; somehow the food has been found to double the world's population since 1900. Even if millions have died in local famines, there has been no world-wide Malthusian catastrophe. The world has undeniably proved able to feed its growing population. If it had not, the population would be smaller. In other words, one fundamental change of recent history is a huge expansion of food production.

Output has been raised in several ways besides bringing new land under cultivation. Down to the 1930s wheat crops were still being successfully introduced to lands where for climatic reasons they had not been grown hitherto. This exploitation of new land was one of the first of the twentieth-century scientific contributions to agriculture comparable in effect to the improvements of earlier times and it was mainly the work of plant geneticists, who evolved new strains of cereals. Such research continues to be important; there is only a finite amount of land in the world, and the more that can grow food, the better. Still greater contributions to world food supplies have come from increasing the production of existing grain-growing areas, and this is largely a consequence of improvements in the chemistry of fertilizers. An unprecedented rate of replacement of nitrogen in the soil is the basic explanation of the huge yields which have now become commonplace in countries with advanced agriculture, and these methods are beginning to be extended to other areas. This is part of a change which far more than the slower transformations of earlier times has the right to be called an "agricultural revolution."

Fertilizers are only part of a story of radical innovation in agricultural chemistry. Effective herbicides and insecticides began to be commercially available in the 1940s and 1950s. At the same time the use of agricultural machinery increased enormously in the developed countries. England had the most mechanized farming in the world in terms of horsepower per acre cultivated in 1939, but English farmers then still did much of their work with horses while combine harvesters (already numerous in the United States) were rare. Now working horses are preserved as interesting curiosities by rich farmers—though there are grounds for thinking that they may be reintroduced for certain types of work where the rising cost of gasoline would not justify the use of a tractor. But the fields are not the only place where the farm has been mechanized. Electricity has brought automatic milking, grain drying, threshing, the heating of animal sheds in winter, and many other changes which have pushed up agricultural productivity by liberating it from weather, the seasons, and the cycle of night and day. Such innovations have reflected the growing control of environment and have also made advanced agriculture less dependent on labor; the agricultural work force has continued to fall while production per acre has risen.

One social result is that subsistence farming is relatively on the retreat. There are probably more subsistence farmers in the world today than in 1900, but only because there are more people. Their relative share of cultivated land and of the value of what is produced has fallen. In Europe the peasant is fast disappearing as he disappeared in Great Britain two hundred and more years ago. But this change is unevenly spread. Subsistence agriculture is still the norm in some countries with large and rapidly growing populations, and in these countries productivity remains low. Just before the First World War the British yield of wheat per acre was already more than two and a half times that of India; by 1968 it was roughly five times India's. Over the same period the United States raised its rice yields from 4.25 to nearly 12 tons an acre while those of Burma, sometimes called the "rice bowl of Asia," rose from 3.8 to 4.2 tons. Another way of looking at these facts is to consider how many families can be fed by one agricultural worker in different countries. In 1968 the answer for Egypt was slightly more than one; for New Zealand the figure was over forty.

Such differences have origins more complicated than the simple presence or absence of technique, but advanced agriculture is usually found in countries advanced in other ways. This has penalized countries where there is most need to increase agricultural productivity because they have found it very difficult to compete with industrial countries in the world commodity markets. Some paradoxes have resulted; the Indians and Chinese, big grain and rice producers, have found themselves buying American and Canadian wheat. The result has been growing disparities between developed and undeveloped countries, and the most striking index of this has been their relative consumption of the world's resources. Roughly half the world's population consumes about six-sevenths of the world's production and the other half consumes the other seventh. Moreover there are wide disparities even among the wealthy nations. There are about six Americans in every hundred human beings; in 1970 they used about forty out of every hundred barrels of oil produced in the world.

Rich and poor societies

The difference between rich and poor societies is much more marked today than ever before and at first sight seems to make nonsense of the thesis that world history is a unity. The division between rich and poor nations has grown more and more marked since 1945. This is not because the poor have grown poorer but because the rich have grown much richer. Even spectacular accelerations of production (Asian countries, for example, augmented their agricultural output between 1952 and 1970 more than Europe and much more than North America) have rarely succeeded in improving the position of poor countries in relation to the rich. There are two reasons: poor countries have been beset by the problems of rising population, and advanced countries began at a higher level. As a result, though their ranking in relation to one another has changed, roughly the same dozen or so countries which enjoyed the highest standards of living in 1950 still enjoy them today, and their lead over the poorer countries has increased.

Generally speaking, countries which are industrialized are richer. In 1970 the three great industrial agglomerations of the world were still, as in 1939, the United States, Europe, and Russia, and the only important Asian industrial society of 1939, Japan, had become almost their equal. No single European country can any longer match the two giants. America's recovery from the Depression began with the approach of war and the beginnings of rearmament; the war and subsequent federal expenditure provided a firm undertone for continued expansion. The result is the greatest industrial economy in the world. But its rate of growth has been nowhere near as rapid as that of Soviet Russia, where according to official figures central planning has succeeded in increasing industrial production at a rate of over 12 percent per annum since 1945.

Much of recent expansion in advanced societies has been in industries which barely existed in 1945—electronics and plastics are examples. But the old basic heavy industries have continued to form their backbone though with changes of emphasis in some instances. The twentieth century has seen a marked transition in advanced countries from coal, which replaced wood in the nineteenth century, to oil and natural gas for the supply of energy. Many mines have been closed, often causing social upheavals. This has happened especially in Great Britain, which ran down another of her old staples, shipbuilding, even before 1939. Other nations—notably Japan in the 1960s—have since moved into the shipping industry. Even a sketch of such changes would have to be very long, but two particular aspects of twentieth-century industrial expansion require comment: its contribution to higher standards of living and its connection with science.

Basic heavy industries, such as power or metallurgy, raise standards of living in a fundamental way. They provide cheaper materials. They improve transport and therefore lower the cost of goods in a different way, or they provide light or fuel to be used as the consumer wishes. But the industrial expansion of the advanced countries has also been characterized recently by an enormous growth in the production of goods directly for the use and pleasure of the individual consumer. Many illustrations could be given of this, but one must suffice. In 1885 there appeared the first machine propelled by an internal combustion engine—that is to say, one in which the energy to drive a piston was produced by heat directly inside the cylinder of an engine instead of being created outside the engine by making steam. Nine years later came a four-wheeled vehicle which is a recognizable ancestor of the modern car, the French Panhard. France and Germany kept a lead in producing cars in the next decade or so; they were few—rich men's toys. This was the automobile's "prehistory." Its history began in the United States when Henry Ford set up a production line for his Model T in 1907. The price of the first one was an unprecedentedly low $950. It was an enormous success. Demand rose so rapidly that by 1915 Ford was producing a million cars a year. He was deliberately planning for a mass market and by 1926 the price was less than $300. This was the beginning of mass consumption of something previously regarded as a luxury. There are now more cars than households in the United States.

Ford's achievement was thus not only technical and financial but cultural. He changed the world by enabling people of modest incomes to enjoy a mobility unavailable to millionaires fifty years earlier. This huge increase in amenity would subsequently penetrate, gradually and in varying degree, all parts of the world. He also ensured a new and rising demand for oil—though transport is not the only reason for this. Finally, his factories carried through

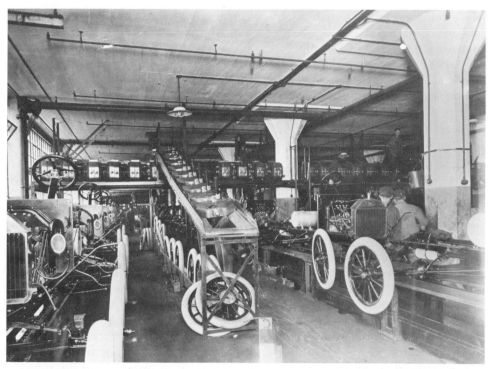

The beginnings of the mass automobile industry. A Ford factory assembly line before the First World War, at the point where wheels and radiators were added to the car. *(Courtesy of the Ford Archives, Dearborn, Michigan)*

a social and technical revolution by their example of what could be done with mass production. Like many great revolutionaries Ford brought together other men's ideas as well as providing his own, but the result was the assembly line. It moved the article under manufacture steadily from worker to worker as each carried out in the minimum necessary time the precisely delimited and, if possible, small task in which he was skilled. Ford realized that such work would be very boring and paid high wages to compensate for this. He thereby contributed to another revolutionary change, the fueling of economic prosperity by high industrial wages which increase purchasing power and therefore demand.

The very real costs of mass production in its psychological effect on the worker were soon apparent, but the principle was fundamental to a wider sharing of the wealth in an industrial economy. It made possible lower prices, which not only satisfied but also increased the demand for consumer goods. The idea steadily spread that goods hitherto thought luxuries could be taken for granted. Rising expectations became a reality for the majority in the developed countries. The flow of consumer goods shattered the last ties that held people to the idea that they lived in a world of stable expectations. Moreover the effect has begun to spread. The spectacle of the wealth of the developed nations is striking in undeveloped countries, where imported cheap consumer goods — transistor radios, for example — often initiate important social changes. In particular, possession of such things is often an important sign of status. They provide an incentive for men and women to seek work where they can get higher wages, and this usually involves leaving the villages in which a majority of mankind lives even today.

SCIENCE AND WORLD CIVILIZATION

Industrial societies were by 1970 dependent on science as never before. Sometimes this was obvious: in the chemistry of some industrial processes, in the use of nuclear plants to generate energy or of computers to control a factory. In other areas — and the production of plastic materials for almost every conceivable requirement is one of the most common — the basic science lay concealed in processes fairly remote from manufacture.

Science's creation of an end product for mass consumption was, moreover, becoming a faster process all the time. The accumulation of technological and scientific skill steadily reduced the time between a discovery and its practical application. This was an important part of the general acceleration of change noticeable in other connections in the last century. The gap between the first use of penicillin and its large-scale manufacture was about three years; general use of the automobile after the principle of the internal combustion engine was grasped was more like half a century.

One reason for this acceleration was structural and economic, the gradual spread of the idea of purposive research. Most practical results of nineteenth-century science were by-products of scientific curiosity, sometimes accidental. By 1900 a few scientists were beginning to see that consciously directed and concentrated research was sensible. Twenty years later large industrial companies had begun to accept the idea that research was a proper call on their investment, albeit a small one. The research departments of some industrial concerns were in time to grow into enormous establishments in their own right as petrochemicals, plastics, electronics, and biochemical medicine made their appearance later in the century. By the middle of it the ordinary citizen of a developed country would be in some difficulty if he wished to lead a life which did not rest on applied science.

The pervasiveness of science, coupled with the impressiveness of its most spectacular achievements, was one of the main reasons for the ever growing importance it came to possess. That importance was reflected and can be measured in monetary terms. The Cavendish laboratory at Cambridge, for example, in which some of the fundamental experiments of nuclear physics were carried out before 1914, then had a grant from the university of roughly $1,500 a year at current rates of exchange. When it was decided during the Second World War to mount a major effort to produce nuclear weapons, the resulting Manhattan Project (as it was called) is estimated to have cost as much as all the scientific research previously conducted by mankind from the beginnings of recorded time.

Such huge sums — and there were to be much larger bills when scientists took up the investigation of space — mark another social fact about science, its increasing importance to governments. Science became a political fact in the twentieth century. Only governments could provide resources on the scale needed for some of the things done after 1945. One usual benefit they sought, unfortunately, was better weapons, and this undoubtedly explains the huge scientific investments of the United States and Russia, which are of comparable magnitude, while the whole of Western Europe's research expenditure is less than a third of Russia's. The mobilization of science in two world wars had shown its importance to war-making power. The increasing interest and participation of governments has not, on the other hand, meant that science has grown more nationalistic; indeed the reverse is true. For purely theoretical and technical reasons science is international, to say nothing of the tradition of international communication among scientists, which is one of their most splendid inheritances from the first great age of science in the seventeenth century.

The general psychological effect of the growth of science has been to create a much wider acceptance of its omnipresence and importance than ever before in history: there are more scientists, more attention given to science in education, and more widely diffused and readily comprehensible scientific information. Yet paradoxically this may have led to some diminution of the wonder felt in earlier times at what science could do. Because of the very success of science, more and more things prove possible, and so there is nothing very surprising about the latest marvel. There is even disappointment when some problems prove recalcitrant. What has undoubtedly grown stronger and more widespread is the master idea of our civilization, the notion that purposive change can be imposed upon nature if sufficient resources are made available. This is an idea which stems from European civilization; for all the early skill shown, for example, by the Chinese in certain technological fields, their tradition proved inadequate to sustain a transformation of nature such as Bacon envisaged and was later proved possible. The science now carried on around the globe is all based on the European experimental tradition.

The changing world of pure science

Science continued in the twentieth century to provide disruptive ideas and implications for traditional, theocentric views of life. They have now spread around the world. This is the high phase of a long process of fundamental intellectual change. Newtonian physics provided a satisfying philosophical framework for a century and a half. It was not until the nineteenth century that this was shattered by the work begun by James Clark Maxwell, the first professor of experimental physics at Cambridge. His work in electromagnetism and thermodynamics opened a great breach in the view of nature which had until then proved adequate for scientific advance, the view that the universe obeyed natural, regular, and discoverable laws of a somewhat mechanical kind and that it essentially consisted of lumps of indestructible matter in various combinations and arrangements. By 1914 Maxwell's theoretical work and the experimental investigation which followed it up had made this concept unacceptable. Instead of lumps of matter, the universe began to be seen as an aggregate of atoms, which were tiny solar systems of particles in particular arrangements. These particles seemed to behave in a way which blurred the established distinction between matter and electromagnetic fields. Moreover the arrangements of particles were not fixed; it appeared that in nature one arrangement might give way to another and thus one element could change into another.

The crucial work which founded modern nuclear engineering was done between 1895 and 1914 by Wilhelm Roentgen who discovered X-rays, A. H. Becquerel who explained radioactivity, J. J. Thomson who identified the electron, Pierre and Marie Curie who isolated radium, and Ernest Rutherford who investigated the atom's structure. Rutherford's work was decisive in establishing that an atom could be "split" because of its structure as a system of particles. Two such particles were soon identified, the proton and the electron; others would not be identified until after 1932 when James Chadwick discovered the neutron. But Rutherford, together with Niels Bohr, had given the scientific world an experimentally validated picture of the atom's structure as a system of particles.

Early twentieth-century science. Lord Rutherford's room and apparatus at the Cavendish Laboratory, Cambridge University, where much of the fundamental work making possible a revolution in physical theory was carried out. *(Copyright, Cavendish Laboratory, University of Cambridge)*

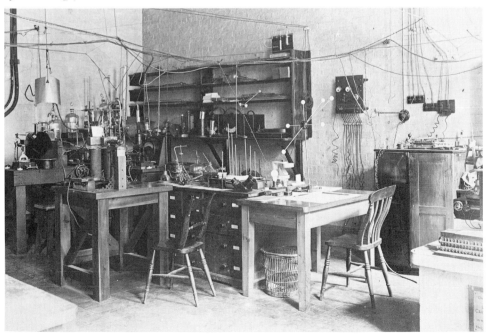

What this radically important experimental work did not do was supply a new theoretical framework to replace the Newtonian one now damaged beyond repair. This was achieved by a long revolution in theory beginning in the last years of the nineteenth century and culminating in the 1920s. It focused on two different sets of problems which gave rise to the relativity and quantum theories. The pioneering work was done by Max Planck and Albert Einstein; they demonstrated experimentally and mathematically that the Newtonian laws of motion could not account for a new fact accepted by scientists: that energy transactions in the material world took place not in an even flow but in bursts — quanta, as they came to be termed. Planck showed that heat from, for example, the sun was not, as Newtonian physics required, emitted continuously; he argued that this was true of all energy emitted by the electron. Einstein argued that light was propagated not continuously but in particles. There quantum theory more or less rested for twenty or so years; Newton's views had been found wanting, but there was nothing to put in their place.

Meanwhile Einstein made his most famous contribution to science in a different way through his work on light, though its importance was not at first grasped. This was his formulation of the relationship between mass and energy: $E = mc^2$, where E is energy, m is mass, and c is the constant speed of light. The importance and accuracy of this theoretical statement were not to be clear until much more work had been done in nuclear physics; scientists would then observe that the relationships resulting when mass-energy was converted into heat-energy in the breaking up of nuclei corresponded exactly to Einstein's formula. In 1905 Einstein also published the work for which he was to be most celebrated, the statement of the theory of relativity. He demonstrated that the traditional distinctions of space and time, and mass and energy could not be consistently maintained. Instead of Newton's three-dimensional physics, he proposed a "space-time continuum" to explain the interplay of space, time, and motion. This was soon to be corroborated by astronomical observation of facts which Newtonian cosmology could not properly explain.

While these advances were being absorbed, theoretical work continued on quantum physics. A major breakthrough finally came in 1925 with the provision of a mathematical framework for what Planck had observed and indeed for nuclear physics. So sweeping was what was achieved by Erwin Schrödinger and Werner Heisenberg, the two mathematicians mainly responsible, that it seemed as if quantum mechanics might be of virtually limitless explanatory power in the sciences. The behavior of atomic particles observed by Rutherford and Bohr could now be accounted for and moreover predictions could be made about what should be found in the nucleus (these were borne out in the 1930s). Quantum mechanics seemed to inaugurate a new age of physics. Ironically one of its consequences was the work of the 1930s, notably that of Enrico Fermi, which made it possible at the outbreak of war to begin work on nuclear weapons.

By mid-century, therefore, much more had disappeared in science than just a set of general laws which had been proved inadequate. (In fact for most everyday purposes Newtonian physics still worked quite adequately.) In physics, from which it had spread to other sciences, the whole notion of a general law was being replaced by the concept of statistical probability as the best that could be hoped for. Not only was the content of science changing but also the concept. Furthermore, the boundaries between sciences collapsed under the onrush of new knowledge made accessible by new theories and new instrumentation. Even one of the traditional fields of science — physics or biology, say — was now beyond the grasp of any single man. The growing complication resulting from bringing physical theory to bear on neurology or mathematics or biology put another barrier in the way of attaining that synthesis of knowledge which had been the dream of the nineteenth century.

Science and attitudes

It would be implausible to suggest that much of what was going on in science filtered through to laymen in any very precise form. Most people continued undisturbed in their accustomed pieties, whether these might be practical, material hedonism, Hinduism, Marxism, or anything else. Yet a tentative assessment must be made of the role of science in changing generally accepted ideas if we are to achieve a balanced view of the history of our culture. At the outset we have to note a distinction between the effect of ideas on intellectual elites, who are of course disproportionately prominent in histories of thought and culture, and their impact, even if in nonsensically distorted forms, on the masses (to which most of us belong) who take their assumptions from the climate of opinion in which they live. The second effect is more important in recent history than earlier because rising literacy and rapid communications have made mass culture more responsive to new ideas than ever before, but the impact of scientific advances on elites is much easier to trace.

Newtonian cosmology had settled down in the eighteenth century into coexistence with Christian religion (and other theocentric modes of thought) and therefore left untroubled the wide range of social and moral beliefs which were tied to this. As the twentieth century went on, science seemed increasingly difficult to reconcile with any fixed belief at all. It appeared to stress the relativism of points of view and the pressure of circumstance in the establishment of truth up to a point at which any unchallengeable assumption or viewpoint seemed ruled out. This was especially obvious in attempts made by the practitioners of the new branch of study, psychology, to investigate human behavior scientifically.

Psychology tended to take one of two paths after 1900. Roughly speaking, one body of work, whatever its exact status and method, took the position that therapy could be pursued and relevant material assembled by interrogating subjects about their wishes, feelings, and thoughts and interpreting this data in accordance with appropriate theories. This is usually termed psychoanalysis. The outstanding figure among many who used this approach

One of Pavlov's dogs; the animal is fitted with a device for the collection of its saliva. A sketch from a paper by the scientist. (*Tass from Sovfoto*)

was Freud. His teaching provides a good example of something which a layman—though not all scientists—would call science having an important and widespread effect both by undermining the confidence of an elite in traditional assumptions and then by being diffused through advanced societies in derivative notions. These took such different forms as new attitudes to sexuality or to responsibility and therefore to punishment.

The other approach is much more mechanistic but generated a body of experimental data at least as impressive as the successes claimed by psychoanalysis. The outstanding name associated with this branch of psychological study is that of the Russian I. V. Pavlov. In a series of celebrated experiments with dogs he established generalizations which with appropriate modification proved applicable to human beings. His most important single discovery was the "conditioned reflex." Essentially he produced this by manipulating one of a pair of variables in his experiment with a dog in order to produce a predicted piece of behavior by a "conditioned stimulus." In the classic experiment the researcher regularly sounded a bell before giving food to a dog. After a time merely sounding the bell without producing the food caused the dog to salivate. Psychologists subsequently explored many refinements and developments of such procedures. Their remarkable work developed into the behaviorist school of psychology, which has not only been the source of a great deal of insight into human action but has also been exploited for a number of purposes (torture has been one of its most depressing applications). The behaviorists made great advances, many of which were put to beneficent use particularly in the treatment of mental illness. But the diffused effect of behaviorism, if an attempt can be made to grasp so shapeless a subject, seems curiously parallel to that of Freudianism in that its bias is toward demolishing the sense of responsibility and individualism which is the heart of European and Christian moral tradition.

RELIGION AND THE STATE

Advances in psychology and other branches of science seem to have contributed importantly to a decline of religious belief. But this decline, often alleged to be characteristic of the contemporary era, needs very careful qualification. People who talk about the waning power of religion usually mean the formal and organized authority of Christian churches. They may go further and point out changes in widely held assumptions which go beyond effects inimical to formal Christianity. They point, for example, to the fact that even India is now a republic which is secular in its constitution. But they do not usually mean that the real power of Islam or Hinduism has declined, or that there have not appeared new religions in other parts of the world which are important, or that states adhering to a particular faith, such as Pakistan, do not exist, or that it is not true that probably more people now than in any earlier time take seriously what is said by the pope. They tend, nevertheless, to feel that in this matter as in others Western society has indicated a path which other societies may shortly be following. This may be true, but it may not.

It is obvious, for example, that the notion of Islamic unity is not dead in the Arab lands. Nor is the destructive power of religion confined to the Middle East or the non-Christian world. When it has been united with strong social forces, religion has produced terrifying massacres in the Indian subcontinent, both during the months of partition in 1947 and since in the struggles which led to the breaking away of East Bengal from Pakistan and the establishment of the new state of Bangladesh. In Ulster the Irish of different churches still bitterly dispute the future of their country in terms drawn from the religious wars of the seventeenth century. Though the hierarchies and leaders of different religions find it appropriate to exchange public courtesies, it cannot be said that religion has ceased to be a divisive force. Whether, on the other hand, the supernatural content of religion is losing its hold and religion is important today merely as a badge of group membership is debatable.

What seems to be true is that within the world whose origins are Christian the decline of sectarian strife has been a concomitant of a general decline of religious belief. Ecumenism, the movement whose most considerable achievement to date was the setting up of the World Council of Churches in 1948, has been easier because all Christians have had a growing sense of living in a hostile environment. The only unequivocal sign of the advance of Christianity has been the growth of the Roman Catholic Church overseas, a matter of largely natural increase, to which attention was drawn in the 1960s by the first papal visits ever made to South America and Asia.

Religious discipline and the notion of a fixed, unchanging moral law have been among the most impressive of mankind's achievements in regulating society. They have both suffered from forces characteristic of the modern world. The other great agent of social order, the state, has done much better. It has emerged from an era of revolutionary change with its powers enhanced by the dangers which were once thought to threaten it. One should not be misled by signs of disillusionment with state power shown by a minority in a few advanced countries; frequently they do not contest the power itself but only the way it is used. The world now contains more states than ever before and more people look to their governments as the ultimate source of their well-being. Even in the countries whose institutions contain important devices for controlling and checking state power, there is a sense that it is stronger and less resistible than it was a century ago.

This has led to some despair. The establishment of national unity and a state structure has not always made for greater freedom in post-colonial countries though whether it has brought greater happiness is more debatable. For all the forms of constitutionalism and democracy new countries adopt, the freedoms they used to guarantee are more conspicuously absent today than ever. The rhetoric of democracy is plentifully employed, which is historically interesting as a tribute, but its substance is often lacking in practice. In part this is because the traditional basis of democracy in individualism is now challenged by communism. But democracy was always a growth successful only in a few countries of Europe or European origin and has rarely been transplanted without failure or a significant mutation. It has proved impossible to work representative and democratic institutions, for example, in new states lacking a solid foundation in habit where there are powerful divisive forces in religious sectarianism or tribalism. In such a setting the imposition of one-party rule and a more authoritarian style of government has often been a way of resisting the fragmentation of the nation once the discipline imposed by a colonial power was withdrawn. There are many more dictators in the world today than in 1939.

It would be unhistorical to deplore this state of affairs (though it may well be morally right to do so); institutions will always reflect circumstances in their working. What is more surprising historically is that there are signs that the state structures of nations in the liberal tradition are increasingly felt to be oppressive and to interfere in the lives of their citizens.

This is in part because the state has been asked to do more and more, and power has been willingly granted to it for this purpose. An age of great wars threw unprecedented power into the hands of governments because huge mobilizations of resources were necessary for survival. Even in peacetime the persistence of international tension has strengthened governments. Yet more notable still is the state's interference with aspects of life thought earlier to be properly of private concern. The coming of welfare services, the participation of government in economic planning as growing industrial and scientific investment was seen to have an important bearing on questions of international relationships have both sucked political action into the nonpolitical sector. Finally, the liberal idea has also suffered from its association with one side of a "cold war" between ideologies and from the respect engendered by other political forms in bringing about modernization. This is hardly surprising; Europe had its enlightened modernizers in the past and they were sometimes despots. Above all, new states have the examples of Russia and China, two great agrarian societies which undertook their own modernization by very authoritarian means.

The role of the urge to modernize in strengthening the state — something prefigured outside Europe in such figures as Mehemet Ali or Kemal Ataturk — was an indication of the new sources from which the state could increasingly draw its moral authority. Instead of resting as it once had done on personal loyalty to a dynasty or supernatural sanction, the authority of the state has come to rest increasingly on the democratic assumption that it was able best to satisfy collective desires. Usually these were for the provision of material improvement but not always. If one idea more than any other validates state authority today it is still nationalism, which remains the motive force of much of world politics. It has proved astonishingly tenacious, as the experience of Communist Europe has shown, and has been successful in mobilizing allegiance as no other force has been able to do. Against it ideologies have not been effective; the forces telling against it and helping to make the whole world one political system have been economics, communications, and technology — not a comparably powerful moral idea or mythology.

The state has also continued to benefit from its possession of the instruments of power. Even a hundred years ago the police and armed forces of a government unshaken by war or revolution virtually assured its survival of any internal challenge. Improved technology has only increased this near certainty. New repressive techniques and weapons, moreover, are now only a small part of the story of state power. The state's intervention in the economy (as consumer, investor, or overt planner) and the improvement of mass communications in a form which leaves access to them highly centralized are also political facts of great importance. They did not begin in 1945. The welfare state was a British reality before 1914, Hitler and Roosevelt made great use of radio (though for very different ends), and interference with economic life is as old as government itself. However, the increase in state power we have witnessed since 1945 in its intense form is very new. When a British foreign secretary said in the late 1940s that he wished to see a world in which a traveler could set off for a foreign country with no need to worry about anything except buying a ticket, without passport, visa, or other officially imposed documentation, he was virtually asking for the return of a state of affairs that had obtained about eighty years earlier.

chapter 39

The Organization of a New World

The end of the Second World War had revealed a revolution in both the economic and political organization of the world, and the era of revolutionary change was far from over. It has been going on ever since. The result is a world still in movement, whose structure is already wholly different from what might have been expected twenty years or so ago. Some recent changes can be connected fairly confidently with forces at work long before the 1940s. They are obviously related, for example, to the energy needs of industrial societies, which have grown steadily for a century or more, or to the triumph of ideas first announced in the French Revolution. But long-range trends are far from being the whole story. Other great changes seem to have more of accident, circumstances, or personality about them.

What is easier to trace in them than the patterns of causation and decisive influence is a simple narrative of how things happened, which is the subject of this chapter. Both the evidence and the perspective to go further than this with confidence are missing. Tracing the steps by which one sort of world turned into another is nonetheless an essential preliminary to historical judgment, which will become easier as the years pass. The earliest of these steps were taken in a world which for most states was still dominated by the prolonged bitterness of Soviet-American antagonism.

THE COLD WAR AT ITS HEIGHT

The opening of the Marshall aid program was almost at once followed by the first and decisive battle of the cold war in Europe, a confrontation over the fate of Berlin. It established the point over which, in Europe, the United States was prepared to fight. The Russian moves which provoked the Berlin crisis were essentially a matter of putting pressure on the Western powers to prevent the appearance of a reunited and economically powerful Germany which was not under Russian influence. But the Western powers pursued the economic restoration of their own zones in the interests of Western Europe as a whole and thus blocked the way to a reunited Germany under Communist control. Following on the Marshall Plan (which of course extended aid to the Western-occupied zones but not to the Russian sector) a currency reform undertaken in the Western zones further cut Germany in two because it meant that the recovery of the eastern half of the country would not proceed as a unit integrated with Western Europe. That the Western powers should get on with the business of putting West German industry on its feet undoubtedly made economic sense, but the decision to do so put East Germany decisively on the other side of the iron curtain.

Currency reform in the Western zones of Berlin divided that city too and thereby prejudiced Communist chances of a political putsch there. The Russians duly responded by interfering with Western communications with Berlin. The Western powers interpreted Russian moves as an attempt to blockade West Berlin and sever it from West Germany. As the dispute over land communications escalated, the British and Americans organized an airlift to supply the city. A trial of strength was thus under way. The Western powers, in spite of the enormous cost of maintaining even such a supply of food, fuel, and medicine as would just keep West Berlin going, announced they were prepared to keep it up indefinitely. The implication was that the Russians could only stop them by force. For the first time since the war American strategic bombers moved back to bases in England. The Russians, on the other hand, probably wanted to demonstrate to the West Berliners that the Western powers could not stay there if the Russians did not want them to. The blockade lasted over a year and the Russians lost. They were neither able to prevent the Allied supply nor to intimidate the West Berliners. They made the best of it by deliberately splitting the city and refusing the non-Communist mayor access to his office. Meanwhile the Western powers had got on with the consolidation of West Germany and had signed a treaty setting up a new organization for Atlantic security. The blockade finally ended in May 1949.

Remarkable though the airlift was as a technical achievement (there was only one airfield and it handled over a thousand aircraft a day for most of the time, with an average daily delivery of 5,000 tons of coal alone), the real significance of the crisis was political. It had shown that neither side wanted to fight but also that all hope of cooperation on the basis of the wartime agreement to create a centrally administered Germany was dead. Henceforth there were to be two Germanies as well as two Europes.

It also began to appear that there might be two worlds. From the treaty on Atlantic security was born in April 1949 the North Atlantic Treaty Organization (NATO), the first cold war creation to transcend Europe. The United States and Canada were members as well as most of the Western European states (only Sweden, Switzerland, and Spain did not belong). It was explicitly a defensive alliance, providing for mutual assistance to any member attacked, and it was another break with the now almost vanished isolationist traditions of American foreign policy.

The Korean War

Though a dangerous phase of the cold war ended in Europe when Russia lifted the Berlin blockade, another soon erupted in Asia. In 1945 Korea

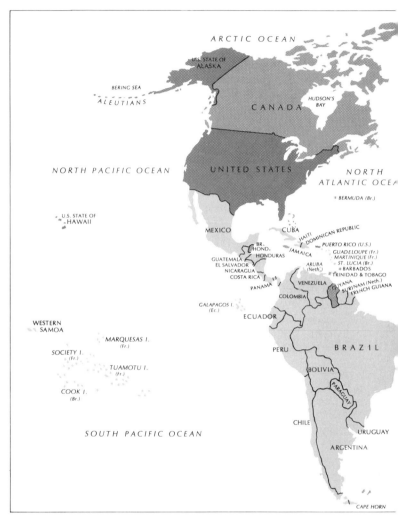

THE WORLD 1975

had been divided, the industrial north and agricultural south being occupied respectively by Russian and American forces. The problem of reunification was eventually referred to the United Nations, which, after fruitless efforts to obtain nationwide elections under its supervision, recognized the regime set up in South Korea as the country's sole lawful government. Meanwhile the Russian zone also produced a government claiming sovereignty over the whole country. In June 1950, after Russia and the United States had both withdrawn their forces, North Korean troops invaded the south. Within two

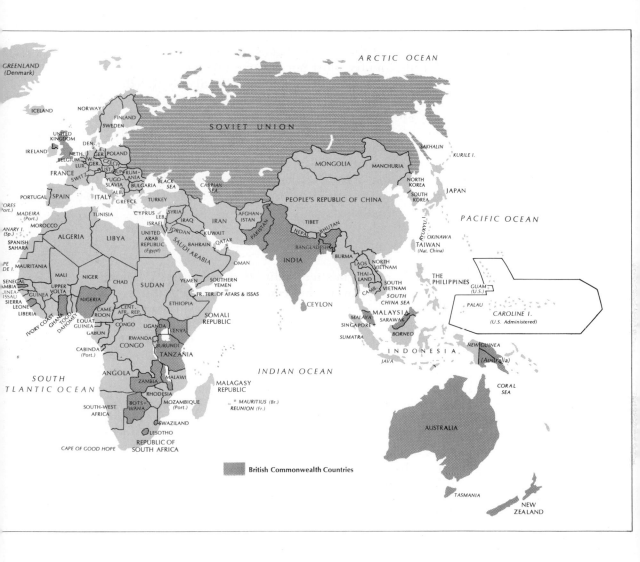

days President Truman intervened, acting in the name of the United Nations, which had voted to resist aggression. The Americans were always to provide the bulk of the United Nations forces in Korea, but other countries sent contingents.

Within a few months it seemed likely that North Korea would be defeated. United Nations forces were operating well north of the former dividing line and nearing the Manchurian frontier. At this point Chinese Communist forces intervened and drove them back. There was now a danger of a much bigger conflict. The Chinese Communists, having driven the Kuomintang from power, ruled the second largest Communist state in the world (the largest in terms of population) and had a nuclear power as an ally.

War between China and the United States did not occur, though Truman's insistence that his country must not become involved in a major war on the Asian mainland could be maintained only by dismissing the commander in chief of the United Nations forces, Douglas MacArthur. By 1953 it began to be clear that although the Chinese might be able to keep the North Koreans in the field, they could not overrun South Korea against American wishes. A new Republican administration in Washington knew the United States had demonstrated its will and capacity to uphold an independent South Korea and felt the real center of the cold war was in Europe rather than in Asia. An armistice was signed in July 1953, though all subsequent efforts to turn this into a formal peace failed.

Global confrontation

Shortly before the Korean armistice Stalin died. It was very difficult to know what his death might mean. In due course it seemed that it marked a break in the continuity of Russian development and policy, but that was not clear at the time. The administration of President Dwight D. Eisenhower, who had taken office earlier in 1953, was as distrustful of Russian intentions as ever. The cold war was entering its most intense phase.

Shortly after Stalin's death his successors revealed that Russia too had the improved nuclear weapon known as the hydrogen bomb. This was something of a memorial to his achievement in assuring Russia her proper status in the postwar world. What was not clear was that this status was bound to cost Russia and the world so much. Russia was now a great industrial power showing the trends in urbanization and population growth which had marked other industrializing nations, but her peoples had been rewarded with precious little except the knowledge of their international strength. Stalin had kept domestic consumption down, and the brutalities of the police system seemed, if anything, to have been intensified after some relaxation during the war. But Stalin had essentially only carried out the repressive policies of Lenin to their logical conclusion. His greater historical stature derives from the results in Russia's new role in world history.

Outside Russia Stalin's major monument was a divided Europe, of which the western half was by 1953 substantially rebuilt thanks to American financial support. Germany was split down the middle; from 1949 the Federal Republic in the west and the German Democratic Republic in the east had moved farther and farther apart. In March 1954 the Russians announced that the East German republic now possessed full sovereignty, and on the following day the West German president signed a constitutional amendment permitting the rearmament of his country. In 1955 a rearmed West Germany entered NATO and the Russian riposte was a military alliance between the Communist states termed the Warsaw Pact. Berlin's future was still in doubt, but it was clear that the NATO powers would fight to resist any unacceptable changes in its status. East Germany had meanwhile agreed to settle an old problem: the line of the Oder-Neisse would be the frontier with Poland and historic Prussia passed under the rule of a Slav state. Hitler's dream of realizing the greater Germany of the nineteenth-century nationalists had been a brief one; his effort to achieve it had ended by destroying Bismarckian Germany.

Two economic systems

It would be improper to attribute to Stalin or any one person another division, which was world-wide after the Communist victory in China, that between what we may call capitalist and socialist economic systems. Yet Stalin's policies contributed significantly to its deepening. The importance of this division lay in its disruption of pre-1939 patterns of world trade; two methods of organizing the distribution of scarce resources divided the world and intercourse between the two economic blocs was henceforth limited. In one the essential determinant of the system was the market—though a market quite different from that envisaged by the old free trade ideology and in many ways a very imperfect one—and in the other political authority was the decisive factor.

Neither economic system remained unchanged, and contacts between them multiplied as the years passed. Nonetheless they were in competition, often as models of economic growth for underdeveloped nations. This competition had been negligible before 1945 but was inflamed by the political struggles of the cold war. It also actually helped to spread the basic political antagonisms. In due course the one system came to be less completely dominated by the United States and the other less completely dominated by Russia than in the 1940s and both contributed to the continuing phenomenon of growth, which is the prevailing theme of world economic history in the 1950s and (a little less markedly) in the 1960s. But the distinction between two economic systems remains fundamental to an understanding of the pattern of world economic development since 1945 for it shut off some possibilities and suggested others.

The entry of China into the socialist economic bloc was of course of great importance but it tended to be seen almost purely in cold war terms and other significances of what had happened were somewhat masked. In fact by the time of Stalin's death there were other signs that the prophecy made a quarter-century before that the center of world politics was shifting away from Europe to the Far East and the Pacific was already realized. Although the German problem persisted as the focus of the cold war, Korea was only the most striking event revealing that the center of gravity of world history had moved decisively from Europe to the Orient.

ASIAN REVOLUTION

The collapse of imperial power in Asia was bound to be followed by further changes as new states came to be aware of their own interests and power. In some instances they only had the shape and unity they possessed because of imperial rule; India's was partially dissolved at the moment of independence; Malaysia and Indochina were to undergo changes. Many new states had important religious or ethnic distinctions within them. Some, such as Singapore and Indonesia, had large numbers of Chinese under their rule and they were often economically in the ascendant. Another shared characteristic which was almost certain to produce tensions and therefore pressure for change was that nearly all these countries had to grapple with fast population growth and economic backwardness. Yet in spite of these difficulties a few very quickly displayed the self-assertiveness of new nations.

India and Pakistan

Within a few years India swallowed the semi-autonomous princely states which had survived during the Raj and the remaining enclaves of French and Portuguese territory. India's relations with other countries quickly turned out to be more difficult, especially those with her neighbor Pakistan. This was mainly because of Kashmir, a princely state in the north with a majority of Muslims but a Hindu prince. When in 1947 Muslims tried to bring about union with Pakistan, the maharajah of Kashmir asked for Indian help and brought his state into the Indian republic. To make matters worse, the spokesmen for the Muslim population of Kashmir were themselves divided. India refused to hold the plebiscite there recommended by the United Nations Security Council and the question became a running sore in Indo-Pakistani relations, some two-thirds of Kashmir remaining in Indian hands while the rest was disputed. Fighting went on until 1949, then broke out again in 1965–1966 and once more in 1969–1970. The Kashmir issue was further complicated by disputes about boundary demarcation, which involved minorities on the wrong side of the border, and about the fair use of the waters of the Indus River.

In its relations with Pakistan (as with the princes and the Portuguese enclaves) the Indian government has shown the ambition of the Congress party to reunite the subcontinent. But the behavior of outside powers has at times cut across efforts at unification. India soon asserted her determination to remain independent of either side in the cold war. In practice this meant warmer relations with Russia and Communist China than with the United States in the 1950s, and indeed Prime Minister Nehru appeared to relish opportunities for criticizing American action. This paralleled the adoption of a mildly socialist program in domestic affairs. It came as a shock therefore to the Indian public to learn in 1959 that armed conflict had been going on for about three years with Chinese forces on the northern borders of India. At the end of 1962 large-scale fighting broke out and Nehru took the improbable step of asking the Americans for military aid; even more improbably, he got it at the same time as he received aid from Russia.

After the achievement of independence Pakistan found herself in a much weaker position than India. She had only a tiny trained civil service (Hindus had joined the civil service under the Raj in much larger numbers

Hunger in India, 1948. A desperate crowd struggles for the small bits of food being distributed. *(Henri Cartier-Bresson/Magnum)*

than Muslims), was divided geographically by India, and almost at once lost her ablest political leader, Mahomed Ali Jinnah. There was another important difference between the two countries: Pakistan was an Islamic state, and the Indian republic was constitutionally secular and uncommitted to any particular religious confession. After a turbulent period a general, Ayub Khan, took power in 1958 and led Pakistan along the path of what was called "guided democracy," which provided village councils in which the masses could vote but superimposed on them a somewhat authoritarian regime. Ayub Khan's policies were to ensure military survival against India and economic development including land reform. They did not prove successful in the long run and in 1972 Pakistan underwent disruption when East Pakistan rebels, acting with Indian encouragement, broke away to set up the new state of Bangladesh. India meanwhile preserved parliamentary forms until 1975, when the Prime Minister deprived them of much of their reality by imprisoning members of the opposition, imposing censorship of the press and radio, and forbidding the full reporting of parliamentary proceedings. Thus India too finally succumbed to the tendency toward authoritarianism which, almost alone among former imperial possessions, she had until then seemed able to resist.

Like other Asian nations, India and Pakistan had to conduct their foreign policies in a world apparently divided into two camps by the cold war. This led Pakistan in the early 1950s to lean toward the non-Communist West. But as the decade went on, a new grouping made its appearance and for a time confused the patterns of diplomacy. This was the association of professedly neutral countries which became known by the vague and sometimes misleading term of the "third world" after a meeting of representatives of twenty-nine African and Asian states at Bandung, Indonesia, in 1954. The group was later enlarged to include Yugoslavia.

In general the third world nations were former colonial territories, poor and needy, more suspicious of the United States than Russia, and more attracted to China than to Russia, but the term is unsatisfactory in that these similarities mask important differences. The coherence of third world politics was not to prove very enduring, and this is not surprising given the huge differences between the neutralist states and their diverging interests. Nevertheless they demonstrated that the weak had power if they chose to use it and that greater states in search of allies would have to take account of it.

In the 1950s the relations of China and Russia with the Bandung countries had already begun to indicate a divergence of interest between the two Communist powers: each wished to claim the leadership of the underdeveloped and uncommitted world. One result was the paradox of Pakistan drawing closer to China (in spite of a treaty with the United States) and India closer to Russia as the 1950s wore on. Pakistan's own border disputes with China were settled amicably, and after the United States declined to supply arms during her 1965 war with India, Pakistan turned to the Chinese. Though she got much less than she had hoped for, this was an example of the new fluidity beginning to mark international affairs in the 1960s.

China as a world power

In retrospect it may be thought notable that the Chinese Communists chose Peking as their capital. It seemed to indicate that China might again be more aware of pressure from her land frontiers in the north than of the threat she had faced for a century from the sea. However this may be, Russia was the first state to recognize the Chinese People's Republic, closely followed by the British, Indian, and Burmese governments.

Given cold war preoccupations elsewhere and the circumstances of the Nationalist collapse, the new China did not immediately face any real threat from the outside to distract her rulers from the long overdue task of modernization. When one did materialize, as the United Nations forces approached the Yalu River frontier between Manchuria and Korea in 1950, the Chinese reaction was strong and immediate: they sent a large army to Korea. But the main preoccupation of the first years of Communist rule was the internal state of the country. This presented formidable problems. Material and physical construction and reconstruction were desperately needed, population pressure on land loomed as seriously as ever, and the moral and ideological void presented by the collapse of the old Chinese culture in the preceding forty years had to be filled.

The peasants were the starting point. For them the establishment of the new republic is not a very significant date. It only punctuated a process of

Rural reform in China required redistribution of land. Here peasants are engaged in surveys preparatory to the reform. *(Eastfoto)*

land reform which had been going on since 1946 and was largely carried out by the peasants themselves, under party leadership, in contrast to the Russian experience. The result was a continuation of the distinctiveness of China's course; collectivization (completed by 1956) was coupled with a social transformation of the villages which gave control of the new units to the peasants themselves. The essential element was the overthrow of the local village leaders and landlords. This was by no means a peaceful process and such persons no doubt made up a large portion of those 800,000 Chinese who were later reported by Mao to have been liquidated in the first five years of the People's Republic. Meanwhile China's First Five-Year Plan (1953–1957) pressed forward a program of industrialization. This depended largely upon Russian help, the only source from which China could draw, and by 1956 it had produced an increase in the Chinese production of manufactured goods and services greater than the increase in the production of food.

China was already acting as a major influence abroad, but her independence was long masked by the apparent unity of the Communist bloc just as her international position was clouded by her continued exclusion from the United Nations, largely the work of the United States. A Sino-Russian treaty in 1950 was the first landmark in foreign relations. It was interpreted abroad—especially in the United States—as evidence that China was entering the cold war on the Russian side. Certainly the regime was Communist and its choices were bound to be confined by the parameters of the cold war. It also used revolutionary and anticolonialist language. Yet in a longer perspective traditional concerns now seem from the start to have had important weight in Chinese policy. At a very early point China desired to reestablish her power within the area it had always tended to fill up. The securing of Manchuria was sufficient motive for Chinese military intervention in Korea, itself long an area of dispute between imperial China and Japan. The occupation of Tibet in 1951 was another incursion into a region which had previously been under Chinese suzerainty; inevitably it called into question border settlements with India which had been established by British force only forty years earlier, an interval hardly significant in Chinese notions of historical time.

The most vociferous demand made in the drive to consolidate the Chinese periphery was for the eviction of the Nationalist government from Taiwan. By 1955 Washington was so deeply committed to the support of the Nationalist regime there that President Eisenhower announced the United States must be prepared to fight not merely to defend Taiwan but also smaller Nationalist-held islands near the Chinese coast. The United States' interest in Chinese affairs tended to crystallize around this issue for over a decade. It seemed at times that the Chinese Nationalist tail was wagging the American dog. Conversely, during the 1950s both the Indian and Russian governments gave diplomatic support to Communist China, insisting that Taiwan was a matter of Chinese internal affairs. It was therefore all the more sensational when the next decade brought about such a deterioration of relations between China and both these powers that armed conflict followed.

The quarrel with India grew out of the initial Chinese occupation of Tibet and that country's reordering as an autonomous region under Chinese sovereignty. The pro-Chinese assumptions of Indian policy were still evident in 1959 when the Chinese further tightened their grasp on Tibet and the Indians discountenanced an attempt by Tibetan exiles to set up a government on Indian soil. But by that time the Chinese advance had provoked a series of territorial disputes, about which the public had not been told. These led to clashes between border guards even in 1959. In the course of discussing these incidents in the following year the Chinese announced that they did not consider the line drawn by a British-Tibetan negotiation in 1914, which had never been formally accepted by any Chinese government, to be the border with India. This was the background of the heavy fighting which broke out between Chinese and Indian forces in the autumn of 1962 when Nehru demanded a Chinese withdrawal from Indian territory. India had defense help not only from the United States but from Russia.

China and Russia

The world was startled when early in 1963 the Chinese Communist party suddenly and bitterly denounced Russia for, on the one hand, giving aircraft to India and, on the other, stopping economic and military aid to China in 1960. The second of these charges indicated a deep background of discord but by no means went to the root of the matter. There were some Chinese Communists, Mao among them, who could remember the consequences of subordinating the Chinese revolution to the international interests of communism, as interpreted by the Russians, as far back as the 1920s. A division had always persisted from those days between Russian and native forces in the leadership of the Chinese party. Mao represented the Sinicizing of Marxism; he envisaged a society different from that which had appeared in Soviet Russia as well as from that which existed in the capitalist countries. However, it was very difficult for outsiders to disentangle these strands because Chinese resentment of Russian policy had to be presented to the rest of the world in Marxist jargon. Almost accidentally, since the new leadership in Russia was engaged in dismantling the Stalin myth, this led the Chinese to become more Stalinist than Stalin in their public pronouncements just when they were pursuing policies of an anti-Stalinist nature at home.

Their dissatisfaction with Russian policy must also be placed in an even deeper historical setting. Well before the foundation of the Chinese Communist party the Chinese revolution had been a movement of national regeneration, one of whose primary aims was the recovery of China's control over her own destiny from the foreigners. The Russians were among those foreigners. There was a long history going back to Peter the Great of Russian encroachment upon the Chinese sphere. It had continued in the Soviet era. The protectorate over Tannu Tuva, for example, was established in 1914 by the tsars; the area was annexed by Russia in 1944. In 1945 Russian armies had entered Manchuria and northern China; they remained in Sinkiang until 1949, in Port Arthur until 1955. Even after the 1955 withdrawal Russia and China shared something like 4,500 miles of frontier (if Mongolia is included) and there was great potential for dispute along its length.

The personal views of Mao Tse-tung must also be taken into account. Although his intellectual formation was Marxist and although he found its categories helpful in explaining his country's predicament, he appears always to have combined with it a certain pragmatism which escaped Marxist dogma through a firm attachment to the lessons of experience. His attitude to knowledge and ideas was predominantly utilitarian and moralistic; he classified the whole complex of phenomena presenting itself to him at any time into contending forces on which human will power could then play to bring about creative change.

Mao's relationship with the Chinese Communist party had not always been smooth. His great opportunity had come when his policy toward the peasantry provided the party with a way ahead after disaster had overtaken it in the cities. After a temporary setback in the early 1930s he had virtually undisputed supremacy among the Chinese Communists from about 1935, which meant that the rural influences within the party were on top at last. There was also an enormous international potential for the new revolutionary strategy Mao had evolved; the notion of a protracted revolutionary war which would be waged from the countryside and carried into the towns was to have a huge influence in other parts of the world lacking the industrial development and revolutionary proletariat required by orthodox Marxism.

The Sino-Russian conflict had undoubtedly been accentuated by the withdrawal of Russian economic and technical help in 1960 just when China was in a particularly bad crisis. Natural disasters, such as floods (said by official sources to have affected 150 million acres of agricultural land), had followed the collapse of a massive economic offensive launched by Mao in 1958 — the Great Leap Forward. Its aim appears to have been to decentralize the economy and society into communes, of which there were some 25,000, thus setting aside centralized planning on the Russian model with its bureaucratic dangers and also calling directly upon the participation of local forces, from which the regime had previously benefited. What happened is obscure, but clearly the Great Leap failed. Mao himself was subsequently somewhat eclipsed until the later 1960s. By then his rivals had managed to put the economy back on the road to modernization. The most striking evidence was the explosion of Chinese nuclear weapons, the first in 1964. This was the expensive admission card to a very exclusive club. But probably more important was the fact that the regime managed to avoid crippling famine (though at a cost of importing Canadian grain) and to keep the loyalty of the people.

Though more slowly than in the early nineteenth century, the Chinese population had continued to rise — and to colossal totals. Reasonable estimates are 545 million in 1950, 685 million ten years later, and 750 million in the mid-1960s; by then China had about one-fifth of the world's population. Demographically China was stronger by the beginning of the 1960s than ever in history and this caused uneasiness abroad, for it seemed that her leaders were at least ready to contemplate the possibility of nuclear war;

their enormous population made it likely that the Chinese would survive in greater measure than the peoples of other countries. More positively, there were signs that Russia was alarmed by the presence of so great and densely populated a power on the border of her most thinly populated regions. Tension between the two great Communist states continued throughout the decade.

Some Chinese Communists were obviously determined to keep the revolution going. Much no doubt turned on the evidence of what had happened in the Soviet Union. The fear that in China too the revolution might become frozen and society rigidify under bureaucratic direction lay behind the Cultural Revolution of 1966–1969, which Mao launched after he reestablished his supremacy with the aid of the army. This huge upheaval, which swept through party and administration, was essentially an attempt to offset the danger that government officials were becoming a new sort of ruling elite. One of the means to stem this was to transform the traditional honor paid to the intellectuals in China by closing the universities and enforcing practical labor on all citizens. The ideological emphasis was upon self-sacrifice and subordination to the thought of Mao Tse-tung. By 1968 the country had been turned upside down as troops of young hotheads calling themselves Red Guards fought officialdom. In the end there were signs that Mao

Cultural revolution. A propaganda photograph of peasants studying quotations from the works of Chairman Mao. Such intensive indoctrination was an important part of the revolution in China and accorded well with the traditional Chinese assumptions about the importance of authoritative moral teaching. *(Eastfoto)*

believed things had gone too far. The army reestablished order and installed new party cadres which reconfirmed Mao's leadership at a party congress. One of the most interesting aspects of this still mysterious episode was its moral preoccupation. What was at stake, Mao clearly felt, was the danger that the revolution might congeal and lose the moral élan which had carried it so far.

Yet Communist China has no more than any other great state been able to escape her history. The continuities of Chinese foreign policy are one mark of this. Another is that Mao himself fits well into the Chinese popular tradition of the ruler-sage. He is presented as a teacher as much as a politician; Western commentators have been amused by the status given to his thoughts in the omnipresent "Little Red Book" (though there have been large areas of the West where similar attention has sometimes been given to the Bible), but the utterances of great teachers have always commanded respect in China. There is also something traditional in Mao's artistic interests; the people admire him as a poet and his poems are praised by qualified judges. No doubt the regime over which he presides benefits also from a more complex inheritance from the Chinese past, a certain attitude to authority. Power has traditionally been sanctioned in China by the notion that the ruler did good things for his people. This has made easier the acceptance of the authorities' action on behalf of the collective good. The Western notion of individualism never had a place in China.

Exported revolution

By 1963 there had appeared within world communism a clear contest between China and Russia for the leadership of revolution. This at first emerged obliquely through differing attitudes to developments in Yugoslavia. But it rapidly developed into a contest for influence inside the Communist movement and in Africa, Asia, and Latin America.

China's competitive patronage of world revolution was mingled with her traditional concerns in Indochina. After the Korean War the Chinese began to supply arms to the Communist guerrilla forces in South Vietnam. In 1953 the French had to give up Cambodia and Laos; in 1954 they lost the battle for a base at Dien Bien Phu in North Vietnam. It was decisive both for French prestige and for the determination of the French electorate to fight. After this it was impossible for the French to maintain themselves in the Red River delta, and a conference at Geneva agreed to partition Vietnam between the French and Vietminh, pending elections which might reunite the country. Although the French hung on for a couple of years, the Geneva conference was the end of French empire in Asia and the beginning of a catastrophic American entanglement in the area. By a bitter irony the cold war would gradually turn the anticolonialist United States of 1945, which had done so much to dismantle its allies' empires, into their replacement in Southeast Asia.

Strains were also appearing in the former Dutch possessions. President Sukarno faced formidable problems in the new Indonesian republic. The most obvious was a wide divergence of political interests, among which those of the Communists and the Muslims were the most obvious. There were the usual problems of overpopulation and underdevelopment and increasing resentment of central authority as the economic situation deteriorated under inflation. By 1957 the central government was in control only of Java, and attempts to employ the time-honored device of distracting opposition by a nationalist campaign (in this case against the continued Dutch occupation of West New Guinea) were not successful.

Under Sukarno's presidency the Indonesian government moved rapidly away from the liberal forms adopted at the birth of the new state toward another kind of "guided democracy." This meant leaning more heavily on Russian support and in 1960 brought the dismissal of parliament. In 1963 Sukarno was made president for life. With American support (usually forthcoming because of fears that Sukarno might turn to China for help) Indonesia absorbed the independent state which had emerged from West New Guinea. Sukarno then turned to confront the new federation of Malaysia, set up in 1957. Attacks were begun on Borneo and Sarawak and eventually on the Malayan mainland. With British help these were repulsed. Although he still enjoyed American support, this failure seems to have been the turning point for Sukarno. Only the distraction of foreign adventure had enabled him to ride the storm at home, where food shortages and inflation were out of control. The details of what followed are obscure, but it seems that Sukarno attempted to forestall his opponents by killing a number of army officers. This antagonized the armed forces, and they then stood back and allowed a popular massacre of Communists, which removed possible support on which he might have relied. Sukarno was then set aside by a military regime in 1966.

American sympathy for Sukarno reflected the belief that the best defense against Communism was the existence of strong and prosperous national regimes. Unfortunately the knowledge that they could depend on American support often removed the incentive to carry out essential reforms to unite people behind these regimes. This was especially true in Vietnam, where the de facto partition had not produced good or stable government in the south. While Buddhists and Roman Catholics quarreled bitterly and the peasants were more and more alienated from the regime by the failure of land reform, an apparently corrupt ruling class seemed able to survive government after government. This was a situation which benefited the Communists. The Vietminh sought reunification on their own terms and maintained from the north support for the Communist underground movement in the south, the Vietcong.

In the late 1950s French influence in Indochina was replaced by American. But by 1960 the Vietcong controlled large areas of the south in defiance of the Saigon government. This was the background to a momentous decision taken by President John F. Kennedy in 1962: he authorized the dispatch not only of financial and material help but also of 4,000 American "advisers" to help the South Vietnamese government put its military house in order. This was the beginning of a road leading to the situation Truman had been determined to avoid—the involvement of the United States in a major war on the mainland of Asia.

Japan's revival

American efforts to obtain influence in Asia led also to safeguarding as long as possible a special position which accrued to the United States from the occupation of Japan. This had been possible because of the Russian delay in declaring war on Japan and the speed of Japan's surrender, which had taken Stalin by surprise. The Americans firmly rejected Russian requests for a share in the occupation they had done nothing to bring about. The results of the American presence were quite unpredictable; the Japanese once more demonstrated their astonishing gift for learning from others only what they wished to learn while safeguarding their own society against fundamental change.

When the war ended in their defeat, the Japanese faced deep and troubling problems. These went far beyond the questions of physical reconstruction and concerned their national identity and purpose. The Westernization of the Meiji era had eventually produced the dream of "Asia for the Asians." This was now blown away by defeat. It had really meant a kind of Japanese Monroe Doctrine and though the slogan might be realized in a different sense by the rolling back of colonialism, Japan was left without an obvious role in that process. Moreover the war had shown Japan's vulnerability; like the United Kingdom, she had depended on shipping and was doomed once she lost control of the sea. The experience of powerlessness was an additional fact for the Japanese to grapple with in the postwar world. Then there were the terms of defeat: the loss of domestic territory to Russia on Sakhalin and the occupation by the Americans. Finally, there was the physical and human destruction to repair.

On the credit side the Japanese had the unshaken central institution of the monarchy; the emperor's prestige was undimmed and indeed had made possible the surrender. The American commander in the Pacific, General MacArthur, believed in the importance of maintaining the monarchy as an instrument of a peaceful occupation and took care to have a new Japanese constitution adopted before republican enthusiasts in the United States could interfere. There was also a great resource in Japanese social cohesiveness and discipline, though for a time it seemed that the American occupation might undermine this by the determination with which it pressed democratic institutions upon the Japanese. This democratic education appeared successful enough by 1951 for a peace treaty to be made between Japan and most of her former opponents except the Russians and Nationalist Chinese. (The Chinese concluded one the following year and the Russians in 1956.) The 1951 treaty restored to the Japanese their full sovereignty including the right to arm themselves for defensive purposes. With it went the cession of virtually all Japanese overseas possessions. Thus Japan emerged from the postwar era stripped of empire but once again in control of her own affairs (although an agreement with the United States provided for the maintenance of American forces on her soil).

This much reduced status was in less than twenty years to be transformed again by two interconnected factors, foreign affairs and economic

Post-war recovery; building supertankers in Japanese yards. *(Consulate General of Japan, New York)*

growth. They had begun to operate even before the peace treaty. The cold war had quite changed the implications of the American occupation. Japan was separated from the territories of Russia and China, the two largest Communist states, by respectively 10 and 500 miles of water; she was only 150 miles from Korea. The spread of the cold war guaranteed Japan even better treatment from the United States, now anxious to display a working example of democracy and capitalism in Asia. It also gave her the protection of the United States nuclear umbrella. While the Korean War went on, Japan had a new importance as a base, and this galvanized her economy. The war put Japanese industrial production back to the level of the 1930s. The United States also became anxious to promote Japanese interests abroad. Finally, these benefits were until 1951 unaccompanied by the burden of defense costs since Japan was forbidden to have armed forces until the peace treaty.

Japan's close connection with the United States, her proximity to the Communist world, and her advanced and stable economy and society all made it natural that before long she should be seen as a potential ally by Washington. The most important early American allies in the Far East had been Australia, New Zealand, and the Philippines (given independence in

1946). In 1954 came the complement to NATO—the Southeast Asia Treaty Organization, or SEATO. It was less effective than its elder brother because Pakistan, Thailand, and the Philippines were the only Asian countries to join; Indonesia and, much more important, India remained aloof.

In seeking such a spread of alliances American policy reflected the new conditions of Pacific and Asian international relations after the British withdrawal from India. The maintenance of British forces east of Suez was to go on a little longer, but the dominions of Australia and New Zealand had discovered during the Second World War that the United Kingdom could not defend them and the United States could. The fall of Singapore in 1942 had been a decisive moment. By the 1960s, though the British supported the Malaysians against the Indonesians, their important colony at Hong Kong survived, they knew, only because it suited the Chinese that it should and they did not pretend any longer to be a great imperial power. If anyone was to play the role of protector of the area against communism, it had to be the United States. On the other hand, there was no question of overcoming the complexities of the new Pacific by simply lining up states in the teams of the cold war. The Japanese peace treaty itself caused great difficulty because the United States saw Japan as a potential anti-Communist force while others— notably Australia and New Zealand—remembered 1941 and feared a revival of Japanese power.

Thus in the early 1960s American policy was much more than the simple expression of ideology. Nonetheless it was unduly influenced by what was believed to be the disaster of the Communist victory in China. The people who felt this pointed to Chinese patronage of revolutionaries as far away as Africa and South America, but such examples were misleading. China's primary revolutionary impact was as an Asian power; what gave her sympathizers and supporters in every Asian country was the fact that in a sense she led all Asians who resented the West. China was bringing to a victorious conclusion at least a hundred years' war of East and West. The revolution in China's position lay in this rather than merely in the adoption of a Western ideology. China was emerging again as a power in her own right after over a century of eclipse and this in the end was bound to make nonsense of the dualist, cold war system. Though at first operating within the former Chinese sphere only, her growing strength was bound to bring about a big change in relative power relationships. The first indication of this was seen in Korea, where American land power was stopped and it became necessary to consider whether air power should be used against China. But the rise of China was also of the most acute importance to Russia, which from one pole of a bipolarized system was gradually becoming the corner of a triangle, to say nothing of losing her unchallenged preeminence in the world revolutionary movement.

THE POSTIMPERIAL ERA IN THE MIDDLE EAST AND AFRICA

The establishment of Israel was the first of three big changes in the Arab world after 1945; the others were the coming to it of the cold war and the huge rise in the world's consumption of oil. The appearance of Israel provided a focus for Arab nationalism. About the injustice of the seizure of what were regarded as Arab lands, the need for the Palestine refugees to return, and the obligations of the great powers and the United Nations to act on their behalf, all the Arab states were able to agree. After their defeat in 1948–1949 they were not for some time disposed again to commit their own forces openly though there were continuing border incidents in the early 1950s; they relied more on raids on Israel from Egyptian and Syrian territory by bands of young guerrilla soldiers recruited from Arab refugee camps.

During this time Israel consolidated her position. A series of armistices in 1949 established de facto borders with Jordan, Syria, and Egypt; they were to last until 1967 though the formal state of war was to last too. The sense of siege gave stability to Israeli politics; the prestige of the party which had brought about the very existence of the new state was scarcely troubled. Helped by a flow of official and unofficial aid from abroad—above all from the United States—the Jews set about the transformation of their land. Within a few years they could show massive progress in bringing barren land under cultivation and establishing industries. The gap between Israel's per capita income and that of the Arab states widened steadily.

In this gap too there was an irritant for Arab nationalism. Although Arab countries received foreign aid, it did not produce in their condition anything like the dramatic change that appeared in Israel. This was largely because the most important Arab states were the poorest. Egypt for example faced, like other underdeveloped countries, grave problems posed by a high rate of population growth and had no oil revenue to help her. This social strain encouraged continuing agitation against the foreigners. The British, who still had a garrison in Egypt, were now blamed for their part in allowing the establishment of Israel. The British government did its best to cooperate with the Arab states because it feared Russian pressure in an area of traditional strategic importance to the United Kingdom.

Arab nationalism and the cold war

One of the weaknesses of Arab nationalism had always been its inability to transcend its own divisions. Within the Arab world the Hashemite kingdoms, the Arabian sheikdoms, and the Europeanized urban states of North Africa and the Levant had both divergent interests and very different historical traditions. Such a lack of cohesion gave added importance to the Israeli issue, which provided a common enemy, and to the appearance in Egypt of a leader who for a time seemed able to unite much of the Arab world. This was a young soldier, Gamal Abdel Nasser, who emerged in 1954 from the military junta which had overthrown the monarchy two years previously.

In the early 1950s strong anti-Western currents were appearing everywhere in the Arab world. In 1951 the king of Jordan was assassinated, and his successor had to demonstrate that he had severed the old special tie with Great Britain if he was to survive. At the other end of the Mediterranean the French had been forced to recognize the complete independence of Morocco and Tunisia soon after the war, and in 1954 an Algerian national rebellion began. This was to become a full-scale war because the French government was not disposed to abandon a country where there were over a million settlers of French blood and where oil had just been discovered in the Sahara. In these circumstances Nasser looked like a possible pan-Arab leader. He presented a program of social reform and nationalism which seemed a model for emerging Arab nations and his anti-Israeli feelings were not in doubt. One of his first successes was the negotiation at last of a treaty with Great Britain which provided for the evacuation of her forces within twenty months. The Americans, increasingly aware of the Russian menace in the Middle East, looked on him with favor as a spotless anticolonialist and potential client.

But Nasser's independence soon led to the waning of his attractiveness in American eyes. The guerrilla raids on Israel from Egyptian territory (the Gaza strip, where the most important Palestinian refugee camps lay) provoked retaliation. The British, French, and Americans had said in 1950 that they would supply no arms to anyone in the area and so Nasser turned to the Communists. This brought the cold war seriously to the Middle East. When Egypt won an arms deal with Czechoslovakia (on the security of her cotton crop) and recognized Communist China, the United States had second thoughts about Nasser.

By way of indicating displeasure, the United States and Great Britain withdrew an earlier offer to finance a cherished project of internal development, a high dam at Aswan on the Nile. As a riposte Nasser seized the assets of the Suez Canal, which was run by a private international company, saying its profits should finance the dam. This action touched the old nerve of British imperial sensibility. For once it seemed possible to pursue in British policy a line which fitted well with both American irritation and anticommunism, and with British friendship with more traditional Arab rulers who looked askance at Nasser. Ironically the loss of India had not made Suez seem less important, for now a new question had arisen, that of the safety of the oil supplies brought through the Canal from the Persian Gulf. The British and French protested; the latter felt they had an additional grievance in Nasser's support for the Algerian insurrection. At this moment, in October 1956, the Israelis suddenly invaded Egypt to destroy, they said, the bases from which guerrillas harassed their settlements. The British and French now claimed that freedom of transit through the Canal was in danger and called for a cease-fire; when Nasser rejected this, they launched first an air attack and then a seaborne invasion of Egypt. Their collusion with the Israeli government was denied but widely credited. By this time the Americans were thoroughly alarmed; they saw a danger of Russian profit from this resurrection of imperialism. Their financial pressure forced the British to accept a cease-fire negotiated by the United Nations.

Though in the long run the Suez affair had little importance, it was disastrous in the short run for Western interests in the Middle East. It also badly distracted the West from events in Eastern Europe, where the Russian army was engaged in crushing a revolution in Hungary. The Anglo-French and Israeli invasions confirmed Arab hatred of Israel and the suspicion that she was indissolubly linked to the West; the Arabs therefore became yet more receptive to approaches from the East. But the essentials of Middle East history continued more or less as before. One was the continued inflammation of Arab nationalism.

Suez had raised Nasser's prestige among Arabs even higher, and one mark of this was the temporary union of Syria and Egypt in the United Arab Republic in 1958. The hitherto pro-Western government of Lebanon was overthrown in the following year; Iraq's monarchy was also swept aside by revolution and a general took power there. But soon the differences between Arab countries asserted themselves. The world watched the curious spectacle of American forces being summoned to Lebanon and British to Jordan for brief periods to help maintain the regimes there. Meanwhile fighting went on sporadically on the Syrian-Israeli border. But the most important event in the Islamic Arab world prior to 1967 was the final success of the Algerian revolution. The intransigence of the French settlers and the bitterness of many soldiers who felt they were asked to do an impossible job nearly brought about a revolution in France herself. A government under General de Gaulle nevertheless opened secret negotiations with the Algerian provisional government in Cairo in June 1960, and in July 1962 France formally granted independence to Algeria.

Libya had become independent under United Nations trusteeship at the end of the war, thus the entire North African coast was now clear of European domination. Suez had only been a flash in the pan. Yet foreign influences still bedeviled Arab history as they had done ever since the Ottoman conquests centuries before. They were now being exercised indirectly, through aid and diplomacy, as the United States and Russia sought to buy friends among the Arab states. Washington labored under the disadvantage of not being able to abandon Israel because of the importance of Zionist sympathy among American voters. Also Arab policy had more and more alienated the United States since 1946. Moscow, on the other hand, had quickly abandoned its initial support of Israel once that had ceased to be a useful weapon with which to embarrass the British. The Russians pursued a steady pro-Arab line and exploited Arab resentment of the survivals of British imperialism still to be found at Aden and in the Persian Gulf. Indeed, by the treatment of their own Jewish people in the later 1960s, the Russians were to earn a certain bonus of Arab approval very cheaply.

Oil

The other factor slowly changing the terms of the Middle Eastern situation was oil. In the 1950s two important developments occurred. One was a much greater rate of oil discovery than hitherto, particularly on the southern shores of the Persian Gulf, in the areas of the small sheikdoms then still under British influence and in Saudi Arabia. The second was the great acceleration of energy consumption in Western countries, especially in the United States, which has gone on ever since. The major beneficiaries of this

Egyptian soldiers throng the streets of Cairo after the Six-Day War carrying death's-head banners and calling for Arab unity. *(Paris Match from Pictorial Parade)*

growing demand were Saudi Arabia, Libya, Kuwait, and then, some way behind, Iraq. There were two important consequences. The great powers which were dependent upon Middle Eastern oil—and this meant the United States, Great Britain, Germany, and increasingly Japan—had to take this dependence into account in their diplomacy in the area. The discoveries also meant big changes in the relative importance of states within the Arab world. None of the three leading oil producers was heavily populated or traditionally a very important Arab state, unless Saudi. abia is thought to have been.

The full impact of these developments was still not apparent in the last Middle East crisis of the decade, that of 1967. This began to mount when a much more extreme Syrian government took power and presented an obvious challenge to Nasser for the leadership of the Arab world. The king of Jordan was also threatened if he did not act in support of the Palestinian guerrilla forces (organized since 1964 as the Palestine Liberation Organization). The Egyptians and Jordanians therefore began to group their forces for an attack on Israel. The Israelis struck first. In a brilliant campaign they destroyed the Egyptian air force and army in the Sinai desert and hurled back the Jordanians. In six days' fighting they acquired frontiers on the Suez Canal, the Golan Heights, and the Jordan River which were infinitely superior to their previous ones for defense, and they announced that they would keep them.

Decolonization in Africa

Only in Algeria was the making of a new post-colonial Africa marked by major bloodshed, though there was plenty of violence in the post-colonial era. The colonial powers in Africa, with the exception of Portugal, ceded their authority peacefully and tried to retain some sort of influence by showing benevolent interest in their former subjects. The new African states had as their principal defining characteristics the boundaries of former colonies. There was not the offsetting influence of great indigenous civilizations to counteract Europe's division of the continent, as there had been in Asia. The result was a Balkanization of Africa, since the doctrine of nationalism, which appealed to Westernized African elites, both fragmented the continent anew and ignored important realities which the theory and practice of colonialism had been able to contain or manipulate. The most important of these realities was the persistence of important tribal and religious divisions.

The economic and social foundations for a prosperous African future were also shaky. The population of Africa is not large; the most populous state, Nigeria, contains about a quarter of the total. The whole continent could not expect to exercise as much weight in international affairs as some individual Asian countries. Colonial regimes too had left behind less cultural and economic infrastructure than in Asia. Rates of literacy were low. Potentially Africa had (and has) important economic resources, especially mineral, but exploiting and marketing them required facilities for which Africans had to turn to the world outside. This would long continue to be the case. In these circumstances it is not surprising that discontent and disillusion sometimes followed the process of decolonization.

In 1945 the only completely independent countries in Africa were Egypt, Ethiopia, and Liberia. The Union of South Africa was a self-governing dominion of the British Commonwealth and is therefore only technically excluded from this category, and a slightly vaguer status also cloaked the virtual independence of the British crown colony of Southern Rhodesia. By 1961, when South Africa was a republic outside the British Commonwealth, twenty-three new states had come into existence and more were to follow. By 1970 only the Portuguese retained their colonial possessions and they were gone five years later.

There were two bad outbreaks of strife during these decades of transformation. In the former Belgian Congo an attempt at secession by the mineral-rich region of Katanga provoked a civil war in which Russian and American influences quickly became entangled and the United Nations strove to restore peace in the early 1960s. Then at the end of the decade came a distressing civil war in Nigeria, hitherto one of the most stable and promising of the new African states. In almost all of them (even the traditional monarchy of Ethiopia) the need, real or imaginary, to suppress open dissent and strengthen central authority for reforming policies led by the 1970s to one-party, authoritarian government or to the interference of the military, paralleling the history of the South American states after the wars of liberation.

The completeness and rapidity of decolonization in Africa and its geographical remoteness, to say nothing of the lack of real power of the new states, tended to focus nationalist resentments not on the former imperial rulers but on the racial division of black and white. Unhappily this division was flagrant in the most powerful African state, the Boer-dominated Union of South Africa. Here resentments which went back as far as the Great Trek in the 1830s had led to the progressive destruction of ties with the British Commonwealth in the years after the First World War. South Africa had entered the second and supplied important forces to fight in it, but even then intransigent Boers had supported a movement favoring cooperation with the Nazis. It was the leader of this movement who became prime minister in 1948. With the steady Boer conquest of power inside South Africa, the prospect of imposing a racial policy which departed from the deep Boer prejudices was inconceivable. The eventual result was a system of separation of the races—apartheid—which embodied and reinforced the systematic reduction of the black African to an inferior status.

This system appealed—on even less excusable grounds than the primitive superstitions of the Boers—to white people elsewhere in Africa. The only country with a similar balance of black and white population and a similar concentration of wealth was Southern Rhodesia, which, to the great embarrassment of the British government, seceded from the Commonwealth in 1965 to begin an evolution toward a society similar to that of South Africa. There was nothing that the African states could effectively do about this, and not much that the United Nations or the United Kingdom could do. An embargo on trade with Rhodesia was decreed, but enforcement was left to individual countries. South Africa and Rhodesia, together with the Portuguese colonies so long as they survived, were increasingly the object of African anger but pursued their way in isolation, South Africa, at least, secure as the richest state on the continent. On a much reduced scale and with different complications for the great powers, there was something like an Israeli-Arab situation in the making south of the Zambezi River by 1970. Five years later, though, the worst had still not occurred. There were even some grounds for hopefulness. The South African government showed itself willing to seek better relations with black African nations and acquiesced in some diminution of the practical rigor of apartheid at home. The most important fact in bringing this about was Portugal's abandonment of her African colonies. This had also the effect of making concessions by Southern Rhodesia more likely because it closed communications with the Indian Ocean which had enabled the regime to escape the full effects of economic sanctions. Perhaps a violent end to white supremacy could, after all, be avoided in southern Africa.

LATIN AMERICA

By the end of the nineteenth century many of the Latin American states had settled down to prosperity and stability. Their upper classes were highly Europeanized; to the original colonial implantation of culture had been added the influence of nineteenth-century France, which had appealed to the

Latin American elites in the post-colonial period. Although manufacturing industry was inconsiderable — almost all of these states were primary producers — Latin America was relatively highly urbanized. In some countries large-scale immigration in the nineteenth century had further emphasized the European characteristics of the towns. But this did not present these countries with the problems of nineteenth-century Europe. The only important revolution in a Latin American state (as opposed to mere changes of personnel between the Wars of Liberation and the Cuban crisis of 1961), the one which overthrew the Mexican dictator Porfirio Díaz in 1911, was carried out essentially by a middle class which felt excluded from the benefits of the regime, not by an industrial proletariat. Indeed it was noticeable that Latin American countries did not appear to share the class conflict which had emerged in industrialized Europe.

Relatively stable, prosperous societies, linked to Europe and North America by dependence upon their capital and markets, thus survived the First World War. Then came the world economic crisis; 1929 was for the Latin American states the doorway to a new and unpleasant era, the beginning of their twentieth century. The collapse of prosperity led to growing nationalist assertiveness, sometimes against other Latin American states, sometimes against the North Americans and Europeans; both Mexico and Bolivia expropriated foreign oil companies. The traditional Europeanized oligarchies were compromised by their failure to meet the problems posed by falling national incomes. From 1930 onward there were military coups in every country except Mexico.

The Second World War brought an improvement as commodity prices again rose. Another of its effects was that it revealed the dependence of Latin America on the United States and Europe for manufactured goods; now there were not enough to go around. In consequence an intensive drive to industrialize gathered speed in many countries. The urban work forces industrialization built up gave rise to a new kind of political power, which entered the lists as a competitor with the military and the traditional elites in the postwar era. It took the form of authoritarian but popular mass movements led by a new kind of strong man. Juan Perón, who came to power in Argentina in 1946, was the most famous, but Colombia in 1957 and Venezuela in 1959 threw up similar regimes. It was striking that Communists had no such conspicuous success among the masses.

Big brother

A significant change in the exercise of the preponderant power of the United States has been another continuing feature of the continent's life since 1900. In the first twenty years of the century the armed forces of the United States intervened directly no fewer than twenty times in the affairs of neighboring republics. The United States even went so far on occasion as to establish protectorates over Haiti and the Dominican Republic. After 1920 there were only two such interventions before the Second World War, in Honduras in 1924 and in Nicaragua two years later. Indirect pressure also declined. Yet after 1950 there was again a change of direction. While Washington had not been unduly alarmed by the earlier manifestations of Latin American nationalism—which always tended to find a target in American policy—it became increasingly concerned lest the hemisphere provide a lodgment for Russian influence. This led to covert operations, for example, to overthrow in 1954 a government in Guatemala which had Communist support and, much more importantly, in support of a conservative revolution against a left-wing government in Chile in 1972.

This was somewhat paradoxical, for at the same time the United States was anxious that the footholds provided for communism by poverty and discontent should be removed. It made available much more economic aid (Latin America had received only a fraction of what had gone to Europe and Asia in the 1950s) and interested itself in governments which proclaimed they sought social reform. Unfortunately whenever such governments moved to eradicate American control of capital by nationalizing American companies, American policy swung around into opposition. Yet acceptable compensation would have required payments on such a scale as to make reform very difficult. On the whole therefore, while it might deplore the excesses of an individual regime, such as that in Cuba before 1958, Washington tended to find itself, as in Asia, supporting conservative interests opposed to social progress. This was not true in every instance; some governments achieved improvements and a notable example was land reform in Bolivia in 1952. But such success was rare. The Indian peasants remained the most oppressed class in Latin America and had virtually no hearing from any regime, whether populist or conservative; both listened only to the towns.

Cuban revolution

In spite of American nervousness, the revolutionary potential for change in Latin America remained low. This was one of the lessons of the sole successful revolution, that carried out with momentous consequences in Cuba.

Cuba was in a number of respects a very exceptional case. One was geographical; the island's position in the Caribbean within a relatively short distance of the United States made it of particular strategic significance. The whole area of the approaches to the Panama Canal Zone had even more importance in American defense than Suez had in British strategy. In the second place, Cuba had been especially badly hit in the depression; she was virtually dependent on one crop, sugar, and that crop had only one important outlet, the United States. This economic tie was only one of several factors which gave Cuba a closer "special relationship" with the United States than any other Latin American country. There were historic connections in American sympathy and help in the struggle for independence before 1898. Until 1934 Cuba's constitution had included special provisions restricting her diplomatic freedom and the United States still has a naval base on the island to this day. There was heavy American investment in urban property and utilities, and Cuba's poverty and low prices made the country an attractive holiday resort for Americans. All in all there was no shortage of reasons for Cuba to produce, as she did, a nationalist movement which was especially anti-American.

Inevitably the United States was seen as the real power behind the conservative postwar Cuban regime. Under the dictator Batista, who came to power in 1952, this in fact ceased to be so; the State Department disapproved of him and cut off aid to his government in 1957. By then a young nationalist doctor, Fidel Castro, had already begun a guerrilla campaign against the dictator. Success came swiftly. In 1959 he became prime minister of a revolutionary Cuba, describing his regime as "humanistic" and specifically not Communist.

Castro's original views are still not known. Perhaps he was himself not clear what he thought. From the start he worked with a wide spectrum of people from liberals to Marxists who wanted to overthrow Batista. This helped to reassure the United States government, which patronized him as a Caribbean Sukarno, while American public opinion idolized him as a romantic figure. But the relationship quickly soured when Castro turned to nationalizing American business concerns, starting with an agrarian reform which required the nationalization of sugar interests. He also denounced Americanized elements in Cuban society which had upheld the old regime. Soon the United States broke off diplomatic relations. Other kinds of pressure followed. Before long the American administration was convinced that Cuba was likely to fall into the hands of Communists, upon whom Castro increasingly relied. It did not help when Khrushchev warned the United States of the danger of acting militarily aginst Cuba and declared the Monroe Doctrine dead; the State Department quickly announced that it was alive. Finally, after Castro had declared himself a Marxist, the United States government decided to promote his overthrow by force.

The plans for ousting Castro were to be carried out by Cuban exiles. All was under way when the presidency changed hands. John Kennedy thus inherited a policy which he had not initiated, but he was not cautious or thoughtful enough to impede its continuation. This was a grave failure because there was much else in the new president's attitude to Latin America, where it had long been obvious that the United States needed to cultivate good will, which promised well. As it was, the possibilities of a more positive approach were blown to pieces by the fiasco known as the Bay of Pigs operation—an invasion of Cuban exiles supported by American money and arms which came to a miserable end in April 1961. Cuban policy now turned in earnest toward Russia. At the end of the year Castro declared himself a Marxist-Leninist.

Thus the cold war was at last truly extended to the Western hemisphere, and it had started badly for the United States, which incurred disapproval everywhere for its attempt to overthrow a genuinely popular and solidly based regime. From then on Cuba was a revolutionary magnet in Latin America. Castro's government pressed forward with policies which, together with American pressure, badly damaged the economy but also showed that the regime was egalitarian and intent on achieving real social reform, even if through an equality of poverty.

The missile crisis

Almost as a by-product of the Cuban revolution came a crisis which gave Cuba a place in world history, and out of it grew the most serious confrontation of the whole cold war and perhaps its turning point.

We do not yet know how it was decided that the Russians should install in Cuba missiles capable of reaching anywhere in the United States and thus roughly doubling the number of American bases or cities which were potential targets. Nor is it known where the initiative came from, though it seems likeliest that it was Russian. But whatever the circumstances, photographic reconnaissance confirmed in October 1962 that the Russians were building missile sites in Cuba. President Kennedy waited for incontrovertible proof and then announced that the United States navy would stop any ship delivering missiles to Cuba and demanded that those already on the island be withdrawn. The Americans boarded and searched one Lebanese ship in the days that followed; Russian ships were only observed. The American nuclear striking force was prepared for war. After a few days and some exchanges of personal letters between Kennedy and Khrushchev, the latter agreed to remove the missiles.

The Cuban missile crisis by far transcended the history of the hemisphere. Its repercussions for the rest of the world are best discussed elsewhere, but it revealed that, although the United States was prepared to promise to refrain from invading Cuba and thus appeared to accept Russian protection of the Castro regime, that state was not really of interest to the Russians except as a pawn in their own game of international chess.

The United States continued its attempt to isolate Cuba from the rest of the hemisphere, but this was ultimately a sterile hope. The appeal of Cuba's revolution seemed for awhile to gain ground among the young in other countries, which did not make Latin American governments more sympathetic toward Castro. Their antipathy increased as he began to make claims that Cuba should be a revolutionary center for the rest of Latin America. In the event, as an unsuccessful attempt in Bolivia showed, this was not likely to prove easy. Cuban circumstances had been very untypical. The hopes entertained of mounting a peasant movement—to start a Vietnam in South America as one revolutionary put it—proved illusory. The official Communists also appear to have deplored this campaign. While there were plenty of materials about for revolution in some places, they were urban rather than rural, and it was urban guerrilla movements in Latin America which within a few years were making the headlines. Though these were spectacular and dangerous, it is not clear that they enjoyed wide popular support. Yet anti-Americanism continued to run high. Kennedy's hopes for a new American initiative based on social reform, his Alliance for Progress, made no headway against the animosity aroused by the United States' treatment of Cuba.

Kennedy's successor, Lyndon Johnson, did no better. Perhaps because he cared less about Latin America than domestic reform and tended to leave hemisphere policy to fellow Texans who were interested in it, the initiative was never recaptured after the initial flagging of the Alliance for Progress.

Even worse, there were fresh signs that the old aim of intervention was still alive in 1965. The scene was the Dominican Republic. Four years earlier American help had assisted in the overthrow and assassination of a corrupt and tyrannical dictator and his replacement by a reforming democratic regime. When this in turn was pushed aside by soldiers acting in defense of the privileged classes, the United States cut off aid; it looked as if, after all, the Alliance for Progress might be used discriminatingly. But aid was restored—as it was to other right-wing regimes—after Johnson took office. When a revolution broke out against the Dominican military dictatorship in 1965, Washington sent 20,000 American troops to put down the rebellion.

New possibilities

By the end of the decade the Alliance for Progress had virtually been forgotten both north and south of the Rio Grande, in part because persistent fears of communism led American policy to put its weight behind Latin American conservatives, in part because Washington had lost interest in Latin America, having plenty of problems elsewhere. One result was a new wave of attacks on American property by governments which did not have to fear the loss of American support while the Communist threat seemed to endure. Chile nationalized the largest American copper company, the Bolivians took over oil concerns, and the Peruvians appropriated plantations owned by Americans. In 1969 a historic meeting of Latin American governments, at which the United States was not represented, explicitly and implicitly condemned much American behavior. When a representative of the president of the United States undertook a tour that year it led to protests, riots, bombings of American property, and requests that he not visit some countries. It was quite like the end of the previous decade when the American vice-president had been mobbed and spat upon by crowds during a good will tour. All in all it looked as if the nationalism of Latin America was entering a new and vigorous period. If Cuba-inspired guerrillas had ever presented a danger, they appeared to do so no longer, and without the spur of an internal threat there was little reason for Latin American governments not to capitalize on anti-American feeling since, in a period when Washington was obviously regretting earlier positive initiatives, they need fear no reprisals. As the fate of Chile showed in 1972, they were only in danger if American policy could make use of disaffected elements among their own countrymen.

What could be seen was that the real problems of Latin America were not yet being met. For all the achievements of an industrialization which had gone very far very rapidly, the continent was threatened by an appallingly fast growth of population. In 1961 it was expected to double in twenty-five years. This was a faster rate of growth than anywhere else in the world. Moreover society still remained deeply divided. There were great discrepancies of wealth and education even in the most advanced Latin American countries, as the slums of rapidly growing industrial cities revealed. Even culture was still a divisive force. To the layers laid down by Indian, slave, colonial, and post-colonial experiences, all of which were reflected strongly in differences of economic level, were now added the distinctions brought by the arrival in the 1950s of the American high-technology culture of consumption, available to the better-off but not to the poor who observed them. Just as in Asia, though perhaps less markedly, the strains of the impact of modern civilization on societies with deep historical roots were obvious, even though Latin America had been undergoing some of them since the sixteenth century.

chapter 40

The End of Bipolarity

THE SUPERPOWERS CHALLENGED

When the series of congresses which followed the Treaty of Vienna of 1815 at last came to an end, the British foreign secretary is said to have been delighted. Things were getting back to normal in diplomacy, he thought, with "each for himself and God for us all." Many people might have echoed him as they contemplated the unrolling of international events in the 1960s. The rigid simplicities of the cold war era then broke down in many ways, and the result was usually to diminish the freedom of action of the two giants who had dominated the world since 1945. The world system of two more or less disciplined blocs in a sea of small fry trying to escape being swallowed by them changed into one in which the blocs showed signs of strain and even disintegration, new quarrels between new states cut across the old ideological divisions, and new competitors for the role of superpower began to emerge.

There is nothing magical about the beginning of a decade and to speak of this as a process of the 1960s only means it came to a head then. Many of the factors which created a new international scene were at work before 1960. Yet they really began to register their effect in a new fluidity of international relations only after 1962 when an important barrier to détente between Russia and the United States was removed. This was because the Cuban missile crisis was the most dangerous confrontation of the cold war and forced both states to contemplate the reality of all-out nuclear conflict and the likely consequences — unacceptable damage to both of them.

Cold war in the post-Stalin era

The death of Stalin in 1953 had produced no obvious change in Russian policy but deepened confusion about it. When after nearly two years it appeared that the Russian leadership was focused on Nikolai Bulganin and Nikita Khrushchev (the first was later to drop into the background), there was still for a time no noticeable clarification. But in both 1955 and 1956 the Russian government announced it was reducing its forces because international tensions had lessened. Also in the latter year V. M. Molotov, Stalin's old henchman and veteran of cold war diplomacy, resigned his post as foreign minister. Above all, news quickly reached the West of a sensational speech made by Khrushchev at a secret session of the Twentieth Congress of

Left Speaks to Left

Lenin founded a tradition that Communists could only cooperate with other socialists for tactical reasons; most of the history of the Bolshevik past is marked by bitter hostility to other left-wing groups, and under Stalin many Marxist socialists in other countries besides Russia were persecuted and killed on the instructions of Moscow. Many remembered this when Khrushchev and Bulganin paid a visit to England in 1956, and they hoped to use the post-Stalin atmosphere to improve this situation. Unfortunately, Russian arrogance and the honest indignation of George Brown, a leading Labour Party M.P., who remembered the Nazi-Soviet Pact of 1939, made a dinner given for the visitors by the Labour Party something less than a success, as the following newspaper report indicates.

To Mr. Brown on Monday night it appeared that Mr. Khrushchev was claiming that Russia alone beat Germany. This was too much for Mr. Brown's volatile nature, and he exclaimed in a tone which brought Mr. Khrushchev's flow of words to an abrupt halt: "God forgive you!" An awful pause followed.

Mr. Krushchev then said to Mr. Brown: "What did you say?" Another awful pause followed. "Don't be frightened," Mr. Khrushchev said. "Say it again."

Mr. Brown again said: "God forgive you!"

the Russian Communist party in which he denounced the misdeeds of the Stalin era and declared "peaceful coexistence" to be the goal of Soviet foreign policy.

All in all 1956 seemed promising, when the atmosphere was suddenly fouled by the Suez invasion and a revolution in Hungary. The first at once led to Russian threats against Great Britain and France; Moscow was not going to jeopardize Arab good will by failing to support Egypt openly. The second event operated in a somewhat more complicated way.

Russia had been almost morbidly sensitive to signs of deviation or dissatisfaction among her satellites ever since 1948, the year she recalled her advisers from Yugoslavia, whose Communist ruler, Marshal Tito, had been showing too much independence. Yugoslavia was expelled from the Cominform, her treaties with Russia and other Communist states were denounced by them, and there followed five years of vitriolic denunciation of "Titoism"

There followed a sharp exchange in which Mr. Khrushchev kept
to his own analysis of the war situation, and Mr. Brown retorted
with anger that British men had been killed in the period of the
Second World War when Soviet Russia and Nazi Germany were
allies.

This outburst of hostility took place before Mr. Gaitskell, Mr. Bevan,
Mr. Sam Watson, and others appealed to the Russians to ease the
lot of Social Democrats who are political prisoners behind the Iron
Curtain. Yesterday Labour members were wondering whether in
all the circumstances this appeal for justice and mercy towards their
political comrades in Central and Eastern Europe could have found
the Russian visitors at their most receptive.

There are some Labour members who doubt whether the dinner
party was the right occasion for this. There are others who wonder
if Mr. Khrushchev would have been less unresponsive to the
appeal if tempers had not been stirred beforehand. But there are
still others who claim that whatever the outcome, the British
Labour party would have betrayed the men and women in prison
overseas if the dinner party had been nothing but an exchange of
genial toasts with the Russians.

From David Ayerst, ed., *The Guardian Omnibus, 1821–1971* (London: Wm. Collins
Sons & Co. Ltd., 1973), p. 660.

by orthodox Communists. The quarrel ended with the Russians climbing
down and asking to reopen diplomatic relations. In 1955 Khrushchev went
to Belgrade to apologize for what had happened and Tito soon paid a return
visit to Moscow.

Yugoslavia's successful survival had been damaging and embarrassing
for Russia and made Soviet policy sensitive to weakness in the Eastern
camp. There had been trouble too in East Berlin in 1953, and in the summer
of 1956 riots marked by anti-Soviet protests had broken out in Poland. Nationalism, it was clear, was still stronger than communism. It was against this
background that riots erupted in Budapest in October and grew into a nationwide movement that led to the withdrawal of Russian forces from the
city and the installation of a new government which promised free elections
and the end of one-party rule. It soon went further, denouncing the Warsaw
Pact and asking the United Nations to take up the Hungarian question. At

The Hungarian resistance broken; the Russians have reasserted their rule and in this picture some show they do not want the photographer to record it. *(Radio Times Hulton Picture Library)*

this point the Russian army returned (with those of other Warsaw Pact countries) and crushed the Hungarian revolution. The United Nations General Assembly recorded—twice—its condemnation of Russia's action.

Unfortunately this episode hardened attitudes on both sides. The Russians were once more made aware of how little they had reconciled the peoples of Eastern Europe and therefore became even more distrustful of Western talk of "liberating" them. Western Europe, on the other hand, was once again reminded of the real face of Russian power and sought to consolidate itself further.

International attention was thus drawn back to Europe where the Russians were much impressed with the potential danger of a rearmed West Germany. They sought to strengthen their own satellite, the German Democratic Republic, and viewed the continued existence of a non-Communist West Berlin occupied by American, British, and French in its territory as a grave weakness. West Berlin's frontiers were open and easily crossed. Its example of prosperity and freedom drew more and more East Germans—especially skilled workers—to defect to the West. This situation led the Russians in 1958 to denounce the arrangements under which the city had been run since 1948; they said they would hand over their sector to the East Germans if better arrangements could not be found. Their threat opened a new round of diplomatic sparring over the fate of Berlin which by 1961 seemed only to have brought Russia and the United States into a new confrontation.

In August of that year the East Germans suddenly erected a wall to cut off the Russian sector of Berlin from the Western zones. They felt driven to this by the huge increase in the number of refugees leaving their half of the city as the atmosphere of crisis deepened; 140,000 crossed the Berlin border in 1959, 200,000 in 1960, and more than 100,000 in the first six months of 1961. The wall immediately raised the temperature of confrontation but in the long run probably helped to lower it. It met the essential concern of the East German state, and Khrushchev was not disposed to maintain his more ex-

East German border guards carry away the body of a young man shot while trying to escape over the Berlin wall, August 1962. *(UPI)*

treme demands when it became clear that the United States would not yield a change in the legal status of Berlin even at the risk of war.

This rhythm was substantially repeated in the Cuban crisis of the following year, but the risk was then far greater. The allies of the United States were not directly concerned, as they had been over a possible change in the German settlement, nor did the Russians give any sign of paying attention to Cuba's interests. It was a much more "pure" confrontation and one in which much more clearly the Russians were forced to give way. While studiously avoiding action or language which might be provocatively dangerous because wounding, and while leaving a simple route of retreat open to the Russians by confining his demands to the essential, President Kennedy nonetheless made no concessions and struck no bargains (such as, for example, would have been implied in acceptance of the Russian demand for a balancing withdrawal of American bombers from Turkey).

It is difficult, even in ignorance of Russian thinking, not to believe that this was a major turn in world history. The prospect of nuclear war as the ultimate price of cold war had been faced and found unacceptable. The Russian withdrawal thereby registered a new era. It was symbolized in one way by inaugurating direct telephone communication between the heads of the two states—the "hot line." So much turned on the possibility of conflict through misunderstanding that some more intimate connection seemed necessary than that provided by ordinary diplomatic channels. It was also clear by then that the American preponderance in weapons remained as great as ever. The new weapon which mattered most for purposes of direct conflict between the two superpowers was the intercontinental ballistic missile; by the end of 1962 it appeared that the Americans had a superiority in this weapon of more than six to one over the Russians. Possibly this helped achieve in August 1963 the first agreement between Great Britain, the United States, and Russia on the restriction of nuclear weapons testing in space, the atmosphere, or under water. Disarmament talks had been pursued without success for many years; this was the first positive achievement of the negotiations.

The Soviet Union

In 1964 Khrushchev was removed from office. It was clear that the Soviet Union had not yet mastered the techniques of orderly political change because colleagues whom he had offended and alarmed set him aside with the connivance of the army. But he was not killed or sent to prison. He was not even sent to run a power station in Mongolia. This was striking and the nature of the regime was such that people accounted it progress.

Undoubtedly the Russian system had undergone some relaxation after Stalin's death. The speech at the Twentieth Congress was itself bound to have effects; it could not be unsaid even if much of it was aimed at diverting criticism from those who (like Khrushchev himself) had been participants in the crimes of which Stalin was accused. Symbolically the body of Stalin was removed from Lenin's tomb, which was regarded as a national shrine. In the next few years there was evidence of what was sometimes called a "thaw" in that marginally greater freedom of expression was allowed to writers and artists and the regime seemed a little more concerned about its appearance in the eyes of the world over such matters as its treatment of Jews. But the motives of Russian rulers remain as obscure as ever and have to be inferred from their behavior.

After Stalin's death and particularly during the era of Khrushchev's ascendancy the party reemerged as a much more independent factor in Russian life. The dominance exercised by the police was reduced and the party undertook much more scrutiny of both policy and administration. Khrushchev's own contribution was to provide a great shaking up of Russian policy on every front. He had a huge failure in agriculture, made a great impact in directing the emphasis of the Russian military toward the strategic rocket services, and undertook many initiatives in foreign affairs. Meanwhile long-term changes rooted in the Stalinist era were also proceeding in Russian society.

In exaggerated and extravagant terms it has been argued that through these developments the United States and Soviet Russia have grown more and more alike and that this similarity has played an important part in making Russian leaders less intransigent. This analysis gives a distorted emphasis to the undoubted truth that they have become the two leading industrial powers of the world. And even that general statement must be qualified by the differences between them. Setting aside the fundamental distinctiveness of two political systems and traditions, there are economic dissimilarities. Russian industrial growth, though very great, is overwhelmingly still a matter of heavy manufacture. The Russian consumer is much less well supplied with manufactured goods than the American, even though since 1953 the government has sought to improve both quantities and qualities of goods available. Another important difference is that Russia has had nothing like the success of the United States in developing her agriculture; paradoxically she has found herself buying American grain.

Yet Russia is regarded—rightly—by many undeveloped countries as a developed nation and a rich one. This is an important qualification of the obvious disparity between the United States and Russia as consumer societies; to the poor, rich and very rich look alike. Two more points should perhaps be made. One is that the comparison present in the minds of Russians is not with the United States but with their own infinitely more impoverished past which is not very remote. The second is that there are sectors in which the comparison of the two industrial systems is by no means as unfavorable to Russia as in that of consumer goods. Russian investment in education, for example, has been so considerable and successful that it has actually achieved a literacy rate very slightly higher than the American one. Health services too, while not commanding investment on the scale of American counterparts, nevertheless provide a very large majority of Soviet citizens with better care than that available to many poor Americans. But such comparisons, which fall easily over the line from quantitative to qualitative judgment, do not alter the basic fact that Russia's per capita national income remains substantially behind that of the United States. There has been a long legacy of backwardness and disruption to eliminate; it was not until 1952 that real wages in Russia even got back to the 1928 level.

What has been achieved, nonetheless, has been a scientific and industrial base which at its best matches that of the United States. The obvious example of this, and one of the great sources of patriotic pride to Soviet citizens, is the exploration of space. There is now so much hardware sailing about in space that it is difficult to recapture the impression made in 1957 when the Russians launched the first satellites. Although American success speedily followed—and comparison is hardly meaningful in what was misleadingly called the "space race" since the two participants often had different goals—Russia's space achievements made it clear that she was in the first rank of powers. The very large size of Russian rockets had a military significance with implications for offensive capabilities, but there was also something in space exploration to feed the Russian imagination and reward Russian patience with other aspects of daily life. It is not too much to say that for some Russians space technology justified the Revolution; it proved Russia was able to do anything another nation could do, and much that only one other could do. Russia was modernized at last.

Whether this meant that she was in some sense becoming a satisfied nation, less prone to disturb the international scene, with leaders more confident and less suspicious of the outside world is an entirely different matter about which only speculation is possible. Certainly the rise of Chinese power suggests they still had plenty to make them anxious. Any such speculation would also at least have to take into account the appearance in the Soviet Union of signs of strain marked in other societies. Dissent and criticism, particularly of restraints upon intellectual freedom, began to manifest themselves much more obviously in the 1960s. So did some symptoms of antisocial behavior, such as hooliganism, corruption, and alcoholism. But these probably held as little potential for significant change as in other countries. Less spectacular facts may turn out to be more important in the long run; later perspectives may reveal that one of the most important watersheds of Russian history was passed in the 1970s when Russians for the first time became a minority in the Soviet Union.

The United States

For obvious reasons changes in the United States since 1945 have been more easily observed than those in the Soviet Union, but this has not always made it easier to discern fundamental trends. Some are obvious. In 1968 the American population passed the 200 million mark and only one in twenty was not native-born; the United States was ceasing to be a nation of immigrants. This growth in population was due to an unexpected increase in births at a time when death rates continued to drop—an unusual pattern among developed countries. More of these Americans than ever lived in cities or the suburbs of cities.

In the middle of the 1950s the United States contained about 6 percent of the world's population and produced more than half the world's manufactured goods. Its immensely successful industrial structure was increasingly dominated by very large corporations, many of them possessing greater resources and wealth than some small states. Concern was more and more drawn to the difficulties of securing the public interest and protecting the consumer's needs in such a structure. But no doubts could be expressed about its ability to create wealth and power. As in Russia the most dramatic evidence of it was space exploration, which reached its climax when an American stepped onto the surface of the moon on July 21, 1969, as millions of people watched the event on their television sets. Though the immense power which brought this about could not do everything that might be asked of it, it was nevertheless the constant of the postwar period. Industrial might sustained the huge military establishment upon which the conduct of American foreign policy rested, notably in its providing a great armory of nuclear weapons.

Not surprisingly economic success deeply affected American politics, not least by the generation of mythologies. President Truman's second administration and those of President Eisenhower were marked by important symbolic struggles and debate about the danger of interference with free enterprise and the threat of socialism. Insofar as this crystallized in legislative proposals, opponents of the New Deal attempted during the Truman years to demolish its agencies and legislation and under Eisenhower to rid the federal government of some of its powers in economic matters. Yet there was much shadowboxing about all this. In the first place government continued to hold and indeed increase its importance as the first customer of the American economy. Since 1945 government spending has been the primary economic stimulant, and hopes of balanced budgets and the ideal of economical, business-like administration, such as bemused the Republicans of the 1950s, always ran aground upon this fact. In the second place the United States is a democracy; whatever the doctrinaire objections to it and however much rhetoric might be devoted to attacking it, some of the welfare state had come to stay because electorates wanted it. These two facts made the old ideal of free enterprise unchecked and uninvaded by the influence of government more unrealistic than ever. They also helped prolong the Democratic coalition put together by Roosevelt. Truman had to face a Republican Eightieth Congress and Republican presidents were elected in 1952, 1956, 1968, and 1972, but they benefited from war weariness and were not able to persuade Americans that they should again elect Republican Congresses. On the other hand, signs of strain in the Democratic bloc were already apparent under Eisenhower—who appealed to some southern states as a conservative figure—and by 1970 something much more like a national conservative party appeared under the Republican banner because Democratic legislation on behalf of the Negro had offended some southerners. This, together with a well-stage-managed diplomacy, gave President Nixon the largest popular vote in American history in 1972.

Governmental trends could not be completely reversed in the postwar era, but different administrations did something to change their emphasis. The Eisenhower years leave an impression that little happened in the domestic history of the United States; it was not part of that president's vision of his office that he should provide a strong policy lead at home. With the election of Kennedy in 1960 the arrival of a new man and a young one by itself helped produce a sense of striking innovation. Much was made at the time of the more superficial aspects of this, but in retrospect it can be seen that not only in foreign policy but in domestic affairs too the eight years of renewed Democratic rule from 1961 were a period of great change, though unhappily not in the ways Kennedy and his vice-president, Lyndon Johnson, anticipated when they took office.

One issue had already begun to emerge, the Negro question. A century after emancipation the American Negro was poorer, more likely to be on relief, less well housed, more often unemployed, and in poorer health than the white American. That this suddenly appeared so intolerable that it became a great political question was due to three facts. One was the transformation of a local southern question into a national problem by Negro migration. Between 1940 and 1960 the Negro population of northern states almost trebled; New York came to have the biggest black population of any state in the Union. Such changes brought the Negro into view; they also revealed that the problem facing him was not only one of legal rights but a complex situation involving economic and cultural deprivation too. The second factor pushing the question forward onto the national stage was the growing importance of the good will of other nations, many of them colored. It was an embarrassment—which Communist propaganda always put to good use—for the United States to display at home so flagrant a contravention of the ideals it espoused abroad. Finally the question was changed by the Negroes themselves; their own action under their own leaders, above all that part inspired by Gandhian principles of passive resistance to oppression, did much to change white attitudes. In the end the position of the black American was radically altered though not to the extent that some had hoped. It was also obvious that bitterness and resentment had not been eliminated but had increased.

The first and most successful phase of the campaign for equal status for the Negro was the struggle to ensure him civil rights, of which the most important were the unhindered exercise of the franchise (always available formally but not in practice in some southern states) and rights to equality of treatment in other ways as set out by Supreme Court rulings in 1954 and 1955. The process began, that is to say, not with legislation but with judicial interpretation. These important first decisions provided that racial segregation within the public school system was unconstitutional and should be brought to an end within a reasonable time. This was to challenge the social system in many southern states. It was to take until 1963 before Negroes were attending public schools together with white children in every state of the Union. By then integration was starting to pose other problems as white parents began to migrate to areas where schools were likely always to have a majority of white pupils.

In 1957 the first civil rights commission was created to oversee this subject, but legislative action to help the Negro was not really important until

Freedom marchers on the third day of their trek from Selma to Montgomery in March 1965. Such marches provided splendid nonviolent propaganda for the civil rights campaign and also appealed to many as an opportunity to participate in a struggle at some cost to themselves, even if only in terms of discomfort. *(UPI)*

after 1961. Kennedy then initiated a program of measures (brought to maturity by his successor) which went beyond the securing of voting rights to attack segregation and the deprivation of many kinds of rights. This legislation followed a successful campaign of Negro sit-ins which itself achieved many important local victories. Yet integration and stricter enforcement of legal equality seemed powerless to touch economic deprivation and the resentment arising from it. This provoked ugly manifestations in riot and arson in what came to be called ghetto areas of great American cities.

More was involved than simply the Negro's plight. Poverty, poor housing, bad schools in run-down urban areas, and crime were symptoms of deep dislocations inside American society among sectors which had escaped the fall-out of wealth produced by the greatest industrial machine in history. Its inequalities were thrown into stark relief by the increasing affluence in which they were set. The Kennedy administration had been aware of these problems and had appealed to Americans to see the removal of such evils as one of the calls of the New Frontier. Lyndon Johnson's administration gave even greater emphasis to social legislation. Johnson's own southern and poor background made him a convinced and convincing exponent of the Great Society in which he discerned America's future. Yet he was to prove a tragically unsuccessful president in spite of great achievements and all his political experience and skill. His great constructive and reforming work came to be overshadowed by an Asian war which grew terrifying enough to appear to confront the United States not only with disaster abroad but with a breakdown of support for government at home.

Vietnam

Under President Eisenhower American policy had come to rest on the dogma that Indochina was essential to American security in Southeast Asia. The elections stipulated by the Geneva agreement in 1954 as the prelude to reuniting Vietnam had never been held, and the United States had therefore become the backer of the conservative Saigon government in the south. The prevailing view was that South Vietnam had to be kept in the Western camp if all the other states of the area—perhaps as far off as the borders of India and Australia—were not to be subverted. Though disposed to be optimistic when he took office, President Kennedy did not question this perspective and began the process of backing up American military aid with "advisers." At the time of his assassination in November 1963 there were about 20,000 of them in South Vietnam. President Johnson took the same view on the importance of Vietnam and felt that what the United States did there would affect the credibility of its pledges to other countries. But the regimes which succeeded one another in Saigon were obviously inadequate, and when Johnson was advised at the beginning of 1965 that South Vietnam might be lost without additional American help, he chose to provide it. Soon after-

American marines in Danang, South Vietnam, 1965. Captured Vietcong are led away, hands tied and bound to each other by the neck. *(UPI)*

ward air attacks were made on targets in North Vietnam and the first American combat units arrived. From that moment the United States' participation soared out of control. In 1968 there were over 500,000 American personnel in Vietnam, and by Christmas that year a heavier tonnage of bombs had been released on North Vietnam than fell on Germany and Japan together in the entire Second World War.

Involvement on this scale was disastrous. It was almost the least of Johnson's worries that the American balance of payments was damaged by the huge costs which were eventually to be borne. Vietnam also took money from badly needed reform projects at home. Worse still was the growing distaste for the war as the weight of effort and the casualties mounted and attempts to negotiate seemed to get nowhere. It was small consolation that the other important participant was Russia, whose costs were also considerable as she supplied arms to North Vietnam. In March 1968 domestic opposition was clearly shown in the primary elections. Too late Johnson drew the conclusion that the United States could not win, restricted bombing, and asked the North Vietnamese to open negotiations again. Dramatically he also announced that he would not stand for reelection in 1968.

Just as the casualties of the Korean War had helped elect Eisenhower in 1952, so the greater casualties of Vietnam—on the battlefield and at home—brought in another Republican president in 1968. Richard Nixon began to withdraw American forces from Vietnam soon after his inauguration. This was one element in a triple strategy of peace making which developed over the next three years. In 1970 North Vietnam and the United States entered into secret negotiations which were accompanied by continuing withdrawals of American ground forces but renewed and intensified bombing of the north. Moreover, American operations were secretly extended also to Cambodia.

The negotiations were tortuous and difficult with the main obstacle to a settlement appearing to be the South Vietnamese government. The United States could not appear to abandon its ally, nor would the North Vietnamese accept terms which would not give the Vietcong some power to harass the Saigon regime. In spite of considerable public outcry the United States briefly resumed bombing at the end of 1972 after a pause for negotiation but for the last time. Soon afterward, on January 27, 1973, a cease-fire was signed in Paris. It was to be riddled with breaches in the next few months.

The war had cost the United States vast sums in money and 56,000 dead. But these were not the largest items in the account. It had also done grave damage to American prestige and diplomatic freedom and had ravaged the country's domestic politics. What had been achieved was the preservation for a while of a shaky South Vietnam, still saddled with internal problems which made its survival uncertain, the infliction of terrible destruction on the peoples and economies of North and South Vietnam alike, and the sacrifice of Cambodia to the Communists.

Sordid as the end of the story was to prove, to disentangle the United States from this morass must be accounted a success. The liquidation of the Vietnamese venture followed other actions which revealed how much the world had changed since the Cuban missile crisis. The most striking of these was Washington's establishment of direct, normal relations with Peking, which was climaxed by President Nixon's visit to China in February 1972. This was not only an attempt to start to bridge what the president described as "16,000 miles and 22 years of hostility"; it was also the first visit any American president ever paid to Asia. Together with a visit to Moscow in May, which was followed by an agreement on arms limitation, it marked something of a watershed in postwar diplomacy. The simplicities of the cold war were now clearly gone however doubtful the future might be. This visit came before the Vietnam settlement and must certainly have been related to it.

China had always loomed in the background of the Vietnamese conflict. Her relations with the struggle were by no means simple; they were complicated by Vietnamese nationalism, Russian intentions, and concern over American policy elsewhere in Asia, particularly in Taiwan. The Vietnamese who sought to unite their country were hardly doing so in order to place it under Chinese direction, for China was an imperial power against which Vietnamese nationalism had struggled in the past. Yet from this confused position China emerged as a member of the United Nations with a seat on the Security Council and opened diplomatic relations at the highest level with the United States. In 1975 her rulers could look out with some complacency on an Asia in which hardly any relics remained of the brief successes of the Western powers in the imperialist era. In that year the thirty years' war in Indochina finally came to an end, with the ousting of a pro-Western government in Cambodia and its replacement by a Communist and nationalist regime whose leaders had been in exile in Peking, and with the final military collapse of South Vietnam and the occupation of Saigon by the northern forces. The 1973 peace had barely lasted long enough for the United States to save its face, and charges of abandoning its ally were hurled at it by the Vietnamese losers. But at last Asians were once more clearly masters of their own destinies.

A MORE FLUID WORLD

Japan: the new Asian power

Another factor which had transformed the Asian balance since 1945 was less violent. This was the still growing economic strength of Japan, which had obvious implications for her place in the balance of power in Asia and the world. By 1970 she had the second highest gross national product in the non-Communist world. She had rebuilt her heavy industrial base and moved with great success into new areas of manufacture, such as electronics and cars, which she produced in greater number than any country except the United States. This was causing resentment among American manufacturers, the supreme compliment. The other side of the account was a population which rose so sharply that Japan's per capita national income at the same moment was only the twentieth largest in the non-Communist world. And in many places there was ample evidence of the costs of economic growth in the destruction of the Japanese environment and the wear and tear of urban life.

Japan had continued to be favored by circumstances (Vietnam helped as had Korea), but men must be available to take advantage of opportunities and Japanese attitudes were an important asset. Great pride and willingness for collective effort were manifested in the postwar era; they sprang from the deep cohesiveness and capacity for subordinating the individual to collective purposes which had always marked Japanese society. These attitudes seemed to survive the introduction of democratic institutions, for which the Americans entertained great hopes. It may be too early to judge the profundity of their adoption; they have, after all, been tried in Japan before. The way in which democracy worked after 1951 was to produce something like one-party rule by the Liberal Democratic party. Irritation with this apparently unshakable predominance expressed itself soon in the emergence of more extreme groupings, some antiliberal. There were signs by the 1960s that such extremism appealed increasingly to youth.

There were also Japanese who found the pace of social change in the 1960s too fast. There was mounting uneasiness over what was happening to traditional values and institutions. The costs of economic growth could be seen not only in the huge urban spread and pollution but also in the emergence of social problems which strained even Japanese custom. Large firms still operated with success on the basis of group loyalties buttressed by traditional attitudes and institutions, but at a different level the Japanese family seemed to be undergoing just the same strains which had so weakened other industrialized societies.

Economic progress also helped change the context of Japan's foreign policy, which in any case moved away in the 1960s from the simplicities of the preceding decade. Economic strength made the yen an important trading currency, which drew Japan into the monetary diplomacy of Europe. Moreover Japan's prosperity involved her in the affairs of many parts of the world. In the Pacific basin she became a consumer of raw materials from Australia and New Zealand. In the Middle East she was a large buyer of oil. In Europe, though her aggregate share of investment was not large, it was thought alarming by some, and Japanese exports of manufactured goods threatened European equivalents. Even food supplies for the large Japanese population involved disputes with other nations; in the 1960s Japan drew 90 percent of her protein requirements from fishing and this led to growing international concern that the Japanese might be over-fishing important grounds.

Such issues changed the atmosphere and content of international relations in the Pacific area, where Japan assumed in the 1960s a position in relation to neighboring countries not unlike that of Germany to central and eastern Europe before 1914. New Zealand and Australia in particular found their economies increasingly and profitably tied to Japanese consumption rather than the old British market. Both of them supplied meat and Australia provided minerals too, notably coal and iron ore. On the Asian mainland the Russians and the South Koreans complained about Japanese fishing, and in the second case this added a new complication to an old story of economic involvement. Korea was Japan's second largest market (the United States was the biggest) and Japanese investment there had begun again after 1951. This revived a traditional distrust; it was ominous to find that South Korean nationalism had so anti-Japanese a tone that in 1959 the South Korean president could urge his countrymen to unite "as one man" not against their northern neighbor but against Japan.

Greater strength also meant greater responsibilities. The withdrawal of American direction was logically rounded off twenty years later when Okinawa was returned to Japan. This was the first of her overseas possessions to be reacquired. There remained to negotiate the question of the Kuriles, still in Russian hands. Taiwan, another former Japanese possession, was unlikely to be returned to her since it was in the possession of the Chinese Nationalists and claimed by the Chinese Communists. There was on the other hand the possibility that the issue of Sakhalin, taken by the Russians in 1945, might be reopened.

All of these questions began to look much more susceptible to investigation in the 1960s because of the great changes brought to the Asian scene by Chinese and Japanese revival. With the advent of the Sino-Soviet quarrel Japan clearly had much greater freedom for maneuver, both toward the United States, her erstwhile patron, and China and Russia. The embarrassments which too close a tie with the Americans might bring were shown as the United States became more deeply involved in Vietnam and political opposition to this grew among the Japanese. Japan's freedom of action was limited in the sense that all three of the other great powers in the area were equipped with nuclear weapons by 1970 (and she of all nations had most reason to know their effect), but there was little doubt of her capacity to produce them within a relatively brief time if required. Altogether the Japanese stance is potentially one which might develop in various different directions. There was clear evidence in 1972 that the possibility of better relations between China and the United States after President Nixon's visit caused some concern in Japan. In a world situation more fluid than it has been since 1941 prediction is hazardous. What is indisputable is that Japan is once more a world power.

The Middle East

Another ambiguous prospect was presented by the Middle East. Time and oil were on the side of the Arabs, but not much else was clear by 1970. The Six Day War in 1967 had solved nothing. It merely exacerbated Arab feeling—there were new waves of refugees—and gave Israel good strategic frontiers. When the Israelis began establishing settlements in their newly won territories, Arab resentment grew even stronger. It was clearly only a matter of years before there was another war, and the identification of American and Russian interests with opposing sides presented the danger that a world war might suddenly blow up out of a local conflict, as in 1914.

At the same time there were a few signs that the decreasing importance of a bipolar structure might bring hopeful changes even here. For one thing the British strove to mend their bridges with the Arabs. This was made a little easier by withdrawal from Aden and was given urgency by Great Britain's need, as the country which more than any other depended on Middle Eastern oil, to improve relations with the Persian Gulf states. The British took the lead in drafting a United Nations resolution to serve as a basis for Arab-Israeli peace; it provided a new starting point by calling for an Israeli withdrawal from occupied territories in return for recognition. Meanwhile efforts were made to improve relations with the Arabs by making a virtue of the economic necessity of withdrawing British forces from the Persian Gulf in 1971. London established closer relations with Saudi Arabia and Iran, and a Union of Arab Emirates was set up with forces trained and armed by Great Britain.

Into this new situation war erupted again in the autumn of 1973. Egypt and Syria supported by all the other Arab states except Jordan attacked Israel and inflicted heavy casualties on the Israelis, who for the first time faced the prospect of military overthrow by the greatly improved forces of their opponents. This did not happen, for Israel was able to retain enough of her former conquests to survive until a cease-fire, but the role of oil diplomacy gave Israel fresh grounds for concern. By announcing restrictions on oil supplies to Europe, Japan, and the United States, the Arab oil producers revealed that the fundamental diplomatic support on which Israel had always been able to rely might not be resistant to pressure forever. By the middle of the decade Israelis had other grounds for concern too: given the United States' abandonment of its allies in Southeast Asia, was it certain that the power whose support had always been taken for granted as the bedrock of Israel's policy would fight, even to protect her from obliteration?

A Europe divided

Even Europe was studded with new question marks by 1970 and they were to be found in both east and west. There had been signs that new problems faced the Russian bloc in Europe ever since the Sino-Soviet rupture. This could be seen in the violence with which Albania, the tiniest of Europe's Communist countries, condemned Moscow and applauded what was done in Peking. But Albania had no frontier with a member of the Warsaw Pact and was thus not likely to have to take account of the Russian army. Yet even within the Russian satellites currents of national independence (which had begun to reemerge in the 1950s) multiplied in the 1960s. This was first clear when Rumania successfully contested the direction of her economy by Comecon. The Rumanians asserted their right to develop their own economy in their own national interest. They soon went further than this by taking up vaguely neutralist positions on questions of foreign policy—though they remained loyal to the Warsaw Pact. Such tendencies were summed up by an Italian Communist as "polycentrism" and showed that the dislocation of the old monolithic unity of communism had gone some way.

But independence had its limits in Eastern Europe. Rumania had no land frontier with a NATO country and had Chinese backing for her inde-

Czech defiance, August 1968; grafitti on a Prague statue equating the Russians with the Nazis. *(Magnum)*

pendent line. A certain skittishness on her part could therefore be allowed. Neither of these conditions held in Czechoslovakia, where in 1968 a Communist government was both deliberately liberalizing its internal structure and developing trade relations with West Germany. After a series of attempts at diplomatic pressure had failed, Warsaw Pact forces invaded Czechoslovakia in August. To avoid a repetition of what had happened in Hungary in 1956, the Czech government did not resist, and the brief attempt to provide an example of "socialism with a human force" (as a Czech statesman had put it) was obliterated.

With the Sino-Soviet quarrel, tremblings within the Eastern bloc, and uncertainty in Washington's Latin American policies, the world as a whole by 1970 might be described as sliding from bipolarity to polycentrism. The process was rapid and surprising. One shock was a revolution in one of the bastions of conservatism in Europe, Portugal, which installed in power a government based on a left-wing military junta powerfully influenced by the formerly banned Communist party. Perhaps the most striking example of the improbabilities of history, though, was to be seen elsewhere in Western Europe, the place where the evolution of a world history had actually begun. By 1970 it was providing a few, if tentative, signs that nationalism's grip on the human potential for organization was loosening.

Western Europe had been made by the war and by Russian policy. These factors not only ended the German problem and therefore French fears but also repeatedly gave the Western countries new reasons to cooperate more closely. The Marshall Plan and NATO had been the first two important steps. In 1950 came the French proposal for a European Coal and Steel Community; this was the first positive move toward integrating West Germany into a new Western European structure and one of the first political expressions of the growing interdependence of national economies which had begun with the process of industrialization.

By that year much had changed in the West. The internal political weakness felt by France and Italy because of the existence of large Communist parties had been overcome by a variety of forces, economic recovery being one of the most important. Both had ended Communist participation in government as early as 1947, thus removing the danger of a coup such as that in Czechoslovakia. In both countries (as in West Germany) anti-Communist opinion had then coalesced about right-wing parties whose essence was Roman Catholicism, an integrating force. Broadly speaking, governments of the right in continental Western Europe pursued similar aims of economic recovery and public welfare from that time onward. One effect was more and more governmental intervention in the economy in France, Italy, and the Benelux countries (Belgium, the Netherlands, and Luxemburg) though less so in West Germany.

The trend to supranational organization in Europe also continued. In 1952 the Coal and Steel Community was set up to develop these industries on a nonnational basis. The most important functional organizations appeared in 1958: the European Economic Community (or Common Market) and Euratom, to coordinate nuclear research. The first offered some faint hope that earlier attempts to unite Europe politically might at last be within sight of success.

The most determined opposition to any evolution toward political union came from France. Objections were expressed most strongly by Charles de Gaulle, who was president from 1958 to 1969. He had returned to politics at a moment of crisis when France seemed threatened with civil war because of divisions over Algeria. De Gaulle carried out an important constitutional reform which gave much more power to the president and in 1961 performed a service to his country as great as had been his wartime role by liquidating France's Algerian commitment. This freed him and France for a more vigorous international role. De Gaulle's view of European consolidation was that it should essentially consist of cooperation on matters of common interest between independent nation states: his thinking remained firmly nationalist and he seemed to see the Common Market as essentially a device for the protection of French economic interests. He was quite prepared to strain the new organization badly to get his way and, in effect, twice vetoed British application to join it.

Wartime experience had left de Gaulle with a deep distrust of the Anglo-Saxons. In 1964 he annoyed the United States by exchanging diplomatic representatives with Communist China. He insisted too that France go ahead with her own nuclear weapons program, declining to be dependent on American patronage and refusing to sign the Test Ban treaty. Finally, after causing it much trouble, he withdrew from NATO. This looked like the coming of polycentrism to the Western bloc, but when de Gaulle resigned in 1969, the major force making for uncertainty and disarray in Western Europe disappeared. However, French policy continued to oppose the evolution of the Common Market in the direction of a more complete cohesion.

Great Britain joined the Common Market in 1972 and the first national referendum in her history confirmed this decision three years later. This was the climax of an era of uncertainty which had lasted almost since 1945. During that time all British governments had failed to achieve a combination of sustained economic growth, increased social services, and high level of employment. The first had always been sacrificed to the last. The vulnerability of the British economy because of its dependence on international trade was a serious handicap.

Because of this relatively poor economic performance—the United Kingdom grew richer but more slowly than other developed countries—British achievements tended to be overlooked. The two outstanding ones were negative: the acceptance of a decline in international power and the implementation of a rapid decolonization without the violence and domestic bitterness visible elsewhere. Among the positive achievements were the creation of the first comprehensive national system of social services and rights to medical treatment in a capitalist economy by a major state, the maintenance of a level of orderliness and social cooperation which still in 1970 made the country attractive to foreigners, and the preservation of her traditional constitutional liberties.

Five years later it was harder to be sure that these achievements could be sustained. In particular there were threats to them in the activities of the Irish Protestant and Catholic hooligans of Ulster, who seemed bent on destroying that province rather than cooperating inside it with their rivals. Here the old threat of lunatic nationalism was as alive as ever and cost the lives of hundreds of civilians and policemen and British soldiers. Nevertheless, there was hope in the decision to enter the Common Market. Though it was unclear what might lie ahead, the adherence of the most insular of European states was striking evidence that Europe, the home of nationalism, might be one of the first regions to transcend it.

chapter 41

In the Light of History

There are deliberately no neat lines dividing periods of history in this book, and now there is to be no neat ending either. Logically of course history cannot have an end; unless we extinguish the human race, someone will always be able to think about its past. History is always unraveling—as this was being written and while it is being read—and a history of the world cannot be pinned down to a finish on a clean chronological boundary.

Nor can it be pinned down in a neat pattern of "significant" topics; what is historically significant will only appear when people in the future start to wonder about what made *their* world. It is the old problem of perspective, of getting things in their right relationship to one another on the same scale. It is all too obvious today that events alter perspective with startling rapidity. In the aftermath of the war which has recently taken place there, the Middle East looks very different from the way it looked in 1967 after the great Israeli victories of that year. To take another example, it turns out that startling changes can come about very quickly in a people's view of an American president: Nixon was driven to resign by political scandal only two years after his triumphant reelection. In nonpolitical history too (or at least history which is not at first sight political) assessments must change with new developments; the Japanese economic miracle of the 1960s now looks less solid in the light of Arab restrictions affecting world oil supplies.

Faced with such difficulties, it is best not to try to do too much and to be content with having a last word at all. Above all, prophecy must be avoided. Prediction is not the historian's business even if he sticks to extrapolation from past trends. This may have a temporary usefulness in clarifying the mind but often because the exercise demonstrates that the trend logically *cannot* continue. The number of scientists in the world, for instance, and expenditure on science cannot continue to increase at the rate of the last couple of centuries because, if it did, the population of the world would within a finite time consist of nothing but scientists. Not dissimilar considerations appear if thought is given to the consumption of energy resources by industrial nations, though in that case recent events show the folly of basing arguments merely on extrapolation from past trends.

The one permissible subject for the historian is the past, and it is reasonable for him to try to see consistency or inconsistency in the relationship of recent events to what has gone before. Here we are back with the difficulties posed by the mass of facts which crowds in on us. The very confusion they present suggests a much more revolutionary period than any preceding it and all that has been said so far about the continuing acceleration of change confirms this. Such an evaluation does not, on the other hand, imply that these more violent and sweeping changes are not consistent with what has gone before. If there is any general trend at all in earlier history, it is twofold—in the direction of a growing unity of human experience and of a growing human capacity to control the environment. It is arguable that recent history can be read so as to confirm that these trends are still operating.

ONE WORLD OR SEVERAL?

So much misuse has been made of the slogan "one world" that it is now little more than a cant term. Insofar as the people who first used it hoped to ease the way to common political action, it also seems exploded. There is just too much conflict and dissension about. In 1931 the Japanese opened the Manchurian campaign, and in the forty-odd years since then there has hardly been a period longer than a few weeks in which someone was not fighting someone else somewhere in the world. Moreover important political divisions, even when they do not break out in overt violence, still produce expensive and dangerous competition: the cold war is an example. This line of thought can be summed up in the observation that although the international institution which emerged in 1945 took the name of the United Nations, it is nevertheless based on the theory that the whole surface of the globe is divided into territories belonging to sovereign states.

Yet this picture of disunity does not quite meet the thesis already set out. The point could be made by thinking about a more remote period. Nobody would dream of denying, for example, that the world of Islam during the European Middle Ages was the scene of struggles between different Muslim rulers and displayed plenty of evidence of strife. Yet Islam was, nonetheless, a unity in another sense. It was a civilization. All over the Islamic world institutions and behavior expressed this by uniformities which were not observable in, say, Inca Peru or Christian Europe. What has been argued in this book is that, for all their frequency and violence, the conflicts of the modern world resemble more and more—though still far from completely—civil wars between contestants sharing a common background rather than battles of civilizations.

At this level the argument can hardly be put without being overstated. More humdrum matters may make the point more exactly. It is obvious, for example, at the level of personal experience. In the days when people of neighboring villages the world around spoke significantly different dialects even if they shared a common language, when their movement in the whole of their lives would only exceptionally take them ten miles from their homes, when even their clothes and tools might provide evidence of significant differences of technology, style, and custom, then the human experience of the world was more highly differentiated than it is now. Nor are these cases the extreme ones. The great physical, racial, and linguistic divisions of the past were much less easily overcome than their equivalents today. It is easy to trace the course of this change in improved communications, mass education, mass production of commonly required artifacts, and so on; much has already been said about such things in these pages. The results are obvious to a traveler in any part of the modern world. Clothes are one visible example. Only rural districts or consciously nationalist regimes now cling to traditional local dress instead of the nearly universal style of shirt-and-trousers. Kilts, kaftans, kimonos are now tourist souvenirs or the carefully preserved relics of a sentimentalized past, and less picturesque traditional clothes tend to be a sign of poverty and backwardness.

The point about nationalist regimes is significant here. When Uganda legislates against the miniskirt or Zaire encourages traditional dancing, it is because common human experience is corrosive of tradition. Conversely, Ataturk forbade Turks to wear the fez and veil, and Peter the Great dressed his courtiers in Western European clothes. These statesmen recognized that more was involved than dress. What was at issue was orientation toward a new range of experience.

The basis of shared experience is now wider than ever before. Human beings have been liberated from differences of climate by electricity, air conditioning, and medicine. All over the world many of them live in cities with electric street lighting and traffic signals, policemen on duty, banks, shops, and so on. In the shops there is a growing likelihood that the same goods will be available as in other countries: toothpaste can be bought anywhere. Men who do not understand one another's language can drive and service the same machines and derive the same or very similar advantages and disadvantages from their use. Everywhere in the world the automobile has imposed in greater or lesser degree the same demands on urban living and everywhere threatens it with the same level of intolerability. The countryside still escapes many of these blessings, but the shared experience is clearly to be seen in the cities.

An effort of historical imagination shows how much we now take for granted unthinkingly. A traveler who went from imperial Rome to imperial Peking would have found contrasts in everything he saw: clothes would have been cut differently and from different materials, the food would have been different, the animals in the streets would have been of different breeds, the weapons of the soldiers and their armor would have been shaped differently. Even the wheelbarrow would have had a different design. A modern American in Peking would find much less to surprise him, even though China's culture is still one of the most resistant to external trends.

The European tradition

It may be argued that shared experience of this kind is peripheral and superficial, that what really matters are more fundamental beliefs, institutions, and attitudes. Such a comment sidesteps the question of the bearing that material experience has on culture, but there is not space to discuss that here. It is easier to reply by pointing to the evidence that ideas and institutions have in fact become more generally spread among mankind.

Not a great deal of practical respect is given to such documents as the United Nations Declaration of Human Rights, but great interest has been shown in drawing them up and signing them. Although many of the signatory nations have little intention of upholding liberal resolutions, nonetheless a decent regard for the opinion of mankind—to borrow a phrase—compels them to pay lip service to common principles. Such principles usually turn out to be derived from the European tradition of civilization (as indeed the notion of a declaration of rights suggests) and this is only one more example of the tendency of the last three centuries for that civilization to extend its influence around the whole world. Whether we regard the European tradition as greedy, aggressive, brutal, and exploitative or as objectively improving, beneficent, and humane is neither here nor there. It was either the master source of the modern world or it was not, and that is all our concern in this study.

The point is not that European ideas and institutions have everywhere replaced traditional ones, for they have not. People still live in worlds shaped by deeply different cultures. Women are not treated in the same way—whether for good or ill is irrelevant—in Islamic and Christian societies. Indians still take astrology into account in fixing the date of a wedding while English people may find the state of public transportation more significant. The philosophy of ancient Asia, or what is taken for it, has a cult attractiveness for a minority of modern Americans, but the roots of American behavior are still to be found, if in any single ideological source, in the confidence of the Enlightenment and the conviction felt by so many early Puritan settlers that they were a people set apart. One could go on and on with such contrasts. Differing traditions even make varying use of shared technology and ideas. Japanese capitalism is not the same thing in its working as British, and the reason lies deep in the different historical traditions of two societies. What remains true is that no other tradition has shown the same vigor and attractiveness in alien settings as the European: it no longer has any competitors as a world shaper.

The dominance of European culture can be seen in the spread of one of its grossest manifestations, its material greed and rapacity. Societies rooted in changeless acceptance of things as they are have taken up the belief that limitless improvement in material well-being is a proper goal and so have assumed much of the mental heritage of an expanding Europe. Often the very idea that willed change is possible is itself deeply subversive. The effect of such ideas has been to impose on top of social institutions of great antiquity and toughness a layer of assumptions and myths drawn from the experience of Western liberalism; republics are common the world over and everyone speaks the language of democracy and proclaims the rights of man. There is also an effort to implant the rationalizing and utilitarian tradition in government and administration and to repeat models of institutions which have been found successful in European countries. One reason why many blacks clamor vociferously against white societies is that they in fact wish to realize the ideals of human rights and dignity which have been evolved by European civilization. Their black cousins in new nations want to share in the benefits made possible by industrialization even when preaching the merits of what is sometimes called "Negritude" or black culture. Ironically they do so just when many raised within the Western tradition are more skeptical than ever about the value of such "benefits."

It is very striking that few cultures have been able to resist altogether this vigorous tradition: even China bows to Marx and science. Some have been more successful in resisting it than others, but almost everywhere the individuality of major traditions of civilization has been much weakened. When modernizers have sought to take some things but not others from the Western mode, they have not found it easy to do so. It is difficult to obtain selective modernity; it typically comes in a package, some of whose contents may be unwelcome. This cohesiveness, together with the relative accessibility of Western material products, explains some of the impression of superficiality which has accompanied modernization in various countries. It is a little like Hellenization in the Near East in the centuries after Alexander. Institutions, ideas, and styles borrowed from Europe often show something of the same lack of real spirit and inspiration that the transplanted Greek ideas did in the Near East. There is the same prevalence of the signs and symbols of material achievement—now dams, universities, steelworks, and airlines instead of baths, theaters, and temples—the same sharing of standard forms of government and administration, the literary and artistic fashions, and even the aesthetic values. English has become a world lingua franca of business and intellectual life as Greek once was. Yet the results often fail to ring true; successfully transplanted though such things seem to have been, they are somehow different in other traditions.

A MATERIAL PROMISE

The inevitable local transformations do not invalidate the claim that the variety of human experience is converging instead of diverging. The subtlest success of European civilization came when it began to convince people in other cultures that through it lay the only road to material success for themselves. What they then seized upon were not only techniques and institutions, not merely such superficialities as clothes and gadgets, but goals and patterns of behavior, and these sometimes produced incongruous and unanticipated results in the recipient societies. The ideas of progress as unlimited material advance, of the right of the individual to assert himself, of nationalism as the determinant of political organization would all produce consequences going far beyond what was expected by the Europeans who confidently conveyed the recipes they believed to underlie their own success. Similarly the introduction of new machines and the building of railways and mines could transform social life in ways no one had willed or envisaged. Yet once Western methods and goals were accepted (as they were eventually by elites in all countries), an irreversible process had begun. Even in the most tightly controlled examples modernization was bound to create new needs and demands.

The prestige and attractiveness of this model of civilization rested at bottom on the power of its techniques and tools to bring about rapid and progressive change, above all in the production of greater material well-being. It was this which underlay a real revolution in the minds of men—the acceptance of the idea that continuous material improvement is possible for large numbers of people. This was the climax of centuries of growing experience in manipulation of the environment. Ironically the idea took root over all the world almost at the moment that misgivings were beginning to be felt about it in its birthplace.

The mastery of environment

There have always been apprehensions about man's interference with nature and his attempts to control it, but until recently they have seemed to rest on nonrational grounds, such as the fear of provoking divine anger or of nemesis. But for most of human history these misgivings were increasingly eroded by the palpable advantages and improvements which such interference brought about. The most obvious form of this was the creation of new wealth; it is undeniable that today more people live longer at a higher standard of living than most of their predecessors.

Some recent critics of our civilization agree that it is supremely efficient at creating material improvement but note that wealth in itself does not remove all man's dissatisfactions and may actually irritate some of them. Pollution, the crowded anonymity of modern cities, and the nervous stress and strain of modern work conditions do much to erase satisfaction with a mere increase of material goods. Scale matters too. Problems have mushroomed in today's cities and may even have grown to the point at which they are insoluble. Still greater misgivings are felt about the threat of overpopulation and the reality of increasing pressure on diminishing energy resources, which could make competition for them more intense and the world therefore more politically unstable. In any case, energy and material resources are now so wastefully and inequitably employed that a new version of the Malthusian disaster seems possible.

We have by no means reached the end (or anything like it) of our capacity to produce food and it is far more likely that the world will run out of other things before the food supply fails, whatever may be the hardships experienced from time to time in specific places. Certainly there would at once be an impossible situation if every nation in the world sought to consume goods other than food at the level of the developed countries today. There is a limit to the food which the individual can consume. There is virtually no limit to the services he can consume in terms of a better environment, medicine, social aids, and the like, and these rest at bottom on energy and material resources. It can no longer seem reasonable to use up natural resources at the rate we have been for the last two or three decades. But we have not yet begun to grasp the social and political changes which must follow from this fact.

The depletion of the world's resources is obviously connected with the greatly accelerated population growth of the last century or so. One of the difficulties here is that there exists to deal with this problem nothing like the knowledge or technique which is available, for example, to put a man on the moon. There are many different methods of restricting family size, but they offer no assured outcome because societies are very complicated things. While population growth has been slowed down in some countries, it is not known whether the conditions which produce this are transferable to other societies and it is unlikely, if they are, that the results will be identical. The impact of sterilization and contraceptive propaganda in India, for example, seems in spite of great efforts to be insignificant.

Continuity and discontinuity

To say whether pessimism or optimism about the future is justified is not (it must be repeated) the historian's job. But he can say whether some historical facts have or have not been taken into account in making a judgment about the present. It is now often urged that man's undoubted success in manipulating the ecosystem is in danger of disappearing because of two interconnected tendencies. One is that new problems often follow rapidly from the solution of older ones and perhaps too rapidly for an answer to be found before irreversible damage is done. Thus we face the problems of depleted natural resources, disturbance of existing ecologies, and the creation of new stresses and dangers, such as those involved in gathering people into great industrial cities. The second tendency is for the achievements of science to outrun our capacities for their social control. Examples are the dangers inherent in the proliferation of nuclear weapons, reduced death rates which lead to disastrous population explosions, and the provision of mass communication before societies are culturally prepared to deal with it critically.

If these observations are correct, then the present age indeed seems to represent a break in historical continuity. They would imply that the progressive power to control the environment, which marked the whole of earlier history and all known prehistory, is at an end. This would be a prospect not to be lightly regarded, but there are no reasons to believe that the process of discovering techniques to meet problems in the past cannot be brought to bear successfully to solve those of the future. There are no grounds either logical or empirical for thinking that the steady accretion of control over nature will not continue. The factor that has changed is simply that scale and acceleration have grown. But this applies to solutions as well as to problems.

The depressing effect of such considerations is bound to be diminished if we reflect that we know of nothing in the nature of the problems now facing the human race which renders them in principle incapable of solution. They may be more urgent and potentially more damaging, but this is only to say that their solution may require more urgent and radical methods, not that they cannot be solved at all. We may have to decide to live in a different way, but we need not assume mankind will be extinguished. There is no reason to conclude that this series of tests will prove fatal to man when earlier ones which he faced with infinitely less resources both mental and technological—the onset of the ice ages, for example—did not. We have plenty of evidence of man's adaptability in the past. The only clear warning which does stand out is that we are likely to be gravely misled about the future if we simply extrapolate past and present trends. We must prepare for discontinuity as well as continuity.

A NEW HORIZON

One huge achievement of the last few years suggests that the capacity of our culture to meet unprecedented challenges is as great as ever. This is the exploration of space, the greatest of man's material triumphs to date. If a symbolic date for a breach in the continuity of history were needed, there is much to be said for July 21, 1969. This was the day when men first stepped onto the surface of the moon and thereby began the latest and greatest extension of their environment. We then truly entered a new phase of history: the story of man on other celestial bodies.

Space technology has deep roots in the imaginations and aspirations of scientists decades ago and in the development of high-powered rockets before and during the Second World War, but our narrative can conveniently begin in October 1957 when Russia launched an unmanned satellite by rocket. This was Sputnik I, nearly two hundred pounds in weight, which orbited the earth emitting radio signals. It was of great political significance because it shattered any illusion that Russian technology lagged far behind American. But what was much more important was that it ended the era when the actual principle of space travel was still in doubt. The space age had clearly begun.

Sputnik I initiated a rapid burst of satellite activity. The United States had started its own space program in 1955 though with much more modest hardware than the Russians. The first American satellite weighed only three pounds; Khrushchev mockingly called it a grapefruit. When an attempt was made to launch it at the end of December 1957 with great attendant publicity, the rocket caught fire instead of taking off and a sad little bleeping from the sands near the launching site was all that resulted. The Americans were soon to have much more impressive success, but within a month of Sputnik I the Russians had launched Sputnik II, an astonishingly successful machine weighing half a ton and carrying the first passenger in space, a black and white mongrel called Laika. For nearly six months Sputnik II orbited the earth, visible to the whole world.

The Russian and American space programs had thus already diverged. Russia's strength lay and would continue to lie in the power and size of her rockets, which could lift big loads. This had military implications more obvious than the equally profound but less spectacular ones which flowed from American concentration on data gathering and sophisticated instrumentation. Thus, although people soon spoke of a "space race" (and one existed in terms of prestige), the contestants were really running toward different goals and with one great exception—the wish to put a man in space—were probably not much influenced by each other's performance except to run harder in the directions they had chosen. The contrast was clear enough when Vanguard, the American satellite which had failed in December 1957, was successfully launched the following March. It went much deeper into space than any predecessor and has provided more valuable scientific information in proportion to its size than any other satellite. It is likely to be going around for another couple of centuries or so.

New achievements followed so quickly that only the main ones need be noted. At the end of 1958 the first satellite for communications purposes was successfully launched. It was American. Information and experience were now making progress faster and faster. In 1960 the Americans scored another "first" by retrieving a capsule after reentry. The Russians soon followed this by orbiting and recovering Sputnik V, a four-and-a-half ton satellite carrying two dogs, who thus became the first creatures to traverse space and return to earth. Finally, on April 12, 1961, a Russian rocket took off carrying the first man to travel in space, Yuri Gagarin. He landed three days later after making one orbit around the earth. The age of man in space had begun four years after Sputnik I.

Possibly spurred by a wish to offset the failure of the Bay of Pigs, President Kennedy proposed in May 1961 that the United States try to land a man on the moon and return him safely to earth before the end of the decade. His reasons for recommending this were interestingly different from the aims which had led the rulers of fifteenth-century Portugal and Spain to back such men as Magellan and da Gama. Kennedy listed four: such a project provided a good national goal; it would be prestigious—"impressive to mankind" were the president's words; it was of great importance for the exploration of space; and finally (somewhat oddly) it was of unparalleled difficulty and expense. Nothing was said of the benefit of advancing science or of the commercial or military advantage. Surprisingly the project met virtually no opposition and Congress soon allocated the first money toward the most expensive technological exercise in history.

During the early 1960s the Russians continued to make spectacular progress in manned space flight. The world was perhaps most struck by their sending a woman into space in 1963, but more technically impressive were the size of their vehicles—a three-man machine was launched in 1964—and the achievement the following year of the first "space walk," or crew member's emergence from the spacecraft and movement outside it while in orbit. The Russians went on to make important advances in arranging rendezvous for vehicles in space and in engineering their docking, but after 1967 the glamour had clearly passed to the Americans. It was in that year too that the first death from space travel occurred when a Russian was killed during reentry. In 1968 the American program achieved a sensational success by sending a three-man vehicle around the moon and transmitting television pictures of its surface. It was now clear that Apollo, as the moon-landing project was named, was going to succeed.

The First Men in the Moon

The veteran reporter Alistair Cooke made it clear in his despatch to the Manchester Guardian *that he found the stage-management on television of the first moon landing less than adequate.*

Then we deserted the excellent simulations from the Grumman Air Base, here, on Long Island, and came to the real thing, a shot, as from the Lumière Bros.' early film, with a bare, off-Broadway set, a perspective of desert, and the white blobs of Armstrong and Aldrin plomping around like little gazelles. This, of course, was the true glory, and only another fourteen hours of it could dim its joy.

In that time, we heard from science fiction men, N.A.S.A. wallahs, the geologists again, and more instant philosophers; and winced through President Nixon's tasteless interlude congratulating the erect astronauts from the tasteful comfort of the White House study.

One science fictioner assured us, minute after soaring minute, that 'This is the Year One. If we don't change our calendars, the historians will. This is Alpha and Omega. This is the Bar Mitzvah. This is the moment of Transition from infancy to adultery—er—to adulthood.' That was worth a replay.

The astronauts continued to bob around on the Sea of Tranquillity while we floundered on the Ocean of Banality.

From David Ayerst, ed., *The Guardian Omnibus, 1821–1971* (London: Wm. Collins Sons & Co. Ltd., 1973), p. 687.

In May 1969 the spacecraft Apollo 10 approached to within six miles of the moon's surface to assess the techniques of the final stage of landing. A few weeks later, on July 16, Apollo 11 carried a three-man crew into space. Their lunar module landed on the moon's surface on July 20. The following morning Neil Armstrong, the commander of the mission, became the first human being to set foot on the moon. President Kennedy's goal set in 1961 had been achieved, with about six months to spare. Other landings were to follow.

The cost had been so great that this wonderful achievement was decried by some who felt that such a huge mobilization of resources was not justifiable because the goal was irrelevant to the real problems of the earth. To some, space travel has seemed to be our civilization's equivalent of the pyramids, a huge investment in the wrong things in a world crying for the allocation of resources to education, nutrition, and mental health — to name only a few pressing needs. It is difficult not to feel some sympathy for such a view at first sight but more difficult to maintain it.

In the first place, much of the scientific and economic effect is hardly quantifiable and may be very far reaching. The techniques of miniaturization used in making control systems, for example, are valuable in other fields, and it cannot be said that they would necessarily have been developed so soon without the investment in space. Nor indeed can we be confident that the resources allocated to space would have been made available for any other great scientific or social goals had they not been used in this way. Our social machinery does not operate like that. But there are also some striking positive characteristics about the programs of the powers engaged in space exploration, which by 1970 included Great Britain and France.

In estimating these achievements the mythical importance of what was happening must not be neglected. Developed societies today — even Communist ones — have shown signs of being unable to generate much interest and enthusiasm among their members for collective purposes except in war. The imagination is not much spoken to by the prospect of adding marginally to the gross national product or of introducing one more refinement into a system of social services, however desirable these things may be. Kennedy's identification of a national goal was shrewd; in the troubled 1960s the United States had much else to concern and divide it, but no one turned up to disrupt the launching of satellites. There is something inspiring about the achievement of a difficult objective at the sacrifice of present goods of other kinds.

This dimension of the space program goes beyond the participating countries. Landing on the moon was the most complete affirmation to that date of the belief that man lives in a universe he can manage. The instruments for doing so are now science and technology; they were once magic and prayer. But there is a continuity in the growing confidence of man through history that he can control the natural world. It cannot be said that landing on the moon is more or less important than, say, the mastery of fire, the invention of agriculture, or the discovery of nuclear power in adding to man's power to enlarge and dominate his environment. But it is emphatically an event of that order.

It is tempting to compare the penetration of space with the last great age of discovery. The time scales are interestingly different. Something like eighty years of exploration were required to take the Portuguese around Africa to India; there were eight between the launching of the first man into space and the arrival of men on the moon. Exploration in space is safer too. It long had no fatalities and in terms of passenger-mile traveled it is still the safest form of transportation known to man, while fifteenth-century seafaring was a perilous business at best. If you did not die of shipwreck, there was a good chance that tropical disease, scurvy, or irritated natives would do you in.

This is not a frivolous point. It indicates something important about the nature of the moon achievement. This is its predictable and cumulative quality, in which it aptly summarizes the whole trend of our scientific society. Apollo was launched from a very wide base, nothing less than the whole aggregate of the scientific knowledge of mankind. The distance to the moon was already known; so were the conditions which would greet men arriving there, most of the hazards they might encounter, the quantities of power and supplies and the nature of the other support systems they would need to return, and even the stresses their bodies would undergo. In part this diminished the tremendous impact of the event. Though things might have gone wrong, there was a widespread feeling that they would not. Since 1969 even more impressive technical operations have been carried out nearer to earth—men living in space for weeks on end—and unmanned satellites have extended the visual exploration of space beyond Jupiter, yet these tremendous achievements have become almost normal, so jaded are our imaginations. However, it is not entirely because of the new familiarity with the idea of space travel, it is also because of the confidence that science can in the end always produce the predicted result.

Another interesting feature of the space effort has been its collective nature. True, there was for a long time only limited cooperation between the two greatest nations concerned, the United States and Russia, and this undoubtedly led to inefficiencies and wasteful duplication of effort. Yet the national programs have been the apotheosis of the collective nature of modern science. Thousands of people in hundreds of laboratories, test stations, and factories made the lunar landing possible. The relative anonymity of the space explorers themselves illustrates the same truth. Though their courage and professional skill cannot be doubted, men like Gagarin and Armstrong are remembered because they were the first to do certain things, not for their enterprise in carrying through their own projects of investigation and discovery. For them to have done that would of course have been impossible. They were the spearhead of a huge process, only in small degree something more than human projectiles whose trajectory was controlled from the ground. No name emerges from a decade of colossal additions to human knowledge and experience of space which will be remembered with the same sense that it sums up an era as do those of Columbus, Magellan, or da Gama.

It was interesting too that at first sight space exploration seemed no more to require changes of outlook or ideology than the great discoveries of the fifteenth and sixteenth centuries. The Apollo landing party planted the American flag on the moon, and an astronaut read aloud from the Bible while orbiting about it. Ten years earlier the Russians had dropped a Lenin pennant to the moon's surface. These symbols of alternative mythologies seemed ominous; nationalism might provoke a scramble for space. And there was the basic fact of national rivalry in the space race itself. Fortunately the worst dangers of competition were avoided and it was soon agreed by treaty that celestial objects were not subject to appropriation by any one state, a stipulation very different in spirit from the treaty of Tordesillas which once divided the newly discovered world between Spain and Portugal. Only a little later too, on July 17, 1975, another major technical feat also provided a symbolic act of cooperation, as American and Russian spacecraft met a hundred and thirty seven miles above the earth, joined themselves together so that their crews could meet and shake hands, and then separated to return safely to the ground.

Space exploration is the most recent step in the increasing mastery of nature, most of which has been achieved in the last few millennia. Those millennia are to be considered against the eons during which prehistoric technology inched forward from the discovery that a cutting edge could be put on a stone chopper and that fire could be mastered. In that era the weight of genetic programing and environmental pressure loomed much larger than conscious control and this must have been true until well into civilized times. The dawning of consciousness that more than this submission to natural forces was possible was the major step in man's evolution after his physical structure settled to become more or less what it is today. The control and use of experience then became possible, and after that, experiment and analysis. There is no need to conclude that this will not still provide man with the toolkit he needs to survive in a world he has made so different from that of even his recent ancestors.

But there are no grounds for unequivocal assertions one way or another, which may seem disappointing to some readers of a history of the world. It should not be. In considering what the future holds the only advantage of being a historian is that one may be a little less surprised by the outcome, whatever it is. Only two general truths emerge from the study of history. One is that things tend to change much more, and more quickly, than one might think. The other is that they tend to change much less, and more slowly, than one might think. Both truths tend to be exemplified by any specific historical situation and so, for good and ill, we shall always find what happens somewhat surprising.

Further Reading

A bibliography should within its limits be exhaustive and list essentials; this essay is not intended to do this and is therefore not a bibliography. It has the humbler aim of offering suggestions and guidance about books to which the reader can turn next for amplification and criticism of theses met in this book and for further basic information about them. It has the secondary purpose (though it might be thought more important) of suggesting books which will actually be enjoyable. From these aims it follows that my suggestions are not always suggestions about the "best" books on particular topics; the "best" history book for one man is far from satisfactory for another and often useful to neither for purposes of study. Utility and interest have been my main considerations in this essay. I have had it in mind to help the reader who wishes to go on just a little beyond what has been said here, and the books I mention seem to me all to be helpful for exactly that purpose. A secondary consideration has been the importance of bringing to notice some of the classic works of history which have deeply shaped historical thinking.

Many books are bound to cut across the boundaries which are employed to divide up a book such as this, and many too do not have a well-defined subject matter, or at least not one which allocates itself easily to a particular category. This presents problems of organization. On the whole it seems to me that a roughly chronological approach is the best one to follow because the most convenient for the reader to use. This essay therefore follows within broad limits the chronological pattern of this book, but the limits are very broad. All the books recommended or mentioned fall into four main classes, as follows:

1. Comprehensive accounts and narratives valuable for their factual content, whether they are best dipped into as works of reference or read straight through.
2. Biographies, monographs, special studies, and interpretative essays to be read for the closer and deeper exploration of individual topics.
3. Classic historical works.
4. Documents or collections of documents which should rapidly deepen a student's response to certain topics. (I have not included volumes of "readings" of the conventional kind because they are usually limited in the interest of comprehensiveness to brief extracts which preclude any real sense of confrontation with remote times and mentalities.)

No books in foreign languages have been mentioned in this essay, and where a foreign book is noted it is given with the date of publication of its translation or, sometimes, of its latest easily accessible edition in English.

One last point should be made before beginning to talk about the literature itself. The essential reference instruments of the historian include a
huge body of works—atlases, encyclopedias, historical and biographical dic-
tionaries, and, above all, bibliographies. Some of these books are of wide
scope, some are narrowly defined. Obviously, all of them are potentially relevant to the history of the world. Many of them already stand on the open or
reference shelves of all libraries of any size, and there is a fair chance that at
least the backs of them are already well known to some readers of this book.
All that can usefully and briefly be said about them is that they should be
used. There are so many that no comprehensive account of them can be giv-
en here and it is hard to think of a useful selection; I therefore mention
none. But there is good reason to draw attention to books mentioned below
which have valuable bibliographical apparatus, and I have done this by putting a dagger (‡) after their titles. Where a paperback edition exists I have
indicated it with an asterisk, but since many titles continue to be made available in paperback the reader may consult *Paperbound Books in Print* for an
up-to-date listing.

EARLY MODERN AND MODERN EUROPE

In this book I have frequently emphasized that it is never wise to lean too heavily on assertions about beginnings and endings of historical periods. A notable example is provided by European history in the fourteenth to sixteenth centuries, where
much debate has gone on about where the Middle Ages ended and Modern (or, now,
"Early Modern") history begins and about the delimitation (and, indeed, definition)
of that elusive concept, the Renaissance. It is reasonable to ask students to make up
their own minds, only urging them to remember that different answers usually reflect
different definitions (explicit or implicit) of what is being talked about. Whatever the
answers adopted, it will also always be worthwhile to read two books which may be
thought classics, in that they did so much to shape debate, even though scholars have
done considerable damage to their arguments. The first is a book over a century old,
Jacob Burckhardt's *The Civilization of the Renaissance in Italy*, and the second a
more modern book by the Dutch historian, J. Huizinga, *The Waning of the Middle
Ages** (1924). Among the most important books contributing to the long debate detonated by the first, there is room for only one here: H. Baron's *The Crisis of the Early
Italian Renaissance** (rev. ed. 1966). A valuable collection of sources is *The Renaissance Philosophy of Man*,* edited by Ernst Cassirer and others (1948). An outstandingly good and lucid integration of cultural with political history over this period is
available in a book by the leading English scholar of the Reformation, A. G. Dickens,
The Age of Humanism and Reformation: Europe in the 14th–16th Centuries*‡
(1972), and its bibliography requires special remarks for its guidance to books on
Renaissance art, a topic which I have deliberately not treated with the amplitude
conventionally given to it. It also provides excellent guidance to the history of the
Church and religion which is the author's special interest. From a Roman Catholic
point of view, one book may nevertheless be mentioned, the third volume of a general history of the Church by P. Hughes entitled *The Revolt Against the Church:
Aquinas to Luther* (1947).

Among general works of reference for the modern era in English first place must be given, unfortunately, to the *New Cambridge Modern History*, whose thirteen volumes (numbered as twelve, though one was so unsatisfactory that it had to undergo an almost immediate and radical revision) contain some outstandingly good summaries of the state of historical opinion and knowledge when they were written, though a few contributions are pedestrian (1957–1968). What is wrong with the series is that its individual volumes are badly coordinated with one another and sometimes badly planned within themselves. This means that, though indispensable, they are less of an achievement and often less useful even now than the old *Cambridge Modern History* (1902–1910), also in twelve volumes, whose outdated approach and focus should not deter the student; it is a work which contains some excellent material and much more information than its successor. It also had good bibliographies (for its day); its successor has none.

There are many short surveys of European history since 1500, or of specific periods since then, which makes this one of the easiest areas to explore without guidance. One which demands mention first of all, though it ranges slightly beyond the area of Europe, is *A History of the Modern World*° by R. R. Palmer and Joel Colton‡ (4th ed. 1971). Helpful books which cover shorter periods include J. R. Hale's *Renaissance Europe 1480–1520*° (1971), which is rather more of an interpretative essay than a factual account; *Europe in the Sixteenth Century*° by H. Koenigsbegred and G. L. Mosse (1968); *The Ancien Regime in Europe* by E. N. Williams (1970); E. J. Hobsbawm's Marxist study of *The Age of Revolution 1789–1848*° (1962); D. Thomson's *Europe Since Napoleon*‡ (1962); and J. M. Roberts' *Europe 1880–1945*° (1970).

They may be supplemented by some of the more important and attractive national histories. For Great Britain, *The Oxford History of England* has nine volumes which divide up the centuries between the Tudors and the Second World War. They are still useful and have good bibliographies though looking more and more out of date, but the most recent, A. J. P. Taylor's *English History 1914–1945*‡ (1965) should certainly be mentioned. For earlier times, G. R. Elton's *England under the Tudors* (2nd ed. 1974) and Conrad Russell's *A Crisis of Parliaments*°‡ (1971) are at the top of their class for the sixteenth century and may be supplemented on the biographical side by the very enjoyable book by Christopher Morris, *The Tudors*° (1955). One figure dominates the biographical discussion of the seventeenth century and may be studied in an old classic work by C. H. Firth, *Oliver Cromwell and the Rule of the Puritans in England*° (1925) and a recent biography by Christopher Hill, *God's Englishman*° (1972). Books which transformed English historians' views of the eighteenth century when they appeared were L. B. Namier's studies of *The Structure of Politics at the Accession of George III* (2nd ed. 1957) and *England in the Age of the American Revolution* (2nd ed. 1961), but the student may find a better starting point in K. B. Smellie's *Great Britain Since 1688* (1962). For the nineteenth century, R. K. Webb's overall survey, *Modern England: From the Eighteenth Century to the Present*° (1968) is first class.

Among other countries France is the best covered in English. Albert Guerard's *France: A Modern History* is the best one-volume survey and has an excellent bibliography (rev. ed. by Paul A. Gagnon, 1969). Within the modern era see also J. B. Wolf's important biography of *Louis XIV* (1968), F. M. Markham's *Napoleon*° (1963) as a starting point for the examination of that remarkable man, and P. Geyl's masterly discussion of the attitudes scholars have taken toward the emperor, *Napoleon, For and Against* (1949). The Revolution cannot be ignored and I suggest three books, the brilliant *Social History of the French Revolution*° by Norman Hampson (1963), G. Lefebvre's textbook of world history in the revolutionary decade called *The*

French Revolution° (2 vols., 1962–1964), and the same author's distillation of scholarship into a small companion in his little book on *The Coming of the French Revolution*° (1947).

On Italy there is a huge bibliography, not least because it was long divided into several states. In the context of world history, I limit myself ruthlessly to pointing out B. Pullan's *A History of Early Renaissance Italy* (1973). No other book in English requires mention in a reading list on this scale until we come to unified Italy, admirably discussed in D. Mack Smith's *Italy: A Modern History*‡ (rev. ed. 1969).

On Spain, a short book by one of the greatest of Spanish historians in this century is the indispensable *Approaches to the History of Spain*° by Jaime Vicens Vives (rev. ed. 1970), and on Spain's great age see J. H. Elliott, *Imperial Spain 1469–1716*‡ (2 vols., 1963, 1970). Her tragic modern era has been explored in one of the masterpieces of twentieth-century historical writing, Gerald Brenan's *The Spanish Labyrinth*° (1950). Finally, a splendid little book in a little but important country, C. Wilson's *The Dutch Republic and the Civilization of the Seventeenth Century*° (1968).

Across the Rhine: from the Reformation to the twentieth century there are three fine volumes by Hajo Holborn which provide the best resource to the beginner. All bear the general title *A History of Modern Germany* and each is subtitled as follows: *The Reformation* (1959), *1648–1840* (1963), *1840–1965* (1969). On the Habsburg monarchy, C. A. Macartney's *The Habsburg Empire 1790–1918*‡ (1969) is huge and authoritative; students may find a short sketch by R. A. Kann, *The Habsburg Empire* (1957), helpful as an appetizer. For the last period of the empire A. J. May's *The Hapsburg Monarchy, 1867–1914*° (1951) is excellent.

On Russia, there is J. Westwood's *Endurance and Endeavour: Russian History 1812–1971*°‡ (1973), and an indispensable work of art, full of information and suggestion to the careful reader, Leo Tolstoy's great novel, *War and Peace.*° On one specific theme, the making of the Russian revolutionary movement, see B. D. Wolfe, *Three Who Made a Revolution*° (rev. ed. 1964).

Among books on economic history which override national boundaries, see the two volumes so far published of the modern part of *The Cambridge Economic History of Europe.* Volume IV is entitled *The Economy of Expanding Europe: The 16th and 17th Centuries* (1967), and Volume VI is *The Industrial Revolution and After* (two parts, 1965). The later volume (in spite of the title of the series) contains some articles on world, American, and Asian economic history, and one part of it has also been reprinted in slightly modified form as a book, the brilliant study by D. S. Landes entitled *The Unbound Prometheus: Technological Change and Industrial Development in Western Europe from 1750 to the Present*°‡ (1969). Its footnotes contain more helpful guidance to further reading than many bibliographies. A more conventional discussion which is a very competent and useful handbook is *The Economic Development of Continental Europe 1780–1870* (1973) by A. S. Milward and S. B. Saul, and there is a brief and excellent survey by W. O. Henderson of *The Industrialization of Europe 1780–1914*° (1969). On the experience of the first industrial nation see two short but excellent books, T. S. Ashton's *The Industrial Revolution 1760–1830*° (1962) and J. D. Chambers' *The Workshop of the World: British Economic History from 1820 to 1880*° (1969). Important background to events inside Europe is also provided by R. Davis, *The Rise of the Atlantic Economies*° (1973). On the ideas of economists, which in modern times became a force in their own right, see in the first place R. L. Heilbroner, *The Worldly Philosophers*° (rev. ed. 1961).

Here are a few more books which escape categorization and are highly stimulating. F. Braudel's *The Mediterranean and the Mediterranean World in the Age of Phil ip II* (2 vols., 1972–4) revolutionized the study of the sixteenth century. G. N. Clark's book on *The Seventeenth Century*° (2nd ed. 1947) is a marvelous collection of essays on different aspects of its civilization. A. Sorel's *Europe and the French Revolution: The Political Traditions of the Old Regime* (1885,° 1969) is a nineteenth-century book still worth reading. Keith Thomas, *Religion and the Decline of Magic*° (1971) is exciting. Harold Nicolson, *The Congress of Vienna*° (1946); P. Robertson, *Revolutions of 1848: A Social History*° (1952); G. Lichtheim, *A Short History of Socialism*° (1970) are all valuable ways into the nineteenth century. I. Berlin's *Karl Marx*° (3rd ed. 1963) is a brilliant short account of his life and thought. A. J. P. Taylor's *The Struggle for Mastery in Europe 1848–1918*° (1954) is the best narrative of international affairs. C. Falls' *A Hundred Years of War: 1850–1950*° (1954) discusses the changing nature of mass industrial war. On eastern Europe see W. H. McNeill's *Europe's Steppe Frontier, 1500–1800* (1964), P. Coles' *The Ottoman Impact on Europe 1350–1699*° (1968), and L. S. Stavrianos' *The Balkans Since 1453* (1956).

THE CREATION OF EUROPEAN WORLD POWER

The best introduction to the phase of discovery and exploration is J. H. Parry's synthesis, *The Age of Reconnaissance*° (1963), but the enthusiasm for the subject is most likely to be encouraged by reading S. E. Morison's *The European Discovery of America* (2 vols., 1971, 1974). D. F. Lach's *Asia in the Making of Europe* (2 vols., 1965) is suggestive, and among the many stimulating historical works we owe to C. Cipolla, his *Guns, Sails and Empires*° (1965) is notable in this context. If we choose one explorer as a way of appreciating the complexity of the forces which focused in early European expansion let it be Columbus, whose biography by S. E. Morison is entitled *Admiral of the Ocean Sea* (1942). On the oceanic empires there are many books, but one which directs interest toward the Eastern seas as well as the Americas is C. R. Boxer's *The Dutch Seaborne Empire 1600–1800* (1965). The early phase of British expansion is examined in another large collective work which maintained a very high level of contributions and had excellent bibliographies for its day, *The Cambridge History of the British Empire‡* (9 vols., 1929–1959); it took thirty years to publish so that much of it has been overtaken by later research, but it is worth exploration. Also on the British Empire, see W. B. Willcox's *Star of Empire: A Study of Britain as a World Power 1485–1945* (1950), and for the later phases of colonial expansion there is a model account in D. K. Fieldhouse, *The Colonial Empires*° (1966), which deals with imperialism substantially since the eighteenth century. On a special but important theme from which much can be learned about the value of an unconventional approach to a well-worn problem, see H. L. Hoskins' *British Routes to India* (1927).

One somber topic in the history of European world management which has attracted a huge volume of publication, most of it polemical, since the early nineteenth century is black slavery and the slave trade. It is ably and broadly surveyed in *Black Mother: The Years of the African Slave Trade* by B. Davidson (1961), and P. D. Curtin has edited and selected accounts by slaves themselves in *Africa Remembered*° (1967). We may bypass at this stage the old and ample debate on the motives of the abolitionists or those who found abolition acceptable and turn more attention to what historians have illuminated about the dimensions of the phenomenon and its effects. The miserable story of the handling of the victims by the slavers has been grippingly told in J. Pope-Hennessy's *Sins of the Fathers: A Study of the Atlantic Slave-Traders 1441–1807* (1967). Among many books dealing with the question of what happened to the slaves when they arrived on the other side of the Atlantic is M. Herskovits' *The*

New World Negro° (1966) and an especially memorable book about Brazil by
G. Freyre, *The Masters and the Slaves*° (1964). On the exploitation of Black Africa in
the post-slavery era, see the case of the Congo, an extreme example, described in
N. Ascherson's admirable book *The King Incorporated* (1963).

THE AMERICAS

An excellent recent popular account of one part of the Spanish conquests is
J. Hemmings' *The Conquest of the Incas*° (1970). An older general account is F. A.
Kirkpatrick's *The Spanish Conquistadores*° (1946). After that, guidance can be found
for this subject in the excellent *Spain in America*° by Charles Gibson (1966). On British America, see J. R. Alden, *Pioneer America*° (1966), L. B. Wright, *The Atlantic
Frontier: Colonial American Civilization 1607–1763*° (1947) for the general background, and R. B. Morris, *The American Revolution Reconsidered*° (1967). A classic
work on early nineteenth-century American civilization is Alexis de Tocqueville's
Democracy in America° (edited by Phillips Bradley, 1944). Beyond this, the mass of
literature on United States history can best be approached by way of the bibliographies of a well-tried textbook, *The Growth of the American Republic*‡ by S. E. Morison et al. (6th ed. 1969). A brief introduction to *Independence in Latin America*°‡ by
R. Graham (1972) provides a list of the main books in English in its reading list.

ASIA IN THE EUROPEAN AGE

A provocative book in its day and still well worth reading is K. M. Panikkar's
*Asia and Western Dominance: A Survey of the Vasco da Gama Epoch of Asian Histo-
ry 1498–1945*° (2nd ed. 1959). Another general book which is essential reading is
East Asia: Tradition and Transformation by J. K. Fairbank, E. O. Reischauer, and
A. M. Craig (1973). For India we have Percival Spear's *India: A Modern History* (rev.
ed. 1972) and L. S. O'Malley's *Modern India and the West* (1941). For the British period as a whole, the student should certainly not miss P. Woodruff's revealing book
about *The Men who Ruled India* (2 vols., 1952–1954). Scholarly study of the nationalist era is now producing many first-rate studies; there is an excellent brief introduction to them in A. T. Embree's *India's Search for National Identity*°‡ (1972).
L. Fischer's *Life of Mahatma Gandhi*° is still useful (1950), and many selections have
been published from the Mahatma's works; some may find *An Autobiography* by
Jawaharlal Nehru (1962) a more immediately attractive document from the nationalist
point of view.

On China's relations with the outside world J. K. Fairbank's study of *The United
States and China*° (3rd ed. 1971) is fundamental reading. See also the collection of
Ssu-yü Têng and J. K. Fairbank, *China's Response to the West: A Documentary Survey 1839–1923*° (1963). One revealing episode is dealt with in V. Purcell's study of
The Boxer Uprising (1963). H. R. Isaacs, *The Tragedy of the Chinese Revolution*°
(2nd ed. 1961) is interesting and important. Overall, the story of Chinese modernization and disruption is treated in a broad setting in *East Asia: Tradition and Transformation* already mentioned. One important thread worth consideration can be taken
up in K. S. Latourette, *A History of Christian Missions in China* (1929).

On modern Japan, a brilliant short history concentrating mainly on the modern
era is R. Storry's *A History of Modern Japan*° (1960). H. Borton's *Japan's Modern
Century* (2nd ed. 1970) is also a good starting point. George Sansom's *The Western
World and Japan*° (1950) remains first-class, though written before much recent research on economic and sociological topics had been done. The *Autobiography of*

Fukuzawa Yuzichi (1966) is an important document, the personal story of a Japanese intellectual's encounter with the Western tradition. On economic history and change, see the succinct *Short Economic History of Modern Japan* by G. C. Allen (rev. ed. 1963).

Southeast Asia has been an area which, for reasons of space, this book has had to neglect, yet it is very important, reflecting as it does the collision of both European and Asian imperialisms and the interplay of major religious and ideological traditions. Its history during the era of European intervention is well discussed in the perspective of a long past in the best introduction to the area's history, *A History of South-East Asia*° by D. G. E. Hall (3rd ed. 1968). Also stimulating is H. G. Q. Wales, *The Making of Greater India: A Study in Southeast Asian Cultural Change* (1950).

Moving westward, there is an admirably clear *History of Modern Iran* by Peter Avery (1965), and B. Lewis' *The Emergence of Modern Turkey*°‡ (2nd ed. 1968) is a very successful compression of a highly complex business. On the Arab countries, see A. H. Hourani's *Syria and Lebanon, a Political Essay* (1946), P. K. Hitti's *The History of the Arabs*° (10th ed. 1970), D. Lerner's *The Passing of Traditional Society, Modernizing the Middle East* (1958), and the magnificent history by Jacques Berque, *Egypt: Imperialism and Revolution* (1972). On that important country, for longer perspectives see also H. H. Dodwell, *The Founder of Modern Egypt* (1931) and P. M. Holt's interesting study, *Egypt and the Fertile Crescent 1516–1922*° (1969).

AFRICA

Historians have done much in recent years using tradition, archaeology, and anthropology to illuminate the history of Africa before effective European penetration of the continent. The books of Basil Davidson are admirable popularizations of this often complex scholarly material and two among them may especially be noted, *The African Past*° (1964), a collection of sources, and *Africa in History: Themes and Outlines*° (rev. ed. 1974). Unfortunately, most of the literature is concerned with specific countries (or with areas which were to emerge later on separate countries) and though there is a great deal of it, it is not easy to discriminate usefully. For that reason, it is important to draw attention to R. Hallett's *Africa to 1875*‡ (1970) for its well-organized bibliography. Two other excellent but much shorter general works are by R. Oliver and J. D. Fage, *A Short History of Africa*° (rev. ed. 1963) and R. Oliver, *The Dawn of African History*° (2nd ed. 1968). On one fascinating and remarkable country, see E. Ullendorf, *The Ethiopians*° (rev. ed. 1973). To the troubled history of South Africa there is an excellent brief introduction in G. Le May's *Black and White in South Africa*° (1971).

WORLD POLITICS IN THE ERA OF WORLD WARS

A good recent addition to a distinguished series (*The Rise of Modern Europe*, edited by W. L. Langer) is O. J. Hale's *The Great Illusion 1900–1914*°‡ (1971), whose bibliography relieves me of the necessity of saying more about the voluminous literature on the background of the First World War. On the war itself, see the cool, competent narrative of C. Falls, *The Great War*° (1959). The inter-war relations of the great powers have produced another flood of historical writing; the most important precaution to be taken is to avoid too narrow a concentration on Europe and, in particular, the German problem. This said, here is a short selection of recommendations (where historians could provide others equally defensible and, they could no doubt say, less idiosyncratic): G. Kennan, *Russia and the West under Lenin and Stalin°* (1961); H. Feis, *The Road to Pearl Harbor°* (1950); D. Borg, *The United States and the Far Eastern Crisis of 1933–1938* (1964); and A. J. P. Taylor, *The Origins of the Second World War°‡* (1961). A special mention must also be made of a unique book, Winston Churchill's own account of *The Second World War* (6 vols., 1948–1953), which for all its highly personal point of view is still the best single narrative of its subject and captivating reading. On the war itself there is another outstandingly good book in the Langer series by Gordon Wright, *The Ordeal of Total War°‡* (1968); once again, the bibliography is excellent.

REVOLUTIONARY FORCES IN THE TWENTIETH CENTURY

The collapse of Russia into revolution can still be approached profitably via M. T. Florinsky's *The End of the Russian Empire°* (1931). On the revolutionaries, the best single book is A. B. Ulman's *The Bolsheviks°* (1965) and there are many biographies of leading individuals. Besides Wolfe's book mentioned above, see the outstandingly important three-volume life of Trotsky by I. Deutscher (° 1954–1963). On the achievements of the revolution at home see J. P. Nettl, *The Soviet Achievement°* (1967) for a brief introduction and L. Schapiro, *The Communist Party of the Soviet Union°* (rev. ed. 1971) for political aspects. Well worth reading is T. H. Von Laue's *Why Lenin? Why Stalin? A Reappraisal of the Russian Revolution 1900–1930°* (1964). For repercussions see K. E. McKenzie, *Comintern and World Revolution 1928–1943* (1964).

Other revolutionary movements with a general impact can be studied in the collection of essays edited by S. J. Woolf under the title *European Fascism°* (1968); F. L. Carsten's *The Rise of Fascism°* (1967); the still outstanding biography of *Hitler: A Study in Tyranny°* by Alan Bullock (1962); and A. J. Nicholl's concise book on *Weimar and the Rise of Hitler°* (1968). Their background can be recalled by reading H. V. Hodson's *Slump and Recovery 1929–1937* (1938) and H. W. Arndt's *The Economic Lessons of the Nineteen Thirties* (1944). An area in which economic forces exercised particularly heavy weight is discussed very lucidly in *Independent Eastern Europe: A History°* by C. A. Macartney and A. W. Palmer (1962).

THE MODERNIZATION OF EUROPEAN THOUGHT

For the most part, bibliographies in books already mentioned must provide guidance for the exploration of intellectual history. About the secularization of European thought, however, and its eventual culmination in a culture in which science played a quite different role from what it played in any other, a little more must be said. Crucial phases in the history of thought were discussed in two exciting books by a French scholar, Paul Hazard. They have been translated and published under the titles *The European Mind 1680–1715°* (1953) and *European Thought in the Eighteenth Century°* (1954). Although there is a danger of duplication here, the approach of P. Gay's notable attempt to reconstruct intellectual history entitled *The Enlightenment: An Interpretation°* (2 vols., 1966–1969) is so different that it is justifiable to direct attention to it. The best thing the student could do next would be actually to read some of the great eighteenth-century authors—Voltaire, Diderot, Condorcet, say—to catch the flavor of the era. The end of its tradition can be caught in a book which is itself a document, Bertrand Russell's *History of Western Philosophy* (1945).

Meanwhile, true scientific thought has its own important history. See overall J. D. Bernal's *Science in History°* (4 vols., 1969), A. C. Crombie's *From Augustine to*

Galileo* (2 vols., 1959), and the stimulating book by A. N. Whitehead, *Science and the Modern World** (1925). On the first great age of scientific advance in the sixteenth and seventeenth centuries, see E. A. Burtt, *The Metaphysical Foundations of Modern Philosophical Science** (1948).

THE LATEST AGE

All books which narrate events since the Second World War tend to be generally overtaken by them. For the most part, it is best to rely on the periodical press to keep up to date and to concentrate on books which provide perspectives in which to view this era.

On cold war origins there is much polemical writing. A good point of departure are the scholarly works of H. Feis, notably *Churchill, Roosevelt, Stalin: The War They Waged and the Peace They Sought** (2nd ed. 1967), *Between War and Peace: The Potsdam Conference** (1960), and *The Atomic Bomb and the End of World War II in the Pacific** (rev. ed. 1966). A strong movement of criticism of American policy is expressed in many books, of which one of the shorter ones is W. A. Williams, *The Tragedy of American Diplomacy** (2nd ed. 1972). More objective is A. Fontaine, *The History of the Cold War** (2 vols., 1968–1969). Away from this debatable area, excellent guidance to the sequence of events can be found in W. Knapp, *A History of War and Peace 1939–1965* (1967) and P. Calvocoressi, *International Politics Since 1945** (1968). For the European story in outline see W. Laqueur, *Europe Since Hitler** (1972), C. Kindleberger, *Europe's Postwar Growth* (1967), and A. Shonfield, *Modern Capitalism** (1965).

As this book has argued, world affairs since 1935 have by no means at any point been completely controlled by the victors of the war. Local and nationalist forces have nowhere done more to force the pace than in the Middle East. On this, see E. Monroe, *Britain's Movement in the Middle East* (1963) and *Backdrop to Tragedy: The Struggle for Palestine* by W. R. Polk and others (1957).

For the post-colonial era in the history of Asia, see S. Schram *Mao Tse-Tung** (1969); A. D. Barnett, *Communist China and Asia** (1960); C. P. Fitzgerald, *The Birth of Communist China** (1966); K. Mahnert, *Peking and Moscow* (1966); and a fine book by a journalist, Edgar Snow's *Red Star Over China** (rev. ed. 1968). H. Tinker's *Ballot Box and Bayonet: People and Government in Emergent Asian Nations* (1964) is stimulating, but one of the most important discussions of the problems of newly independent societies is brought out in G. Myrdal's massive *Asian Drama: An Inquiry into the Poverty of Nations** (3 vols., 1968). On India in particular, see L. I. and S. H. Rudolph, *The Modernity of Tradition* (1967). For independent Africa see books already mentioned, and J. Hatch, *A History of Postwar Africa** (1965).

PRONUNCIATION KEY

a	act, bat, marry	i	if, big, mirror, furniture	p	pot, supper, stop	ə	occurs only in unaccented syllables and indicates the sound of
ā	aid, cape, way						
â(r)	air, dare, Mary	ī	ice, bite, pirate, deny	r	read, hurry, near		a *in* alone
ä	alms, art, calm						e *in* system
				s	see, passing, miss		i *in* easily
b	back, cabin, cab	j	just, badger, fudge	sh	shoe, fashion, push		o *in* gallop
							u *in* circus
ch	chief, butcher, beach	k	kept, token, make	t	ten, butter, bit		
				th	thin, ether, path		
d	do, rudder, bed	l	low, mellow, all	th̸	that, either, smooth	ᵊ	occurs in unaccented syllables before **l** preceded by **t, d,** or **n,** or before **n** preceded by **t** or **d** to show syllabic quality, as in
e	ebb, set, merry	m	my, simmer, him				
ē	equal, seat, bee, mighty			u	up, love		
		n	now, sinner, on	û(r)	urge, burn, cur		
ēr	ear, mere	ng	sing, Washington				
				v	voice, river, live		**cra·dle** (krā′dᵊl)
f	fit, differ, puff	o	ox, box, wasp				**red·den** (red′ᵊn)
		ō	over, boat, no	w	west, away		**met·al** (met′ᵊl)
g	give, trigger, beg	ô	ought, ball, raw				**men·tal** (men′tᵊl)
		oi	oil, joint, joy	y	yes, lawyer		
		o͝o	book, poor				
h	hit, behave, hear	o͞o	ooze, fool, too	z	zeal, lazy, those		
hw	white, nowhere	ou	out, loud, prow	zh	vision, mirage		

FOREIGN SOUNDS

A as in French **a·mi** (A mē′) [a vowel intermediate in quality between the **a** of *cat* and the **ä** of *calm,* but closer to the former]

KH as in German **ach** (äKH) or **ich** (iKH); Scottish **loch** (lôKH) [a consonant made by bringing the tongue into the position for **k** as in *key, coo,* while pronouncing a strong, rasping **h**]

N as in French **bon** (bôN) [used to indicate that the preceding vowel is nasalized. Four such vowels are found in French: **un bon vin blanc** (OEN bôN vaN bläN)]

OE as in French **feu** (fOE); German **schön** (shOEN) [a vowel made with the lips rounded in the position for **o** as in *over,* while trying to say **a** as in *able*]

R as in French **rouge** (Ro͞ozh), German **rot** (Rōt), Italian **ma·re** (mä′Re), Spanish **pe·ro** (pe′Rô) [a symbol for any non-English **r**, including a trill or flap in Italian and Spanish and a sound in French and German similar to KH but pronounced with voice]

Y as in French **tu** (tY); German **ü·ber** (Y′bər) [a vowel made with the lips rounded in position for o͞o as in *ooze,* while trying to say **ē** as in *east*]

ᵊ as in French **Bas·togne** (bA stôn′yᵊ) [a faint prolongation of the preceding voiced consonant or glide]

Abbreviations used in the Index: b. = born; d. = died; r. = reigned; fl. = flourished.

The pronunciation notation is adapted from *The Random House Dictionary of the English Language,* by permission of Random House, Inc.

Index

Abdul-Hamid (äb'd o͝ol hä mēd'), Ottoman sultan (r. 1876–1909), 833
aborigines, Australian, 588, 723
Académie des Sciences (A kA dä mē' dä syäns'), 594
Acadia, 582
advertising, 777
Afghanistan, 539, 732
Africa: and Asia, European conquest, 559–566; imperialism, late 1800s, 730–732; partition, 732–735; WWII spread in, 857; decolonization, 925–926
Age of Discovery, 555–559
agriculture: early modern Europe, 485–487; Caribbean, 571; revolution in, 619–621; overseas, 621–623; Russia, 787, 810; production, 887–889
Alaska, 687, 724
Albania, 777, 949
Albert, Prince Consort of England (1819–1861), 702
Alembert, Jean d' (dA län beR') (1717–1783), 608
Alexander I, tsar of Russia (r. 1801–1825), 677, 678
Alexander II (Tsar Liberator) of Russia (r. 1855–1881), 680, 681, 787
Algeria, 729, 733, 734, 922, 923, 951
Algiers, battle of, 529
Alliance for Progress, 930–931
Allies, WWI, 794; intervention in Russia, 801–802
Almanach Royale (Al mA nA' roi al'), 544
alphabet, Turkish, 839
Alsace and Lorraine, 779, 791, 805
American Revolution, 636–640
Americas: European settlement, 566–578; Spanish imperialism, 567–568; Spanish colonial system, 569–571
Amritsar (əm rit'sər), 872
Anabaptists, 507
anarchists, 773
Anglo-Persian Oil Co., 840
Annam, 767, 878
Anne, queen of England (r. 1702–1714), 535
Anschluss, 850–851
anticlericalism and Enlightenment, 609–610
apartheid, 926

Apollo moon mission, 961–963
Arabi Pasha (ə rä'bä pä'shä) (1839–1911), 832
Arab League, 881
Arabs (*see also* Islam): revolt, 835–836; organization of lands, 836–838; war with Israel, 881–882; nationalism and cold war, 921–923
Argentina, 927
Aristotle (ar'i stot'əl) (384–322 B.C.), 599
Armada (1588), 531–532
arms control, 785, 822
Armstrong, Neil (1930–   ), 964
art, interwar years, 842
Articles of Confederation (1781), 641
Asia (*see also* China; Far East; Japan): and Africa, European conquest of, 559–566; response to Western imperialism, 759–760
Aswan high dam, 922
Atlantic, battle of, 854, 859–860
Atlantic Charter, 856
Augsburg, League of (ouks'bo͞oRKH'), 534
Augsburg, Treaty of, 532
Australasia, 592
Australia: aborigines, 588, 723; rabbits and sheep in, 591; convicts shipped to, 592; becomes Commonwealth, 718; in WWII, 858; post-WWII, 919, 920; relations with Japan, 947
Austria (*see also* Austria-Hungary; Habsburgs): vs. Russia, 552–553; and Polish partition, 553; revolution, 666; isolation, 669; Anschluss, 850–851
Austria-Hungary: Dual Monarchy begins, 671; government, 786; annexes Bosnia, 790, 791; and start of WWI, 793; Dual Monarchy ends, 802, 805
Ayub Khan, Mohammed (ä yo͞ob' kän') (1907–1974), 910
Aztecs, 568, 723

Bacon, Francis (1561–1627), 600, 603, 60̶
Balboa, Vasco Nuñez de (1475–1517), 567
Balfour Declaration, 836
Balkans, 790–791
Balkan Wars 793, 833
Baltic states, Russian takeover, 854
Bandung conference, 910

Bangladesh, 898, 910
banking, 487, 489
Basutoland, 721
Batista, Fulgencio (bə tē′stə) (1901–1973), 929
Bayle, Pierre (pē âr′ bāl′), (1647–1706), 605
Bay of Pigs, 929
Beccaria, Cesare (che′zä ʀe′ bek′kä rē′ä) (1738–1794), 608
Becquerel, A. H. (bek′ə rel′) (1852–1908), 894
Belgian Congo, 734, 735
Belgium, 512, 513, 664, 734, 735, 793, 794
Belsen concentration camp, 861
Bengal (beng gôl′, beng′gəl), 564, 565, 566; partition, 762, 763
Bentham, Jeremy (1747–1832), 608, 785
Berlin blockade and airlift, 903
Berlin Wall, 936–938
Bessarabia (bes′ə rā′bē ə), 854
Bevin, Ernest (1881–1951), 870
Bibliolatry, 595, 598
Bill of Rights: England, 519; U.S., 643
Bismarck, Otto von (1815–1898), 669, 671, 673, 777, 786, 791
Black Dragon Society, 818
Black Hole of Calcutta, 565
blacks: after emancipation, 695, 696; and civil rights, 942–943
blockade: of Germany, WWI, 798; of Berlin, 903
Boers, 719–722
Boer War, 721–722
Bohemia, 779, 786
Bohr, Niels, (1885–1962), 894, 895
Bolívar, Simón (1783–1830), 714
Bolivia, 927, 928, 931
Bolsheviks, 774, 800
books (see also press; printing), Index of prohibited, 594, 604
Borneo, 917
Bosnia, 790, 791
Boston Massacre, 638
Boston Tea Party, 638
Bourbons (bŏŏr′bənz), 510, 522, 526, 534; restoration, 663–664
Boxer Rebellion, 748–749
Brahe, Tycho (tē′kō brä′hē) (1546–1601), 602
Brazil, 566, 569, 581, 714, 715
Breda, Treaty of (brā dä′), 582
Brest-Litovsk, Treaty of, 801
Bright, John (1811–1889), 634
Britain, see England; Great Britain
British East India Co., 562, 563, 564, 566, 586, 592; end of, 725–726, 728

Bruno, Giordano (1548–1600), 604
Buchenwald concentration camp, 861
Bulganin, Nikolai (nik′ə lī′ bŏŏl gä′nin) (1895–1975), 933
Bulgaria, 777, 794, 833
bureaucracy (see also government), early modern state, 524
Burke, Edmund (1729–1797), 612, 653
Burma, 560, 747, 767, 858, 863, 875
Burma Road, 830

Calicut, 557, 558, 561
California: gold, 673; Russian settlements, 678
Calvin, John (1509–1564), 507–508
Cambodia, 767, 878, 916, 946
Canada: settlement, 574, 576, 577; British in, 582, 583; Quebec Act, 638, 639; becomes Dominion, 718
Canadian Pacific Railway, 718
Cape Colony, 718, 720, 721
capitalism, vs. socialism, 907
Caribbean colonies, 571–572
Cartesians (kär tē′zhənz), 604
Castro, Fidel (1927–   ), 929, 930
casualties: WWI, 794, 798, 802–803; WWII, 861, 866, 867, 868; Indian independence and partition, 874; Chinese revolution, 912
Catherine II (the Great), tsarina of Russia (r. 1762–1796), 547–549, 609, 680
Catholic Church (see also church; papacy; Reformation; religion): Spanish colonies, 569, 571, 590; and French Revolution, 649–650; turn of the century, 780; and Latin American population, 887; growth, 899
Cavour, Camillo (kä mēl′lô kä vōōʀ′) (1810–1861), 669, 671
Central Powers, WWI, 794
Ceylon, 561, 566
Chadwick, James (1891–1974), 894
Chamberlain, Neville (1869–1940), 851
Champlain, Samuel de (1567–1635), 574
Charles I, king of England (r. 1625–1649), 516–517
Charles II, king of England (r. 1660–1685), 519, 563, 582
Charles X, king of France (r. 1824–1830), 663
Charles V, Holy Roman Emperor (r. 1519–1555), 505, 512, 527, 528–529, 560
Charles II, king of Spain (r. 1665–1700), 534
Chartism, 700–701
Ch'ên Tu-hsiu (chun′ dōō′shyōō′) (1879–1942), 818, 821
Chiang Kai-shek (chyäng′ kī′shek′), (1887–1975), 823, 825, 828, 875

child labor, 631–633

Chile, 928, 931

China: diplomacy, 525; Europeans in, 558, 559, 560; cultural interplay with Europe, 586–587; emigration from, 712; and European imperialism, 730, 740–744; social upheaval, 744–746; semicolonialism, 746–747; reform, 747–749; revolutionary movement, 749–751; and Japanese aggression, 750, 758–759, 818–819; republic, 817–818; May 4th movement, 819–820; communism, 820–822; civil war, 828–829; Japanese attack, 829–830; and cold war origins, 869; completion of revolution, 875–877; People's Republic inaugurated, 877; population, 887; and Korean War, 905–906; border conflict with India, 908, 913; as world power, 911–913; relations with Russia, 912, 913–916; exported revolution, 916–917; seated in UN, 946; U.S. resumes relations with, 946

Chinese Communist party, 821; and Kuomintang, 822–825

Chinese Eastern Railway, 828

Chinese National People's Party, 817

Chinese Soviet Republic, 828

Christendom vs. nationalism, 500

church, Russian, 540

Churchill, Winston (1874–1965), 854, 856, 860, 863, 868, 869

Church of England, 508, 509

cities (see also urbanization): and religion, 630; early 1900s, 772

civilization: Aztec, 567–568; and science, 892–898; choice of one world or several, 954–955; European tradition, 955–957; material promise, 957–960; continuity and discontinuity, 959–960; and space exploration, 960–965

civil rights, 942–943

Clemenceau, Georges (klä män sō') (1841–1929), 804, 806

Clive, Robert (1725–1774), 565

Cobden, Richard (1804–1865), 634

Cochin-China, 878

cold war: origins, 868–871; at its height, 902–907; and Arab nationalism, 921–923; in Western Hemisphere, 929–931; in post-Stalin era, 933–938

collectivization: Russia, 810; China, 912

Colombia, 717, 927

Columbus, Christopher (1451–1506), 566

Combined League Society, 750

Comecon, 949

Cominform, 870, 934

Comintern, 807, 821

commerce (see also trade), early modern Europe, 487–490

Common Market, 951–952

Commonwealth, and English Civil War, 517–518

communalism, 763–766

communism (see also Russia): Taiping society, 745; Chinese, 820–822; Islam, 838

Communist Manifesto (Marx), 676

Comte, Auguste (ō gyst' kôNt) (1798–1857), 785

concentration camps, WWII, 861–862

conditioned reflex, 898

The Condition of the English Working Class (Engels), 629

Confederate States of America, 693, 694

Confederation of the Rhine, 658

Congo, 734, 925

Congress of Berlin (1878), 790

Congress party, 874, 908

conquistadors, 567–568

conservatism, 653; industrial, 775

Constitution: U.S., 641–643, 694; France, 649

Constitutional Convention (1787), 641

containment, U.S. policy of, 870

Continental Congress, 638

contraception: and population, 618, 887; and women's role in society, 777

Convention (France), 647

Cook, Captain James (1728–1779), 592

Copernicus, Nikolaus (nik'ə lā'əs kō pûr'ni-kəs) (1473–1543), 602, 603

Corn Laws, 634–635; Repeal crisis, 698, 777

Cortés, Hernán (er nän' kôr tez'), (1485–1547), 567–568, 723

Cossacks, 538, 539, 540

Council for Mutual Economic Assistance, 870

Counter Reformation, 510–513

Cranmer, Thomas (1489–1556), 509

creed of Manchester, 634

Crete: Ottoman conquest, 535; Greek governor in, 777; union with Greece, 833; German takeover, 856

Crimea, 553

Crimean War, 667–669, 680

Cromwell, Oliver (krom'wəl, -wel'), (1599–1658), 517, 518, 533, 581

Cuba, 566, 567, 715; independence, 717, 739; revolution, 928–929; missile crisis, 930–931, 938

cubism, 842

Cultural Revolution, 915

culture: American colonies, 576–577; interplay, and world trade, 586–592; diffusion, 709–710

Curie, Marie (kyōō rē') (1867–1934), 894

Curie, Pierre (1859–1906), 894
customs administration, China, 745, 822
customs union, Germany, 635
Cyprus, 535
Czechoslovakia: post-WWI, 804, 805; German seizure, 851; Communist coup in, 870, 950

dadaism, 842
Darkest England, 630
Darwin, Charles (1809–1882), 781–782
Debs, Eugene (1855–1926), 844
Declaration of Human Rights, 956
Declaration of Independence, 639, 691
Declaration of the Rights of Man and the Citizen, 649
The Decline and Fall of the Roman Empire (Gibbon), 608
de Gaulle, Charles (də gōl', də gôl'), (1890–1970), 854, 923, 951–952
Denmark, 852
Descartes, René (rə nā' dā kärt') (1596–1650), 521, 604
despotism, enlightened, 521–523
Dewey, John (1859–1952), 818
Dialogue on the Two Great Systems of the World (Galileo), 603
diamonds, in South Africa, 721
Díaz, Porfirio (dē'äs) (1830–1915), 927
Diderot, Denis (dē'də rō') (1713–1784), 608
Dien Bien Phu (dyen' byen' fōō'), battle of, 916
diplomacy, origins, 525–526
Directory (France), 649
Discovery, Age of, 555–559
Disraeli, Benjamin (1804–1881), 698
A Doll's House (Ibsen), 775
Dominican Republic, 715, 717, 927, 931
Dual Monarchy, *see* Austria-Hungary
Dupleix (dy pleks'), French governor of India (1742–1754), 564
Dutch East India Co., 561
Dutch West India Co., 572
Dynasticism, Western Europe, 526–535

East Asian Cultural Union, 750, 759
Eastern Question, 540, 664, 679–680
economy: early modern Europe, 483–494; Russia, and serfdom, 545–547; American colonies, 577; world, and gold in California, 673, 706–710; Japan, 757; Russia, 787; France vs. Germany, 787; WWI, 797; post-WWI Europe, 804; Soviet Russia, 808; post-WWI recovery and collapse, 813–815; Japan (1930s), 825–826; capitalist vs. socialist, 907; and government, U.S., 941–942; Japan, 946–947

ecumenism, 899
Egypt: and French empire 729; British protectorate, 732, 838; birth of modern, 831–832; and Suez crisis, 921–922; and UAR, 923; wars with Israel, 924, 949
Einstein, Albert (1879–1955), 895
Eisenhower, Dwight D. (1890–1969), 866, 906, 912, 941, 944, 945
El Alamein (el ä'lä män'), battle of, 859
Elba, Napoleon exiled to, 660
Eleven Years' Tyranny, 516–517
Elizabeth I, queen of England (r. 1558–1603), 509, 531, 540, 580, 583
emancipation: of Russian serfs, 680–681; of American slaves, 681; abolitionist campaign for, 691; proclaimed by Lincoln, 693–694; of women, 775–777
emigration from Europe, 710–712
empire (*see also* imperialism): transatlantic, first effects of, 578; trade, war, and, 580–586; crumbling of, 871–882
enclosure acts, 620
Encyclopédie (äɴ sē klô pä dē') (Diderot and d'Alembert), 608
Engels, Frederick (1820–1895), 629
England (*see also* Great Britain): population change, 485; overseas trade, 490–492; Reformation in, 508–509; beginnings of modern, 513–518; parliamentary monarchy, 519–520; and Spanish Armada, 531–532; United Kingdom formed (1707), 534
enlightened despotism, 521–523
Enlightenment, 605–606; and reform, 606–609; and anticlericalism, 609–610; limits of, 610; romantic vision, 611–612
environment: science and control of, 783–784; mastery of, 958–959
epidemics, 617; Great Plague, 485
Erasmus (i raz'məs), 503
Essay on Population (Malthus), 615
Estates General, 645, 646
Ethiopia, 730, 734; Italy invades, 845; liberation, 857; government, 925
Europe: early modern, economy of, 483–494; Western, dynasticism in, 526–535; Eastern, changing patterns of state in, 535–554; Age of Discovery, 555–559; Napoleonic stamp on, 657–659; world power and influence, 703–710; emigration, 710–712; overseas nations, 710–723; changes and challenges, 1900s, 771–779; pre-WWI alliances, 791–792; post-WWI rebuilding, 802–815; economic recovery and collapse, 813–815; post-liberal years, 841–845; imbalance of power, 845; post-WWII, 863, 867 868, 949 951;

Western, supranational organization, 951–952; tradition of, 955–958
European Coal and Steel Community, 951
European Economic Community (Common Market), 951–952
evolution, 781–782
exploration and discovery, 555–559
extermination factories, WWII, 861–862

factory, development of, 627
Faraday, Michael (1791–1867), 782
Far East (see also China; Japan): European imperialism in, 735; clashes, post-WWI, 816–830; end of empires in, 871–872
fascio di combattimento (fä'shô dē kôm bät'tē-men'tô), 811
Fascism, 810–813; and beginning of WWII, 850
February Revolution, 665
Fermi (fûr'mē) Enrico (1910–1954), 895
feudalism, abandonment of, 620, 621
Final Solution, Hitler's, 861, 882
Finns, 104; war with Russia, 854
Five-Year Plans: Russia, 810; China, 912
Florida acquired from Spain, 687
food supply and population, 887–889
Ford, Henry (1863–1947), 890
foreign policy: Louis XIV, 533–534; Russia, 678–680; Japan, 1930s, 826
foreign trade, Russia, 547
Formosa, 561, 747, 877
France: wars of religion, 509–510; challenges to authority, 518; absolute monarchy, 520–521; reform, 523–524; ascendancy, 533–534; vs. England in India, 564–566; Caribbean colonies, 572; North American colonization, 576; Enlightenment, 609; agriculture, 620–621; crisis, 643–645; Revolution, 646–653; return to monarchy, 653–657; Napoleonic stamp on Europe, 657–659; imperial government, 659–660; after Napoleon, 663–664; February Revolution, 665; revolution of 1848, 666; Second Empire, 669, 671; empire, 729; in Indochina, 767–768; income tax, 775; nationalism, 779; economy, vs. Germany, 787; entente with Britain, 792–793; and start of WWI, 793; and coming of WWII, 850–852; Third Republic ends, Vichy government set up, 852, 853–854; allied invasion of, 860; at end of WWII, 863; casualties post-WWII, 868; and Vietnam, 878, 916; and Arab nationalism, 922–923; policy under de Gaulle, 951–952
Franche Comté (fRäNsh kôn tä'), 527, 533, 534
franchise, see suffrage

Franciscans (Gray Friars), 560
Francis I, king of France (r. 1515–1547), 528
Franco, Francisco (1892–1975), 850
Franco-Prussian War, 671, 681, 777
Frederick II, Holy Roman Emperor (r. 1212–1250), 522, 609
Frederick I (Great Elector), king of Prussia (r. 1701–1713), 550
Frederick II (the Great), king of Prussia (r. 1740–1786), 551, 553
Frederick William I, king of Prussia (r. 1713–1740), 551
freemasons, 594
free trade, 634–635, 709
French Revolution, 643–652
Freud, Sigmund (1856–1939), 842–843, 897
friendly societies, 701
Fronde, 519, 521

Gagarin, Yuri (1934–1968), 961, 964
Galileo Galilei (gal'i lā'ō gal'i lā'ē) (1564–1642), 603
Gama, Vasco da (vä'skō də gam'ə, gä'mə) (c. 1460–1524), 556
Gandhi, Mohandas K. (gän'dē) (Mahatma) (1869–1948), 872–874
Garibaldi, Menotti (gar'ə bôl'dē) (1840–1903), 763
Genoa, 658, 661
George III, king of England (r. 1760–1820), 740
George V, king of England (r. 1910–1936), 766
Georgia, obtained by Russia, 678
German Communist party, 846
German Social Democratic Party, 774, 846
Germany: Habsburg-Bourbon disputes over, 532; Enlightenment, 609; customs union, 635; Napoleonic stamp on, 658; revolutions (1848), 666; Austrian hegemony ends, 669; unification, 669, 671; Second Reich, 671; colonial population, 739; Marxism in, 774; nationalism, 779; economy, vs. France, 787; reinsurance treaty with Russia, 791; and start of WWI, 793; surrender, 802; Fascism in, 813; post-WWI economy, 814–815; interwar years, 843–844; alliance with Italy, 845; Nazi takeover, 847–849; and beginning of WWII, 850–852; invasion of Russia, 854, 856; at end of WWII, 863; and Berlin blockade, 903; east vs. west, 906–907
Gibbon, Edward (1737–1794), 608
Gladstone, William Ewart (1809–1898), 698, 832
Glorious Revolution, 520

Goa, 560, 590

gold: California, 673; Transvaal finds, 722

government (*see also* bureaucracy; politics; state): and early capitalism, 490; absolute monarchy, 500–501; colonial areas, 591; imperial, 659–660; and economy, U.S., 941–942

Government of India Act, 874

Grand Alliance, 534

Gray Friars (Franciscans), 560

Great Britain (*see also* England): Raj, *see* Raj; Caribbean colonies, 572; North American colonization, 574–576; turn toward empire, 581–582; Enlightenment, 608; agriculture, 619–620; industrialization, 627–628; and American Revolution, 636–640; war with Napoleon, 656–657; constitutional revolution, 697–698; reform, 698–700; popular' demands, 700–701; as center of economic world, 708; emigration from, 712; dominions, 717–718; imperialism, 724–725; protectorate in Egypt, 732, 832, 838; colonial population, 739, 771; annexation of Burma, 747; alliance with Japan, 759; strikes and demonstrations, early 1900s, 773; conservatism, 775; and Irish nationalism, 779; end of isolation, 792–793; and start of WWI, 793; and organization of Arab lands, 836–838; mandates, 837; move toward welfare state, 846; and coming of WWII, 850–852; at end of WWII, 863; and establishment of Israel, 880–882; and Berlin blockade, 903; and Arab nationalism, 922–923; mends fences in Middle East, 948; joins Common Market, 952

Greater Antilles, 571

Great Exhibition (1851), 698

Great Leap Forward, 914

Great Northern War, 544

Great Rebellion, 517

Great Resettlement, 710

Great Society, 943

Great Trek, 720

Greece: new kingdom, 664; nationalism, 777; in WWI, 794; German takeover, 856

Guadalcanal, battle of, 859

Guadeloupe (gwä′dəl ōōp′), 572

Guatemala, 928

guillotine, 647

Habsburg, house of (haps′bûrg), 526, 527–528; enlightened despotism, 522, 523; competition for Italy, 528–530; empire divided, 529–530; and Peace of Westphalia, 532; vs. Hohenzollerns, 551–552; becomes Danu-bian, 669; and Magyar nationalism, 786; end of, 805

Habsburg empire vs. Ottoman empire, 835

Haiti, 715, 927

Harvey, William (1578–1657), 600

Hawaii, U.S. annexation of, 738

Heisenberg, Werner (1901–   ), 895

Hejaz (hə jaz′), 835, 836

heliocentricity, 602

Henry VII, king of England (r. 1485–1509), 526

Henry VIII, king of England (r. 1509–1547), 508, 583

Henry IV, king of France (r. 1572–1610), 509–510

heresy, and Reformation, 503–510

Herrero (hə rär′ō), German massacre of, 734

Hinduism, 564

Hindus, 726, 762–763, 873–875

Hiroshima (hir′ō shĕ′mə, hi rō′shi mə), bombing of, 860

Hitler, Adolf (1889–1945), 847, 849, 850, 856, 860, 861, 900

Hobbes, Thomas (hobz) (1588–1679), 519–520

Ho Chi Minh (hō′ chĕ′ min′) (1890–1969), 878

Hohenzollern dynasty (hō′ən zol′ərn), 550–552

Holy Alliance, 663, 668

Holy Roman Empire, 528, 534

Honan movement (hō′nan′), 823–824

Honduras, 927

Hottentots (hot′ən totz′), 588

Hudson, Henry (d. 1611), 574

Huguenots (hyōō′gə nots′), 518, 519, 521

humanism, 503

Hume, David (hyōōm) (1711–1776), 608

Hundred Days of Reform (1898), 747–748

Hungary: Ottoman defeat of, 535, 536; revolution (1848), 666, 678; post-WWI, 804; revolt, 922, 934, 935–936

Hung Hsiu-ch'üan (hōong′ shyōō′chyän′) (d. 1864), 745, 746

Hu Shih (hōō′ shoE′) (1891–1962), 818

Hussein (hōō sān′), king of Hejaz (r. 1916–1924), 835, 836

Hussein, sherif of Mecca (r. 1908–1916), 834

Ibsen, Henrik (1828–1906), 775, 818

immigration, U.S., 1800s, 696

Imperial Conference (1926), 872

imperialism: Spain in Americas, 567–568; Britain, 724–729; France, 729; late 1800s, 730; U.S., 735, 738–739

Index of prohibited books, 594, 604

India: Portuguese in, 559–560; Raj in, *see* Raj; Mogul empire at its peak, 388–389; British in, 760–762; nationalism, 762–763; communalism, 763–766; independence and partition, 874–875; border conflict with China, 908, 913; relations with Pakistan, 908–910

Indian Communist party, 872

Indian Mutiny (1857), 728, 760, 761

Indian National Congress, 762–763, 766, 873

Indians: colonial enslavement of, 569, 590; revolt, 637; Mexican, 715–716; Canadian, 722; U.S., 722, 723

India Office, 874

Indochina, 747, 767–768, 858; *see also* Vietnam

Indonesia, 560, 561, 768, 877–878, 916–917

industrial expansion and living standards, 890–892

industrialization: early, 492–493; Russia, 546–547, 810; new scale of, 623–628; Japan, 816–817; China, 820, 912

Industrial Revolution, 623–628

infant mortality, 886

inflation: early modern Europe, 493–494; post-WWI, 813

Inquisition, 512, 594, 604; Spanish, 511–512; in Western Hemisphere, 571, 590; condemnation of Galileo, 603

International: Second, 774; Third, 807

International Workingmen's Association, 677

Iran (i ran'): oil flow from, 838; new name for Persia, 840; and cold war origins, 869; WWII occupation, 879

Iraq (i rak'): British mandate in, 837; oil from, 838, 924; in WWII, 857; WWII occupation, 879; monarchy ends, 923

Ireland: famine (1846), 665; home rule demands, 701; nationalism, 779; divisiveness of religion in, 898–899

iron, and industrialization, 623–624

irrigation, Egypt, 832

Islam (is läm'), Western lands, 831–840

Ismail Pasha, khedive of Egypt (1830–1895), 831–832

isolationism, U.S., 683–685

Israel, establishment of, 880–882; and Arab nationalism, 921; and Suez crisis, 922; Six-Day War, 924, 948; and renewal of warfare, 949

Italy: dynastic competition in, 528–530; Enlightenment, 608; Napoleonic stamp on, 658; revolution (1848), 666; Austrian hegemony ends, 669; emigration from, 712; colonial population, 739; outbreaks, 773; nationalism, 786; in WWI, 794; Fascism in,

810–813; invades Ethiopia, 845; alliance with Germany, 845; allied invasion of, 860; at end of WWII, 863

Ivan III (the Great), tsar of Russia (r. 1462–1505), 539

Ivan IV (the Terrible), tsar of All the Russias (r. 1547–1584), 538, 539, 540

Jackson, Andrew (1767–1845), 690

Jacobin club, 664

Jagellion dynasty (yä gel'yən), 537

Jamaica, 581, 583

James I, king of England (r. 1603–1625), 515–516, 562, 574

James II, king of England (r. 1685–1688), 520, 582

Japan: Portuguese trade with, 560, 561; Dutch trade with, 561; emigration from, 712; early 1800s, 751–753; opening of, 753–755; Meiji Restoration, 755–758; aggressive nationalism, 758–759; as new great power, 788; and start of WWI, 794; post-WWI ascendancy, 816–817; aggression in China, 818–819; and Versailles settlement, 819; in Manchuria, 825–828; and "China incident," 829–830; attack on Pearl Harbor, 856–857; in WWII, 858–859; surrender, 860; and Chinese revolution, 875, 876–877; postwar revival, 918–920; as new Asian power, 946–948

Java, 561

Jefferson, Thomas (1743–1826), 691

Jesuits, 510, 522, 559, 590, 610

Jews, and Spanish Inquisition, 511, 512; emigration, 712; in Palestine, 835, 836, 837; Nazi pogroms against, 849; and Hitler's Final Solution, 861–862; and establishment of Israel, 880–882

Jinnah, Mahomed Ali (mə hom'əd ä lē' jin'ə) (1876–1948), 910

Johannesburg, 721

Johnson, Lyndon (1908–1972), 930, 931, 942, 943, 944–945

Joseph II, Holy Roman Emperor (r. 1765–1790), 523

journalism, early modern Europe, 598

July Monarchy, 664

June Days (1848), 666, 667, 673, 676

Kansas, statehood, 692

Kant, Immanuel (1724–1804), 605, 609

Kashmir (kash'mēr, kash mēr'), 908

Kazan (kə zan'), 539

Kemal Ataturk, Mustafa (kə mäl' ä tä tʏʀk') (c. 1880–1938), 839, 900

Kennedy, John F. (1917–1963), 917, 929, 930, 938, 942, 943, 944, 961
Kepler, Johann (1571–1630), 602
Keynes, J. M. (1883–1946), 804
Khrushchev, Nikita (ni kē′tə krōōsh′chôf) (1894–1971), 929, 930, 933, 935, 938, 939, 960
King's Evil, 592
King William's War, 534
Kipling, Rudyard (1865–1936), 731
Korea, 758–759, 947–948
Korean War, 903–906, 911
Kuchuk Kainarji (kōō chōōk′ kī′när jē′), Peace of, 552, 553
Kuomintang (kwō′min tang′; *Chin.* gwô′min′-däng′), 817; and Chinese Communist party, 822–825; and civil war, 828–829; defeat, 875–877
Kurds, 837
Kuwait, 924

labor: and industrialization, 630–633; strikes and demonstrations, Britain, early 1900s, 773
laissez faire (les′ā fâr′), 634, 841
land, as commodity, 486
language: Medieval Europe, 480; Western Hemisphere, 578; French, as lingua franca of intellectuals, 609; India, 726; French, in Egypt, 831
Laos, 767, 878, 916
las Casas, Bartolomé de (bär tô′lô me′ **ㅑㅑe** läs kä′säs) (1474–1566), 569
Latin America: Spanish sovereignty ends, 712–714; problems of independence, 715–716; hemisphere relations, 716–717; population, 887; post-WWII, 926–932
law: early modern Europe, 500; Napoleonic codes, 659
League of Nations, 805–806; and Japanese aggression in Manchuria, 827; and organization of Arab lands, 836–837; and Italy's invasion of Ethiopia, 845
learned societies, 594
Lebanon, 879, 923
Leeward Isles, 572
Lend-Lease Act (1941), 856, 863
Lenin, Nikolai (nik′ə lī′ len′in) (1870–1924), 800, 801, 807, 808, 809
Leopold II, king of Belgium (1865–1909), 735
Leopold II, Holy Roman Emperor (r. 1790–1792), 609
Lepanto (li pan′tō), battle of, 529
Lesser Antilles (an til′ēz), 583

Lettres persanes (le′tʀə peʀ sän′) (Montesquieu), 608
Leviathan (Hobbes), 519
Lexington, battle of, 639
liberalism, 663, 666, 775
Liberia, 730, 734
Libya, 923, 924
Life of Jesus, 781
Lincoln, Abraham (1809–1865), 693, 694
Lister, Joseph (1827–1912), 782, 784
Li Ta-chao (lē′ dä′jou′) (1888–1927), 821
literacy: Russia, 545; early modern Europe, 594–598; Japan, 755; and manipulation of public opinion, 777; Ottoman Near East, 834; Africa, 924; Russia vs. U.S., 939
Lithuania, 535, 536–537
"Little Red Book," 916
living standards and industrial advances, 890–892
Lloyd George, David (1863–1945), 804, 806
Locarno Pact (1925), 843
Locke, John (1632–1704), 605, 608, 643
Long March, 828–829
Louis XIII (lōō′ē), king of France (r. 1610–1643), 518
Louis XIV, king of France (r. 1643–1715), 518, 520–521, 533–534
Louis XV, king of France (r. 1715–1774), 523
Louis XVI, king of France (r. 1774–1792), 644
Louis XVII, king of France (r. 1793–1795), 663
Louis XVIII, king of France (r. 1814–1824), 663
Louisiana Purchase (1803), 686–687
Louis Philippe, king of France (r. 1830–1848), 663–664, 665
Loyola, Ignatius (loi ō′lə) (1491–1556), 510
Lucknow (luk′nou), siege of, 728
Lusitania, liner, 798
Luther, Martin (1483–1546), 504–507
Lyell, Charles (lī′əl) (1797–1875), 781

Macao (ma kou′), 560, 561, 747
MacArthur, Douglas (1880–1964), 906, 918
Macartney, George, First Earl of (1737–1806), 740, 743
Macaulay, Thomas Babington (1800–1859), 770
Magna Carta, 502
Magyars (mag′yärz), 786, 790–791
Mahomed Ali Jinnah, *see* Jinnah
Maine, U.S.S., 738
Malaya, 858, 879
Malaysia, 561, 917

Malthus, Thomas (mal'thəs) (1776–1834), 615, 771

Manchu dynasty (man choo'), 740, 749–751

Manchukuo (man'choo'kwō'), 827

Manchuria, 759, 825–828, 912, 913

Mandate of Heaven, 741, 746, 751

Manhattan Project, 892

Manifest Destiny, 738

Manifeste du Surréalisme (mA nē fest' dy sy rā A lēs'mə), 842

Maoris (mä'ō rēz), 723

Mao Tse-tung (mou' dzə dŏong') (1893–), 821, 823, 824; and civil war in China, 828–829; and Communist takeover, 876, 877; and relations with Russia, 913–916

March on Rome, 812

Maria Theresa, Habsburg queen (1717–1780), 523, 551–552, 609

Marshall Plan, 870–871, 951

Martinique, 572

Marx, Karl (1818–1883), 630, 676–677, 785

Marxism, 677, 774, 821, 913

Mary, queen of England (Bloody Mary), (1516–1558), 509, 512

Mary, queen of England (wife of William III) (r. 1689–1694), 520, 534

Maryland settlement, 575

Massacre of the Innocents, 236

mass production, 890–892

Matabeles (mat'ə bē'lēz), 723, 734

mathematics, 1600s, 600

Maxwell, James Clark (1831–1879), 893–894

May 4th movement, 819–820

Mazzini, Giuseppe (joo zep'pe mät tsē'nē) (1805–1872), 663, 673, 761–762, 763

Medici (med'i chē), 528

medicine: and population growth, 617; and nursing, Crimean War, 668

Mehmet Ali (me met' ä lē'), pasha of Egypt (1769–1849), 729, 831, 900

Meiji Restoration (mā'jē'), 755–758

Mesopotamia (mes'ə pə tä'mē ə) in WWI, 795

Metternich, Clemens, Prince (met'ər niKH) (1773–1859), 664, 666

Mexican War, 688

Mexico, 567–568, 715–716, 927

Middle East: post-WWII, 879; postimperial era, 920–924; situation in, 948–949

Midway, battle of, 858–859

Mill, John Stuart (1806–1873), 761, 818

Miranda, Francisco de (1750–1816), 713

Missouri Compromise, 690–691

Mitsui (mit soo'ē), House of, 752

Mogul empire (mō'gul, gəl), 564, 728

Molotov, V. M. (mol'ə tôf') (1890–), 933

Moluccas (mō luk'əz), 560, 561

monarchy: absolute, 500–501, 520–521; Parliamentary, 519–520

money, 487, 489

money economy, 488

Monroe Doctrine, 678, 716, 717, 738–739

Montenegro, 777

Montesquieu, Baron de la Brède (mon'təskyoo'; *Fr.* môn tes kyoE') (1689–1755), 498, 608

Morocco, 733, 792, 793

Mukden incident (mook'den'), 827

Muslim League, 873, 874

Muslims: in India, 564, 726; and communalism, 763–766; vs. Hindus, 873–875

Mussolini, Benito (1883–1945), 811, 812, 845, 850, 860, 879

Nagasaki (nä'gə sä'kē), bombing of, 860

Nantes, Edict of (nants; *Fr.* näNt), 510, 521

Naples, 518, 519, 528

Napoleon Bonaparte (r. 1804–1813): and return of monarchy, 653–657; stamp on Europe, 657–659; abdication and exile, 660; Egypt expedition, 729

Napoleon III, Emperor of France (1808–1873), 669, 671

Nassar, Gamal Abdel (1918–1970), 921–923

Natal, 720, 721

National Assembly, 646

nationalism: and liberalism, 663; and revolutions of 1848, 666–667; and Crimean War, 667–668; aggressive, in Japan, 758–759; India, 762–763; and mass politics, 777–779; Magyar, 786; revolutionary, 790; Arab, 838; Turkish, 839; Latin America, 931–932

Nationalist China, *see* Kuomintang

National Socialist German Workers' party (Nazi), 847

native peoples, and Europeanization, 722–723

natural selection, 782

Navigation Act, 581

Near East, Ottoman, and WWI, 834–835

Negro question, U.S., 942–943

Nehru, Jawaharlal (nä'roo) (1889–1964), 908, 913

Nelson, Horatio (1758–1805), 724

Netherlands: agricultural advances, 486; overseas trade, 490–492; freedom from Spain, 512–513, 530–531; and war with France, 533; and Peace of Utrecht, 534; seaborne empire, 560–562; colonies, 572, 574, 576, 580–581; in Indonesia, 768, 877–878

Neutrality Proclamation, 683

New Amsterdam, 572, 582

New Deal, 844, 941

New Economic Policy (NEP), 809

New England colonies, 575–576
New Frontier, 943
New Guinea, 858
Newton, Isaac (1642–1727), 603–604, 608
New Youth, 818, 821
New Zealand, 718, 723, 919, 920, 947
Nicaragua, U.S. intervention in, 717, 927
Nicholas I, tsar of Russia (r. 1825–1855), 678, 680
Nigeria, 925
Nightingale, Florence (1820–1910), 668
Nixon, Richard (1913–   ), 941, 945, 948
Normandy, allied landing in, 860
North America, colonization, 568, 573–578
North Atlantic Treaty Organization (NATO), 903, 949, 951
Norway, German conquest of, 852
Nova Scotia (Acadia), 582
nuclear engineering, 894

oil: increasing influence of, 838; in Persia, 840; and Japanese attack on Pearl Harbor, 857; and Middle East situation, 922–924, 948–949; expropriation in Latin America, 927
Okinawa, 948
Omdurman (om'doōr män'), battle of, 706
On the Revolutions of the Celestial Orbs (Copernicus), 602
Open Door Policy, 819
Opium Wars, 708, 743
Orange Free State, 721
Organization for European Economic Co-operation, 870
The Origin of Species (Darwin), 781–782
Ottoman empire, 529; decline, 535–536; and France, 729; Young Turks movement, 833–834; and WWI, 834–835; vs. Habsburg empire, 835; end of, 839

Pakistan, 874–875, 898, 908–910
Palestine, 834–838
Palestine Liberation Organization, 924
Palmerston, Henry John Temple, Viscount (1784–1865), 698
Panama, 567
Panama Canal Zone, 717, 739
Pan-American Congress (1889), 716
papacy, temporal powers curbed, 780
Papal States, 522, 535, 780
Paris: Peace of (1763), 579; Treaty of (1783), 640, 683, 688; German capture of, 852; Commune, 648, 673–675, 677; June Days (1848), 666, 667, 673, 676
Parlement of Paris, 518, 609
Parliament of Religion (1893), 762

parochialism and Enlightenment, 608
Passchendaele (pas'kn dä'lə), battles of, 800
Pasteur, Louis (1822–1895), 784
Pavlov, I. V. (pav'lôf) (1849–1936), 897–898
Pax Britannica, 585, 706
peaceful coexistence, 934
Pearl Harbor, attack on, 857
Pedro I, emperor of Brazil (r. 1822–1831), 714
Peel, Sir Robert (1788–1850), 635, 698
peninsulares (pe nēn'soō lä'ʀes), 571, 713
People's Charter, 700
periodicals, 598
Perón, Juan (wän' pə rōn') (1895–1974), 927
Perry, Matthew (1794–1858), 755
Persia, war with Russia, 724; revival of, 840
Peru, 568, 931
Pescadores (pes'kə dôr'ēz), 747
Pétain (pā taʌ'), Henri Philippe (1856–1951), 852
Peter (the Great) tsar of Russia (r. 1682–1725), 542–545, 548, 549
Peter III, tsar of Russia (r. 1762), 547
Philip II, king of Spain (r. 1556–1598), 512, 529, 530, 531, 580
Philippines, 568, 583, 730, 738, 858, 919–920
philosophes, 608–610
Philosophical Transactions, 601
Pilgrims, 577
Pizarro, Francisco (pi zär'ō) (c. 1478–1541), 568
Planck, Max (mäks' plängk') (1858–1947), 895
Plantagenets (plan taj'ə nits), 441–442
Plassey (plä'sē), battle of, 565
Poland, 535, 536–538; alliance with Russia, 540; partitions of, 553–554; revolutions against Russia, 673, 678; emigration from, 712; resurrected, 802, 804, 805; and coming of WWII, 851–852
politics (*see also* bureaucracy; government): U.S., 695–696; and suffrage for women, 775–776; mass, and nationalism, 777–779
politiques, 509
Poltava, battle of, 544
polycentrism, 949, 950–951
Pompadour, Madame de (pôn pa doōr') (1721–1764), 498
Pontiac, Ottawa chief, 637
Pope, Alexander (1688–1744), 603
popular sovereignty, in France, 654
population: early modern Europe, 484–485; and agriculture, 486–487; Russia, 546; American colonies, 577; changes, 615–619; cities in industrial age, 628–629; U.S., 696; and wealth, Latin America, 716; colonial,

739; 1900, 771–772; Egypt, 832; post-WWII, 885–887; Africa, 925
Port Arthur, 747, 759, 866, 913
Portugal: trade with Japan, 405; exploration, 470–472; overseas trade, 490–491; under Spain, 512, 518; eastern empire, 559–560; slave trade, 588–589; Brazilian independence from, 714; in WWI, 794; WWII neutrality, 857; and decolonization in Africa, 925, 926; revolution in, 951
Potocki (pô tôts'kĕ), Count (d. 1692), 538
Potosí, 568
Potsdam conference, 869
poverty: U.S., late 1800s, 696–697; 1900, 772
press: censorship, 654; and public opinion, 777
Principia (Newton), 603
Principles of Geology (Lyell), 781
printing, and spread of knowledge, 586, 594, 598
propaganda warfare, 798
protectionism and free trade, 634–635
Protestantism, 503–510, 590
Prussia: enlightened despotism, 522–523; under Hohenzollerns, 550–552; and partition of Poland, 553; and German unification, 669, 671
Ptolemy of Alexandria (tol'ə mē) (fl. 2nd century A.D.), 599
public opinion and mass politics, 777
Pugachev (pōō gä chôf') (1742?–1775), 548
Punch, 717
Punjab (pun jäb'), 726
Puritanism, 517–518, 575
Puritan Revolution, 519

quantum theory, 895
Quebec Act (1774), 638

races, interbreeding in colonies, 569–571, 591
Radziwill clan, 538
railroads, 623, 626–627; transcontinental, 696, 718; in India, 726
Raj (räj), 562–566, 725–729, 760–766, 872–875
raskol (rə skôl'), 540
realpolitik, 499, 532
Red Guards, 915
Red Turbans, 744
Reflections on the Revolution in France (Burke), 653
reform: and Enlightenment, 606–609; China, 747–749; vs. revolution, 772–775
Reform Act (1832), 697, 698
Reformation, 500, 503–510; and literacy, 595, 598

reinsurance treaty, Germany and Russia, 791
relativity theory, 895
religion (see also Hinduism): French wars of, 509–510; 1600s, 593–594; and science, 604–605; and Enlightenment, 609–610; and urbanization, 630; early 1900s, 779–781; and science, 781–785; and state, 898–901
Renaissance, 501–502, 519
republicanism, 641–642
Restoration (1660), 519
revisionists, 774
revolution: Industrial, 623–628; American, 636–640; French, 643–652; contagion of (1848), 664–667; ebbing of, 672–675; constitutional, in Britain, 697–702; Chinese, 744–751, 875–877; vs. reform, 772–775; agricultural, 888; Asian, 907–920; Cuban, 928–929
Reza Khan (rə zä' kän'), shah of Iran (1877–1944), 840
Rhodesia, 925, 926
Richelieu, Armand Jean Du Plessis, Cardinal (rē shə lyoE') (1585–1642), 532, 533
Risorgimento (rē sôr'jē men'tô), 794, 810
Roentgen, Wilhelm (wil'helm rent'gən, -jən) (1845–1923), 894
Romanticism, 611–612, 653
Roosevelt, Franklin (rō'zə velt') (1882–1945), 844, 856, 863, 868, 900, 941
Roosevelt, Theodore (1859–1919), 717
Rousseau, Jean Jacques (zhäN zhäk rōō sō') (1712–1778), 611–612
Royal Academy, 594
Royal Society, 601
Rumania, 668, 777, 794, 854, 949–950
Russia: enlightened despotism, 522; emergence of power, 538–540; Romanov aristocracy, 540–542; under Peter the Great, 542–545; economy and serfdom, 545–547; under Catherine the Great, 547–549; vs. Austria, 552–553; and partition of Poland, 553; serfdom and agriculture, 621; Napoleon's invasion of, 656; conservatism, 677–680; emancipation of serfs, 680–681; war with Persia, 724; takeover of Chinese territory, 746, 747; war with Japan in Manchuria, 759; population, 1900, 771; revolution (1905), 773, 786; Bolsheviks, 774; nationalism within empire, 777; internal problems, 786–787; reinsurance treaty with Germany, 791; and start of WWI, 793; October Revolution, 800–801; Allied intervention in, 801–802; and Versailles settlement, 806; Comintern, 807; beginnings of Soviet regime, 808–810; and Kuomintang, 825; interwar policy, 846;

and coming of WWII, 851–852; war with
Finland, 854; German invasion, 854, 856;
at end of WWII, 863; post-WWII, 865–
867; U.S. containment policy toward, 870;
and Berlin blockade, 903; and Korean War,
904; China's relations with, 912, 913–916;
and Arab nationalism, 922–923; and Cuban
revolution, 929; and Cuban missile crisis,
930–931; and cold war in post-Stalin era,
933–938; internal status, 938–940; space
exploration, 960–965
Russian Communist party Twentieth Congress,
933–934, 938
Rutherford, Ernest (1871–1937), 894, 895

St. Helena, Napoleon exiled to, 660
Saint-Simon, Claude (klôd saɴ sē môɴ′)
(1760–1825), 675–676
Salonika, battle of, 795
Sarajevo, (sar′ə yä′vō), 793
Saratoga, battle of, 639
Sarawak, 917
Satsuma rebellion (sä′tsoō mä′), 758
Saudi Arabia, 837, 924, 948
Savoy, House of, 535, 669
Schrödinger, Erwin (1887–1961), 895
science: and agricultural advances, 486; early
modern Europe, 598–599; new view of,
600; and religion, 604–605, 781–785; and
civilization, 892–893; changing world of,
893–896; and attitudes, 896–898
scientists, 601, 783
sea power and imperial supremacy, 583–585
Second International, 774
Serbia, 777, 791, 793
serfs, 538; Russian, 545–547, 680–681
Seven Years' War, 551, 565, 566, 577, 579,
582, 644
Shantung (shan′tung′, -toong′), 819
Shintoism, 757–758
ships and shipping: and overseas trade, early
modern Europe, 490–492; gun-carrying,
558–559; merchant vs. naval, 583–585;
steam-powered, 623, 626; and British-In-
dian ties, 726; WWI U-boat attacks, 798;
and WWII battle of the Atlantic, 859
Siam, 560, 561, 730
Siberia, 539, 724
Sierra Leone (sē er′ə lē ō′nē), 589
Sikhs (sēks), 564
silver mining, 568
Sind, 726
Six-Day War, 924, 948
slavery: Spanish colonies, 569, 590; West
Indies, 572; and world power, 588–589; in

United States, 688–693; in Brazil, 715;
in South Africa, 719
slave trade, 558, 585, 586; Europe, early
Middle Ages, 377; early modern Europe,
491–492; Caribbean, 572; British, 582, 583
Slovakia, 779
slums, early 1900s, 772
Smith, Adam (1723–1790), 606, 608, 615
Sobieski, John (sô byes′kē), king of Poland (r.
1674–1696), 536, 538
socialism, 675–677; Marxist, 774
socialists vs. communists, 807–808
society: Europe, 494–498; Poland, 538; Russia, 548; rich and poor, 889–892; industrial,
and science, 892–898
Society for the Study of Self-Strengthening,
747
Society of Jesus, 510
Somma, battle of, 794
South Africa, Union of, 718–722, 925, 926
Southeast Asia, 766–768
Southeast Asia Treaty Organization (SEATO),
920
Soviet Union, see Russia
space exploration, 940, 941, 960–965
space-time continuum, 895
Spain: and Counter Reformation: 511–512;
challenges to authority, 518–519; en-
lightened despotism, 522; ascendancy, 530–
532; and Peace of Utrecht, 534; colonial
system, 569–571; Caribbean colonies, 571–
572; emigration from, 712; sovereignty in
Latin America ends, 712–714; revolt, Bar-
celona, 773; WWII neutrality, 857
Spanish American War, 738–739
Spanish Civil War, 850, 851, 862
The Spectator, 498, 598
Spencer, Herbert (1820–1903), 818
Sputnik (spoōt′nik), 960, 961
Stalin, Joseph (stä′lin) (1879–1953), 809–
810, 825, 851, 863, 866, 868, 881, 906
Stalingrad, battle of, 859
Stamp Act (1765), 638
Stamp Act Congress, 638
The Star-Spangled Banner, 685
state (see also bureaucracy; government):
growth of power, 500–501; Renaissance,
501–502, 519; Counter Reformation, 510–
513; early modern, 524; Eastern Europe,
535–554; and religion, 898–901
statistics, age of, 483–484
steam power, and industrialization, 625–627
stock companies, joint, 487, 489
stock exchanges, 487, 489
strikes, early 1900s, 773
Stuart dynasty, 515–518

submarines: WWI, 798, 799–800; WWII, 859–860

Sudan, 732

Suez Canal, 729, 732, 831; protection of, 835, 838, 879; Egyptian seizure of, 922–923

suffrage: post-Napoleonic France, 664; for British freeholders, 697; for women, 775–776

Sugar Act (1764), 638

Sukarno, Achmed (äk'med sōō kär'nō) (1901–1970), 878, 916–917

Sun Yat-sen (sōōn' yät'sen') (1866–1925), 750, 751, 767, 817, 819, 822, 823

superpowers: post-WWII, 865–867; challenges to, 933–946

surrealism, 842

suttee, 726

Swaraj (swə räj'), 763

Sweden, 532, 537, 544, 857

Switzerland, 507–508, 857

Syllabus of Errors (1864), 780

Syria: and France, 729, 837; in WWII, 857; independence, 879; and UAR, 923; war with Israel, 949

szlachta (shläkн'tä), 538

Taiping Rebellion (tī'ping'), 745–746

Taiwan (tī'wän'), 912

Tannu Tuva (tan'ōō tōō'və), 913

Tatars (tä'tərz), defeat, 539

taxes: Renaissance state, 502, 518–519; Russia, 548; American colonies, 637–638; prerevolutionary France, 644; and conservatism, Britain, 775; on income, 775

technology, science, 782

Terror (France), 647–648

Texas, annexation of, 688

Third International, 807

third world, 910

Thirty Years' War, 532, 537, 580

Thomson, J. J. (1856–1940), 894

Tibet, 912, 913

Time of Troubles, 539, 540

Tito (Josip Broz) (1892–   ), 934, 935

Titoism, 934–935

Tokugawa shogunate (tō'kōō gä'wä), 751–753

Tordesillas, treaty of (tôr'tнe sē'lyäs), 965

trade (*see also* commerce): overseas, 490–492; war, empire, and, 580–586; China's terms of, 743–744

Trafalgar, battle of, 657, 713

Transcaspia, 724

Transjordan, 837

transport: and agricultural revolution, 623; steam powered, 623, 626; India, 726

Transvaal, 721

Treblinka extermination factory, 861

Trent, Council of (1545), 510

Triple Alliance, 791

Tripoli, 739; battle of (1560), 529; Italian conquest of, 732–733, 833

Trotsky, Leon (1877–1940), 809

Truman Harry (1884–1972), 868, 869–870, 881, 905, 906, 941

Truman Doctrine, 869–870

Tudor dynasty, 508–509, 526–527

Tunis, 529, 729, 733

Turks, war with Russia, 553

Turkey: vs. Russia, 678–680; war with Balkan states, 777; and start of WWI, 794; allied attack on Dardanelles, 795; war with Egypt, 832; new, 838–840

Tuscany, 609

twenty-one demands, 819

U-boats, *see* submarines

unemployment: 1840s, 665; new phenomenon of, 772

Union Indochinoise (In'dō shēn woz'), 767

Union of Arab Emirates, 949

United Arab Republic, 923

United Kingdom, *see* England; Great Britain

United Nations: organization of, 864–865; and establishment of Israel, 881; and Korean War, 904–906; and Congo civil war, 925; mainland China seated in, 946

United States: settlement and independence, 575–578; agriculture, 621–623; Revolutionary War, 636–640; new nation, 640; Constitution, 641–643; heritage, 682–683; foreign policy, 683–688; slavery in, 688–693; War Between the States, 693–697; hemisphere relations, 716–717; conquest of Philippines, 730; imperialism, 735, 738–739; population, 1900, 771; as new great power, 788; in WWI, 798; post-WWI recovery and collapse, 814–815; and China incident, 830; interwar years, 844–845; Germany declares war on, 856; Japan attacks Pearl Harbor, 856–857; at end of WWII, 863; and Berlin blockade, 903; and Korean War, 903–906; in Vietnam, 916, 917; and Arab nationalism, 921–923; as Latin America's big brother, 927–928; and Cuban revolution, 928–929; and Cuban missile crisis, 930–931; resumes relations with China, 940; internal status, 940–944; and war in Vietnam, 944–946; space exploration, 960–965

universe, understanding of, 601–604

universities: religious ties, 594; in India, 726; in China, 820

urbanization: early modern Europe, 485; in industrial age, 628–633
Utrecht, Peace of (yoo'trekt), 534, 792

Valois dynasty (val'wä; *Fr.* va lwa'), 526, 527, 528–530
Vanguard satellite, 961
Venezuela, 567, 572, 716, 927
Venice, 525, 535, 658, 661
Verdun (vûr dun'; *Fr.* ver doen'), battle of (WWI), 794
Versailles (ver sī'), palace of, 521, 533, 671; Treaty of, 804–806, 819
Vesalius (vi sä'lē əs) (1514–1564), 599
Victoria, queen of England (r. 1837–1901), 699, 701–702, 760, 784
Vienna: Ottoman sieges, 535, 536; Treaty of, 661, 663; revolution (1848), 666
Vietcong, 917
Vietminh (vyet'min'), 878, 916
Vietnam, 767; republic set up, 878–879; partition, 916; U.S. presence in, 916, 917; war, 944–946
vikend, 839
Virginia Company, 574
Virginia settlement, 574, 575
Vladivostok, 678, 724, 746, 759
Volkerwanderung (foel'kər vän'də roong), 712
Voltaire (vōl târ') (1694–1778), 606, 609, 610

Wahhabi sect (wə hä'bē), 763
War Between the States, 693–696
warfare: trade, empire, and, 580–586; civilized, 785–786
War of 1812, 685–686, 738
War of Jenkins' Ear (1737), 490, 582
War of the Austrian Succession, 551, 582
War of the League of Augsburg, 534, 582
War of the Roses, 527
War of the Spanish Succession, 534
Warsaw, grand duchy of, 659
Warsaw Pact, 906, 935, 936, 947, 948
Wars of Religion, 509, 531
Washington, George (1732–1799), 640, 641, 689; Farewell Address, 683–684, 689, 690

Waterloo, battle of, 660
wealth: and suffrage, France, 664; and population, Latin America, 716
Wealth of Nations (Smith), 606, 608, 615
weaponry: early modern state, 524; in Age of Discovery, 558–559; WWI, 794
Weimar Republic (vī'mär), 843
West Indies, 571–572
West New Guinea, 917
Westphalia, Peace of, 532–533
Wilhelm II, German emperor (r. 1888–1918), 779
William III, king of England (r. 1689–1702), 520, 534
William (the Silent), prince of Orange (1533–1584), 512
Wilson, Woodrow (1856–1924), 802, 804, 805–806, 836
Windward Isles, 572
women: early modern Europe, 497–498; and nursing services, Crimean War, 668; in Taiping society, 745; early 1900s, 775–777
Workers' and Soldiers' Soviet, 800
World Council of Churches, 899
world powers, 579–580; China as, 911–913
world trade, 585–586; and cultural interplay, 586–592
World War I: prologue, 788–793; Sarajevo and after, 793; nature of, 794–798; 1917, 798–800; and Russian Revolution, 800–802; postwar rebuilding, 802–815
World War II, 841; beginnings, 850–852; expansion, 852–856; U.S. involvement, 856–857; spread to Pacific, 857–860; balance sheet, 860–863
World Zionist Congress, 881

Yorktown, battle of, 640
Young Turk movement, 833–834
Yüan Shih-kai (yvän' shē'kī') (1859–1916), 751, 817, 819
Yugoslavia, 804, 856, 866, 869, 934–935

Zionism, 881
Zulus, 720, 723, 734
Zwingli, Huldreich (hool'drikh tsving'lē, zwing'lē) (1484–1531), 507

About the Author

J. M. ROBERTS is Fellow and Tutor of Merton College, Oxford, a graduate of that university, where he also received his doctorate in 1953. His areas of specialization are French and Italian history of the eighteenth and nineteenth centuries and twentieth-century world history. He is a fellow of the Royal Historical Society and member of the Association européenne de l'histoire contemporaine. Professor Roberts was a member of the Institute for Advanced Study at Princeton in 1960 and has taught at the University of South Carolina (1961) and Columbia University (1963). He is editor of the *English Historical Review* and author of *French Revolution Documents* (1966), *Europe 1880–1945* (1967), *The Mythology of the Secret Societies* (1972), and *The Paris Commune from the Right* (1973). His articles and reviews have appeared in a number of professional and popular journals, among them the *Revue de l'histoire moderne et contemporaine, Bulletin of the Institute of Historical Research, The Times Literary Supplement, History Today, Spectator, New Statesman,* and *The Listener.*

A Note on the Type

The text of this book is set Linofilm in Caledonia, originally a Linotype face designed by W. A. Dwiggins. It belongs to the family of printing types called "modern face" by printers—a term used to mark the change in style of type-letters that occurred around 1800. Caledonia borders on the general design of Scotch Modern, but is more freely drawn than that letter.

The book was composed by The Clarinda Co., Clarinda, Iowa. Printed and bound by American Book-Stratford Press, Inc., Saddle Brook, N.J. Color inserts by New York City Press, Inc., New York, N.Y.